American Regional Cuisine

American
Regional Cuisine

Ai The Art Institutes℠

With photography by Cynthia Holling-Morris

JOHN WILEY & SONS, INC.

LIBRARY OF CONGRESS CATALOGING-IN-PUBLICATION DATA:
American regional cuisine / the Art Institutes; with photography by Cynthia Holling-Morris.
         p. cm.
  Includes bibliographical references and index.
  ISBN 0-471-40544-2 (cloth : alk. Paper)
  1. Cookery, American. I. Art Institutes.
 TX715.A50847 2001
 641.5973—dc21   2001026947

Printed in the United States of America.

10 9 8 7 6 5 4 3 2 1

Book design by Richard Oriolo

Contents

Foreword

by Martin Yan

In my travels, I've crisscrossed the world, experiencing different cultures and tasted their dishes. And I must say that the United States is one of the most diverse nations with respect to culture, people, history, and food. Some say the American national cuisine is like a melting pot of many ethnic cuisines; some describe it as a mixed salad with distinct ingredients. Regardless of which analogy you prefer, each American regional cuisine is a special treat, combining its unique local history and culture with distinct regional ingredients. It's not by chance that certain parts of the country maintain a particular taste or flavor in their dishes. Regional cuisines reflect the characteristics of the locale.

From one U.S. coast to the other, from ocean to mountain, valley to plain, I've noticed that each region's dishes tell a story and are like mirrors. A recipe evolves along with the communities and, with each adaptation, the dish absorbs and reflects much of the environment. For example, the cuisine of New England is an adaptation of English cuisine, the local ingredients such as turkey, lobster, and clams giving the region its well-known Boston brown bread, clam chowder, and Maine boiled lobster. In the Great Plains, where wheat is the staff of life, you'll find wheat and honey buns, colaches, and wheat beer. You can actually taste the wet weather typical of the Pacific Northwest in its apples and berries. In the Southwest, you'll find foods flavored by fiery spices because of their abundance in the region. Head over to my home state of California and you'll taste the freshness of the seasons and the experimental spirit of the people, whose recipes use a wide range of readily available ingredients—asparagus, lettuce, artichoke, bok choy, lemongrass, tomato, and more.

I've had the pleasure of gaining illuminating perspective on each region I've visited just from taking a bite of its food. The Cajun and Creole region, home of my good friend Paul Prudhomme, is a marvelous blend of French, Spanish, Italian, German, Native American, African, and West Indian traditions. For a taste of the Asian blends, such as Chinese, Japanese, Filipino, Korean, Indian, and Thai, it's back to California and the Pacific Northwest. It's an enjoyable journey for the mind and taste buds when traveling the United States.

Travel among these pages—enjoy! What follows is insight into and details of what makes each American culinary region unique. Each chapter contains not only recipes but also historical and cultural information, as well as a guide to ingredients specific to that region. And to top it off, once you prepare these dishes and take a bite, the flavors and tastes will reinforce everything you read. It's a history, anthropology, and cooking class all in one!

Martin Yan is a master chef and corporate chef of Chef Martin Yan's CreAsian. He has written more than 24 cookbooks and is the host of *Yan Can Cook* on PBS. Chef Yan is the founder of the Yan Can International Cooking School in the San Francisco Bay area.

Acknowledgments

The Art Institutes wishes to thank the following contributors for their efforts on behalf of American Regional Cuisine:

Chris DeJohn, CEC, AAC

John R. Fisher, CEC, AAC

Klaus Friedenreich, CMC

Michael Nenes, CEC, CCE

Gary J. Prell, CEC, CCE, AAC

Doug Zimmerman, CEC

In addition, we are grateful for the beautiful work of photographer Cynthia Holling-Morris, her assistant Richard Christian, and photo stylist Michael Pizzuto, CCE. Karl Schiemann, our HACCP consultant, provided invaluable assistance with the recipes. Karen Overfield, Ed.D., Vice President, Curriculum and Instruction was instrumental during the production and editing process. And the project could not have been completed without the recipe contributions of the Art Institute Culinary Program directors and faculty:

The Art Institute of Atlanta

Sarah Gorham, CEC–Chef Director

James W. Paul, CSC, FMP–Assistant Academic Director

Joe Costa, CEC
Caroline Edenfield

The Illinois Institute of Art - Chicago
Michael L. Carmel, CCE, CEC, M.AD. ED.–Chef Director

The Art Institute of Dallas
Charles J. Boley, CMC CCE–Chef Director

The Art Institute of Colorado
Christopher DeJohn, CEC, AAC, CCE–Chef Director

The Art Institute of Fort Lauderdale
Klaus Friedenreich, CMC–Chef Director

The Art Institute of Houston
Michael Nenes, CEC, CCE–Chef Director
Lawrance Matson, CWC, MBA
Joseph Bonaparte, CCC, MHM
Kimberly Joyner

The Art Institute of Los Angeles
Richard E. Battista, CEC, CEPC, CCE–Chef Director
Joseph Zoellin, CEC, CCE
Kurt Struwe, CEC, CCE

The Art Institute of Los Angeles-Orange County
Paul Yarmoluk–Chef Director

The Art Institutes International Minnesota
William G. Niemer, B.A., MSU–Chef Director

The New York Restaurant School
Brendan Keenan–Chef Director

The Art Institute of Philadelphia
Joseph E. Shilling, B.S., A.O.S.–Chef Director

The Art Institute of Phoenix
Bill Sy, MBA, CEC, AAC–Chef Director
Walter Leible, CMC, AAC–Assistant Director

The Art Institute of Seattle
John R. Fisher, CEC AAC–Chef Director

The Art Institute of Washington
John Harrison–Chef Director

Finally, we wish to thank the following companies for the supplies and equipment used in the photography for American Regional Cuisine: Coosemans-Denver, Inc; JDSR Produce; Nobel Sysco; Seattle Fish Company; The Restaurant Source; Le Grueís Flowers and Gifts; Royal Doulton; Steelite International; Homer Laughlin China; Syracuse China; Rosenthal USA Limited; and Mikasa.

Introduction

American Regional Cuisine is written with great pride in our country, the professionalism of our culinarians, and the incredible foods that are bountiful from coast to coast. Few countries can boast the diverse selection of high-quality indigenous ingredients found in the United States. These ingredients, combined with America's varied cultures and colorful history, have led to a worldwide reputation for creative and purposeful cuisine. The geographical diversity represented by The Art Institutes' culinary programs and their associated culinary educators, located in every region of the country, provides a unique breadth of knowledge of American regional cuisine. The recipes, specialized skills, and procedures presented in this book are authentic and unique to each region. They have been, in many cases, handed down from generation to generation of our faculty of professional chefs. We are pleased to present this book to professional culinarians, students, and home gourmets. It documents the history and culture that led to the development of American regional cuisine and identifies the vast and wide variety of foods indigenous to our great country.

The cuisine of the United States is not homogenous. It is derived from a blending of many cultures and ethnic backgrounds that coexist in specific regions throughout the country. Each region possesses a unique history and culture and a variety of ingredients that make its cuisine distinct.

The principles and foundations of cooking were developed and practiced in Europe, Asia, and Africa, and other countries long before the development of American regional cuisine as we know it today. The European immigrants, who brought their cooking skills to America, applied their basic culinary principles to the ingredients at hand. In the 1900s, as the palate of the typical American became more sophisticated, many European-trained chefs immigrated to the United States to take jobs in the growing restaurant and hotel industries. In time, Americans began to cook professionally, and, in many cases, trained under these European chefs. Thus, even today, French is the language of cooking taught to students of the culinary arts. A vocabulary of cooking terms used in this book can be found in the Glossary.

Knowledge of basic cooking principles is essential to proper preparation of the recipes presented in this book. When learning to play a musical instrument, one must first learn how to read notes. Likewise, when learning to cook, one must first learn how to prepare stocks and sauces and to become proficient with the fundamental techniques of cooking before one can expect to create attractive and tasty dishes.

The chapters present the cuisine of 11 culinary regions. The regional recipe chapters are presented in an order representing the arrival of the first American colonists and the approximate routes they took as they explored and settled what eventually became the United States. The states included in each chapter are selected and grouped based on similarities of the cultures and backgrounds of their residents and their cuisine, as well as how the indigenous ingredients of the area are utilized in the cooking of the region. A notable culinary professional of the region introduces each chapter. He or she offers a local perspective of the region's cuisine and a philosophy of how ingredients should be selected and used in the recipes. Following this introduction, a historical overview of the development of the region's cuisine addresses how various cultures and ethnic backgrounds influenced its growth and evolution. Information about typical ingredients and dishes and a selection of representative regional recipes follow. It will be of interest to the reader to discover that many ingredients typically associated with the cuisine of other countries, such as tomatoes, potatoes, and peppers, are actually native to America, only later transported and popularized elsewhere.

Some important tips for using this book are outlined below:

- It is important to understand that to yield a superior dish, one must start with high-quality ingredients. Good results cannot be obtained with substandard ingredients.

- Some ingredients called for in the recipes are highly specific to a region and may be difficult to obtain elsewhere. Many such recipes are followed by Chef Tips, which indicate suitable substitutions for these items.

- All herbs called for in recipes should be fresh unless specified as dry.

- All butter called for in recipes should be lightly salted unless specified as sweet to indicate unsalted butter.

- It is recommended that both white and black pepper be ground fresh in the level of coarseness called for in the recipes. Ground pepper loses its strength over time, making it difficult to judge the quantity needed.

- When citrus juice is called for in the recipes, it should be squeezed from fresh fruit rather than reconstituted from concentrate.

- Many of the cooking times indicated in the recipes are approximations. The altitude, type of cookware, and amount of heat applied are all variables that affect the required cooking time. Professional cooks use these times as a guideline while determining the doneness of the dish using all appropriate means.

The recipes are written using a format aligned with the Hazard Analysis and Critical Control Point (HACCP) food safety program, as recommended by the U.S. Food and Drug Administration (FDA). HACCP is a food handling, preparation, and reporting process intended to prevent the formation and transmittal of food-borne illness. Critical Control Points (CCPs) are indicated by the icon 🍲 to identify steps where the potential for growth of bacteria, toxins, or viruses is high. The CCPs identified with certain steps contain time and temperature handling procedures that can significantly reduce or negate the transmission of food-borne illnesses.

Remember, if you are serving food to others, their health is in your hands—literally. One does not intend to make another person sick, but it can and will happen if sanitation and safety guidelines are not followed. The preventive nature of HACCP food safety procedures helps to significantly reduce the formation and transmission of food-borne illnesses and yields higher-quality dishes with a longer life span.

More on Hazard Analysis and Critical Control Points (HACCP)

There are many ways people can contract a food-borne illness. The four most common types of food-borne illness are infection, intoxication, toxin-medicated infection, and viral infection. The popular belief that it takes 24 hours to become ill is incorrect. Some symptoms can begin in minutes while others may take as long as 50 days. The impact of food-borne illnesses also varies widely from person to person. Some illnesses can lead to short-term nausea and diarrhea, whereas others can cause serious health problems leading to hospitalization and even death. We always recommend a preventive approach, as opposed to a reactive approach, when dealing with food safety issues. Professional culinarians have a civic, ethical, and moral responsibility to ensure that the food they handle, cook, and serve is safe to eat. The material in this book is not exhaustive, nor is it intended to replace information that exists in food safety manuals. If the indicated CCPs are observed and followed, however, the opportunity to transmit food-borne illnesses is significantly reduced.

Basic Critical Control Points include the cooling, reheating, holding, and storing of foods as well as the minimum internal temperatures of cooked meat, fish, and eggs. The number-one cause of food-borne illness is improperly cooled food, which is a factor in almost 55 percent of reported incidents. The following CCPs should always be adhered to:

- **Cooling**—Foods should be cooled from 140ºF (60ºC) to 70ºF (21.1ºC) or lower within 2 hours. Cool from 70ºF (21.1ºC) to 41ºF (5ºC) within an additional 4 hours for a total cooling time of 6 hours or less.

- **Reheating**—When reheating foods of any kind, they should be brought to a temperature of 165ºF (73.9ºC) within 2 hours and maintained at that temperature for at least 15 seconds before serving.

- **Hot Holding**—Food to be held hot until needed should maintain a temperature of 140ºF (60ºC) or higher.

- **Cold Storage**—Refrigerate foods at 41ºF (5ºC) or lower.

- **Danger Zone**—A temperature range between 41ºF (5ºC) and 140ºF (60ºC). If foods are held in the danger zone, technically, they should be discarded after 4 hours; however, for safety's sake, we recommend discarding them after 2 hours.

- **Cooking Temperature**—The final internal temperature a particular protein item should reach for at least 15 seconds before serving varies from item to item. The FDA revises these temperatures from time to time; therefore, we recommend that professional culinarians update their knowledge of food safety regularly.

  - Pork, game meats, ground beef, and chopped, flaked, or minced meats or fish are required to reach a minimum internal temperature of 155ºF (68.3ºC) for 15 seconds or more.

- Chicken, other poultry items, and stuffed foods are required to reach a minimum internal temperature of 165ºF (73.9ºC) for 15 seconds or more.

- Eggs, fish, and beef and lamb items that are not ground are required to reach a minimum internal temperature of 145ºF (62.8ºC) for 15 seconds or more.

- Raw fish intended to be served raw, as in sushi, is required to be frozen at –4ºF (-20ºC) for at least 7 days in order to kill parasites that naturally live in the flesh of many species of fish.

Cross contamination is another frequent cause of food-borne illnesses. Good personal hygiene practices significantly reduce the hazards of such transmission. The following practices are highly recommended for all culinarians.

- Use sanitizing solutions on all work surfaces to kill bacteria and viruses that are easily carried from one food to another via knives, cutting boards, door handles, plates, dirty towels, sink faucets, and handles.

- Change food-handling gloves often and wash hands before putting on clean gloves. Gloves should be considered single-use items. Use them for one task and one task only. Contrary to public opinion, gloves do not need to be worn at all times. Gloves should be worn when handling food that will not be cooked further or is served in its raw state. Glove use is also warranted when the food handler has to protect a cut.

- Wash hands often. Handwashing is the single most important step in reducing opportunities of food-borne illnesses from cross contamination. Wash vigorously with soap for a minimum of 20 seconds in warm to hot running water. Nailbrushes should also be used to get under and around nails. Dry hands with clean paper towels or with an air-drying system.

The professionalism, creativity, and imagination of today's American chefs cannot be underestimated. Although American regional cuisine is still relatively young, from a global perspective, the passion and respect for food that exists among our professionals, students, and home gourmets is unsurpassed. We hope you enjoy using this book and its collection of recipes as a complete reference and guide to American cuisine.

Noel Cullen

ON THE CUISINE OF NEW ENGLAND

New England is a distinctive region of America. It is known for the rocky coastline of Maine, the White Mountains of New Hampshire, the rolling green mountains and dairies of Vermont, the fertile farms and orchards of Connecticut. Massachusetts and Rhode Island offer gateway ports, centers of commerce and manufacturing like Boston and Newport. This region is the source from which the rest of our great nation has sprung. From colonial times to the present, New England has been a region known for its food.

Seasons in New England are intense, the changes dramatic. New England's northern latitude makes for a short growing season. When summer herbs and leaf vegetables are scarce, New Englanders focus on root vegetables and winter squash.

From the rocky coast come shellfish of great variety and high quality. The rivers, bays, and oceans produce an abundance of seafood of many varieties. The hills and valleys of New England are home to some of America's oldest fruit orchards and vegetable and grain farms. There is a berry patch in every section of New England. The woodlands are abundant in sugar maples, mushrooms, and fiddlehead ferns. For generations, New Englanders have been masters at making cider, cheese, jams, and preserves—and the list goes on.

Noel Cullen was president of the American Culinary Federation, the nation's oldest and largest association for professional chefs and cooks. He is presently an associate professor at Boston University.

New England

The influence of New England cuisine is significant due to its connection with the arrival of the Pilgrims at Plymouth Rock in 1620. Many consider it the foundation of American regional cuisine. The terrain the Pilgrims found on landing was much different from their home, for which they named New England. The coastline was windswept, rocky, and irregular. Inland, the Pilgrims found dense forests, large rivers and streams, icy lakes, mountains, and fertile valleys. The weather proved a radical departure from what they were used to in England—severe, long, and cold winters, with a much shorter spring-to-fall growing season.

Upon landing in the New World, the colonists immediately realized that survival would be their first concern. Without help from the local Native Americans, survival would not have been possible. The Native Americans taught the colonists how to cultivate beans, squash, and corn as well as how to forage in the forests for fruits, roots, and greens. They also introduced the colonists to the diverse plant and animal life that thrived in the region. Without the methods learned from the Native Americans and techniques such as drying, curing, and smoking brought from the Old World to preserve their food through the winter, the colonists would never have survived their first winter in the New World.

Most of the original colonists were Puritans, known for their strict interpretation of the Bible. Their religious austerity made finding sustenance for the winter even more challenging due to their habit of collecting and using the bare minimum of foods to sustain themselves and their families. This austerity eventually led to the simple but hearty food style we know today as New England cuisine. As time went on, the colonists, even the strict Puritans, could not help but partake in the bountiful variety of meat, fish, seafood, vegetables, and fruits that existed in the region.

Many of the original dishes were cooked in a single pot or baked together in a casserole for practical reasons. Examples of single-pot and casserole dishes adapted from the Native Americans are succotash, chowder, stew, hash, and baked beans. Dishes such as roasted fish and meat were eaten plain, with few accompaniments. Traditional English desserts such as cobbler, pie, pudding, and custard were still served, but ingredients like molasses and maple syrup were substituted for sugar.

The holiday tradition of Thanksgiving has its roots in the New England region. In 1621, Massachusetts governor William Bradford proclaimed this feast as a day of observance. Two schools of thought exist with regard to the origin of Thanksgiving. The first explanation is that it was a feast shared by the colonists with the Native Americans as thanks for their assistance in helping the colonists survive their first winter in the New World. The second explanation is that the feast was a celebration of a military victory over those same Native Americans. Although for many decades the turkey has been the mainstay of the Thanksgiving feast, it is unknown whether or not turkey was actually served during the first Thanksgiving celebration in Massachusetts. Pumpkin pie and cranberries, two products indigenous to New England, are also traditional accompaniments to the Thanksgiving meal. Thanksgiving was declared a national American holiday by Abraham Lincoln in the 1860s, and is now celebrated annually on the third Thursday of November.

A milestone in American history was the Boston Tea Party, which occurred in 1773. The story began in 1767, when the English passed the Townshend Act, which established a three-pence tax on each pound of tea purchased in the American colonies. This tax, considered heavy as well as an infringement of their rights, greatly angered the colonists. In 1773, the British

Parliament passed the Tea Act, which legalized the British right to impose such taxes on the colonists. The Tea Act actually provided the financially unstable British East India Tea Company an exclusive monopoly on selling tea to the colonies at prices so low that they undercut the tea smugglers. This infuriated the colonists and, on the night of 16 December 1773, Paul Revere, Samuel Adams, and their compatriots dressed like Native Americans, boarded three English ships in Boston Harbor, and dumped 342 chests of tea into the water. This defiant act was one of the preemptive moves signaling the start of the War of Independence.

Throughout the war, Americans continued their boycott of tea, perhaps one reason why today Americans prefer coffee instead. After the war ended, American companies established their own relationships with Chinese tea producers. Two such entrepreneurs were George Huntington Hartford and George Gilman, who imported tea from China to the new United States, eliminating the middlemen and offering tea to their customers at a greatly reduced price. Their business grew to be the Great Atlantic and Pacific Tea Company. It later evolved into one of America's first supermarkets, the A&P, which is still in business today.

In sharp contrast to the American supermarket is the story of the country store, which also has its origins in New England. The country store traditionally carried something for everyone—gas, newspapers, flour, homemade jams and preserves—and functioned as a postal service. Penny candy, a favorite among children, is still available in the remaining country stores; however, the candy is now rarely sold for a penny apiece, as the name still implies. Common crackers, a New England tradition, are still made with the original recipe and in the original machines from 1828. They are generally sold in bags stored in large wooden barrels. The main commodity associated with country stores was friendliness. The country store tradition in New England is today being quickly replaced by 24-hour convenience markets.

The American Independence Day holiday, observed on 4 July, commemorates the signing of the Declaration of Independence. This holiday, in both small towns and large cities, typically concludes with a feast shared by the entire community, smaller groups, or individual families. The feast includes informal, homegrown dishes that are straightforward and in season. In New England, coastal communities traditionally serve salmon with a dill mayonnaise accompanied by corn on the cob, new potatoes, and fresh spring green peas; inland, lamb was the traditional dish. However, since the end of World War II in 1945, grilled chicken, steaks, hamburgers, and hot dogs are often substituted throughout the region. Regardless of whether the celebration is by the sea or inland, dessert is usually a summer specialty such as strawberry shortcake, blueberry pie, or slices of watermelon.

In the 1800s, when immigrants, particularly those from Ireland, Italy, and Portugal, began to arrive en masse in New England, the culinary customs they brought from their homelands were incorporated into the local cuisine and cooking style. Single-pot dishes such as meat and seafood stews, which were commonly eaten in Europe, were adapted to the local ingredients. Braised and pickled beef, a mainstay of Britain and Ireland, became the popular dish called New England boiled dinner. Irish immigrants became so enamored with potatoes from America that they took them back to Ireland. Potatoes are still so popular there that many believe that they originated in Ireland, even though that is not the case.

Today, the culinary traditions of New England grow richer and richer as more cultures are integrated and add to the diversity of the cuisine. New influences currently come from the Middle East, the Far East, and Latin America. However, the roots of the region run deep, and Thanksgiving and the Fourth of July remain important traditional holidays celebrated throughout the nation.

Typical New England Ingredients and Dishes

Apple: The first American apple orchard was planted in 1625 by the Reverend William Blaxton. Originally, the only apples growing in the New England region were crab apples. When the Pilgrims planted the apple seeds they had brought with them from Europe, they discovered the resulting varieties were different from the fruits they remembered. Unknown to the Pilgrims, cross-pollination was the cause of the change in the fruit. Over time, experiments with the crossbreeding of apples created thousands of varieties. Some of the first produced in the New England region included Lady in 1628, Roxbury Russet in 1630, Pomme Grise in 1650, Baldwin in 1740, Porter in 1800, Mother in 1844, and Wright in 1875.

Barbecue: Unlike in the Deep South, Tex-Mex, and Central Plains cuisines, to barbecue, a New Englander, means to grill quickly over a fire made from charcoal briquettes, lump charcoal, or hardwood, or simply to cook on a gas or propane grill. In the New England region, the terms *barbecue* and *grill* are used interchangeably.

Blueberry: A small, dark-blue fruit common to the New England region. Maine has a reputation for producing the finest-quality blueberries in America. Blueberries are eaten raw, made into jams and jellies, and used as an ingredient in pies, cobblers, cakes, and breads.

Bluefish: A fish common to the coast of Cape Cod and Nantucket in the summer. This round fish has a blue-silver skin and dark, oily flesh. Bluefish is well suited for smoking, broiling, and sautéing, but it must be used quickly, as its freshness rapidly decreases.

Boston Brown Bread: A colonial bread traditionally served on Saturday evenings with baked beans. Boston brown bread is made from cornmeal, molasses, and both rye and whole wheat flours, and is steamed within a large can or mold.

Chowder: Originally, this dish was served on sea voyages and was made with dried cod, hard biscuits, water, and potatoes, and cooked in a large, black cauldron kettle. On land, clams and milk were typically added to the chowder. Throughout recent history, New England clam chowder has been a creamy soup made with clams, onions, and potatoes. It usually does not include celery, peppers, or other vegetables. Other well-known varieties of clam chowder are Manhattan clam chowder, which has tomatoes and, sometimes, vegetables added to the broth, and Vermont clam chowder, which is usually even more spartan than the New England style and utilizes just a clear broth with clams, onions, and potatoes.

Cider: A hard alcoholic beverage made from fermented apples. It was common until the nineteenth century, when the temperance movement began a campaign against alcohol consumption. Prior to the nineteenth century, cider and beer were consumed instead of the unreliable and sometimes polluted local well water.

Clam: New England clams are available in two main varieties: soft- and hard-shell. The soft-shell clam is best either steamed or fried. Care must be taken because soft-shell clams tend to have more sand than the hard-shell variety. The longneck like siphon on the clams contributes to their nicknames—pisser, gaper, and squirt. Small hard-shell clams are referred to as *littlenecks*, medium-size clams as *cherrystones*, and large-size clams as *quahogs*. These clams are eaten raw, steamed, and in New England clam chowder. Other varieties of clams include the razor clam and the surf or bar clam. Breaded, deep-fried clams are a popular dish in New England and are found at many pubs and restaurants.

Clambake: A New England tradition adopted from the Native Americans. Clams, lobsters, and corn are cooked on top of a seaweed bed over a fire built in a large, stone-lined pit dug in the sand and covered with a tarpaulin cloth. Today, crabs, mussels, fish, chicken, and sausage as well as potatoes and other vegetables are found at a clambake, but the cooking process remains basically the same.

Cobbler: A baked deep-dish fruit pie with a biscuit or pie crust. Cobbler is typically sprinkled with sugar before serving.

Cod: A fish so important to New England that the region's largest cape, Cape Cod, was named after it. The first commercial codfishing started about 1623 just north of Boston, Massachusetts, on Cape Ann. Codfish was important for its trade value. Ships carried salt cod to Africa, picked up slaves and took them to the Caribbean, and, to complete the triangle, carried sugar from the Caribbean to New England. Cod is a bottom-feeding fish and usually weighs between 2½ and 10 pounds.

Common Cracker: Round nuggetlike crackers. Originally from Vermont, the recipe for these crackers is attributed to Charles Cross in 1828, who was said to have made them by hand, distributing them himself from a wagon. Stores that sold cheese provided these crackers to their customers. Today, common crackers are still made in Vermont and can be found in most country stores. They are typically eaten with aged cheddar cheese or crumbled into a bowl of clam chowder.

Concord Grape: A cross between European and native varieties of grapes. The Concord grape is large, deep purple in color, and known for its high juice content. Mainstay American products such as Welch's Grape Juice, grape jelly, and wines produced by Manischewitz and Mogen David all use the Concord grape as the main ingredient. The most popular use of the Concord grape is in the peanut butter and jelly sandwich, usually referred to as a *PB&J*.

Coral: Roe inside the lobster's body that, when cooked, turns from black to orange. The coral is frequently chopped and used in the stuffing for baked lobster or eaten plain with steamed or boiled lobster.

Cranberry: A tart red berry cultivated in New England since the early 1800s. Captain Henry Hall conducted the first experiments for commercial cranberry-growing techniques. He discovered that covering the vines with sand promotes rapid growth. Cape Cod and the island of Nantucket are known as the home of the cranberry.

Cull: A lobster with only one claw.

Fiddlehead Fern: The young, edible, coiled fronds of ferns that emerge during springtime. Fiddlehead ferns are aptly named, as they look like violin scrolls. In New England, they are available for approximately two weeks only, sometimes between April and early May. They are rich green in color and are about 2 inches long and 1½ inches in diameter; their flavor is similar to asparagus. The ferns are usually served as a side dish or used raw in salads. They must be washed carefully before using. Fiddlehead ferns are also found in other parts of the country.

Fig Newton: A cookie that was the product of a machine invented by James Mitchell in 1891. This invention allowed for a machine to pipe out hollow cookie dough while simultaneously filling it with a fig jam. The cookie was a huge success and the company went on to become Nabisco Brands, located in Cambridgeport, Massachusetts. The Fig Newton was named after the nearby town of Newton.

Graham Bread: A bread first made in Massachusetts by a nineteenth-century health advocate named Sylvester Graham. Graham bread was originally made with unsifted whole wheat flour, including the kernel, and mixed with nothing but water and yeast. The product we know today as graham crackers is also named after Sylvester Graham, but it bears little resemblance to the original bread.

Johnnycake: A cornmeal pancake made without a leavening agent, eggs, or butter; typically, it does not even have a sweetener. No one is really sure where or how the name originated, but there are many theories. One version is that the name is a variation on the pronunciation of journey cake or Shawnee cake, while another version has the name deriving from the joniken cake from northern England.

Lobster: An icon of New England cuisine. The Maine lobster is larger than its European cousin and possesses a rich, sweet flavor. In Old English, lobster means spidery creature. From time to time, the Maine lobster molts and sheds its shell, allowing the lobster to increase in weight up to 50 percent more than its original size. It takes the Maine lobster almost five years to grow to 1 pound (.45kg); therefore, large lobsters can sometimes be up to ten years old. When the Pilgrims arrived in New England, they reported lobsters up to 4 feet long and weighing up to 40 pounds. Contrary to popular belief, larger lobsters are not necessarily tougher than smaller lobsters—it is the cooking time that determines whether a lobster will be tender or tough. Lobster is referred by different names in the industry depending on its weight: *chicken lobster* equals 1 pound (.45kg); *heavy chicken* equals 1–1⅛ pounds (.45kg-.51kg); *quarter* equals 1⅛–1¼ pounds (.51kg-.56kg); *select* equals 1¼ –1¾ pounds (.56kg-.79kg); deuce equals 1¾–2 pounds (.79kg-.91kg); *heavy select* equals 2–2¼ pounds (.91kg-1.02kg); *small jumbo* equals 2¼–2½ pounds (1.02kg-1.13kg); and jumbo exceed 2½ pounds (1.13kg). The term *in the rough* is a local term indicating the conditions under which lobster is eaten. Eating lobster in the rough is usually done outdoors on a table with little more than lobster crackers and napkins.

Maple Sugar: A crystallized form of maple syrup. If a recipe calls for maple sugar, maple syrup can be substituted, but use half of the amount indicated in the recipe. (See *maple syrup*.)

Maple Syrup: Prior to the introduction of the honeybee by the Europeans, the only natural sweetener in New England was maple syrup. This sugar is actually the sweet sap from a variety of maple trees indigenous only to North America. Even after molasses and other sugars became available, New Englanders still preferred maple syrup as their sweetener of choice. The best-quality maple syrup is tapped from trees with a lot of leaves on their branches. New England and Canadian trees are known for their high-quality sap and produce the best maple syrup in America. Today, maple syrup is commonly used as a topping for pancakes and waffles. Care should be taken when purchasing maple syrup, as many maple-flavored syrups are available. These flavored syrups typically contain 10 percent or less of actual maple syrup and have little resemblance to pure maple syrup, which is sometimes hard to get and always expensive.

Molasses: A sap product derived during the processing of sugar cane into sugar. Molasses was first imported to America from the West Indies. It is commonly found in two varieties: light and dark. Light molasses is used as a syrup, while the dark or blackstrap molasses is used primarily as an ingredient in recipes.

Mussel: The black mussel found off the coast of New England is the same species as that found in the Mediterranean. A beard is attached to the mussel; this needs to be removed prior to cooking. Depending on the diet of the mussel, the flesh can be tan, coral, or pink in color. Mussels are commonly used in soups, stews, and pasta as well as eaten steamed with a variety of sauces.

Necco Wafers: Created in 1849 by Oliver Chase, the machine used to make these round, wafer-like candies was the first American candy machine. The company, founded in Cambridge, Massachusetts, went on to become the New England Confectionery Company (NECCO) and is still in business today, producing in excess of 4 billion Necco wafers each year.

Oyster: In the days of the colonists, oysters thrived along the east coast of America. However, they were harvested extensively, depleting many of the oyster beds by the early nineteenth century. Recently, due to the efforts of environmentalists and the advancement of technology, many of the oyster beds in New England have been repopulated, and oysters are again available for consumption. Oysters are generally named after the water they live in, such as Cape Cod Wellfleets and Cotuits. Oysters are typically eaten raw or on the half shell in New England. Folklore says eating raw oysters boosts virility.

Paquette: A female lobster with black, fertilized eggs under the tail. These very small eggs are in a cluster and referred to as *berries*. Paquettes have up to 10,000 eggs.

Parker House Roll: A yeast-raised, white-flour, soft roll with a cleft in the center. The commonly told story is that the baker at the restaurant in Boston's Parker House Hotel invented this roll in the mid-nineteenth century.

Periwinkle: A small mollusk with a spiral shell usually measuring less than 1 inch across. Periwinkles attach themselves to piers, pilings, and coastline rocks in either salt or fresh water. These mollusks are referred to as *winkles* and *sea snails*.

Popover: An American variation of English Yorkshire pudding. Popovers are a type of muffin or bread made by pouring a batter of eggs, milk, and flour into butter that has been heated in a muffin pan.

Pumpkin: A hardy squash the colonists learned of from the Native Americans. This squash is one of the foods that helped them survive their first winter in the New World. Pumpkin is also the main ingredient in pumpkin pie, which is a traditional dessert for the Thanksgiving meal.

Scallop: The white and sometimes pink muscle of a bivalve that thrives off the coast and in the bays of New England. Sea scallops are larger than bay scallops and are best cooked quickly by broiling, grilling, or sautéing. These large scallops are well suited for making brochettes. Bay scallops are much smaller, very tender, and have a sweet, delicate flavor; they are popular marinated for salads. Cape Cod and Nantucket Island in Massachusetts are well known for their high-quality bay scallops. Scallops harvested in America typically come removed from the shell and without the roe—unlike how Europeans are used to seeing them. Shell-on scallops, also referred to as *pink scallops,* are starting to become more available in America. They allow the diner to enjoy the roe as well as the muscle.

Scrod: A baby cod or a codfish of another variety weighing less than 2 pounds (.91kg) (see *cod*). The term *scrod* is commonly claimed to have been invented by the Parker House restaurant in an attempt to market their cod dish as made with the youngest, freshest cod available.

Sea Urchin: A spiny black crustacean foraged off of the coast of New England. Sea urchins are not nearly as popular in America as they are in Japan, but their popularity is increasing as more and more people enjoy the sushi trend. The edible part of the sea urchin is the orange roe inside the spiny shell; it has an unusually strong, nutty flavor. Wear gloves while handling sea urchins to protect the hands. The roe can be removed with a spoon after laterally slicing the sea urchin in half with a knife.

Tea Bag: An American innovation started in 1908 by John Sullivan, who began to offer samples of his teas in little hand-sewn cloth sacks.

Toll House Cookie: A chocolate chip cookie first made in 1930 by Ruth Wakefield, who, with her husband, ran the Toll House Inn in Whitman, Massachusetts. The cookies became so popular that the Nestlé Company printed her recipe on every bar of semisweet chocolate they sold. Today, the Toll House cookie is the official state cookie of Massachusetts.

Tomalley: The liver of the lobster, which turns from green to red when cooked. Many New Englanders consider tomalley a delicacy.

Turkey: A large fowl indigenous to the New World. Wild eastern turkeys were domesticated by the Mexicans. The conquistadors took them to Europe; from there, they were taken to other parts of the world. Today's domesticated turkeys are much different than the wild turkeys with which the Pilgrims were familiar, as special breeding produces exceptionally large breasts. Benjamin Franklin once suggested that the turkey be America's national bird.

Vermont Cheddar Cheese: Made in the English tradition, Vermont cheddar cheese is a common product of the typical New England farm. Cheese production in New England originated as a means to store milk in a less perishable form as well as a way to earn extra income by selling the cheese in local country stores. The cheese is usually made in small wheels measuring approximately 18 inches across; it is protected by wax, a dry cloth, and a dry rind. Small businesses in Vermont, such as the Grafton Village Cheese Company, Shelburne Farms, and Crowley Cheese, are recognized leaders in the field of handcrafted, high-quality cheddar cheeses.

Sample Menus from the Cuisine of New England

MENU ONE

Butternut Squash Soup

Clams Casino

Roasted Turkey Roll with Cranberry Sauce · Green Bean Casserole · Glazed Turnips

· Sweet Potato and Horseradish Gratin

MENU TWO

Cod Cakes with Tartar Sauce

Maine Lobster Salad

New England Boiled Dinner with Horseradish Sauce

MENU THREE

New England Clam Chowder

Mesclun Salad with Cranberries, Apples, and Cider Vinaigrette

Shepherd's Pie · Glazed Turnips

Butternut Squash Soup

YIELD: 6 PORTIONS · PORTION SIZE: 8 OUNCES

25 ounces (709g) butternut squash, peeled, cubed

7½ ounces (213g) Granny Smith apples, peeled, cubed

10 fluid ounces (300ml) white chicken stock, prepared (see page 517)

5 fluid ounces (148ml) heavy cream, hot

1¼ ounces (37g) butter

salt, to taste

white pepper, ground, to taste

cinnamon, nutmeg, allspice (optional), to taste

2 tablespoons (30ml) sour cream

Place the squash, apples, and white chicken stock into a saucepot and bring to a boil.

Reduce the heat and simmer apples approximately 45 minutes or until the squash is tender. Do not allow the simmering soup to fall below 140°F (60°C).

Purée the soup in a blender or food processor or, if a coarse texture is desired, a food mill.

Return the soup to the saucepot and bring back to a boil. Reduce the heat to a simmer and add the hot cream and butter.

Season to taste with salt, white pepper, and either cinnamon, nutmeg, or allspice.

SERVING/HOLDING

Carefully ladle the soup into hot soup bowls or plates.

Garnish each portion with a dollop of sour cream in the center of the soup.

Hold the soup at 140° (60°C) or higher.

COOLING/STORING

Pour the remaining soup into smaller metal containers.

Cool the soup from 140°F (60°C) to 70°F (21.1°C) or lower within 2 hours. Cool from 70°F (21.1°C) to 41°F (5°C) within an additional 4 hours for a total cooling time of 6 hours or less.

Cover the soup; label, date, and store under refrigeration at 41°F (5°C) or lower.

New England Clam Chowder

2 ounces (60g) bacon, cut into small dice

4 ounces (120g) onions, cut into small dice

1½ ounces (45g) all-purpose flour

2 cups (480ml) milk, scalded

2 cups (480ml) clam juice

1½ pounds (720g) potatoes, peeled, cut into small dice

salt, to taste

black pepper, ground, to taste

2 cups (480ml) clams, chopped

½ cup (120ml) light cream

parsley, chopped, as needed

CHEF TIPS *New England clam chowder is a cream soup made with clams, onions, and potatoes. It does not include celery, peppers, or other vegetables commonly added in regions outside New England.*

Cook the bacon in a saucepot over medium heat until the fat is fully rendered and the bacon is crisp.

Add the onions to the bacon fat and sauté over medium-high heat for approximately 2–3 minutes or until they become translucent.

Stir in the flour and cook over low heat for 5 minutes while stirring frequently.

Add hot milk and clam juice to incorporate.

Add the potatoes.

Season to taste with salt and black pepper.

Bring to a boil, reduce the heat, cover, and simmer for approximately 10-15 minutes or until the potatoes are tender. Do not allow the simmering soup to fall below 140°F (60°C).

Add the chopped clams and light cream. Cook over medium heat for 5 additional minutes or until the potatoes are tender and the clams are cooked.

SERVING/HOLDING

Carefully ladle the chowder into hot soup bowls or plates.

Garnish each portion of soup by sprinkling with chopped parsley.

🥣 **Hold** the chowder at 140°F (60°C) or higher.

COOLING/STORING

Pour the remaining soup into smaller metal containers.

Cool the soup from 140°F (60°C) to 70°F (21.1°C) or lower within 2 hours. Cool from 70°F (21.1°C) to 41°F (5°C) within an additional 4 hours for a total cooling time of 6 hours or less.

Cover the soup; label, date, and store under refrigeration at 41°F (5°C) or lower.

Cod Cakes with Tartar Sauce

YIELD: 6 PORTIONS · PORTION SIZE: 6 OUNCES

8 ounces (240g) codfish fillets

12 ounces (360g) mashed potatoes

1 large egg

salt, to taste

white pepper, ground, to taste

vegetable oil for frying, as needed

6 leaves green leaf lettuce

1 lemon, cut into 6 wedges

1 plum tomato, cut into 6 wedges

12 ounces (360g) tartar sauce (recipe follows)

CHEF TIPS *You may want to add some powdered instant potatoes to the mix if the mashed potatoes are too moist.*

Poach the cod in simmering liquid until it becomes tender and reaches a minimum internal temperature of 145°F (62.8°C) for at least 15 seconds.

Drain the fish and transfer it to a bowl.

Break the fish into pieces and cool from 140°F (60°C) to 70°F (21.1°C) or lower within 2 hours. Cool from 70°F (21.1°C) to 41°F (5°C) within an additional 4 hours for a total cooling time of 6 hours or less.

Combine the mashed potatoes, egg, and reserved cod.

Season to taste with salt and white pepper.

Shape the mixture into cakes, each approximately 2 ounces (60g) in weight and ¾ to1 inch (1.905-2.54cm) thick.

Heat the vegetable oil in a sautoir pan and pan-fry the patties on both sides until they are golden brown and reach a minimum internal temperature of 165°F (73.9°C) for at least 15 seconds.

Drain the cakes on absorbent paper towel.

SERVING/HOLDING

Place a green lettuce leaf on the center of each plate.

Place 2 codfish cakes on the plate.

Garnish each portion with a lemon wedge and a tomato wedge.

Serve the cakes with approximately 2 ounces (57g) tartar sauce on the lettuce liner.

Hold the codfish cakes at 140°F (60°C) or higher.

COOLING/STORING

Cool the codfish cakes from 140°F (60°C) to 70°F (21.1°C) or lower within 2 hours. Cool from 70°F (21.1°C) to 41°F (5°C) within an additional 4 hours for a total cooling time of 6 hours or less.

Cover the codfish cakes and tartar sauce; label, date, and store under refrigeration at 41°F (5°C) or lower.

TARTAR SAUCE

YIELD: 6 PORTIONS · PORTION SIZE: 2 OUNCES

8 ounces (240g) mayonnaise, prepared

¾ fluid ounces (22ml) lemon juice

1½ ounces (45g) dill pickles, finely chopped

1½ ounces (45g) capers, chopped

1 ounce (30g) onions, finely chopped

1½ large eggs, hard-boiled, chopped

salt, to taste

white pepper, ground, to taste

Worcestershire sauce, to taste

Tabasco sauce, to taste

Mix the mayonnaise, lemon juice, dill pickles, capers, onions, and hard-boiled eggs in a bowl.

Blend until all of the ingredients are thoroughly incorporated.

Season to taste with salt, white pepper, Worcestershire sauce, and Tabasco sauce.

Chill well before using.

Hold under refrigeration at 41°F (5°C) or lower.

COOLING/STORING

Cover the sauce; label, date, and store under refrigeration at 41°F (5°C) or lower.

Maine Lobster Salad

YIELD: 6 PORTIONS · PORTION SIZE: 6 OUNCES

4 ounces (120g) mayonnaise, prepared

½ fluid ounce (15ml) lemon juice

3 ounces (90g) celery, minced

1 ounce (30g) green onions, minced

salt, to taste

black pepper, ground to taste

1 pound (480g) lobster meat, cooked, drained

12 leaves green leaf lettuce

1 lemon, cut into 6 wedges

2 plum tomatoes, cut into 6 wedges each

6 lobster claws, cooked

CHEF TIPS *You can substitute crabmeat for the lobster meat.*

Combine the mayonnaise, lemon juice, celery, and green onions in a bowl.

Season to taste with salt and black pepper.

Cut the cooked lobster meat into small dice, taking care to remove and discard any bits of shell or cartilage. Carefully fold the lobster meat into the mayonnaise mixture.

Allow the salad to chill for at least 30 minutes under refrigeration at 41°F (5°C) or lower until needed.

SERVING/HOLDING

Place 2 lettuce leaves in the shape of a cup in the center of each chilled plate.

Carefully scoop approximately 4 ounces (113g) of the lobster salad into the center of each lettuce liner.

Garnish each portion of salad with 1 lemon wedge and 2 tomato wedges, shaped into leaves.

Remove lobster claws from their shells and place one on top of each mound of salad.

Hold under refrigeration at 41°F (5°C) or lower.

COOLING/STORING

Cover the salad and garnishes; label, date, and store under refrigeration at 41°F (5°C) or lower.

Clams Casino

YIELD: 6 PORTIONS · PORTION SIZE: 6 OUNCES

4 ounces (120g) bacon, diced

4 ounces (120g) onions, diced

4 ounces (120g) red bell peppers, diced

4 ounces (120g) green bell peppers, diced

6 ounces (180ml) butter, melted

6 ounces (180g) bread crumbs, dried

salt, to taste

black pepper, ground, to taste

Worcestershire sauce, to taste

CLAMS

2½ dozen cherrystone clams

1 lemon, cut into 6 wedges

CHEF TIPS *You may want to top the clam with a piece of bacon when broiling.*

Cook the bacon over medium heat until the fat is completely rendered and the bacon is crisp.

Add the onions and peppers to the bacon and sauté over medium-high heat for approximately 2–3 minutes or until the onions become translucent and the peppers are tender.

Add melted butter and bread crumbs.

Season the breadcrumb mixture to taste with salt, black pepper, and Worcestershire sauce.

Cool the breadcrumb mixture from 140°F (60°C) to 70°F (21.1°C) or lower within 2 hours. Cool from 70°F (21.1°C) to 41°F (5°C) within an additional 4 hours for a total cooling time of 6 hours or less.

Open the clams with a clam knife and discard the top half of the shell. Loosen the meat from the lower shell with the clam knife.

Place the clams on a baking sheet and top each clam with a tablespoon of the breadcrumb mixture.

Broil the clams until they are thoroughly cooked, the breadcrumb mixture is crisp, and the clams reach a minimum internal temperature of 145°F (62.8°C) for at least 15 seconds.

SERVING/HOLDING

Serve 5 clams on each hot plate or sizzle platter.

Garnish each portion with a lemon wedge.

Hold the clams at 140°F (60°C) or higher.

COOLING/STORING

Cool the clams from 140°F (60°C) to a temperature of 70°F (21.1°C) or lower within 2 hours. Cool from 70°F (21.1°C) to 41°F (5°C) within an additional 4 hours for a total cooling time of 6 hours or less.

Cover the clams; label, date, and store under refrigeration at 41°F (5°C) or lower.

Mesclun Salad with Cranberries, Apples, and Cider Vinaigrette

YIELD: 6 PORTIONS · PORTION SIZE: 6 OUNCES

VINAIGRETTE

9 fluid ounces (270ml) vegetable oil

3 fluid ounces (90ml) cider vinegar

salt, to taste

black pepper, ground, to taste

SALAD

1 pound (480g) mixed baby lettuce

2 ounces (60g) dried cranberries

1 ounce (30g) carrots, cut into julienne

3 ounces (90g) Granny Smith apples, peeled, cored, sliced

2 ounces (60g) almonds, slivered, toasted

Prepare the vinaigrette by briskly whisking the oil and vinegar together in a bowl.

Season the dressing to taste with salt and black pepper.

Place the baby greens in the bowl and toss until the lettuce is thoroughly coated.

Add the cranberries and carrots and toss together.

SERVING/HOLDING

Carefully place a portion of the dressed salad into the center of each chilled plate.

Toss the sliced apples in the bowl with the residual dressing left from the baby greens.

Place 2–3 apple slices in a fan shape adjacent to the baby lettuce.

Garnish each salad by sprinkling toasted almonds on top.

Hold under refrigeration at 41°F (5°C) or lower.

COOLING/STORING

Cover the salad and dressing; label, date, and store under refrigeration at 41°F (5°C) or lower.

Baked Stuffed Maine Lobster

YIELD: 6 PORTIONS · PORTION SIZE: 8 OUNCES

3 live chicken lobsters, 1¼ pounds (591g) each

3 ounces (90g) onions, cut into small dice

3–5 ounces (90–150g) butter, melted

3 cups (720g) breadcrumbs, fresh

2 ounces (60m) sherry

salt, to taste

pepper, to taste

½ teaspoon (2g) paprika

CHEF TIPS *Other seafood items such as scallops, shrimp, or extra lobster meat are sometimes added to the stuffing.*

Split the live lobsters in half with a sharp, pointed knife from head to tail. Lay the lobsters flat and remove the intestinal vein, stomach, and tomalley from the body. If desired, reserve the tomalley for use in the stuffing under refrigeration at 41°F (5°C) or lower until needed.

Add the onions to 1 tablespoon of melted butter and sauté over medium-high heat for approximately 2–3 minutes or until the onions become translucent.

Mix the breadcrumbs, onions, butter, and remaining ingredients in a bowl. Add tomalley, if desired.

Toss until the ingredients are thoroughly incorporated.

Generously fill the cavity of the lobsters with the stuffing and place them on a baking sheet.

Bake the lobsters in a preheated 450°F (232.2°C) oven for approximately 15–20 minutes or until they reach a minimum internal temperature of 145°F (62.8°C) for at least 15 seconds.

SERVING/HOLDING

Serve 1 stuffed lobster on each hot plate or sizzle platter.

Garnish each portion with a lemon wedge wrapped in cheesecloth.

Hold the stuffed lobsters at 140°F (60°C) or higher.

Cool the stuffed lobster from 140°F (60°C) to 70°F (21.1°C) or lower within 2 hours. Cool from 70°F (21.1°C) to 41°F (5°C) within an additional 4 hours for a total cooling time of 6 hours or less.

Cover the stuffed lobsters; label, date, and store under refrigeration at 41°F (5°C) or lower.

New England Boiled Dinner with Horseradish Sauce

YIELD: 6 PORTIONS · PORTION SIZE: 12 OUNCES

48 ounces (1.4kg) corned beef, trimmed

2 tablespoons (30g) pickling spice

3 cloves garlic, peeled

14 ounces (420g) or 12 small white onions, peeled

14 ounces (420g) or 12 small turnips

24 ounces (720g) or 12 new red potatoes, peeled

16 ounces (480g) carrots, peeled, cut into large dice

24 ounces (720g) green cabbage, cut into 4-ounce (113g) wedges

1½ tablespoons (22g) parsley, chopped

2 fluid ounces (60ml) horseradish sauce (recipe follows)

Place the corned beef in a large stockpot with enough cold water to cover the beef by 1 inch (2.54cm).

Tie the pickling spice and garlic in a cheesecloth bag and add to the cold water. Bring to a boil, lower the heat, cover, and simmer very gently for 2–3 hours or until the beef is fork-tender and reaches a minimum internal temperature of 155°F (68.3°C) for at least 15 seconds.

Do not allow the simmering beef to fall below 140°F (60°C).

Approximately 30 minutes before the meat is done, add the onions, turnips, potatoes, and carrots.

Continue simmering for approximately 20–25 minutes or until they are almost tender.

Remove the corned beef, wrap it in foil (along with any vegetables that are also done), and reserve at 140°F (60°C) or higher until needed.

Add the cabbage and cook for approximately 10 minutes or until the cabbage and the remainder of the vegetables are tender.

Drain the vegetables from the liquid and reserve at 140°F (60°C) or higher until needed.

SERVING/HOLDING

Slice the corned beef perpendicular to the meat's natural grain into ¼-inch (.64cm) slices.

Serve approximately 7 ounces (198g) of corned beef on each hot plate.

Decoratively place 2 onions, 2 turnips, 2 potatoes, 3 or 4 pieces of carrot, and 1 wedge of cabbage on each plate.

Garnish each portion by sprinkling chopped parsley on top.

Serve each portion with a side dish of horseradish sauce.

Hold the corned beef and vegetables at 140°F (60°C) or higher.

COOLING/STORING

Cool the corned beef and vegetables from 140°F (60°C) to 70°F (21.1°C) or lower within 2 hours. Cool from 70°F (21.1°C) to 41°F (5°C) within an additional 4 hours for a total cooling time of 6 hours or less.

Cover the corned beef and vegetables; label, date, and store under refrigeration at 41°F (5°C) or lower.

HORSERADISH SAUCE

YIELD: 6 PORTIONS · PORTION SIZE: 2 OUNCES

1 ounce (30g) butter

4 ounces (120g) onion, finely chopped

1½ ounces (45g) all-purpose flour

16 fluid ounces (480ml) milk, warm

1½ teaspoon (7g) salt

½ teaspoon (3g) dry mustard

¼ teaspoon (1g) white pepper, ground

1 tablespoon (15g) horseradish root, peeled, grated

CHEF TIPS *The sauce can also be made cold with mayonnaise, horseradish, sour cream, and parsley.*

Melt the butter in a medium saucepan over medium-high heat.

Add the onions and cook for approximately 5 minutes or until they become tender and translucent.

Stir in the flour and cook over low heat, stirring frequently, for 3 minutes.

Reduce the heat to low and gradually whisk in the warm milk.

Bring to a boil, reduce the heat, and simmer.

Add the salt, dry mustard, and white pepper and continue to cook over low heat, stirring frequently, for 5 more minutes or until the sauce has thickened.

Remove from the heat and stir in the grated horseradish.

SERVING/HOLDING

Hold the sauce at 140°F (60°C) or higher.

COOLING/STORING

Cool the sauce from 140°F (60°C) to 70°F (21.1°C) or lower within 2 hours. Cool from 70°F (21.1°C) to 41°F (5°C) within an additional 4 hours for a total cooling time of 6 hours or less.

Cover the sauce; label, date, and store under refrigeration at 41°F (5°C) or lower.

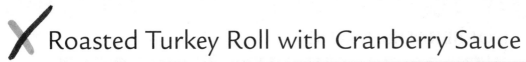

Roasted Turkey Roll with Cranberry Sauce

3 pounds (1.4kg) turkey breast lobe, skinless

salt, to taste

black pepper, to taste

4½ ounces (130ml) egg whites

4 ounces (120g) toasted croutons

¾ ounce (21g) fresh sage, chopped

¾ ounce (21g) fresh parsley, chopped

1 ounce (30g) fresh thyme, chopped

turkey bones, as needed

8 ounces (240g) onions, cut into julienne

4 ounces (120g) celery, cut into julienne

4 ounces (120g) carrots, cut into julienne

2 ounces (60g) butter

16 fluid ounces (473ml) white stock, prepared (see page 517)

2 tablespoons (30g) cornstarch

24 ounces (720g) cranberry sauce (recipe follows)

Sweat the vegetables in the butter, add the herbs and croutons and cool. Add the egg whites and mix.

Butterfly the turkey breast into a rectangle shape and place it between two pieces of parchment paper or plastic wrap.

Pound the breast gently with a tenderizing mallet until it is approximately ¼ inch (.64cm) thick.

Season the meat to taste with salt, black pepper and herbs. Place vegetable mixture neatly in center.

Roll the turkey breast to form a tight 3–4-inch (7.62cm-10.16cm) roll. Truss the roll as you would a roast.

Season the turkey roll to taste with salt and black pepper.

Place the roasting pan in a preheated 450°F (232.2°C) oven roast for 15 minutes to sear the top. Turn the roll and cook an additional 15 minutes to sear the other side.

Reduce the temperature to 350°F (176.7°C). Cook for approximately 30–40 minutes, until the turkey reaches a minimum internal temperature of 165°F (73.9°C) for at least 15 seconds.

Remove the turkey from the oven and allow to rest for at least 10 minutes before slicing at 140°F (60°C) or higher.

Deglaze the pan with white stock. Combine cornstarch with water to create slurry. Reserve at 140°F (60°C) or higher for use.

Remove from heat and strain the juice from the roasting pan.

SERVING/HOLDING

Slice the turkey roll into ¼ inch (.64cm) slices.

Place 3 slices of the turkey in the center of each hot plate.

Carefully ladle approximately 1 ounce (15ml) of deglazed liquid over half the turkey and around the plate.

Serve each portion with approximately 4 ounces (120ml) of cranberry sauce.

Hold the turkey and deglazed liquid at 140°F (60°C) or higher.

Hold the cranberry sauce under refrigeration at 41°F (5°C) or lower.

COOLING/STORING

Cool the turkey and deglazed liquid from 140°F (60°C) to 70°F (21.1°C) or lower within 2 hours. Cool from 70°F (21.1°C) to 41°F (5°C) within an additional 4 hours for a total cooling time of 6 hours or less.

Cover the turkey, deglazed liquid, and cranberry sauce; label, date, and store under refrigeration at 41°F (5°C) or lower.

CRANBERRY SAUCE

YIELD: 6 PORTIONS · PORTION SIZE: 4 OUNCES

6 ounces (180g) sugar

1½ fluid ounces (45ml) orange juice

3 fluid ounces (90ml) water

12 ounces (360g) cranberries

½ teaspoon (2g) cinnamon, ground

1½ teaspoons (7g) orange zest

Combine the sugar, orange juice, and water in a saucepan and bring to a boil.

Add the cranberries and ground cinnamon. Reduce the heat and simmer for approximately 15–20 minutes or until the cranberries burst.

Add the orange zest and continue to simmer for 5 additional minutes or until the sauce is reduced to the desired consistency.

Remove from the heat.

Cool the cranberry sauce from 140°F (60°C) to 70°F (21.1°C) or lower within 2 hours. Cool from 70°F (21.1°C) to 41°F (5°C) within an additional 4 hours for a total cooling time of 6 hours or less.

SERVING/HOLDING

Reserve the cranberry sauce under refrigeration at 41°F (5°C) or lower.

COOLING/STORING

Cover the cranberry sauce; label, date, and store under refrigeration at 41°F (5°C) or lower.

Shepherd's Pie

15 fluid ounces (450ml) lamb stock, prepared (see page 515)

1 ounce (30g) dried wild mushrooms

1½ pounds (720g) new red potatoes, cut into medium dice

4 cloves garlic, minced

8 ounces (240g) sweet butter

1½ ounces (45ml) crème fraîche

1 fluid ounce (30ml) heavy cream

1 ounce (30g) green onions, finely chopped

1½ tablespoons (22g) parsley, chopped

salt, to taste

black pepper, ground, to taste

4 ounces (120g) onions, chopped

6 ounces (180g) button mushrooms, sliced

1½ pounds (720g) ground lamb

1 ounce (30g) all-purpose flour

4 fluid ounces (120ml) dry sherry

1 teaspoon (5g) dried thyme

15 ounces (450g) corn kernels

CHEF TIPS

1. *Crème fraîche is a cultured cream made with heavy cream and buttermilk. It is available commercially in most specialty food markets. To make crème fraîche from scratch, mix 3 quarts (2.8L) of heavy cream with 1 cup (237ml) of buttermilk and place in a sterilized jar. Seal well and allow to rest at room temperature for 24–36 hours, then refrigerate the crème fraîche until needed. If the jar is not properly sterilized, the resulting product is potentially hazardous and can result in an outbreak of foodborne illness.*

2. *If a milder flavor is desired, substitute beef stock and ground beef for the lamb stock and ground lamb.*

3. *Some chefs prefer mashed as a topping rather than diced potatoes.*

Bring the lamb stock to a boil and add the wild mushrooms. Remove from the heat and let rest for 30 minutes.

Place the potatoes and garlic in a large saucepan and cover with water. Bring to a boil. Cook until the potatoes are tender, remove from the heat, and mash until smooth.

Stir into the mashed potatoes, one-third of the butter, crème fraîche, heavy cream, green onions, and parsley. Mix until the ingredients are thoroughly incorporated.

Season the potatoes to taste with salt and black pepper.

Hold the potatoes at 140°F (60°C) or higher until needed.

Heat half of the remaining butter in a sautoir pan over medium-high heat and sauté the onions and button mushrooms for 3–4 minutes or until the onions become translucent.

Add the ground lamb and continue to cook until it is browned and reaches a minimum internal temperature of 165°F (73.9°C) for at least 15 seconds.

Strain the wild mushrooms from the beef stock and finely chop. Reserve the stock and mushrooms until needed.

Sprinkle the flour over the lamb mixture and stir until incorporated.

Cook while stirring over medium heat for 3 minutes.

Add the sherry and the reserved wild mushrooms and stock.

Continue to cook over medium heat, stirring, until the mixture thickens slightly.

Add the thyme. Season to taste with salt and black pepper.

Melt the remaining butter in another sautoir pan over medium heat and add the corn kernels. Sauté the corn for approximately 5 minutes or until it is tender. Season to taste with salt and black pepper.

Spoon the lamb mixture into a lightly greased baking dish or casserole and spread the mixture evenly on the bottom of the dish.

Spread the sautéed corn kernels over the lamb.

Spread the potatoes over the corn kernels. Bake in a preheated 350°F (176.7°C) oven for 45 minutes or until lightly browned on top and until the casserole reaches a minimum internal temperature of 165°F (73.9°C) for at least 15 seconds.

SERVING/HOLDING

Serve the shepherd's pie by carefully spooning approximately 12 ounces (340g) onto the center of each hot plate. Be careful to spoon deep to the bottom of the casserole to ensure that all of the layers are served with each portion.

Hold the pie at 140°F (60°C) or higher.

COOLING/STORING

Cool the shepherd's pie from 140°F (60°C) to 70°F (21.1°C) or lower within 2 hours. Cool from 70°F (21.1°C) to 41°F (5°C) within an additional 4 hours for a total cooling time of 6 hours or less.

Cover the shepherd's pie; label, date, and store under refrigeration at 41°F (5°C) or lower.

Baked Acorn Squash

YIELD: 6 PORTIONS · PORTION SIZE: 4 OUNCES

1½ pounds (720g) acorn squash

½ teaspoon (2g) salt

¼ teaspoon (1g) black pepper, ground

2 ounces (60ml) butter, melted

3–4 drops lemon juice

2 fluid ounces (60ml) cold water

3¾ ounces (113g) light brown sugar

Wash the acorn squash and slice lengthwise into 6 large wedges.

Remove and discard the seeds from the squash.

Place the squash wedges on a baking sheet or in a roasting pan and sprinkle with salt and black pepper.

Combine the butter, lemon juice, and water in a bowl and brush the inside of each piece of squash with the mixture until coated thoroughly.

Sprinkle the inside of each piece with brown sugar.

Put a small amount of water in the bottom of the cooking pan. Tent with aluminum foil, and bake the squash in a preheated 350°F (176.7°C) oven for approximately 20–30 minutes or until tender. Remove foil and brush with pan drippings until brown.

SERVING/HOLDING

Hold the squash at 140°F (60°C) or higher.

COOLING/STORING

Cool the squash from 140°F (60°C) to 70°F (21.1°C) or lower within 2 hours. Cool from 70°F (21.1°C) to 41°F (5°C) within an additional 4 hours for a total cooling time of 6 hours or less.

Cover the squash; label, date, and store under refrigeration at 41°F (5°C) or lower.

Green Bean Casserole

YIELD: 6 PORTIONS · PORTION SIZE: 6 OUNCES

CASSEROLE

1½ pounds (720g) green beans, washed, stems and tips removed

1½ ounces (45g) butter

3 ounces (90g) mushrooms, sliced

salt, to taste

black pepper, ground, to taste

FRIED ONIONS

2¼ ounces (68g) onions, thinly sliced

1½ cups (360g) all-purpose flour

black pepper, ground, to taste

salt, to taste

Cook the green beans in boiling salted water until tender. Shock the beans in an ice-water bath and reserve under refrigeration at 41°F (5°C) or lower until needed.

To prepare the fried onions, soak the onions in ice water for 1 hour.

Drain the onions thoroughly and toss in flour, pepper, and salt mixture until they are thoroughly coated.

Shake off the excess flour and deep-fry in a preheated 375°F (190.6°C) fryer until they are golden brown and crispy.

Hold the onions at 140°F (60°C) or higher until needed.

Melt the 1½ ounces (45g) butter in a pan and briefly sauté the mushrooms over medium-high heat until they are tender and thoroughly heated.

Add the green beans and toss until incorporated and heated thoroughly.

SERVING/HOLDING

Place the beans and mushrooms into a casserole dish.

Top with deep-fried onions and serve immediately.

Hold the beans and onions at 140°F (60°C) or higher.

Cool the beans and onions from 140°F (60°C) to 70°F (21.1°C) or lower within 2 hours. Cool from 70°F (21.1°C) to 41°F (5°C) within an additional 4 hours for a total cooling time of 6 hours or less.

Cover the beans and onions; label, date, and store under refrigeration at 41°F (5°C) or lower.

Glazed Turnips

YIELD: 6 PORTIONS · PORTION SIZE: 4 OUNCES

18 ounces (540g) turnips, cut in large dice

4 fluid ounces (120ml) chicken stock, prepared

2 ounces (60g) butter

salt, to taste

black pepper, ground, to taste

1 teaspoon (5g) sugar (optional)

COOKING

Place the turnips in sauté pan with stock and butter.

Cover the pan, stir occasionally, and simmer until liquid has evaporated (10–15 minutes).

Season to taste with salt and black pepper. Add sugar if needed, and stir until incorporated.

SERVING/HOLDING

Hold the turnips at 140°F (60°C) or higher.

COOLING/STORING

Cool the turnips from 140°F (60°C) to 70°F (21.1°C) or lower within 2 hours. Cool from 70°F (21.1°C) to 41°F (5°C) within an additional 4 hours for a total cooling time of 6 hours or less.

Cover the turnips; label, date, and store under refrigeration at 41°F (5°C) or lower.

Boston Baked Beans

YIELD: 6 PORTIONS · PORTION SIZE: 4 OUNCES

1 pound (480g) dried navy beans

½ pound (240g) salt pork

5 ounces (150g) onions, cut into medium dice

32 fluid ounces (960ml) water

4 cloves garlic, minced

8 ounces (227g) tomato concassée

1 teaspoon (5g) salt

2 teaspoons (10g) black pepper, ground

4 tablespoons (60g) dry mustard

2 ounces (60g) maple sugar

4 ounces (120g) molasses

2 bay leaves

3 tablespoons (44ml) cider vinegar

Cover the beans with cold water and soak overnight under refrigeration at 41°F (5°C) or lower.

Drain the beans and sort, discarding off-colored and broken beans.

Divide the salt pork in half.

Remove and discard the rind from one half of the salt pork and cut it into into ½-inch (1.27cm) squares.

Cut the other half of the salt pork into ¾–1-inch (1.9cm–2.54cm) thick strips with the rind attached.

Line the bottom of an earthenware pot or casserole dish with the squares of salt pork and the onions. Place the soaked beans on top of the salt pork and onions.

Bring the water to a boil in a saucepan and add the remaining ingredients.

CHEF TIPS *The colonists first learned to cook dried beans from the Native Americans, who depended on beans as a food staple The Native Americans slow-cooked beans with maple sugar and bear fat inside deer hides in underground pits. As the dish evolved, the beans were cooked with salt pork and molasses in a bean pot, often overnight. The Puritans' belief in minimal work on the Sabbath led to the widespread practice of making beans on Saturday for consumption on Sunday. Another interesting way to serve beans is to rebake them inside a baby pumpkin or acorn squash.*

It is traditional to serve Boston brown bread with beans. Many types of beans can be used for Boston baked beans. The authentic bean is the pea bean, although some believe it is the Jacob's cattle, yellow eye, soldier's, navy, or great northern bean. Once cooked, all the types of beans mentioned have similar results. This recipe was tested using navy beans, but it works with any small dried white bean. Maple syrup can be substituted for maple sugar, but only half the quantity should be used.

Reduce the heat and simmer for 1 minute.

Mix well and pour the mixture over the beans in the casserole dish.

Score the strips of salt pork crosswise, approximately every inch (2.54cm), without cutting through the strips, to prevent the strips from curling while cooking.

Place the strips on top of the beans and liquid. Cover the pot and place in a preheated 250°F (121.1°C) oven.

Bake the beans for approximately 5 hours. Check the beans occasionally (first after 2 hours, then every hour), to be sure the liquid is just barely covering the beans. Add more water as needed.

After 5 hours, remove the cover from the casserole and cook for an additional 1 hour.

Remove and discard the strips of salt pork and stir the beans before serving.

SERVING/HOLDING

Hold the beans at 140°F (60°C) or above.

COOLING/STORING

Cool the beans from 140°F (60°C) to 70°F (21.1°C) or lower within 2 hours. Cool from 70°F (21.1°C) to 41°F (5°C) within an additional 4 hours for a total cooling time of 6 hours or less.

Cover the beans; label, date, and store under refrigeration at 41°F (5°C) or lower.

Corn Bread

YIELD: 6 PORTIONS · PORTION SIZE: 4 OUNCES

6 ounces (180g) yellow cornmeal

6 ounces (180g) all-purpose flour

2¼ ounces (68g) sugar

¾ teaspoon (4g) salt

¾ ounce (21g) baking powder

3 ounces (90g) sweet butter, melted

7½ fluid ounces (225ml) milk

3 large eggs, beaten

butter, softened, as needed

Place cornmeal, flour, sugar, salt, and baking powder in a mixer and mix thoroughly with the paddle attachment.

Add the butter, milk, and eggs and mix for 1 minute on low speed until a smooth batter forms.

Pour the batter into a small, well-greased (with softened butter) baking pan.

Bake in a preheated 400°F (204.4°C) oven for 25–30 minutes or until the corn bread is golden brown and reaches a minimum internal temperature of 145°F (62.8°C) for at least 15 seconds. Test for doneness by inserting a skewer or knife into the bread. If it comes out clean and free of batter, the bread is done.

SERVING/HOLDING

Wait approximately 5 minutes before unmolding.

Cut the corn bread into pieces and serve warm, or cool and use in other preparations.

Hold the cornbread at 140°F (60°C) or higher.

COOLING/STORING

Cool the cornbread from 140°F (60°C) to 70°F (21.1°C) or lower within 2 hours. Cool from 70°F (21.1°C) to 41°F (5°C) within an additional 4 hours for a total cooling time of 6 hours or less.

Cover the corn bread; label, date, and store under refrigeration at 41°F (5°C) or lower.

Rhode Island Johnnycakes

12 ounces (360g) yellow cornmeal

4 ounces (120g) sugar

1 teaspoon (5g) baking soda

2 teaspoons (10g) cream of tartar

salt, to taste

16 fluid ounces (480ml) buttermilk

1 large egg, beaten

2 tablespoons (30ml) molasses

2 tablespoons (30ml) butter, melted

Preheat the griddle or small sauté pan.

Sift the cornmeal, sugar, baking soda, cream of tartar, and salt together in a mixing bowl and make a well in the center.

Combine the buttermilk, egg, molasses, and butter and pour into the well made in the dry ingredients.

Mix until a smooth batter forms.

Lightly grease the griddle with softened butter.

Pour the mixture on the griddle in 3-ounce (90g)quantities.

Cook johnnycakes on one side for 2½ minutes, flip and, cook for 2½ minutes longer, until they reach a minimum internal temperature of 145°F (62.8°C) for at least 15 seconds.

SERVING/HOLDING

Hold the johnnycakes at 140°F (60°C) or higher.

COOLING/STORING

Cool the johnnycakes from 140°F (60°C) to 70°F (21.1°C) or lower within 2 hours. Cool from 70°F (21.1°C) to 41°F (5°C) within an additional 4 hours for a total cooling time of 6 hours or less.

Cover the johnnycakes; label, date, and store under refrigeration at 41°F (5°C) or lower.

Sweet Potato and Horseradish Gratin

YIELD: 6 PORTIONS · PORTION SIZE: 6 OUNCES

2¼ pounds (1kg) sweet potatoes

1½ cups (360ml) heavy cream

3 ounces (90g) horseradish root, peeled, grated

¾ teaspoon (4g) nutmeg, ground

salt, to taste

black pepper, ground, to taste

1 cup breadcrumbs, dried

1 ounce (30g) butter, softened

Bake the sweet potatoes in a preheated 400°F (204.4°C) oven for approximately 45 minutes or until tender.

Cut potatoes in half and scoop out interior; reserve.

Heat the cream in a heavy-bottomed saucepan over medium heat and simmer for approximately 10 minutes or until the volume of liquid reduces by half.

Remove cream from the heat and stir in the horseradish and nutmeg.

Season to taste with salt and black pepper.

Combine horseradish cream and sweet potatoes.

Spread mixture into baking dish or casserole.

Cover with breadcrumbs and dot with softened butter.

Bake in a preheated 350°F (176.7°C) oven for 30 minutes or until golden and reaches a minimum internal temperature of 165°F (73.9°C) for at least 15 seconds.

SERVING/HOLDING

Hold the sweet potato casserole at 140°F (60°C) or higher.

COOLING/STORING

Cool the sweet potato casserole from 140°F (60°C) to 70°F (21.1°C) or lower within 2 hours. Cool from 70°F (21.1°C) to 41°F (5°C) within an additional 4 hours for a total cooling time of 6 hours or less.

Cover the sweet potato casserole; label, date, and store under refrigeration at 41°F (5°C) or lower.

Popovers

YIELD: 6 PORTIONS · PORTION SIZE: 2 OUNCES

vegetable oil, as needed

8 ounces (240g) all-purpose flour

½ tablespoon (7g) salt

8 fluid ounces (240ml) milk

1 fluid ounce (30ml) butter, melted

3 large eggs

CHEF TIPS *Popovers are a form of Yorkshire pudding. They are often made with rendered beef fat instead of the melted butter called for in this recipe.*

Oil a standard muffin pan and reserve until needed.

Mix the flour and salt together in a bowl and gradually add the milk and melted butter. **Mix** until a smooth batter forms.

Add the eggs one at a time and mix well until the mixture is frothy, approximately 12–15 minutes.

Heat the prepared muffin pan in a 425°F (218.3°C) oven for 3–4 minutes.

Remove the pan and pour the batter into the muffin pan, filling each compartment three-quarters to the top.

Put the muffin pan into the hot 425°F (218.3°C) oven and bake for 15 minutes.

Reduce the oven's heat to 350°F (176.7°C) and bake for an additional 25–40 minutes until the popovers are brown and crisp on the outside and reach a minimum internal temperature of 145°F (62.8°C) for at least 15 seconds.

SERVING/HOLDING

Remove the popovers from the pan and serve immediately.

Hold the popovers at 140°F (60°C) or higher.

COOLING/STORING

Cool the popovers from 140°F (60°C) to 70°F (21.1°C) or lower within 2 hours. Cool from 70°F (21.1°C) to 41°F (5°C) within an additional 4 hours for a total cooling time of 6 hours or less.

Cover the popovers; label, date, and store under refrigeration at 41°F (5°C) or lower.

Blueberry Cobbler

YIELD: 6 PORTIONS · PORTION SIZE: 6 OUNCES

TOPPING

> 11 ounces (330g) bread flour
>
> ½ teaspoon (2g) salt
>
> 1½ tablespoon (22g) baking powder
>
> 2 ounces (60g) sweet butter
>
> 13 fluid ounces (390ml) heavy cream

COBBLER

> 8 ounces (240g) sugar
>
> 3 tablespoons (44g) cornstarch
>
> ¼ teaspoon (2g) cinnamon, ground
>
> ¼ teaspoon (2g) nutmeg, ground
>
> 8 fluid ounces (240ml) water
>
> 22 ounces (660g) blueberries, fresh or frozen

GARNISH

> 6 scoops vanilla ice cream

Prepare the cobbler topping by rubbing the flour, salt, baking powder, sweet butter, and heavy cream together until the ingredients are well blended and stick together to form very small pellets.

Reserve under refrigeration at 41°F (5°C) or lower until needed.

In a heavy-bottomed saucepan, combine the sugar, cornstarch, cinnamon, and nutmeg.

Gradually stir in the water.

Bring the mixture to a boil, stirring constantly.

Remove from the heat and reserve at 140°F (60°C) or higher until needed.

Place the blueberries in a 10-inch (25.4cm) cake pan.

Pour the reserved hot liquid over the berries.

Bake uncovered in a preheated 400°F (204.4°C) oven for 10 minutes.

Remove from the oven and place the cobbler topping on top of the blueberries in random piles.

Continue baking for approximately 15 minutes or until the topping is golden brown and baked throughout.

SERVING/HOLDING

Serve the cobbler warm with a scoop of vanilla ice cream on the side.

Hold the cobbler at 140°F (60°C) or higher.

COOLING/STORING

Cool the cobbler from 140°F (60°C) to 70°F (21.1°C) or lower within 2 hours. Cool from 70°F (21.1°C) to 41°F (5°C) within an additional 4 hours for a total cooling time of 6 hours or less.

Cover the cobbler; label, date, and store under refrigeration at 41°F (5°C) or lower.

Joseph E. Shilling

ON THE CUISINE OF THE MID-ATLANTIC STATES

The warmth and comfort of the foods from the Mid-Atlantic stir the soul. The rolling hills of the Appalachia, the coast of the Atlantic Ocean, the waterways of the Chesapeake and Delaware Bays, the fertile valleys of New York, Pennsylvania, New Jersey, and Maryland contribute the indigenous foods that define the cuisine of this region.

The primary ethnic influence is found in the Old World techniques and ingredients contributed by the Dutch, German, and English settlers. Paired with the Iroquois reliance on small game, fish, corn, and beans, these distinct cultures have fused to create a uniquely American style.

Maryland blue crabs, with their sweet meat, have made the crab cake a menu standard; the original steamer Ipwich clams from Long Island have been embellished with a variety of flavors to tantalize the taste; the bluefish, with its rich flesh, has been interpreted in numerous regional staples: smoked, stuffed, pan-fried.

It was the influences of the Native Americans that brought to our table the tender roasted tom turkey and the juicy meat of New York duckling so often used for celebrations. The migratory fowl gorging on the native vegetation of the East Coast developed the deep and complex flavor associated with the game of the region.

The vast array of agricultural products of the Mid-Atlantic afford the cook opportunity for a wide range of self-expression. Sweet summer corn becomes a spicy corn salsa, New Jersey peaches enhance slowly roasted caramelized peach-crusted pork, and the grapes of New York have been bottled into robust Merlots and Cabernets.

The greatest enjoyment of having grown up in the region is to have sampled game such as venison, bear, and wild turkey from the moutains and brook trout from the clear streams. The butter-soaked sweet ears of corn, the fresh rhubarb pies, and the spiced apple butter on hot baked breads were staples of our table.

Fresh, delicious, exciting, and bountiful describe the foods and the creations that bring the Mid-Atlantic region to the forefront of gastronomical success.

Joseph E. Shilling, C.E.C., is the chef owner of Your Private Chef, an in-your-home cooking school and caterer, and chef owner of Chef's Creation, a gourmet line of canned goods and savories, in Philadelphia.

The Mid-Atlantic States

Delaware

Maryland

New Jersey

New York

Pennsylvania

Virginia

West Virginia

The Mid-Atlantic region, with its mild climate, abundance of river valleys with rich soil, and extensive coastline, made a perfect environment for the orchards and farms established by the settlers who immigrated to America from England, Germany, the Netherlands, and other European countries.

When the colonists arrived in the Mid-Atlantic region, they discovered that over 40 rivers fed into Chesapeake Bay, where the mix of fresh and salt water was home to an amazing quantity and variety of seafood. The colonists quickly learned from the Native Americans how to gather oysters and blue crabs from Chesapeake Bay, which in the local native language meant "great shellfish bay." Oysters, a familiar food to the European settlers, were found in such quantity that the colonists not only consumed them but also used the shells for brickmaking as well as embedding them in the ground to make paths. Enthusiasm for the abundant blue crabs, however, took a little longer to catch on. In the seventeenth century, even the starving settlers in Jamestown refused to eat the local crabs until commanded to do so by their leaders. In time, the blue crab became a delicacy prepared and enjoyed in a variety of ways.

Toward the end of the seventeenth century, William Penn, founder of Pennsylvania, invited Europeans seeking religious freedom to settle in his colony. Many people, beginning with the Mennonites, accepted his invitation. The Mennonites were followed by the Amish and the Moravians, who arrived in Philadelphia and moved beyond the Delaware River. These German-speaking people soon became known as the best farmers in the region. Over time, many of these settlers continued their migration west; however, those who remained in Pennsylvania became known as the Pennsylvania Dutch, not because they were from Holland but because the name of their language, Deutsche, sounded like the word *Dutch*. Many of the Pennsylvania Dutch settled in and around Lancaster, Pennsylvania, where their descendants still live today. Although the Amish people retain their religious commitment to a plain and simple life, the Mennonites and Moravians embrace some technology. The food prepared by these groups is referred to as "plain and plenty" and is generally hearty and thriftily prepared. Pennsylvania Dutch specialties include chicken pot pie, scrapple, boova shenkel, and schnitz und knepp, among a variety of hearty soups and stews.

In sharp contrast to the Pennsylvania Dutch and their simple lifestyle were the wealthy English gentry who settled and built expansive estates in what are now Delaware, Virginia, and Maryland. The extravagant palates of these aristocratic settlers were satisfied with the rich and abundant foods in the region. Many of the manors owned slaves from the Deep South who brought with them the cooking traditions of the Southern culture, which were subsequently merged with the foods indigenous to the Mid-Atlantic. Smoked ham, deviled crabs, and greens are but a few examples of dishes with a Southern influence that are popular today in the Mid-Atlantic. A traditional sporting event in the eighteenth century that was popular with these English gentlemen was the fox hunt, held each spring and fall. The hunt breakfast was typically served at noon, after the hunt concluded, and featured a table rich with regional culinary dishes. Many of the items were prepared with a Southern flair and included scrambled eggs with cream, sausage with apples, creamed sweetbreads with oysters, baked country ham, and biscuits, spoonbread, and hominy. No hunt breakfast was complete without bourbon punch and mint juleps.

In the late eighteenth century, after the War of Independence, presidential influence began to affect Mid-Atlantic cuisine. America's first president, George Washington, was an accomplished farmer as well as a gourmet and was one of the first to use fertilizer on his fields and to pen his animals to control the feeding process. As president, Washington entertained frequently and lavishly at his estate in Mount Vernon, Virginia, dining with dignitaries both American and international. Although the modern concept of American regional cuisine was years away, Washington adhered to its principles by preparing and serving foods that were either raised on his farm or were indigenous to the surrounding area. Accounts of meals served at Mount Vernon include dishes made from fresh sturgeon from the Potomac River and wild pigs from the forests. Dinner was served each day at three o'clock. Wild game and ham were served daily and were always accompanied by fresh fruits and vegetables. After meals, brandy made with fruit from the area's orchards was poured.

Thomas Jefferson, also an accomplished farmer and epicurean, was America's third president. Before becoming president, Jefferson served as the American emissary to France and, as such, lived in Paris for a number of years. While in France, Jefferson learned many of the customs and acquired a taste for French wine and food. In 1801, he brought his own French-trained chefs to the President's House, now called the White House, to take charge of food preparation. An experienced statesman and diplomat, Jefferson believed successful international relations could be accomplished through a table set with fine wines and good food. Toward this objective, Jefferson's table always included a generous variety of dishes incorporating ingredients indigenous to the Mid-Atlantic and from his Monticello estate. Jefferson is credited with bringing the French technique for making ice cream to America and was also one of the first Americans to grow tomatoes, now one of the region's most notable corps.

Andrew Jackson, John Quincy Adams, James Madison, and James Monroe, who all had extensive gardens at the White House, continued the gardening tradition of American presidents. Over the years, American presidents popularized many foods and regional dishes. Eleanor Roosevelt served hot dogs to King George VI of England. Theodore Roosevelt coined the phase "good to the last drop" while drinking a cup of coffee at the Maxwell House in Nashville, Tennessee; the phrase eventually became the slogan for the Maxwell House brand of coffee. John F. Kennedy carried a thermos of New England fish chowder with him on the campaign trail, while Lyndon Johnson popularized Texas barbecue. Most recently, Ronald Reagan influenced the Jelly Belly jelly bean craze that swept America. George H. W. Bush had the opposite effect on broccoli after admitting that he did not like the vegetable.

Contained within the Mid-Atlantic region is New York City, which, according to many culinarians, is a region in itself. Since the city's beginning, it has been a magnet, attracting immigrants from all over the world. The huge variety of cultures and ethnic backgrounds that make up this melting pot is the reason why New York City is considered one of the dining capitals of the world. By the end of the nineteenth century, chefs from the city's posh restaurants and hotels carried on European culinary traditions while creating many of America's most famous dishes, such as eggs Benedict, vichyssoise, and lobster Newburg. New York City also laid the way for many more modest dishes, like cheesecake, pizza, and the blue plate special made famous in the city's luncheonettes, diners, and steakhouses. The ethnic makeup of New York's five boroughs also significantly influenced the city's cuisine. The Italian and Chinese influence is seen in Little Italy and Chinatown in downtown Manhattan, while the Lower East Side is home to Russian, Polish, German, and Ukrainian Jews, who brought the delicatessen to America. Harlem offers the culinary influences of African Americans, Caribbeans, and Puerto Ricans. Astoria, in the borough of Queens, claims to be home to more Greeks than any other city except Athens, Greece, and Melbourne, Australia. Brighton Beach, in Brooklyn, is home to Russian immigrants. More recent immigrant populations come from Asian, Middle Eastern, and Latin American cultures, who in turn added to New York City's culinary history as well as that of the entire Mid-Atlantic region. New York City is one of the few places in the world where so many ethnic backgrounds and cultures have had such significant impact on cooking style and foods. One can experience the foods and culinary traditions of the entire world simply by walking the streets—a complete culinary journey without ever leaving the city.

The delicatessen, a type of Jewish food store, emerged in the Mid-Atlantic region in the late 1800s. During this period, thousands of Jewish immigrants from Eastern Europe settled in Manhattan's Lower East Side and many opened stores, called *delicatessens*, that sold their favorite foods. As many of these deli owners were of German heritage, products typically found in delicatessens included hams and dried beef as well as Jewish foods such as pastrami, corned beef, pickled tongue, and gefilte fish. Many of the German items traditionally made with pork, like salami and frankfurters, were made with beef to make them kosher for the largely Jewish clientele. The term *kosher* means "permitted" or "ritually correct"; foods so described conform to the Kashruth—the Jewish dietary laws. Some of the many rules, which are observed by Orthodox Jews, are that meat and dairy products cannot be eaten together, or even stored together, and that consuming pork and shellfish is prohibited. The laws of Kashruth also prescribe how to make food fall in line with the dietary laws. In order for meats to be called kosher, animals must be slaughtered a certain way while under the strict supervision of a rabbi. The food prepared and served in today's delicatessens has changed little over time. One dish still closely associated with the deli is a hot pastrami or corned beef sandwich on rye bread, served with mustard and pickles.

The Mid-Atlantic was the birthplace of many of America's foodservice innovations. The automat, a type of self-service cafeteria that started in Philadelphia in 1908, featured a large variety of foods portioned on single-service plates and held inside a bank of small compartments with little doors. Customers could buy as many portions of food as desired by placing the correct amount of change in each compartment, then opening the door and removing the plate. The automat, in a sense, was one of the first vending machines dedicated to foodservice. Over the years, with the rise in popularity of the quick-service industry, the automats went into decline. The last known automat, located in New York City, finally closed its doors in 1990.

The diner was a casual type of café common in the Mid-Atlantic from the 1930s to 1950s. The diner concept began in 1872 with the first mobile lunch wagon. A wagon was pulled around by a horse while the vendor sold sandwiches and pies to blue-collar workers. In the early 1900s, the mobile lunch wagons were exchanged for abandoned trolley cars that were converted into small restaurants and permanently located in one spot. By the 1930s, diners were manufactured in the style of railroad dining cars, and many expanded their hours from strictly a lunch operation to 24-hour-a-day service. Patrons could expect a wide variety of offerings, from a simple cup of coffee or plate of pie to breakfast to a full dinner. One of the greatest contributions diners made to American regional cuisine was the blue plate special, a large plate of meatloaf with mashed potatoes and either peas or green beans. The blue plate special eventually evolved into a daily special and was the forerunner of the chef's specials common to many restaurants today. The decline of the diner started in the 1960s with the introduction of the quick-service restaurant industry and the availability of take-out food. However, today diners are being reborn as theme restaurants and are once again becoming popular places to dine.

Delmonico's, America's first freestanding fine dining restaurant, opened in New York City in 1831. Heavily influenced by French cuisine, Delmonico's established many of America's modern dining trends. Aside from being the first restaurant not connected to a hotel, Delmonico's was the first to utilize a menu from which the customers could choose and pay for what they consumed only. Some of America's most famous culinary innovations were invented at Delmonico's, including lobster Newburg, baked Alaska, eggs Benedict, and chicken à la king. Delmonico's operated for almost 100 years.

The food takeout concept also was born in the Mid-Atlantic. Originally, takeout was simply the process of bringing home leftovers after dining out in a restaurant. Around the 1930s takeout became specific to Chinese restaurants in the Mid-Atlantic as a result of the huge portions they served—and diners rarely finished. The leftovers were typically placed in small, white cardboard boxes with the symbol of a red dragon on the side and wire handles connected to the top for carrying. Eventually, Chinese takeout extended to the food-to-go concept. Today, *takeout* refers to both leftovers and food-to-go.

Delmarva is the 200-mile-long peninsula shared by Delaware, Maryland, and Virginia. Due to the temperate weather conditions created by the Chesapeake and Delaware bays, many of the region's early settlers became egg farmers, as chickens thrived in the climate. In 1923, an egg farmer decided to renew her entire egg-laying flock after only two years and to sell the two-year-old chickens, called *broilers*, to local butchers. The butchers saw that these chickens were extremely tender and flavorful and, at a time when young chickens were typically rare and considered a luxury, found a strong demand for them. By the early 1990s, the Delmarva Peninsula was producing over 11 million broilers per week. Today, Sussex County in Delaware produces more broilers than any other county in America.

Immigrants from all over the world have been attracted to the large cities of the Mid-Atlantic and, over the years, played an important role in influencing the cuisine of the region. Foods like doughnuts, pretzels, and ice cream, once considered international treats, are now deeply embedded in American regional cuisine. The orchards and farms established generations ago by European immigrants, which produced fruits and vegetables in abundance, gave rise to the American canning industry, led by Campbell's of Camden, New Jersey, and H.J. Heinz of Pittsburgh, Pennsylvania. The region's orchards, farms, and seafood are still an important part of the Mid-Atlantic agricultural business, supplying produce, meats, seafood, and canned goods to the world.

Typical Mid-Atlantic Ingredients and Dishes

Apple Butter: A butterlike fruit spread made by the Pennsylvania Dutch. Apple butter is made by cooking down peeled apples in cider flavored with spices until it has a buttery consistency. Making apple butter is often a traditional social event involving groups of Pennsylvania Dutch women. Although this type of spread can be made with any fruit, the apple variety is the most popular.

Bagel: A popular bread brought to the Mid-Atlantic by Jewish immigrants from Eastern Europe. Among the several accounts regarding its origin, the most plausible tells us that the bagel was created in Vienna, Austria, around 1683 when the Turks captured the city. As the story goes, Polish soldiers were asked to come to the assistance of the Austrians and successfully recaptured the city. After the battle, some of the Polish soldiers stayed in Vienna and opened a coffeehouse, where they prepared and sold a pastry shaped like a stirrup to symbolize the stirrups used by the Polish calvary. Supporting this account of the bagel's origin is the German word for stirrup, *buegel*, which possibly is the word from which *bagel* is derived.

Today, bagels are one of the most popular breads in America. Traditional bagels are hand-shaped, boiled, then baked to attain their chewy texture. However, the bagels found in many of America's new bagel shops are fashioned by machines, mixed with a variety of flavorings or toppings, and cooked with a modified process.

Bagel Chip: Made from stale bagels sliced very thin, seasoned with products such as garlic, salt, herbs, and cheese, and baked until crisp. Bagel chips are a common substitute for potato chips in the mid-Atlantic region. (See *bagel*.)

Beef on Weck: A sandwich from western New York that dates back to 1837. Beef on weck is made from thinly sliced, very lean roast beef served on a German caraway-seed roll encrusted with salt. The German name for the roll is *kummelweck*, which is shortened in the name for the sandwich. The roll is typically moistened in beef juices and filled with roast beef sliced to order. The sandwich should be served with horseradish sauce on the side.

Beefsteak Tomato: Often thought to be a unique variety of tomato, beefsteak tomatoes are actually a certain size of tomato. Tomatoes of any variety that grow to at least 3 inches in diameter can be correctly referred to as *beefsteak*. The Brandywine variety, which typically grows quite large before ripening, is frequently big enough to be called beefsteak. Large beefsteak tomatoes are well known for their excellent balance of sweetness and tartness, which is due to their being kept on the vine through the hottest days of the summer.

Beet Egg: An Amish preparation in which eggs are hard-boiled in a seasoned liquid derived by cooking beets. When done, the eggs turn a purplish-red color. The first use of colored eggs for the Easter holiday is traceable to the Amish immigrants who settled in the Mid-Atlantic region.

Bialy: A doughy, chewy bread made from wheat flour, salt, yeast, and water. It is commonly found in delicatessens in the Mid-Atlantic region. After the dough is shaped into a loaf, an indentation is made in the middle; it is then sprinkled with either chopped onions or poppyseeds and baked until crisp and golden brown. The bialy is named after the Polish town of Bialystock and, although the bread is said to be of Polish heritage, other breads almost identical to the bialy are found around the world, including the onion bread in the United States.

Bloody Mary: An alcoholic beverage first served at the King Cole Bar at the St. Regis Hotel in New York City. It is now traditionally served during Sunday brunch. The Bloody Mary is made with vodka and tomato juice and mixed with horseradish and spicy seasonings. The nonalcoholic version is aptly named the Virgin Mary.

Blue Crab: A common species of crab indigenous to the Mid-Atlantic and found in abundance in the Chesapeake Bay area from April through December. Blue crabs, which are marketed and sold in both their hard- and soft-shell stages, can be easily identified by their oval shell, colored anywhere from dark blue to blue-green to brown. The underside of the blue crab is cream colored with scarlet markings. Crab dishes from the Chesapeake Bay area are among the region's most popular dishes. Blue crabs are used for a variety of regional preparations, including plain steamed crabs, crabmeat frittata, and—one of the most popular preparations—crab cakes.

The meat from blue crabs is available in three basic types. The large pieces of meat from the muscles that operate the legs are referred to as *lump meat*. The small pieces of meat from the body section are called *flake meat*. Blue crabmeat can also be obtained from the claws. Special packs with a combination of the three types of meat are sold as well. Terminology associated with blue crabs is briefly described below.

Apron: A flap located on the underside of the bodies of blue crabs. When cleaning blue crabs, the apron is pried away from the crab's body in order to remove the intestinal vein, which is normally pulled out when the apron is removed.

Deadman's Fingers: The spongy yellow matter found in a blue crab's body. The crab's gills and intestines, along with the deadman's fingers, should be discarded when cleaning blue crabs.

Jimmies: Male blue crabs. Jimmies are a little meatier than their female counterparts.

Peelers: Crabs that have grown their new soft shell underneath and have split the hard shell on top. Peelers are kept in separate tanks and watched carefully until they completely shed their shell. Within just a few short hours, the soft shell will begin to harden if the crab is left in the water after molting.

Soft Shell: A stage in the life of blue crabs when they begin to molt and shed their shells. Typically around the first of May in the Chesapeake Bay area, both male and female blue crabs lose their shell and begin to form a new one as they grow and mature. Blue crabs molt up to 22 times before reaching full maturity and a size between 5 (12.7cm)and 7(17.78cm) inches. Knowing exactly when the crabs are molting is one of the specialized skills of an experienced crabber. The difficulty involved with predicting the exact time is one reason why soft-shell blue crabs are so highly regarded in the region. Soft-shell crabs are graded by the size of the shell span. Hotel crabs are 4–4½ inches (10.16–11.43cm), prime crabs are 4½–5 inches, jumbo crabs are 5–5½ inches (12.7–13.97cm), and whale crabs are 5½ inches (13.97cm) and larger. Soft-shell crabs are a delicacy in the Mid-Atlantic and are generally pan-fried and eaten whole. A Chesapeake Bay specialty is to pan-fry a soft-shell crab and serve it warm in a sandwich with lettuce, tomatoes, and mayonnaise.

Sooks: Female blue crabs. Sooks are a little less meaty than their male counterparts.

Tomalley: The yellow-colored liver of the blue crab. The tomalley is edible and considered by many the delicacy of the blue crab.

Boova Shenkel: A recipe prepared by the Pennsylvania Dutch. The literal translation is "boys' legs." Boova Shenkel is a beef stew with half-moon–shaped potato-filled dumplings that look like short, thick legs.

Brownie: A classic American dessert said to have been created by mistake. Although the story is not confirmed, many accounts say that, shortly after World War I, a librarian named Brownie Schrumpf apparently forgot to include baking powder while preparing a chocolate cake. She served the failed, unrisen cake to her guests anyway—and the rest is history. During the Great Depression, brownies gained popularity as a quick, easy-to-make dessert. They served as an excellent alternative for working mothers who no longer had time to bake regular cakes. In the Mid-Atlantic, brownies are frequently served warm and topped with vanilla ice cream and chocolate syrup.

Button Mushroom: In 1896, the first commercial mushroom cultivation began in the Brandywine Valley near Philadelphia. William Swayne is noted as having first experimented with the cultivation of mushrooms and discovered that a rich mix of soil and horse manure made for ideal mushroom-growing conditions. Swayne also constructed the first house designed specifically to grow mushrooms. Today, mushrooms are grown in 36 states, but Pennsylvania has the largest cash crop, accounting for almost half of America's mushroom crop. Button mushrooms are the most common mushrooms consumed in America and are recognized by their firm white exterior and smooth skin.

Campbell's Soup: Shortly after the Civil War, the Anderson and Campbell Preserve Company, located in Camden, New Jersey, opened and soon became a pioneer in the mass-marketed canned produce industry. In 1897, a chemist named John T. Dorrance joined the organization with the idea of duplicating European-style soups in concentrated form, canning them, and marketing them to homemakers as a convenient, easy-to-make soup. The first soup varieties made by Campbell's were tomato, consommè, vegetable, chicken, and oxtail. In 1900, Campbell's condensed soups won a gold medal at the Paris Exhibition.

Challah: A traditional Jewish holiday bread commonly found in Mid-Atlantic delicatessens. Challah is a braided white yeast bread enriched with eggs and sprinkled with poppyseeds. Eastern European Jews who immigrated to the Mid-Atlantic region in the late nineteenth century brought challah with them. Although this bread was originally reserved for the Jewish Sabbath and religious holidays, today it is available year-round.

Chestnut: Chestnut trees are indigenous to the United States. Prior to the 1950s it was one of the most important trees from Maine to South Florida and played a central part in eastern rural economics. Although chestnuts have many culinary uses, people living in the Mid-Atlantic enjoy them most as a street food snack. The chestnuts are roasted over a charcoal grill and sold hot from a vendor's cart; their distinctive smoky aroma can be recognized many blocks away. Eating freshly roasted chestnuts is a New York holiday tradition while viewing the large Christmas tree and watching the ice skaters at Rockefeller Center. Due to the high cost of chestnuts today, few vendors sell them, except during the Christmas holidays.

Chicken Pot Pie: A traditional dish made by the Pennsylvania Dutch and found in restaurants all over Pennsylvania. Chicken pot pie is stewed chicken combined with pot pie noodles, which are squares of dough cooked in broth and baked in small pie or casserole dishes.

Clear Toy: An artisan style of lollipop made by the Pennsylvania Dutch. Clear toys are made from cooked sugar that is colored and poured into handcrafted molds shaped like miniature figures from German folktales. The artisan process used to make clear toys yields an exceptionally clear and brilliant color, similar to that of colored glass. Traditionally, clear toys are hung on Christmas trees as ornaments, then given as gifts to the children, who eat them on Epiphany.

Crab Boil: A special mix of herbs and spices used to season blue crabs as well as other seafood. Crab boil can be found pre-blended in products such as Old Bay Seasoning. However, many families use their own recipe for crab boil, which is passed from generation to generation and considered as valuable as heirlooms. It is said that the taste for spicy seafood in the Mid-Atlantic came from the Caribbean slaves brought to work on the region's plantations. They prepared blue crabs with the peppery seasoning common to their homeland. Many crab boil recipes include cayenne pepper and red chili powder, which give a spicy flavor to the meat as well as enhancing the dark red color of the cooked crabs. (See *Old Bay Seasoning*.)

Crab Cake: A popular Mid-Atlantic preparation featuring blue crabmeat, which is used by itself mixed with egg, fresh breadcrumbs, herbs, and spices, then formed into cakes and pan-fried. Chefs from the Mid-Atlantic agree that the best crab cakes are made only from fresh lump crab in pieces as large as possible, and that smaller cakes tend to come out better than larger ones. The history of crab cakes dates back as early as the mid-1600s, when the founder of Maryland, Lord Baltimore, is said to have eaten his first crab cake.

Egg Cream: A nonalcoholic beverage traditionally served at New York luncheonette counters. An egg cream contains neither eggs nor cream; it is made with chocolate syrup, milk, and seltzer water, which causes the mixture to foam like beaten eggs.

Eggs Benedict: A dish first made by the chef at Delmonico's in New York City. The recipe calls for two toasted English muffins, each topped with a slice of grilled ham, a poached egg, and hollandaise sauce. It is said that the dish was created for a regular customer named

Benedict who was bored with the regular menu. The chef met the needs of his customer by creating the egg dish, which is still popular today.

Fastnacht: A rectangular piece of dough, slit down the center and deep fried, considered a forerunner of today's doughnut. The slit allows the fastnacht to cook evenly, which could also be the reason why modern doughnuts have a hole in the center. Fastnachts are typically dunked in coffee before being eaten. They are also frequently served filled with jam or topped with molasses.

Frankfurter: Commonly referred to as *hot dogs*, frankfurters are made in the German tradition of fine sausages. They are a type of sausage made from an emulsified forcemeat of pork or beef that is lightly smoked. They are eaten on a oval bun with ketchup, mustard, or pickle relish. One of the most popular street foods in the United States, frankfurters are commonly sold from carts by street vendors and are also the traditional food eaten at baseball games and other American sporting events. In 1939, Eleanor Roosevelt served hot dogs at their home in Hyde Park, New York, to King George VI of England. The king enjoyed them so much he had a second helping. Today, chicken, turkey, and vegetarian hot dogs are available as well.

Funnel Cake: A deep-fried snack originally enjoyed by Pennsylvania Dutch farmers, who ate them as a midmorning snack. Funnel cakes are made by pouring a batter through a funnel into hot fat, then swirling strips before they fully cook. The process results in a crisp, doughnutlike pastry with a squiggly shape like that of a snail. Funnel cakes are typically sprinkled with powdered sugar and sometimes topped with molasses or syrup before they are eaten.

Gibson: An alcoholic beverage named after the famous illustrator Charles Dana Gibson. The drink, created at the Player's Club in New York City in the 1930s, is essentially a gin martini garnished with a pickled onion instead of an olive.

Hero: Called "the sandwich so big you have to be a hero to eat it," a hero sandwich should be made using a French roll at least 12 inches long. The word hero is also thought to be derived from the phonetic Anglicization of the Greek word "gyro." Typical fillings include just about any combination of sliced deli meats and cheeses topped with thinly sliced tomatoes and onions. To prepare the hero sandwich, first split the roll and scoop out some of the bread from the inside to make room to stack the meat and cheese. Moisten the bread with olive oil and spread mustard and mayonnaise on each piece. Finally, fill the bread with the deli meats and cheeses and top with tomatoes and onions. Additional condiments, such as pickles, peppers, and olives, should be served on the side. Several cities lay claim to originating the hero sandwich, including Atlantic City, Baltimore, New York, and San Francisco. Heroes go by different names in different regions. For example, in Pennsylvania the hero is called a hoagie, in New Jersey a submarine, and in New England it's a blimp, torpedo, or grinder. The name *hero* is, however, the original. The name *submarine* became popular during World War II, as the sandwich resembles an underwater vessel.

Hershey's Chocolate: The largest confectionery company in the world, Hershey's Chocolate, was founded by Milton Hershey in rural Pennsylvania in the late 1890s. After failing in a variety of businesses, Hershey noticed an unfilled demand for chocolates and went to Europe to learn the secret of making milk chocolate. He soon returned to Pennsylvania, but without a recipe, and began to experiment on his own, eventually coming up with a recipe that would change chocolate manufacturing forever. Hershey's recipe required extra cocoa butter, which led to a surplus of cocoa powder, a byproduct that helped establish the company's success. In 1907, Hershey introduced the individually foil-wrapped chocolate kiss—an immediate hit. Today, Hershey's Chocolate uses 175,000 gallons of milk every day for chocolate production and is the single largest user of almonds in the United States.

Ketchup: Also referred to as *catsup*, this tomato spread or condiment was popular long before Americans began to enjoy the tomato as a fruit or ingredient in recipes. Ketchup was first used by the British and was brought to the Mid-Atlantic by the colonists. The word *ketchup* originally came from a Malaysian term meaning a savory sauce. In 1872, the Heinz and Noble Company started to bottle walnut and tomato ketchup. By 1890, ketchup had become so popular that Heinz dedicated a large percentage of the firm's resources to bottling it. By 1905, Heinz was selling over 5 million bottles per year. Today, Heinz produces and sells over 50 percent of the world's supply of tomato ketchup.

Lebanon Bologna: A ready-to-eat sausage developed by the Pennsylvania Dutch of Lebanon County. Lebanon bologna is a somewhat spicy beef sausage made form 90 percent lean beef seasoned with black pepper and sugar. The sausages are hung in wooden smoke-houses for 2½ days and smoked very slowly. The moist, reddish-brown sausage is typically thinly sliced and eaten with bread as a sandwich. Sometimes, Lebanon bologna is cut into strips and served hot with a cream sauce, similar to the way dried beef was eaten by the settlers of years past.

Lox: Derived from the German word *lachs*, meaning salmon. Lox is a salt-cured side of salmon, usually sliced paper-thin, and is a common item found in delicatessens in the Mid-Atlantic. Lox is often referred to as *smoked salmon*, but is actually cured rather than smoked. The most frequent use for lox is as a topping for a bagel spread with cream cheese. The cream cheese in the sandwich not only holds the lox in place but also helps cut the saltiness of the fish.

Manhattan: An alcoholic beverage named after the Manhattan Club in New York City, where it was first made in 1874 in honor of New York's governor. The drink uses bourbon, America's only indigenous distilled spirit, combined with sweet vermouth and angostura bitters. It is garnished with a slice of orange and a maraschino cherry.

Marshmallow: A sticky, sweet confection brought to the Mid-Atlantic region by the colonial settlers. Marshmallows were originally made from the roots of a common garden plant called mallow or marshmallow shrub and were first used for culinary purposes by the early Romans. The extraction of the mallow from the roots of the shrub was a long and involved process. The process was simplified over the years by replacing the mallow with gum arabic and, these days, gelatin. Although marshmallows are frequently associated with gatherings around a campfire, Americans use them for a variety of other culinary purposes, including cake frosting, ice cream toppings, and the favorite dessert of campers—s'mores.

Matzoh: An unleavened bread that resembles a cracker. It is eaten by Jews during the Passover, or Pesach, holiday. The story of matzoh dates back to the time of Moses and the Egyptian pharaoh. When the pharaoh decided to release the Jews from bondage in Egypt, they left so quickly that their bread did not have enough time to rise. They took the dough with them and baked it under hot desert sun into thin, flat, crisp sheets. Matzoh is used during Passover instead of regular bread in remembrance of this historical and religious event. Matzoh is also used to make matzoh balls for matzoh ball soup, another traditional Passover food.

McClure Bean Soup: A tradition with roots dating back to the American Civil War. During the war, soldiers survived on a diet primarily composed of hardtack (a hard, stale biscuit) and dried pork or beef. However, sometimes bean soup with a little meat in it was served. The soup was welcomed by the soldiers to break up the monotony of their regular diet. After the war, the bean soup was served at get-togethers and reunions and, eventually, public events. The first public bean soup event was held in McClure, Pennsylvania, in 1891. The festival is still held today and is attended by the descendants of the Civil War veterans.

New York Cheesecake: A cake, made from cream cheese, that is a popular American dessert. It was first served at Lindy's restaurant in New York City in the 1940s. Traditional New York cheesecake is a tall cake with a smooth cream cheese filling and a graham cracker crust. It is often topped with fresh fruit, such as cherries or strawberries.

Nova Scotia Lox: A lightly cured version of lox that is much more delicate in flavor than regular lox. Nova Scotia lox is typically made using salmon from the North Atlantic and is usually a little more expensive than regular lox. Nova-style smoked salmon is used similarly to lox but, due to its mild flavor, is more commonly eaten plain as an appetizer with condiments, such as capers and diced onions. (See *lox.*)

Old Bay Seasoning: Developed by a German immigrant named Gustav Brunn, Old Bay Seasoning is a crab boil spice mixture. Although the actual recipe for the seasoning blend is a secret, it does contain cloves, pimento, ginger, and celery salt, among other spices. (See *crab boil*.)

Oyster: When European settlers arrived in the Mid-Atlantic, they were pleased to find large oysters growing in abundance in the waters along the seaboard. By the 1820s, almost every city along the coast had oyster parlors where, for less than ten cents, one could enjoy his fill of oysters prepared in a variety of ways. By the mid-1800s, the oyster populations in Long Island Sound and Chesapeake Bay began to diminish. The first attempts at aquaculture were made about this time by ingenious American oystermen who were able to grow their own oysters. They prepared a bed of old oyster shells in Chesapeake Bay and the East River of New York so that the new oysters had something to attach themselves to. This feat of engineered oyster cultivation was the forerunner to today's modern aquaculture techniques, without which the American oyster supply would have long since disappeared. Because oysters filter about a hundred gallons of water every day, their flavor tends to take on the characteristics of the water where they grow, so even oysters of the same species can have different tastes. Only one species inhabits the waters of the Eastern Seaboard. The various names attached to them indicate the name of the growing area from which they are harvested, including Blue Point, Chesapeake Bay, Chincoteague, Kent Island, Pine Island, and St. George. Brief descriptions of the oysters indigenous to the Mid-Atlantic are listed below.

Blue Point Oysters: Originally the name for the internationally renowned oysters that came from Great South Bay in New York. Today, Blue Point is a generic term used to describe any oyster with a mild flavor that comes from the Mid-Atlantic.

Chesapeake Bay Oyster: A variety of oyster indigenous to the bay with the same name. Chesapeake Bay oysters are small in size, with a round shell. They are well known for their exceptionally sweet flavor.

Chincoteague Oyster: A variety of oyster named after the Chincoteague Bay of Maryland and Virginia. The Chincoteague oyster is small to medium in size, with shells that are flat and round in shape. These oysters are well known for their sweet yet salty flavor and distinctive aftertaste.

Kent Island Oyster: A variety of Chesapeake Bay oyster with a medium-sized shell and oval shape. Kent Island oysters are well known for their plump meat and sweet, clean flavor.

Pine Island Oyster: A variety of oyster from Oyster Bay Harbor in Long Island, New York. Pine Island oysters are well known for their intense sweet and salty combination of flavors.

St. George Oyster: A variety of Chesapeake Bay oyster with a smooth, dark shell and a symmetrical shape. St. George oysters are well known for their sweet flavor and tender texture.

Oyster Stew: Sometimes referred to as *oyster soup*, oyster stew is a thin, creamy broth made from oyster liquor (the watery brine inside the oyster) and either milk or cream. Traditional oyster stew is made by simmering milk or cream with aromatics in one pan while the oysters are gently simmered for just a few minutes in their own liquor in a separate pan; then the two are combined. Folklore tells us that oysters simmered in milk are a sure cure for insomnia.

Pan Puddin: Popular among the Pennsylvania Dutch, pan puddin is a traditional item prepared after butchering a hog. After the butchering is completed and all of the primary and secondary cuts used, the bones and head of the animal are cooked to remove the scrap pieces of meat. They are then mixed with a variety of meats such as liver, kidneys, and hearts and cooked in the broth made from the bones and meat. The mixture is seasoned and poured into molds, where resting allows the fat to rise to the top and seal the loaf. Pan puddin is typically used as a spread for toast, pancakes, and waffles.

Perdue Chicken: A well-known brand of broiling chicken produced by the Perdue family on the Delmarva Peninsula in Salisbury, Maryland. In 1930, at the age of ten, Frank Perdue, the son of a Maryland egg farmer, received 50 chickens to care for from his father. When he took over the family business in 1950, Frank was already known for successfully cross-breeding chickens as well as for having developed a special all-natural diet, which he fed to them. The feed combined corn and soybeans with minerals from ground oyster shells and marigold petal extract. Although the marigold petal extract does not add vitamins to the birds, it is responsible for their distinctive yellow-gold skin color. In 1991, Frank's son Jim took over the family business. Today, Perdue Farms is the second largest poultry producer in the United States.

Philadelphia Pepper Pot: This soup was invented by the cook for General George Washington's troops at Valley Forge, Pennsylvania, during the War of Independence. In an attempt to raise the morale of his troops, Washington ordered his cook to prepare a dish the soldiers would like. The cook, however, only had a few pounds of tripe, some vegetables, and some peppercorns. The cook prepared soup from these ingredients and, as the story goes, it did indeed fortify the soldiers and give them courage. The spicy tripe soup became known as Philadelphia pepper pot and was one of the first 21 varieties of soup canned by Campbell's.

Philly Cheese Steak: A sandwich originating in Philadelphia that is typically sold by a street vendor. A true Philly cheese steak is made from shaved slices of rib eye that are cooked on a grill with diced onions and served on a hard roll topped with Cheeze Whiz. Optional toppings are usually available from the vendor and include relish, peppers, ketchup, and hot sauce. The traditional accompaniment to a Philly cheese steak is a cherry cola.

Pizza: The first pizza originated in Naples, in the southern part of Italy, and was essentially a piece of dough topped with tomato sauce and baked. In 1905, an Italian immigrant named Gennaro Lombardi opened the first American pizza parlor in New York City and began to serve what would become one of the most popular dishes in the history of American cuisine—the pizza pie. Over the years, pizza has actually become more American than Italian and has little resemblance to its Italian counterpart. The gas oven, for the most part, eventually replaced the original practice of cooking pizza in a wood-fired oven, and homemade doughs were replaced with commercially prepared ones. In most regions of the United States today, pizza is associated with quick-service restaurants that specialize in home delivery. However, in many cities in the Mid-Atlantic, the pizzeria is still a real treat, holding to the many traditions of quality passed down through the generations.

Portobello Mushroom: A very large variety of the crimini mushroom whose top is fully opened. Portobello mushrooms, grown in abundance near Kennett Square, Pennsylvania, have a coarse skin with a dark brown color and frequently grow to between 4 and 8 inches in diameter. Due to their size, portobello mushrooms are often used in vegetarian cooking and are meaty enough to be grilled and served like a hamburger or steak. Although portobello mushrooms represent only a fraction of the Mid-Atlantic mushroom crop, their popularity is rapidly growing.

Pretzel: A piece of dough twisted into a shape with three holes in the center, then baked crisp and topped with salt. The first pretzel factory in the United States, the Sturgis Pretzel House, is located in the heart of the Pennsylvania Dutch region near Lititz, Pennsylvania. For the Pennsylvania Dutch, the twist of the pretzel symbolizes the bond of marriage, and the three holes in the center represent the Holy Trinity. Children of the region who said their prayers were traditionally given pretzels by their parents as a reward.

Pumpernickel: A bread commonly found in delicatessens and made in a fashion very similar to rye bread. Pumpernickel bread is different from rye bread only in the addition of molasses or caramel, which gives the bread its dark brown color, and the use of unsifted (unbolted) rye flour for its grainy texture. (See *rye bread*.)

Reuben: A popular American sandwich, said to have been invented by a man named Reuben or at a deli in New York City called Reubens. Regardless of which Reuben actually invented the sandwich, it has remained a deli icon for many years. The Reuben sandwich is made with corned beef, Swiss cheese, sauerkraut, and Russian dressing, all grilled between two pieces of rye bread.

Rivel: A thrifty soup, made by the Pennsylvania Dutch, consisting of a simple broth with rice-shaped bits of dough. The bits are made by rubbing a ball of pasta dough through a sieve over the simmering broth.

Rye Bread: A bread commonly found in delicatessens throughout the Mid-Atlantic. Jewish-style rye bread is made from a mixture of ground rye grain and wheat flour. German-style rye bead uses rye flour only. Rye breads are frequently prepared with caraway seeds that are either sprinkled on top of the dough or mixed into it before baking. Jewish rye bread usually uses a sourdough starter as a leavening agent, which gives it a distinctive, slightly sour flavor.

Sauerbraten: A dish, originally from Germany, brought to the Mid-Atlantic by Mennonite and Amish immigrants. Sauerbraten is made with beef cured with sugar and vinegar, then braised in gravy thickened with crushed gingersnaps.

Schmaltz: A Yiddish term referring to pure, rendered chicken fat. Schmaltz is typically found in Jewish delicatessens and is used for cooking in a manner similar to butter. Sometimes schmaltz is flavored with apples, onions, and seasonings to give it additional flavor and is used as a spread. Schmaltz is the fat used in preparing a traditional Jewish spread called chopped chicken liver, which is a type of pâté common to delicatessens in the Mid-Atlantic.

Schmear: Derived from the Yiddish word *shmirn*, meaning "to smear and grease" or, more commonly, "to ask for a dab of something." *Schmear* is commonly used in New York delis by customers asking for mustard to be spread lightly on a sandwich or cream cheese on a bagel.

Schnitz und Knepp: A traditional dish of the Pennsylvania Dutch. Schnitz und knepp is a simple stew that combines dried apples with smoked ham and is topped with steamed dumplings. If made properly, the apples become soft and plump and the dumplings light and fluffy.

Scrapple: A form of pan puddin made popular by the Amish immigrants of the Mid-Atlantic. Scrapple is the same as pan puddin except that cornmeal or buckwheat flour is added to the meats as they cook. The traditional way to cook prepared scrapple is to cut slices about ½ inch thick and pan-fry them until golden brown. Scrapple is frequently served at breakfast with poached eggs. (See *pan puddin*.)

Shad: A member of the herring family. Female shad are considered better-tasting than their male counterparts; all shad are known for their numerous bones. The fish, which have a rich, oily flesh and delicate flavor, are seasonal and inhabit the rivers of New England and the Mid-Atlantic region in the spring, when the fish returns from the ocean to spawn.

Shad Roe: The roe produced by shad just before spawning. It is considered a delicacy and has a distinctive, nutty flavor. The roe is prone to burst and needs to be very gently simmered in flavored liquid. After just a few minutes, the roe can be sliced and served over a cooked shad fillet or used as an ingredient in other recipes.

Shoofly Pie: The most famous of all Pennsylvania Dutch pies. Shoofly pie, also referred to as *pie cake* or *molasses cake*, is a crumbly mixture made from brown sugar, flour, cinnamon, and butter baked over a layer of molasses in a pie shell. There are many accounts of how the name *shoofly pie* originated. One is that the molasses in the pie was so sweet that one had to shoo the flies away from it. Another account tells us *shoofly* is derived from the French word for cauliflower, *choufleur*, due to the way the crumb topping resembles cauliflower.

Smithfield Ham: The result of a patented process for curing and smoking Virginia hams. The hams are cured for a minimum of 6 to 12 months in Smithfield, Virginia, before being cooked. Before they can be used, they must be soaked in water for 12 to 24 hours to remove excess salt.

Smoked Sable: A smoked black codfish common in delicatessens of the Mid-Atlantic. Smoked sable is frequently sliced thin and served on bread with onions, salty black olives, and sweet butter.

Smoked Whitefish: A common item in delicatessens. Smoked whitefish can be identified by its shiny golden skin and mild flavor. It is frequently served as a salad by making a paste of it and adding chopped red onions and seasonings. Smoked whitefish is also sliced and served with pickled onions.

Tomato: Originally tomatoes were used only as ornamental plants due to the belief in the early 1800s that they were poisonous. Tomatoes were one of the first and most successful products canned by the Anderson and Campbell Company in 1870 and used in the first soup the company canned in 1897, Campbell's Beefsteak Tomato Soup. Tomatoes did not become popular until the very late 1800s, when French and Italian immigrants began to use them frequently in recipes. Ketchup, first made commercially by the Heinz and Nobel Company, also helped to build the popularity of the tomato among Americans.

By the early 1900s, tomato consumption surpassed that of apples and potatoes. Even today, tomatoes are the second most consumed products in the fruit and vegetable category, just behind potatoes. Tomatoes are an important fruit crop in the Mid-Atlantic and are grown in abundance in New Jersey. Today, 20 percent of the New Jersey tomato crop is devoted to canned pizza and spaghetti sauce, while the majority of the crop comprises over 25 table varieties including Rutgers, Brandywine, Mountain Spring, Sunbright, and Old Flame varieties, to name a few.

Vichyssoise: A chilled potato and leek soup invented by Chef Louis Diat at the Ritz-Carlton Hotel in New York City. Although the name sounds French, vichyssoise is definitely an American innovation. If prepared properly, the soup is smooth and creamy, with the delicate flavor of the leeks coming through in a subtle way. Vichyssoise should be served extremely cold and garnished with nothing but minced chives.

Sample Menus from Mid-Atlantic Cuisine

MENU ONE

Split Pea Soup

Corn Crêpes with Smoked Shrimp and Asparagus

Shaker-Style Turkey Cutlets · Glazed Carrot Sticks · Buttery Homemade Noodles

MENU TWO

Buffalo Chicken Wings

Open-Face Soft-Shell Crab Sandwich

Pennsylvania Pork Roast · Croquette Potatoes

MENU THREE

Manhattan Clam Chowder

Waldorf Salad

Chicken with Dill Dumplings · Spinach Timbales · Spaghetti Squash

Split Pea Soup

YIELD: 6 PORTIONS · PORTION SIZE: 8 OUNCES

2 ounces (60g) butter

2 ounces (60g) onions, cut into fine dice

4 ounces (120g) celery, cut into fine dice

4 ounces (120g) carrots, cut into fine dice

16 ounces (480g) split peas

1 ham bone with some meat attached

48 fluid ounces (1.4L) white chicken stock prepared (see page 517)

salt, to taste

black pepper, ground, to taste

8 ounces (240g) croutons, prepared

CHEF TIPS *If a thicker consistency is desired, purée half of the soup in a blender or food processor before adding the diced ham. Return the puréed soup to the pot and mix well. Then add the diced ham and continue with the remainder of the recipe's steps.*

Heat the butter in a saucepot over medium-high heat. Sweat the onions, celery, and carrots in the butter for approximately 4 minutes or until the onions become translucent.

Add the split peas, ham bone, and white chicken stock to the vegetables and bring to a boil.

Reduce the heat and simmer for 30–40 minutes or until the split peas are tender. Add water or additional stock as needed if the soup becomes too thick. Do not allow the simmering soup to fall below 140°F (60°C).

Remove the ham bone and remove any meat that is still attached. Dice the meat and place it back into the soup.

Season to taste with salt and black pepper.

SERVING/HOLDING

Carefully ladle the soup into hot soup bowls or plates.

Garnish each portion with small, crisp croutons.

Hold the soup at 140°F (60°C) or higher.

Pour the remaining soup into small metal containers.

Cool the soup from 140°F (60°C) to 70°F (21.1°C) or lower within 2 hours. Cool from 70°F (21.1°C) to 41°F (5°C) within an additional 4 hours for a total cooling time of 6 hours or less.

Cover the soup; label, date, and store under refrigeration at 41°F (5°C) or lower.

Manhattan Clam Chowder

YIELD: 6 PORTIONS · PORTION SIZE: 8 OUNCES

7 ounces (210g) clams, chopped, juice reserved

water, as needed

2 ounces (60g) bacon, cut into small dice

2 ounces (60g) onion, cut into small dice

2 cloves garlic, minced

2 ounces (60g) celery, cut into small dice

1½ ounces (45g) green bell peppers, cut into small dice

1½ ounces (45g) red bell peppers, cut into small dice

1 ounce (30g) carrots, cut into small dice

1 tablespoon (15g) shallots, minced

8 ounces (240g) tomato concassée

5 ounces (150g) potatoes, cut into small dice

¼ teaspoon (1g) basil, minced

1 tablespoon (15g) parsley, minced

¼ teaspoon (1g) red pepper, ground

¼ teaspoon (1g) black pepper, ground

Add enough water to the 7 ounces of reserved clam juice to equal 6 fluid ounces (180ml). Reserve under refrigeration at 41°F (5°C) or lower until needed.

Cook the diced bacon in a sautoir pan over medium heat until the bacon is crisp and the fat is completely rendered.

Remove the bacon and reserve at room temperature until needed.

Sauté the onions, garlic, celery, red and green bell peppers, carrots, and shallots in the rendered bacon fat for 4–5 minutes or until the onions are translucent and the vegetables are tender.

Stir in the reserved clam juice and water mixture (6 ounces [180ml]), additional clam juice (24 ounces [720ml]), tomatoes, potatoes, basil, parsley, and red and black pepper.

Bring to a boil, reduce the heat, cover, and simmer for 20–25 minutes or until the vegetables are tender. Do not allow the simmering soup to fall below 140°F (60°C).

SERVING/HOLDING

Carefully ladle the chowder into hot soup bowls or plates.

Hold the soup at 140°F (60°C) or above.

COOLING/STORING

Pour the remaining chowder into small metal containers.

Cool the chowder from 140°F (60°C) to 70°F (21.1°C) or lower within 2 hours. Cool from 70°F (21.1°C) to 41°F (5°C) within an additional 4 hours for a total cooling time of 6 hours or less.

Cover the chowder; label, date, and store under refrigeration at 41°F (5°C) or lower.

Buffalo Chicken Wings

YIELD: 6 PORTIONS · PORTION SIZE: 12 OUNCES

64 ounces (1.9kg) or 24 chicken wings

3 ounces (90g) butter

3 fluid ounces (90ml) Tabasco sauce

1 fluid ounce (30ml) cider vinegar

salt, to taste

black pepper, ground, to taste

GARNISH

6 fluid ounces (180ml) blue cheese dressing, prepared

6 ounces (180g) celery, cut into sticks

CHEF TIPS *This Mid-Atlantic chicken wing preparation is popular in bars and casual dining establishments throughout the region. Buffalo chicken wings are said to have first been prepared by Theresa Belissimo at the Anchor Bar in Buffalo, New York. Buffalo wings are made by separating the two sections of the chicken wing at the joint, then deep-frying them. Typically, Buffalo chicken wings are served with fresh celery sticks and blue cheese dressing, which is said to help soothe the effects of the spicy sauce.*

Many types of hot pepper sauce can be used with this recipe, all of which claim to be the original hot sauce. Some brands of hot sauce that we have found to work exceptionally well are Crystal, Franks, and Tabasco sauces; however, dozens of other brands are available to choose from. The type and brand of hot pepper sauce greatly affect the heat and flavor of this dish. Sometimes cayenne pepper is used as a substitute for the hot pepper sauce.

Separate and discard the tips of the chicken wings. Cut the wings at the joints to form 48 pieces.

Deep-fry the wings in a preheated 375°F (190.6°C) fryer, using the basket method. Do not overload the baskets. If needed, cook the wings in small batches.

Cook until the chicken is golden brown and reaches a minimum internal temperature of 165°F (73.9°C) or higher, or until needed.

Degrease the wings on absorbent paper towel. Reserve the chicken wings at 140°F (60°C) for at least 15 seconds.

Heat the butter in a sauteuse pan over medium heat.

Mix in the Tabasco sauce and vinegar, and sauté the wings until hot and thoroughly coated with the sauce.

Season to taste with salt and black pepper.

Carefully spoon approximately 2 ounces (60ml) of blue cheese dressing into ramekins or small bowls and place them in the center of each hot plate.

Place 8 pieces of the chicken wings in a fan shape on the lower half of the plate.

Arrange 2 or 3 celery sticks in a fan shape pointing in the other direction.

🍲 **Hold** the chicken wings at 140°F (60°C) or higher.

COOLING/ STORING

🍲 **Cool** the chicken wings from 140°F (60°C) to 70°F (21.1°C) or lower within 2 hours. Cool from 70°F (21.1°C) to 41°F (5°C) within an additional 4 hours for a total cooling time of 6 hours or less.

Cover the chicken wings, celery sticks, and blue cheese dressing; label, date, and store under refrigeration at 41°F (5°C) or lower.

Corn Crêpes with Smoked Shrimp and Asparagus

YIELD: 6 PORTIONS · PORTION SIZE: 10 OUNCES

CRÊPES

3 large eggs

6 fluid ounces (180ml) milk

3 ounces (90g) all-purpose flour

1½ teaspoons (7ml) vegetable oil

3 ounces (90g) corn kernels, steamed, finely chopped

salt, to taste

white pepper, ground, to taste

CORN SALAD

3 fluid ounces (90ml) olive oil

1 fluid ounce (30ml) white wine vinegar

1 teaspoon (5g) parsley, chopped

9 ounces (270g) corn kernels, steamed

1 ounce (30g) red bell peppers, cut into small dice

1 ounce (30g) yellow bell peppers, cut into small dice

1 ounce (30g) green bell peppers, cut into small dice

salt, to taste

black pepper, ground, to taste

GARNISH

24 ounces (720g) or 36 asparagus tips

10 ounces (300g) or 36 shrimp, peeled

½ cup (120g) apple-wood chips, soaked

8 fluid ounces (240ml) hollandaise sauce (see page 521)

Place the eggs and milk in a bowl and whisk together. Add the flour and continue to mix until a smooth batter forms.

Adjust the consistency of the batter with additional flour or water as needed to achieve a nappé consistency. Add the oil and chopped corn kernels; season to taste with salt and white pepper.

COOKING

Heat a steel crêpe or nonstick pan over medium-high heat. Carefully ladle approximately 1 ounce (28g) of the batter into the center of the hot pan and spread the batter out by moving the pan in the air.

Cook the crêpe until it is lightly browned on one side. Turn the crêpe over and lightly brown the other side. Stack the crêpes as they are cooked, loosely wrap them in plastic wrap, and reserve under refrigeration at 41°F (5°C) or lower until needed. The batter should make at least 12 crêpes.

Mix the olive oil, vinegar, and parsley together in a bowl and add the steamed corn kernels and red and green bell peppers. Mix until the vegetables are thoroughly coated with the dressing.

Season the salad to taste with salt and black pepper and reserve under refrigeration at 41°F (5°C) or lower until needed.

Blanch the asparagus spears, shock in an ice bath, drain, and reserve under refrigeration at 41°F (5°C) or lower until needed.

Lightly pan-smoke the shrimp with the soaked apple-wood chips for approximately 3–4 minutes or until the shrimp are fully cooked and reach a minimum internal temperature of 145°F (62.8°C) for at least 15 seconds.

Cool the shrimp from 140°F (60°C) to 70°F (21.1°C) or lower within 2 hours. Cool from 70°F (21.1°C) to 41°F (5°C) within an additional 4 hours for a total cooling time of 6 hours or less. Reserve under refrigeration at 41°F (5°C) or lower until needed.

SERVING/HOLDING

Fill each of the crêpes with 2 asparagus spears and 3 smoked rock shrimp. Roll the crêpes into cylinders.

Place 2 crêpes on each plate and top with approximately 1 ounce (30g) of hollandaise sauce.

Lightly brown the sauce under a salamander or in a broiler.

Garnish each portion with approximately 2 ounces (60g) of the reserved corn and pepper salad.

Hold the shrimp, crêpes, and corn and pepper salad under refrigeration at 41°F (5°C) or lower.

COOLING/STORING

Cover the shrimp, crêpes, and corn and pepper salad; label, date, and store under refrigeration at 41°F (5°C) or lower.

Open-Face Soft-Shell Crab Sandwich

YIELD: 6 PORTIONS · PORTION SIZE: 10 OUNCES

2 large eggs

12 fluid ounces (360ml) half-and-half

16 ounces (480g) all-purpose flour

salt, to taste

black pepper, ground, to taste

6 soft-shell blue crabs, jumbo grade, cleaned

12 fluid ounces (360ml) clarified butter

½ cup (120ml) sour cream

2 fluid ounces (60ml) ketchup

1½ tablespoons (22ml) horseradish

1 tablespoon (15g) parsley, chopped

¼ teaspoon (1ml) Tabasco sauce

6 thick slices crusty white bread

5 fluid ounces (150ml) olive oil

2 fluid ounces (60ml) red wine vinegar

6 ounces (180g) iceberg lettuce, cut into chiffonnade

2 lemons

CHEF TIPS *To clean soft-shell crabs:*

1. *Rinse them under cold water several times.*
2. *If the crab is alive, stick a sharp paring knife into the body between the eyes.*
3. *Using scissors, cut off the front part of the crab's head—about ½ inch (1.27cm) behind the eyes.*
4. *Remove the sand bag from behind the mouth and discard.*
5. *Lift the shell at each of the pointed ends and remove the white gill sacks from each side and discard.*
6. *Gently pull the apron from the bottom rear of the crab. The intestinal vein should pull away from the crab with the apron.*
7. *Wash the crabs again in cold salted water before cooking.*

Floured soft-shell crabs are also excellent deep fried. They are frequently served plain with just a little tartar sauce and a lemon wedge.

Combine the eggs and half-and-half. Beat well.

Season the flour to taste with the salt and black pepper.

Dip the cleaned crabs in the half-and-half mixture.

Dredge each crab in the seasoned flour; shake off the excess flour.

Heat the clarified butter in a sautoir pan over medium heat and sauté the crabs for approximately 2–3 minutes per side or until they are thoroughly cooked and reach a minimum internal temperature of 145°F (62.8°C) for at least 15 seconds.

Drain on absorbent paper towels and reserve at 140°F (60°C) or higher until needed.

Combine the sour cream, ketchup, horseradish, parsley, and Tabasco sauce in a bowl and season to taste with salt and black pepper.

Spread the sauce mixture on the top of each slice of bread.

Prepare vinaigrette dressing by briskly whisking the olive oil and vinegar together in a bowl. Season to taste with salt and black pepper.

SERVING/HOLDING

Place 1 slice of bread on each cold plate.

Toss the iceberg lettuce with the vinaigrette and top each slice of bread with approximately 2 ounces (60g) of the dressed lettuce.

Place 1 reserved crab on top of each sandwich.

Squeeze the juice of 1 lemon over the crab sandwiches.

Cut the remaining lemon into 6 wedges and garnish each sandwich with a lemon wedge.

Hold the cooked crabs at 140°F (60°C) or higher.

Hold the sauce and lettuce under refrigeration at 41°F (5°C) or lower.

COOLING/STORING

Cool the crabs from 140°F (60°C) to 70°F (21.1°C) or lower within 2 hours. Cool from 70°F (21.1°C) to 41°F (5°C) within an additional 4 hours for a total cooling time of 6 hours or less.

Cover the crab, sauce, and lettuce; label, date, and store under refrigeration at 41°F (5°C) or lower.

Waldorf Salad

24 ounces (720g) apples, peeled, cored, cut into julienne

1 teaspoon (5ml) lemon juice

2 ounces (60g) walnuts, chopped

1 ounce (30g) celery root, cut into julienne

6 fluid ounces (180ml) heavy cream

2 tablespoons (30g) sugar

4 ounces (120g) mayonnaise, prepared

12 leaves leaf lettuce

2 ounces (60g) walnuts, toasted

1 lemon, cut into 6 wedges

CHEF TIPS *A variety of excellent substitutions exist for the traditional ingredients used in Waldorf salad. Fresh pears can be used in place of the apples, or a combination of pears and apples can be used, if desired. The walnuts can be replaced with just about any nut, but pecans are the most common substitute.*

Toss the apples with the lemon juice.

Stir in the 2 ounces of walnuts and celery root. Reserve under refrigeration at 41°F (5°C) or lower until needed.

Combine the cream and sugar and whisk to soft peaks.

Gently fold the mayonnaise into the whipped cream.

Toss the fruit and nut mixture in the cream until the ingredients are thoroughly incorporated.

Cover and reserve under refrigeration at 41°F (5°C) or lower for at least 2 hours or until needed.

SERVING/HOLDING

Place 2 lettuce leaves in the shape of a cup in the center of each cold plate.

Carefully scoop approximately 6 ounces (180g) of the Waldorf salad into the butter lettuce cup.

Garnish the salad by sprinkling toasted walnuts on top of the salad.

Serve each portion with a lemon wedge.

Hold the Waldorf salad under refrigeration at 41°F (5°C) or lower.

COOLING/STORING

Cover the salad; label, date, and store under refrigeration at 41°F (5°C) or lower.

Pennsylvania Pork Roast

YIELD: 6 PORTIONS · PORTION SIZE: 14 OUNCES

48 ounces (1.4kg) boneless pork shoulder roast

2 tablespoons (30ml) vegetable oil

4 fluid ounces (120ml) brown stock, prepared (see page 515)

4 ounces (120g) leeks, cleaned, cut into 1-inch (2.54cm) lengths

1 teaspoon (5g) dried basil

1 teaspoon (5g) dried marjoram

1 bay leaf

salt, to taste

black pepper, ground, to taste

16 ounces (480g) acorn squash, cut into 6 wedges, seeded

8 ounces (240g) parsnips, peeled, sliced

12 ounces (360g) carrots, peeled, sliced

8 ounces (240g) mushrooms, washed, sliced

4 fluid ounces (120ml) cold water

1 ounce (30g) all-purpose flour

Trim some of the fat from the pork. Heat the vegetable oil in a roasting pan over medium-high heat and sear all sides of the roast until it is thoroughly browned. Reserve until needed.

Drain and discard the fat and return the roast to the pan. Add the brown stock, leeks, basil, marjoram, and bay leaf.

Season the liquid to taste with salt and black pepper.

Bring the liquid to a boil and reduce the heat. Roast for 1–1½ hours. Do not allow the simmering roast to fall below 140°F (60°C).

Add the squash, parsnips, and carrots. Bring the liquid back to a boil, reduce the heat, cover, and simmer an additional 30 minutes. Do not allow the simmering roast to fall below 140°F (60°C).

🥣 **Add** the mushrooms, return the liquid to a boil, reduce the heat, and continue to cook, uncovered, until the vegetables are done and the roast is fork tender and reaches a minimum internal temperature of 155°F (68.3°C) for at least 15 seconds.

🥣 **Remove** the roast and the vegetables from the liquid and reserve at 140°F (60°C) or higher until needed.

Skim and discard the fat from the liquid. Bring the liquid to a boil.

Combine the cold water and flour to make a slurry and whisk in as much of the slurry as needed to thicken the liquid to the desired consistency.

Cook the sauce, stirring constantly, until fully thickened.

Season to taste with salt and black pepper.

SERVING/HOLDING

Slice the pork roast into ½-inch-thick (1.27cm) slices and shingle approximately 8 ounces (227g) of the sliced pork into the center of each hot plate.

Decoratively arrange approximately 4 ounces (120g) of the reserved vegetables around each portion of the slice pork.

Carefully ladle approximately 2 ounces (60ml) of the sauce over half of the pork and around the plate.

🥣 **Hold** the pork roast, vegetables, and sauce at 140°F (60°C) or higher.

COOLING/STORING

🥣 **Cool** the pork roast, vegetables, and sauce from 140°F (60°C) to 70°F (21.1°C) or lower within 2 hours. Cool from 70°F (21.1°C) to 41°F (5°C) within an additional 4 hours for a total cooling time of 6 hours or less.

Cover the pork roast, vegetables, and sauce; label, date, and store under refrigeration at 41°F (5°C) or lower.

Chicken with Dill Dumplings

YIELD: 6 PORTIONS · PORTION SIZE: 12 OUNCES

2 chickens, 2¾ pounds (1.2kg) each, boned, cut into 9 pieces each (whole breast in 3 pieces)

salt, to taste

black pepper, ground, to taste

3 tablespoons (45ml) vegetable oil

1 tablespoon (15g) butter

2 ounces (60g) celery, chopped

2 ounces (60g) onion, chopped

½ ounce (15g) all-purpose flour

16 fluid ounces (480ml) white chicken stock, prepared (see page 517)

12 fluid ounces (360ml) heavy cream

¾ tablespoon (11g) dill, chopped

DUMPLINGS

9 ounces (270g) all-purpose flour

1 teaspoon (5g) baking powder

¼ teaspoon (1g) baking soda

1 teaspoon (5g) salt

3 tablespoons (44ml) sweet butter, melted

6 fluid ounces (180ml) buttermilk

1½ tablespoons (21g) dill, chopped

48 fluid ounces (1.4L) white chicken stock, prepared (see page 517)

Wash and dry the chicken pieces and season them to taste with salt and black pepper. Heat the oil in a sautoir over medium-high heat. Sear the chicken pieces on both sides until golden brown.

Place the seared chicken in a roasting pan and place in a preheated 300°F (148.9°C) oven for approximately 30–40 minutes or until it reaches a minimum internal temperature of 165°F (73.9°C) for at least 15 seconds. Reserve at 140°F (60°C) or higher until needed.

Heat the butter in a sautoir pan over medium heat and cook, stirring constantly, until it becomes light brown.

Add the chopped celery and onions and sauté approximately 3–4 minutes or until the onions become translucent.

Reduce the heat to low, add the first quantity of flour, and cook, stirring frequently, for 5 minutes.

Slowly whisk in the white chicken stock.

Bring to a boil, reduce the heat, and simmer for 30 minutes. Do not allow the simmering sauce to fall below 140°F (60°C).

Stir in the cream and continue to simmer over low heat for 5 additional minutes.

Strain the sauce into a baking dish or casserole, discarding the onions and celery.

Fold the ¾ tablespoon (11g) dill into the sauce, add the reserved cooked pieces of chicken, and hold in a warm oven. Reserve at 140°F (60°C) or higher until needed.

Prepare the dumplings by sifting together the second quantity of flour, baking powder, baking soda, and salt in a bowl.

Add the melted butter and buttermilk and blend until smooth.

Fold in the 1½ tablespoons (21g) chopped dill. Reserve the batter under refrigeration at 41°F (5°C) or lower until needed.

Bring the 48 ounces (1.4L) of white chicken stock to a boil in a saucepot. Reduce the heat to a simmer and spoon the dumpling mixture into the stock one tablespoon at a time.

Cover and simmer for five minutes. Do not allow the simmering stock to fall below 140°F (60°C).

With a slotted spoon, turn the dumplings over, cover, and cook for an additional five minutes. Do not allow the simmering stock to fall below 140°F (60°C).

Remove the cover and poach the dumplings until they are puffed and cooked in the center. Drain well.

SERVING/HOLDING

Place 1 piece of white meat and 2 pieces of dark meat in the bottom third of each hot plate.

Top the chicken with approximately 2 ounces (60ml) of the sauce.

Garnish each portion with 2 or 3 dumplings and serve immediately.

Hold the chicken, sauce, and dumplings at 140°F (60°C) or higher.

🥣 **Cool** the chicken, sauce, and dumplings from 140°F (60°C) to 70°F (21.1°C) or lower within 2 hours. Cool from 70°F (21.1°C) to 41°F (5°C) within an additional 4 hours for a total cooling time of 6 hours or less.

Cover the chicken, sauce, and dumplings; label, date, and store under refrigeration at 41°F (5°C) or lower.

Shaker-Style Turkey Cutlets

YIELD: 6 PORTIONS · PORTION SIZE: 10 OUNCES ·

2¼ pounds (1kg) turkey breast, cut into 12 cutlets, 3 ounces (85g) each

salt, to taste

black pepper, ground, to taste

all-purpose flour, as needed

2 ounces (60g) clarified butter

¾ ounce (22g) shallots, finely diced

6 fluid ounces (180ml) dry white wine

15 fluid ounces (450ml) brown stock, prepared (see page 515)

6 ounces (180g) tomato concasseé

½ ounce (14g) butter

1½ tablespoons (22g) parsley, chopped

Prepare the turkey cutlets by pounding them evenly to approximately ¼ inch (.64cm) thick. Pat dry.

Season the cutlets to taste with salt and black pepper.

Dredge in flour and shake off the excess.

🥣 **Heat** the clarified butter over medium-high heat in a sautoir pan. Sauté the turkey cutlets approximately 2–3 minutes on each side until they are golden brown and reach a minimum internal temperature of 165°F (73.9°C) for at least 15 seconds. Reserve the cutlets at 140°F (60°C) or higher until needed.

Discard the excess fat from the pan and return to medium-high heat. Add the shallots and sauté for 1 minute.

Deglaze the pan with white wine and add the veal jus lié. Reduce the liquid to a nappé consistency.

Add the tomatoes and cook until all of the ingredients are thoroughly incorporated and hot.

Remove from the heat, stir in the butter, and season to taste with salt and black pepper.

SERVING/HOLDING

Shingle 3 turkey cutlets on the lower third of each hot plate.

Carefully ladle approximately 2 ounces (60ml) of the sauce over half the turkey and around the plate.

Garnish each portion by sprinkling with chopped parsley.

Hold the turkey cutlets and sauce at 140°F (60°C) or higher.

COOLING/STORING

Cool the turkey cutlets and sauce from 140°F (60°C) to 70°F (21.1°C) or lower within 2 hours. Cool from 70°F (21.1°C) to 41°F (5°C) within an additional 4 hours for a total cooling time of 6 hours or less.

Cover the turkey cutlets and sauce; label, date, and store under refrigeration at 41°F (5°C) or lower.

Sautéed Scallops with Fresh Herb Tartar Sauce

TARTAR SAUCE

- 6 ounces (180g) mayonnaise, prepared
- 2 tablespoons (30g) onion, finely chopped
- 1 teaspoon (5g) lemon zest
- 4 teaspoons (20ml) lemon juice
- 1 teaspoon (5g) dill, chopped
- 1 teaspoon (5g) thyme, chopped
- 1 teaspoon (5g) parsley, chopped

SCALLOPS

- 1½ ounces (45g) butter, melted
- ½ teaspoon (2g) black pepper, ground
- ¼ teaspoon (1g) paprika, sweet
- 40 ounces (1.2kg) sea scallops
- ½ teaspoon (2g) salt
- 1 lemon, cut into 6 wedges

CHEF TIPS *This preparation is also well suited to pan-smoking, but be careful not to oversmoke the scallops, as they will become bitter. A mere 30–45 seconds of smoke is sufficient to impart distinctive flavor to the scallops. More is unnecessary.*

Prepare the tartar sauce by combining the mayonnaise, onions, lemon zest, lemon juice, and chopped herbs. Mix thoroughly until all the ingredients are incorporated. Reserve under refrigeration at 41°F (5°C) or lower until needed.

Combine the melted butter, pepper, and paprika.

Remove and discard the muscles from the scallops. Season the scallops with salt.

Heat the butter mixture in a sautoir pan over medium-high heat and sauté the scallops, turning and brushing them frequently with the butter mixture from the pan, until they are opaque in color and reach a minimum internal temperature of 145°F (62.8°C) for at least 15 seconds.

SERVING/HOLDING

Place approximately 6 ounces (180g) of scallops on the center of each hot plate.

Carefully spoon some of the butter used to cook the scallops over the top of each portion. Serve with lemon wedges.

🥣 **Hold** the scallops at 140°F (60°C) or higher.

COOLING/STORING

🥣 **Cool** the scallops from 140°F (60°C) to 70°F (21.1°C) or lower within 2 hours. Cool from 70°F (21.1°C) to 41°F (5°C) within an additional 4 hours for a total cooling time of 6 hours or less.

Cover the scallops; label, date, and store under refrigeration at 41°F (5°C) or lower.

Spaghetti Squash

YIELD: 6 PORTIONS · PORTION SIZE: 4 OUNCES

48 ounces (1.4kg) or 1 spaghetti squash

8 ounces (240g) butter

salt, to taste

black pepper, ground, to taste

Cut the squash in half lengthwise and place on a baking sheet lined with parchment paper.

Bake in a preheated 350°F (176.7°C) oven for approximately 30–45 minutes or until the squash is tender.

Cool the squash from 140°F (60°C) to 70°F (21.1°C) or lower within 2 hours. Cool from 70°F (21.1°C) to 41°F (5°C) within an additional 4 hours for a total cooling time of 6 hours or less.

With a fork, gently scrape out the flesh of the squash. It will come out in strings like spaghetti and should have a yellow color.

Heat the butter in a sauteuse pan over medium heat.

Toss the spaghetti squash until it is thoroughly coated with the butter and hot.

Season to taste with salt and black pepper.

SERVING/HOLDING

Hold the spaghetti squash at 140°F (60°C) or higher.

COOLING/STORING

Cool the squash from 140°F (60°C) to 70°F (21.1°C) or lower within 2 hours. Cool from 70°F (21.1°C) to 41°F (5°C) within an additional 4 hours for a total cooling time of 6 hours or less.

Cover the squash; label, date, and store under refrigeration at 41°F (5°C) or lower.

Spinach Timbales

YIELD: 6 PORTIONS · PORTION SIZE: 4 OUNCES

12 ounces (360g) spinach, blanched, squeezed dry

3 ounces (90g) Granny Smith apples, peeled, cored, sliced, blanched

2 large eggs

6 fluid ounces (180ml) milk

3 ounces (90g) breadcrumbs

salt, to taste

black pepper, ground, to taste

Combine all the ingredients in a food processor, except for the salt and pepper.

Process until the ingredients are thoroughly incorporated and puréed.

Season the mixture to taste with salt and black pepper.

Pour the mixture into 6 buttered 4-ounce (120ml) timbale molds.

Bake the timbales in a water bath in a preheated 325°F (162.8°C) oven for approximately 20 minutes or until they are firm and set and reach a minimum internal temperature of 145°F (62.8°C) for at least 15 seconds.

SERVING/HOLDING

Remove the timbales from the oven, dry the molds, and invert one on each hot plate.

Carefully remove the mold, leaving the molded spinach intact on the plate.

Hold the spinach timbales at 140°F (60°C) or higher.

COOLING/STORING

Cool the spinach timbales from 140°F (60°C) to 70°F (21.1°C) or lower within 2 hours. Cool from 70°F (21.1°C) to 41°F (5°C) within an additional 4 hours for a total cooling time of 6 hours or less.

Cover the spinach timbales; label, date, and store under refrigeration at 41°F (5°C) or lower.

Glazed Carrot Sticks

YIELD: 6 PORTIONS · PORTION SIZE: 4 OUNCES

3 fluid ounces (90ml) clarified butter

10 fluid ounces (300ml) white chicken stock, prepared (see page 517)

24 ounces (720g) carrots, cut into sticks

salt, to taste

black pepper, ground, to taste

Melt the butter in a pan over medium heat. Add the white chicken stock.

Add the carrots and cover the pan.

Sweat the carrots for 4–5 minutes.

Bring the carrots to a boil, reduce the heat, cover, and simmer over low heat for 5–6 minutes or until the carrots are almost tender.

Remove the cover and increase the heat to medium-high.

Reduce the liquid to a syrupy consistency. If the carrots are done before the glaze forms, remove the carrots with a spoon, and reserve at 140°F (60°C) or higher until needed. When the liquid is done, return the carrots to the pan and toss until hot and thoroughly coated.

Season to taste with salt and black pepper.

SERVING/HOLDING

Hold the carrots at 140°F (60°C) or higher.

COOLING/STORING

Cool the carrots from 140°F (60°C) to 70°F (21.1°C) or lower within 2 hours. Cool from 70°F (21.1°C) to 41°F (5°C) within an additional 4 hours for a total cooling time of 6 hours or less.

Cover the carrots; label, date, and store under refrigeration at 41°F (5°C) or lower.

Matchstick Potatoes

YIELD: 6 PORTIONS · PORTION SIZE: 4 OUNCES

32 ounces (960g) russet potatoes, peeled

salt, to taste

white pepper, ground, to taste

Cut the potatoes into allumette strips using a French knife or mandoline and place them in a bowl of cold water. Rinse the starch from the potatoes by washing them thoroughly under cold running water.

Thoroughly drain and dry the potatoes on absorbent paper towels.

Deep fry the potatoes in a preheated 350°F (176.7°C) fryer using the basket method in two stages. First, fry the potatoes until they are soft and form a skin. Remove the potatoes from the fryer and let the fat return to its original temperature. For the second step, toss the potatoes, still in the fryer basket, and place them back into the hot fat. Continue to cook until the potatoes are crisp and have a golden straw color.

Drain the fried potatoes well on absorbent paper towels and season to taste with salt and white pepper.

Be careful when handling the cooked matchstick potatoes, as they are delicate once fully cooked and break easily.

SERVING/HOLDING

Hold the matchstick potatoes at 140°F (60°C) or higher.

COOLING/STORING

Cool the matchstick potatoes from 140°F (60°C) to 70°F (21.1°C) or lower within 2 hours. Cool from 70°F (21.1°C) to 41°F (5°C) within an additional 4 hours for a total cooling time of 6 hours or less.

Cover the matchstick potatoes; label, date, and store under refrigeration at 41°F (5°C) or lower.

Croquette Potatoes

YIELD: 6 PORTIONS ·· PORTION SIZE: 4 OUNCES

32 ounces (960g) potatoes, peeled, quartered

water, as needed

2 ounces (60g) butter, softened

2 egg yolks

salt, to taste

white pepper, ground, to taste

flour, as needed

egg wash, as needed

dry breadcrumbs, finely ground, as needed

CHEF TIPS *Freezing the piped potato cylinders makes the standard breading procedure much easier, as frozen potatoes are quite hard. Be sure to properly cool the potatoes before placing them in the freezer.*

The cylinder-shaped croquette potatoes are called for in classic cuisine, but any shape is acceptable in American regional cuisine.

Boil the potatoes in a saucepot of boiling salted water until they are tender. Drain thoroughly.

Place the potatoes on a baking sheet lined with parchment paper and dry in a preheated 300°F (148.9°C) oven for approximately 10–15 minutes.

Process the potatoes through a food mill or meat grinder while still hot.

Add the butter and egg yolks to the mashed potatoes and mix thoroughly until the ingredients are incorporated.

Season the potatoes to taste with salt and white pepper.

Place the potatoes in a pastry bag with a large round tip and pipe long sausage shapes onto a baking sheet lined with parchment paper or dusted with flour.

Cool the potatoes from 140°F (60°C) to 70°F (21.1°C) or lower within 2 hours. Cool from 70°F (21.1°C) to 41°F (5°C) within an additional 4 hours for a total cooling time of 6 hours or less.

Once the potatoes are thoroughly chilled, cut the potato shapes into 3-inch-long (7.6cm) cylindrical pieces.

Coat the potato cylinders with the standard breading procedure by dredging them in flour, dipping them in egg wash, then coating them with breadcrumbs.

Deep fry the croquettes in a preheated 375°F (190.6°C) fryer using the basket method or until they are golden brown and reach a minimum internal temperature of 165°F (73.9°C) for at least 15 seconds.

Degrease on absorbent paper towels.

SERVING/HOLDING

✍ **Hold** the croquette potatoes at 140°F (60°C) or higher.

COOLING/STORING

✍ **Cool** the croquette potatoes from 140°F (60°C) to 70°F (21.1°C) or lower within 2 hours. Cool from 70°F (21.1°C) to 41°F (5°C) within an additional 4 hours for a total cooling time of 6 hours or less.

Cover the croquette potatoes; label, date, and store under refrigeration at 41°F (5°C) or lower.

Buttery Homemade Noodles

YIELD: 6 PORTIONS · PORTION SIZE: 6 OUNCES

8 large eggs

2 teaspoons (10g) salt

24 ounces (720g) all-purpose flour

32 fluid ounces (960ml) white chicken stock, prepared (see page 517)

4 tablespoons (60g) butter

4 tablespoons (60g) parsley, chopped

salt, to taste

black pepper, ground, to taste

Combine the eggs and 2 teaspoons of salt in a bowl.

Using a fork, stir in the flour.

Form the dough into a ball and knead for 2–3 minutes until it becomes smooth.

Cover the dough and let rest for 10 minutes under refrigeration at 41°F (5°C) or lower until needed.

Roll the dough into a large rectangle approximately ⅛ inch (.32cm) thick. Let the dough rest for an additional 5 minutes.

Dust the top of the dough with a little flour and roll it up like a jelly roll.

Slice the dough crosswise into noodles ¼ inch (.64cm) thick.

Bring the white chicken stock to a boil in a saucepot. Reduce the heat and add the noodles.

Simmer the noodles for approximately 2–3 minutes or until tender. Drain thoroughly and reserve at 140°F (60°C) or higher until needed.

Heat the butter in a sauteuse pan over medium heat.

Add the noodles and toss until they are thoroughly coated with butter and hot.

Sprinkle with parsley and toss until incorporated.

Season to taste with salt and pepper.

SERVING/HOLDING

Hold the noodles at 140°F (60°C) or higher.

COOLING/STORING

Cool the noodles from 140°F (60°C) to 70°F (21.1°C) or lower within 2 hours. Cool from 70°F (21.1°C) to 41°F (5°C) within an additional 4 hours for a total cooling time of 6 hours or less.

Cover the noodles; label, date, and store under refrigeration at 41°F (5°C) or lower.

Scalloped Sweet Potatoes

YIELD: 6 PORTIONS · PORTION SIZE: 6 OUNCES

16 ounces (480g) sweet potatoes

2 ounces (60g) butter

2½ ounces (75g) light brown sugar

1 teaspoon (5g) nutmeg, grated

½ teaspoon (2g) salt

4 fluid ounces (120ml) heavy cream

2 ounces (60g) walnuts, chopped

15 ounces (450g) apples, peeled, cored, sliced

Wash the sweet potatoes and place the unpeeled potatoes in a saucepot of cold salted water.

Bring to a boil and cook for approximately 30–40 minutes or until tender.

Drain the potatoes and let cool slightly until they can be handled safely.

Peel the potatoes, keeping them whole.

⚕ **Slice** the potatoes approximately ½ inch (1.27cm) thick and hold at 140°F (60°C) or higher until needed.

Melt the butter in a saucepan over medium heat and, when it begins to foam, stir in the brown sugar, nutmeg, and salt.

Lower the heat and slowly cook the mixture until the sugar dissolves and forms a syrup.

Stir in the heavy cream and remove from the heat.

Place a layer of the sliced sweet potatoes in a baking or casserole dish and scatter some of the chopped walnuts over the top of the sliced potatoes.

Spoon some of the syrup over the top, then layer some of the sliced apples on top of the potatoes.

Continue the layering process until all of the sweet potatoes, nuts, syrup, and apples have been used. The final layer should be apples.

Cover and bake in a preheated 350°F (176.7°C) oven for 30 minutes.

Uncover and continue to cook for approximately 15 minutes until the potatoes are fully cooked and the apples are browned.

SERVING/HOLDING

⚕ **Hold** the sweet potatoes at 140°F (60°C) or higher.

COOLING/STORING

⚕ **Cool** the sweet potatoes from 140°F (60°C) to 70°F (21.1°C) or lower within 2 hours. Cool from 70°F (21.1°C) to 41°F (5°C) within an additional 4 hours for a total cooling time of 6 hours or less.

Cover the sweet potatoes; label, date, and store under refrigeration at 41°F (5°C) or lower.

Apple Brown Betty

YIELD: 6 PORTIONS · PORTION SIZE: 6 OUNCES

24 ounces (720g) fresh breadcrumbs, coarsely ground

6 ounces (180g) butter

4 large Winesap or Rome Beauty apples

8 ounces (240g) sugar

½ teaspoon (2g) cinnamon, ground

½ teaspoon (2g) nutmeg, ground

12 fluid ounces (360ml) heavy cream

1 teaspoon (5g) sugar

½ fluid ounce (15ml) dark rum

CHEF TIPS *Apple brown betty is a traditional Mid-Atlantic dessert made with apples. It is a casserole layered with sliced apples, fresh bread-crumbs, butter, cinnamon, and nutmeg, then baked until the apples are cooked and the crumb topping is golden brown. Apple brown betty is usually served hot with ice cream or whipped cream, which is sometimes flavored with rum. Throughout the region, the recipe for Brown Betty varies from area to area, taking on differ-ent characteristics from those who prepare it.*

Toast the breadcrumbs in a preheated 350°F (176.7°C) oven until golden brown. Divide the breadcrumbs into 3 parts and reserve at room temperature until needed.

Cut the butter into small pieces approximately ½ inch (1.27cm) square. Divide into 4 parts and reserve under refrigeration at 41°F (5°C) or lower until needed.

Peel and core the apples and cut them into thin slices. Divide into 2 parts and reserve under refrigeration at 41°F (5°C) or lower until needed.

Combine the sugar, cinnamon, and nutmeg. Divide into 3 parts and reserve at room tempera-ture until needed.

Lightly butter a 2-quart (1.9L) casserole or baking dish and arrange in it layers, using the reserved ingredients in the following order: crumbs, butter, apples, spices, butter, crumbs, but-ter, apples, spices, crumbs, butter, spices.

Pour ½ cup (120ml) heavy cream over the top of the casserole.

Bake the casserole for 30 minutes in a preheated 375 °F (190.6°C) oven or until the apples are tender and the crumb topping is nicely browned.

Whip the remaining heavy cream with the sugar and rum until it forms stiff peaks.

Carefully spoon approximately 6 ounces (180g) of the warm brown betty into the center of each hot plate. Make sure to spoon to the bottom of the casserole to ensure that each portion receives all of the layers.

Garnish each portion of the brown betty with a dollop of the rum whipped cream.

Hold the brown betty at 140°F (60°C) or higher.

COOLING/STORING

Cool the brown betty from 140°F (60°C) to 70°F (21.1°C) or lower within 2 hours. Cool from 70°F (21.1°C) to 41°F (5°C) within an additional 4 hours for a total cooling time of 6 hours or less.

Cover the brown betty and whipped cream; label, date, and store under refrigeration at 41°F (5°C) or lower.

Deborah R. Vantrece-Berry

ON THE CUISINE OF THE DEEP SOUTH

Travel through the South, on roads named with route numbers, not street names; spend a Sunday afternoon conversing with the matrons of the church about the many children they've raised and who makes the best sweet potato pie; smell the peanuts boiling at the little shack on the side of the road—now you have touched upon a small nibble of the Deep South. Southern dishes are not just made of ingredients; they are made of history, experiences, and heirloom recipes.

For me, the cuisine of the Deep South is a combination of inheritance, travel, and learned knowledge. Raised in Kansas City, Missouri, born to a family full of good cooks with lineage from Arkansas and Louisiana, good food was something I took for granted. Early on, without much scope for comparison, I classified food simply as good or bad and did not expand to more sophisticated reasoning about regions, influences, or style.

Southern cuisine is what I know. It comprises ingredients, flavors, and tastes that represent comfort—a cuisine full of experience, flavor, and, at its height, sophistication.

Spend hours picking greens, cleaning chitterlings, or in the smokehouse, and you will literally feel the history of the South running through your veins. You start with the freshest, purest ingredients and you understand that there are no shortcuts. Discovering ways of preparing southern dishes with healthfulness in mind but without compromising flavor is the challenge. Using creativity to give the bounty of the South a more international appeal, style, and attitude is the fun part.

My personal style of Southern cooking is in a category of its own. It has been referred to as *New Southern, New Soul*, and *International*. I prefer to call it *twisted*. It's a new take on familiar, traditional Southern ingredients, products, and recipes. It's a blend of the many cultures of today's South and reflects its influences. Jokingly, it's Escoffier meets the Southern belle.

For me, Southern cuisine is about hospitality, the fellowship of breaking bread, and tradition. It's about the marriage of the old and new South, roots whose plants are now blossoming. This is the culinary South.

Deborah R. Vantrece-Berry is the owner of Edible Art Café and Gourmet Caterer's in Atlanta, Georgia. She is a graduate of The Art Institute of Atlanta.

The Deep South

The roots of Southern cuisine predate the arrival of the
English and Spanish in the Americas. As in most other areas of the United States, the cuisine was heavily influenced by the Native Americans of the region. When the settlers founded James Cittie, later called Jamestown, they encountered the Powhatan tribe of the Algonquian Native Americans and shared a dish of succotash, venison, and berries. The Native Americans' diet included meat and seafood cooked over open fires, thought of by many as the original barbecue. Game stews, sweet potatoes, cymlings (squash), pumpkins, and maize (corn) were also staples of the local cuisine. The Native Americans introduced the settlers to corn and taught them to cultivate it. The corn that colonists grew did not resemble the corn of today but was more like what we now call Indian corn, with starchy

multicolored kernels that required slow cooking in order to become edible. The whole kernels were also boiled in lye solution, then hulled, washed, and dried to create hominy, an ingredient used in succotash (see page 123). The settlers brought with them boar, sows, and the seeds of carrots and turnips. These foods, as well as the indigenous foods of the region, particularly corn and pork, became essentials in the cuisine of the Deep South.

Many new foods began to be used in the cooking of the region. Varieties of meat and seafood as well as beans, onions, greens, berries, and stone fruits were incorporated into local dishes. After the Carolinas were founded in 1670, the first wave of settlers moved south and west, eventually crossing the Appalachian Mountains into Kentucky. Immigrants and their cultures began to shape the cuisine of the Deep South region.

As the lands were settled, the Great Philadelphia Wagon Road connected them. This road, called the Philly Road, was completed in the 1750s and became the first road to link Philadelphia to South Carolina. The immigrants traveling down the Philly Road were of Irish, Scottish, Welsh, English, and German descent. From Augusta, Georgia, wagons left the Philly Road and followed the nation's second road, the Upper Federal Road, through Georgia and Alabama to bring goods to market towns like Columbus, Mississippi.

Rice cultivation began in South Carolina in the early 1700s. By 1725, rice was also a major crop in Arkansas, Louisiana, Mississippi, and Texas. It was exported by the ton to England. Charleston became an affluent port full of wealthy plantation owners in the rice production business. Rice became a staple used frequently in the cooking of the Low Country—an area of South Carolina that extends from Orangeburg to the coast and from the North Carolina border to Georgia's Savannah River. Southerners stirred the grain into casseroles, soups, breads, and puddings. The familiar dish red beans and rice had its beginnings here. Chicken Country Captain, a curried chicken dish named after a British army officer who allegedly brought the recipe to the Low Country from India, is another famous local recipe. Pilau, another well-known regional rice dish, involves simmering rice in an aromatic broth. The Civil War, hurricanes, and the end of slavery took their toll on the rice business in South Carolina. By the end of the 1800s, most rice production had moved to Texas, California, Arkansas, and Mississippi.

Foods from this region contain elements of French, Spanish, African, and English culture and tradition. The French Huguenots brought sauces, gratins, and meat dishes to the area. The Spanish brought figs, pomegranates, and peaches to the Low Country 100 years before the Carolinas were founded. The Spanish also brought red beans and rice and pilaus to the region. Low Country dishes include Sally Lunn bread, benne (sesame seed) wafers, Huguenot torte, and Chicken Country Captain.

A second wave of immigrants split off the Philly Road in North Carolina in the 1790s to settle in the Blue Ridge Mountains and the valleys and plateau regions of Tennessee. In the early 1800s, the Natchez Trace was carved out of the wilderness to link Natchez on the Mississippi River to Nashville. It was created so merchants traveling downstream could get home again. By the time it was completed, the steamboat had been invented and, soon after that, the steam locomotive ushered in the Industrial Revolution. These historical benchmarks helped further diversify the Southern diet and lifestyle.

The Old South can be defined temporally as the pre–Civil War period from 1820 to 1860 and geographically as comprising North Carolina, South Carolina, Georgia, Mississippi, and Alabama. Arkansas became part of the United States with the Louisiana Purchase and received statehood in 1836. Its tie to the Deep South was its main crop, cotton. During the pre–Civil War period, the main cash crop in all of the Southern states, from North Carolina to Texas, was cotton. Other crops flourished in South Carolina, which grew rice, indigo, and tobacco. Sugar, wheat, grains for distilling, sheep for wool, and cattle for meat were regular mainstays of the Deep South. Today, the states of Arkansas, Kentucky, and Tennessee are included in the culinary region of the Deep South.

The tobacco and cotton plantations led the economic growth of the Deep South and, in turn, provided the materials for the industrialization of the North. With the plantations came the slaves. The rice plantation owners in South Carolina first enslaved the indigenous Native American tribes. When they rebelled, the colonists began importing slaves from Africa. The Africans had a profound influence on the Southern diet. They brought with them yams, sesame seeds, okra, peanuts, and black-eyed peas as well as their own cooking methods and styles.

The smokehouse was an integral component of every plantation. A shallow pit was dug in the center of the earthen floor inside the dark smokehouse. Pork was rubbed with salt and placed in a wooden box to cure for about six weeks. It was then hung from the ceiling or placed on shelves around the edges of the smokehouse. The butchered meat was then smoked over a slow-burning fire flavored with corncobs and apple wood.

Poultry was also an important part of the Southerner's diet. Most plantations kept a variety of domesticated fowl, including chickens, ducks, geese, pigeons, and turkeys. Chickens were the most popular due to their high yield of meat and their ease of care.

The slaves of the Deep South were such good cooks that they were even more sought after than French chefs. Slaveholder Robert Q. Mallard, in the mid-1800s, said, "My slaves possess so much natural genius that they completely distanced French cooks in the production of wholesome, dainty, and appetizing food."

The slave cooks' style was dramatically different when they cooked for their own families, as they were provided only the "waste" after preparing the finer cuts of meat for their masters.

Pork fat was rendered into lard and the hog's skin was fried and called *cracklings*. Fried hog's intestine was called *chitterlings*. Other ingredients commonly used by slaves included hoofs, ears, tails, and brains.

The term *soul food* refers to what slaves cooked for their own families, and that "came from the soul" or from one's memory. Soul food recipes were typically handed down through the generations by word of mouth. The term also refers to Southern food that is spicier, saltier, and sweeter than typical Southern cuisine and is of African heritage.

The New South, or Reconstruction Era, began with the emancipation of the slaves after the Civil War. By 1900, the expansion of Southern railways, cotton textiles, tobacco and forest products, and the iron, steel, and coal industries were the benchmarks of the New South. During the 1920s, cotton was still the region's main cash crop, others being rice, sugar, and tobacco. The cultivation of apples, peaches, peanuts, pecans, and soybeans also emerged about this time. President Roosevelt's New Deal allowed Southern farmers to replace 50 percent of their topsoil-depleted cotton acreage with soybeans, peanuts, hay, wheat, and truck crops. Truck crops included fruits such as peaches, apples, grapes, watermelon, cantaloupe, and blueberries.

Vegetable varieties in the South are endless, with major cultivation of mixed greens, squash, tomatoes, peppers, cucumbers, cabbage, onions, and beans. The only tea grown in America comes from Wadmalaw Island, South Carolina. Other primary crops include sweet potatoes, peanuts, sweet corn, mushrooms, eggplant, and okra. Agriculture items of importance are chickens, turkeys, eggs, beef cattle, milk, hogs, goats, and catfish. Seafood from the shores of North Carolina to Georgia to Mississippi includes tilapia, pompano, red snapper, flounder, grouper, mullet, shad, trout, striped bass, shrimp, stone crabs, scallops, oysters, crawfish, clams, and soft-shell crabs.

The people from the islands off the South Carolina and Georgia coastlines mainly speak Gullah, a creole language combining seventeenth- and eighteenth-century English, with West African languages. Words such as *goober* for "peanut" and *gumbo* for "okra" are Gullah. Gullah cooking is similar to that of the Low Country, except that Gullah cooks tend to use rendered pork fat instead of butter. Gullah cooks are also known for their seafood and shellfish dishes.

Icons of the cuisine of the Deep South region include Southern Fried Chicken with Creamy Pepper Gravy (page 116), Hoppin' John Salad with Pecan Vinaigrette (page 110), Buttermilk biscuits (page 125), Brunswick Stew (page 112), and, of course, Carolina Pulled Pork Barbecue (page 114). Other notable regional dishes include burgoo from Kentucky, Frogmore stew from St. Helena Island, South Carolina, and shrimp Awendaw from Awendaw Island, South Carolina. Vidalia onions, mint juleps, country ham, grits, and red-eye gravy are also popular regional specialties.

Dutch, French, Spanish, English, German, African, and Native American gastronomy enriched the Deep South's style of cooking and made food a central feature of Southerners' lives. Throughout the region's history, Southern hospitality has revolved around Sunday dinners and public feasts. It is worth noting that what the rest of the country refers to as *lunch*, Southerners call *dinner*, and their evening meal is called *supper*. Public feasts, such as barbecues, oyster roasts, and Low Country boils, attract crowds of people. No matter the purpose, Southerners are known for their hospitality and culinary delights.

Typical Deep South Ingredients and Dishes

Ambrosia: A chilled salad or dessert, frequently served in the Deep South, made with diced fruit, nuts, marshmallows, and coconut.

Baby Lima Bean: A New World bean named for its origin in Lima, Peru. Baby lima beans are different from the larger variety of lima bean, the Fordhook; they are pale green, plump, and have a kidney-shaped curvature. Baby lima beans are available from June to September and need to be shelled just before use. They are also available frozen and canned.

Banana Pudding: A vanilla custard dessert, frequently served in the Deep South, topped with sliced bananas and vanilla wafer cookies.

Barbecue: A barbecue is a piece of equipment also known as a *grill*. Barbecue is also a cooking technique utilized for meat. In the Deep South region, pork and chicken are the meats most commonly barbecued, whereas in Tex-Mex cooking, beef barbecue is preferred. Barbecue in the Deep South is generally seasoned with a dry rub, then slowly cooked over a fire, which gives it a smoky taste. Basting with a wet rub (made of an acid, such as vinegar, and spices) to keep the meat moist is highly recommended.

Barbecue Sauce: Used to baste barbecued meat and as an accompanying sauce. Regional preferences differ; however typical ingredients include onions, garlic, mustard, tomatoes, brown sugar, and, often, vinegar.

Benne Wafer: *Benne* is another name for sesame seed, the main ingredient in this crisp, nut-flavored cookie. Other ingredients are pecans and brown sugar.

Bibb Lettuce: Born in Frankfort, Kentucky, in 1865, this lettuce is named for Judge Jack Bibb, who propagated it in his greenhouse. It as also known as *limestone lettuce* because the alkaline limestone soil of the area was credited in helping produce the superior lettuce. This lettuce has small, round, loosely formed heads with soft, buttery-textured leaves.

Biscuit: A small, round quick bread leavened with baking powder or baking soda and cream of tartar. When made properly, biscuits are tender and light, with a savory flavor. They are usually served, smothered with gravy, for breakfast or as an accompaniment to fried chicken at dinner.

Black-Eyed Pea: This small, tan bean, with its distinctive black eye, was brought to the Deep South with African slaves. Black-eyed peas, also called *cowpeas*, are sold fresh, dried, frozen, and canned.

Bourbon: This distilled spirit is made from corn and was invented in the 1700s by the Baptist minister Elijah Craig of Bourbon County, Kentucky. Bourbon, also called *straight whiskey*, is the only distilled spirit to originate in the United States.

Bourbon Ball: A confection made from ground cookies, nuts, and sugar, and usually spiked with bourbon or rum.

Brunswick Stew: Attributed to the people of Brunswick, Georgia, this stew traditionally used squirrel as its primary meat. Today, it contains smoked pork or chicken and is sometimes seasoned with a ham bone. Brunswick stew is hearty and thick, somewhere between soup and stew in its consistency. The traditional vegetables included are tomatoes, onions, celery, carrots, potatoes, lima beans, and corn.

Burgoo: A thick stew made from barbecued meat or mutton and vegetables. This dish usually has a shot of bourbon added to it—a token of its Kentucky origins.

Butter Bean: A regional name for lima bean.

Catfish: A freshwater, bottom-feeding fish indigenous to the rivers and lakes of the Deep South. The wild variety, which used to be eaten mainly by Southerners, has recently been replaced by the farm-raised variety, now popular across America. Belzoni, Mississippi, is recognized as the catfish capital of the world and is famous for its high-quality farm-raised catfish, which have a fresh, subtle taste and no fishy odor.

Chicken Country Captain: A traditional Low Country dish made by simmering chicken smothered in tomato gravy flavored with curry. Chicken Country Captain is typically served over rice.

Chitterling: The small intestine of a hog. After being cleaned, chitterlings are simmered until tender. They are usually fried and added to soups or served with sauce. They are also used as a casing for sausage.

Chow-Chow: Its roots are unclear (Native American, British, or Chinese), but chow-chow is a familiar condiment in the Deep South region. More often than not, it includes cabbage and green tomatoes, which are boiled in pickling brine and flavored with a hint of mustard.

Coca-Cola: The Deep South region's original beverage. In 1886, an Atlanta pharmacist named John Styth invented Coca-Cola, as a prescription medicine to cure headaches and hangovers. Coca-Cola was originally made from the kola nut and the coca plant. Later, carbonated water was added to the recipe. Asa Candler purchased the syrup rights in 1888 and eliminated the coca leaf ingredient, then registered the trade name known worldwide today as Coca-Cola.

Corn: The Native Americans introduced this staple to the colonists of the Deep South region. At the time, corn was tough and required slow cooking to become edible. Now every part of the corn plant can be used. The kernels are the most versatile part—used whole in side dishes and popcorn, cooked in ground forms such as cornmeal and cornstarch, and transformed altogether into corn syrup, bourbon, and whiskey. The stalks and cobs are fed to cattle and other animals. The husks are the only authentic wrap for tamales. Even the silks are used—brewed as a medicinal tea. Corn is primarily a summer crop, but it is readily available throughout the year frozen and canned.

Cornmeal: Ground dried corn kernels. The old-fashioned grinding technique involved water-powered stone mills. The modern approach employs steel rollers. Both methods can be controlled to vary the texture of the resulting meal. Cornmeal is sold in several color varieties—white, yellow, and the increasingly popular blue—each of which has its own characteristic flavor nuances.

Corn Pone: The first corn bread. The word *apone* is a Native American term meaning "baked." These cakes are made from water and cornmeal and baked in ashes. From this simple recipe, an assortment of breads was developed, including hushpuppies, spoonbread, cracklin' bread, johnnycakes, and hoecakes.

Country Ham: A dry ham that is salt-cured for up to 3 months and aged for up to 12 months. It is produced in the Deep South states of Kentucky, Tennessee, North Carolina, and Georgia. After the curing process, which can take up to 40 days, the salt is rinsed off and the ham slowly smoked over a hardwood fire before being aged. The salt used to cure country ham draws out the moisture in the meat, yielding a firm, flavorful finished product. Country ham is different from canned or water-added ham. With these hams, the salt is dissolved with the cure and injected into the meat. The entire process takes as little as 24 hours.

Cowpea: A broad category of peas that includes black-eyed peas and blue-hulled peas.

Cracklings: The crisp fried, brown skin of roasted pork. Cracklings are sold packaged and eaten as a snack. They are also used as an ingredient in corn bread.

Deviled: In the Deep South, *deviled* indicates a dish that contains mustard, Worcestershire sauce, Tabasco sauce, and peppers. Deviled eggs are a commonly served appetizer or hors d'oeuvre.

Divinity: A Deep South regional confection made from white fudge, corn syrup, or molasses combined with stiffly beaten egg whites. Even richer variations are formed by the addition of nuts, chocolate, coconut, and other goodies.

Fatback: A fresh, unsmoked, and unsalted layer of fat from a hog's back.

Frogmore Stew: Named after a town on St. Helena Island, South Carolina. Frogmore stew is a Gullah dish of crab, shrimp, sausage, and corn cooked with spicy seasonings.

Greens: The edible leaves of plants such as collard, mustard, turnip, beet, watercress, poke sallet, spinach, kale, ramp, and dandelion. Greens are usually sautéed with salt pork or bacon or steamed.

Grits: Ground from hominy to a coarse, medium, or fine texture, grits are typically made into a soft, savory cornmeal mush. Coarse-ground grits are cooked for 30–60 minutes. Medium-grind grits are packaged as "quick grits," which take only 5 minutes to cook. Finely ground grits are sold as "instant grits" and are boiled for 1 minute. Grits are commonly used as a side dish during breakfast. On the Southern coast, grits are often served with seafood.

Hoecakes: Also referred to as johnnycakes, these flat griddlecakes are made from cornmeal, salt, and boiling water. Tradition has it that they were created by slaves, who cooked the mixture on their hoes under the hot sun while they worked in the fields.

Hominy: Corn kernels boiled in a lye solution, then hulled, washed, and dried. Hominy is usually sold whole in cans. It is an ingredient commonly found in succotash. When ground, hominy is referred to as *hominy grits*. (See *grits*.)

Hoppin' John: First made by African slaves on the South Carolina plantations, this dish is made from black-eyed peas cooked with salt pork and combined with rice. Hoppin' John was traditionally served on New Year's Day to ensure good luck and prosperity, but it is now served year-round. Collard greens and corn bread usually accompany hoppin' John. The greens are said to represent money and the corn bread signifies gold. This recipe is made with black-eyed peas and represents the soldiers who died in the Civil War.

Hushpuppies: Hushpuppies were first made in the town of Nouvell near New Orleans, shortly after 1727, by a group of nuns who sailed from France to New Orleans. The nuns converted cornmeal into a delicious food that they named *croquettes de maise*. The origin of the term *hushpuppy* has many accounts. One is based on an aquatic reptile called the salamander found in the South, which was referred to as a *water dog* or *water puppy*. Salamanders were deep-fried with cornmeal dough and formed into sticks. It is said that they were called hushpuppies because eating such lowly food was not something a Southern wife would want known to her neighbors. Another account follows the Civil War era, when army cooks would toss scraps of corn batter from frying fish to hungry dogs, saying, "Hush, puppies." In yet another tale, it is said that the fried cornmeal cakes kept the dogs from barking and revealing the location of a Southern battalion during the Civil War.

Iced Tea: A Southern drink that is served at any time of the day. Iced tea became popular at the St. Louis World's Fair in 1904, when Richard Blechynden found that he could not sell his hot tea in the summer's heat. He transformed the drink into an iced version sweetened with sugar. It was an instant success.

Mint Julep: An alcoholic beverage made by crushing mint with a spoon and mixing it with sugar, bourbon, and crushed ice. Mint juleps are typically served in a silver tumbler and are traditionally drunk during the Kentucky Derby.

Muscadine: A slipskin purple grape that grows only in the Deep South, of which it is native. It is mainly eaten as a fruit but actually was the grape used for the first American-made wine.

Okra: An unusual and versatile vegetable, originally from Ethiopia. It can be prepared by several methods—frying, boiling, stewing, and baking. Okra's characteristic property is that, when cooked, it exudes a substance that acts as a thickening agent; this is its function in gumbo. When buying fresh okra, look for small pods, less than 4 inches long, with a bright green color. Okra is also available frozen, canned, breaded, and frozen breaded.

Oyster Roast: A popular Low Country event similar to a clambake in the Northeast. Bushels of oysters are dumped into a roasting kettle and covered with a burlap sack, then placed over hot coals to cook. Once cooked, the oysters are served on newspaper-lined picnic tables and are pried open with special knives.

Peanut: South Americans originally cultivated this nut over 5000 years ago. They were taken from South America to Africa by the Spanish explorers. The African slaves, in turn, brought the high-protein peanuts to North America. Slave traders used peanuts to provide sustenance to the Africans on the long overseas voyage. Today, peanuts are grown primarily in the Deep South region. The peanuts grown in Georgia are used primarily for peanut butter and peanut oil. The peanuts grown in Virginia are for eating raw or as cocktail nuts.

Pecan: This relative of the hickory nut has a fat content of over 70 percent, which is higher than any other nut. The trees were brought east from Texas by Thomas Jefferson to his estate in Monticello, Virginia. Most pecans are grown in Georgia now, but they can also be found in Oklahoma, Texas, and Virginia. The trees prefer temperate climates. Sold shelled and packaged, pecans are available year-round. They are typically eaten as a snack and are used in both sweet and savory dishes.

Pecan Pie: The best known pecan dessert. The colonial settlers who transplanted the trees combined the nuts with molasses or corn syrup and eggs to make "transparent pie." In Kentucky, pecan pie is spiked with bourbon.

Pilau: A rice dish associated with South Carolina but with roots in Persia. Long-grain rice is simmered in an aromatic broth until cooked and nearly dry. Some pilaus call for meat or seafood in a manner similar to Spanish paella.

Poke Sallet: The leaves of the perennial pokeweed plant, which grows wild in the eastern

United States. The plant can reach a height of 10 feet and bears small, white flowers that eventually become purple berries. The berries and roots are poisonous. The young leaves must be washed, boiled, and washed again. Once cooked, poke sallet resembles spinach but tastes like asparagus.

Ramp: A wild onion that resembles a large scallion. Found between February and June over a considerable range—from the Carolinas to Canada—it has an assertive garlic and onion flavor. Ramps are used both raw and cooked.

Red-Eye Gravy: This gravy marries ham with biscuits, and mashed potatoes with fried chicken. The gravy is made from pan drippings and flecks of ham, a few spoonfuls of coffee, and water. It is cooked until thick and is usually served with ham, biscuits, or corn bread, or used as a sauce with grits or other breakfast foods.

Salt Pork: A salt-cured layer of fat from a hog's sides and belly. Salt pork should be blanched before using.

Scuppernong: A variety of muscadine grape with a tawny skin. Scuppernong is used primarily as a snack or to make sweet wine.

She-Crab Soup: A flour-thickened cream soup prepared exclusively from female crabs, due to their superior flavor. The roe (crab eggs) is usually added to enhance the flavor. Hard-boiled eggs can be used as a substitute for the crab roe.

Silver Queen Corn: A hybrid corn that is sweet, tender, and white in color. Silver Queen corn matures beginning in July and remains in season for only about 30 days. It is the preferred corn in the Deep South region.

Spoonbread: A type of corn bread that is similar to a soufflé. This bread is found today all over the Deep South region.

Succotash: A dish Native Americans served to the first American colonists. It is a cooked dish of lima beans, corn kernels, sweet peppers, and, sometimes, meat. The name is a contraction of a Native American word meaning "boiled whole kernels of corn."

Sweet Potato: A large edible root found by European colonists in America. Sweet potatoes belong to the morning glory family and come in two varieties. The first has a light yellow skin and a pale yellow flesh. Despite its name, it is not sweet. Its texture is crumbly. The second variety has a thicker, dark orange skin and an orange, sweet flesh that cooks to a moist texture. Store sweet potatoes in a cool, dry place; never refrigerate. Prepare them by baking, boiling, sautéing, or frying.

Vidalia Onion: Sweet onions brought from Texas 65 years ago and grown only in a small number of counties around Vidalia, Georgia. The soil in this region yields a milder, sweeter onion than those grown in Texas or Hawaii. The peak growing season is late spring, and every onion is set, clipped, harvested, and sized by hand.

Sample Menus from the Cuisine of the Deep South

MENU ONE

Fried Green Tomatoes with Roasted Tomato Sauce
Carolina Pulled Pork Barbecue · Creamy Southern Coleslaw ·
Succotash of Corn, Hominy, and Baby Lima Beans

MENU TWO

Tuskegee Peanut Soup
Southern Fried Chicken with Creamy Pepper Gravy and Buttermilk Biscuits ·
Squash Casserole · Grits Soufflé with Roasted Garlic and Cheddar Cheese

MENU THREE

Vidalia Onion Tart with Red Bell Pepper Sauce
Hoppin' John Salad with Pecan Vinaigrette
Pan-Fried Catfish with Corn Relish · Southern Hushpuppies

Tuskegee Peanut Soup

YIELD: 6 PORTIONS · PORTION SIZE: 8 OUNCES

3 ounces (90g) butter

2 ounces (60g) celery, cut into small dice

2 ounces (60g) carrots, cut into small dice

2 ounces (60g) leeks, cut into small dice

2 ounces (60g) yellow onions, cut into small dice

1 teaspoon (5g) garlic, minced

½ ounce (14g) all-purpose flour

48 fluid ounces (1.4L) white chicken stock, prepared (see page 517)

6 ounces (180g) peanut butter

1 teaspoon (5g) salt

½ teaspoon (2g) white pepper, ground

¼ teaspoon (1g) cayenne pepper

4½ ounces (135g) peanuts, toasted and chopped

1 tablespoon (15g) chives, chopped

CHEF TIPS *The Tuskegee Institute, located in Tuskegee, Alabama, was founded in 1881 by Booker T. Washington to provide high-quality education to African American students. George Washington Carver, the head of agriculture at the school, conducted extensive research on peanuts, among other foods and agricultural products, during his tenure. Over 40 years, Carver developed thousands of recipes using peanuts. Peanut soup is one example of the work begun by Carver at Tuskegee in the early 1900s.*

Melt the butter in a heavy-bottomed saucepot over medium-high heat. Sweat the diced celery, carrots, leeks, and onions for approximately 5 minutes or until the onions become translucent. Add the minced garlic and continue to cook for 5 additional minutes.

Add the flour and stir until it is incorporated. Gradually blend in the white chicken stock, stirring constantly. Bring to a boil, then reduce the heat to a simmer. Simmer 15 minutes. Do not allow the simmering soup to fall below 140°F (60°C).

Remove from the heat and blend in the peanut butter, salt, white and cayenne pepper, and three-quarters of the chopped peanuts.

Purée in a food processor or blender for approximately 3 minutes or until very smooth. Strain through a fine sieve.

Adjust the seasonings to taste.

Bring the soup back to a boil. Reduce the heat to a simmer.

SERVING/HOLDING

Carefully ladle the soup into hot bowls or soup plates. Garnish each portion with the remaining chopped peanuts and chopped chives.

Hold the soup at 140° (60°C) or above.

COOLING/STORING

Pour the remaining soup into small metal containers.

Cool the soup from 140°F (60°C) to 70°F (21.1°C) or lower within 2 hours. Cool from 70°F (21.1°C) to 41°F (5°C) within an additional 4 hours for a total cooling time of 6 hours or less.

Cover the soup; label, date, and store under refrigeration at 41°F (5°C) or lower.

Shrimp Awendaw with Grit Cakes

YIELD: 6 PORTIONS · PORTION SIZE: 8 OUNCES

1 ounce (30g) butter, divided in half

18 shrimp, 16/20 count, peeled, tail on, deveined

2 ounces (60g) shallots, chopped

1 clove garlic, minced

3 ounces (90g) red bell peppers, cut into small dice

4 ounces (113g) country ham, cut into julienne

12 fluid ounces (360ml) dry white wine

22 fluid ounces (660ml) heavy cream

1½ ounces (43g) Parmesan cheese, grated

6 ounces (180g) peaches, peeled, seeded, cut into medium dice

white pepper, ground, to taste

6 grit cakes (recipe follows)

2 ounces (60g) scallions, sliced on the bias

CHEF TIPS *This type of preparation using shrimp is frequently found along the Atlantic coastline of the Carolinas. This particular recipe is said to have originated in Awendaw Island, South Carolina.*

Country hams come in many varieties, each with a distinctive flavor. One of the most frequently used country hams is Smithfield Ham from Virginia. Similar country-style hams manufactured in the Deep South region include Talmadge and Hatfield hams from Georgia and Stadler and Watuga hams from North Carolina.

Just about any type of fruit can be used in place of peaches, depending on availability and desired flavor.

Melt half the butter in a large sauté pan over medium-high heat. Add the shrimp and sauté for approximately 2 minutes or until the shrimp reach a minimum internal temperature of 145°F (62.8°C) or higher for at least 15 seconds.

Remove the shrimp and reserve at 140°F (60°C) or higher until needed.

Add the remaining butter to the sauté pan. Sauté the shallots, garlic, red bell peppers, and ham over medium-high heat for 2 minutes.

Add the white wine and reduce the volume by half.

Add the heavy cream and reduce the volume of liquid by two-thirds.

Stir in the grated cheese and diced peaches.

Season to taste with white pepper and return the reserved shrimp to the sauce.

Place 1 prepared grit cake on each hot plate. Decoratively place 3 shrimp on top of each grit cake and carefully ladle 2 ounces (60 ml) of sauce onto each portion.

Garnish the appetizers with the sliced scallions.

Hold the shrimp and sauce at 140°F (60°C) or higher.

COOLING/STORING

Cool the shrimp, sauce, and grit cakes from 140°F (60°C) to 70°F (21.1°C) or lower within 2 hours. Cool from 70°F (21.1°C) to 41°F (5°C) within an additional 4 hours for a total cooling time of 6 hours or less.

Cover the shrimp, sauce, and grit cakes; label, date, and store under refrigeration at 41°F (5°C) or lower.

GRIT CAKES

YIELD: 6 PORTIONS · PORTION SIZE: 3 OUNCES

48 fluid ounces (1.4L) water

2 teaspoons (10g) salt

½ teaspoon (2g) white pepper, ground

16 ounces (480g) quick grits

1¼ ounce (38g) red bell peppers, cut into brunoise

1 ounce (30g) Parmesan cheese, grated

all-purpose flour, as needed

salt, to taste

white pepper, ground, to taste

peanut oil, as needed

Bring the water, salt, and white pepper to a boil in a large saucepot.

Stir in the quick grits and reduce the heat to low.

Cook over low heat for approximately 10 minutes, stirring occasionally, until the grits become thick.

Remove the grits from the heat and stir in the red bell peppers and grated cheese.

Pour onto a greased half-size sheet pan.

 Cool the grits from 140°F (60°C) to 70°F (21.1°C) or lower within 2 hours. Cool from 70°F (21.1°C) to 41°F (5°C) within an additional 4 hours for a total cooling time of 6 hours or less. Reserve under refrigeration until needed.

Cut the chilled grits into 1½-inch (3.81cm) rounds with a round cutter.

Season some flour to taste with salt and white pepper. Dredge the grit cakes in the seasoned flour and shake off the excess.

Heat approximately ½ inch (1.27cm) of peanut oil in a sautoir pan and pan-fry the grit cakes until they are golden brown on both sides and reach a minimum internal temperature of 165°F (73.9°C) for at least 15 seconds.

Degrease the cakes on absorbent paper towels and serve immediately.

COOLING/STORING

Cool the grit cakes from 140°F (60°C) to 70°F (21.1°C) or lower within 2 hours. Cool from 70°F (21.1°C) to 41°F (5°C) within an additional 4 hours for a total cooling time of 6 hours or less.

Cover the cakes; label, date, and store under refrigeration at 41°F (5°C) or lower.

Fried Green Tomatoes

YIELD: 6 PORTIONS · PORTION SIZE: 6 OUNCES

21 ounces (620g) green tomatoes

½ teaspoon (2g) salt

¼ teaspoon (1g) black pepper, ground

4½ ounces (135g) all-purpose flour

3 large eggs, beaten

6 ounces (180g) yellow cornmeal, coarsely ground

vegetable or peanut oil, as needed

salt, to taste

9 fluid ounces (270ml) roasted tomato sauce (recipe follows)

1 teaspoon (5g) parsley, minced

1 teaspoon (5g) thyme, minced

1 teaspoon (5g) rosemary, minced

Slice the tomatoes into ¼-inch-thick (.64 cm) slices.

Combine the salt and black pepper with the flour.

Dredge the tomatoes in seasoned flour, then in the beaten eggs, and, last, in the cornmeal. Make sure each slice of tomato is thoroughly coated.

Heat the oil in a sautoir pan to medium-high. Pan-fry a few slices of tomato at a time for approximately 2 minutes on each side or until they are golden brown.

Remove the tomatoes from the hot oil and degrease on absorbent paper towels.

Season to taste with salt.

SERVING/HOLDING

Hold the fried green tomatoes at 140°F (60°C) or higher.

Shingle 3 slices of fried green tomato in a circular pattern in the center of each hot plate.

Drizzle roasted tomato sauce around the tomatoes.

Mix the minced fresh herbs and sprinkle over the tomatoes as a garnish.

COOLING/STORING

Cool the fried green tomatoes from 140°F (60°C) to 70°F (21.1°C) or lower within 2 hours. Cool from 70°F (21.1°C) to 41°F (5°C) within an additional 4 hours for a total cooling time of 6 hours or less.

Cover the fried green tomatoes and sauce; label, date, and store under refrigeration at 41°F (5°C) or lower.

ROASTED TOMATO SAUCE

YIELD: 6 PORTIONS · PORTION SIZE: 1½ OUNCES

40 ounces (1.2kg) Roma tomatoes

3 ounces (90g) red onion, cut in half

¼ teaspoon (1g) thyme, chopped

¼ teaspoon (1g) rosemary, chopped

½ tablespoon (7ml) olive oil

salt, to taste

white pepper, ground, to taste

CHEF TIPS *Once the roasted tomato sauce is finished, it can be placed in plastic squeeze bottles and held in a bain marie at the proper holding temperature until needed. The plastic squeeze bottles allow the sauce to be presented on the plates more precisely than with a ladle.*

Toss the tomatoes, onions, and herbs in the olive oil.

Place on sheet pan with a parchment liner and roast in 350°F (176.7°C) oven for 45 minutes.

Purée the roasted vegetables in a food processor until the mixture has a smooth consistency.

Push the purée through a medium sieve or chinois.

Place the purée in a small saucepot and bring to a boil. Turn the heat down to a simmer and season to taste with salt and white pepper.

SERVING/HOLDING

 Hold the sauce at 140°F (60°C) or higher until needed.

COOLING/STORING

 Cool the sauce from 140°F (60°C) to 70°F (21.1°C) or lower within 2 hours. Cool from 70°F (21.1°C) to 41°F (5°C) within an additional 4 hours for a total cooling time of 6 hours or less.

Cover the sauce; label, date, and store under refrigeration at 41°F (5°C) or lower.

Vidalia Onion Tart with Red Bell Pepper Sauce

YIELD: 6 PORTIONS · PORTION SIZE: 8 OUNCES

8 ounces (240g) or 1 sheet puff pastry dough, thawed

12 ounces (360g) shallots, peeled

3 cloves garlic, peeled

2 fluid ounces (60ml) olive oil

5 ounces (150g) red onions, peeled, sliced whole

9 ounces (270g) leeks, cleaned, white part only, cut into julienne

10 ounces (300g) Vidalia onions, peeled, cut into julienne

3 large eggs, beaten

13 fluid ounces (390ml) heavy cream

1 teaspoon (5g) salt

½ teaspoon (2g) white pepper, ground

2 ounces (60g) chives, minced

18 fluid ounces (540ml) red bell pepper sauce (recipe follows)

Line a 10-inch (25cm) tart pan with the puff pastry sheet.

Trim the overhang to 1 inch (2.54cm) beyond the rim of the tart pan.

Dock the dough by repetitively poking it with a fork.

Bake the unfilled tart shell in a preheated 375°F (190.6°C) oven for 10–15 minutes or until the dough is cooked and golden brown. Reserve the crust at room temperature until needed.

Toss the shallots and garlic in 1 tablespoon of the olive oil.

Wrap the shallots and garlic loosely in aluminum foil and roast in a 350°F (176.7°C) oven for approximately 20 minutes or until they become soft. Reserve until needed.

Heat 1 tablespoon (30ml) of the olive oil in a sauté pan over medium heat and slowly caramelize the whole slices of red onions. The red onions should be handled gently so that they retain their round shape for use as a garnish for the finished product. When the red onion slices are browned, arrange them in the reserved tart shell.

Gently squeeze out the layers of the shallots and arrange in the tart shell around the sliced red onions.

Sauté the leeks and Vidalia onions in the remaining olive oil for approximately 5–10 minutes or until the onions become transparent. Reserve until needed.

Mash the roasted garlic in a bowl. Add the eggs, heavy cream, salt, white pepper, and chives. Mix until the ingredients are completely blended.

Pour the mixture into the tart over the red onions and bake at 350°F (176.7°C) for 15 minutes. The tart must reach a minimum internal temperature of 145°F (62.8°C) for at least 15 seconds and should begin to brown on top.

Loosely cover the tart with aluminum foil and bake an additional 45 minutes or until set.

Let rest at least 5 minutes before serving.

SERVING/HOLDING

Cut the tart into 6 wedges and serve on hot plates with red bell pepper sauce.

Hold the tart at 140°F (60°C) or higher.

COOLING/STORING

Cool the tart from 140°F (60°C) to 70°F (21.1°C) or lower within 2 hours. Cool from 70°F (21.1°C) to 41°F (5°C) within an additional 4 hours for a total cooling time of 6 hours or less.

Cover the tart; label, date, and store under refrigeration at 41°F (5°C) or lower.

RED BELL PEPPER SAUCE

30 ounces (900g) red bell peppers, stemmed and seeded

4 ounces (120g) shallots, peeled

2 cloves garlic, peeled

1 fluid ounce (30ml) olive oil

2 teaspoons (10ml) sugar

salt, to taste

white pepper, ground, to taste

1 ounce (30g) cornstarch

2 fluid ounces (60ml) water

CHEF TIPS *Once the red bell pepper sauce is finished, it can be placed in plastic squeeze bottles and held in a bain marie at the proper temperature until needed. The plastic squeeze bottles allow the chef to decorate the plates more precisely than a ladle would.*

Roast the red bell peppers, shallots, and garlic in a 350°F (176.7°C) oven for approximately 35 minutes or until the skin of the red peppers begin to loosen and bubble.

Remove from the oven and peel the red peppers. Discard the skin.

Place the red peppers, garlic, shallots, and olive oil in a food processor or blender and purée.

Add the sugar.

Continue to purée until smooth.

Place the purée in a small saucepot and bring to a boil. Turn the heat down to a simmer and season to taste with salt and white pepper.

Make a slurry by combining the cornstarch and water, and gradually add to the sauce to thicken as needed.

SERVING/HOLDING

Hold the sauce at 140°F (60°C) or higher until needed.

COOLING/STORING

Cool the sauce from 140°F (60°C) to 70°F (21.1°C) or lower within 2 hours. Cool from 70°F (21.1°C) to 41°F (5°C) within an additional 4 hours for a total cooling time of 6 hours or less.

Cover the sauce; label, date, and store under refrigeration at 41°F (5°C) or lower.

Hoppin' John Salad with Pecan Vinaigrette

SALAD

> 4 ounces (120g) long-grain white rice
>
> 8 fluid ounces (240ml) water
>
> 16 ounces (480ml) black-eyed peas
>
> 2 tablespoons (30g) butter
>
> 1 tablespoon (15g) parsley, chopped
>
> salt, to taste
>
> black pepper, ground, to taste
>
> 5 ounces (150g) red bell peppers, skinned, seeded, cut into brunoise
>
> 8 ounces (240g) green beans, blanched, shocked, cut into 1½-inch pieces on the bias

VINAIGRETTE

> 2 fluid ounces (60ml) apple cider vinegar
>
> ½ teaspoon (2g) brown sugar
>
> 3½ ounces (105g) pecans
>
> ½ teaspoon (2g) rosemary, chopped
>
> ½ teaspoon (2g) thyme, chopped
>
> 8 fluid ounces (240ml) vegetable oil

GARNISH

> 12 ounces (360g) mixed baby lettuce

Cover the rice with the water in a small saucepot. Bring to a boil and reduce the heat to a simmer.

Cover and simmer for 20 minutes or until the rice is cooked and all of the liquid is absorbed. Fluff the rice with a fork.

Cool the rice from 140°F (60°C) to 70°F (21.1°C) or lower within 2 hours. Cool from 70°F (21.1°C) to 41°F (5°C) within an additional 4 hours for a total cooling time of 6 hours or less.

Reserve under refrigeration at 41°F (5°C) or lower until needed.

Prepare the black-eyed peas by boiling them in a small saucepot of salted water for approximately 45–60 minutes or until tender.

Drain the water from the peas and add the butter and chopped parsley. Season to taste with salt and black pepper.

Cool the black-eyed peas from 140°F (60°C) to 70°F (21.1°C) or lower within 2 hours. Cool from 70°F (21.1°C) to 41°F (5°C) within an additional 4 hours for a total cooling time of 6 hours or less.

Reserve under refrigeration at 41°F (5°C) or lower until needed.

Combine the chilled rice and black-eyed peas, red peppers, and green beans. Mix and reserve until needed.

Purée the vinegar, brown sugar, pecans, and herbs in a blender or food processor.

Slowly drizzle in the oil until the dressing is thoroughly blended.

Adjust seasoning to taste with salt and black pepper.

Toss three-quarters of the dressing with the rice and pea mixture and the remaining dressing with the baby greens.

SERVING/HOLDING

Place a bed of dressed greens on each chilled plate. Press the hoppin' John mixture into a 1-cup (240g) mold. Unmold the hoppin' John over the baby greens.

COOLING/STORING

Cover hoppin' John mixture and baby greens; label, date, and store under refrigeration at 41°F (5°C) or lower.

Brunswick Stew

YIELD: 6 PORTIONS · PORTION SIZE: 12 OUNCES

hickory chips, soaked, as needed

16 ounces (480g) pork butt

2 44-ounce (1320g) fryer chickens, boned, cut into 6 pieces each

8 fluid ounces (240ml) water

24 ounces (720ml) tomato sauce

24 ounces (720g) diced tomatoes with juice

12 ounces (360g) russet potatoes, peeled, cut into medium dice

4 ounces (120g) onions, cut into small dice

8 ounces (240g) corn kernels

8 ounces (240g) butter beans or baby lima beans, fresh or frozen

1 teaspoon (5g) black pepper, ground

¼ teaspoon (1g) cayenne pepper

4 fluid ounces (120ml) Worcestershire sauce

1 teaspoon (5g) salt

Tabasco sauce, to taste

Prepare a smoker with the soaked wood chips.

Cut the pork butt into 2 or 3 pieces to enhance the smoke flavor. Place the pieces of pork butt into the smoker. Allow to smoke for 1 hour at 250°F (121.1°C). Add the chicken pieces and smoke an additional 30 minutes. The pork must reach a minimum internal temperature of at least 145°F (62.8°C) for at least 15 seconds and the chicken 165°F (73.9°C).

Remove the meat and cut to a medium dice. Hold the meat at 140°F (60°C) or higher until needed.

Combine the water, tomato sauce, and diced tomatoes in a heavy-bottomed saucepot. Add the potatoes and onions. Bring to a boil and turn the heat down to a simmer.

Cover and simmer over medium heat for 15 minutes. Do not allow the simmering stew to fall below 140°F (60°C).

Add the remaining ingredients and reserved pork and chicken. Bring back to a boil and turn the heat down to a simmer, stirring often. Simmer slowly for at least 1 hour, stirring occasionally. Do not allow the simmering stew to fall below 140°F (60°C).

Season to taste with Tabasco sauce.

SERVING/HOLDING

Carefully ladle the Brunswick stew into hot bowls or plates. Each portion should receive 2 pieces of chicken and an even amount of pork and vegetables.

Hold the stew at 140°F (60°C) or higher.

COOLING/STORING

Cool the stew from 140°F (60°C) to 70°F (21.1°C) or lower within 2 hours. Cool from 70°F (21.1°C) to 41°F (5°C) within an additional 4 hours for a total cooling time of 6 hours or less.

Cover the stew; label, date, and store under refrigeration at 41°F (5°C) or lower.

Carolina Pulled Pork Barbecue

YIELD: 6 PORTIONS · PORTION SIZE: 12 OUNCES

1½ tablespoons (22g) kosher salt

1 tablespoon (15g) black pepper, ground

36 ounces (1kg) pork butt, boned, trimmed to 65–70% lean

16 fluid ounces (480ml) Carolina barbecue sauce (recipe follows)

6 fluid ounces (177ml) water

24 ounces (720g) creamy southern coleslaw (see page 122)

24 ounces (720g) potato salad (see page 128)

Mix the salt and black pepper together and rub the exterior of the pork butt with the mixture.

Roast the pork butt at 300°F (148.9°C) for approximately 2–3 hours until it is fork tender and reaches a minimum internal temperature of at least 145°F (62.8°C) or higher for 15 seconds.

Remove the roast from the oven and let it rest for 25 minutes, loosely covered. Hold the pork at 140°F (60°C) or higher.

Pull the meat apart to create a shredded effect.

Place the shredded pork in a medium saucepot with half the barbecue sauce and the water.

Bring to a boil and turn the heat down to a simmer. Simmer for 1 hour, stirring occasionally. Do not allow the simmering pork to fall below 140°F (60°C).

SERVING/HOLDING

Serve the pork on hot plates with 4 ounces (120g) each of coleslaw and potato salad. Serve the remaining sauce on the side.

Hold the pork and sauce at 140°F (60°C) or higher.

COOLING/STORING

Cool the pork and sauce from 140°F (60°C) to 70°F (21.1°C) or lower within 2 hours. Cool from 70°F (21.1°C) to 41°F (5°C) within an additional 4 hours for a total cooling time of 6 hours or less.

Cover the pork and sauce; label, date, and store under refrigeration at 41°F (5°C) or lower.

CAROLINA BARBECUE SAUCE

YIELD: 2 CUPS · PORTION SIZE: 2½ OUNCES

4 fluid ounces (120ml) cider vinegar

5 fluid ounces (150ml) water

2 ounces (60g) whole-grain mustard

½ teaspoon (2g) paprika

3 ounces (90ml) honey

1 teaspoon (5g) salt

1 tablespoon (15ml) Worcestershire sauce

1½ teaspoons (7ml) Tabasco sauce

½ teaspoon (2g) chili powder

1 teaspoon (5g) black pepper, ground

1 tablespoon (15ml) lemon juice

3 ounces (90g) onion, cut into small dice

1 tablespoon (15g) garlic, minced

Combine all the ingredients in a small saucepot and bring to a boil.

Reduce the heat to a simmer. Simmer for 40 minutes. Do not allow the simmering sauce to fall below 140°F (60°C).

SERVING/HOLDING

Hold the sauce at 140°F (60°C) or higher until needed.

COOLING/STORING

Cool the sauce from 140°F (60°C) to 70°F (21.1°C) or lower within 2 hours. Cool from 70°F (21.1°C) to 41°F (5°C) within an additional 4 hours for a total cooling time of 6 hours or less.

Cover the sauce; label, date, and store under refrigeration at 41°F (5°C) or lower.

Southern Fried Chicken with Creamy Pepper Gravy and Buttermilk Biscuits

YIELD: 6 PORTIONS · PORTION SIZE: 12 OUNCES

2 44-ounce (1320g) fryer chickens, boned, cut into 9 pieces each (whole breast in 3 pieces)

8 fluid ounces (240ml) buttermilk

1 teaspoon (5g) salt

8 ounces (240g) all-purpose flour

2 teaspoons (10g) paprika

salt, to taste

black pepper, ground, to taste

vegetable or peanut oil, as needed

GRAVY

2 fluid ounces (60ml) vegetable oil

2 ounces (60g) all-purpose flour

8 fluid ounces (240ml) half-and-half

8 fluid ounces (240ml) milk

1 teaspoon (5g) salt

2 teaspoons (10g) black pepper, coarsely ground

¼ teaspoon (1g) cayenne pepper

1 teaspoon (5ml) Worcestershire sauce

12 buttermilk biscuits (see page 125)

Soak the prepared fryer chickens in the buttermilk and salt for at least 30 minutes under refrigeration at 41°F (5°C) or lower until needed. For extra-juicy chicken, soak the pieces overnight.

Combine the flour and paprika and season to taste with salt and black pepper.

Remove the chicken pieces from the buttermilk and liberally coat them with the seasoned flour.

CHEF TIPS *The following are cooking techniques for "real" Southern fried chicken propounded by recognized experts on the Deep South region. These techniques are often the subject of hot debate.*

John Martin Taylor: *"The deeper the fat, the better"; pieces should not touch as they fry and should sear on all sides as they enter the hot fat.*

Edna Lewis: *Fry the white meat first in a blend of home-rendered lard and churned butter. Add a piece of smoked ham to the hot fat for extra flavor.*

Camille Glenn: *Do not dip the chicken in milk, crumbs, or batter—just a generous coating of seasoned flour. Lard makes the crispiest chicken, but vegetable shortening is fine as well.*

Jeanne Voltz: *Fried chicken requires a generous amount of fat and moderately high heat to prevent greasiness.*

Bill Neal: *Marinate the chicken pieces in buttermilk for at least 2 hours before use, then coat them with seasoned flour and fry in a blend of lard and peanut oil.*

Craig Claiborne: *Soak the chicken pieces in milk and Tabasco sauce, coat them in seasoned flour, and pan-fry them in a blend of lard and butter in a cast-iron skillet.*

Let the chicken rest under refrigeration at 41°F (5°C) or lower until the flour is a pastelike consistency. This is an important step for crisp fried chicken.

Preheat the oil a heavy-bottomed skillet or in a deep-fat fryer to 350°F (176.7°C).

Deep or pan-fry the chicken for approximately 25–30 minutes or until done and the internal temperature reaches a minimum of 165°F (73.9°C) or higher for at least 15 seconds. Dark meat takes longer to cook than white, so for all the chicken to be done at the same time, cook the dark meat for approximately 10 minutes before adding the white meat.

Remove the chicken from the fat and drain on absorbent paper towels. Hold the chicken at 140°F (60°C) or higher until needed.

To prepare the gravy, make a roux with 2 ounces (60ml) of oil and 2 ounces (60ml) of flour. If the chicken was pan-fried, drain off all the fat from the skillet except for 2 ounces (60ml) and use that in place of the oil called for in the recipe.

Cook the roux over low heat for 10–12 minutes or until it has a slightly nutty aroma and a light tan color.

Add the half-and-half and cook over medium-high heat for 3 minutes.

Add the milk and cook an additional 3 minutes.

Add the salt, black pepper, cayenne pepper, and Worcestershire sauce. Reduce the heat to low and simmer for approximately 20 minutes or until thick and smooth. Do not allow the simmering sauce to fall below 140°F (60°C).

Adjust the seasonings to taste. If the sauce is too thick, add more milk.

SERVING/HOLDER

Place 1 piece of white chicken and 2 pieces of dark chicken on each hot plate. Top each portion of chicken with approximately 2 ounces of creamy pepper gravy. Serve each portion with 2 buttermilk biscuits.

Hold the chicken and sauce at 140°F (60°C) or higher.

COOLING/STORING

Discard the remaining breading items.

Cool the chicken and sauce from 140°F (60°C) to 70°F (21.1°C) or lower within 2 hours. Cool from 70°F (21.1°C) to 41°F (5°C) within an additional 4 hours for a total cooling time of 6 hours or less.

Cover chicken and sauce; label, date, and store under refrigeration at 41°F (5°C) or lower.

Pan-Fried Catfish with Corn Relish

YIELD: 6 PORTIONS · PORTION SIZE: 12 OUNCES

4 ounces (120g) cornmeal, finely ground

4½ ounces (135g) all-purpose flour

1½ teaspoons (7g) salt

1 teaspoon (5g) black pepper, coarsely ground

¾ teaspoon (4g) paprika

48 ounces (1.4kg) or 6 catfish, cut into 8-ounce fillets

vegetable or peanut oil, as needed

24 ounces (120g) corn relish (see recipe page 126)

Mix the cornmeal, flour, and seasonings.

Dredge the catfish in the cornmeal mixture, thoroughly coating the fillets.

Fill a sautoir pan or skillet with ½ inch (1.27cm) of oil and heat on medium-high.

Pan-fry 3 catfish fillets at a time for approximately 3 minutes on each side until they are golden brown and reach a minimum internal temperature of 145°F (62.8°C) for at least 15 seconds.

Remove the fillets from the fat and drain on absorbent paper towels.

SERVING/HOLDING

Serve each catfish fillet on a hot plate with ½ cup (120g) corn relish.

Hold at 140°F (60°C) or higher until needed.

COOLING/STORING

Cool the catfish from 140°F (60°C) to 70°F (21.1°C) or lower within 2 hours. Cool from 70°F (21.1°C) to 41°F (5°C) within an additional 4 hours for a total cooling time of 6 hours or less.

Cover the catfish and relish; label, date, and store under refrigeration at 41°F (5°C) or lower.

Glazed Country Ham with Vidalia Onion and Cola Sauce

2–3 pounds (1–1.5kg) or 1 country ham, bone in

whole cloves, as needed

2 ounces (60g) light brown sugar

1 fluid ounce (30ml) cola

1½ teaspoons (7g) dry mustard

3 fluid ounces (90ml) apple cider vinegar

16 ounces (480ml) Vidalia onion and cola sauce (recipe follows)

CHEF TIPS *This is one way of preparing a traditional Southern-style country ham. The most important consideration is the choice of the ham itself. It needs to be a cured ham with the bone in.*

Country hams come in many varieties, each with a distinctive flavor. One of the most frequently used country hams is Smithfield Ham from Virginia. Similar country-style hams manufactured in the Deep South region include Talmadge and Hatfield hams, from Georgia, and Stadler and Watuga hams, from North Carolina. Canned hams and water-added hams typically yield less meat due to their high water content and have a much different flavor due to the different process used to manufacture them.

Preheat an oven to 300°F (148.9°C).

Remove the skin and most of the fat from the outside of the ham, leaving just a thin layer of fat on the ham's topside.

Score the remaining layer of fat diagonally in both directions to a depth of about ⅛ inch (.32cm), making diamond patterns.

Stud the center of each diamond with a whole clove.

Place the ham in a shallow roasting pan.

Cover securely with aluminum foil and bake for approximately 20 minutes per pound. The ham must reach a minimum internal temperature of 145°F (62.8°C) for at least 15 seconds.

Remove the ham and increase the oven temperature to 375°F (190.6°C).

Combine the brown sugar, cola, and dry mustard. Spoon the glaze evenly over the top of the ham.

Return the ham to the oven and bake approximately 30 minutes or until it browns. Baste occasionally.

Remove the ham. Deglaze the pan with the vinegar. Reserve this liquid for addition to the Vidalia onion and cola sauce.

Slice the ham thinly and serve approximately 8 ounces (240g) on each hot plate. Serve the slices of ham with 2 ounces (60ml) of hot Vidalia onion and cola sauce.

Hold the ham and sauce at 140°F (60°C) or higher.

COOLING/STORING

Cool the ham and sauce from 140°F (60°C) to 70°F (21.1°C) or lower within 2 hours. Cool from 70°F (21.1°C) to 41°F (5°C) within an additional 4 hours for a total cooling time of 6 hours or less.

Cover the ham; label, date, and store under refrigeration at 41°F (5°C) or lower.

VIDALIA ONION AND COLA SAUCE

YIELD: 6 PORTIONS · PORTION SIZE: 2½ OUNCES

½ ounce (14g) clarified butter

10 ounces (300g) Vidalia onions, cut into julienne

2 ounces (60g) raisins

8 fluid ounces (240ml) cola

2 teaspoons (10ml) white wine vinegar

2 fluid ounces (60ml) water

3 fluid ounces (90ml) dry white wine

1 quart (960ml) white chicken stock, prepared (see page 517)

salt, to taste

black pepper, ground, to taste

1½ teaspoons (7g) cornstarch

2 tablespoons (30ml) water

Heat the clarified butter in a pan over medium-high heat. Caramelize the onions by cooking them until they are evenly browned. Do not stir the onions too often, as they will sweat instead of brown.

When onions are brown, add the raisins, cola, vinegar, and water. Bring to a boil and reduce the heat to low.

Simmer until almost dry. Do not allow the simmering sauce to fall below 140°F (60°C).

Add the white wine and reduce the volume of liquid by one-quarter.

Add the white chicken stock and reduce the volume of liquid by half over medium heat. Do not allow the sauce to fall below 140°F (60°C).

Season the sauce to taste with salt and black pepper.

Mix the cornstarch with the water to create a slurry and blend it into the sauce.

Bring the sauce to a boil and reduce the heat to low. Simmer for 10 minutes.

SERVING/HOLDING

Hold the sauce at 140°F (60°C) or higher.

COOLING/STORING

Cool the sauce from 140°F (60°C) to 70°F (21.1°C) or lower within 2 hours. Cool from 70°F (21.2°C) to 41°F (5°C) within an additional 4 hours for a total cooling time of 6 hours or less.

Cover the sauce; label, date, and store under refrigeration at 41°F (5°C) or lower.

Creamy Southern Coleslaw

YIELD: 6 PORTIONS · PORTION SIZE: 4 OUNCES

8 ounces (240g) mayonnaise, prepared

16 ounces (480g) green cabbage, shredded

4 ounces (120g) carrots, shredded

4 ounces (120g) raisins

3½ fluid ounces (104ml) lemon juice

½ tablespoon (7g) Dijon mustard

¼ teaspoon (1ml) Tabasco sauce

¼ teaspoon (1g) cayenne pepper

1 teaspoon (5ml) cider vinegar

1 ounce (30g) sugar

salt, to taste

black pepper, ground, to taste

Combine all the ingredients and mix until thoroughly combined.

Reserve under refrigeration at 41°F (5°C) or lower at least 1 hour or until needed.

SERVING/HOLDING

Hold at 41°F (5°C) or lower until needed

COOLING/STORING

Cover the coleslaw; label, date, and store under refrigeration at 41°F (5°C) or lower.

Succotash of Corn, Hominy, and Baby Lima Beans

YIELD: 6 PORTIONS · PORTION SIZE: 4 OUNCES

16 ounces (480ml) water

8 ounces (240g) baby lima beans, fresh or frozen

5 ounces (150g) corn kernels, fresh

2 ounces (60g) shallots, chopped

1 ounce (30g) butter

10 ounces (300g) canned hominy, drained

1 fluid ounce (30ml) white wine

4 fluid ounces (120ml) heavy cream

½ tablespoon (7g) parsley, chopped

salt, to taste

white pepper, ground, to taste

Bring the water to a boil in a small saucepot.

Add the baby lima beans. Return the water to a boil and reduce the heat to a simmer.

Cover and simmer over low heat for 10 minutes. Drain and reserve beans until needed.

Sauté the corn and shallots in half of the butter over medium heat for 3 minutes.

Add the hominy and reserved lima beans.

Toss until combined. Add the white wine and reduce the volume of liquid by half over medium heat.

Add the heavy cream and reduce the volume of liquid by half over medium heat.

Remove the succotash from the heat and stir in the remaining butter and parsley.

Season to taste with salt and white pepper.

SERVING/HOLDING

Hold the succotash at 140°F (60°C) or higher.

COOLING/STORING

Cool the succotash from 140°F (60°C) to 70°F (21.1°C) or lower within 2 hours. Cool from

70°F (21.2°C) to 41°F (5°C) within an additional 4 hours for a total cooling time of 6 hours or less.

Cover the succotash; label, date, and store under refrigeration at 41°F (5°C) or lower.

Squash Casserole

12 ounces (360g) zucchini, cut into ½-inch rondelles

12 ounces (360g) yellow crookneck squash, cut into ½-inch rondelles

2 ounces (60g) onion, chopped

1 large egg, beaten

8 ounces (240g) sharp cheddar cheese, grated

½ tablespoon (7g) sugar

¾ teaspoon (4g) salt

¼ teaspoon (1g) white pepper, ground

2½ ounces (75g) breadcrumbs, coarsely ground

1 fluid ounce (30ml) butter, melted

CHEF TIPS *Sautéing the vegetables may give better results than boiling.*

Bring a medium saucepot of water to a boil. Boil the zucchini, yellow squash, and onions, covered, for 15 minutes. Drain and reserve the vegetables until needed.

Combine the reserved vegetables and onions with the egg, cheese, sugar, salt, and white pepper.

Pour into a greased casserole dish and top with the breadcrumbs.

Drizzle the melted butter over the breadcrumbs and place in a preheated 375°F (190.6°C) oven for approximately 30–45 minutes or until the casserole is golden brown and reaches a minimum internal temperature of 145°F (62.8°C) for at least 15 seconds.

SERVING/HOLDING

Hold the casserole at 140°F (60°C) or higher.

COOLING/STORING

Cool the squash casserole from 140°F (60°C) to 70°F (21.1°C) or lower within 2 hours. Cool from 70°F (21.1°C) to 41°F (5°C) within an additional 4 hours for a total cooling time of 6 hours or less.

Cover the casserole; label, date, and store under refrigeration at 41°F (5°C) or lower.

Buttermilk Biscuits

YIELD: 6 PORTIONS · PORTION SIZE: 2 BISCUITS

10 ounces (300g) cake flour

2¼ teaspoons (11g) baking powder

½ teaspoon (2g) baking soda

1 teaspoon (5g) salt

2 ounces (60g) solid vegetable shortening, chilled

1 ounce (30g) butter, chilled, cut into small dice

9 fluid ounces (270ml) buttermilk

CHEF TIPS *The amount of liquid in biscuit recipes is frequently given as a range. The dough must be handled with a light touch and kneaded just until it reaches the correct feel. Some bakers press their biscuit dough flat with their hands, while others use a rolling pin. Biscuits can be cut with a glass, jelly jar, or biscuit cutter. The best secret of biscuit production is the flour. White Lily flour, milled in Knoxville, Tennessee, is a soft winter red wheat ground to a fine powder and sifted through fine silk cloths. This type of flour is lower in gluten than northern varieties and is perfect for baking tender Southern-style biscuits. Cake flour can be substituted if White Lily flour is unavailable.*

Preheat the oven to 450°F (232.2°C).

Sift the dry ingredients together into a large bowl.

Blend or cut the shortening and butter into the flour by rubbing the ingredients lightly between the fingers, incorporating the fat into the flour. Continue to rub until the dough resembles coarse cornmeal.

Stir in the buttermilk with a fork, lifting and combining until the dough is soft.

Gather the dough together with your hands and knead lightly on a clean surface dusted with flour until the dough is no longer sticky.

Roll the dough with a rolling pin to ½ inch thick.

Dip a 2-inch round cutter in flour and cut rounds from the sheet of dough.

Place the rounds on a heavily greased sheet pan and bake for approximately 15 minutes or until light brown.

SERVING/HOLDING

Serve immediately.

COOLING/STORING

Cover the biscuits; label, date, and store under refrigeration at 41°F (5°C) or lower.

Corn Relish

20 ounces or 4 ears (600g) corn on the cob

6 ounces (180g) tomato concassée

2 scallions, sliced on a bias

4 ounces (120g) red onion, cut into brunoise

8 ounces (240g) green bell peppers, cut into brunoise

2 tablespoons (30g) parsley, chopped

¼ teaspoon (1g) garlic, minced

2 fluid ounces (60ml) cider vinegar

1 teaspoon (5g) sugar

salt, to taste

black pepper, ground, to taste

Blanch the ears of corn for 10 minutes in boiling water. Drain and reserve until cool enough to handle.

Cut the kernels from the ears of corn. Cool the corn kernels from 140°F (60°C) to 70°F (21.1°C) or lower within 2 hours. Cool from 70°F (21.1°C) to 41°F (5°C) within an additional 4 hours for a total cooling time of 6 hours or less.

Reserve the prepared tomatoes, scallions, onions, bell peppers, parsley, and garlic under refrigeration at 41°F (5°C) or lower until needed.

Once the corn is thoroughly chilled, mix with the prepared vegetables, vinegar, and sugar.

Season to taste with salt and black pepper.

SERVING/HOLDING

Hold the relish at 41°F (5°C) or lower.

COOLING/STORING

Cover the relish; label, date, and store under refrigeration at 41°F (5°C) or lower.

Grits Soufflé with Roasted Garlic and Cheddar Cheese

YIELD: 6 PORTIONS · PORTION SIZE: 4 OUNCES

6 ounces (180ml) grits

6 fluid ounces (180ml) water

6 fluid ounces (180ml) milk

2 ounces (60g) sweet butter

salt, to taste

¼ teaspoon (1ml) Tabasco sauce

4 ounces (120g) sharp cheddar cheese, grated

2 cloves garlic, roasted, minced

4 large eggs, separated

1 teaspoon (5g) sugar

Combine the grits, water, milk, butter, and salt in a heavy-bottomed saucepot. Bring to a boil and reduce the heat to a simmer.

Simmer, stirring constantly, for 8 minutes.

Remove from the heat and add the Tobasco sauce, grated cheese, and roasted garlic.

Whip the egg whites to soft peaks in a mixing machine. Add the sugar and continue to whip until stiff peaks form.

Whisk the egg yolks and add to the grits mixture, stirring constantly.

Gently fold the egg whites into the grits mixture.

Pour the mixture into a buttered casserole or baking dish.

Bake at 350°F (176.7°C) for approximately 40 minutes or until the soufflé is set and brown on top and reaches a minimum internal temperature of 145°F (62.8°C) for at least 15 seconds.

SERVING/HOLDING

Hold the grits soufflé at 140°F (60°C) or higher.

COOLING/STORING

Cool the grits soufflé from 140°F (60 °C) to 70°F (21.1°C) or lower within 2 hours. Cool from 70°F

(21.1°C) to 41°F (5°C) within an additional 4 hours for a total cooling time of 6 hours or less.

Cover the soufflé; label, date, and store under refrigeration at 41°F (5°C) or lower.

Potato Salad

YIELD: 6 PORTIONS · PORTION SIZE: 4 OUNCES

1½ pounds (680g) chef potatoes, cooked, cut into medium dice

2 large eggs, hard-boiled, cut into small dice

2 ounces (57g) green bell peppers, cut into small dice

1 pimento, cut into small dice

2 ounces (57g) celery, cut into small dice

salt, to taste

black pepper, ground to taste

2 ounces (57g) mayonnaise, prepared

1 ounce (28g) mustard

cayenne pepper, to taste

Boil the potatoes until they are fork tender.

Drain the potatoes and place them on a sheet pan lined with parchment paper.

Place in a preheated 350°F (176.7°C) oven for approximately 10-15 minutes to dry them out.

Cool the potatoes from 140°F (60°C) to 70°F (21.1°C) or lower within 2 hours. Cool from 70°F (21.1°C) to 41°F (5°C) within an additional 4 hours for a total cooling time of 6 hours or less.

While the potatoes are cooling, prepare the eggs and vegetables as indicated and mix them with the remaining ingredients.

Cover the mixture and reserve under refrigeration at 41°F (5°C) or lower until needed.

Once the potatoes are thoroughly cooled, fold them lightly into the reserved vegetable mixture.

SERVING/HOLDING

Hold at 41°F (5°C) or lower until needed.

COOLING/STORING

Cover the potato salad; label, date, and store under refrigeration at 41°F (5°C) or lower.

Southern Hushpuppies

YIELD: 6 PORTIONS · PORTION SIZE: 4 OUNCES

15½ ounces (465g) cornmeal

5½ fluid ounces (165ml) buttermilk

2 large eggs, beaten

2 ounces (60g) red onion, cut into small dice

2 ounces (60g) fresh corn kernels

1 tablespoon (15g) parsley, chopped

1 tablespoon (15g) sugar

1½ teaspoons (7g) salt

1½ teaspoons (7g) baking powder

frying fat, as needed

Preheat a deep-fat fryer to 325°F (162.8°C).

Combine all of the ingredients except the frying fat and mix until smooth.

Using a scoop or ladle, drop approximately 2 ounces (60g) of the hushpuppy batter into the center of the fryer. Be careful not to overload it.

Deep-fry the hushpuppies for approximately 5 minutes or until golden brown.

Remove the hushpuppies from the fat and degrease on absorbent paper towels.

SERVING/HOLDING

Hold the hushpuppies at 140°F (60°C) or higher.

COOLING/STORING

Cool the hushpuppies from 140°F (60°C) to 70°F (21.1°C) or lower within 2 hours. Cool from 70°F (21.1°C) to 41°F (5°C) within an additional 4 hours for a total cooling time of 6 hours or less.

Cover the hushpuppies; label, date, and store under refrigeration at 41°F (5°C) or lower.

Pecan Pie

YIELD: 6 PORTIONS · PORTION SIZE: 1 SLICE

FILLING

4 large eggs, beaten

5 ounces (150g) light brown sugar

2 ounces (60g) butter, softened

8½ ounces (255ml) light corn syrup

½ teaspoon (2g) salt

1 tablespoon (15ml) vanilla extract

10 ounces (300g) pecans, chopped

1 pecan pie crust (recipe follows)

TOPPING

8 fluid ounces (240ml) whipping cream

2 ounces (60g) powdered sugar

CHEF TIPS *If you make more than 1 pie, it is advisable to divide the pecans evenly between the pie shells and then strain the liquid over the top. Straining the liquid assures there is less foam in the baking process.*

Mix all the filling ingredients together and pour the mixture into a prepared pie shell.

Bake in a preheated 400°F (204.4°C) oven for 15 minutes.

Reduce the heat to 350°F (176.7°C) and continue to bake for an additional 30 minutes or until the filling is firm and reaches a minimum internal temperature of 145°F (62.8°C) for at least 15 seconds.

Remove the pie from the oven and let rest at least 30–45 minutes before serving.

While the pie is resting, prepare the topping by whipping the cream with the powdered sugar in a small mixing machine on high speed. Be careful not to overmix the cream, as this small amount can turn to butter in a very short period.

SERVING/HOLDING

Slice the pecan pie into 6 wedges. Serve each wedge on a chilled plate. Pipe a small rosette of sweetened whipped cream through a pastry tube with a star tip onto the top of each piece of pie.

Hold the pie, sauce, and whipped cream under refrigeration at 41°F (5°C) or lower until needed.

COOLING/STORING

Cool the pecan pie from 140°F (60°C) to 70°F (21.1°C) or lower within 2 hours. Cool from 70°F (21.1°C) to 41°F (5°C) within an additional 4 hours for a total cooling time of 6 hours or less.

Cover the pie and whipped cream; label, date, and store under refrigeration at 41°F (5°C) or lower.

PECAN PIE CRUST

YIELD: 1 PIE CRUST

8 ounces (240g) butter, or shortening

16 ounces (480g) pastry flour

¼ teaspoon (1g) salt

4 fluid ounces (120ml) cold water

Break shortening or butter into flour to form large nuggets the size of walnuts.

Dissolve salt in water.

Add cold water to flour and shortening and mix just enough to form a dough.

Allow dough to rest 1 hour.

Roll out dough for a 9-inch pie.

Bake for 5–8 minutes in a preheated 425°F (218.3°C) oven.

COOLING/STORING

Cool the pie crust from 140°F (60°C) to 70°F (21.1°C) or lower within 2 hours. Cool from 70°F (21.1°C) to 41°F (5°C) within an additional 4 hours for a total cooling time of 6 hours or less.

Cover the pie crust; label, date, and store under refrigeration at 41°F (5°C) or lower.

Allen Susser

ON FLORIBBEAN CUISINE

It requires much more than cooking skills to be a chef. It calls for imagination, balance, and flexibility. And it requires working with a medium—fresh food—that is as fickle and difficult as any. For me, pride comes from envisioning and capturing our resources for inclusion in my cuisine. In South Florida, I find a mosaic of cultural influences, the strongest coming from the nearby Caribbean and from Latin America, though reaching as far as Africa, India, and Southeast Asia.

Ingredients travel. My market basket is always changing to reflect the seasonality of ingredients. The selection of ingredients must obviously reflect the architecture of the land. In South Florida, we have water on three sides as well as a subtropical climate. My menu captures the unique aquaculture and agriculture of the region. The foodstuffs include wonderful local fresh fish and seafood, tropical and citrus fruits, and Latin vegetables and tubers. My New Era cuisine emcompasses the foods, cultures, and techniques of our world village. The threads of these broad, diverse flavors are fused by a careful, deliberate, and knowledgeable hand into a single cuisine. My philosophy and food are inseparable: simple, direct, and powerful flavor!

Allen Susser is the James Beard Foundation award-winning owner and head chef of Miami's renowned Chef Allen's Restaurant.

Floribbean Cuisine

Floribbean cuisine, also known as *new era cuisine,* **has** emerged as one of America's most innovative regional cooking styles. The fresh flavors, combinations, and tastes of Floribbean cuisine are representative of the variety and quality of foods indigenous to Florida and the Caribbean Islands. Regional chefs often make a commitment to using locally grown foods and the fish and seafood of the abundant fresh and salt waters of the area.

The cooking style and techniques used in Florida today are highly influenced by those of Cuba, Jamaica, and the Bahamas. This current movement is, however, only a little more than a decade old. The roots of Floribbean cuisine are traced back much farther in time to the exploration of the New World by the Spanish.

In the early 1500s, with the arrival of Ponce de Leon, Spanish culture began to affect the Florida area. From that time until now, Spanish cooking traditions and flavors have heavily influenced the foods of Florida. Hernando de Soto, another Spaniard, brought cattle and pigs with him on his voyage to the New World. From this introduction of livestock to Florida, the Spanish are given credit for many recipes using meat in a region that formerly depended entirely on fish and game. In return for livestock, the Native Americans taught the Spanish about local fruits and vegetables, including hearts of palm, malanga, yuca, and plantains. The Native Americans also taught the Spanish how to catch and prepare the ample seafood indigenous to the waters of the Florida region.

Spain was not the only European nation that found Florida attractive. In the early 1560s, the French Protestant Jean Ribault explored the Florida region. Two years later, Rene Goulaine de Laudonniere established Fort Caroline at the mouth of the St. Johns River, near present-day Jacksonville. The French approach to cooking was blended with the existing Spanish style to form the basis of Floribbean cuisine.

In the mid-1600s, slaves from Africa began to influence the cooking styles of the Florida region. Over the years, the Spanish conquistadors brought many thousands of slaves from Africa to Florida and the Caribbean Islands. The slaves typically existed on a diet of yams, eggplant, sesame seeds, and okra. They brought with them the skills and knowledge to grow, cook, and prepare these types of foods. In time, these foods and cooking influences merged into the region's cuisine, as the slaves cooked not only for themselves but also for their owners. Many of today's regional specialties, like peas and okra (page 167), came from this period.

In the mid-1700s, a group of Minorcans, people of Catalan descent from the Spanish Balearic Islands, were brought to the Florida region as indentured laborers. Once established in the St. Augustine area, their foods and cooking influenced the existing Florida cuisine, particularly in the use of peppers.

Key West was also settled about this time, mainly by civil war refugees from the Bahamas. Their contributions to Floribbean cuisine included conch salad, seasoned rice and peas, and steamed pudding. Key lime pie (page 176) was created in Key West, the outermost of the Florida Keys. It combines native Key limes and condensed milk, used because of the limited availability of fresh milk on the island.

The British gained control of Florida in the early 1760s in exchange for Havana, Cuba, which they had captured from Spain a few years earlier. The Spanish evacuated Florida after the exchange, leaving the region virtually empty of European settlers. Although British rule of the Florida region lasted only 20 years, the regional cooking style was affected. The British evacuated Florida in turn after the American revolution. Spanish colonists as well as settlers from the newly formed United States came pouring into the region, lured by generous land grants.

The Anglo-American influence began with the descendants of settlers from New England who relocated to Georgia and Florida just before the War of Independence. The settlers brought with them their taste for sweets and rice. By 1840, the people of Florida were concentrating on developing their territory and gaining statehood. The population began to escalate significantly, with freed African-American slaves making up almost half the population. These new settlers from the Southern colonies introduced a style of cooking that is referred to as *soul food*, sometimes called *country cooking* and *cracker cooking*. Soul food is rustic, simple food and, until recently, was the predominant cooking style in the Florida area. It combines typical English blandness with piquant Spanish flavors. The result is food that is not as spicy as that associated with Southwest cuisine. Cracker cooking is literally defined as cuisine from residents of Florida or Georgia.

The development of industries throughout Florida prompted the construction of roads and railroads on a large scale. The year-round railroad workers and their families had a significant impact on Floribbean cuisine. The railroad workers who came from other parts of the United States prepared New England clam chowder with stone crab and substituted mangos for apples in their pies. These cooks, in many respects, earned the right to be called the parents of Floribbean cuisine by combining indigenous ingredients of the Florida region with traditional recipes, handed down from generation to generation, in other styles.

Beginning in the 1870s, residents from the northern states visited Florida as tourists to enjoy the state's natural beauty and mild climate. The tourists drove the development of lavish winter resorts from Palm Beach to Miami Beach, nicknamed the Gold Coast. By the 1920s, a large Jewish population began to settle in Florida, bringing with them delicatessens and kosher markets.

Probably the greatest influence on Floribbean cuisine began in the 1950s with the large migration of Cubans to South Florida. Cuba is just 90 miles off the coast and is the largest of the Caribbean Islands. Today, the largest number of Cubans outside of Havana resides in Florida, many in an area of Miami dubbed "Little Havana." The Cubans no doubt feel culinarily at home because many of their native ingredients are indigenous to Florida. In addition, Cuba was under Spanish rule for many years. The Spanish influence on Floribbean cuisine was significant in Cuba as well. Typically, Cubans mixed the Spanish flavors of tomatoes, garlic, onion, and peppers with Caribbean ingredients such as conch, plantain, coconut, guava, and mango. The Cuban influence on Floribbean cuisine is tasted in lime-marinated grilled fish and seafood, as in the recipes on pages 155 and 160, seafood stews spiced with chiles, and salads that include many exotic fruits and vegetables, like those on pages 150 and 152.

Today, new influences affect the foods and cooking styles enjoyed in Florida as the regional cuisine continues to evolve. Large populations from Haiti, Nicaragua, the Dominican Republic, Brazil, and other Central and South American countries exist in Florida. In addition, a Southeast Asian influence is beginning to be seen as more and more people immigrate to Florida from Indonesia, Cambodia, and Vietnam.

The culinary history of Florida is one of immigration and adaptation. Even the area's prominent Native American tribe, the Seminoles, immigrated to Florida from other regions of America. An important feature of Floribbean cuisine is its continuing evolution in response to the constant influx of new immigrants. With the characters and flavors of the cooking in Florida being shaped by so many influences, it is no wonder that the Floribbean style has emerged as one of the finest and most creative cuisines in America.

Typical Floribbean Ingredients and Dishes

Alcaporado: A Cuban-style beef stew cooked with raisins and olives.

Annatto: Sometimes referred to as *achiote seeds*, annatto seeds, from the tropical annatto tree, are used commercially as a natural orange coloring agent for butter and cheese. Annatto is also a useful ingredient when sautéing, as it imparts a vibrant yellow-orange tint to the protein being prepared. The seeds are available both dried and crushed and can be used to flavor oil. Annatto oil can be drizzled over meat and shellfish for both color and subtle flavoring and can be added to salad dressings as a flavoring agent.

Arroz con Pollo: A Cuban chicken and rice dish frequently served in South Florida restaurants. Arroz con pollo can be served as an entrée with a little broth or as a hearty soup.

Arroz Marillo: Cuban-style saffron rice. Arroz marillo is, typically, long-grain rice cooked with saffron. Due to the high cost of saffron, turmeric is frequently used as a substitute.

Avocado: Dating back to almost 8000 B.C., the avocado originates from Mexico and was considered an aphrodisiac by the Incas and Aztecs. Avocado trees have been known to produce up to 400 fruits per year. Avocados can be left on the tree for almost six months. Those grown in South Florida are often called *alligator pears* because their skin resembles an alligator hide. The buttery-flavored avocado is rich in vitamin A and potassium and unusually high in fat. Florida avocados typically have a higher water content and milder flavor than avocados from California.

Banana Leaf: The leaf from the banana tree, frequently used as a wrapper for cooking food in the Florida region. This technique imparts the flavor of the banana to other foods. Banana leaves are typically available in Latin, Caribbean, and Asian specialty markets.

Banana Pepper: Also known as the Hungarian wax chile. Banana peppers are large, usually 3–5 inches in length, with ranges in flavor from mild to medium hot. Banana peppers are known for their distinctive waxy texture.

Black Bean: Also referred to as *black turtle bean* and *frijole negro*. Black beans are the dried bean variety most commonly prepared in the Florida region as well as in the Caribbean and Central and South America. Black beans are actually not black at all but a dark purple color. They are a staple starch for many of the Hispanic cultures represented in the Florida region. Black beans are frequently made into soup or served with rice.

Bolichi: A popular Cuban dish in the Florida Keys. Bolichi is a marinated pot roast rolled with hard-boiled eggs. In South America, a similar preparation for pot roast is called *matambre*.

Bollito: A Cuban preparation combining black-eyed peas and garlic rolled into a ball and deep-fried.

Boniato: A tuber that is similar in appearance to a sweet potato. Boniato has white or yellow flesh with a somewhat bitter flavor. The flesh is typically a little less sweet than that of a normal sweet potato, and it is drier and fluffier when cooked. Boniato can be prepared by boiling, baking, deep-frying, roasting, steaming, or sautéing.

Calabaza: Also referred to as a *West Indian pumpkin*. Calabaza is a large Cuban squash with a round shape, similar to a pumpkin, or a pear shape. It is rarely smaller than a honeydew melon. The skin of the calabaza is usually orange in color, but sometimes it is green or striped. Calabaza is typically sold halved or in slices due to its large size. The orange flesh has a flavor similar to pumpkins or butternut squash, but is sweeter and moister.

Callaloo: A vegetable that is similar in appearance to kale, Swiss chard, and spinach. It was a favorite of the African slaves brought to the Caribbean and is now commonly used in South Florida. Substitutes include spinach and kale.

Cassava: Another name for yuca. (See *yuca*.)

Chayote: A light-green pear-shaped member of the squash family and a staple of Hispanic cuisine for centuries. Chayote came to Florida with settlers and slaves from the West Indies and has a flavor similar to zucchini. In the southern states, chayote is referred to as *mirliton*. The large seed in the center of the chayote needs to be removed before using. Chayote is frequently stuffed and baked or cut into cubes that are seasoned and used as an ingredient in salads and appetizers. Chayote is usually available from August through November and can be stored under refrigeration for up to a month.

Chorizo: A spicy Spanish sausage made with pork and seasonings. Traditionally, chorizo of Spanish origin is made with smoked pork, while the Mexican tradition calls for fresh pork. The casing is removed before cooking.

Citrus Fruit: Florida is one of the largest producers of citrus fruits in the world. Almost 80 percent of the orange juice consumed in the United States is made from Florida oranges. Florida also produces grapefruit, limes, lemons, and tangerines. Some of the more exotic citrus fruits from the region include kumquats, tangelos, pomelos, and calamondins. Citrus fruit should be chosen by weight rather than color; the heavier the fruit, the more juice it contains.

Coconut: The large, hairy fruit of the coconut palm tree. The flesh of the fruit is white in color and lines the inside of the shell. When selecting coconuts, shake them to ensure that there is liquid inside the shell.

Coconut Milk: A combination of equal parts of water and shredded fresh coconut meat, simmered until foamy. The mixture is then strained through cheesecloth to retain as much liquid as possible. Canned coconut milk makes an excellent substitute for fresh.

Conch: A large mollusk found in the coral reefs off the coast of South Florida and around the Florida Keys. Conch meat has a flavor similar to sweet clams and is typically used to make chowder or fritters. Conch shells are large, attractive, and whorled—the kind that children hold to their ear to hear the sound of the ocean.

Cubanella Pepper: The cubanella pepper is a large, lemon-yellow, rather mild pepper that is available at most Hispanic specialty markets. It can grow almost to the size of a green bell pepper.

Empanada: A small half-moon–shaped pastry, usually stuffed with a meat, fish, or cheese filling. Empanadas are typically served hot as hors d'oeuvres or appetizer.

Escabeche: A method of pickling frequently used to prepare fish or vegetables. Escabeche is typically served as an appetizer, light entrée, or side dish. It is best served at room temperature after resting under refrigeration overnight. The resting process allows the full extraction of flavors of the ingredients.

Flan: A traditional Cuban dessert similar to French crème caramel. Flan is also commonly served in the Southwest and Tex-Mex regions. The Cuban-style preparation of flan flavors the custard with almonds, coconut, or rum. It is frequently served with plantains or black beans.

Grouper: A fish found in the waters of the Caribbean, the Gulf of Mexico, and the North and South Atlantic. Grouper generally range in size from 5 to 15 pounds but can sometimes be as large as 600 pounds. There are many species; however, the most popular include the black, tiger, yellowmouth, comb, and graysby varieties. Grouper is known for its excellent sweet flesh that is both lean and firm, making the fish suitable for baking, broiling, frying, poaching, and steaming.

Guava: A round fruit, usually 2–6 inches in diameter. The thick skin of the fruit, which is edible, is a greenish white, yellow, or red color when the fruit is ripe. The small seeds embedded in the flesh of the fruit are frequently removed by passing the flesh through a sieve. It is said that the flavor of guava is similar to strawberries. Guava is eaten raw or cooked in jellies and pastes. It is also used as a base for glazes and custards.

Hearts of Palm: Also referred to as *swamp cabbage*, hearts of palm are the tender inner parts of the stem of the sabal or cabbage palm tree. They are somewhat rare and expensive because the palm tree must be destroyed in order to obtain them. Hearts of palm have a white to ivory color and many concentric layers. Their delicate flavor is somewhat reminiscent of an artichoke. Hearts of palm are typically served in salad preparations and can be eaten either raw or cooked.

Jamaican Pimiento: A highly aromatic pea-sized berry commonly known as *allspice*. When the Spaniards arrived in the Caribbean, they discovered the berry and named it Jamaican pepper or pimiento, the word for pepper in Spanish. The Jamaican pimiento has a flavor that tastes like a combination of cinnamon, nutmeg, and cloves. Generally, the whole berries are referred to as *allspice* and, when ground, *pimiento*.

Jerk Chicken: A Caribbean chicken recipe. The chicken is seasoned with a special blend of spices called *jerk seasoning* and Jamaican peppers, and slow-cooked in deep pits or earthenware pots. The name *jerk* is derived from the Native American word *charqui*, meaning sun-dried beef or jerky. Today, the term *jerk* refers to a particular way of seasoning and cooking meats and seafood, typically accomplished with a dry spice rub or wet marinade. Jerk chicken can also be prepared with excellent results on a grill or in an oven.

Key Lime: One of the two main varieties of lime available in the United States. Lime trees were first planted in the Florida Keys in 1835. The fruit from these trees were small, yellowish limes with a highly aromatic, tart flavor, similar to very tart lemons. The Key lime is smaller than the more common Persian lime and rounder, with a color more yellow than green. When substituting Persian limes for Key limes, use one Persian lime for every three Key limes called for in the recipe.

Litchi: A small, oval fruit with a hard red shell; it is frequently referred to as a nut. The fruit contains one large seed surrounded by sweet white flesh. Litchi is available fresh as well as in cans. The litchi is generally prepared by drying the fruit, which gives it a nutty, raisinlike flavor. Litchi is also spelled *litchee* and *lychee*, depending on the region.

Manchego Cheese: A Spanish sheep's-milk cheese that has a full, mellow flavor and is ivory to yellow in color and semifirm to hard in texture. Manchego cheese is prepared in a variety of ways, including dry salting, curing, and soaking in olive oil. Each of the preparation techniques used to make Manchego cheese results in a different color, flavor, and texture.

Malanga: A root vegetable with a shape like a long yam. Malanga has pinkish flesh and patchy, thin brown or beige skin.

Mango: A sweet fruit with a pale to deep yellow flesh. When ripe, the skin of the mango is green to a rosy red color. Select mangos with smooth skin that is free of pits. When they are ripe, the surface should yield to light pressure, similar to an avocado. Mangos are aromatic when ripe and are said to have a flavor similar to a very sweet peach. To remove the pulp, peel and cut away the fruit from the fibrous seed. Green, unripe mangos are frequently used in the Florida region to prepare chutneys and relishes.

Moros y Cristianos: A traditional Spanish dish, popular among the Cubans in South Florida, that is made with black beans and rice. The name *moros y cristianos* is Spanish for *Moors and Christians*. It symbolizes the conflict between the dark-skinned Moors, who invaded Spain in the eighth century, and the white-skinned Christians, who, after being dominated for hundreds of years, eventually overthrew them. Moros y cristianos is typically served as a side dish with meat and fried plantains.

Paella: A classic Spanish rice dish that became popular in Cuba and South Florida when the Spanish colonized the regions. Paella, in Florida, features chorizo and shellfish cooked with Valencia rice in a large cooking vessel commonly referred to as a *pallero* or a paella.

Papaya: A sweet melonlike fruit that often has bright yellow-pink to yellow-orange flesh within a smooth, thin skin whose colors range from deep orange to green. In the Florida region, papaya is frequently eaten on the half-shell with just a squeeze of lime. Papaya is also used in chutneys, sauces, desserts, and salads. The small, spicy edible seeds are a grayish-black color and are often used in salad dressings or as a garnish.

Passion Fruit: A small fruit with a brownish-purple skin that is wrinkled like a walnut. Passion fruit are typically about the size of a golf ball and have yellow-colored flesh that is said to taste like a combination of pineapple, guava, and lemon. To determine if a passion fruit is ripe, shake the fruit and listen for the sound of liquid moving under the skin.

Picadillo: A popular Cuban preparation featuring a highly seasoned and spicy beef hash. Picadillo is typically served with black beans, rice, and fried plantains.

Pickapeppa Sauce: A hot pepper sauce, similar to Tabasco sauce, that is made in the St. Augustine area of Florida.

Pink Bean: A smooth, reddish-brown dried bean frequently prepared in the Florida region. Pinto beans are a common substitute.

Plaintain: A member of the banana family that is used extensively in South Florida and Cuba. Unlike bananas, plantains are almost never eaten raw. They vary in size and generally have a starchy, somewhat nutty flavor when the peel is green to yellow. When the peel is yellow to black, the fruit has a sweet flavor similar to a banana and can be served as a vegetable or dessert. Plantains are often used as a starch instead of potatoes and to make tostones, which frequently substitute for bread or rolls during a meal. Plantains are also deep-fried and salted and served like chips as a snack or garnish.

Red Snapper: One of the most popular species of fish in the Florida region and around the country. Red snapper is a soft-fleshed fish with a remarkable flavor that requires little to no seasoning before cooking. Ranging from 2 to 6 pounds, snapper is available in many varieties, including yellowtail, blackfin, gray, and mahogany. Pacific red snapper, from the West Coast, is not a snapper at all but a variety of ling cod.

Sangria: A wine-based beverage made with fruit and sugar. The name derives from the Spanish word for blood. The Spanish colonists first brought sangria to the Florida region. Typically, sangria was made by the Spanish priests. Its fruity flavor makes it an excellent accompaniment to the spicy fare of the region.

Seville Orange: Also referred to in Florida as *bitter* or *sour orange*. Seville oranges are smaller than regular oranges and have a rough, thin orange and yellow skin. The flesh and juice are darker than typical Florida oranges and have a very tart flavor. Seville oranges are frequently used in the preparation of orange marmalade. The juice is used to marinate meats, and the rind is used to make the liqueur curaçao and orange flower water. If Seville oranges are not available, combine regular orange juice with a little lime juice as a substitute.

Shrimp: Many believe that the American shrimping industry was born in the Florida region and that it quickly spread north along the Georgia coast to the Carolinas and west to the Gulf of Mexico. Today, American shrimp consumption is second only to that of canned tuna fish, among seafoods. Several varieties of shrimp are caught along Florida's coastline; they are typically named after their color. The most popular varieties are pink, white, and brown shrimp. The colors differ with diet; however, all shrimp shells turn pink once they are cooked.

Sofrito: *Sofrito* is derived from the Spanish word *sofreir*, meaning "to fry lightly." Sofrito is an essential flavoring agent made by cooking salt pork, ham, onion, garlic, and oregano in oil. It can be prepared in large amounts and stored in the refrigerator until needed.

Sour Orange: Another name for Seville orange. (See *Seville orange.*)

Spiny Lobster: Also referred to as the *rock lobster*. Spiny lobsters inhabit the warm waters off the Florida coast and are aptly named, as the forward segment of their shell is covered with spines. Unlike the Maine lobster, almost all the meat of the spiny lobster is concentrated in the tail section, with some additional meat located in the small claws. Spiny lobster is frequently served baked, stuffed with crabmeat and other fish, and flavored with lime. The tail meat is also broiled and served plain with just a little seasoned butter.

Star Fruit: Also referred to as *carambola*. Star fruit is a small yellow-green to golden-orange fruit appropriately named for its star-shaped cross sections. The flesh of the fruit has a tart, crisp flavor somewhat like a tart apple, and the thin, waxy skin is edible. Star fruit is frequently used in salad preparations and as a garnish for other dishes.

Stone Crab: A species of crab indigenous to the waters of Biscayne Bay near Miami, Florida. Typically, only the oversized, black-tipped claws of the crabs are eaten. The stone crab season generally runs from October to May. The population is diminishing, so fishermen catch the crabs and remove the smaller of their two claws. They are then returned to the water, where in a period of 18 to 24 months, they grow a new claw. The stone crab claws are cooked, cracked, and served with simple drawn butter to enhance the flavor of the meat, similar to how New Englanders enjoy eating Maine lobster.

Tamarind: The sticky, dry pod of the tamarind tree, sometimes referred to as *Indian date*. Tamarind has a taste similar to plums, yet much more sour. It is frequently used as an ingredient in chutney. Tamarind is also used in place of lime or lemon juice in recipes that require a sweet and sour tang with extra body. Tamarind paste can usually be purchased in Caribbean specialty markets.

Yuca: Also referred to as *cassava*, yuca is a sweet, buttery, and starchy tuber shaped like an elongated sweet potato. It has a barklike skin and hard white flesh. Yuca is used in preparations much as a potato is, and is frequently prepared as fritters or used in stews. Coating the skin with olive oil helps retain the yuca's moisture as well as helping it cook faster.

NEW ENGLAND DISHES STARTING IN
THE UPPER LEFT AND CONTINUING
CLOCKWISE: Maine Lobster Salad;
Clams Casino; Sweet Potato
and Horseradish Gratin; Baked
Stuffed Maine Lobster.

NEW ENGLAND DISHES STARTING IN THE UPPER LEFT AND CONTINUING CLOCKWISE: Baked Acorn
Squash; Blueberry Cobbler; Butternut Squash Soup; Roasted Turkey Roll with Cranberry Sauce and
Green Bean Casserole.

COMMON INGREDIENTS
OF MID-ATLANTIC
CUISINE

MID-ATLANTIC DISHES
STARTING IN THE UPPER
LEFT AND CONTINUING
CLOCKWISE: Sautéed
Scallops with Fresh Herb
Tartar Sauce, Glazed
Carrot Sticks, and
Matchstick Potatoes;
Manhattan Clam
Chowder; Open-Face
Soft-Shell Crab
Sandwich; Scalloped
Sweet Potatoes.

MID-ATLANTIC DISHES
STARTING AT THE TOP
AND CONTINUING
CLOCKWISE:
Pennsylvania Pork
Roast; Split Pea Soup;
Shaker-Style Turkey
Cutlets with Spinach
Timbales and Buttery
Homemade Noodles;
Corn Crêpes with
Smoked Shrimp and
Asparagus; Apple
Brown Betty.

COMMON INGREDIENTS OF
THE DEEP SOUTH

DEEP SOUTH DISHES STARTING IN THE UPPER LEFT
AND CONTINUING CLOCKWISE: Brunswick Stew;
Hoppin' John Salad with Pecan Vinaigrette;
Vidalia Onion Tart with Red Bell Pepper Sauce;
Fried Green Tomatoes with Roasted
Tomato Sauce.

DEEP SOUTH DISHES STARTING IN THE UPPER LEFT AND CONTINUING CLOCKWISE: Pecan Pie;
Shrimp Awendaw with Grit Cakes; Grits Soufflé with Roasted Garlic and Cheddar Cheese;
Glazed Country Ham with Vidalia Onion and Cola Sauce.

COMMON INGREDIENTS OF
FLORIBBEAN CUISINE

FLORIBBEAN DISHES STARTING
IN THE UPPER LEFT AND
CONTINUING CLOCKWISE:
Stuffed Chayote with
Mushrooms; Whole Poached
Fish; Ceviche of Scallops with
Floribbean Slaw.

FLORIBBEAN DISHES
STARTING AT THE TOP AND
CONTINUING CLOCKWISE:
Key Lime Pie; Tropical Fruit
Salad with Avocado
Dressing; Floribbean
Grouper and White Rice
and Tomatoes; Floribbean
Slaw.

COMMON INGREDIENTS OF
CAJUN AND CREOLE
CUISINES

CAJUN AND CREOLE DISHES STARTING IN THE
UPPER LEFT AND CONTINUING CLOCKWISE:
Tomato and Haricot Vert Salad; Chicken
and Sausage Jambalaya; Fried Okra,
Cajun Fish Beignet.

CAJUN AND CREOLE DISHES STARTING IN THE UPPER LEFT AND CONTINUING CLOCKWISE: Oysters Rockefeller; Blazing Hushpuppies; Paneéd Chicken and Fettuccine with Creole Collard Greens; Apple Bread Pudding with Caramel Sauce and Crunchy Pralines.

COMMON INGREDIENTS OF THE CENTRAL PLAINS

CENTRAL PLAINS DISHES
STARTING IN THE UPPER LEFT
AND CONTINUING CLOCKWISE:
Deep-Dish Chicken and Sausage
Pie with Buttermilk Biscuits;
Central Plains Cheesecake;
Planked Whitefish with
Horseradish Crust and Red
Cabbage Braised in Cider and
Beer; Wheatberry and Toasted
Sunflower Seed Salad.

CENTRAL PLAINS DISHES
STARTING IN THE UPPER LEFT
AND CONTINUING CLOCKWISE:
Pan-Seared Steak with Maytag
Blue Cheese, Brussels Sprouts
with Mushrooms and Central
Plains Smashed Potatoes; Beet
and Apple Salad with
Horseradish Vinaigrette;
Kansas City Barbecue Ribs;
Morel and Goat Cheese Tart
with Red Bell Pepper Coulis.

COMMON INGREDIENTS
OF TEX-MEX CUISINE

TEX-MEX DISHES STARTING IN THE
UPPER LEFT AND CONTINUING CLOCKWISE:
Escabeche of Vegetables; Tortilla Soup;
Shrimp Tacos with Guacamole and
Pico de Gallo; Homemade Tamales
with Red Pepper Coulis.

TEX-MEX DISHES STARTING IN THE UPPER LEFT AND CONTINUING CLOCKWISE: Mole de Pollo; Jalapeño Corn Bread; Caldo de Res; Chicken Flautas, Chiles Rellenos with Tomatillo Salsa, Refried Beans, and Colache.

COMMON INGREDIENTS
OF ROCKY MOUNTAIN
CUISINE

ROCKY MOUNTAIN
DISHES STARTING IN
THE UPPER LEFT AND
CONTINUING CLOCKWISE:
Buffalo Consommé with
Anasazi Bean Custard;
Roasted Garlic
Potatoes, Barbecued
Montana Quail with
Barley Salad; Charred
Corn and Quinoa
Soufflé with Mountain
Crawdads.

ROCKY MOUNTAIN DISHES
STARTING IN THE UPPER
LEFT AND CONTINUING
CLOCKWISE: Marinated
Colorado Dried Bean
Salad with Red Bean
Crêpes; Garlic and
Rosemary Roasted Leg of
Lamb with Pan Gravy, Red
Chared Casserole,
Caramelized Onions, and
Sweet Potato Dumplings;
Red Potato, Corn, and
Chorizo Chowder; Rocky
Mountain Trout in
Cornmeal Crust with
Horseradish Butter Sauce,
Warm Rocky Mountain
Slaw, Cayenne and Honey-
Glazed Carrots, and
Indian Flat Bread.

COMMON INGREDIENTS OF
THE AMERICAN SOUTHWEST

AMERICAN SOUTHWEST DISHES STARTING
IN THE UPPER LEFT AND CONTINUING
CLOCKWISE: Tamale Tart with Roast
Garlic Custard; Ensalada de Nopalitos;
Spicy Pork Empanadas; Quail, Roasted
Pepper, and Avocado.

AMERICAN SOUTHWEST DISHES STARTING IN THE UPPER LEFT AND CONTINUING CLOCKWISE: Chile-Rubbed Bass with Cilantro Cream, Ancho Chile Mayonnaise, and Southwestern Coleslaw; Buñuelos with Honey Syrup; Baked Goat Cheese with Roasted Peppers, Pine Nuts, and Corn; Calabacitas con Maize and Achiote Rice with Wild Mushrooms and Queso Fresco.

COMMON INGREDIENTS OF CALIFORNIA AND HAWAIIAN CUISINES

CALIFORNIA AND HAWAIIAN DISHES STARTING IN THE UPPER LEFT AND CONTINUING CLOCKWISE: San Francisco Cioppino; Baby Greens with Warm Goat Cheese and Walnut Vinaigrette; Deep-Fried Monterey Bay Calamari with Lemon Butter Sauce, Monterey-Style Penne Pasta with Calamari and Baby Artichokes.

CALIFORNIA AND HAWAIIAN DISHES STARTING IN THE UPPER LEFT AND CONTINUING CLOCKWISE: Chilled Castroville Artichoke with Confetti Vinaigrette; Rosemary Focaccia; Sautéed Petaluma Duck Breast with Port Wine Reduction, Chinese Long Beans with Sesame Seeds, and Spicy Roasted Eggplant; Strawberry Shortcake with Cornmeal Biscuits.

PACIFIC NORTHWEST DISHES STARTING IN THE UPPER LEFT AND CONTINUING CLOCKWISE: Cardamon Cornmeal Waffles; Alaskan King Crab Legs with Champagne Sauce; Buckwheat Soba Noodle Salad with Grilled Mushrooms; Steelhead with Asparagus and Butter Sauce and Mashed Potato and Wheatberry Cakes.

COMMON INGREDIENTS OF PACIFIC NORTHWEST CUISINE

PACIFIC NORTHWEST DISHES STARTING IN THE UPPER LEFT AND CONTINUING CLOCKWISE: Warm Flourless Chocolate Cake with Espresso Sauce; Oven-Roasted Vegetables; Chilled Blackberry Yogurt Soup; Roasted Ellensburg Lamb Rack with Thyme–Merlot Sauce and Green Beans cooked with Summer Savory.

Sample Menus from Floribbean Cuisine

<u>M E N U   O N E</u>

Key West Conch Chowder

Hearts of Palm Salad

Floribbean Grouper with Black Bean, Jicama, and Corn Salsa ·

Peas and Fresh Okra · White Rice with Tomatoes

<u>M E N U   T W O</u>

Black Bean Soup

Ceviche of Scallops with Floribbean Slaw

Roasted Pork with Prune Sauce and Mango Chutney · Stuffed Chayote with Mushrooms

· Spicy Orange Carrot Sticks · Rice and Peas

<u>M E N U   T H R E E</u>

Chicken with Ginger and Tamarind

Tropical Fruit Salad with Avocado Dressing

Shrimp with Roasted Garlic and Papaya with Avocado Salsa ·

Candied Sweet Potatoes · Stewed Pink Beans

Key West Conch Chowder

YIELD: 6 PORTIONS · PORTION SIZE: 10 OUNCES

1 pound (480g) conch meat

lime or lemon juice, as needed

1 clove garlic, crushed

4 ounces (120g) celery, cut into small dice

1 pound (480g) carrots, cut into small dice

8 ounces (240g) onion, cut into small dice

7 ounces (210g) green bell pepper, cut into small dice

2 pounds (960g) chef potatoes, peeled and diced

4 ounces (120g) tomato concassée

2½ quarts (2.4L) clam juice

1 sprig thyme

2 bay leaves

2 ounces (60g) bacon, diced

1 teaspoon (5ml) Tabasco sauce

salt, to taste

black pepper, ground, to taste

CHEF TIPS *Celebrity chef Norman Van Aken says, "Conch chowder is to Key West what cioppino is to San Francisco." This unique mollusk is so intertwined with the folklore and diet of Key Westerners that the people who were born and raised there in the late 1800s became known as conchs (konks).*

Conch meat has a rich, exotic, clamlike taste and can be used in salads, fritters, and chowders. Conch meat is almost always purchased frozen, even in Florida. Try to select Grade A quality conch and be sure to check for freezer burn, which can be identified by ice crystals formed on the meat or by off-white colored spots. Do not buy the conch if you see indications of freezer burn.

Conch meat can be extremely tough, even if you dice it very small. We recommend grinding conch meat in a meat grinder using a medium die. Before grinding, cut away and discard any orange flaplike meat attached to the conch.

Thoroughly wash the conch in lime or lemon juice.

Grind the conch in a meat grinder using a medium die. Store covered in a refrigerated unit at 41°F (5°C) or lower until needed.

Reserve the prepared vegetables under refrigeration at 41°F (5°C) or lower until needed.

COOKING

Combine conch and clam juice with the thyme and bay leaves. Cook over low heat for 30 minutes and to a temperature of 145°F (62.8°C) for at least 15 seconds.

In a separate sauté pan, render the bacon.

Add the garlic, celery, carrots, onion, and green pepper to the bacon and rendered fat and cook for 2–3 minutes.

🍲 **Add** the cooked vegetables to the conch, along with the potatoes and tomatoes. Bring to a boil and turn the heat down to a simmer, making sure the soup does not fall below 140°F (60°C).

Simmer the soup until the potatoes are tender.

About 10 minutes before removing the soup from the heat, add the Tabasco sauce and season to taste with salt and freshly ground pepper.

The potatoes should thicken the soup adequately. If a thicker consistency is desired, use a corn-starch slurry.

SERVING/HOLDING

Carefully ladle the conch chowder into hot soup plates.

Sprinkle the top with a few additional drops of Tabasco sauce and serve immediately.

🍲 **Hold** the chowder at 140°F (60°C) or above.

COOLING/STORING

Pour the remaining chowder into small metal containers.

🍲 **Cool** the remaining chowder in an ice bath from 140°F (60°C) to 70°F (21.2°C) or lower within 2 hours. Cool from 70°F (21.1°C) to 41°F (5°C) within an additional 4 hours for a total cooling time of 6 hours or less.

Cover the chowder; label, date, and store in refrigerated unit at a product temperature of 41°F (5°C) or lower.

Black Bean Soup

YIELD: 6 PORTIONS · PORTION SIZE: 10 OUNCES

8 ounces (240g) dried black beans

32 fluid ounces (960ml) water

16 fluid ounces (480ml) brown beef stock, prepared (see page 515)

1 ham hock, smoked

2 fluid ounces (60ml) dry sherry

salt, to taste

black pepper, ground, to taste

24 ounces (720g) rice, prepared, hot

4 ounces (120g) green onion, chopped

4 ounces (120g) ham, cooked, cut into small dice

CHEF TIPS *As a garnish, you may wish to use garlic, red and green peppers, chopped onion, and sour cream; they add a pleasing look and more flavor to the presentation of the soup.*

Rinse and sort the black beans, removing and discarding any stones.

Cover the beans with several inches of cold water and soak overnight under refrigeration.

Drain the beans and place them in a large pot.

COOKING

Cover the beans with the water and brown beef stock. Add the smoked ham hock. Bring the mixture to a boil and turn the heat down to a simmer. Simmer approximately 2 hours or until the beans are tender. Do not let the simmering soup fall below 140°F (60°C).

Add additional water as needed to maintain the original volume of water during the simmering process.

Remove the ham hock and let it cool just long enough to be safely handled.

Remove the skin from the ham hock and discard. Cut the meat into fine brunoise and discard the bones.

Purée approximately half of the beans in a blender or food processor.

Return the puréed beans to the pot and add the diced ham hock meat and the sherry.

Reheat gently and season to taste with salt and pepper. Maintain the internal temperature at 165°F (73.9°C) or higher for 15 seconds.

Carefully place a mold of ½ cup (120g) cooked rice in the center of each hot soup plate. Ladle the black bean soup around the rice and top with chopped green onions and diced ham.

Hold the soup at 140°F (60°C) or above.

Pour the remaining soup into smaller metal containers.

Cool the remaining soup in an ice bath from 140°F (60°C) to 70°F (21.1°C) or lower within 2 hours. Cool from 70°F (21.1°C) to 41°F (5°C) within an additional 4 hours for a total cooling time of 6 hours or less.

Cover the soup; label, date, and store in a refrigerated unit at a product temperature of 41°F (5°C) or lower.

Ceviche of Scallops with Floribbean Slaw

YIELD: 6 PORTIONS · PORTION SIZE: 8 OUNCES

4 ounces (120g) red bell pepper, whole

4 ounces (120g) green bell pepper, whole

1 pound (480g) sea scallops

4 fluid ounces (120ml) lime juice

½ teaspoon (2g) black pepper, ground

2 fluid ounces (60ml) lemon juice

½ teaspoon (2g) coriander, ground

2 fluid ounces (60ml) orange juice

2–3 bay leaves

2 fluid ounces (60ml) olive oil

1 ounce (30g) cilantro, chopped

salt, to taste

6 portions Floribbean slaw (recipe follows)

Roast the whole bell peppers. Remove the stem and seeds, then skin and dice the flesh. Reserve until needed.

Clean the scallops and remove the attached muscle. Slice the scallops ⅛ inch (.32cm) thick. Reserve under refrigeration, maintaining a temperature of 41°F (5°C) or lower.

COOKING

Mix all the ingredients together, except the scallops and slaw, in a stainless-steel or glass bowl. Season to taste with salt. Gently toss the sliced scallops in the mixture.

Marinate the mixture for 45–60 minutes, maintaining a temperature of at least 41°F (5°C) or lower.

When the scallops turn a solid white color and become firm in texture from the acids in the marinade, marination is complete.

Remove the scallops from the marinade and hold both until needed under refrigeration, maintaining a temperature of 41°F (5°C) or lower.

Place approximately 4 ounces of Floribbean slaw in the center of each service plate. Carefully place 4 ounces of the sliced marinated scallops around the base of the slaw. Drizzle a little of the marinade over the top and around the perimeter of the plate.

COOLING/STORING

Cover the ceviche; label, date, and store under refrigeration unit at a product temperature 41°F (5°C) or lower.

FLORIBBEAN SLAW

YIELD: 6 PORTIONS · PORTION SIZE: 4 OUNCES

6 ounces (180g) carrots, cut into julienne

3 ounces (90g) red bell peppers, cut into julienne

3 ounces (90g) green bell peppers, cut into julienne

3 ounces (90g) green cabbage, cut into julienne

6 ounces (180g) summer squash, cut into julienne

2 ounces (60g) red bell peppers, cut into small dice

2 ounces (60g) green bell peppers, cut into small dice

2 ounces (60g) mayonnaise, prepared

2 ounces (60ml) sour cream

1 ounce (30g) cilantro, chopped

salt, to taste

Reserve the prepared vegetables under refrigeration until needed.

COOKING

Mix all the ingredients together in a bowl and marinate for approximately 30–60 minutes. Reserve under refrigeration, maintaining a temperature of 41°F (5°C) or lower.

COOLING/STORING

Cover the slaw; label, date, and store in the refrigerator at 41°F (5°C) or lower.

Chicken with Ginger and Tamarind

1½ pounds (720g) chicken meat, cut into tenders or strips

6½ fluid ounces (195ml) lemon juice

3½ fluid ounces (104ml) lime juice

3 cloves garlic, chopped

14 ounces (420g) onions, chopped

1 tablespoon (15g) ginger root, peeled and grated

4 ounces (120g) red bell peppers, cut into julienne

4 ounces (120g) yellow bell peppers, cut into julienne

2 fluid ounces (60ml) vegetable oil

4 ounces (120g) tamarind paste

8 fluid ounces (240ml) water

salt, to taste

black pepper, ground, to taste

1 fluid ounce (30ml) olive oil

CHEF TIPS *Ginger and tamarind have always been two of the favorite flavoring agents in the Caribbean Islands. With the increased immigration of Caribbean natives to South Florida, the popularity of ginger and tamarind has increased there as well. This recipe combines these two unique flavors in one preparation.*

To make tamarind juice, steep the pods in a bowl of hot water until the sour brown juice can be easily squeezed out or strained. If tamarind paste is available, mix 1 teaspoon paste to 6 ounces water and adjust the flavor with more paste or water as needed. If tamarinds are not available, lemon juice or vinegar will make a fairly close substitute.

Rinse and pat dry the chicken meat. Rub the chicken pieces with the lemon and lime juice. Reserve the chicken under refrigeration at a product temperature of 41°F (5°C) or lower.

Reserve the prepared vegetables under refrigeration at a product temperature of 41°F (5°C) or lower.

COOKING

Heat the vegetable oil over medium heat in a sautoir pan.

Place the chicken in the hot oil in small batches, lightly browning and removing the chicken pieces to absorbent towels as they are done. Be sure to let the pan reheat between batches so that the chicken browns rather than steams.

Once all the chicken pieces are browned and removed from the pan, degrease the pan.

Reduce the heat slightly and add the garlic. Stir the garlic and add the onions. Cook the onions until they are lightly colored.

Stir in the ginger root.

Add the tamarind paste and water.

Season to taste with salt and black pepper.

Return the chicken pieces to the pan and bring to a simmer. Cover the pan and reduce the heat. Simmer until chicken is tender and reaches an internal temperature of 165°F (73.9°C) or higher for 15 seconds.

In a separate bowl, toss the peppers in the olive oil and season to taste with salt and black pepper.

SERVING/HOLDING

Place approximately 2 ounces (60g) of the dressed peppers in the center of each plate. Top the peppers with approximately 4 ounces (120g) of the hot chicken mixture.

Hold the chicken at 140°F (60°C) or above.

COOLING/STORING

Cool the remaining chicken from 140°F (60°C) to 70°F (21.1°C) or lower within 2 hours. Cool from 70°F (21.1°C) to 41°F (5°C) within an additional 4 hours for a total cooling time of 6 hours or less.

Cover chicken and peppers; label, date, and store under refrigeration unit at a product temperature of 41°F (5°C) or lower.

Tropical Fruit Salad with Avocado Dressing

YIELD: 6 PORTIONS · PORTION SIZE: 8 OUNCES

DRESSING

- 7 ounces (210g) avocado, peeled and pitted
- 5 fluid ounces (180ml) sour cream
- 2 fluid ounces (60ml) lime juice
- 1 tablespoon (15ml) honey
- 1 dash Tabasco sauce
- 1 pinch salt

SALAD

- 14 ounces (420g) red leaf lettuce
- 7 ounces (210g) avocado, thinly sliced
- 2 bananas, thinly sliced
- 1 pound (480g) pineapple rings, fresh or canned
- 8 ounces (240g) mango, cut into medium dice
- 8 ounces (240g) papaya, sliced
- 8 ounces (240g) white seedless grapes
- 4 ounces (120g) pecans or toasted almonds, chopped

CHEF TIPS *The seeds of the papaya may also be used as a garnish. If other tropical fruits are available, such as carambola, oranges, or pink grapefruit, they can be used in place of grapes. A slice of banana bread makes an excellent accompaniment for this salad.*

Chill all the dressing ingredients before using.

Line a large serving platter or chilled individual plates with red lettuce. Reserve under refrigeration until needed.

Reserve the prepared fruit under refrigeration at a product temperature of 41°F (5°C) or lower.

COOKING

Place the chilled dressing ingredients in a blender.

Blend until smooth. Reserve under refrigeration at 41°F (5°C) or lower.

SERVING/HOLDING

Arrange the prepared fruit in a circular fashion on the platter or plates, beginning with the avocado on the outside.

Follow the same procedure with the bananas, pineapple, and mango.

Arrange the sliced papaya last, with seedless grapes in the center.

Sprinkle the chopped nuts on top as a garnish.

Present the salad and dressing separately or, before serving, carefully ladle the dressing over the fruit in a decorative fashion, leaving some fruit exposed.

Hold the salad at 41°F (5°C) or below.

COOLING/STORING

Cover the fruit and dressing; label, date, and store in a refrigerated unit at a product temperature of 41°F (5°C) or lower.

Hearts of Palm Salad

YIELD: 8 PORTIONS · PORTION SIZE: 8 OUNCES

2 pounds (960g) hearts of palm, fresh, cut into medium dice

8 ounces (240g) red bell pepper, cut into small dice

8 ounces (240g) green bell pepper, cut into small dice

8 fluid ounces (240ml) lemon juice

2 oranges, sections plus juice

2 teaspoons (10g) tarragon, chopped

4 ounces (120g) mayonnaise, prepared

2 fluid ounces (60ml) honey

salt, to taste

black pepper, ground, to taste

6 leaves Bibb lettuce

1 ounce (30g) walnuts, chopped

CHEF TIPS *Hearts of palm are also referred to as swamp cabbage because they come from the cabbage palm tree and usually grow in swamps in southern Florida. Fresh hearts of palm are frequently available in Cryovac bags in many of America's regions and last up to two weeks in a refrigerator. Canned hearts of palm may be substituted for fresh.*

🥣 **Reserve** the prepared vegetables under refrigeration at 41°F (5°C) or lower until needed.

COOKING

Combine the lemon juice with the diced hearts of palm. Add the juice created by sectioning the oranges, reserving the sections for the salad's garnish.

Add the peppers, tarragon, mayonnaise, and honey to the hearts of palm. Season to taste with salt and pepper. Refrigerate until needed at 41°F (5°C) or lower.

SERVING/HOLDING

Place a Bibb lettuce leaf liner on each of the chilled plates. Place approximately 8 ounces (240g) of the hearts of palm salad on top of each lettuce liner. Garnish the salads with the reserved orange sections and sprinkle the top with chopped walnuts.

🥣 **Hold** the salad at 41°F (5°C) or below.

Whole Poached Fish

YIELD: 6 PORTIONS · PORTION SIZE: 8 OUNCES

3 pounds (1.4kg) red snapper, cleaned, heads and tails intact

8 cloves garlic, minced

21 ounces (630g) onion, finely chopped

72 fluid ounces (2.1L) water

8 fluid ounces (240ml) lime or lemon juice

2 ounces (60g) jalapeño, seeded and minced

2 tablespoons (30g) salt

24 fluid ounces (720ml) dry white wine

2 ounces (60g) jalapeño, whole

6 cloves garlic

1½ teaspoons (7g) allspice berries

3 bay leaves

1½ teaspoons (7g) dried thyme

CHEF TIPS *Although this preparation calls for red snapper, other fish can be used. Striped bass, yellow snapper, black bass, and redfish make excellent substitutions.*

Prepare the fish by removing the excess scales and the viscera. Wash, cover, and refrigerate the fish, maintaining an internal temperature of 41°F (5°C) or lower, until needed.

Refrigerate the prepared garlic and onions until needed at 41°F (5°C) or lower.

COOKING

Prepare a marinade with 48 fluid ounces (1.4L) of the water, 2 tablespoons (30ml) of the lime or lemon juice, 1 seeded and minced jalapeño, the minced garlic cloves, and the salt. Place the marinade in a dish or pan deep enough to hold the whole fish.

Add the fish to the marinade. Cover and marinate for 1 hour under refrigeration at 41°F (5°C) or lower.

Drain the fish and discard the marinade.

Combine the wine, remaining water, onion, whole jalapeño, whole garlic cloves, remaining lime or lemon juice, allspice berries, bay leaves, and thyme in a large sautoir pan.

Bring the mixture to a boil. Reduce the heat and simmer for 5 minutes.

Add the fish and continue to poach until it reaches an internal temperature of 145°F (62.8°C) or higher for 15 seconds.

SERVING/HOLDER

Serve the fish, using the poaching liquid as the sauce. This preparation of whole poached fish can be served, if desired, with boiled green bananas, cooked white rice, and deep-fried plantains.

Hold the sauce and fish at 140°F (60°C) or above.

COOLING/STORING

Pour the remaining sauce into small metal containers.

Cool the remaining sauce and fish from 140°F (60°C) to 70°F (21.1°C) or lower within 2 hours. Cool from 70°F (21.1°C) to 41°F (5°C) within an additional 4 hours for a total cooling time of 6 hours or less.

Cover the fish and sauce; label, date, and store under refrigeration at a product temperature of 41°F (5°C) or lower.

Shrimp with Roasted Garlic and Papaya with Avocado Salsa

36 shrimp, 16/20 size

2 bulbs garlic, whole

2 ounces (60g) celery, finely chopped

7 ounces (210g) onion, finely chopped

22 ounces (660g) papayas

basil, chopped, to taste

thyme, chopped, to taste

4 ounces (120g) butter or margarine

2¼ cups (600ml) dry white wine

1 bay leaf

32 ounces (960ml) fish stock (see page 518) or white chicken stock, prepared (see page 517)

16 ounces (480ml) whipping cream

salt, to taste

black peppercorns, ground, to taste

8 ounces (240g) avocado salsa (recipe follows)

CHEF TIPS *This recipe combines the flavors of garlic, papaya, and avocado salsa to yield an unexpected great taste. This unique dish, prepared with a Caribbean flair, sets these sautéed shrimp apart from more conventional preparations.*

Peel and devein the shrimp. Cover and refrigerate until needed at 41°F (5°C) or lower.

Cut the tops off the garlic bulbs and wrap the bulbs in aluminum foil. Roast them in a 375°F (190.6°C) oven for approximately 30–45 minutes.

Reserve the chopped celery and onion in the refrigerator at 41°F (5°C) or lower.

Cut the papayas in half, remove the seeds, and peel. Slice the papayas into long, thin strips and toss in a bowl with the basil and thyme. Reserve under refrigeration until needed at 41°F (5°C) or lower.

COOKING

Melt 2 tablespoons (30ml) of the butter or margarine in a medium saucepan.

Squeeze the pulp from the roasted garlic bulbs into the butter. Add the celery and onions. Cook the vegetables until the onions are translucent.

Add 16 fluid ounces (480ml) of the white wine, bay leaf, and stock to the cooked garlic and onions. Reduce liquid to half its original volume over high heat. Stir in the cream and reduce to a nappé consistency.

Melt the remaining 2 tablespoons (30ml) butter in another large skillet.

🥄 **Add** the shrimp and sauté them for approximately 4 minutes or until they are pink in color and reach an internal temperature of 145°F (62.8°C) or higher for 15 seconds. Add the remaining white wine during last 2 minutes of cooking.

Season to taste with salt and black pepper.

SERVING/HOLDING

Carefully spoon approximately 2 ounces (60ml) of the sauce into the center of each hot plate. Decoratively place some papaya strips in the center of each plate around the sauce. Top the papaya with approximately 1¼ ounces (38g) of avocado salsa and place 6 cooked shrimp around the perimeter.

🥄 **Hold** the shrimp and sauce at 140°F (60°C) or above.

COOLING/STORING

Pour the remaining shrimp and sauce into small metal containers.

🥄 **Cool** the remaining shrimp and sauce from 140°F (60°C) to 70°F (21.1°C) or lower within 2 hours. Cool from 70°F (21.1°C) to 41°F (5°C) within an additional 4 hours for a total cooling time of 6 hours or less.

Cover the shrimp and the sauce; label, date, and store under refrigeration at a product temperature of 41°F (5°C).

AVOCADO SALSA

5½ ounces (165g) avocado, peeled and seeded, cut into small dice

2 ounces (60g) cubanella pepper, minced

1 tablespoon (15g) cilantro, chopped

8 ounces (320g) plum tomatoes, peeled

½ teaspoon (2g) cumin, ground

1 tablespoon (15ml) lime juice

1 dollop sour cream

1 tablespoon (15g) red onion, minced

CHEF TIPS *Avocados in south Florida are often referred to as alligator pears. The buttery-flavored avocado is rich in vitamin A and potassium. The red onions add a measure of sweetness to the tart salsa. Florida avocados typically have a higher water content than avocados from California, and a much milder flavor. If Florida avocados are not available, the California variety can easily be substituted. If cubanella peppers are not available, substitute 1 seeded and diced jalapeño.*

Reserve the prepared vegetables under refrigeration at 41°F (5°C) or lower.

Combine all ingredients except the lime juice, sour cream, and red onions in a bowl.

Mix well, but keep chunky.

COOKING

Sprinkle some of the lime juice over the salsa for a tart flavor as well as to keep avocado from oxidizing and discoloring. Store under refrigeration until needed at 41°F (5°C) or lower.

Blend the lime juice into the salsa just before serving.

SERVING/HOLDING

Garnish the salsa by topping with a small dollop of sour cream and minced red onions.

Hold the salsa at 41°F (5°C) or lower.

COOLING/STORING

Cover the salsa; label, date, and store in a refrigerated unit at a product temperature of 41°F (5°C) or lower.

Floribbean Grouper with Black Bean, Jicama, and Corn Salsa

YIELD: 6 PORTIONS · PORTION SIZE: 12 OUNCES

6 grouper fillets, 4–5 ounces (120–150g) each

MARINADE

4 fluid ounces (120ml) lime juice

4 ounces (120g) cilantro, coarsely chopped

1 tablespoon (15g) garlic, minced

salt, to taste

black pepper, ground, to taste

1 tablespoon (15g) sugar

8 fluid ounces (240ml) olive oil

SAUCE

1 pound (480g) papaya, peeled, seeded, cut into medium dice

3 tablespoons (44g) ginger root, peeled and minced

32 fluid ounces (960ml) fish stock or white chicken stock, prepared (see page 517)

2 tablespoons (30g) shallots, minced

1 tablespoon (15g) garlic, minced

2 tablespoons (30ml) lime juice

2 tablespoons (30ml) honey

salt, to taste

1 lime, cut into 6 wedges

6 springs cilantro

20 ounces (532g) black bean, jicama, and corn salsa (recipe follows)

🥣 **Refrigerate** the grouper fillets until needed at 41°F (5°C) or lower.

🥣 **Reserve** the prepared fruit, vegetables, and herbs for the sauce under refrigeration at 41°F (5°C) or lower until needed.

COOKING

Combine all the marinade ingredients, except the olive oil, in a food processor and process thoroughly.

With the processor running, slowly drizzle the olive oil through the feed tube into the mixture. Continue to process until a fairly thick emulsion forms.

In a large saucepan, combine the papaya, ginger, stock, shallots, and garlic. Bring to a boil and reduce the heat to a simmer. Continue to simmer until the papaya is very soft—approximately 30–40 minutes. Do not let the simmering sauce fall below 140°F (60°C).

Purée the sauce and pass it through a chinois. Add the lime juice and honey, then season to taste with salt.

Hold the sauce 140°F (60°C) or higher until needed.

Coat the grouper fillets with the marinade. Grill the fillets until they are cooked and reach an internal temperature of 145°F (62.8°C) or higher for 15 seconds. Be careful not to overcook the fish fillets, as they become dry and tough.

SERVING/HOLDING

Carefully spoon approximately 2 fluid ounces (60ml) of the sauce into the center of each hot plate. Place the grouper on the plate over half the sauce.

Garnish the plates with a lime wedge, a cilantro sprig, and approximately 3 ounces (90g) black bean, jicama, and corn salsa.

Hold the fish and sauce at 140°F (60°C) or above.

COOLING/STORING

Cool the remaining fish and sauce from 140°F (60°C) to 70°F (21.1°C) or lower within 2 hours. Cool from 70°F (21.1°C) to 41°F (5°C) within an additional 4 hours for a total cooling time of 6 hours or less.

Cover the fish and the sauce; label, date, and store in refrigerated unit at a product temperature of 41°F (5°C) or lower.

BLACK BEAN, JICAMA, AND CORN SALSA

4 ounces (120g) red onion, minced

1 clove garlic, peeled and minced

8 ounces (240g) corn, roasted, kernels removed

4 ounces (120g) jicama, peeled, cut into small dice

1 ounce (30g) serrano chile, seeded and minced

2 ounces (60g) black beans, cooked or canned

1 tablespoon (15ml) lime juice

2 fluid ounces (60ml) extra-virgin olive oil

salt, to taste

CHEF TIPS *To roast corn over charcoal, prepare a moderately hot charcoal fire. Pull back the husks on each ear but do not remove them. Carefully remove the silk, then smooth the husks back over the ears of corn. Secure the husks by tying the tips with butcher's twine. Turn ears frequently to ensure even heat distribution while grilling. The corn can also be roasted in a 400°F (204.4°C) oven for approximately 55–60 minutes if desired.*

Reserve the prepared vegetables under refrigeration for a product temperature of 41°F (5°C) or lower.

COOKING

Combine all the ingredients in a bowl and allow the salsa to marinate overnight under refrigeration at a product temperature of 41°F (5°C) or lower. This allows all the flavors to integrate.

SERVING/HOLDING

Hold the salsa at 41°F (5°C) or lower.

COOLING/STORING

Cover the salsa; label, date, and store under refrigeration at a product temperature of 41°F (5°C) or lower.

Roasted Pork with Prune Sauce and Mango Chutney

YIELD: 6 PORTIONS · PORTION SIZE: 10 OUNCES

MARINADE

4 black peppercorns, cracked

½ teaspoon (2g) cloves, ground

2 sprigs oregano

1 ounce (30g) salt

½ fluid ounce (15ml) olive oil

½ fluid ounce (15ml) cider vinegar

PORK ROAST

48 ounces (1.4kg) pork roast, butt or loin

1 fluid ounce (30ml) olive oil

8 fluid ounces (240ml) dark rum

8 ounces (240g) prunes, pitted and diced

16 fluid ounces (480ml) beer

2 ounces (60g) brown sugar

8 ounces (240g) ham, cut into small dice

8 ounces (240g) Spanish olives, pimiento stuffed, sliced

salt, to taste

black pepper, ground, to taste

18 ounces (540g) mango chutney (recipe follows)

CHEF TIPS *If you reduce the meat part of the portion size to 4 ounces (120g), you can yield 12 servings.*

Mix all the marinade ingredients in a bowl. Reserve until needed.

Cover the pork roast with the marinade and refrigerate 1-2 hours at a product temperature of 41°F (5°C) or lower.

Remove the meat from the marinade.

COOKING

Heat the olive oil in a small roasting pan and sear the pork roast on all sides until thoroughly browned. Place the pork in a preheated 375°F (190.6°C) oven.

Roast the pork for approximately 1 hour, turning from time to time to promote even cooking.

In a separate saucepot, bring the rum, diced prunes, and beer to a boil.

Add the brown sugar and simmer until the prunes are soft.

Place mixture in a blender or food processor and purée. Return to the saucepot and add the diced ham and sliced olives. Hold the sauce until needed at a minimum temperature of 140°F (60°C).

Once the roast reaches an internal temperature of 155°F (68.3°C) or higher for at least 3 minutes and is fork tender, remove the pork from the pan and hold the pork at 140°F (60°C) or above.

Deglaze the pan with a little water and stir this liquid into the sauce. Finish the sauce by seasoning to taste with salt and black pepper.

SERVING/HOLDING

Slice the pork and decoratively place approximately 8 ounces (240g) on each hot plate. Top the sliced pork with 2 ounces (60g) of the sauce and garnish with approximately 3 ounces (90g) of mango chutney.

COOLING/STORING

Pour the remaining sauce into smaller metal containers.

Cool the remaining pork and sauce from 140°F (60°C) to 70°F (21.1°C) or lower within 2 hours. Cool from 70°F (21.1°C) to 41°F (5°C) within an additional 4 hours for a total cooling time of 6 hours or less.

Cover the pork and sauce; label, date, and store in refrigerated unit at a product temperature of 41°F (5°C) or lower.

MANGO CHUTNEY

YIELD: 2¼ CUPS

8 ounces (240g) mango, peeled, cut into strips

2 ounces (60g) onion, chopped

8 ounces (240g) Granny Smith Apples, peeled, cored, and chopped

½ clove garlic, minced

¼ teaspoon (1g) ginger root, peeled and minced

4 fluid ounces (120ml) apple cider vinegar

2 ounces (60g) sugar

¼ teaspoon (1g) cinnamon, ground

2 ounces (60g) dark brown sugar

⅛ teaspoon (½g) cloves, ground

½ teaspoon (2g) allspice, ground

½ teaspoon (2g) mustard seeds, ground

¾ teaspoon (4g) black pepper, ground

1 ounce (30g) raisins

salt, to taste

1 ounce (30g) currants

¼ teaspoon (1g) cayenne pepper

CHEF TIPS *Despite what you may have heard, there is no mystery to preparing chutney. This recipe is easy to make and much better than most commercial chutney products. This chutney tastes best if stored in sterilized jars or canned for at least 1 month prior to using, but it can be enjoyed sooner.*

Mix all the ingredients in a bowl and reserve overnight under refrigeration at 41°F (5°C) or lower.

COOKING/COOLING

Place the mixture in a small heavy-bottomed saucepot. Bring the mixture to a boil, then reduce the heat to a simmer. Simmer for approximately 30 minutes or until the mixture is syrupy.

Cool the chutney from 140°F (60°C) to 70°F (21.1°C) or lower within 2 hours. Cool from 70°F (21.2°C) to 41°F (5°C) within an additional 4 hours for a total cooling time of 6 hours or less.

Spicy Orange Carrot Sticks

YIELD: 6 PORTIONS · PORTION SIZE: 3 OUNCES

24 ounces (720g) carrots, cut into julienne

6 fluid ounces (180ml) orange juice

1 tablespoon (15g) light brown sugar

¼ teaspoon (1g) ginger, ground

salt, to taste

black pepper, ground, to taste

1 tablespoon (15g) parsley, chopped

CHEF TIPS *This is a tasty preparation for carrots, meant to be used as a side dish. The combination of flavors from the orange juice, brown sugar, and ginger makes the carrots sweet and spicy at the same time.*

Reserve the prepared carrots under refrigeration at 41°F (5°C) or lower until needed.

COOKING/HOLDING

Combine the orange juice, brown sugar, ginger, and carrots in a medium saucepan.

Cover and cook over medium-high heat until the carrots are tender, with just a little crisp left.

Season the carrots to taste with salt and black pepper.

Toss the carrots with the chopped parsley.

COOLING/STORING

Cool in shallow pan with a product depth of less than 2 inches (5cm). Cool the carrots from 140°F (60°C) to 70°F (21.1°C) or lower within 2 hours. Cool from 70°F (21.1°C) to 41°F (5°C) within an additional 4 hours for a total cooling time of 6 hours or less.

Cover the carrots; label, date, and store under refrigeration at a product temperature of 41°F (5°C) or lower.

Peas and Fresh Okra

YIELD: 6 PORTIONS · PORTION SIZE: 4 OUNCES

16 ounces (480g) black-eyed peas or pigeon peas

4 ounces (120g) salt pork, cut into small dice and rendered

8 ounces (240g) okra, fresh or frozen

salt, to taste

black pepper, ground, to taste

CHEF TIPS *Dried peas can be substituted if fresh peas are not available. When using dried peas, used half the amount listed in the recipe and soak overnight in water under refrigeration. Increase the cooking time for the dried peas to 1–1½ hours. If fresh okra is not available, frozen will suffice, but it should be completely thawed before using.*

Clean and shell the peas and reserve.

COOKING

Place the peas in a heavy-bottomed saucepan. Cover with water and add the salt pork.

Bring to a boil and cook 30–40 minutes or until the peas are tender.

Slice the okra into ¼-inch (.64cm) rounds and place on top of the cooked peas.

Cover the saucepan and remove it from the heat, allowing the okra to cook in the steam from the peas. Let the okra and peas rest, covered, for approximately 7 minutes or until the okra is tender yet a little crisp.

Season to taste with salt and black pepper.

SERVING/HOLDING

Strain out any excess liquid and serve immediately.

Hold the vegetables at 140°F (60°C) or higher.

COOLING/STORING

Cool in a shallow pan with a product depth of less than 2 inches. Cool the peas and okra from 140°F (60°C) to 70°F (21.1°C) or lower within 2 hours. Cool from 70°F (21.1°C) to 41°F (5°C) within an additional 4 hours for a total cooling time of 6 hours or less.

Cover the vegetables; label, date, and store in a refrigerated unit at a product temperature of 41°F (5°C) or lower.

Stuffed Chayote with Mushrooms

16 ounces (480g) chayote, split, seed removed

2 fluid ounces (60ml) olive oil

2 cloves garlic, minced

2 ounces (60g) Spanish onion, finely diced

8 ounces (240g) shiitake mushrooms, washed and sliced

7 ounces (210g) green bell peppers, cut into medium dice

8 ounces (240g) tomato concassée

4 sprigs parsley, chopped

Tabasco sauce, to taste

salt, to taste

black pepper, ground, to taste

2 ounces (60g) manchego cheese, grated

CHEF TIPS *Manchego cheese is a Spanish-style sheep's-milk cheese. If manchego cheese is not available, a mild feta cheese can be used as a substitute. Goat cheese is also frequently used to make stuffed chayote.*

Put the prepared chayote in a heavy-bottomed pot and add about 1 inch (2.54cm) of boiling salted water. Cover tightly, reduce the heat, and boil for approximately 10–15 minutes or until slightly tender.

Remove the chayote and reserve until needed.

COOKING

Heat the olive oil in a sauté pan over medium-high heat. Add the garlic and cook for 1 minute. Add the onions, mushrooms, and green peppers. Continue to cook until the moisture evaporates.

Turn the heat down to low and add the tomato concassée and chopped parsley.

Season the stuffing to taste with Tabasco sauce, salt, and black pepper. Let the mixture cool slightly.

Spoon the stuffing into the chayote halves and top with the grated cheese.

Bake in a preheated 350°F (176.7°C) oven until the chayote is tender and thoroughly heated.

SERVING/HOLDING

Remove the stuffed chayote from the oven and serve immediately.

🍴 **Hold** the vegetables at 140°F (60°C) or higher.

COOLING/STORING

🍴 **Cool** in a shallow pan with a product depth of less than 2 inches (6cm). Cool the stuffed chayote from 140°F (60°C) to 70°F (21.1°C) or lower within 2 hours. Cool from 70°F (21.1°C) to 41°F (5°C) within an additional 4 hours for a total cooling time of 6 hours or less.

Cover the chayote; label, date, and store in a refrigerated unit at a product temperature of 41°F (5°C) or lower.

Corn and Sweet Pepper Sauté

YIELD: 6 PORTIONS · PORTION SIZE: 12 OUNCES

20 ounces (600g) corn kernels, cut from 6 ears

4 ounces (120g) green bell peppers, diced

4 ounces (120g) red bell peppers, diced

2 ounces (60g) butter or margarine, melted

4 fluid ounces (120ml) half and half

salt, to taste

black pepper, ground, to taste

Reserve the prepared vegetables under refrigeration at 41°F (5°C) or lower until needed.

COOKING

Heat the butter in a large sautè pan.

Add the corn and bell peppers to the pan, cover, and cook over medium heat for 2 minutes.

Reduce the heat to low and add the half-and-half. Season to taste with salt and black pepper and cook, uncovered, over low heat for an additional 5-7 minutes or until the liquid is absorbed. Stir frequently during cooking

SERVING/HOLDING

Serve immediately.

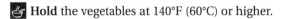 **Hold** the vegetables at 140°F (60°C) or higher.

COOLING/STORING

 Cool in a shallow pan with a product depth of less than 2 inches. Cool the corn from 140°F (60°C) to 70°F (21.1°C) or lower within 2 hours. Cool from 70°F (21.1°C) to 41°F (5°C) within an additional 4 hours for a total cooling time of 6 hours or less.

Cover vegetables; label, date, and store in refrigerated unit at a product temperature of 41°F (5°C) or lower.

Stewed Pink Beans

YIELD: 6 PORTIONS · PORTION SIZE: 5 OUNCES

12 ounces (360g) dried small pink beans

cold water, as needed

SOFRITO

2 tablespoons (30ml) vegetable oil

2 ounces (60g) salt pork, cut into small dice

4 ounces (120g) ham, cut into small dice

½ teaspoon (2g) dried oregano leaves

2 onions, finely chopped

6 cloves garlic, minced

4 cilantro leaves, finely chopped

BEANS

64 fluid ounces (1.9L) cold water

8 ounces (240g) West Indian pumpkin (calabaza) or domestic pumpkin, peeled, cut into medium dice

8 ounces (240g) white potatoes, peeled, cut into medium dice

4 tomato concassée

1 Scotch bonnet or jalapeño chile, seeded and minced

1 tablespoon (15ml) white vinegar

salt, to taste

black pepper, ground, to taste

CHEF TIPS *This dish can be made with virtually any variety of dry beans. The West Indian pumpkin is typically available in specialty markets in south Florida. Regular pumpkins are an excellent substitute. If pumpkins are not available at all, try using yams.*

The procedure uses an important element of Latin and Caribbean cooking—sofrito. The term is derived from the Spanish word sofreir, meaning to fry lightly. Sofrito is an essential flavor element and can be prepared in large amounts and stored in the refrigerator until needed.

Rinse the pink beans under cold running water. Place them in a container, cover with cold water, and soak them overnight under refrigeration at 41°F (5°C).

Drain the beans and discard any that did not swell.

SOFRITO

Heat the oil over medium heat in a large sauté pan.

Add the salt pork and ham and cook in the hot oil until browned.

Add the oregano, stir, and continue to cook for 30 seconds. Then add the onions, garlic, and cilantro.

Reduce the heat to low and cook, stirring frequently, until the onions are soft. Hold the sofrito at 140°F (60°C) until needed.

BEANS

Place the pink beans in a large saucepot and cover with the cold water. Bring to a boil and turn the heat down to a simmer.

Simmer 30 minutes. Do not allow the simmering beans to fall below 140°F (60°C).

Add the diced pumpkin and potatoes and simmer an additional 30 minutes or until the beans are almost tender. Do not allow the simmering beans to fall below 140°F (60°C).

Mash some of the pumpkin and potato against side of pan.

Add the sofrito mixture, the tomatoes, and the minced chile.

Simmer approximately 30 more minutes or until the liquid thickens. Do not allow the simmering beans to fall below 140°F (60°C).

Add the vinegar.

Season to taste with salt and black pepper.

SERVING/HOLDING

Serve the beans immediately.

Hold the beans at 140°F (60°C) or higher.

COOLING/STORING

Cool in a shallow pan with a product depth of less than 2 inches (5cm). Cool the beans from 140°F (60°C) to 70°F (21.1°C) or lower within 2 hours. Cool from 70°F (21.1°C) to 41°F (5°C) within an additional 4 hours for a total cooling time of 6 hours or less.

Cover the beans; label, date, and store in refrigerated unit at a product temperature of 41°F (5°C) or lower.

Rice and Peas

4 ounces (120g) dried kidney beans

2 ounces (60g) green onion, finely chopped

1 sprig thyme, minced

1 clove garlic, minced

16 fluid ounces (480ml) coconut milk

12 ounces (360g) raw long-grain rice

1 teaspoon (5g) salt

½ tablespoon (7g) sugar

CHEF TIPS *This Jamaican rice preparation has no peas in it. A Jamaican cook who always referred to kidney beans as "Jamaican peas" coined the name rice and peas many years ago. The dish came to south Florida with the influx of Jamaican immigrants, and the name stuck.*

Rinse the kidney beans under cold running water. Place them in a container, cover with cold water, and soak them overnight under refrigeration at 41°F (5°C).

Reserve the prepared green onions, thyme, and garlic under refrigeration until needed.

Drain the soaked beans.

COOKING

Combine the soaked beans and coconut milk and cook over medium heat until the beans are tender but not mushy.

Add the garlic, onion, thyme, rice, salt, and sugar.

Cook, covered, over medium heat, stirring once or twice, until the rice reaches the desired texture and absorbs the liquid.

Add water if additional moisture is necessary during cooking.

SERVING/HOLDING

Serve immediately.

Hold the rice and beans at 140°F (60°C) or higher.

COOLING/STORING

Cool in a shallow pan with a product depth of less than 2 inches (5cm). Cool the rice and beans from 140°F (60°C) to 70°F (21.1°C) or lower within 2 hours. Cool from 70°F (21.1°C) to 41°F (5°C) within an additional 4 hours for a total cooling time of 6 hours or less.

Cover the rice and beans; label, date, and store under refrigeration at a product temperature of 41°F (5°C) or lower.

White Rice with Tomatoes

YIELD: 6 PORTIONS · PORTION SIZE: 4 OUNCES

3 ounces (90g) butter or margarine

8 ounces (320g) onion, finely chopped

12 ounces (360g) raw long-grain rice

24 fluid ounces (720ml) cold water

2 teaspoons (10g) salt

12 ounces (360g) tomato concassée

½ teaspoon (2g) black, ground pepper

CHEF TIPS *Some chefs add more seasonings such as hot sauce, garlic, and hot chiles to this recipe.*

Melt 4 tablespoons of the butter in a sautoir pan over medium heat.

Add the onion and cook for approximately 1 minute. Stir in the rice and cook, stirring, until the rice is coated with the butter.

Add water and salt. Bring to a boil and reduce the heat to a simmer.

Cover and cook 15–20 minutes until all the water is absorbed.

Melt the remaining butter in a separate saucepot over medium heat. Add the tomatoes to the butter and cook an additional minute.

Stir the butter, pepper, and tomatoes into the rice.

SERVING/HOLDING

Serve immediately.

Hold the rice at 140°F (60°C) or higher.

COOLING/STORING

Cool in a shallow pan with a product depth of less than 2 inches (5cm). Cool the rice from 140°F (60°C) to 70°F (21.1°C) or lower within 2 hours. Cool from 70°F (21.1°C) to 41°F (5°C) within an additional 4 hours for a total cooling time of 6 hours or less.

Cover the rice and tomatoes; label, date, and store under refrigeration at a product temperature of 41°F (5°C) or lower.

Candied Sweet Potatoes

YIELD: 6 PORTIONS · PORTION SIZE: 5 OUNCES

2 ounces (60g) butter or margarine

32 ounces (960g) sweet potatoes

cold water, as needed

salt, to taste

2 ounces (60g) brown sugar

¼ teaspoon (1g) nutmeg, grated

4 fluid ounces (120ml) water

Grease a 2-quart casserole dish with some of the butter. Reserve until needed.

COOKING

Wash the sweet potatoes. Place them in a large saucepot and cover with cold water and salt. Boil the sweet potatoes until they are tender.

Drain the sweet potatoes and cool slightly. Peel the potatoes and cut them into slices ¼–½ inch (.64–1.27cm) thick.

Layer the slices of sweet potato in the buttered casserole dish. Dot each layer with the remaining butter and sprinkle each layer with brown sugar and nutmeg.

Add the additional water and bake in a preheated 350°F (176.7°C) oven until top is crisp, approximately 45 minutes.

SERVING/HOLDING

Serve immediately.

Hold the sweet potatoes at 140°F (60°C) or higher.

COOLING/STORING

Cool in a shallow pan with a product depth of less than 2 inches (5cm). Cool the sweet potatoes from 140°F (60°C) to 70°F (21.1°C) or lower within 2 hours. Cool from 70°F (21.1°C) to 41°F (5°C) within an additional 4 hours for a total cooling time of 6 hours or less.

Cover the sweet potatoes; label, date, and store under refrigeration at a product temperature of 41°F (5°C) or lower.

Key Lime Pie

YIELD: 6 PORTIONS · PORTION SIZE: ⅙ PIE

CRUST

4½ ounces (135g) graham cracker crumbs

1½ ounces (45g) sugar

1½ fluid ounces (45ml) butter, melted

FILLING

15 fluid ounces (450ml) sweetened condensed milk

6 egg yolks

6 fluid ounces (180ml) Key lime juice

1 tablespoon (15ml) lime zest

TOPPING

8 fluid ounces (240ml) whipping cream

2 ounces (60g) powdered sugar

CHEF TIPS *The Key lime is one of the two main varieties of lime available in the United States. The Key lime is smaller than the more common Persian lime and is rounder, with a color more yellow than green. Outside of Florida and Mexico, where it is called limón, the Key lime is usually available only in Hispanic specialty markets.*

Key lime pie became popular in the Florida Keys in the 1850s. The first Key lime pies were baked in a pastry crust and topped with a meringue, but now they are frequently baked in a graham cracker crust and served with a whipped cream topping. Key lime pie can also be served frozen, if desired.

If true Key limes are not available, the juice from regular Persian limes will suffice, but the pie should be called a lime pie rather than a Key lime pie.

Mix the graham cracker crumbs and sugar in a bowl.

Add the melted butter and combine until the mixture resembles wet sand.

Press the mixture into a 9-inch (229cm) pie pan.

Mix the sweetened condensed milk with the egg yolks in a bowl.

Blend in the Key lime juice and lime zest.

Pour the mixture into the pan with the pie crust.

Bake in a preheated 350°F (176.7°C) oven for approximately 15 minutes or until the filling is set. Be careful not to overbake the pie.

COOLING/STORING

Cover the pie; label, date, and store under refrigeration at a product temperature of 41°F (5°C) or lower.

Prepare the topping by whipping the cream with the powdered sugar in a small mixing machine on high speed. Be careful not to overmix the cream, as this small amount can turn to butter in a very short period.

Pipe the whipped cream decoratively through a pastry tube onto the pie.

Slice the finished pie into 6 portions and serve.

John Folse

ON CAJUN AND CREOLE CUISINE

Imagine a huge cast-iron pot filled with vegetables, meats, and grains. Each ingredient is unique. Some combinations are as familiar as a dark Cajun roux, while others are strange and unfamiliar. What will the dish taste like once the marriage of ingredients is complete?

Now, imagine the cast iron pot is Louisiana and the ingredients represent the seven homelands (Native America, France, Spain, Germany, England, Africa, and Italy) whose peoples merged to become the Cajuns and Creoles—the source of Louisiana's culinary heritage. The traditions range from the swamp floor pantry of the Cajun trappers to the lavish tables of the Creole royalty.

The history of the Bayou State is rich and flavorful, much like its cuisine. Louisiana's culinary and cultural heritage has developed over several centuries, evolving by way of cultivating new ideas and adding ingredients to the culinary melting pot.

Creoles were knowledgeable about fine wines and food, and their cooking was inventive and refined. They used lots of seasoning and spice while combining the influences of each of the seven nations. Gumbo and jambalaya are probably the two most distinctive creations of the Creole kitchen.

The Cajuns utilized that which was indigenous to the area. Their cuisine is characterized by the use of wild game, seafood, wild vegetation, and herbs. Most famously known for the institution of one pot meals that contain a variety of ingredients gathered from the swamp floor pantry, the Cajuns also introduced to Louisiana their form of jambalaya, gumbo, fricassee, sauce piquante, and stuffed vegetable dishes, such as eggplant and mirliton.

Through this development, the cultural and culinary heritage of Louisiana was created. The Cajuns and Creoles evolved in their own way and at their own pace, contributing recipes, traditions, and beliefs to the cast-iron pot. This gradual growth, a key ingredient in history, added to the flavor of Bayou heritage and, like a seafood gumbo simmering over a low flame in a cast-iron pot, the seven cultural groups melded to produce a culinary and culture masterpiece called Louisiana.

Chef John Folse, a native of Louisiana, is owner and CEO of Chef John Folse & Company.

Cajun and Creole Cuisines

Cajun and Creole cooking styles are widely recognized as two of America's oldest and richest regional cuisines. Each is full of culture and history dating back almost 300 years, with roots and traditions in classic French cuisine— which, of course, is significantly older. Cajun and Creole cuisines are in a class by themselves in their molding of the rich and diverse cooking methods of several cultures into a singular taste and philosophy.

Around 1755, French Acadians, religious exiles from Brittany and Normandy, were expelled in turn from Nova Scotia, Canada. Many settled in the swamps, bayous, and marshes of Louisiana. Cajun country, also referred to as *Acadiana,* runs approximately 300 miles from the marshes of the Gulf coast to Texas and includes the inland prairies, accounting for almost one-third of Louisiana. Because the

Acadians were isolated from New Orleans, eventually a new dialect came to be—Cajun French—a mixture of words from French, Canadian French, Native American, and African languages. The word Cajun itself is a corruption of Acadian.

The term *Cajun* describes both a geographical area and the people who live in or come from that region. In the swamp country, the Cajuns had to rely on local resources, such as fish, shellfish, and wild game, for sustenance. Native Americans taught them how to exploit the swamps, bayous, and surrounding forests for agricultural and hunting purposes. The Cajuns learned how to cook with indigenous ingredients. Among the many dishes attributed to their culture are crawfish étouffée, gâteau de sirop, and alligator gumbo. The Cajun culture is well known for their hospitality as well as cuisine that is earthy and robust. It is a Cajun custom to always throw in a little extra, whether it's a few extra shrimp in the étouffée or 13 cookies in a dozen at the local bakery. *Lagniappe* is the term in southern Louisiana referring to this hospitality and means "something extra."

The Cajuns developed variations of jambalaya, grillades, fricassees, stews, gumbos, and other dishes identified with southern Louisiana. Cajuns also enhanced the sausage making of the local Germans. The boucherie, a traditional daylong Cajun event, centers on the slaughter and butchering of a hog. Every possible part of the animal is utilized in one preparation or another, many of which are made that day, including boudin, cracklings, head cheese, tasso, chaudin, and sausages. Today, the Cajuns are famous for the andouille, boudin, and tasso that enhance their flavorful dishes.

One distinctive dish that emerged from the combination of French, Native American, African, and Southern cultures and cooking techniques is gumbo, a New Orleans signature dish (see page 202). The French soup bouillabaisse heavily influenced gumbo. The Cajuns combine oil or animal fats and flour over heat to form a thickening agent, the roux, which is a classic French approach to thickening soups and sauces. The roux used in gumbo has since been modified and expanded by various cultures to create numerous colors and tastes. The Africans contributed the vegetable okra and the Native Americans added filé powder to gumbo, both of which serve as additional thickening agents. The French contributed to Cajun cooking the use of mirepoix, a combination of aromatic vegetables frequently used in French cooking, but adapted the vegetables to those indigenous to the region. Today, this combination of onions, celery, and green peppers is still widely utilized in Cajun cooking and is referred to as the *holy trinity*.

The Germans brought their knowledge of sausage making to the New World and utilized a wide assortment of meat and dairy products. They helped establish the boucherie and the tradition of fine sausage making in southern Louisiana. They brought with them not only pigs but chicken and cattle as well. Before the arrival of the Germans, a steady supply of milk and butter was seldom available in southern Louisiana. The Italians contributed red gravies, garlic, and breadcrumbs. These ingredients became local cooking staples, used to create dishes featuring artichokes, eggplant, and mirliton (a type of squash).

The Creoles were Europeans who traveled to New Orleans via one of the American colonies in the late 1600s for the opportunity to establish communities and traditions in the New World. The term *Creole* is derived from the Spanish word *criollo*, which, roughly translated, means "native to a place." The Creoles are generally believed to be people of French or Spanish descent. In the state of Louisiana, the name *Creole* is claimed by two groups of people. White Creoles are those who can trace their lineage to aristocratic French or Spanish ancestry. These immigrants were generally wealthy and educated, bringing with them a variety of celebrated European dishes. Black Creoles, former slaves who often took the same last name as their former owners, trace their lineage in the same fashion. Both black and white Creoles maintained high standards for food and service throughout the nineteenth century. It was not uncommon for a typical Creole dinner or brunch to have at least seven courses. Today, the term *Creole* is used to describe not only people and their culture but also a style of cooking associated with the Louisiana region.

Creole cuisine was most profoundly influenced by the French, Spanish, German, Italian, Native American, West Indian, and African-American cultures. When the French settlers began to arrive, it was the Choctaw tribe that introduced them to many foods of the area, including corn-based breads and cereals, squash (particularly mirlitons), bay leaves, and dried beans. The Choctaw used persimmons in syrups and chokecherries to season smoked meats. One of the greatest contributions to Creole cuisine that came from the Choctaws is powdered sassafras leaves. Referred to as *filé powder*, this spice acts as a thickening agent.

The influences of these cultures on Creole cooking brought us some of America's tastiest dishes. The Spanish culture is credited with the incorporation of tomatoes and spices in many Creole recipes. In the early 1800s, the Spanish residents of Louisiana began cooking with tomatoes. At that time, many in Europe believed the New World tomato to be poisonous. It was the Spanish who proved otherwise with the special flavors their dishes attained. Spanish paella, traditionally a seafood and rice dish, evolved into the Creole rice dish called jambalaya (see page 204).

African Americans have also had a profound influence on the cooking style of the region. In Louisiana, African Americans were first slaves and later farmers. When they cooked, they combined ingredients such as rice, beans, and green leafy vegetables with traditional African ingredients such as okra, yams, onions, and garlic. They also favored a cooking technique called *slow roasting* and extended this idea of continuous cooking to traditional French roux. African-American cooks added fresh herbs, onions, garlic, and tough pork or chicken to the traditional butter and flour base and simmered it over low heat all day long. They then added this aromatic mixture to a variety of sauces, soups, and other local dishes. The people enslaved from the West Indies introduced another slow cooking technique, braising, which also transformed Creole cuisine. This method was later used by others to make gumbo.

The Creoles' sophisticated cuisine combines delicate sauces with robust flavors, making it one of America's most unusual regional cuisines. Today, many extravagant Creole dining experiences—notably, Sunday brunches featuring course after course—have disappeared; however, the dishes and preparations live on.

The basic differences between Cajun and Creole cuisines can be simply stated. Cajun cuisine is a country style of cooking, using more animal fats and meats than does the Creole style. Creole cuisine is a citified style of cooking, more closely associated with New Orleans than the rest of the state. The Spanish and French influences on Creole cuisine have made it more refined than the Cajun cooking style. Both Cajun and Creole cooking, however, share many ingredients and spices, such as filé powder and hot pepper sauce, as well as the holy trinity of vegetables.

Celebrations have always been a large part of the Cajun and Creole culture. Most notable is Mardi Gras, an event that began in 1699 when Pierre Lemoyne d'Iberville proclaimed a small piece of land on the Mississippi River near New Orleans Pointe du Mardi Gras in honor of Shrove Tuesday. Mardi Gras (French for "Fat Tuesday") is the day before Ash Wednesday and the first day of Lent. Fat Tuesday celebrates the arrival of the three kings who traveled to pay homage to the Christ Child. The first Mardi Gras parade was recorded in 1872 and introduced the traditional Mardi Gras colors—purple, representing justice; green, symbolizing faith; and gold, for power. Mardi Gras is cause for celebration in the entire region, but most notably in New Orleans. One traditional event is the Running of the Mardi Gras. Participants search for food while on horseback, collecting crawfish, chickens, and pigs, all as part of a relay race to assemble the ingredients needed to prepare Mardi Gras gumbo. Carnival is a period of celebration associated with Mardi Gras. The word *carnival* can be interpreted in Latin as "putting away the meat" and is a celebration to prepare for fasting before the Easter holiday.

The coffeehouse and trading post that opened in Jackson Square in New Orleans in 1791 was called the French Market. At the time, the French Market was a center for business and society in the New Orleans area. Everything was available, from herbs and vegetables to slaves. The bar located inside the French Market was a gathering place where soldiers, businesspeople, and the aristocracy gathered and drank coffee. In 1812, a hurricane destroyed the original French Market; however, an improved market was quickly erected that featured a variety of meats and poultry stalls. Today, the market is three city blocks long and houses a yearlong farmer's market where the region's freshest produce is bought and sold, as are products indigenous to the region.

New Orleans is known for its characteristic cuisines and for its many outstanding dining establishments. Antoine's, which opened in 1840, was the first restaurant in New Orleans. It is widely recognized as a New Orleans institution and has been owned by the same family for five generations. It is said that during Prohibition, patrons of Antoine's could enjoy a cup of coffee laced with illegal cognac; this was served in a tall, white pedestal cup designed by the chef to disguise its content. The coffee drinks served at Antoine's are still considered one of their finest specialties.

Typical Cajun and Creole Ingredients and Dishes

Absinthe: An alcoholic beverage also referred to as the "green goblin." Absinthe is an anise-flavored liqueur originally from Switzerland but made famous in Paris. At one point, the beverage was so popular that men carried vials of absinthe hidden in compartments built into their walking canes. Absinthe was banned in America in 1912 because the aromatic herb, wormwood, used in its distillation process was discovered to be a narcotic. The addictive properties of absinthe were no doubt a factor in its huge popularity. Absinthe was the liqueur used in the original preparation of oysters Rockefeller, made famous at Antoine's, and the Sazerac cocktail. After the ban of absinthe, Pernod was used to make the oyster dish and Herbsaint to make the Sazerac. Absinthe is now a generic term for any liqueur with an anise or licorice flavor.

Alligator: A large reptile indigenous to the swamps, rivers, and marshes of Louisiana. Alligator meat, a Cajun specialty, is high in protein while low in fat and cholesterol. It is said to be as tasty and tender as chicken. The choicest cuts of alligator are the tail and jaw sections, although the legs and body meat can be eaten as well, with a little tenderizing. Alligator meat needs to be trimmed of all fat and tendons before it is cooked to prevent it from becoming tough.

Andouille Sausage: Originally brought to Louisiana by the Acadians. Andouille is now a well-known Cajun sausage made from pork butt, shank, pork fat, and spicy seasonings and smoked slowly over pecan wood and sugar cane. Authentic Andouille sausage is stuffed into beef middle casings, making the finished product about 1½ inches (3.81cm)in diameter. Once cooked, the sausage is very dark to almost black in color. Andouille is the preferred sausage for making jambalaya and gumbo and is used as an accompaniment for red beans and rice.

Bananas Foster: Named after Dick Foster, who in the 1950s helped clean up New Orleans French Quarter. The popular dessert is prepared tableside and was made famous at a New Orleans restaurant named Brennan's. The dish consists of bananas cooked in a mixture of butter, brown sugar, cinnamon, rum, and banana liqueur. It is served hot, right out of the pan, with a scoop of vanilla ice cream. Brennan's saw the dessert as an opportunity to use bananas, which were frequently shipped into the port of New Orleans from Central and South America. Today, Brennan's claims to use over 35,000 pounds of bananas each year in the preparation of their classic dessert.

Beignet: French for "fritter." Beignets are diamond-shaped, raised doughnuts without the hole in the middle. They are typically topped liberally with powdered sugar before serving.

Blackened Redfish: A dish invented in 1979 by chef Paul Prudhomme at his restaurant K-Paul in New Orleans. Blackened redfish became so famous that it is now considered the icon of Cajun cooking. Prudhomme's method of preparing the fish involves seasoning it with his own custom blend of Cajun spices and cooking it at a super-hot temperature. The dish was so popular at one time that redfish was placed on the endangered species list.

Blue Crab: Although it is not as well known for blue crabs as Chesapeake Bay, Louisiana is the primary exporter of blue crabs to the Mid-Atlantic region. Blue crabs in Louisiana are available in both hard- and soft-shell varieties. The meat is also available packaged by the size of the pieces. Backfin and jumbo lump are the most popular as well as the most expensive forms of blue crabmeat. A New Orleans specialty is a fried soft-shell crab po' boy sandwich, frequently sold by street vendors and restaurants.

Boudin Blanc: A well-known regional sausage made from ground pork and organ meat, rice, and spices and cooked in a casing made from the pig's intestines. Cajun-style boudin is spicier than the French boudin, where its roots are, and does not use milk in its preparation. Boudin blanc is sold commercially and is frequently eaten as a snack. The sausage is typically warmed and held in a napkin. The meat is squeezed from the casing into the mouth. The tough casing is discarded after the contents are consumed.

Boudin Rouge: This sausage is made with the fresh blood of a slaughtered pig in place of the rice used in boudin blanc. Boudin rouge is similar in nature to blood pudding from France, which is made in the same fashion. Because fresh blood is used in the preparation of boudin rouge, it may not be sold commercially in the United States. However, many Cajuns still prepare this sausage during the traditional boucherie and reserve it for personal consumption.

Bread Pudding: Considered by many the apple pie of Louisiana, bread pudding is a dessert that combines the influences of the French, with their bread, and the Germans, with their eggs and dairy products. A number of "authentic" regional recipes for bread pudding exist; all start with leftover French bread, which is soaked in milk and eggs, combined with ingredients such as nuts, raisins, nutmeg, and cinnamon, and baked in an oven. "Traditional" sauces are as numerous as "authentic" recipes for bread pudding; however, whiskey or caramel sauces are frequently used as the topping.

Brown Meunière Sauce: A brown butter sauce popular in New Orleans and the Louisiana region. Meunière sauce is essentially the same as the French sauce beurre noisette and is used to top both meat and fish dishes. It is made by adding demi-glace sauce and cayenne pepper to brown butter, giving it a spicy flavor and a nutty aroma.

Café au Lait: Coffee made with the addition of ground chicory root and served with steamed milk. Café au lait became popular during the Civil War and remains a Louisiana specialty.

Cane Syrup: The concentrated sap of the sugar cane plant, sometimes referred to as *light molasses*. Cane syrup is made by crushing sugar cane to extract the juice, which is treated with chemicals to remove the impurities, then boiled. The syrup is processed to allow the cropping out of the sugar crystals. The technique is progressive so that the first syrup produced, molasses, can yield an additional crop of crystals, brown sugar. The syrups derived from sugar cane vary in color from light brown to almost black and can be blended from different varieties of cane. Cane syrup is frequently substituted for maple syrup and molasses in Cajun and Creole preparations.

Chicory: The root of a variety of Belgian endive that when mature, is dried, roasted, and ground. When mixed with coffee beans and brewed, chicory imparts a bittersweet, somewhat nutty flavor to the coffee. Napoleon's troops first added chicory to coffee to stretch their dwindling supply of coffee beans. The first French settlers of the region brought this coffee-making tradition to Louisiana. Chicory is also added to warm milk and served after dinner as a sleep inducer. It is also frequently added to gravies, soups, and dark breads to add an element of richness and color.

Crab and Shrimp Boil: A bouquet garni of spices used for cooking seafood. It is packaged and sold in New Orleans in netted bags or in concentrated liquid form. Crab or shrimp boil is used to flavor the water in which crabs, shrimp, or crawfish are boiled.

Cracklings: A Cajun specialty, typically prepared during a boucherie. Cracklings are small pieces of pork skin that are fried and seasoned and eaten as a snack.

Crawfish: Sometimes referred to as *mudbug* or *crawdad*, this small freshwater crustacean is similar in appearance to a miniature lobster. Freshwater crawfish are frequently confused with their saltwater cousins, the crayfish. All the edible meat from crawfish comes from the tail, as the claws and legs are too small to yield any significant amount of meat. Crawfish are found in the region's swamps, ditches, bayous, lakes, and ponds and are generally available from December through May. Due to the small quantity of meat in the tail section, one should cook 7 pounds (3.18kg) of crawfish to yield 1 pound (.45kg) of meat. For a seafood boil, a typical person will consume 4 to 5 pounds of whole crawfish. Crawfish are best cooked in boiling salted water flavored with spices and herbs.

Creole Cream Cheese: A version of the French fromage blanc, or fresh white cheese, frequently found in markets and restaurants in Louisiana. This fresh-made cream cheese is rarely found outside Louisiana. It is said that a certain type of beneficial bacteria used to make Creole cream cheese is indigenous to the region and the results cannot be duplicated elsewhere. Creole cream cheese is eaten as a snack or served with any meal. It is frequently eaten with sugar and strawberries or plain—just seasoned with salt and pepper.

Creole Mustard: A distinctive locally made mustard that uses spicy, dark mustard seeds that are marinated in vinegar before use. Creole mustard is quite pungent and is similar to horseradish. It is frequently used in remoulade sauce and served with ham and po' boy sandwiches.

Creole Tomato: A locally grown tomato that has a very thin skin, low acidity level, and an extremely high juice content. Vine-ripened Creole tomatoes are known for their sweet aroma and characteristic taste. The sweet taste of the Creole tomato is attributed to Louisiana's fertile soil and humid air. The tomato is typically in season between June and August. However, due to their delicate nature, these tomatoes are rarely shipped outside of the region. Creole tomatoes should never be stored under refrigeration, as the cold temperature will diminish their natural sweet flavor.

Crescent City Breakfast: The typical New Orleans breakfast, which includes beignets and café au lait. As many of the restaurants and cafés in New Orleans are open around the clock, it is not uncommon to see people eating a Crescent City breakfast at any hour of the day or night. One famous restaurant where the Crescent City breakfast is served is the Café du Monde in the French Quarter.

Dirty Rice: A Creole rice dish much better known in New Orleans than in the rest of Louisiana. Dirty rice gets its name from the livers and giblets that are added to the rice preparation, which results in dark-colored rice. Dirty rice typically has diced celery, onions, and peppers (see *the holy trinity*) included in the recipe.

Eggs Hussard: A brunch dish, inspired by eggs Benedict, that was created at Brennan's, a New Orleans restaurant. Eggs Hussard tops toasted English muffins with sliced Canadian bacon, marchand de vin sauce, poached eggs, and cayenne-flavored hollandaise sauce. Eggs Hussard is typically served with grilled tomatoes.

Étouffée: A French word meaning "smothered" or "braised." In Louisiana cooking, étouffée is generally a preparation made with crawfish, crab, or shrimp and slowly cooked in a thick sauce made with seafood stock, tomatoes, onions, celery, peppers, and seasonings. Étouffée is typically served over rice with hot pepper sauce. Although étouffée is a Creole innovation, it is quite common in Cajun country as well.

Filé Powder: A powder with thickening properties, discovered by the Choctaw tribe of Native Americans. Filé powder is made from sassafras leaves, which are dried, ground, and passed through a sieve. Filé powder is commonly used as an aromatic thickening agent for gumbos.

Frog: Of the many species of frog indigenous to the Louisiana region, the Creole Frog, commonly referred to as the *bullfrog*, is the most frequently eaten. Typically, the legs are the best cut of frog for eating. They are usually broiled, fried, or sautéed.

Gâteau de Sirop: A traditional spice cake found all over Louisiana. Gâteau de sirop is typically sweetened with cane syrup, topped with icing made from brown sugar, and garnished with pecan nuts.

Grillade: A thinly sliced piece of fresh pork or veal, pan-fried and cooked with sliced onions, peppers, celery, and tomatoes. The origins of grillades are not known for certain but are said to lie in the traditional boucherie. Grillades were cooked in cast-iron pans over fires and were served all day long with grits or rice. Today, grillades are frequently served with grits for brunch at many of Louisiana's restaurants.

Gumbo: A type of hearty soup or stew frequently served in the Louisiana region. It is commonly thought that gumbo is a Louisiana version of the French fish soup called *bouillabaisse* and was first made by the French settlers using local fish and seafood. Over time, the dish evolved to include hot peppers, contributed by the Spanish settlers; okra, contributed by the Africans; and filé powder, contributed by the Native Americans. The term *gumbo* is derived from an African word, *gombo*, meaning "okra." Okra is a vegetable used in gumbo that acts as a thickening agent for the dish. Gumbo blends and balances all the varied ethnic influences that have shaped present-day Louisiana cooking—the Spanish love of rice and spices, the Southern fondness for okra, the French technique of making roux, and the Caribbean art of combining seasonings. In New Orleans and southeastern Louisiana, tomatoes are added and cooked in the pot with the gumbo. In southwestern Louisiana, the favorite recipe is gumbo ya ya, which is a chicken and andouille sausage gumbo thickened with only roux—no okra or tomatoes. Gumbo is traditionally served with or over rice.

The Holy Trinity: A mirepoix-style combination of vegetables that includes onions, green bell peppers, and celery. This trio of vegetables is used in most Cajun and Creole preparations.

Jambalaya: A rice dish derived from the Spanish dish paella, which Spanish settlers brought with them to Louisiana in the early 1700s. The Spanish immigrants adapted their recipe to local ingredients. Oysters and crawfish replaced the clams and mussels and andouille sausage replaced the ham. Originally, the dish was named jambon à la yaya after an African word for rice—*yaya*. Over the years, jambalaya has evolved into one of America's most famous and popular rice dishes and is made today with whatever products are available. However, pork, chicken, and andouille sausage are the most frequently used ingredients.

King Cake: A cake traditionally served in the New Orleans area during the Mardi Gras celebration. King cake is a brioche ring filled with a mixture of nuts and topped with icing in the colors of Mardi Gras—purple, green, and gold. Typically, a small prize is hidden inside the cake. The person who finds the prize in their portion is expected to make a donation to charity. This tradition dates back to medieval Europe, where King cake was served on January sixth (King's Day or Twelfth Night) and had gold coins hidden inside. Today, King cake is also used to select the king and queen of the Mardi Gras celebration.

Mirliton: A light-green, pear-shaped vegetable also referred to as *chayote* in other regions of the United States. The mirliton came to Louisiana with settlers and slaves from the West Indies and has a flavor similar to squash. Mirliton is usually available from August through November and can be stored under refrigeration for up to a month. It can be prepared using a variety of cooking techniques; however, mirliton stuffed with breadcrumbs and seafood is among the most popular preparations.

Mock Turtle Soup: A preparation of turtle soup made without actual turtle meat. (See *turtle.*)

Moussa: A cornmeal mush frequently used as a substitute for rice. In the 1800s, when rice was not readily available in Louisiana, gumbo was served over moussa.

Muffuletta: A sandwich common in Louisiana that is made by slicing a round loaf of Italian bread horizontally and stuffing it with meats or seafood. The muffuletta is dressed with a tangy salad made from green and black olives and then sliced into quarters. Muffuletta sandwiches were developed in the early 1900s by Italian grocers who sold a lunch plate with bread, assorted meats and cheeses, and a zesty olive salad. One day, a worker who bought the lunch plate sliced the bread in half and piled all the ingredients into it, creating a huge sandwich. *Muffuletta* is the Sicilian name for the loaf of bread topped with sesame seeds that was typically served with the lunch plate the grocers sold. When the grocers started selling the sandwiches, they wrapped them in the paper that the bread came in, which was labeled *muffuletta*, and the sandwiches in turn began to be called by the same name.

Okra: A green bullet-shaped vegetable with ridges and one tapered end. Okra seeds apparently were brought to Louisiana hidden in the hair of Congolese slaves in the early 1700s. The shortened name used by the slaves for this vegetable was *gombo*. The famous Louisiana dish gumbo gets its name from this African word for okra. When cooked, the white okra seeds produce a glutinous substance that acts as a natural thickening agent. When okra is in season, it generally replaces filé powder as the thickening agent in gumbo.

Pecan Praline: A candy invented by Marechal du Plessis Praslin in seventeenth-century France. The confection was originally made with almonds and called *amande rissolée dans le sucre*. It is, essentially, one or two kinds of nuts that are coated with butter and caramelized sugar and left to harden into a candy. When the French arrived in Louisiana, they substituted the local pecans for the almonds called for in the recipe. Pecan Pralines are typically served in the New Orleans area after dinner with a cup of coffee.

Po' Boy: The most popular sandwich in Louisiana. The po' boy is related to similar sandwiches from other parts of the United States that go under the names *hoagy, grinder, submarine,* and *hero*. The po' boy was created in the late nineteenth century by Madame Begue, who sold the sandwiches at her stall at the French Market. She split a loaf of French bread, filled it with seafood or meat, and dressed the sandwich with lettuce, tomatoes, butter, and mayonnaise. It is said that the name *po' boy* came from the unemployed men who wandered the French Market looking for work, who would beg her to "please give a sandwich to a po' boy."

Popcorn Rice: Also referred to as *wild pecan rice*. This long-grain rice is milled in such a way that most of the bran layer is left on. Popcorn rice is grown only in the parish (county) of New Iberia, Louisiana. This variety of rice has nothing in common with either wild rice or pecans, but it has a distinctive taste and nutty aroma when cooked.

Providence Rice: Home-grown rice cultivated in the local ponds and swamps of Cajun Louisiana for over 250 years. The reference to providence comes from the saying "it's up to the providence or the grace of God" to see the rice harvested. Louisiana is America's third largest rice-producing state, right behind California and Arkansas, and its population consumes more rice per capita than any other state. Southwestern Louisiana grows over 80 percent of the state's rice crop. The regional preference is for medium-grain white rice with a high gluten content. The remainder of Louisiana prefers long-grain or extra long-grain rice.

Ramos Gin Fizz: An alcoholic beverage named after Henry Ramos of the Imperial Cabinet Saloon in New Orleans. Although Ramos did not invent the cocktail, he brought the drink to its height of popularity. Orange-flower water, a derivative of the orange tree blossom, is essential in making an authentic Ramos Gin Fizz.

Red Beans and Rice: A dish typically served on Mondays. As folklore has it, Monday was always laundry day for homemakers. A pot of red beans and rice could be left to simmer on the stove for many hours and, when the laundry was done, so were the red beans and rice. Others say that the dish was served on Mondays to make good use of the ham bone left from Sunday's dinner. Still others say that the "red and white," as the dish is called, allows for the alcohol consumed over the weekend to be absorbed by the red beans and rice. Red beans are not a unique species of dried bean—just red kidney beans cooked in the Louisiana tradition.

Remoulade Sauce: A spicy sauce commonly served with seafood. Louisiana remoulade is a mayonnaise-based sauce flavored with Creole mustard, finely diced vegetables, and herbs and spices. A number of regional recipes for remoulade exist. Each chef adds his or her own signature flavors through the selection of condiments and seasonings added to the sauce's mayonnaise base.

Root Beer: A nonalcoholic soft drink created by a chemist named Ed Barq in 1898. Barq used his expertise in creating flavors to make his soft drink. Root beer became popular in the Gulf Coast region, as it went well with many of the local dishes, such as po' boys, red beans and rice, and fried seafood. A Southern tradition is to consume a handful of peanuts while drinking a root beer. Today, the people of New Orleans drink twice as much root beer as other Americans do.

Roux: A classic French thickening agent made by combining equal parts of flour and butter and cooking prior to use. The cooking process gradually colors the roux, which begins as a white roux, changes to blond roux, then darkens to brown or dark roux, depending on the cooking time. In Creole cuisine, roux is typically cooked to the brown to dark stages and used to thicken dishes like gumbos and stews. Sometimes animal fats, such as bacon or duck, are substituted for the butter for a lighter flavor. In Cajun cuisine, roux is usually made with vegetable oil or animal fat instead of butter and cooked to a dark caramel color. The dark roux used in Cajun and Creole cuisines helps provide richness and depth of flavor to the dishes.

Sazerac: A New Orleans saloon that opened in 1852 and was named after the famous French cognac. The popularity of the drinking establishment was attributed to a cocktail called the Sazerac, which contained bitters, sugar, lemon, and absinthe. When absinthe was banned, a liqueur called Herbsaint, also referred to as "the spirit of New Orleans," was used in its place to make the cocktail.

Seafood Boil: A common event in Louisiana and on the Mississippi Gulf Coast, where crab, shrimp, or crawfish are boiled in a deep pot with herbs and spices. The herbs and spices are tied inside a cheesecloth sack and include bay leaves, allspice, cloves, mustard seeds, coriander seeds, dill seeds, and pepper. Seafood boils are typically held outdoors and the seafood is eaten on tabletops lined with newspapers. Once the seafood is consumed, the newspapers, with the shells and all, is rolled up and discarded.

Sugar Cane: A type of giant perennial grass that grows to 6 feet in height and is one of the largest cash crops in Louisiana. Sugar cane first came to Louisiana in the mid-1700s from the

West Indies. It is used primarily to make molasses, white and brown sugar, and cane syrup, a sweetening agent frequently used in Cajun and Creole recipes. (See *cane syrup*.)

Sweet Potato: Commonly referred to in the region as "Louisiana yam." However, sweet potatoes are not yams at all. They are simply called *yams* by the locals to help differentiate the tubers from other varieties of sweet potatoes. This variety of sweet potato was discovered in the early 1700s by the Dutch explorer Antoine Simon le Page du Pratz, who represented France at the time. Louisiana yams should not be refrigerated but kept in a warm, dry place. They store well for up to four weeks and are best prepared by baking, boiling, frying, or sautéing. Candied yams are a favorite among the locals.

Tabasco Sauce: One of the most famous hot pepper sauces, currently available in over 100 countries. Tabasco sauce was formulated over 130 years ago by New Orleans banker Edward McIlhenny, who was given a gift of pepper seeds by a friend returning from a trip to Mexico. During the Civil War, the McIlhennys were forced to abandon their home in Louisiana. Upon their return after the war, they found that everything was destroyed except the hearty pepper plants. In 1868, McIlhenny began to experiment with the fruits of the plants and eventually invented a flavorful sauce made by mashing the peppers with salt, storing the mash in a crock for 30 days, then adding French wine vinegar and storing for an additional 30 days. The resulting sauce was an immediate success. Although the methods and procedures for making Tabasco sauce have evolved, the sauce still contains only three ingredients—peppers, salt, and vinegar. The name *Tabasco* is a Mexican term meaning "land where soil is humid." One small bottle of Tabasco sauce contains 720 drops. Tabasco sauce is best added to food after it is removed from the heat.

Tasso: A chunk of pork liberally seasoned with filé powder, garlic, and red pepper. Tasso is cured and smoked for two to three days and used as a flavoring agent for a variety of other preparations. Tasso is rarely eaten on its own due to its heavy salt and smoke flavor. Tasso is typically made at home from a piece of meat left over from a traditional boucherie.

Turtles: Until the middle of the 1990s, turtles were abundant in the Louisiana region and their meat was commonly sold at stalls in New Orleans's French Market. Due to a diminishing population, turtle meat is now available only through farms. Turtle was most frequently used to prepare soup, which was made as a clear broth, a cream soup, or thick like a stew. The fat from female turtles has long been considered a delicacy. Today, mock turtle soup is frequently prepared, substituting veal, duck, or beef for the hard-to-find turtle meat.

Wild Pecan Rice: (See *popcorn rice*.)

Sample Menus from Cajun and Creole Cuisines

MENU ONE

White Bean Soup

Cajun Fish Beignet and Cajun Red Remoulade Sauce

Paneéd Chicken and Baked Cheese Grits · Creole Collard Greens · Sautéed Tomatoes

MENU TWO

Tomato and Haricot Vert Salad

Shrimp and Chicken Étouffée · Red Beans and Rice

MENU THREE

Oysters Rockefeller

Chicken and Sausage Jambalaya

Fried Okra

Creole Onion Soup

YIELD: 6 PORTIONS · PORTION SIZE: 10 OUNCES

36 ounces (1kg) onions, thinly sliced

2 fluid ounces (60ml) clarified butter

4 fluid ounces (120ml) olive oil, 80/20 blend

4 ounces (120g) all-purpose flour

1 teaspoon (5g) salt

½ teaspoon (2g) cayenne pepper

3 bay leaves

½ teaspoon (2g) dried thyme

1 tablespoon (15g) garlic, minced

½ teaspoon (2g) dried basil

48 fluid ounces (1.4L) brown chicken stock, prepared (see page 515)

4 ounces (120g) cheddar cheese, grated

4 ounces (120g) Parmesan cheese, grated

12 ounces (360g) croutons

In a medium rondeau over high heat, caramelize the onions in the clarified butter until golden brown. Add the oil and sprinkle in the flour while stirring slowly. Stir constantly for approximately 10 minutes to make a blond roux.

Add the salt, cayenne pepper, bay leaves, thyme, garlic, and basil. Cook for approximately 10 minutes, stirring frequently.

Add the chicken stock and stir thoroughly, blending the roux into the stock. Bring to a boil (at least 165°F or 73.9°C), then reduce heat to medium-low. Cook uncovered, stirring frequently, for approximately 1 hour. Do not allow the simmering soup to fall below 140°F (60°C). Remove bay leaves.

When ready to serve, add the cheeses to the soup, stirring until they are blended into the soup and completely melted.

SERVING/HOLDING

Ladle 10 ounces (300ml) of the soup into 8-inch rimmed soup bowls, being careful not to splash the rim.

Sprinkle ¼ cup (60g) of the croutons into each bowl and serve.

🥣 **Hold** the soup at 140°F (60°C) or above.

COOLING/STORING

Pour the remaining soup into smaller metal containers.

🥣 **Cool** the remaining soup in an ice bath from 140°F (60°C) to 70°F (21.1°C) or lower within 2 hours. Cool from 70°F (21.1°C) to 41°F (5°C) within an additional 4 hours for a total cooling time of 6 hours.

Cover the soup; label, date, and store under refrigeration at 41°F (5°C) or lower.

White Bean Soup

YIELD: 6 PORTIONS · PORTION SIZE: 10 OUNCES

12 ounces (360g) Great Northern beans

4 ounces (120g) onion, chopped

2 ounces (60g) green onion, chopped

2½ ounces (75g) green bell pepper, chopped

1 ounce (30g) celery, chopped

2 tablespoons (30g) parsley, chopped

1 tablespoon (15g) garlic, chopped

1 fluid ounce (30ml) olive oil

128 ounces (3.8L) cold water or white chicken stock, prepared (see page 517)

1 ham hock

8 ounces (240g) smoked sausage, chopped

2 teaspoons (10g) salt

½ teaspoon (2g) white pepper, ground

¼ teaspoon (1g) cayenne pepper

¼ teaspoon (1g) red pepper flakes, crushed

¼ **teaspoon (1g) dried thyme**

2 bay leaves

¼ **teaspoon (1g) dried basil**

Soak the Great Northern beans overnight. Drain.

COOKING

Sweat the vegetables in the olive oil in a medium saucepot. Add the beans, water or stock, ham hock, smoked sausage, and seasonings.

Bring to a simmer and cook over low heat for approximately 3 hours or until the beans are tender. Do not allow the simmering soup to fall below 140°F (60°C).

Remove the ham hock, cool, and reserve until needed.

Remove the meat from the ham hock bone and cut the meat into ½-inch (1.27cm) pieces.

Put 24 fluid ounces (720ml) of the soup into a blender and purée.

Pour the purée back into the saucepot. More soup can be pureéd and added, depending on the consistency preferred. The more pureé added, the smoother the texture.

Add the chopped ham pieces back into the soup. Simmer for approximately 15–20 minutes or until the soup is slightly thickened.

SERVING/HOLDING

Hold the soup at 140°F (60°C) or above.

COOLING/STORING

Pour the remaining soup into smaller metal containers.

Cool the remaining soup in an ice bath from 140°F (60°C) to 70°F (21.1°C) or lower within 2 hours. Cool from 70°F (21.1°C) to 41°F (5°C) within an additional 4 hours for a total cooling time of 6 hours.

Cover the soup; label, date, and store under refrigeration at 41°F (5°C) or lower.

Cajun Fish Beignet

YIELD: 6 PORTIONS · PORTION SIZE: 3 OUNCES

18 ounces (540g) whitefish fillet

salt, to taste

white pepper, ground, to taste

lemon juice, as needed

BEER BATTER

4½ ounces (135g) all-purpose flour

4½ ounces (135g) cornstarch

¾ teaspoon (4g) baking soda

1½ teaspoons (7g) powdered sugar

3 teaspoons (15g) salt

½ teaspoon (2g) white pepper, ground

1 teaspoon (5g) paprika

6 fluid ounces (180ml) beer

6 fluid ounces (180ml) water

SERVING

all-purpose flour, as needed

18 fluid ounces (540ml) Cajun red
remoulade sauce (recipe follows)

CHEF TIPS *This recipe shows that seasoning both the marinade and the coating adds depth of flavor. A light coating, such as the one used in this recipe, is appropriate for all delicate whitefish fillets.*

Here are tips for making moist batters:

- *For a puffier batter, use baking powder. Avoid brands that contain aluminum salts.*
- *To make a lighter batter, include 1 tablespoon of vegetable oil as a part of the liquid.*
- *Mix the batter just until combined. Do not overmix.*

As an alternative preparation method, the fish fillets can be breaded instead of battered. Pearly meal is the name for a local mixture of half yellow cornmeal and half corn flour. Pearly meal makes a crust that is crunchier than white flour, but not as hard as pure cornmeal.

A typical whitefish fillet used in the New Orleans area is flounder. Other fish that can easily be substituted include sole, yellowtail, sand dab, and turbot.

Line a sheet pan with paper towels and reserve until needed.

Preheat a deep-fat fryer to 375°F (190.6°C).

Remove any bones and skin from the whitefish fillets. Cut fish into strips measuring ½ inch (1.27cm) x ½ inch (1.27cm) x 2 inches (5cm) (goujonettes). Hold the fish under refrigeration or in an ice bain marie to maintain 41°F (5°C) until needed.

Season the fish with salt and pepper, sprinkle with lemon juice, and refrigerate at least 30 minutes before cooking.

Prepare beer batter by sifting all the dry ingredients into a bowl. Add the beer and water, then stir. The consistency should be a nappé, similar to a crêpe batter.

COOKING

Dredge the whitefish strips in flour, shake off the excess, and dip them in the beer batter, coating the fish thoroughly. Deep-fry until golden brown and with an internal temperature of 145°F (62.8°C) for 15 seconds.

Remove the fried fish and degrease on the paper towel–lined sheet pan. Hold at 140°F (60°C) or higher.

SERVING/HOLDING

Carefully place 3 ounces (90g) of the fish beignets on the serving plate.

Using a squeeze bottle, squeeze approximately 3 ounces of the red remoulade sauce around the beignets.

COOLING/STORING

Discard any unused batter. Wrap the leftover fish in plastic, date, and label.

Seal the remoulade sauce, label, and date.

Store fish and sauce under refrigeration at 41°F (5°C) or lower.

CAJUN RED REMOULADE SAUCE

YIELD: 6 PORTIONS · PORTION SIZE: 3 OUNCES

5 ounces (150g) red bell pepper, roasted and peeled, cut into small dice

1 ounce (30g) dill pickle, cut into small dice

1 ounce (30g) capers, chopped

¼ ounce (7g) parsley, chopped

½ ounce (15g) green onion, chopped

4 ounces (120g) serrano chile, diced

6 ounces (180g) mayonnaise, prepared

½ fluid ounce (14ml) lemon juice

salt, to taste

black pepper, ground, to taste

1 dash cayenne pepper

Place all ingredients into a blender and blend thoroughly. Adjust the seasoning as needed and refrigerate until needed.

COOLING/STORING

Cover the remoulade sauce; label, date, and store under refrigeration at 41°F (5°C) or lower.

Oysters Rockefeller

36 oysters, half shell

4 ounces (120g) green onion with tops, chopped

3 ounces (90g) celery, finely diced

1½ ounces (45g) parsley, chopped

3 ounces (90g) spinach, chopped

6 ounces (180g) butter, sweet

⅓ teaspoon (2g) dried tarragon

1 tablespoon (15g) Pernod

3 ounces (90g) breadcrumbs

½ teaspoon (2g) salt

black pepper, ground, to taste

1 dash Tabasco sauce

12 ounces (360g) rock salt

2 lemons, cut into 6 wedges each

Wash and shuck oysters and reserve under refrigeration at 41°F (5°C) or lower.

Reserve the prepared vegetables under refrigeration at 41°F or (5°C) or lower.

COOKING

Melt the butter in a large skillet over medium-high heat. Add the green onion and celery and cook for 4 minutes. Add the parsley, spinach, and tarragon and continue to cook for an additional 4 minutes.

CHEF TIPS *Do not overcook fresh spinach. When fresh spinach wilts, it is done. A longer cooking time allows the spinach to exude acids, leaving a bitter flavor.*

To open oysters:

1. *Wash the oysters with a scrub brush under cold, running water. Make sure to thoroughly clean the joint where the shells connect, as this area collects a large amount of sediment.*
2. *Place the oyster in a towel with the joint end sticking slightly outside the towel.*
3. *Put an oyster knife firmly into the joint and twist, popping the joint open.*
4. *Move the knife to the inside of the top shell and scrape the meat from the top shell.*
5. *Remove the top shell and discard.*
6. *Slide the knife between the oyster meat and the bottom shell to loosen the meat. Take care not to damage the oyster meat or to lose any of the flavorful oyster liquor (the natural liquid found in the oyster).*
7. *Open the oysters as close to use as possible.*
8. *Store the oysters on a bed of shaved ice until needed.*

Add Pernod, breadcrumbs, salt, black pepper, and Tabasco sauce. Adjust seasonings to taste.

Cool the mixture. Place approximately ½ ounce (1.27cm) of the mixture on top of each oyster.

Place the oysters on a bed of rock salt and bake in a 375°F (190.6°C) oven for approximately 10 minutes. Cook the oysters to a minimum internal temperature of 145°F (62.8°C) for at least 15 seconds.

Place 2 ounces (60g) of the rock salt on the bottom of each hot service plate.

On each plate, position 6 of the baked oysters in a circle around 2 lemon wedges in the center. Serve immediately.

COOLING/STORING

Cool the remaining oysters from 140°F (60°C) to 70°F (21.1°C) or lower within 2 hours. Cool from 70°F (21.1°C) to 41°F (5°C) within an additional 4 hours for a total cooling time of 6 hours.

Tomato and Haricot Vert Salad

YIELD: 6 PORTIONS · PORTION SIZE: 10 OUNCES

SALAD

8 ounces (240g) fennel, cleaned, sliced paper-thin

6 ounces (180g) haricots verts, ends removed, blanched

40 ounces (1.2kg) tomatoes, peeled, seeded, cut into julienne

salt, to taste

black pepper, ground, to taste

1 tablespoon (15ml) olive oil

1 tablespoon (15g) chives, minced

2 ounces (60g) chervil leaves

3 basil leaves, cut into chiffonnade

VINAIGRETTE

3 tablespoons (44g) mayonnaise, prepared

2 tablespoons (30ml) red wine vinegar

1 tablespoon (15ml) lemon juice

1 tablespoon (15g) Dijon mustard

1 clove garlic, mashed with salt

8 fluid ounces (240ml) olive oil

salt, to taste

white pepper, ground, to taste

Place all the salad ingredients in a bowl. Reserve under refrigeration until needed.

In a blender, mix the mayonnaise, vinegar, lemon juice, mustard, and garlic.

While the blender is running, slowly drizzle in the oil until the dressing is smooth and thick. Season to taste with salt and white pepper.

SERVING/HOLDING

Hold the salad and dressing separately under refrigeration, maintaining 41°F (5°C) until ready to plate. Toss together and serve.

COOLING/STORING

Cover the salad and dressing; label, date, and store under refrigeration at 41°F (5°C) or lower.

Chicken and Andouille Sausage Gumbo

YIELD: 6 PORTIONS · PORTION SIZE: 12 OUNCES

SEASONING MIX

- ½ **teaspoon (2g) salt**
- ½ **teaspoon (2g) black pepper, ground**
- ½ **teaspoon (2g) cayenne pepper**
- ½ **teaspoon (2g) white pepper, ground**
- ½ **teaspoon (2g) paprika**
- ½ **teaspoon (2g) onion powder**
- ½ **teaspoon (2g) garlic powder**

GUMBO

- 24 **ounces (720g) boneless chicken breast**
- 12 **ounces (360g) onion, chopped**
- 6 **ounces (180g) green pepper, chopped**
- 6 **ounces (180g) celery, chopped**
- 12 **ounces (360g) okra, sliced**
- 6 **ounces (180g) green onion, chopped**
- 2 **ounces (60g) flat-leaf parsley, minced**
- 9 **ounces (270g) all-purpose flour**
- 8 **fluid ounces (240ml) vegetable oil**
- 6 **ounces (180g) lard**
- 72 **fluid ounces (2.4L) white chicken stock, prepared (see page 517)**
- 16 **ounces (480g) Andouille sausage, cut into bite-size pieces**
- 2 **teaspoons (10g) garlic, minced**
- ¾ **tablespoon (11g) salt**
- ¾ **tablespoon (11g) black pepper, ground**
- ¾ **tablespoon (11g) cayenne pepper**
- 2 **ounces (60g) filé powder**
- 32 **ounces (960g) cooked rice, hot**

CHEF TIPS *Gumbo comes in many varieties, but every one uses certain fundamental cooking techniques. First, most gumbos have a roux base that is cooked slowly to a rich brown, giving gumbo much of its characteristic thick texture and smoky taste. To prevent the roux from burning once it is done, add the cold vegetables all at once.*

Filé powder, when used to thicken gumbo, should be added only after the gumbo is finished and removed from the heat. Once filé powder is stirred in, the soup cannot be reheated as the filé will either turn stringy or solidify at the bottom of the pot. Let the gumbo stand in the pot for 5 minutes after adding the filé powder for the best results.

Combine all seasoning mix ingredients. Set aside.

Remove skin from the boneless chicken breasts and discard.

Cut chicken into bite-size pieces. Place the chicken pieces on a parchment-lined baking sheet and sprinkle liberally with the prepared seasoning mix. Refrigerate at 41°F (5°C) for at least 30 minutes before using.

Reserve the prepared vegetables under refrigeration at 41°F (5°C) or lower.

COOKING

Put the flour in a plastic bag, add the seasoned chicken meat, close the bag, and shake, coating all of the pieces thoroughly.

Remove the chicken. Shake in a colander to remove any excess flour. Reserve the excess flour to use a roux.

Heat the vegetable oil over medium-high heat. Add the chicken meat in small batches, stirring until browned and crisp on all sides. Remove and reserve.

Loosen any browned bits stuck to the bottom of the pan. Strain the fat to remove the particles and return to the pan. Add the lard to the fat and place over medium-low heat.

Add the reserved flour and cook, whisking frequently, for approximately 45 minutes or until a smooth mahogany-colored roux forms.

Remove the roux from the heat and add the onion, green peppers, and celery all at once. Stir to blend and prevent browning.

Cook the onions, peppers, and celery until they are wilted and the onions are translucent.

Stir in the stock very slowly in small batches. Thoroughly combine the stock with the roux each time before adding more. Once all the stock is added, bring the liquid to a full boil, then reduce the heat to a simmer.

Add the sausage, garlic, salt, black pepper, and cayenne.

Add the browned chicken meat and simmer for 24 minutes, making sure the chicken reaches at least 165°F (73.9°C).

Add the okra and cook for an additional 20 minutes.

Remove from heat and stir in the filé powder, green onion, and parsley.

Let rest 5 minutes before serving.

Adjust the seasoning. Hold the gumbo at 140°F (60°C) or above.

Place ½ cup (120g) of hot cooked rice in each hot soup plate and ladle 8 fluid ounces (240ml) of the soup carefully over it.

COOLING/STORING

Cool the remaining gumbo in an ice bath from 140°F (60°C) to 70°F (21.1°C) or lower within 2 hours. Cool from 70°F (21.1°C) to 41°F (5°C) within an additional 4 hours for a total cooling time of 6 hours or less.

Cover the gumbo; label, date, and store in a refrigerated unit at a product temperature of 41°F (5°C) or lower.

Chicken and Sausage Jambalaya

YIELD: 6 PORTIONS · PORTION SIZE: 12 OUNCES

1½ chickens

1 tablespoon (15ml) olive oil

12 ounces (360g) pork butt, cut into ½-inch cubes

6 ounces (180g) onion, diced

4½ ounces (135g) green bell pepper, diced

4½ ounces (135g) green onion tops, chopped

¾ ounce (23g) garlic, chopped

⅜ ounces (11g) parsley, chopped

4½ ounces (135g) ham, chopped

18 ounces (540g) Andouille sausage, cut into bite-size pieces

¾ ounce (23g) salt

¾ teaspoon (4g) black pepper, ground

⅜ teaspoon (2g) cayenne pepper

3 bay leaves

3 cloves

⅜ teaspoon (2g) dried thyme

⅜ teaspoon (2g) dried basil

CHEF TIPS *One of the secrets of great jambalaya is the way fat rendered from the chicken or sausage coats and seals the rice, helping it keep its texture during the long cooking process while absorbing the flavors that surround it. This cooking process is similar to the technique for making rice pilaf. Some jambalaya recipes call for the rice to be browned before adding the liquid. By using both dried and fresh herbs, intense and diverse flavors are imparted to the jambalaya.*

When preparing jambalaya, cook the meats over medium heat, stirring constantly, until they are thoroughly browned. This process takes around 15 minutes. When the meats are browned, remove them from the pan and brown the vegetables in the same manner. Add the seasonings after the vegetables are browned and cook for 5 minutes more to build the flavors on top of one another.

18 ounces (540g) raw rice

48 fluid ounces (1.4L) white chicken stock, prepared (see page 517)

Wash, dry, and cut the chicken into 8 pieces. Reserve until needed under refrigeration at a unit temperature of 41°F (5°C) or below.

COOKING

In a large, heavy-bottomed saucepot, heat the oil over medium-high heat. Brown the chicken pieces thoroughly. As the pieces brown, remove them and reserve until needed.

Thoroughly brown the cubed pork butt. As the pieces brown, remove them and reserve until needed.

Add the onion, bell pepper, green onion, and garlic and cook for approximately 15 minutes, stirring frequently, or until the vegetables are thoroughly browned. Add the parsley and ham and reduce the heat to low.

Add the sausage and seasonings and continue to cook, stirring frequently, for 5 additional minutes. Add the reserved chicken pieces, rice, and chicken stock. Mix gently.

Bring to a boil, cover the pot, and turn the heat down to very low. Cook, covered, for 45 minutes. From time to time, uncover and stir gently to prevent the rice from drying out.

Adjust the seasoning to taste and continue to cook until the jambalaya reaches 165°F (73.9°C) or higher for 15 seconds.

SERVING

Place approximately 1 cup (240g) of the jambalaya in each hot soup plate.

COOLING/STORING

Cool the remaining jambalaya in an ice bath from 140°F (60°C) to 70°F (21.1°C) or lower within 2 hours. Cool from 70°F (21.1°C) to 41°F (5°C) within an additional 4 hours for a total cooling time of 6 hours or less.

Cover the jambalaya; label, date, and store under refrigeration at 41°F (5°C) or lower.

Shrimp and Chicken Étouffée

YIELD: 6 PORTIONS · PORTION SIZE: 12 OUNCES

¾ fluid ounce (22ml) olive oil

1½ ounces (45g) all-purpose flour

4½ ounces (135g) onion, cut into small dice

3 ounces (90g) celery, cut into small dice

3 ounces (90g) green bell pepper, cut into small dice

¾ ounce (22g) garlic, minced

12 ounces (360g) shrimp, 21/25 count

12 ounces (360g) chicken, leg and thigh meat

1½ ounces (45g) butter

12 fluid ounces (360ml) white chicken stock (see page 517) or fish stock, (see page 518), prepared

1½ fluid ounces (4ml) tomato sauce (see page 517)

¾ teaspoon (45g) paprika

¼ teaspoon (1g) cayenne pepper

⅓ teaspoon (2g) dried basil

salt, to taste

black pepper, ground, to taste

12 fluid ounces (360ml) cream, reduced by half

1½ ounces (45g) green onion, tops, sliced

¾ ounce (22g) parsley, chopped

6 portions creole rice (see page 215)

Make a pale roux with the oil and flour. Reserve until needed.

Reserve the prepared vegetables until needed.

Cook the shrimp to an internal temperature of 145°F (62.8°C) or higher for 15 seconds. Douse in an ice bath to stop the cooking process. Peel and devein the shrimp. Reduce their temperature from 140°F (60°C) to 70°F (21.1°C) or lower within 2 hours. Cool from 70°F (21.1°C) to 41°F (5°C) within an additional 4 hours for a total cooling time of 6 hours.

Bone the pieces of chicken and dice the meat. Reserve under refrigeration to maintain 41°F (5°C) until ready to cook.

Melt the butter in a large skillet over medium-high heat. Sauté the onion, celery, bell pepper, and garlic until soft, but do not brown.

Add the roux, stock, tomato sauce, paprika, cayenne pepper, basil, and seasoning. Bring to a boil, then reduce the heat to a simmer. Simmer for 30 minutes, being careful not to let the temperature fall below 140°F (60°C). Add more stock or water as necessary if the liquid becomes too thick.

Add the chicken and simmer for an additional 8 minutes or until the chicken reaches a minimum internal temperature of 165°F (73.0°C). Add the shrimp and cream and continue to simmer for 5 minutes or until the shrimp reaches an internal temperature of 145°F (62.8°C). Add the green onions and parsley and cook for about 1 minute.

Adjust the seasonings to taste with salt and black pepper.

SERVING

Place approximately ½ cup (120g) of creole rice on the center of each heated plate.

On the bottom half of the plate and on top of half the rice, ladle 12 ounces (360ml) of the étouffée. Take care to spoon equal amounts of shrimp and chicken onto each plate.

COOLING/STORING

Cool the remaining étouffée in an ice bath from 140°F (60°C) to 70°F (21.1°C) or lower within 2 hours. Cool from 70°F (21.1°C) to 41°F (5°C) within an additional 4 hours for a total cooling time of 6 hours or less.

Cover the étouffée; label, date, and store in a refrigerated unit of 41°F (5°C) or lower.

Paneéd Chicken and Baked Cheese Grits

SEASONING MIX

3 fluid ounces (90 ml) ketchup

2¼ fluid ounces (75ml) Creole mustard

1½ tablespoons (22g) white pepper, ground

1½ tablespoons (22g) cayenne pepper

5 tablespoons (74g) paprika

¾ teaspoon (4g) dried thyme

⅓ teaspoon (2g) dried sage

⅓ teaspoon (2g) dried basil

BREADING

7 large eggs

3 tablespoons (44ml) vegetable oil

5 ounces (150g) breadcrumbs, ground fine

40 ounces (1.2kg) chicken breast, boned and evenly flattened

1½ tablespoons (22g) salt

vegetable oil, as needed

6 portions Creole collard greens (see page 211)

6 portions sautéed tomatoes (see page 210)

6 portions baked cheese grits (see page 218)

Line a sheet pan with paper towels.

COOKING

Combine the ingredients of the seasoning mix in a small bowl and mix thoroughly.

Combine the eggs and 3 tablespoons (45ml) of the vegetable oil in a pan. Beat well.

Combine 2 tablespoons (30g) of the seasoning mix with the breadcrumbs and blend in a food processor. Reserve until needed.

Spread an even layer of the seasoning mix over both sides of the chicken, then soak the chicken for 15–30 minutes in the egg mixture.

In a large skillet, heat about ¼ inch (64cm) vegetable oil to at least 300°F (148.9°C).

Remove the chicken from the egg mixture and drain the excess batter from the chicken.

Dredge the chicken pieces in the breadcrumbs, thoroughly coating them. Shake off the excess and gently place in the hot oil. Pan-fry until golden brown and reaches an internal temperature of 165°F (73.9°C). Drain on paper towels.

SERVING

Place approximately 6 ounces (180g) of the cheese grits at the top center of each hot plate.

To the left of the cheese grits, place 2 ounces (60g) of collard greens, twisted to add height.

To the right of the cheese grits, spoon 3 ounces (90g) of the sautéed tomatoes.

On the bottom half of all three, fan out 6 ounces (180g) of chicken breast. Serve immediately.

COOLING/STORING

Discard the remaining breading items.

Cool the remaining chicken from 140°F (60°C) to 70°F (21.1°C) or lower within 2 hours. Cool from 70°F (21.1°C) to 41°F (5°C) within an additional 4 hours for a total cooling time of 6 hours.

Cool the cheese grits in shallow pans with a product depth of 2 inches (5cm) or less from 140°F (60°C) to 70°F (21.1°C) or lower within 2 hours. Cool from 70°F (21.1°C) to 41°F (5°C) within an additional 4 hours for a total cooling time of 6 hours or less.

Cover the chicken and cheese grits; label, date, and store in a refrigerated unit at 41°F (5°C).

Sautéed Tomatoes

YIELD: 6 PORTIONS · PORTION SIZE: 3 OUNCES

½ ounce (15g) butter

2 ounces (60g) onion, chopped

1 ounce (30g) green bell pepper, chopped

18 ounces (540g) tomatoes, peeled, seeded, cut into wedges

salt, to taste

black pepper, ground, to taste

sugar, to taste

Melt the butter in a sauté pan and add the onion and bell pepper. Sauté until the onions are translucent.

Add the tomatoes. Cook until heated thoroughly.

Season to taste with salt, black pepper, and sugar.

SERVING/HOLDING

Serve immediately.

COOLING/STORING

Cool in shallow pan with a product depth of less than 2 inches (5cm) and cool from 140°F (60°C) to 70°F (21.1°C) or lower within 2 hours. Cool from 70°F (21.1°C) to 41°F (5°C) within an additional 4 hours for a total cooling time of 6 hours or less.

Cover the tomatoes; label, date, and store in refrigerated unit at a product temperature of 41°F (5°C) or lower.

Creole Collard Greens

YIELD: 6 PORTIONS · PORTION SIZE: 2 OUNCES

12 ounces (360g) or 2 bunches collard greens, cut into ½-inch (1.27cm) strips

1½ ounces (45g) butter

salt, to taste

pepper, to taste

lemon, to taste (optional)

Trim and wash the collard greens. Blanch them in boiling salted water. Shock in an ice-water bath and drain them thoroughly.

Place in a plastic container, wrap, label, and refrigerate until needed.

COOKING

Melt the butter in a sauté pan and sauté the greens. Season with salt and pepper to taste. Serve with a squeeze of lemon if desired.

COOLING/STORING

Cool in shallow pan with a product depth of less than 2 inches (5cm) and cool from 140°F (60°C) to 70°F (21.1°C) or lower within 2 hours. Cool from 70°F (21.1°C) to 41°F (5°C) within an additional 4 hours for a total cooling time of 6 hours or less.

Cover the collard greens; label, date, and store in a refrigerated unit at a product temperature of 41°F (5°C) or lower.

Fried Okra

18 ounces (540g) okra

8 ounces (240g) all-purpose flour

3 large eggs, beaten

8 ounces (240g) breadcrumbs

olive oil, as needed

salt, to taste

black pepper, ground, to taste

CHEF TIPS *The best okra pods are less than 3 inches (7.5cm) long. More mature okra tends to be fibrous and difficult to digest. Do not cook okra in cast-iron cookware, as it reacts with the metal and turns an unappetizing black color.*

Trim, wash, and dry the okra. Reserve under refrigeration until needed.

Coat the okra by dredging them in the flour, dipping them into egg wash, and thoroughly coating them with finely ground breadcrumbs.

COOKING

Fill a large sauté pan with ½ inch (1.27cm) of olive oil. Heat the oil to 350°F (176.7°C).

Pan-fry the okra until golden brown. Drain on paper towels.

SERVING/HOLDING

Season to taste with salt and black pepper. Serve immediately.

COOLING/STORING

Cool in a shallow pan with a product depth of less than 2 inches (5cm) and cool from 140°F (60°C) to 70°F (21.1°C) or lower within 2 hours. Cool from 70°F (21.1°C) to 41°F (5°C) within an additional 4 hours for a total cooling time of 6 hours or less.

Cover the fried okra; label, date, and store in a refrigerated unit at a product temperature of 41°F (5°C) or lower.

Red Beans and Rice

YIELD: 6 PORTIONS · PORTION SIZE: 8 OUNCES

24 ounces (720g) dried red beans

9 ounces (270g) bacon, cut into julienne

6 ounces (180g) onion, cut into small dice

1½ ounces (45g) green onion, with tops, chopped

1½ ounces (45g) green bell pepper, cut into small dice

¾ tablespoon (11g) garlic, minced

1½ tablespoons (22g) parsley, minced

1 ham hock

1 pinch cayenne pepper

1½ bay leaves, broken into quarters

1 pinch dried thyme

1 pinch dried basil

48 fluid ounces (1.4kg) cold water

¾ teaspoon (4g) salt

⅓ teaspoon (2g) black pepper, ground

6 portions Creole rice (recipe follows)

CHEF TIPS *The rich taste of authentic slow-cooked beans comes from the careful balance of spices and from the marrow of the ham bone seeping into the natural gravy. The ham selected for red beans and rice should be baked rather than country or smoked. Smoked ham is too salty and unbalances the seasoning.*

Bean dishes are popular in Creole cooking because they take seasoning well, are inexpensive, and the quantity of meat can be varied according to budget. These bean dishes were enriched by the arrival of immigrants and chefs from the Caribbean, with their love of seasoning, and Italian chefs, whose way with beans made them masters of Creole bean cooking.

Soak the red beans in cold water overnight under refrigeration.

Drain the soaked beans and reserve until needed.

COOKING

Sweat the bacon in a sauté pan. Add the vegetables, garlic, and parsley, and sweat an additional 2–3 minutes.

Add the beans, ham hock, garlic, parsley, and spices and cover with cold water. Bring to a boil and lower the heat to a simmer. Do not let the beans drop below 140°F (60°C).

Cook the beans until they are tender and a natural thick gravy forms. Add water toward the end of cooking to adjust the consistency if the beans appear too dry. Season to taste with salt and black pepper.

SERVING/HOLDING

🥣 **Hold** the beans at 140°F (60°C) or higher.

Reserve the beans until needed. Place approximately ½ cup (120g) of Creole rice into the center of each hot bowl and carefully ladle about 8 ounces (240g) of the beans over it.

Serve immediately.

COOLING/STORING

🥣 **Cool** in a shallow pan with a product depth of less than 2 inches (5cm) and cool from 140°F (60°C) to 70°F (21.1°C) or lower within 2 hours. Cool from 70°F (21.1°C) to 41°F (5°C) within an additional 4 hours for a total cooling time of 6 hours or less.

Cover the beans; label, date, and store in refrigerated unit at a product temperature of 41°F (5°C) or lower.

CREOLE RICE

YIELD: 6 PORTIONS · PORTION SIZE: 4 OUNCES

16 fluid ounces (480ml) white chicken (see page 517) or vegetable stock, prepared (see page 519)

1½ ounces (45g) onion, cut into small dice

¾ ounce (23g) butter

8 ounces (240ml) white long-grain rice, washed twice

1½ bay leaves

salt, to taste

black pepper, ground, to taste

Heat the stock in a medium saucepot and reserve until needed.

COOKING

Sweat the onions in the butter in a sautoir pan.

Add the rice and stir to coat with the butter.

Add the hot stock and seasonings.

Bring the liquid to a boil. Cover the pan, transfer it to a 350°F (176.7°C) oven, and cook it for 18–20 minutes or until the liquid is absorbed and the rice is tender.

Remove the lid and fluff the rice with a fork.

SERVING/HOLDING

Hold the Creole rice at 140°F (60°C) or higher.

Dirty Rice

½ ounce (15g) butter, sweet

6 ounces (180g) chicken livers, cleaned, chopped

1 ounce (30g) shallots, finely diced

salt, to taste

black pepper, ground, to taste

½ ounce (15g) green onions, finely diced

¼ ounce (7g) parsley, minced

14 ounces (420g) cooked white rice

Melt the butter in a sauté pan and sauté the chicken livers and shallots until tender and falling apart and the livers reach 165°F (73.9°C). Season with salt and pepper.

Add green onions and parsley. Add the cooked white rice and mix thoroughly.

COOLING/STORING

Cool in shallow pan with a product depth of less than 2 inches (5cm) and cool from 140°F (60°C) to 70°F (21.1°C) or lower within 2 hours. Cool from 70°F (21.1°C) to 41°F (5°C) within an additional 4 hours for a total cooling time of 6 hours or less.

Cover the rice; label, date, and store in a refrigerated unit at a product temperature of 41°F (5°C) or lower.

Blazing Hushpuppies

YIELD: 12 PORTIONS · PORTION SIZE: 6 EACH

12 ounces (360g) self-rising flour

1½ cups (360g) cornmeal

1 tablespoon (15g) cayenne pepper

12 ounces (360g) onion, finely chopped

1 large egg

16 fluid ounces (480ml) beer

3 tablespoons (44g) green onion, finely chopped

Preheat a deep fryer to 375°F (190.6°C).

Line a sheet pan with paper towels and reserve.

COOKING

Mix together the flour, cornmeal, and cayenne pepper. Add the onions.

Add the egg and beer to this mixture and blend until it makes a light batter. Stir the green onions into the batter.

Drop 6 tablespoons (90ml) of batter into the deep fryer at a time. The hushpuppies will turn themselves.

SERVING/HOLDING

Remove the hushpuppies from the oil when medium brown and place on the paper towel–lined sheet pan.

Serve immediately or hold the hushpuppies at 140°F (60°C) or higher.

COOLING/STORING

Cool in a shallow pan with a product depth of less than 2 inches (5cm) and cool from 140°F (60°C) to 70°F (21.1°C) or lower within 2 hours. Cool from 70°F (21.1°C) to 41°F (5°C) within an additional 4 hours for a total cooling time of 6 hours or less.

Cover the hushpuppies; label, date, and store in a refrigerated unit at a product temperature of 41°F (5°C) or lower.

Baked Cheese Grits

1½ tablespoons (22g) garlic, chopped

3 ounces (90g) butter

salt, to taste

black pepper, ground, to taste

4½ ounces (135g) Longhorn cheddar cheese, grated

10 ounces (300g) yellow grits, prepared, hot

3 large eggs

6 fluid ounces (180ml) milk

Prepare six 3-inch (7.6cm) plating rings by covering one side with aluminum foil and placing the covered side on the bottom of a baking dish.

COOKING

Sauté the garlic lightly and reserve until needed.

Add the butter, salt, pepper, sautéed garlic, and cheese to the prepared grits. Mix until the butter and cheese melt. Remove from the heat.

Beat the eggs and milk together in a small bowl and incorporate into the grits mixture.

Fill each of the prepared rings with ½ cup (120g) of the cheese grits and place in a preheated 350°F (176.7°C) oven. Cook the molds until they reach an internal temperature of 145°F (62.8°C) for at least 15 seconds.

SERVING/HOLDING

Remove the foil and carefully push the molded grits onto hot plates.

Hold the baked cheese grits at 140°F (60°C) or higher.

COOLING/STORING

Cool in a shallow pan with a product depth of less than 2 inches (5cm) and cool from 140°F (60°C) to 70°F (21.1°C) or lower within 2 hours. Cool from 70°F (21.1°C) to 41°F (5°C) within an additional 4 hours for a total cooling time of 6 hours or less.

Cover the grits; label, date, and store in a refrigerated unit at a product temperature of 41°F (5°C) or lower.

Apple Bread Pudding with Caramel Sauce and Crunchy Pralines

YIELD: 12 PORTIONS · PORTION SIZE: 4 OUNCES

6 ounces (180g) brioche or croissant, 2 days old

1½ fluid ounces (45ml) butter, melted

16 fluid ounces (480ml) milk

4 large eggs

6 ounces (180g) sugar

¾ fluid ounce (22ml) vanilla extract

1½ ounces (45g) raisins

¾ fluid ounce (22ml) brandy

8 ounces (240g) apples, peeled and cored, sliced

powdered sugar, as needed

12 portions caramel sauce (recipe follows)

12 portions crunchy pralines (recipe follows)

Slice the bread into ⅛-inch (.32cm) slices and coat them with the melted butter. Place them in a bowl and reserve until needed.

Butter a 9-inch (22.9cm) cake pan and line it with parchment paper. Reserve until needed.

Place the milk in a saucepan, bring to a boil, and reserve hot.

Place the eggs, sugar, and vanilla in a large bowl and mix well. Slowly temper with the hot milk and pour the mixture over the bread.

Soak the raisins in the brandy for 30–40 minutes.

Fold in the apples and raisins soaked in brandy. Pour the mixture into the buttered cake pan.

COOKING

Place the pan in a hot-water bath and bake in a preheated deck oven at 350°F (176.7°C) for approximately 1 hour, allowing a light crust to form on top.

Garnish by sprinkling with powdered sugar.

Place 1–2 ounces (30–60ml) of sauce on a chilled plate. Place a portion of bread pudding on the sauce and drizzle additional sauce over the top of each portion.

Sprinkle pralines on bread pudding and sauce before serving.

Cool in a shallow pan with a product depth of less than 2 inches (5cm) and cool from 140°F (60°C) to 70°F (21.1°C) or lower within 2 hours. Cool from 70°F (21.1°C) to 41°F (5°C) within an additional 4 hours for a total cooling time of 6 hours or less.

Cover the bread pudding; label, date, and store in a refrigerated unit at a product temperature of 41°F (5°C) or lower.

CARAMEL SAUCE

YIELD: 12 PORTIONS · PORTION SIZE: 2 OUNCES

16 ounces (480g) sugar

4–6 drops lemon juice

12 fluid ounces (360ml) heavy cream

milk, as needed

Combine the sugar and the lemon juice in a heavy-bottomed pot. Place the pot over medium heat and cook the sugar until it melts.

Using a pastry brush dipped in water, wash down the sides of the pot to eliminate undissolved sugar crystals.

Continue to cook the sugar until it is golden to medium brown. The darker the sugar, the more pronounced the caramel flavor will be. Remove the caramel from the heat immediately to prevent overcooking.

Let the caramel cool slightly for approximately 5 minutes, stirring frequently so the caramel does not harden.

Bring the heavy cream to a boil while the caramel cools. Carefully stir the heavy cream into the caramel very slowly until all the caramel is dissolved.

Let the sauce cool. Adjust the consistency with a little milk if the sauce is too thick.

COOLING/STORING

🍲 **Cool** in a shallow pan with a product depth of less than 2 inches (5cm) and cool from 140°F (60°C) to 70°F (21.1°C) or lower within 2 hours. Cool from 70°F (21.1°C) to 41°F (5°C) within an additional 4 hours for a total cooling time of 6 hours or less.

Cover the caramel sauce; label, date, and store in a refrigerated unit at a product temperature of 41°F (5°C) or lower.

CRUNCHY PRALINES

YIELD: 12 PORTIONS · PORTION SIZE: 2 OUNCES

24 ounces (720g) brown sugar

3 tablespoons (45g) butter

6 fluid ounces (180ml) water

24 ounces (720g) pecans

Line a sheet pan with parchment paper and reserve until needed.

COOKING

Combine the brown sugar, butter, and water in a saucepan over medium heat. Stir to dissolve the sugar. Continue to stir for 3–4 minutes.

When the mix begins to boil at 234°F (1122°C), add the pecans and continue to stir for about 5 minutes.

Remove from the heat. Drop the pecans by the spoonful onto a sheet pan lined with parchment paper. Let cool. Remove from the paper with a thin knife. Reserve until needed.

COOLING/STORING

Store candies in an airtight container; label, date, and store in a cool, dry area free of humidity.

Michael Foley

Being born in and now living and cooking in the Midwest after having traveled the globe, I can easily say this region's heritage of food and drink is one of the world's most interesting. The key to cooking success here is to use the Midwest's history and its fascinating agriculture, husbandry, and aquaculture base to advantage, and to apply modern cooking methods to a vast repertoire of flavor opportunities. Recipes from the Central Plains are steeped in those of the region's Native American tribes. With hundreds of ethnic influences from the colonial period right down to our present changing demographics, the prize goes to those who respect the Midwest's origins and demand to keep its food sources strong and healthy. This region is gifted with a more extensive inventory of meat, fish, poultry, game, rice, grains, legumes, fruits, vegetables, and herbs than any other in the United States. It is our work as cooks and chefs, professionals and amateurs, to spread this word.

Nowhere is there a better supply of tree fruit and berry fruit. Meats, game, and poultry are staples of the Central Plains. You may think fish is found only on the coasts, but you are wrong. The lakes, streams, and rivers of the region supply more than ample varieties of fish. There is hardly a market in season that cannot supply all kinds of mushrooms. Whether farming practices are organic, sustainable, or traditional, the Central Plains boasts of basic foodstuffs. What a picture of variety, seasonality, and high quality. And we must sing the praise of our bounty.

Michael Foley is the owner of Printer's Row Restaurant in Chicago, Illinois

The Central Plains

Known as the land of milk and grain, the Central Plains region is the breadbasket and main source of food crops for the United States. As elsewhere in America, the culinary story of the Central Plains begins with an exchange of knowledge and ideas between the Native Americans and the pioneers, settlers, and immigrants of the region. The first Europeans to travel through the Central Plains were the French fur traders, known as *mountain men*, in the 1600s. Although they were not settlers, they did establish outposts in the region. These outposts were significant because only here could the mountain men obtain food and supplies. Typically, the only foods available in the outposts were indigenous to the local area. Relatively few changes occurred in the Central Plains over the next century and a half. In 1849, gold was discovered in California and the Oregon and

Santa Fe trails opened, signaling the start of the land rush. European immigrants and people from other parts of America began to settle in the Great Plains to farm, ranch, build towns, and work on the railroads.

Between 1820 and 1914, over two million Scandinavians immigrated to America. The Norwegians were the first to arrive and began to work along the East Coast as loggers, fishermen, and farmers. Soon, many moved inland, where they found the weather and lands of the Midwest and Central Plains similar to Norway. Around 1840, the Norwegians settled in the area of the upper Mississippi Valley—specifically, the region that today makes up much of Minnesota and Wisconsin. Following the Norwegians, many immigrants from Sweden and Denmark also arrived to settle in the Central Plains. As this westward migration took place, the Mississippi River quickly became a dividing line that separated the "civilized" East and the "untamed" West. The Central Plains, with the Mississippi River running through the middle, lured new residents with hopes of agricultural wealth and great prosperity.

The immigrants from Northern Europe who settled throughout the Central Plains first learned how to harvest corn and wild rice from the Native Americans. Native Americans also taught the immigrants techniques for hunting the abundant wild game of the region, including pheasant, quail, grouse, wild turkey, deer, and buffalo. The settlers also learned how to fish in the many rivers and lakes, which contain walleye, yellow perch, trout, and pike and are home to many varieties of duck, geese, and other waterfowl. Most important, the vast lands were well suited for farming and for grazing livestock. The new agricultural techniques were quickly adapted by the Scandinavians and the new foods integrated into their daily diet. Rustic stews, like the chicken and sausage pie on page 252, breads, and the root vegetables that were the traditional foods of Scandinavians in Northern Europe, became dietary staples. The Scandinavians also brought to the area many other traditional food favorites from the Old Country, such as cheese, sausage, smoked fish and meat, and, of course, beer. An example of a recipe that includes a combination of Old Country ingredients is Wisconsin cheese and beer soup (see page 234).

As the western migration expanded, people from Eastern Europe began to settle in the Central Plains, which also reminded them of their homelands. Germans, Poles, Austrians, and more Scandinavians settled in Illinois and Iowa as well as Minnesota and Wisconsin. They farmed the land and raised dairy cattle as their primary source of income. Wisconsin became a popular destination of German and Swedish immigrants. Cheese production began in Wisconsin in the 1830s. Cheddar cheese was made in the English tradition and other cheeses from the Old Country, such as brie, ricotta, Limburger, mozzarella, feta, and gouda, were made as well. Two of the three cheeses invented in America, brick and Colby, were invented in the 1870s. Today, there are over 200 cheese-making plants in Wisconsin alone. Wisconsin is also the number-one dairy-producing state in the country, producing milk, butter, and excellent domestic cheese.

Germans and Bohemians who immigrated to the region brought the art and the love of beer. The extensive prairies and farmlands of the Central Plains were perfect for growing wheat, oats, barley, rye, and corn, which are the grains used to produce beer. The region's major trade areas of St. Louis, Milwaukee, Chicago, Cincinnati, St. Paul, and Kansas City became home to America's first breweries. By the end of the nineteenth century, thousands of breweries had sprung up and begun to produce unique beer products. The great beer industry went into decline during Prohibition, which began in 1920. In 1933, when Prohibition ended, only about 400 of the original breweries were able to reopen for business. At one point, Milwaukee, Wisconsin, was dubbed "the city of suds" due to its dozens of breweries. Although many of the original brewers no longer operate in Milwaukee, residents still enjoy the traditions and culture that beer brewing left behind.

Another popular product made from grain grown in the Central Plains is cereal. Ready-to-eat cereal was invented by Dr. John Harvey Kellogg of Battle Creek, Michigan, in 1894. While experimenting with foods in the sanitarium where he worked, he made a ready-to-eat cereal from wheat that had been shredded. He tried the same process with corn and from that created Corn Flakes. Today, most ready-to-eat cereals are fortified with vitamins and minerals to make them more nutritious than their predecessors.

German immigrants also brought to the region their expertise in sausage making. Not only were they experts in sausage production, they were inventive as well. The German farmers of the Central Plains region originated sausage varieties such as knackwurst, bratwurst, liverwurst, Mettwurst, and Thuringer, which are all still popular products today. The Germans also built smokehouses to smoke hams, bacon, and fish from the region's lakes and rivers. Today, it is difficult to tell where German ingredients and cooking styles leave off and American ones begin. Over the years, the styles have blended and merged.

By the mid-1800s railroads had connected the East with the West and the Central Plains became a major hub for connections to each coast. Cities like Kansas City, Chicago, and St. Louis played an important role in cross-country commerce. During this time, Chicago became the leader in the transportation of cattle to the East Coast. Men like Adolphus Swift and George A. Hormel developed methods of keeping food refrigerated in rail cars so that quality and sanitary conditions could be maintained during the long trip. Chicago and Kansas City became known as the "home of meat and potatoes." Great steaks and other cuts of beef soon became associated with these cities of the Central Plains. The seared steak with Maytag blue cheese (see page 260) is one such example.

Chicago's stockyards emerged in the late 1800s. With them came a huge migration of newly freed slaves from the South as well as Irish, Italian, and Polish immigrants seeking new opportunities in the big cities of the Central Plains. Small ethnic communities sprang up throughout cities like Chicago, providing a great deal of ethnic and cultural diversity. Even though the stockyards are no longer there, ethnic neighborhoods still exist within Chicago. Pilsen, known for its Hispanic culture; Andersonville, for its Swedish heritage; the area around Eighteenth Street and Wentworth, for its Asian culture; and Devon Avenue, home to Jewish, Pakistani, Indian, and Arab cultures, all remain vital communities of rich cultural diversity. Little Ukraine is an area dominated by people of Russian descent; Hyde Park on the south and west sides of Chicago is the home of many African Americans and great soul food. An Italian community exists around Taylor Street on the southwest side and there is an Irish community farther south in an area known as Bridgeport. The Greeks settled in Greek Town, located near the West Loop. Today, more Poles live in Chicago than in Warsaw, the capital of Poland.

All these cultures have contributed to the cuisine found in Chicago today. The diverse and rich food network in Chicago allows one, on any given day, to sample an array of foods ranging from Swedish pancakes to pirogi, Italian ice to corned beef and cabbage. Borscht, spanikopita, barbecue, whitefish, sausage, tacos, and dim sum are all available, along with local beer made at Goose Island Brewery on Chicago's north side. This ethnic and cultural diversity has allowed Chicago to grow into one of America's great food cities.

Some of the greatest chefs in the world reside and cook in Chicago. Their ranks include Charlie Trotter, Rick Bayless, Rick Tramonto, Gail Gand, Michael Foley, Jean Joho, Jean Banchet, and Arun Sampavat, just to name a few. Restaurateur Richard Melman's company Lettuce Entertain You has become a restaurant empire renowned from coast to coast.

These famous chefs and restaurateurs have helped support today's market farmers, who grow and sell crops only for urban farm markets and restaurants featuring high-quality ingredients. These farmers usually do not have contracts with supermarkets or food processors. They typically follow the principle of "farm to table," indicating that, at the very most, the products are less than a day off the vine or out of the ground from when they are sold. These market farmers, who do not use insecticides or pesticides as growing aids, are said to produce organic products.

The lands, waters, and cultural diversity of the Central Plains have added a wealth of culinary knowledge and culture to what we know today as American regional cooking.

Typical Central Plains Ingredients and Dishes

All-Purpose Flour: Red winter wheat flour with a protein level of 11–12 percent. Hudson Cream Flour from Kansas is one of the best-recognized brands of high-quality all-purpose flour. The patented process requires sifting at least 12 times, with the last sifting through fine silk. Of 100 pounds of wheat kernels, Hudson Cream accepts only 62 pounds for use in its all-purpose flour. The rest is used for animal feed.

Bigos: A rich and heartily flavored Polish hunter's stew made from fresh pork, bacon, kielbasa sausage, mushrooms, and sauerkraut. The preparation time for this dish can take up to three days if the recipe is followed according to tradition.

Black Walnut: Grown in Missouri, black walnuts are about the same size as the more common English walnut but have a dark shell with well-defined ridges. The nutmeat is quite oily and possesses an earthy, pungent taste different from the sweet flavor of the English variety. Black walnuts are more frequently used as a cooking ingredient than as a snack nut because the flavors permeate any recipe in which they are used as an ingredient. Due to the popularity and rarity of hardwood made from black walnut trees, these nuts are becoming hard to find and very expensive.

Brick Cheese: One of three cheeses invented in America. Swiss-born John Jossi invented brick cheese in the late 1870s. His recipe begins the same as German Limburger cheese but is altered by lowering the moisture content of the curds by pressing them between two bricks—hence the name. The results are much milder in flavor than brick cheese's German counterpart, with a much less offensive smell. These attributes caused it to be nicknamed "married man's Limburger."

Cheddar Cheese: The most popular cheese in America. Wisconsin devotes about half its annual cheese production to the cheddar variety. Cheddar comes in two colors and many flavors. Americans west of the Mississippi River seem to prefer their cheddar an orange color, made by adding an extract of the annato seed to the milk during production, while Americans east of the Mississippi prefer cheddar white, or uncolored. The flavors are identical. Flavor variations of cheddar cheese are usually based on how long the cheese is aged. Mild cheddar is aged less than four months; aging between four and ten months creates a medium-sharp flavor; and more than ten months results in a sharp flavor. The color of the wax found on cheddar denotes its age—clear wax for mild cheddar, red wax for medium-sharp, and black wax for sharp.

Corn: A crop for over 5000 years in the Western Hemisphere, corn was the bedrock on which ancient civilizations, such as the Maya and the Inca, were built. Today, the greatest amount of corn is grown in the Central Plains. Over 85 percent of all corn is called *dent* *corn* and is used primarily to feed animals and livestock, making it an important American commodity. The remaining corn harvested in the Central Plains is called *hidden corn* and is used to make products such as ethanol, corn syrup, corn oil, cough drops, and toothpaste. Corn is a very popular American staple, with over 3 pounds of shucked corn consumed each year per person.

Corn Dog: A snack food that became popular at state fairs throughout the Central Plains. It is a hot dog on a stick, dipped in a thick cornmeal batter and deep-fried. It is usually eaten off the stick with yellow mustard.

Fish Boil: A Scandinavian feast that is an annual event in Door County, Wisconsin. A huge cauldron kettle of water is brought to boil over an outdoor fire. Whitefish, potatoes, onions, and lots of salt are the main ingredients. The large amount of salt allows the impurities in the broth to rise to the surface and overflow into the fire.

Holupka: A Russian term for the stuffed cabbage rolls that are commonly found in the Little Ukraine neighborhood of Northwest Chicago.

Honey: A major product of the Central Plains, primarily North and South Dakota, which produce in excess of 60 million pounds of honey each year. The most popular types are clover and blossom, which are light in color and mildly sweet in flavor. Wildflower honey is much darker than and not as sweet as clover honey. Wildflower honey is excellent for cooking, as it provides dishes a distinct honey flavor without adding extra sweetness. Clover honey should be used when sweetness is a desired outcome in a recipe.

Jerusalem Artichoke: The bulb of the perennial sunflower plant, also referred to as *sunchoke*. The Spanish conquistadors first brought this American food to Europe, where the French popularized it as a vegetable. Oddly enough, the Jerusalem artichoke is not nearly as popular in the United States as it is in Europe. This vegetable needs to be cooked before being eaten to avoid digestive gas. Jerusalem artichokes are sometimes sliced and served in salads.

Kielbasa: A Polish type of cured sausage with garlic flavoring, usually cooked by boiling or grilling. Today, kielbasa sausage is so common that it is hardly considered an ethnic food.

Kringle: An oval-shaped coffeecake with a rich, buttery flavor. The recipe is Danish in heritage and was passed down through the generations from Scandinavians who settled in the Wisconsin area.

Kutia: A sweet pudding made from wheat for the traditional meatless Polish meal served on Christmas Eve. Folklore tells us that if a spoonful of kutia flung at the ceiling sticks, the family's harvest and luck will be good in the coming year.

Lefse: A flat bread of Norwegian origin made by the farm women of Western Minnesota. The dough, which contains potatoes, is rolled extremely thin with a special rolling pin called a *lefse roller*. The bread is cooked on a griddle top and served with butter and cinnamon sugar.

Lutefisk: A Scandinavian style of prepared fresh cod. To prepare lutefisk, cod fillets are soaked in a lye solution made with the ashes of birch wood. The cod is then air-dried. This method of preserving fish is somewhat primitive but very effective. Fish preserved in this manner can remain unspoiled for years in regions with cold climates.

Maytag Blue Cheese: The signature product of a family-owned cheese-making business in Iowa that began operations in 1941. The method adopted by the Maytag family for making blue cheese was patented by a scientist at Iowa State University and used the milk from Holstein cows. Unlike most blue cheeses, Maytag blue cheese is aged five months, giving it a creamy and tangy flavor considered by many cheese experts to rival the famous Italian Gorgonzola and French Roquefort cheeses. Maytag blue cheese is noted as the first artisan cheese in America. Today, many artisan cheese-makers meet the demand by Americans for the quality and character of old-fashioned foods.

Morel: A tan to black fungus with a cone-shaped, umbrella-capped stem that grows primarily in the deep-wooded forests of Michigan. Similar to the French and Italian truffles, morels are found growing out of the roots of oak, elm, and ash trees, covered by decaying leaves. Their growing patterns are inconsistent and unpredictable, making them scarce as well as expensive. Typically, the fresh morel season lasts but a few short weeks. Most locals familiar with morels gladly share their recipes—but never their secret about where the prized mushrooms can be located.

Muskellunge: Sometimes referred to as *muskie*, the largest of the pike fish. Muskellunge have been known to grow as large as 70 pounds (31.8kg). They have very sharp teeth and are vicious fighters, making them a favorite among anglers.

Oblaten: The first course of the traditional meatless Polish meal served on Christmas Eve. Oblaten, also referred to as the *holy wafer*, is a thin bread elaborately stamped prior to baking.

Paczki: A filled doughnut of Polish heritage, usually served during Lent. Paczki are traditionally filled with raspberry preserves, but nowadays they are made with a variety of fruit fillings.

Persimmon: A Native American fruit that grows in Southern Indiana, Illinois, and Missouri. These persimmons are much smaller than the more common Asian variety. The American variety of persimmon is about the size of a golf ball and somewhat squat in shape. It has a vibrant orange color and a deep green crown. The flavor is sweet and chalky.

Pike: A freshwater fish. There are six species, many of which are found in the rivers and lakes in the Central Plains. The largest of the pike is the muskie or muskellunge. The most common is the Great Northern pike, usually weighing between 4 and 10 pounds (1.8 and 4.5kg).

Pirogi: A filled dumpling of Polish heritage. The flour dough of traditional pirogi is usually filled with ground, seasoned pork, sauerkraut, farmer's or cottage cheese, or sweet fruit, such as cherries or apples. Pirogis are typically fried in bacon fat or oil.

Popcorn: A popular snack food consumed by Americans—over 14 gallons (52.9L) per person per year. Most popcorn is produced in the state of Indiana. Charles Cretors of Chicago invented the first machine that could make enough popcorn to make it a viable street concession. Two other Chicagoans, Frederick and Louis Ruckheim, sweetened the popcorn with molasses, added peanuts, and put a small toy in each package of popcorn. We know this product today as Cracker Jack. Gourmet popcorn came to be in the 1960s, when Orville Redenbacher of Indiana trademarked a hybrid variety of popcorn that was lighter and fluffier than normal popcorn as well as leaving virtually no kernels unpopped after cooking. Popcorn expands to 44 times its original volume when cooked.

Processed Cheese: A cheese product made by milling cheddar cheese into shreds and cooking it. The cheese is then colored and shaped in a mold that resembles a block of cheese. The most common processed cheese is called *American cheese* and was invented by James L. Kraft in the early 1900s. This cheese became quite popular in World War I, when it was used extensively as a food for soldiers. Kraft improved the original product twice, first by slicing the block prior to packaging and then again in 1965, when individually wrapped slices were first marketed. Although American cheese is somewhat bland and predictable in taste, it is the most commonly consumed cheese product in America.

Rullepolse: A type of cured, spiced, and pressed beef flank made by the Danish descendants of Elk Horn, Iowa, one of the few places in the United States where this dish can be found.

Sausage: The Central Plains are considered the home of sausage in the United States. The state of Illinois produces and butchers the most hogs, so it is logical, given the region's heavy influence by Danish, Bavarian, and Scandinavian immigrants, that sausage making is popular there. Some of the most famous sausages in America have German and Polish heritage. Sheboygan bratwurst, Usingers Thuringer sausage, Polish sausage, kielbasa, knackwurst, beerwurst, and liverwurst are just a few famous recipes for sausage that have made their mark in the Central Plains.

Sorghum: A canelike grass plant, originally from Africa, that grows well in the Central Plains. A sweet, dark syrup is extracted from the plant and used in a fashion similar to molasses or honey. The use of sorghum as a sweetener dates back to the days of the pioneers.

Sunflower: A perennial plant that dates as far back as 3000 B.C. It was a major crop in the

Central Plains for Native Americans as well as for the European settlers in the region. Sunflower seeds grown for oil are solid black in color. Sunflower seeds grown for eating are striped. Sunflowers also produce a bulb that is used as a vegetable (see *Jerusalem Artichoke*). Fargo, North Dakota, is known as the sunflower capital of the United States.

Tart Cherry: Also known as the *transparent* or *pie cherry*. Tart cherries are grown primarily on the shores of Northern Michigan. The variety, previously called the *Montmorency cherry*, was brought to the United States about 100 years ago and is the only tart cherry produced here today. These cherries are light and clear but so sour they are hard to eat right from the tree. Once combined with sugar, they make excellent pies, cobblers, and preserves.

Walleye: Walleye pike is not a pike at all, but a perch. It is sometimes referred to in the foodservice industry as *yellow* or *blue pike*. Walleye is an excellent mild-tasting fish with a delicate flesh that is bright white in color.

Waterfowl: So many waterfowl fly over the Central Plains in the fall that it is sometimes called "flyover country." A large variety of ducks and geese migrate south for the winter from Canada and stop to rest and eat in the Central Plains. Duck and geese are a large part of the diet for the residents of the Central Plains.

Wheat: A grain brought to America by the European colonists. However, due to growing difficulties, wheat was not a major crop until the end of the nineteenth century, when Turkey Red Winter Wheat began to grow well in the Central Plains. The growth and development of wheat crops in the Central Plains are attributed to Mennonite farmers from the Ukraine, who, with land provided from the Santa Fe Railroad in 1875, began farming along the rail lines in Kansas. Today, Kansas alone produces enough wheat in one year to make 30 billion loaves of bread and grows over 200 varieties of red winter wheat. In the Dakotas and parts of Oklahoma, durum, a spring wheat and common crop, is used to make semolina flour for pasta.

Wheatberry: The whole kernel produced by the wheat plant. Wheatberries are usually served in salads, made into cereal, or toasted and ground and used as a coating or recipe ingredient.

Wheat Flour: A starch milled from the whole kernel of the wheat plant. Wheat flour comes in two varieties—that made from winter wheat, like all-purpose flour, and that made from spring wheat, like semolina. Wheat flour is used primarily for making bread but has a variety of additional uses and purposes. The many types of wheat flour are distinguished based on protein content. Bread flour has the highest protein content, referred to as the *gluten strength*, and cake flour has the lowest protein content.

Wild Rice: The long, thin brown grain we know in the United States as wild rice is not really rice at all. The grains are the seeds of an aquatic plant that commonly grows in the lakes of

Wisconsin and Minnesota. These seeds were originally harvested by the Ojibway and Chippewa tribes. The European settlers and immigrants who stayed in this region quickly adopted wild rice into their diet. This is the only cereal grain indigenous to North America and is usually harvested for about two weeks in August. California is also a major producer of wild rice.

Yellow Perch: A species of freshwater fish from the lakes and rivers of the Central Plains. Yellow perch is known for its especially sweet-tasting flesh. However, it is not readily available due to a ban recently imposed to protect the species from extinction.

Sample Menus from the Cuisine of the Central Plains

MENU ONE

Wisconsin Cheese and Beer Soup

Planked Whitefish with Horseradish Crust and Red Cabbage Braised in Cider and Beer

Morel and Goat Cheese Tart with Red Bell Pepper Coulis

Roast Pork Loin with Apple and Corn Bread Stuffing and Brandy Sauce ·

Brussels Sprouts with Mushrooms

MENU TWO

Wheatberry and Toasted Sunflower Seed Salad

Pan-Seared Steak with Maytag Blue Cheese

Wild Rice with Black Walnuts

Cheddar Potato Fries

MENU THREE

Clear Chicken Soup with Sage Dumplings

Beet and Apple Salad with Horseradish Vinaigrette

Deep-Dish Chicken and Sausage Pie with Buttermilk Biscuits · Prairie Sunchoke Gratin

· Macaroni and Cheese

Wisconsin Cheese and Beer Soup

YIELD: 6 PORTIONS · PORTION SIZE: 10 OUNCES

4 ounces (120g) butter

2 ounces (60g) onion, cut into small dice

1 ounce (30g) celery, cut into small dice

1 ounce (30g) red bell peppers, cut into small dice

4 ounces (120g) all-purpose flour

2 teaspoons (10g) dry mustard

1 pinch paprika

½ teaspoon (2g) thyme, ground

2 tablespoons (30ml) Worcestershire sauce

12 fluid ounces (360ml) beer or lager

32 fluid ounces (960ml) white chicken stock, prepared (see page 517)

16 fluid ounces (480ml) milk

16 ounces (480g) kielbasa or smoked sausage, cooked

salt, to taste

white pepper, ground, to taste

16 ounces (480g) Wisconsin sharp cheddar cheese, grated

2 ounces (60g) green onions, chopped

CHEF TIPS *When adding cheese to a hot liquid, make sure the liquid is between 140°F (60°C) and 185°F (85°C). If the temperature of the liquid is too hot, the cheese will not melt but curdle.*

Wisconsin cheese and beer soup is traditionally served with a warm soft pretzel.

Melt the butter over medium heat. Add the onions, celery, and peppers and sweat for 5 minutes or until the onions are translucent.

Add the flour and stir to make a roux. Cook for 1 minute over medium heat.

Add the seasonings, Worcestershire sauce, and beer, stirring constantly. Cook for an additional 1 minute.

Blend the chicken stock into the roux, stirring constantly. Bring the soup back to a boil and simmer for 30 minutes. Do not allow the simmering soup to fall below 140°F (60°C).

Heat the milk in a separate saucepot and add to the soup.

Cut the smoked sausage on the bias into slices ¼ inch (.64cm) thick. Add to the soup.

Cook over medium heat for 10 minutes.

Season to taste with salt and white pepper.

Remove from the heat and allow the temperature of the soup to drop below 185°F (85°C). Stir in the cheese.

Stir constantly until the cheese is melted.

SERVING/HOLDING

Serve the soup in hot bowls or soup plates. Garnish each portion with chopped green onions. Additional grated cheddar can also be used as a garnish if desired.

Hold the soup at 140°F (60°C) or higher.

COOLING/STORING

Pour the remaining soup into small metal containers.

Cool the soup from 140°F (60°C) to 70°F (21.1°C) or lower within 2 hours. Cool from 70°F (21.1°C) to 41°F (5°C) within an additional 4 hours for a total cooling time of 6 hours or less.

Cover the soup; label, date, and store under refrigeration at 41°F (5°C) or lower.

Clear Chicken Soup with Sage Dumplings

YIELD: 6 PORTIONS · PORTION SIZE: 10 OUNCES

8 ounces (240g) dark chicken meat

6 egg whites, beaten

4 ounces (120g) onion, chopped

2 ounces (60g) carrot, chopped

2 ounces (60g) celery, chopped

1 bay leaf

1 sprig thyme

2 teaspoons (10g) kosher salt

1 teaspoon (5g) white pepper, ground

1 teaspoon (5g) poultry seasoning

1 tablespoon (15ml) lemon juice

72 fluid ounces (2.2L) white chicken stock, prepared (see page 517)

2 ounces (60g) carrots, cut into brunoise

2 ounces (60g) celery, cut into brunoise

12 sage dumplings (recipe follows)

CHEF TIPS *If the raft from the soup breaks up or the soup is too cloudy, beat 4–5 egg whites together with 1 cup crushed ice. Temper the hot liquid into the egg white mixture and slowly return the soup to a simmer. A second raft should form, reclarifying the soup.*

Grind the chicken meat in a food processor until smooth. Reserve under refrigeration at 41°F (5°C) or lower until needed.

Beat the egg whites with a whisk until they are frothy. Combine the chicken meat, onion, carrot, and celery with the egg whites.

Mix in the seasonings and lemon juice.

Place 64 fluid ounces (1.9L) of the cold chicken stock in a small stockpot and blend in the meat mixture.

Slowly bring the liquid to a boil, stirring the bottom occasionally. Once the liquid comes to a boil, immediately reduce the heat and simmer at 185°F (85°C). A raft will soon form on the surface. Once the raft forms and appears solid, make a small hole in it to allow steam to escape. *Do not stir the soup from this point on.*

Simmer the soup for 1 hour. Do not allow the simmering soup to fall below 140°F (60°C).

While the soup is simmering, blanch the brunoise carrots and celery in the remaining chicken stock. Hold the vegetables at 140°F (60°C) or higher until needed. Do not add this stock to the soup, as it will make the soup cloudy.

Strain the soup through a conical strainer laced with a double mesh of rinsed cheesecloth. Be careful not to break the raft when ladling the liquid out of the stockpot. Adjust the seasoning to taste with salt and white pepper.

SERVING/HOLDING

Carefully ladle the soup into hot soup cups. Garnish each portion with 2 sage dumplings and some of the reserved brunoise carrots and celery.

Hold the soup at 140°F (60°C) or above.

COOLING/STORING

Pour the remaining soup into small metal containers.

Cool the soup from 140°F (60°C) to 70°F (21.1°C) or lower within 2 hours. Cool from 70°F (21.1°C) to 41°F (5°C) within an additional 4 hours for a total cooling time of 6 hours or less.

Cover the soup; label, date, and store under refrigeration at 41°F (5°C) or lower.

SAGE DUMPLINGS

YIELD: 6 PORTIONS · PORTION SIZE: 2 DUMPLINGS

2 ounces (60g) salt pork, cut into small dice

2 ounces (60g) onion, cut into small dice

16 ounces (480g) French bread, cubed

2 fluid ounces (60ml) milk

3 large eggs, beaten

1 tablespoon (15g) sage, cut into chiffonade

salt, to taste

white pepper, ground, to taste

5½ ounces (165g) all-purpose flour

64 fluid ounces (1.9L) white chicken stock, prepared (see page 517)

Cook the salt pork in a pan or skillet over medium heat until it is brown and the fat is completely rendered. Pour off all the fat except for 1 tablespoon.

Add the onions to the salt pork and sauté in the salt pork fat over medium-high heat until they are translucent.

Add the bread cubes and continue to cook for approximately 3–5 minutes or until they are soft.

Add the milk, beaten eggs, and sage.

Season to taste with salt and white pepper.

Gradually add the flour until the mixture thickens.

Cool the dumpling mixture for 10 minutes.

Form balls with a 2-inch (5cm) diameter.

Bring the chicken stock to a boil and reduce the heat to a simmer.

Cook the dumplings in the simmering chicken stock until firm to the touch. Do not allow the simmering stock to fall below 140°F (60°C).

Remove the dumplings from the stock, using a spider or slotted spoon.

SERVING/HOLDING

Hold the dumplings at 140°F (60°C) or higher until needed.

COOLING/STORING

Cool the dumplings from 140°F (60°C) to 70°F (21.1°C) or lower within 2 hours. Cool from 70°F (21.1°C) to 41°F (5°C) within an additional 4 hours for a total cooling time of 6 hours or less.

Cover the dumplings; label, date, and store under refrigeration at 41°F (5°C) or lower.

Morel and Goat Cheese Tart with Red Bell Pepper Coulis

YIELD: 6 PORTIONS · PORTION SIZE: 8 OUNCES

TART SHELLS

16 ounces (480ml) all-purpose flour

1 teaspoon (5g) salt

1 teaspoon (5g) thyme, minced

½ cup (120g) butter or shortening

1 tablespoon (15ml) water

FILLING

4 ounces (120g) leeks (white part only), cut into small dice

2½ ounces (75g) shallot, minced

2 fluid ounces (60ml) olive oil

2 fluid ounces (60ml) dry sherry

1 tablespoon (15ml) garlic, minced

10 ounces (300g) fresh morels, trimmed or 2 ounces (60g) dried morels

½ teaspoon (2g) thyme, chopped

salt, to taste

black pepper, ground, to taste

16 fluid ounces (480ml) heavy cream

4 large eggs, beaten

½ teaspoon (2g) nutmeg, ground

6 ounces (180g) goat cheese, crumbled

18 fluid ounces (540ml) roasted red bell pepper coulis (recipe follows)

6 sprigs thyme

CHEF TIPS *If fresh morel mushrooms are unavailable or too expensive, dried morels can be substituted. The dried mushrooms need to be reconstituted prior to using. Boil a small pot of water, add the dried mushrooms, cover, and remove from the heat. Steep the mushrooms 4–5 minutes and remove from the hot water. Generally, the mushrooms expand to 5 times their dried weight, so to get 10 ounces (283g) of reconstituted mushrooms, use just 2 ounces (57g) of dried. The water that the mushrooms steep in is flavorful and can be used in a variety of soups and sauces. In addition, dried forest mushroom mix is available at a very reasonable cost.*

Prepare the tart shells by sifting the dry ingredients together into a bowl.

Blend or cut the butter or shortening into the flour by rubbing the ingredients lightly between the fingers to incorporate the fat into the flour. Continue to rub until the dough resembles a course cornmeal.

Stir in the water with a fork, lifting and combining until the dough is soft.

Gather the dough together with your hands and knead lightly on a clean surface dusted with flour until the dough is no longer sticky.

Roll the dough with a rolling pin to ¼ inch (.64cm) thick.

Dip a 5-inch (127cm) round cutter in flour and cut rounds from the sheet of dough.

Press the rounds of dough into 4-inch (100cm) tart molds

Reserve the tart shells under refrigeration at 41°F (5°C) or lower until needed.

Sauté the leeks and shallots in the olive oil over high heat. When the onions begin to brown, deglaze with a little sherry and stir briefly. Continue this process until the onions caramelize and are thoroughly browned. Do not stir too frequently, as the onions will sweat rather than caramelize.

Add the garlic and cook an additional 1 minute.

Wash the morels at least 5–6 times with fresh water each time or until all the dirt is rinsed away. Trim the stems and dice the morels into ¼-inch (.64cm) pieces.

Add the morels to the onions with the remaining sherry and thyme. Reduce the liquid over medium-high heat until almost dry.

Season the mixture to taste with salt and black pepper.

Mix the heavy cream, eggs, and nutmeg together in a bowl. Add the morel mixture and mix until all ingredients are incorporated.

Carefully ladle the mixture evenly into the reserved tart shells.

Sprinkle goat cheese evenly on top of each tart.

Bake the tarts on a sheet pan on the bottom rack of a preheated 400°F (204.4°C) oven for 5 minutes.

Reduce the heat to 325°F (162.8°C). Move the tarts to the middle of the oven and bake for 10–15 minutes or until they are set and reach a minimum internal temperature of 145°F (62.8°C) for at least 15 seconds.

Let the tarts rest at room temperature at least 10 minutes before serving.

SERVING/HOLDING

Serve each morel tart on a hot plate over a bed of approximately 3 fluid ounces (90ml) roasted red bell pepper coulis. The tart can be served whole or cut into smaller pieces. Garnish each tart with a sprig of fresh thyme.

Hold the morel tarts at 140°F (60°C) or higher.

COOLING/STORING

Cool the tarts from 140°F (60°C) to 70°F (21.1°C) or lower within 2 hours. Cool from 70°F (21.1°C) to 41°F (5°C) within an additional 4 hours for a total cooling time of 6 hours or less.

Cover the tarts; label, date, and store under refrigeration at 41°F (5°C) or lower.

RED BELL PEPPER COULIS

YIELD: 6 PORTIONS · PORTION SIZE: 3 OUNCES

30 ounces (900g) red bell peppers, stemmed and seeded

4 ounces (120g) shallots, peeled

2 cloves garlic, peeled

1 fluid ounce (30ml) olive oil

½ teaspoon (2g) thyme, chopped

2 teaspoons (10g) sugar

4 fluid ounces (120ml) heavy cream

salt, to taste

white pepper, ground, to taste

CHEF TIPS *When a cornstarch slurry is added to the sauce after bringing it to a boil, the natural liquid is not as prone to separate from the coulis as it starts to cool on the plate. However, the slurry does add a slightly starchy flavor to the coulis.*

Roast the red bell peppers, shallots, and garlic cloves in a 350°F (176.7°C) oven for approximately 35 minutes or until the skin of the red peppers begins to loosen and bubble.

Remove from the oven and peel the red peppers. Discard the skin.

Place the red peppers, garlic, shallots, and oil in a food processor or blender and purée.

Add the thyme and sugar.

Continue to purée until smooth.

Place the purée in a small saucepot, blend in the heavy cream, and bring to a boil. Turn the heat down to a simmer and season to taste with salt and white pepper.

SERVING/HOLDING

Hold the sauce at 140°F (60°C) or higher until needed.

COOLING/STORING

Cool the sauce from 140°F (60°C) to 70°F (21.1°C) or lower within 2 hours. Cool from 70°F (21.1°C) to 41°F (5°C) within an additional 4 hours for a total cooling time of 6 hours or less.

Cover the sauce; label, date, and store under refrigeration at 41°F (5°C) or lower.

Planked Whitefish with Horseradish Crust and Red Cabbage Braised in Cider and Beer

YIELD: 6 PORTIONS · PORTION SIZE: 8 OUNCES

6 3 x 6 x ½-inch (1.27cm) cedar planks

2 fluid ounces (60ml) corn oil

32 ounces (960g) or 6 whitefish, cut into 5-ounce (150g) fillets, skinned and boned

salt, to taste

black pepper, ground, to taste

zest and juice of one orange

3 tablespoons (45ml) horseradish

8 ounces (240g) butter

3½ ounces (105g) dill, chopped

3½ ounces (105g) breadcrumbs

18 ounces (540g) red cabbage braised in cider and beer (recipe follows)

Soak the cedar planks in water for at least 2 hours before proceeding.

COOKING

Remove the planks and brush with the corn oil.

Season the fillets with salt and pepper and place each of them on a cedar plank.

Mix the orange juice, orange zest, horseradish, butter, dill, and breadcrumbs together with the paddle attachment of a mixer. When thoroughly combined, remove from the mixer. Spread approximately 2 ounces (60g) of the mixture on each whitefish fillet.

Bake the fillets for approximately 10–15 minutes in a preheated 350°F (176.7°C) oven or until they are done and reach a minimum internal temperature of 145°F (62.8°C) for at least 15 seconds.

CHEF TIPS *Planking is a method of cooking fish that the settlers of the region learned from the Native Americans. Fish is tied to large pieces of driftwood and placed vertically next to a fire, where they cook slowly until done. Today, planking is accomplished by placing a fish fillet on a soaked plank of wood—usually cedar, which gives off a tasty and unique flavor. The fillet is then cooked, plank and all, on a grill over a fire or even by baking in an oven.*

The cedar planks used in this preparation are easy to find at a local building supply store. Cedar roof shingles are usually smooth on one side and the perfect shape for a fish fillet of this size. Make sure to purchase the untreated variety, as some shingles come with a chemical fire retardant that leaves an unpleasant aftertaste on the fish. The shingles are inexpensive. It is recommended, for sanitary reasons, that they not be reused. The whitefish called for in this Central Plains recipe can be walleye, pike, or yellow perch. However, the procedure described yields excellent results with any type of round fish or large flatfish, such as halibut and turbot. Small flatfish, like sole and flounder, should be avoided, as they are too delicate and tend to absorb too much flavor from the wooden planks.

Serve the whitefish fillets on hot plates on a small mound of approximately 3 ounces (85g) red cabbage braised in cider and beer.

 Hold the whitefish and cabbage at 140°F (60°C) or higher.

COOLING/STORING

 Cool the whitefish and cabbage from 140°F (60°C) to 70°F (21.1°C) or lower within 2 hours. Cool from 70°F (21.1°C) to 41°F (5°C) within an additional 4 hours for a total cooling time of 6 hours or less.

Cover the whitefish and cabbage; label, date, and store under refrigeration at 41°F (5°C) or lower.

RED CABBAGE BRAISED IN CIDER AND BEER

YIELD: 6 PORTIONS · PORTION SIZE: 3 OUNCES

4 ounces (120g) bacon, diced

4 ounces (120g) butter

16 ounces (480g) onions, thinly sliced

32 ounces (960g) red cabbage, shredded

8½ ounces (255g) pippin apples, cored and sliced

1 tablespoon (15g) sugar

2 fluid ounces (60ml) red wine vinegar

8 fluid ounces (240ml) white chicken stock, prepared (see page 517)

1 teaspoon (5g) caraway seeds

6 fluid ounces (180ml) dark beer

4 fluid ounces (120ml) apple cider

1 tablespoon (15g) cornstarch

salt, to taste

black pepper, ground, to taste

CHEF TIPS *Granny Smith apples can be substituted for the pippin apples if they are not available.*

Sauté the bacon in a sautoir pan or skillet over medium-high heat until it is crisp.

Add the butter and melt. Add the onions and sauté for about five minutes or until they are translucent.

Add the red cabbage and continue to cook, stirring frequently, for another 3 minutes.

Add the rest of the ingredients, except for the cornstarch and seasonings. Bring to a boil and turn the heat down to a simmer.

Cover and simmer for approximately 30 minutes or until the cabbage is soft and tender. Do not allow the simmering cabbage to fall below 140°F (60°C).

Make a slurry by mixing the cornstarch with a small amount of water. Blend the slurry into the braising liquid and bring to a boil. Reduce the heat to a simmer.

Season to taste with salt and black pepper.

SERVING/HOLDING

Hold the cabbage at 140°F (60°C) or higher.

COOLING/STORING

Cool the cabbage from 140°F (60°C) to 70°F (21.1°C) or lower within 2 hours. Cool from 70°F (21.1°C) to 41°F (5°C) within an additional 4 hours for a total cooling time of 6 hours or less.

Cover the cabbage; label, date, and store under refrigeration at 41°F (5°C) or lower.

Beet and Apple Salad with Horseradish Vinaigrette

YIELD: 6 PORTIONS · PORTION SIZE: 8 OUNCES

40 ounces (1.2kg) large beets, unpeeled

4 fluid ounces (120ml) red wine vinegar

2 ounces (60g) sugar

32 fluid ounces (960ml) water

8½ ounces (255g) green apples, cored

DRESSING

1 tablespoon (15g) brown or grain mustard

2 tablespoons (30ml) horseradish

2 fluid ounces (60ml) raspberry vinegar

6 fluid ounces (180ml) olive oil

salt, to taste

black pepper, to taste

1½ ounces (45g) green onions, sliced

6 leaves butter lettuce

Cook the beets in the red wine vinegar, sugar, and water until tender.

Shock the cooked beets in an ice-water bath and peel.

Julienne the beets and the apples and reserve under refrigeration at 41°F (5°C) or lower until needed.

Combine the mustard, horseradish, and raspberry vinegar and place in a food processor or blender. Slowly drizzle in the oil while the machine is running. Process until the dressing emulsifies.

Season to taste with salt and black pepper.

Toss the reserved beet and apple mixture and the green onions with the dressing.

SERVING/HOLDING

Serve approximately 8 ounces (240g) of the salad on each cold plate over a crisp lettuce leaf.

Hold the beet and apple salad under refrigeration at 41°F (5°C) or lower.

Cover the salad and dressing; label, date, and store under refrigeration at 41°F (5°C) or lower.

Wheatberry and Toasted Sunflower Seed Salad

YIELD: 6 PORTIONS · PORTION SIZE: 8 OUNCES

6 ounces (180g) wheatberries

8 ounces (240g) Israeli couscous

2¼ ounces (68g) sunflower seeds

3½ ounces (105g) green onions, sliced

1½ ounces (45g) red bell peppers, cut into brunoise

2 ounces (60g) yellow crookneck squash, cut into brunoise

2 ounces (60g) zucchini, cut into brunoise

5½ ounces (165g) cucumber, peeled and seeded, cut into brunoise

1 teaspoon (5g) garlic, minced

2 tablespoons (30g) Italian parsley, chopped

DRESSING

3 fluid ounces (90ml) champagne vinegar

1 tablespoon (15g) Dijon mustard

1 teaspoon (5g) dill, chopped

2 fluid ounces (60ml) lemon juice

zest from 1 lemon

2 ounces (60ml) olive oil

8 ounces (240g) yogurt

6 leaves red leaf lettuce

Cook the wheatberries and couscous in separate saucepots of boiling water until tender. Drain.

Cool the wheatberries and couscous from 140°F (60°C) to 70°F (21.1°C) or lower within 2 hours. Cool from 70°F (21.1°C) to 41°F (5°C) within an additional 4 hours for a total cooling time of 6 hours or less.

Reserve under refrigeration at 41°F (5°C) or lower until needed.

Toast the sunflower seeds on a sheet pan in a preheated 375°C (190.6°C) oven for approximately 10–12 minutes. Reserve until needed.

Combine the wheatberries, toasted sunflower seeds, couscous, vegetables, garlic, and parsley in a large bowl.

Prepare the dressing by combining the remaining ingredients, except lettuce, in a separate bowl. Whisk vigorously until completely blended.

SERVING/HOLDING

Mix enough of the dressing into the wheatberry and vegetable mixture to bind it. Mix gently until all the ingredients are thoroughly coated.

Place a lettuce leaf on each cold plate.

Carefully spoon approximately 8 ounces (240g) of the salad mixture on top of each lettuce leaf.

Hold under refrigeration at 41°F (5°C) or lower.

COOLING/STORING

Cover the salad and dressing; label, date, and store under refrigeration at 41°F (5°C) or lower.

Kansas City Barbecue Ribs

YIELD: 6 PORTIONS · PORTION SIZE: 12 OUNCES

72 ounces (2.2kg) baby back ribs

12 ounces (360g) seasoning mix
(recipe follows)

SAUCE

6 ounces (180g) light brown sugar

1 teaspoon (5g) chili powder

1 teaspoon (5g) dry mustard

1 teaspoon (5g) ginger, ground

1 tablespoon (15g) garlic, minced

½ teaspoon (2g) allspice, ground

¼ teaspoon (1g) paprika

¼ teaspoon (1g) mace, ground

¼ teaspoon (1g) black pepper, ground

8 fluid ounces (240ml) cider vinegar

6 fluid ounces (180ml) molasses

2 teaspoons (10ml) liquid smoke

32 fluid ounces (960ml) ketchup

2 fluid ounces (60ml) water

wood chips, soaked, as needed

CHEF TIPS *If a smoky flavor is not desired, the ribs can be cooked in a combination oven at 275°F (135°C) or a traditional oven at 325°F (162.8°C). Numerous varieties of baby back ribs are available on the market. Some of the region's most notable ribs come from the pork-producing states of Kansas, Missouri, Iowa, and Illinois. To be classified as baby back ribs, the entire rack of ribs should not exceed 1¾ pounds. Larger racks are simply called back ribs.*

Remove the thin, transparent skin from the backside of the rib racks. This is easily done by scraping the corner of the bone on the small side of the rack on the backside. Lift the skin and pull. The skin should separate from the rack in one piece. Discard the skin.

Rub the ribs liberally with the seasoning mix.

Cover and reserve under refrigeration at 41°F (5°C) or lower for at least 24 hours or until needed.

Prepare the sauce by placing all the barbecue sauce ingredients in a small saucepot.

Bring to a boil, stirring constantly, and turn the heat down to a simmer.

Simmer for 1 hour. Do not allow the simmering sauce to fall below 140°F (60°C).

Cool the sauce from 140°F (60°C) to 70°F (21.1°C) or lower within 2 hours. Cool from 70°F (21.1°C) to 41°F (5°C) within an additional 4 hours for a total cooling time of 6 hours or less.

Cover the sauce; label, date, and store under refrigeration at 41°F (5°C) or lower.

COOKING

Prepare a smoker with the soaked wood chips.

Coat the ribs liberally with half the barbecue sauce.

Place the rib racks into the smoker. Allow to smoke for 2 hours at 250°F (121.1°C), basting every 20 minutes with the extra barbecue sauce. The ribs must reach a minimum internal temperature of at least 155°F (68.3°C) for at least 15 seconds.

Reheat the remaining sauce to 165°F (73.9°C) and reserve until needed.

SERVING/HOLDING

Cut the rib racks in half and serve 1–2 pieces on each hot plate, depending on their size. Serve the remaining barbecue sauce on the side.

Hold the ribs and sauce at 140°F (60°C) or higher.

COOLING/STORING

Cool the ribs and sauce from 140°F (60°C) to 70°F (21.1°C) or lower within 2 hours. Cool from 70°F (21.1°C) to 41°F (5°C) within an additional 4 hours for a total cooling time of 6 hours or less.

Cover the ribs and sauce; label, date, and store under refrigeration at 41°F (5°C) or lower.

SEASONING MIX

4 teaspoons (20g) black pepper, ground

4 teaspoons (20g) lemon pepper

2 teaspoons (10g) cayenne pepper

4 teaspoons (20g) chili powder

4 teaspoons (20g) dry mustard

4 ounces (120g) dark brown sugar

3 teaspoons (15g) garlic powder

½ teaspoon (2g) cinnamon, ground

2 teaspoons (10g) seasoned salt

Blend all the ingredients.

Reserve until needed.

COOLING/STORING

Cover the seasoning mix; label, date and store at room temperature in a sealed container.

Deep-Dish Chicken and Sausage Pie with Buttermilk Biscuits

44 ounces (1.3kg) whole fryer chicken

48 fluid ounces (1.4L) white chicken broth, prepared (see page 517)

1 tablespoon (15g) salt

SUPRÊME SAUCE

4 ounces (120g) butter

4 ounces (120g) all-purpose flour

8 fluid ounces (240ml) heavy cream

salt, to taste

white pepper, ground, to taste

GARNISH

24 pearl onions

4 ounces (120g) carrots, cut obliquely

5 ounces (150g) red bell peppers, cut into small dice

5 ounces (150g) corn kernels, fresh

9 ounces (270g) red bliss potatoes, quartered

4 ounces (120g) asparagus tips

5 ounces (150g) peas, fresh or frozen

8 ounces (240g) button mushrooms, quartered

4 ounces (120g) bacon, diced

¼ teaspoon (1g) thyme, chopped

2 tablespoons (30g) sage, chopped

2 tablespoons (30g) parsley, chopped

12 ounces (360g) kielbasa, beer, or smoked sausage

2 tablespoons (30ml) water

1 large egg

12 ounces (360g) buttermilk biscuit dough (recipe follows)

Place the whole chicken in a small stockpot. Cover with the chicken broth. Add the salt and bring to a boil. Reduce the heat to a simmer.

Simmer for 45 minutes, until the chicken reaches a minimum internal temperature of 165°F (73.9°C) for at least 15 seconds. Do not allow the simmering broth to fall below 140°F (60°C).

Remove the chicken from the stockpot. Strain the broth and reserve.

Let the chicken cool to the point where it can be handled and carefully separate the meat from the bones and skin. Reserve the meat and discard the bones and skin.

Hold the chicken meat and reserved broth at 140°F (60°C) or higher until needed.

Using the same stockpot, make a roux with the butter and flour.

Cook over low heat for 10 minutes.

Make a velouté sauce by slowly adding the reserved broth, stirring constantly until thoroughly blended.

Bring to a boil, stirring frequently, and reduce the heat to a simmer.

Simmer for 30–45 minutes. Do not allow the simmering sauce to fall below 140°F (60°C).

Turn the velouté sauce into a suprême sauce by blending in the heavy cream. Season to taste with salt and white pepper.

Strain through a conical strainer lined with rinsed cheesecloth.

Cool the suprême sauce from 140°F (60°C) to 70°F (21.1°C) or lower within 2 hours. Cool from 70°F (21.1°C) to 41°F (5°C) within an additional 4 hours for a total cooling time of 6 hours or less.

Blanch all the vegetables separately and shock in an ice-water bath. Reserve under refrigeration at 41°F (5°C) or lower until needed.

Sauté the bacon in a sautoir pan or skillet over medium-high heat until crisp.

Add the reserved vegetables, herbs, reserved chicken meat, and enough of the reserved suprême sauce to bind the ingredients.

Slice the kielbasa or smoked sausage on a bias, ¼ inch (.64cm) thick, and add to the vegetable mixture.

Heat the mixture over medium heat until it reaches a minimum internal temperature of 165°F (73.9°C) for at least 15 seconds.

Divide the mixture equally into 6 soup bowls or soufflé dishes.

Prepare an egg wash by mixing the egg with 2 tablespoons (30ml) of water.

Brush the outside rim of the soup bowls or soufflé dishes with the egg wash.

Cut circles from the biscuit dough that are approximately ¼ inch (.64cm) larger in diameter than the bowls. Place one circle over each bowl and brush the tops with the remaining egg wash. Gently press the overlapping dough onto the outside rim of the bowls so that the dough adheres to the surface.

Bake the pies in a prehreated 425°F (218.3°C) oven for approximately 20–30 minutes or until the crusts are golden brown and the pies reach a minimum internal temperature of 165°F (73.9°C) for at least 15 seconds.

SERVING/HOLDING

Let the pies rest at least 10 minutes before serving.

Hold the pies at 140°F (60°C) or above.

COOLING/STORING

Cool the pies from 140°F (60°C) to 70°F (21.1°C) or lower within 2 hours. Cool from 70°F (21.1°C) to 41°F (5°C) within an additional 4 hours for a total cooling time of 6 hours or less.

Cover the pies; label, date, and store under refrigeration at 41°F (5°C) or lower.

BUTTERMILK BISCUIT DOUGH

YIELD: 6 PORTIONS · PORTION SIZE: 2 OUNCES

18 ounces (540g) cake flour

1 teaspoon (5g) baking powder

1 teaspoon (5g) baking soda

1 teaspoon (5g) salt

⅓ cup (72g) vegetable shortening, solid, chilled

⅓ cup (72g) butter, chilled, cut into small dice

8 fluid ounces (240ml) buttermilk

Sift the dry ingredients into a large bowl.

Blend or cut the shortening and butter into the flour by rubbing the ingredients lightly between the fingers to incorporate the fat into the flour. Continue to rub until the dough resembles a course cornmeal.

Stir in the buttermilk with a fork, lifting and combining until the dough is soft.

Gather the dough together with your hands and knead lightly on a clean surface dusted with flour until the dough is no longer sticky.

Roll the dough with a rolling pin to ¼ inch (.64cm) thick.

SERVING/HOLDING

Reserve the dough under refrigeration at 41°F (5°C) or lower until needed.

Roast Pork Loin with Apple and Corn Bread Stuffing and Brandy Sauce

CORN BREAD

4 ounces (120g) cornmeal

4 ounces (120g) all-purpose flour

½ tablespoon (7g) baking powder

½ teaspoon (2g) salt

2 tablespoons (30g) sugar

6 ounces (180ml) buttermilk

2 tablespoons (30ml) vegetable oil

1 large egg, beaten

STUFFED PORK LOIN

64 ounces (1.9kg) pork loin, center cut, boneless

salt, to taste

black pepper, ground, to taste

1 fluid ounce (30ml) olive oil

2 ounces (60g) celery, cut into small dice

4 ounces (120g) onions, cut into small dice

6½ ounces (194g) pippin apples, peeled, cored, cut into medium dice

4 fluid ounces (120ml) apple cider

2 teaspoons (10g) thyme, chopped

1 teaspoon (5g) rosemary, chopped

2 teaspoons (10g) sage, chopped

2 fluid ounces (60ml) olive oil

12 fluid ounces (360ml) brandy sauce (recipe follows)

CHEF TIPS *Granny Smith apples can be substituted for pippin apples if they are not available.*

Prepare the corn bread by combining all the dry ingredients in a mixing bowl. Combine the wet ingredients in a separate bowl, then add to the dry ingredients.

Stir until combined. The batter should be slightly lumpy.

Pour the corn bread batter into a greased 6-inch (15cm) cake pan.

Bake at 350°F (176.7°C) for approximately 30 minutes or until done.

Reserve until needed.

🪔 **Trim** 10 ounces (283g) of meat from the pork loin and grind through a meat grinder using a small die. Reserve under refrigeration at 41°F (5°C) or lower until needed.

🪔 **Split** the remaining pork loin lengthwise and season to taste with salt and pepper. Reserve under refrigeration at 41°F (5°C) or lower until needed.

Heat 1 ounce (30g) olive oil in a sautoir pan or skillet and sauté the celery, onions, and apples until the onions are translucent.

Add the fruit and vegetable mixture to the ground pork.

Crumble the reserved corn bread and add 2 cups (480g) to the ground pork mixture.

Mix the remaining ingredients, except the 2 ounces (60ml) olive oil and the brandy sauce, into the ground pork. The mixture should be moist. Adjust the consistency as needed with apple cider.

Spread the mixture evenly down the center of the two pieces of pork loin.

Place the two pieces of pork together and truss every few inches.

Season the outside of the pork loin to taste with salt and black pepper. If desired, the pork loin can be seasoned with additional fresh herbs before roasting.

Heat the olive oil in a sautoir pan or skillet over medium-high heat.

Sear the pork loin on all sides until thoroughly browned.

🪔 **Place** the seared pork loin in a preheated 350°F (176.7°C) oven and roast for approximately 1 hour or until it is done and reaches a minimum internal temperature of 150°F (65.6°C) for at least 15 seconds.

🪔 **Remove** from the oven and wrap with aluminum foil. Continue cooking in the oven until an internal temperature of 155°F (68.3°C) for 15 seconds is reached.

SERVING/HOLDING

Let the pork loin rest for at least 15 minutes before serving.

Reserve the pan drippings and add to the brandy sauce.

Remove the strings from the pork loin and cut it into ½-inch (1.27cm) slices.

Place 2–3 slices of pork on each hot plate.

Top with approximately 2 fluid ounces (60ml) of brandy sauce.

 Hold the pork loin and sauce at 140°F (60°C) or higher.

COOLING/STORING

Cool the pork loin and brandy sauce from 140°F (60°C) to 70°F (21.1°C) or lower within 2 hours. Cool from 70°F (21.1°C) to 41°F (5°C) within an additional 4 hours for a total cooling time of 6 hours or less.

Cover the pork loin and brandy sauce; label, date, and store under refrigeration at 41°F (5°C) or lower.

BRANDY SAUCE

YIELD: 6 PORTIONS · PORTION SIZE: 2 OUNCES

1 fluid ounce (30ml) clarified butter

1 ounce (30g) shallots, chopped

3 fluid ounces (90ml) applejack brandy

8 fluid ounces (240ml) apple cider

1 sprig thyme

16 fluid ounces (480ml) demi-glace sauce, prepared

2 ounces (60g) sweet butter

salt, to taste

black pepper, ground, to taste

Heat the clarified butter in a small saucepot over medium-high heat.

Sweat the shallots in the hot butter for 2 minutes or until they are translucent.

Add the brandy and reduce until almost dry.

Add the apple cider and the thyme and reduce the volume of liquid by half.

Add the demi-glace sauce and simmer until a nappé consistency is reached. Do not allow the simmering sauce to fall below 140°F (60°C).

Remove the sauce from the heat and stir in the sweet butter.

Strain and adjust the seasoning to taste with salt and black pepper.

SERVING/HOLDING

Hold the sauce at 140°F (60°C) or higher.

COOLING/STORING

Cool the sauce from 140°F (60°C) to 70°F (21.1°C) or lower within 2 hours. Cool from 70°F (21.1°C) to 41°F (5°C) within an additional 4 hours for a total cooling time of 6 hours or less.

Cover the sauce; label, date, and store under refrigeration at 41°F (5°C) or lower.

Pan-Seared Steak with Maytag Blue Cheese

YIELD: 6 PORTIONS · PORTION SIZE: 6 OUNCES

4 ounces (120g) Maytag blue cheese

STEAK

2 pounds, 4 ounces (1kg) top loin, cut into 6-ounce (180g) steaks

salt, to taste

black pepper, ground, to taste

2 fluid ounces (60ml) vegetable oil

Season the steaks to taste with salt and black pepper.

Heat the vegetable oil in a sautoir pan or skillet over medium-high heat.

Sear in the steaks in the hot oil until brown on both sides.

If cooking to medium rare, finish cooking in the pan until the steaks reach a minimum internal temperature of 145°F (62.8°C) for at least 15 seconds.

For medium to well done, complete the cooking process in a preheated 350°F (176.7°C) oven for 5–10 minutes or until the desired internal temperature is attained and a minimum internal temperature of 155°F (68.3°C) is reached for at least 15 seconds.

SERVING/HOLDING

Place each steak on a hot plate and top with ¾ ounce (22g) of the blue cheese. Place the prepared plates under a broiler or salamander for approximately 30 seconds before serving to soften and brown the blue cheese.

Hold the steaks at 140°F (60°C) or higher.

COOLING/STORING

Cool the steaks from 140°F (60°C) to 70°F (21.1°C) or lower within 2 hours. Cool from 70°F (21.1°C) to 41°F (5°C) within an additional 4 hours for a total cooling time of 6 hours or less.

Cover the steaks and blue cheese; label, date, and store under refrigeration at 41°F (5°C) or lower.

Brussels Sprouts with Mushrooms

YIELD: 6 PORTIONS · PORTION SIZE: 4 OUNCES

24 ounces (720g) Brussels sprouts

2 ounces (60g) bacon, diced

4 ounces (120g) butter

4 ounces (120g) onion, cut into small dice

1 teaspoon (5g) garlic, minced

6 ounces (180g) mushrooms, quartered

salt, to taste

white pepper, ground, to taste

Trim the bottom of the Brussels sprouts and score an X into the bottom of each with a pairing knife.

Cook the Brussels sprouts in boiling salted water until tender in the center.

Shock the Brussels sprouts in an ice-water bath and reserve under refrigeration at 41°F (5°C) or lower until needed.

Sauté the bacon over medium-high heat in a sautoir pan or skillet until it is crisp.

Add the butter, onions, and garlic and sauté for approximately 5 minutes or until the onions are translucent.

Add the mushrooms and sauté for an additional 5 minutes or until the mushrooms are cooked.

Cut the Brussels sprouts in half and add to the onions and mushrooms.

Season to taste with salt and white pepper and sauté until thoroughly heated.

SERVING/HOLDING

Hold the Brussels sprouts at 140°F (60°C) or higher.

COOLING/STORING

Cool the Brussels sprouts from 140°F (60°C) to 70°F (21.1°C) or lower within 2 hours. Cool from 70°F (21.1°C) to 41°F (5°C) within an additional 4 hours for a total cooling time of 6 hours or less.

Cover the Brussels sprouts; label, date, and store under refrigeration at 41°F (5°C) or lower.

Corn Pudding

2 ounces (60g) butter

4 ounces (120g) onion, minced

1 ounce (30g) green bell pepper, minced

1 ounce (30g) red bell pepper, minced

½ teaspoon (2g) garlic, minced

¼ ounce (7g) green onion, finely chopped

32 fluid ounces (960ml) milk

1 tablespoon (15g) sugar

5¾ ounces (173g) corn kernels

6 ounces (180g) yellow cornmeal

2½ ounces (75g) cheddar cheese, grated

salt, to taste

white pepper, ground to taste

cayenne pepper, to taste

Melt the butter in a sauté pan and sauté the onions, peppers, garlic, and green onions over medium-high heat until the onions become translucent.

Add the milk, sugar, and corn kernels.

Bring to a boil and reduce the heat to a simmer

Slowly stir in the cornmeal. Simmer over low heat, stirring frequently, for 3–5 minutes or until the mixture has the consistency of cream of wheat.

Add the grated cheddar cheese and stir until thoroughly blended.

Season to taste with salt, white pepper, and cayenne pepper. Put into an ovenproof pan.

Bake in a preheated 350°F (176.7°C) oven for 30–45 minutes or until puffy and brown on top.

SERVING/HOLDING

Hold the corn pudding at 140°F (60°C) or higher.

COOLING/STORING

Cool the corn pudding from 140°F (60°C) to 70°F (21.1°C) or lower within 2 hours. Cool from 70°F (21.1°C) to 41°F (5°C) within an additional 4 hours for a total cooling time of 6 hours or less.

Cover the corn pudding; label, date, and store under refrigeration at 41°F (5°C) or lower.

Prairie Sunchoke Gratin

YIELD: 6 PORTIONS · PORTION SIZE: 6 OUNCES

24 ounces (720ml) sunchokes, peeled, cut into ¼-inch (.64cm) slices

1 tablespoon (15ml) sunflower or olive oil

4 ounces (120g) onion, minced

1 tablespoon (15g) garlic, minced

1 sprig thyme, chopped

3½ ounces (105g) green onion, cut into small dice

12 fluid ounces (360ml) heavy cream

2 teaspoons (10g) cornstarch

salt, to taste

white pepper, ground, to taste

butter, as needed

½ ounce (14g) breadcrumbs, coarsely ground

3 ounces (90g) Parmesan cheese, grated

1 teaspoon (5g) paprika

CHEF TIPS *Sunchokes are the bulbs of perennial sunflower plants. They are also referred to as Jerusalem artichokes.*

Blanch the prepared sunchokes in a saucepot of boiling salted water for 1 minute.

Shock the sunchokes in an ice-water bath. Drain and reserve under refrigeration at 41°F (5°C) or lower until needed.

Heat the oil in a sauté pan over medium-high heat.

Add the sunchokes, onions, garlic, thyme, and green onions. Sauté for approximately 2 minutes.

Reserve 2 tablespoons (30ml) of the heavy cream and add the remainder to the pan. Bring the liquid to a boil.

Mix the cornstarch with the reserved cream to make a slurry and add to the boiling mixture. Stir until incorporated and reduce the heat to a simmer.

Simmer over low heat for 3 minutes.

Season the liquid to taste with salt and white pepper.

Place the mixture in a buttered casserole or soufflé dish.

Mix the breadcrumbs and the cheese together. Sprinkle over the top of the sunchoke mixture and top with paprika.

Bake in a preheated oven at 400°F (204.4°C) for approximately 20 minutes or until set.

SERVING/HOLDING

Let the sunchoke gratin rest at least 10 minutes before serving.

Hold the sunchoke gratin at 140°F (60°C) or higher.

COOLING/STORING

Cool the sunchoke gratin from 140°F (60°C) to 70°F (21.1°C) or lower within 2 hours. Cool from 70°F (21.1°C) to 41°F (5°C) within an additional 4 hours for a total cooling time of 6 hours or less.

Cover the sunchoke gratin; label, date, and store under refrigeration at 41°F (5°C) or lower.

Central Plains Smashed Potatoes

YIELD: 6 PORTIONS · PORTION SIZE: 6 OUNCES

2 teaspoons (10g) salt

48 ounces (1.4kg) red potatoes, washed and quartered

4 fluid ounces (120ml) milk

8 ounces (240g) butter

white pepper, ground, to taste

4 ounces (120g) sour cream

2 tablespoons (30g) chives, chopped

CHEF TIPS *Smashed potatoes are typically a little lumpy from the potato skins that are beaten into the mixture.*

Bring 6 quarts (5.68L) of water to a boil in a large saucepot. Add the salt and potatoes.

Boil uncovered for approximately 20–30 minutes or until the potatoes are tender.

Drain the potatoes and place them on a sheet pan. Dry the potatoes in a preheated 350°F (176.7°C) oven for 2–3 minutes.

Remove the potatoes from the oven and place them in a mixing machine. Using the paddle attachment, beat the potatoes on medium speed for 1 minute.

Add the remaining ingredients and beat until thoroughly incorporated.

SERVING/HOLDING

Hold the potatoes at 140°F (60°C) or higher.

COOLING/STORING

Cool the potatoes from 140°F (60°C) to 70°F (21.1°C) or lower within 2 hours. Cool from 70°F (21.1°C) to 41°F (5°C) within an additional 4 hours for a total cooling time of 6 hours or less.

Cover the potatoes; label, date, and store under refrigeration at 41°F (5°C) or lower.

Macaroni and Cheese

½ tablespoon (7g) salt

6 ounces (180g) elbow macaroni

1 ounce (30g) butter

2 tablespoons (30g) all-purpose flour

12 fluid ounces (360ml) milk

¼ teaspoon (1g) cayenne pepper

⅓ teaspoon (2g) dry mustard

½ teaspoon (2ml) Worcestershire sauce

6 ounces (180g) sharp cheddar cheese, grated

butter, as needed

1 ounce (30g) breadcrumbs, fresh

½ teaspoon (2g) paprika

Bring 4 quarts (3.79L) of water to a boil in a large saucepot. Add the salt and the macaroni.

Boil uncovered, stirring frequently, for approximately 10–12 minutes or until the pasta is al dente.

Drain the macaroni and cool under cold running water. Reserve until needed.

Melt the butter in a medium saucepot over low heat. Add the flour to make a white roux. Cook over low heat for 2 minutes.

Whisk in the milk and bring back to a boil, stirring constantly.

Add the cayenne pepper, dry mustard, and Worcestershire sauce. Cook for 15 minutes over low heat, stirring frequently.

Remove from the heat and add two-thirds of the grated cheese. Stir until smooth.

Add the reserved macaroni and mix until thoroughly coated.

Butter a casserole dish or individual soufflé cups. Pour the macaroni mixture into the dishes.

Combine the breadcrumbs, paprika, and remaining cheese and mix. Sprinkle the mixture over the macaroni and cheese.

Bake in a preheated 400°F (204.4°C) oven for 20 minutes or until golden brown on top.

Let the macaroni and cheese rest at least 5 minutes before serving.

⚙ Hold the macaroni and cheese at 140°F (60°C) or higher.

COOLING/STORING

⚙ Cool the macaroni and cheese from 140°F (60°C) to 70°F (21.1°C) or lower within 2 hours. Cool from 70°F (21.1°C) to 41°F (5°C) within an additional 4 hours for a total cooling time of 6 hours or less.

Cover the macaroni and cheese; label, date, and store under refrigeration at 41°F (5°C) or lower.

Wild Rice with Black Walnuts

YIELD: 6 PORTIONS · PORTION SIZE: 6 OUNCES

64 fluid ounces (1.9L) white chicken stock, prepared (see page 517)

12 ounces (360g) raw wild rice

1½ tablespoons (22ml) walnut oil

2 ounces (60g) onions, cut into small dice

1 ounce (30g) celery, cut into small dice

½ tablespoon (7g) garlic, minced

2 ounces (60g) black walnuts, chopped

1 tablespoon (15g) parsley, chopped

salt, to taste

black pepper, ground, to taste

CHEF TIPS *Black walnuts from Missouri are about the same size as the more common English walnut, but they have a dark shell with well-defined ridges. The nutmeat is quite oily and possesses an earthy, pungent taste different from the sweet flavor of the English variety. If black walnuts are not available, English walnuts make an excellent substitute.*

Bring the chicken stock to a boil in a medium saucepot. Add the wild rice and gently boil for 30–45 minutes or until tender. Be careful not to undercook the rice. It will appear as though the grains have exploded as they become fully cooked.

Drain the rice, reserving the remaining chicken stock.

⚙ Cool the chicken stock from 140°F (60°C) to 70°F (21.1°C) or lower within 2 hours. Cool from 70°F (21.1°C) to 41°F (5°C) within an additional 4 hours for a total cooling time of 6 hours or less.

Cover the chicken stock; label, date, and store under refrigeration at 41°F (5°C) or lower. Use the chicken stock for another preparation.

Heat the walnut oil over medium-high heat in a medium saucepot. Sauté the onions, celery, and garlic until the onions are translucent.

Add the black walnuts and sauté for 1 additional minute.

Add the cooked wild rice and parsley. Toss.

Season to taste with salt and black pepper.

SERVING/HOLDING

Hold the wild rice at 140°F (60°C) or higher.

COOLING/STORING

Cool the wild rice from 140°F (60°C) to 70°F (21.1°C) or lower within 2 hours. Cool from 70°F (21.1°C) to 41°F (5°C) within an additional 4 hours for a total cooling time of 6 hours or less.

Cover the wild rice; label, date, and store under refrigeration at 41°F (5°C) or lower.

Cheddar Potato Fries

YIELD: 6 PORTIONS · PORTION SIZE: 6 OUNCES

32 ounces (960g) russet potatoes, cut into 8 full-length wedges

seasoned salt, to taste

black pepper, ground, to taste

6 ounces (180g) sharp cheddar cheese, grated

6 ounces (180g) bacon, cooked, chopped

4 ounces (120g) sour cream

4 ounces (120g) green onion, diced

CHEF TIPS *Cheddar potato fries can also be baked if a lower fat content is desired. Toss the potato wedges lightly with a little corn oil and bake in a 400°F (204.4°C) oven until cooked. Continue to follow recipe from "Degrease" step.*

Deep-fry the potatoes in a preheated 325°F (162.8°C) deep-fat fryer. Fry until the potatoes are tender on the inside and crisp on the outside.

Degrease the fried potatoes on absorbent paper towels. Season to taste with salt and black pepper.

Place the potatoes on a sheet pan and top with the grated cheese.

Bake in the oven or under a salamander until the cheese is melted.

Remove from the oven.

SERVING/HOLDING

Serve the potato wedges garnished with the bacon bits, sour cream, and green onions.

Hold the fries at 140°F (60°C) or higher.

COOLING/STORING

Cool the cheddar fries from 140°F (60°C) to 70°F (21.1°C) or lower within 2 hours. Cool from 70°F (21.1°C) to 41°F (5°C) within an additional 4 hours for a total cooling time of 6 hours or less.

Cover the cheddar fries; label, date, and store under refrigeration at 41°F (5°C) or lower.

Central Plains Cheesecake

YIELD: 12 PORTIONS · PORTION SIZE: 5 OUNCES

CRUST

> 8 ounces (240g) graham crackers, ground
>
> 2 ounces (60g) sugar
>
> 2 ounces (60g) butter, melted
>
> ½ teaspoon (2ml) vanilla extract
>
> butter, softened, as needed

FILLING

> 24 ounces (720g) cream cheese
>
> 6 ounces (180g) sugar
>
> 4 fluid ounces (120ml) cherry purée
>
> 4 ounces (120g) cherries, dried
>
> zest from 1 lemon
>
> 5 large eggs
>
> 5 egg yolks
>
> ¾ tablespoon (11g) cornstarch
>
> 2½ fluid ounces (74ml) heavy cream

CHEF TIPS *For a more intense fruit flavor, macerate the dried cherries in brandy or cherry liqueur before adding to the cake batter. Strawberries and blueberries make excellent substitutes for the cherries called for in this recipe.*

Blend the graham cracker crumbs and the sugar in a food processor until incorporated. Add the melted butter and vanilla and process until the mixture sticks together. When you press the mixture together in your hands, it should hold its shape.

Press the graham cracker mixture into a buttered 9-inch (22.86cm) or 10-inch (25.4cm) springform or cake pan. There should be enough graham cracker mixture for a ½-inch (1.27cm) layer on the bottom of the cake pan and a depth of about ¼ inch (.64cm) up the sides.

Reserve the crust under refrigeration at 41°F (5°C) or lower until needed.

Put the cream cheese and sugar in the bowl of a mixing machine and beat on medium-low speed with the paddle attachment for approximately 10 minutes or until thoroughly blended.

Add the cherry purée, dried cherries, and lemon zest. Blend for an additional 1 minute.

Beat the eggs and egg yolks in a separate bowl and blend the eggs into the cheese mixture just until the ingredients are incorporated. Do not over mix.

Dissolve the cornstarch into the cream and mix into the cheese and egg mixture.

Pour the finished batter into the cake pan with the graham cracker crust so that the batter comes within ½ inch (1.27cm) from the top. Do not overfill, as the cake will rise.

Place the cheesecake in a deep hotel pan.

Place the pan with the cake in a preheated 350°F (176.7°C) oven. Fill the pan with hot water so that the water level comes about halfway up the side of the cake pan.

Bake for approximately 60–80 minutes or until the center of the cake is firm and reaches a minimum internal temperature of 145°F (62.8°C) for at least 15 seconds. Test the cake for doneness by inserting a metal skewer into the center. If the skewer comes out clean, the cake is done; if the skewer has batter remaining on it, the cake is not yet done.

When the cheesecake is done, place it on a wire rack to cool for at least 1 hour before refrigerating.

Reserve under refrigeration at 41°F (5°C) or lower overnight or until thoroughly chilled.

SERVING/HOLDING

Remove the springform pan or, if using a round cake pan, briefly place the pan in hot water in order to loosen the bottom and sides.

Cut the cake into 12 slices.

COOLING/STORING

Cover the cheesecake; label, date, and store under refrigeration at 41°F (5°C) or lower.

Michael Nenes

TEX-MEX CUISINE

Guacamole, pico de gallo, dessert of praline candies or flan, the unexpected delicacy of green sauces and tomatillos, enchiladas verde con pollo, chicken flautas or beef fajitas, they are all Tex-Mex cuisine. This colorful, spicy, adventurous, larger than life cuisine is a merging of cultures between Texas and Mexico, Mexican-Americans cooking Mexican food with the ingredients they had at hand. The focus is on fresh, seasonal ingredients and products that are indigenous to Texas and Mexico. The flavors are clean and simple; many say it is the only truly American cuisine.

Tex-Mex is explicitly not the cuisine of Mexico, a proud and separate tradition. The fundamentals of Tex-Mex are the three staves of life for the vaquero and the American cowboy: beans, beef, and corn. The building blocks of Tex-Mex are chili, chiles, cheese, and cheaper cuts of beef, small, pungent onions, cumin, cilantro, tart tomato, tomatillos, masa harina (cornmeal), beans, and rice. The hallmarks of real, honest Tex-Mex are a devotion to rural roots, the strict adherence to tradition, the uncompromising use of only those ingredients, fresh as can be, and in only those combinations hallowed by time, that are native to its South Texas and Border birthplace.

Michael Nenes has owned and operated successful restaurants in Fairbanks, Alaska; Vail, Colorado; and Houston, Texas. He is a former Executive Chef of Chez Eddy Restaurant in Houston, Texas, the original "Heart Healthy" restaurant.

Tex-Mex Cuisine

Tex-Mex cooking began in the southwestern corner of Texas near San Antonio and has been described as the only food that is truly native to the United States. The cuisine merges the Texas and Mexican cultures and, although Tex-Mex cooking was originally regarded as a poor man's Mexican cuisine, today it has become sophisticated while still adhering to many south-of-the-border traditions. Tex-Mex is the cooking of Mexican-style food with the ingredients found also in the Texas region, such as corn, pinto beans, tomatoes, and chile peppers. Additionally, when we think of Texas, longhorn cattle, cowboys, chuck wagon cooking, and Lone Star chili frequently come to mind. The beef and chilis we associate with the cuisine of Texas are remnants of the state's Spanish and Mexican heritage. Over the centuries, these flavorful introductions have influenced the eating habits of not only Texans but all Americans.

From the early sixteenth century to the 1800s, the Spanish conquistadors ruled the Texas region. The Spanish came to Texas in search of a shorter route to the Far East and with hopes of finding treasure while they "civilized" and Christianized the natives. Once the Spanish started building missions in Texas, they began to import European foods. They had local access to wild cattle, hogs, and sheep, and they imported corn and other small grains. This constituted the regional cuisine for close to 300 years. The territory was ceded to Mexico in 1821.

In that year, the Mexican government took control of the region and adopted a policy encouraging immigrants from the United States to settle in the region. When Anglo-Americans started settling in Texas in the early 1800s, they brought their favorite kinds of cattle, hogs, sheep, and poultry with them. They found wild cattle left by the Spanish from the missions, along with buffalo, turkey, and deer, so meat was always plentiful. The settlers had to grow most of the other foods that they consumed. Almost every family had a garden that provided corn, white potatoes, and an abundance of sweet potatoes. Oats were the only small grain that grew well in the Texas climate except rye, which was grown, but not in large quantities. The early Texans consumed large quantities of corn—fresh corn in season and dried corn in the winter. Cornmeal was available year round once mills were built. The production of wheat did not become popular until the late 1800s.

Texas earned its independence from Mexico in 1836 and was an independent republic for ten years before joining the United States in 1846. At that time, the state possessed two distinct regions—the highly settled east, with its seaports and plantations, and the wild western frontier. In the east, the leading port of Galveston reflected European and Southern influences in its culture and cuisine. However, foods such as salt, coffee, sugar, and wheat flour still had to be imported. Many of these staples were brought from New Orleans to Galveston. In contrast, log cabins were the common dwellings on the western frontier and foods such as stewed game were mainstays of the local diet.

Texas is as large as all of New England, New York, Pennsylvania, Ohio, and Illinois combined. With more than 267,000 square miles, it occupies about 7 percent of the total area of the United States. In addition to beef, the state produces a variety of fresh produce and seafood. It is also well known for its ruby red grapefruit, melons, pecans, and figs.

Five distinct regions of Texas exist today, all settled by pioneers from different parts of the Americas and Europe, with different food heritages.

Northeastern Texas: The early Americans, Europeans, and Mexicans in this region traded cooking techniques and learned from the Native Americans how to plant corn and cook with wild plants. The settlers also supplemented indigenous foods with produce grown from seeds brought when they settled in the region. Wheat, for example, is grown in northern Texas, particularly in the panhandle, which is the southern extension of the Great Plains. When wheat flour became inexpensive, corn bread in Texas gave way to biscuits. Farming became a major activity of the region and remains so today. Pork, chicken, and local vegetables continue to be traditional food favorites.

Deep East Texas: Many residents from the southern United States—from Alabama, Georgia, Mississippi, and Louisiana—settled in Deep East Texas. Some were "poor whites," who existed on wild berries, fruits, edible weeds, and game. Others were plantation owners, who brought the tradition of fine foods and Southern hospitality to their Texas plantations. Cajun and Creole cookery naturally became part of Deep East Texas cuisine. Shrimp from the Gulf of Mexico, for example, was used in jambalayas. Rice crops and the associated milling, over the years, have become important agricultural activities in Deep East Texas, where rice grows in the low, marshy coastal plains near the Gulf of Mexico. Texmati rice, introduced in 1970, is a crossbreed of white, long-grain, and Native American aromatic rice.

Central Texas: Stephen Austin and 300 of his followers whom he brought to his colony originally settled Central Texas. The local fare was that of the original Anglo settlers and the Germans who immigrated to the region. Toward the latter part of the 1800s, more Germans, Czechs, and Poles began moving to Central Texas, greatly influencing the foods and cuisine of the region. This cultural addition brought sausage making, meat smoking, and a German dish called *Wiener Schnitzel*. Wiener Schnitzel is considered by many the predecessor of the Texas favorite chicken-fried steak (see page 305). Texas barbecue also has its origin in Central Texas.

South Texas: Today, this region is influenced primarily by the cuisines of Mexico and Spain. Starting in the mid-1850s, the cooking style of the Mexicans became quite popular in South Texas. Tacos, guacamole (see page 298), enchiladas, and tortillas (see pages 291, 308) became the daily foods of many settlers. They used Mexican chiles and Spanish spices, such as cumin, for flavoring. Tex-Mex cooking is attributed primarily to this region. On the Gulf coast, seafood is as much a part of traditional Texas cuisine as chili and chicken-fried steak. More than 100 million pounds of shrimp, oysters, crabs, and finfish are harvested annually from the Gulf of Mexico. Catfish and trout are caught in the rivers and cultivated in ponds. Another Texas favorite from this region is the ruby red grapefruit. This natural mutation, which was discovered in 1929, is said to have occurred due to the intense radiation of the strong Texas sun. The area where ruby red grapefruits are grown is called the Magic Valley because the environment provides the perfect growing conditions for these special grapefruits.

West Texas: Texas ranches were established to raise beef cattle on land granted to Mexican families by the king of Spain. The well-known Texas longhorns were descendants of the wild cattle left by the Spanish in the sixteenth century and were popular because they could withstand the extreme weather in the deserts of West Texas. Until the discovery of oil in West Texas, cattle production for beef was the biggest industry in the state. Although the longhorns were well suited to the region, they did not produce the best-tasting meat. Today, beef is still the primary meat of the region; however, the ranchers mainly raise Hereford, Brahma, and Angus cattle. Other meats are now being raised in West Texas, including bison, ostrich, and emu. West Texas adopted a basic food—beans—from the Mexicans. Thus, beef, beans, corn bread, and tortillas are staple foods of West Texas.

One contribution to American cooking from the Tex-Mex region is chuck wagon cooking. The chuck wagon is one of the symbols of the American cowboy. After the Civil War, the country's appetite for beef fueled the long cattle drives from the ranges of the Southwest to the Midwest, where cattle were shipped to the eastern markets and abroad. The chuck wagon first came into use in the 1860s to supply the long cattle drives from Texas to the railheads in Kansas. A Texas cattleman named Charles Goodnight is given credit for the efficient design of the chuck wagon. Originally designed as a military supply wagon, the chuck wagon was a kitchen on wheels, with compartments designed like cupboards and a tailgate that served as a workstation. *Chuck* was a cowboy word for "food." During the long trip, three meals a day had to be provided for the dozen or so cowboys and the trail boss. The chuck wagon cook was called a *cookie* or *coosie,* from the Spanish word *cocinero*, meaning "male cook." The coosie or cocinero was usually an aging cowboy hired for his ability to drive a wagon rather than his culinary skills. He was the complete boss of the wagon and everything that pertained to it and he acted as the doctor, barber, and undertaker as well. He was usually paid more than the other hands because the success of the camp and the drive depended greatly on him. A cowhand earned about a dollar a day; the cook made twice that. The abilities of the coosies varied greatly; it was common for cowboys to retaliate against cooks with little talent. Cooking was usually done over an open fire, and tough cuts of beef were often slowly smoked in a pit or cooked in a Dutch oven, a stewpot with a tight-fitting lid made of cast iron. Favorites included grilled steaks, smoked brisket, and biscuits. Mexican vaqueros (Mexican for "cowboy") introduced their favorite foods—chili, beans, and tortillas—to chuck wagon cooking. Famous recipes such as Texas barbecue, cowboy steaks, chicken-fried steak, and chili (see page 309) originated on the cattle drives. However, today, the only chuck wagons found are those on cattle-drive theme vacations and ones used as props for catered events.

The evolution of food and cooking in Texas continues today. As more and more immigrants from around the world settle in the state, new flavors and cooking techniques continue to influence the cuisine of the various regions in Texas. Tex-Mex cuisine is truly an American original.

Typical Tex-Mex Ingredients and Dishes

Ancho Chile: A dried poblano chile. It measures 3–4 inches (7.62cm–10.16cm) long and has a dark, reddish-brown color. It is the sweetest of all the dried chiles and has a slightly fruity flavor. Ancho chiles are frequently ground and used as the basis for commercial chili powders. In 1912, a pharmacologist named Wilbur Scoville came up with an index for measuring the heat of chiles in a food product. The heat index comprised Scoville units ranging from 1 to 300,000. However, a simpler scale, called the Scoville scale, is often utilized; this ranks heat levels from 1 to 10, with 1 being the mildest and 10 being the hottest. The heat of ancho chiles is rated at 1000–1500 Scoville units and is placed at about 1 on a scale of 1 to 10. The typical substitute for ancho chiles is pasilla peppers.

Anticuchos: A Tex-Mex shish kabob generally made with sirloin chunks marinated in jalapeño and tomato and skewered and grilled over a mesquite wood fire.

Arroz: Spanish for "rice." In cooking, it usually refers to long-grain white rice. Arroz is a staple of Tex-Mex regional cooking.

Barbacoa: In Spanish, *barbacoa* means "food cooked over or adjacent to an open fire." In Tex-Mex cooking, it is a Mexican-style shredded beef made from the cow's head. Barbacoa is typically served with pico de gallo and freshly made corn or flour tortillas.

Barbecue: A term derived from the Spanish word *barbacoa*, meaning "food cooked over or adjacent to an open fire." True Texas barbecue is a method of cooking meat in a closed container or in the ground using a low-temperature fire that emits a sweet smoke. A tradition in Texas for over 100 years, barbecue is usually made from tougher cuts of beef, such as the brisket, and is served with a ketchup-based sauce seasoned with vinegar and spices.

Bolillo: A Mexican roll used for sandwiches. Bolillos are usually about 6 inches (15.25cm) in length.

Boracho: A cooking term indicating the inclusion of beer in a recipe—for example, in frijoles borachos, which means "beans cooked with beer" in Spanish.

Burrito: A large flour tortilla filled with any number of ingredients. Burritos are formed by tucking the ends of the tortilla inside as it is rolled to seal in the filling. They are usually eaten with condiments such as salsa, lettuce, tomato, cheese, and guacamole. Deep-fried burritos are called *chimichangas.*

Cascabel Chile: A dried chile approximately 1½ inches (3.8cm) in diameter and shaped like an acorn. Cascabel chiles have a distinctive flavor and are dark orange to red in color, with medium heat. The seeds of the cascabel chile rattle in the pod, which explains the literal translation of its name, "jingle bell."

Chicken-Fried Steak: An original Texas recipe made with tenderized round steak or cubed steak coated with egg and flour and pan-fried. Local Texans usually refer to chicken-fried steak by the abbreviation CFS. Chicken-fried steak is traditionally served with "the works"—white cream gravy, mashed potatoes, fresh corn kernels or green beans, and biscuits.

Chile Relleno: *Relleno* is Spanish for "stuffed." Authentic Tex-Mex chiles rellenos are fresh, large poblano chiles that are stuffed with cheese and dipped in egg batter. They are then pan-fried in oil and usually served with refritos and arroz. Today, a variety of other Tex-Mex recipes frequently use the name *chiles rellenos* for stuffed foods, including jalapeño poppers. However, the similarity is in name only.

Chili: A Tex-Mex adaptation of an American Southwest dish of meat (usually beef or pork) that is slowly simmered in a sauce made from dried chiles and spices. In Tex-Mex cooking, beans are never included, as Texans feel it dilutes the flavor of the meat and chiles. Chili is the official state dish of Texas.

Chimichanga: A deep-fried burrito. (See *burrito*.)

Chorizo: A spicy Mexican sausage made with pork and seasonings. Traditionally, chorizo of Mexican origin is made with fresh pork, while the Spanish tradition calls for smoked pork. The casing is usually removed before cooking.

Churro: A light, crisp pastry dough made from cornmeal and sugar. The dough is piped out of a pastry bag into strips and deep-fried until golden brown. Churros are served sprinkled with cinnamon sugar.

Cilantro: A highly aromatic herb related to parsley; it is used extensively in Tex-Mex cooking. Cilantro is also referred to as *Chinese parsley*. The leaves of the herb are usually finely chopped and used as a condiment or as an ingredient in Tex-Mex recipes. The stems can be chopped and used in soups, beans, or anything that is simmered. The seeds of the plant are known as *coriander* and, when dried, are referred to as *cumin* or *comino*.

Comal: A round, flat griddle used to make tortillas. It is usually made of either cast iron or unglazed earthenware.

Comino: Another name for cumin. (See *cilantro, coriander*.)

Coriander: The undried seeds of the cilantro plant, which are produced when the plant is at full maturity. The dried seeds are called *cumin* or *comino*.

Cumin: Ground, flat, dried seeds of the cilantro plant. When the dried seeds are ground to a fine, powdery consistency, the spice is referred to as *cumin* or *comino*. (See *cilantro, coriander*.)

Enchilada: A corn tortilla rolled with a filling made from cheese, beans, chicken, pork, or beef. Enchiladas are typically smothered with a thin red chili sauce, referred to as *enchilada* *sauce*, topped with cheddar cheese, and baked in an oven until the cheese is completely melted.

Escabeche: A method of pickling that is frequently used to prepare fish or vegetables. Escabeche is typically served as an appetizer, light entrée, or side dish. It is best served at room temperature after resting under refrigeration overnight. The resting process allows the full extraction of flavors from the vegetables.

Fajita: An original Tex-Mex recipe made by grilling marinated skirt steak, then slicing it and serving it with smoked strips of green chiles and tortillas. Fajitas originated along the Rio Grande on the Texas-Mexico border and were typically eaten by cattle wranglers. The skirt steak (the diaphragm muscle of the steer) is the traditional cut of meat utilized for fajitas. Skirt steaks were originally the discards given to the cowboys after cattle were slaughtered. The presentation of fajitas with sizzling bell peppers and onions on a smoking hot cast-iron plate is utilized mainly by theme restaurants and in no way is a part of true Tex-Mex fajitas. However, although it is not authentic, this serving method can be dramatic. Other people associate fajitas with a taco or the strips of meat that go into the taco. However, this too, is not authentic.

Flan: A Tex-Mex dessert similar to French crème caramel. Flan is either made as a pie and cut into slices to serve or made in individual cups.

Flauta: A white or yellow corn tortilla stuffed with beef, chicken, or pork. Flautas are rolled and pan- or deep-fried until crisp. They are usually about ¾ inch (1.9cm) in diameter and served two or three to a plate. Flautas are typically topped with cheese, sour cream, and guacamole.

Frijoles: Spanish for "beans." Typically, *frijoles* refers to pinto beans grown in the southwestern states. In restaurants, unless they are referred to as *boracho* or *ranchero frijoles*, you will typically be served refritos or refried beans. (See *refried beans*.)

Gebhardt's Chili Powder: A brand-name chili powder from San Antonio, Texas. Gebhardt's chili powder features ground, dried chiles enhanced with herbs and spices. An extensive variety of chili powders is available in the region, varying widely in heat and flavor. Tex-Mex cooking professionals generally choose to blend their own chili powder by grinding a special mix of dried chiles in a coffee grinder. This technique is used to bring an exact flavor to a given recipe by carefully balancing the different flavors of various chiles.

Green Chile: This is the California green chile, also referred to as the Anaheim chile, which is planted and grown in the state of Texas. Although it is the same plant as that grown in California, the Texas variety is generally much hotter, similar to the Big Jim chiles grown in Colorado. They are bright green, 4–8 inches (10.16cm–20.32cm) long and 1–1½ inches

(2.54cm–3.81cm) in width. The heat of Texas green chiles is rated with 1000–1500 Scoville units and usually placed at 1 or 2 on a scale of 1 to 10.

Guacamole: An avocado mixture made from the fruit's flesh. Guacamole is usually blended with lemon or lime juice, diced onion, tomato, and chopped cilantro. It is used as a condiment in numerous Tex-Mex dishes.

Gulf Shrimp: A Texas shellfish that spawns in the Gulf of Mexico. Several types are caught along the 375-mile coastline, each named for its color. Two of the most popular are the Gulf white shrimp and the gulf brown shrimp. The color differences are due to different diets; however, all shrimp shells turn pink once they are cooked.

Jalapeño: A fairly spicy, small chile that turns from green to red as it matures. Jalapeños average about 2 inches (5cm) in length. Like most chiles, the heat comes mainly from the seeds. The heat of jalapeño peppers is rated with 2500–5000 Scoville units and placed at about 2 on a scale of 1 to 10. The typical substitute for jalapeño peppers is serrano chiles. The jalapeño is the most frequently used pepper in Tex-Mex cooking.

Jicama: A crisp and crunchy root vegetable with a thick brown skin that must be removed prior to use. The flavor of jicama is similar to a mild apple crossed with a potato, which makes it excellent for use in salads and salsas. Unlike apples, the flesh of jicama does not turn brown after it is peeled. Jicama is generally available from November to June.

Masa: Spanish for dough. In the Tex-Mex region, masa is plain corn flour dough made from dried corn, which is cooked in lime water, then cooled. Masa is most commonly used to make tamales and tortillas.

Masa Harina: A commercial dried masa that has been processed into a fine powder. To make the dough for tamales, reconstitute the powder by adding water to the masa and blending. (See *masa*.)

Mole: Derived from the Aztec word *molli*, meaning a concoction, stew, or sauce. Mole is more than just a Mexican chocolate sauce; it is a special, complex dish woven together with dried chiles, nuts, seeds, vegetables, spices, and chocolate. There are as many styles of mole as the imagination can conjure. Each local area has its own version of mole, from Texas to Arizona to Mexico. The more common varieties are green mole, made with tomatillos, and red mole, made with pumpkin seeds. Mole is frequently made as a sauce and used to braise meat and poultry items.

Nopales: The whole paddles or pads of the prickly pear cactus. *Nopalitos* are cactus pads that are already peeled and cut into julienne; they are generally available in cans and jars. Some say the cactus pads have a flavor similar to green bell peppers, while others say nopales taste like green beans. They are commonly used in the region as an ingredient in salads. Nopalitos should be rinsed several times under cold water before using.

Pico de Gallo: The literal translation is "beak of the rooster." Pico de gallo is an uncooked salsa made from tomatoes, onions, serrano chiles, and cilantro, all cut into a very small dice. Pico de gallo is typically used as a condiment or topping for a variety of Tex-Mex recipes, such as tacos and tostadas. Frequently it is served with tortilla chips as an appetizer.

Pinto Bean: The most commonly used bean in Tex-Mex cooking. The pinto bean, a variation of the kidney bean, is a pinkish-beige color and slightly streaked. Once pintos are cooked, the variegations of color disappear. Pinto beans are the main ingredient in refritos or refried beans, a starch commonly served with Tex-Mex and Southwestern cuisine.

Poblano Chile: A large, dark-green chile often confused with the pasilla chile, which is, in fact, a dried chilaca chile. When poblano chiles are dried, they are referred to as *ancho chiles*. Poblano chiles are mild to moderately hot and have a full flavor. They are usually 3–6 inches (7.62cm–15.24cm) long and 3–4 inches (7.62cm–10.16cm) in width. The heat of poblano chiles is rated at 1000–1500 Scoville units and placed at about 1 on a scale of 1 to 10. They are commonly the chile of choice when making chiles rellenos.

Pollo: Spanish for chicken.

Queso: Spanish for cheese. In Tex-Mex cooking, cheddar is the most frequently used cheese. One of the most distinct differences between Tex-Mex and American Southwest foods is the selection of cheese. In American Southwest cuisine, fresh goat cheese or queso fresco is used for traditional dishes. In Tex-Mex cooking, cheddar and Monterey Jack are the cheeses of choice.

Queso Blanco: Spanish for "white cheese." Queso blanco is the Mexican cheese Monterey Jack was named after. It was popular as an economical product that could be made with little equipment and even when only a small amount of milk could be obtained.

Ranchero: A Tex-Mex cooking term referring to the addition of tomatoes, bell peppers, and garlic in a recipe. *Ranchero* is usually used to describe a cooked salsa or a cooking technique, as in *frijoles rancheros*. *Ranchero* is sometimes confused with *boracho*. However, ranchero does not have beer as an ingredient.

Refried Beans: A well-known recipe frequently served in the Tex-Mex region. Refried beans are commonly referred to as *refritos* and are usually made from pinto beans. The Spanish word *refritos* means well fried but is frequently misinterpreted as refried or twice fried. Typically, pinto beans are cooked and drained, then mashed with hot lard or bacon fat, seasonings, and (sometimes) chiles. Despite their name, refried beans are fried only once. A cast-iron frying pan produces the best results. However, a nonstick pan will also work.

Salsa: Spanish for "sauce." In Tex-Mex cooking, however, the term generally refers to a tomato-based condiment. If the salsa is uncooked, such as pico de gallo, it is classified as *salsa cruda* or *salsa fresca*. If the salsa is blended finely in a food processor, it is usually called chile or picante sauce.

Serrano Chile: A small, fresh, hot chile measuring about 1½ inches (3.8cm) long. As it matures, it turns from dark green to red, then to yellow. Usually, the smaller a serrano chile is in size, the hotter it is. The serrano chile is usually used when making pico de gallo. Similar to jalapeño chiles, serranos are a great source of vitamin C. Serrano chiles are the most frequently used pepper in Tex-Mex cooking after jalapeños.

Star Ruby Grapefruit: Invented by Dr. Robert Hensz of Texas A&M University in 1966. This grapefruit, with its bright ruby-red flesh, is the result of a mutation induced by radiation, making it the first commercial grapefruit produced by artificial means.

Taco: A folded, grilled or deep-fried corn tortilla typically filled with meat such as pork, beef, or chicken. Tacos are usually topped with lettuce, tomatoes, and cheese and served with pico de gallo.

Tamale: A traditional Tex-Mex recipe whose name is derived from the ancient Aztec word *tamalli*. Tamales are made from masa dough and typically filled with shredded pork or beef. They are usually 5–6 inches (12.7cm–15.24cm) long and about 1 inch (2.54cm) thick. The tamale is wrapped in a soaked corn husk, steamed, and topped with red chili. Tamales are a Hispanic holiday tradition throughout Texas and are always served at Christmas and New Year.

Tequila: An alcoholic beverage distilled from the sap of the blue agave plant, which grows in the red, volcanic soil of the Mexican state of Jalisco, near the town of Tequila. Tequila is the primary ingredient in the popular margarita drink. The liquor comes in four categories: blanco (white or silver, bottled immediately after it is distilled), joven abocado (gold, enhanced by coloring and flavoring), reposado (rested two months to one year in oak barrels), and anejo (aged at least one year in oak barrels).

Texmati Rice: A crossbreed of white and basmati rice. Texmati is an aromatic variety of rice that smells like popcorn when cooking, and has a delicious nutty taste, not bland like ordinary rice. It cooks up light and fluffy every time. It was developed at a research facility in Alvin, Texas.

Tomatillo: A small, green Mexican fruit of the tomato family. Tomatillos are rough to the touch and are covered with a brown husk. They are mainly used in making fresh and cooked salsas. The tomatillos are simmered, then blended in a food processor with spices. Tomatillo sauce is called *salsa verde*.

Tortilla: Spanish for "little cakes," which the conquistadors thought the Native American recipe resembled. Before the European colonists introduced wheat flour to the region, tortillas were made exclusively from the corn grown by the Native Americans and were the staple food for the entire population. In Tex-Mex cooking, tortillas are a round, thin bread made of either corn flour or wheat flour. Once the dough, called *masa*, is made, the tortillas are formed in a tortilla press or are hand-shaped by patting the dough into thin round shapes. Tortillas are then cooked quickly on a hot skillet or griddle, called a *comal*. They are eaten by themselves or with other Tex-Mex dishes. Corn tortillas are usually about 6 inches (15.24cm) in diameter, much smaller than their flour counterparts, which can be as large as 24 inches (60.96cm) around. Tortillas are also used to wrap a variety of Tex-Mex foods, such as beans, meats, and vegetables, and eaten like a taco. (See *masa*.)

Tostada: Literally, "toasted chip." Tostadas are served as an appetizer or snack, usually with a fresh salsa. According to experts in San Antonio, the self-proclaimed Tex-Mex capital of the world, with the addition of toppings such as beans, meats, or cheese, tostadas should be referred to as *nachos*.

Sample Menus from Tex-Mex Cuisine

MENU ONE

Tortilla Soup

Starburst Spinach Salad with Poppy-Seed Vinaigrette

Lone Star Chicken-Fried Steak with Cream Gravy · Mashed Potatoes

MENU TWO

Frijoles Alla Charra

Quesadillas with Jicama Salsa

Mole de Pollo · Arroz à la Mexicana

MENU THREE

Caldo de Res

Homemade Tamales with Red Pepper Coulis

Chicken Flautas · Chiles Rellenos with Tomatillo Salsa · Refried Beans · Colache

Tortilla Soup

YIELD: 6 PORTIONS · PORTION SIZE: 10 OUNCES

3 ounces (90g) onion, peeled and quartered

8 ounces (240g) Roma tomatoes, quartered

1 fluid ounce (30ml) vegetable oil

12 fluid ounces (360ml) white chicken stock, prepared (see page 517)

½ corn tortilla, chopped

1⅓ cloves garlic, chopped

1 ounce (30g) ancho chile, stemmed, seeded, toasted, finely chopped

⅓ bay leaf

⅔ teaspoon (4g) cumin, ground

12 fluid ounces (360ml) brown beef stock, prepared (see page 515)

3 ounces (90ml) tomato sauce

salt, to taste

black pepper, ground, to taste

2 ounces (60g) cheddar or Jack cheese, grated

1 ounce (30g) avocado, peeled, pitted, cut into medium dice

6 ounces (180g) corn tortillas, cut into thin strips, deep-fried

CHEF TIPS *If desired, shredded chicken meat can be added to the other garnishes.*

Rub the onions and the tomatoes with the vegetable oil. Grill on all sides until thoroughly charred. Alternatively, char on a sheet pan underneath a broiler.

Place the onions, tomatoes, and 4 fluid ounces (120ml) of the chicken stock in a blender and process until smooth. Reserve until needed.

Heat the remaining oil in a large saucepot. Add the chopped tortilla, garlic, and ancho chile and sauté for 3–4 minutes. Add the bay leaf, cumin, remaining chicken broth, and beef stock. Bring to a boil.

Stir in the blended tomato mixture and add the tomato sauce. Simmer for 30 minutes. Do not allow the simmering soup to fall below 140°F (60°C).

Season to taste with salt and black pepper. Strain through a coarse strainer if desired. Taste and adjust seasoning as needed.

SERVING/HOLDING

Serve the soup in hot bowls or soup plates, garnishing each portion with the grated cheese, diced avocado, and crisp fried tortillas.

Hold the soup at 140°F (60°C) or higher.

COOLING/STORING

Pour the remaining soup into small metal containers.

Cool the remaining soup from 140°F (60°C) to 70°F (21.1°C) or lower within 2 hours. Cool from 70°F (21.1°C) to 41°F (5°C) within an additional 4 hours for a total cooling time of 6 hours or less.

Cover soup; label, date, and store under refrigeration at 41°F (5°C) or lower.

Caldo de Res

YIELD: 6 PORTIONS · PORTION SIZE: 10 OUNCES

8 ounces (240g) beef shank or chuck

5 ounces (150g) corn kernels, fresh

3 ounces (90g) red potatoes, peeled

3 ounces (90g) carrots, peeled

3 ounces (90g) onions, skinned

12 ounces (360g) collard greens

5 ounces (150g) zucchini

32 fluid ounces (960ml) water

2 bay leaves

salt, to taste

black pepper, ground, to taste

1 fluid ounce (30ml) lime juice

serrano chile, minced, as needed

cilantro, chopped, as needed

CHEF TIPS *If the flavor of the collard greens is very strong, blanch them before adding to the soup. Cabbage or mustard greens are good substitutes for the collard greens.*

Rinse the beef under cold running water.

Place the beef and all the whole vegetables in a large saucepot with the cold water. Add the bay leaves, salt, and pepper and bring to a boil.

Reduce the heat and simmer until all of the ingredients are cooked and tender. Do not allow the simmering soup to fall below 140°F (60°C). The meat must reach a minimum internal temperature of 145°F (62.8°C) or higher for at least 15 seconds.

As the vegetables become tender, remove them from the saucepot and cut them into 1-inch (2.54cm) cubes. Reserve until needed. When the meat is tender, remove it and reserve until needed.

Once all of the ingredients are removed, discard the bay leaves and strain the beef stock.

Reduce the broth until it is very flavorful.

Remove any fat or cartilage from the beef. Dice the meat in to ½-inch (1.27cm) cubes.

Return the diced meat and vegetables to the broth and bring to a simmer. Do not allow the simmering soup to fall below 140°F (60°C). Taste and adjust the seasoning with salt and black pepper as needed.

SERVING/HOLDING

Carefully ladle the soup into hot bowls or soup plates.

Garnish each portion with a little lime juice, serrano chile, and chopped cilantro. Serve immediately.

Hold the soup at 140°F (60°C) or above.

COOLING/STORING

Pour the remaining soup into small metal containers.

Cool the remaining soup from 140°F (60°C) to 70°F (21.1°C) or lower within 2 hours. Cool from 70°F (21.1°C) to 41°F (5°C) within an additional 4 hours for a total cooling time of 6 hours or less.

Cover soup; label, date, and store under refrigeration at 41°F (5°C) or lower.

Frijoles Alla Charra

YIELD: 6 PORTIONS · PORTION SIZE: 10 OUNCES

8 ounces (240g) dried pinto beans

64 fluid ounces (1.9L) white chicken stock, prepared (see page 517)

2 ounces (60g) pork butt, cut into medium dice

2 ounces (60g) bacon, cut into medium dice

4 ounces (120g) onion, cut into medium dice

1 clove garlic, minced

2 ounces (60g) poblano chile, charred, cut into small dice

4 ounces (120g) tomato concassée

⅓ teaspoon (2g) salt

⅓ teaspoon (2g) dried oregano

⅓ teaspoon (2g) cumin, ground

⅔ ounce (20g) cilantro, chopped

CHEF TIPS *For a little variety, add 4 ounces (120g) each medium-diced carrots and celery. To prepare frijoles borrachos, substitute 8 fluid ounces (240ml) of beer for 8 fluid ounces (240ml) of chicken stock. To prepare frijoles fronterizos, substitute 8 ounces (240g) of chorizo sausage for the pork and bacon called for in the recipe.*

Soak the pinto beans overnight under refrigeration.

COOKING

Drain the beans and place them in a saucepot with 64 fluid ounces (1.9L) of chicken stock.

Add the diced pork and bring to a boil. Reduce the heat and simmer for approximately 1 hour or until the pork is tender. Do not allow the simmering beans to fall below 140°F (60°C).

Sauté the bacon in a sauté pan and remove when crisp. Reserve until needed.

Sweat the onions, garlic, and poblano chile in the bacon fat. Stir in the tomato concassée and bring to a boil. Remove from the heat and add the mixture to the simmering beans.

Add the salt, oregano, and cumin and simmer for another 30 minutes or until the beans are tender. Do not allow the simmering beans to fall below 140°F (60°C).

When done, adjust the seasonings as needed and stir in the chopped cilantro.

Carefully ladle the soup into hot bowls or soup plates and serve immediately.

Hold the beans at 140°F (60°C) or above.

Pour the remaining beans into small metal containers.

Cool the remaining beans from 140°F (60°C) to 70°F (21.1°C) or lower within 2 hours. Cool from 70°F (21.1°C) to 41°F (5°C) within an additional 4 hours for a total cooling time of 6 hours or less.

Cover soup; label, date, and store under refrigeration at 41°F (5°C) or lower.

Quesadillas with Jicama Salsa

YIELD: 6 PORTIONS · PORTION SIZE: 6 OUNCES OR 1 QUESADILLA

2 ounces (60g) butter

2 ounces (60g) onion, sliced

12 ounces (360g) green chiles, roasted, peeled, seeded, chopped

4 ounces (120g) chorizo, skin removed, sliced

12 ounces (360g) potatoes, cooked, peeled, sliced

salt, to taste

black pepper, ground, to taste

12 flour tortillas (recipe follows)

12 ounces (360g) Monterey Jack or queso blanco, grated

18 ounces (840g) jicama salsa (recipe follows)

CHEF TIPS *Commercially prepared flour tortillas can easily be substituted for the homemade version called for in this recipe. 8-10 inch flour tortillas are an appropriate size for this appetizer.*

Quesadillas are typically grilled on a flat top griddle. If a griddle is not available, they can be cooked in a sauté pan over an open flame. Quesadillas can also be prepared by baking or broiling in an oven.

The jicama salsa and corn tortilla cylinders should be made in advance of the quesadillas and reserved until needed.

Heat the butter in a sauté pan. Add the onions and chiles and sauté until the onions are translucent.

Add the sliced chorizo and sauté until it reaches an internal temperature of 155°F (68.3°C) or higher for at least 15 seconds.

Remove excess fat. Add sliced potatoes, season to taste with salt and black pepper, and sauté until golden brown.

Divide the sausage and potato mixture among 6 of the flour tortillas and spread evenly. Sprinkle each with 2 ounces (60g) of grated cheese, top with another flour tortilla, and press together. Grill the quesadillas on each side for 30–60 seconds or until hot, crisp, and golden brown.

SERVING/HOLDING

Spoon approximately 3 ounces (90g) of jicama salsa in the center of each hot plate.

Cut each quesadilla into eighths. Serve immediately.

Hold the quesadillas at 140°F (60°C) or higher.

Cool from 140°F (60°C) to 70°F (21.1°C) or lower within 2 hours. Cool from 70°F (21.1°C) to 41°F (5°C) within an additional 4 hours for a total cooling time of 6 hours or less.

Cover the quesadillas and salsa; label, date, and store under refrigeration at 41°F (5°C) or lower.

FLOUR TORTILLAS

YIELD: 6 PORTIONS · PORTION SIZE: 1 TORTILLA

8¾ ounces (263g) all-purpose flour

⅓ teaspoon (2g) salt

⅓ teaspoon (2g) baking powder

2⅓ ounces (70ml) shortening, melted

4 fluid ounces (120ml) water

Mix all the dry ingredients together.

Mix in the shortening a little at a time until thoroughly incorporated. Mix in enough water to make a stiff dough.

Cover the dough and allow it to rest for 20 minutes.

COOKING

Heat a cast-iron skillet or comal over medium-high heat.

Pinch off a piece of dough about the size of a golf ball. Dust both your hands and the dough with a little flour. Place the dough ball on a lightly floured surface and flatten it into a circle about ½ inch (1.27cm) thick. Using a rolling pin, roll it out into a circle about ⅛ inch (.3cm) thick and 8 inches (20cm) in diameter.

Immediately place the tortilla in the hot skillet and cook it for 30–40 seconds or until the tortilla starts to bubble on top. Turn it over and cook an additional 20 seconds.

Remove the tortilla from the pan and keep it warm between towels until needed.

COOLING/STORING

Cover the tortillas; label, date, and store under refrigeration at 41°F (5°C) or lower.

JICAMA SALSA

6 ounces (180g) jicama, peeled, cut into small dice

6 ounces (180g) pineapple, cut into small dice

2 ounces (60g) red bell peppers, cut into small dice

1 clove garlic, minced

½ ounce (14g) serrano chile, minced

⅓ ounce (9g) cilantro, chopped

½ fluid ounce (15ml) lime juice

salt, to taste

black pepper, ground, to taste

Combine all the ingredients in a bowl.

Season to taste with salt and black pepper.

Reserve until needed under refrigeration at a product temperature of 41°F (5°C) or lower.

COOLING/STORING

Cover salsa; label, date, and store under refrigeration at 41°F (5°C) or lower.

Homemade Tamales with Red Pepper Coulis

12 ounces (360g) pork, butt roast

6 ounces (180g) beef, chuck roast or bottom round

1 ounce (30g) ancho chiles

½ ounce (14g) garlic, minced

8 ounces (240g) lard

¼ ounce (7g) cumin, ground

⅛ ounce (3g) black pepper, ground

½ teaspoon (2g) dried oregano

salt, to taste

5 ounces (160g) corn husks

24 ounces (720g) masa or ¾ pound (360g) masa harina, reconstituted

¼ ounce (7g) chili powder

¼ ounce (7g) paprika

¾ ounce (21g) garlic powder

18 fluid ounces (540ml) red pepper coulis (recipe follows)

Place the pork and beef in a roasting pan, cover, and cook in a 300°F (148.9°C) oven for approximately 4 hours or until the meats are fork tender.

Once the meats are fork tender and reach a minimum internal temperature of 155°F (68.3°C) or higher for at least 15 seconds, remove them from the heat, and pull or shred the meat.

Hold the meats at 140°F (60°C) or higher until needed.

Remove the stems from the ancho chiles and split open the pods along one side. Rinse the chiles under cold running water. Rinse the seeds from the chiles and discard them.

CHEF TIPS *The shredded beef and pork can also be prepared by simmering the meats in water until fork tender. If using this technique, be careful to not allow the simmering liquid to fall below 140°F (60°C) and make certain that meats reach a minimum internal temperature of 155°F (68.3°C) for at least 15 seconds. A chicken filling can be made by boiling chicken with seasonings such as cumin, chili powder, garlic, and salt. Once cooked, the chicken meat should be removed from the bones and shredded. Simply substituting refried beans for the shredded meat can make bean tamales. A thin slice of jalapeño or a strip of fried bacon can be added to the beans for extra flavor, if desired.*

Making genuine, homemade Tex-Mex–style tamales is a three-day process—one day to prepare the meat filling, a second day to prepare and roll the tamales, and a third day to steam and serve them. However, a number of techniques are used today to speed this process. One method we recommend, if time is of the essence, is to substitute coarsely ground pork and/or beef for the roast meats used in the filling. The ground beef can be quickly cooked, seasoned, and cooled. Then the seasoned ground meat can be used to fill the tamales without the lengthy resting period needed to make the traditional shredded meat filling.

Place the chiles in a pot of water, cover, and simmer for 15 minutes.

Remove the chiles from the water and scrape the pulp from the skin. Discard the skin. Chop the pulp and reserve both the pulp and liquid until needed.

Sauté the minced garlic in 2 tablespoons (30g) of the lard.

Combine the cooked meat, sautéed garlic, chile pod pulp, cumin, black pepper, and oregano. Season to taste with salt.

Cool the meat from 140°F (60°C) to 70°F (21.1°C) or lower within 2 hours. Cool from 70°F (21.1°C) to 41°F (5°C) within an additional 4 hours for a total cooling time of 6 hours or less. Once cool, shred the meat.

Cover the meat; label, date, and store under refrigeration at 41°F (5°C) or lower. Refrigerate overnight to allow the flavors to develop and to permeate the meats.

COOKING–DAY 2

Soak the corn husks in water for at least 2 hours. Separate them one by one and stack them ready for use.

Prepare the dough by combining the masa or reconstituted masa harina with the remaining lard, chili powder, paprika, and garlic powder. Adjust the consistency of the dough as needed with the reserved liquid used to simmer the ancho chiles.

Combine this mixture with your hands until it is thoroughly mixed. The more air that is incorporated into the masa dough, the better, as it will result in moist and fluffy tamales. It is impossible to overmix this dough.

Place an unbroken corn husk on a tray or work surface in front of you with the small end away from you.

Using a spatula or masa spreader, spread approximately 1–2 tablespoons (15–30g) of the masa dough on the corn husk in such a way that it covers the lower two-thirds and right 4 inches (10cm) of the husk. The masa should be spread thick enough so that you cannot see through to the husk.

Place the desired amount of the reserved meat filling in the middle of the masa. The amount of meat filling is a matter of personal preference.

Seal each tamale by rolling it over, starting from the right side where the masa and meat are. The unspread side covers the outside of the tamale and holds it together.

Fold the unfilled end at the top over to the middle. Tie the tamale, if necessary, with thin strips torn from a soaked corn husk.

Cover the tamales; label, date, and store overnight under refrigeration at 41°F (5°C) or lower.

COOKING—DAY 3

Set up a steamer in a large saucepot with an elevated bottom and tight-fitting lid. Add water to the saucepot until it reaches just under the elevated bottom. Place the tamales on the elevated bottom, standing them shoulder to shoulder with the open ends facing up. Cover the saucepot and steam for about 1 hour or until the masa peels away from the husk and the internal temperature of the tamales reaches 165°F (73.9°C) for at least 15 seconds.

Check the water level in the saucepot from time to time and add additional water as needed in order to keep the pot from boiling dry.

Let the tamales rest for 10–15 minutes before serving. This allows them to become firm.

SERVING/HOLDING

Remove the tamales from their corn husks. Fold the corn husks and place one on each hot serving plate. Place 2 or 3 tamales, depending on size, on top of the husks and top with heated red pepper coulis.

Hold the tamales at 140°F (60°C) or higher.

COOLING/STORING

Cool the tamales and red pepper coulis from 140°F (60°C) to 70°F (21.1°C) or lower within 2 hours. Cool from 70°F (21.1°C) to 41°F (5°C) within an additional 4 hours for a total cooling time of 6 hours or less.

Cover the tamales and sauce; label, date, and store under refrigeration at 41°F (5°C) or lower.

RED PEPPER COULIS

YIELD: 6 PORTIONS · PORTION SIZE: 3 OUNCES

10 ounces (300g) red bell peppers, stemmed and seeded

¼ ounce (7g) onion, finely diced

34 fluid ounces (1020ml) water

1 fluid ounce (30ml) white wine

1 ounce (30ml) cornstarch

salt, to taste

white pepper, ground, to taste

Place the peppers, onion, 32 fluid ounces (960ml) of the water, and white wine over medium heat and simmer until the peppers and onions are tender.

Cool slightly and purée until smooth.

Combine cornstarch and the remaining 2 ounces (60ml) water to create a slurry. Return purée to heat, and gradually add the slurry mixture as needed.

Season to taste with salt and white pepper and strain.

COOLING/STORING

Cool the red pepper coulis from 140°F (60°C) to 70°F (21.1°C) or lower within 2 hours. Cool from 70°F (21.1°C) to 41°F (5°C) within an additional 4 hours for a total cooling time of 6 hours or less.

Cover the coulis; label, date, and store under refrigeration at 41°F (5°C) or lower.

Shrimp Tacos with Guacamole and Pico de Gallo

YIELD: 6 PORTIONS · PORTION SIZE: 6 OUNCES OR 2 TACOS

4 ounces (120ml) vegetable oil

8 ounces (240g) onion, cut into small dice

4 ounces (120g) green bell peppers, cut into julienne

10 ounces (300g) red bell peppers, cut into julienne

2 cloves garlic, minced

6 ounces (180g) serrano chile, minced

24 shrimp, 16/20 count, peeled and deveined

salt, to taste

black pepper, ground, to taste

12 flour or corn tortillas, prepared

18 ounces (540g) iceberg lettuce, cut into chiffonade

12 ounces (360g) guacamole (recipe follows)

18 ounces (540g) pico de gallo (recipe follows)

6 fluid ounces (180ml) sour cream

6 ounces (180g) cheddar cheese, grated

Heat the oil in a sauté pan over medium heat.

Add the onions and cook until they are translucent and tender.

Add the peppers and cook an additional 2 minutes or until they are limp but not soft.

Add the garlic and serrano chile.

Add the shrimp and cook them approximately 3–5 minutes, until they are firm and reach a minimum internal temperature of 145°F (62.8°C) or higher for at least 15 seconds.

Adjust the seasoning to taste with salt and black pepper.

SERVING/HOLDING

Fill the corn or flour tortillas with the shrimp mixture, ensuring that each taco receives 2 of the shrimp. Fold the tortillas into a taco shape and arrange 2 tacos per plate over a bed of shredded lettuce.

Top the tacos with guacamole, pico de gallo, sour cream, and grated cheese.

Hold the tacos at 140°F (60°C) or higher.

COOLING/STORING

Cool the tacos from 140°F (60°C) to 70°F (21.1°C) or lower within 2 hours. Cool from 70°F (21.1°C) to 41°F (5°C) within an additional 4 hours for a total cooling time of 6 hours or less.

Cover the tacos, guacamole, pico de gallo, sour cream, and cheese; label, date, and store under refrigeration at 41°F (5°C) or lower.

GUACAMOLE

12 ounces (360g) avocado

¾ fluid ounce (22ml) lemon juice

1 jalapeño, seeded and minced

4 ounces (120g) tomato concassée

1½ ounces (45g) onion, finely diced

3 tablespoons (44g) cilantro, chopped

salt, to taste

black pepper, ground, to taste

Peel and pit the avocado. Place the avocado flesh in a bowl and mash to a chunky consistency.

Add the remaining ingredients and mix thoroughly.

COOLING/STORING

Cover the guacamole so that the plastic is touching the spread; label, date, and store under refrigeration at 41°F (5°C) or lower until needed.

CHEF TIPS *Guacamole should be mixed by hand. Use a fork to blend the ingredients until the mixture has a chunky consistency. Do not use a blender or food processor, as the consistency will be too thin. For a more distinctive appearance, split the avocado, remove the seed, and, with a paring knife, cut through the flesh, making ¼-inch (.64cm) slices both vertically and horizontally down to the skin. Using a tablespoon, scoop the sliced flesh out of the skin. The result is a small dice that can then be mixed gently with the other ingredients.*

Guacamole naturally oxidizes and turns brown if stored overnight. To reuse the guacamole, carefully skim the oxidized portion away and discard. Do not mix it in. To prevent oxidation, a little lemon juice can be spread over the top of the guacamole before storing.

PICO DE GALLO

8 ounces (240g) tomato, cut into brunoise

8 ounces (240g) onion, cut into brunoise

1 ounce (30g) garlic, minced

1 ounce (30g) serrano chile, cut into brunoise

1 ounce (30g) cilantro, chopped

1 fluid ounce (30ml) lime juice

salt, to taste

black pepper, ground, to taste

Combine all ingredients, adjusting the seasoning to taste with salt and black pepper.

COOLING/STORING

Cover the pico de gallo; label, date, and store under refrigeration at 41°F (5°C) or lower until needed.

Starburst Spinach Salad with Poppy-Seed Vinaigrette

YIELD: 6 PORTIONS · PORTION SIZE: 7½ OUNCES

2 Texas ruby red grapefruit

8 ounces (240g) spinach, torn into bite-sized pieces

11 ounces (330g) strawberries, stemmed, cut in half

VINAIGRETTE

2 tablespoons (30ml) strawberry vinegar

1 tablespoon (15g) sugar

1 tablespoon (15g) onion, chopped

¼ teaspoon (1g) salt

2 fluid ounces (60ml) vegetable oil

1 teaspoon (5g) poppy seeds

Finely grate 1½ teaspoons (22g) peel from the grapefruit and reserve until needed.

Peel the grapefruits and remove the fruit sections over a bowl, reserving the juice and sections for the salad dressing.

Combine the grapefruit sections, spinach, and strawberries in a bowl. Toss gently and reserve until needed.

Prepare the salad dressing by combining the reserved grapefruit juice, strawberry vinegar, sugar, onion, and salt. Place in a blender and process until smooth.

Slowly drizzle in the oil through the hole in the lid while the blender is running and process until the dressing has thickened.

Remove from the blender and stir in the poppy seeds.

Toss the spinach and fruit with the poppy-seed dressing and carefully place the spinach on chilled plates.

Garnish the salads by decoratively arranging the grapefruit sections and strawberries on top.

Serve immediately.

COOLING/STORING

Cover the salad and dressing; label, date and store under refrigeration at 41°F (5°C) or lower.

Braggin' Rights Brisket

YIELD: 6 PORTIONS · PORTION SIZE: 8 OUNCES

48 ounces (1.8kg) beef brisket, untrimmed

2 teaspoons (10g) black pepper, ground

1 teaspoon (5g) cayenne pepper

1 teaspoon (5g) onion salt

½ teaspoon (2g) dry mustard

hickory, pecan, or mesquite chips, soaked, as needed

2 tablespoons (10g) salt

18 fluid ounces (540ml) barbecue sauce (recipe follows)

CHEF TIPS *Hardwoods such as hickory, pecan, and oak burn slowly and thus are the best for slow smoking. Mesquite, although aromatic and great for grilling, burns too hot to be used for barbecue and leaves an oily taste to the meat. Notwithstanding, mesquite is still commonly used in West Texas. True Texas barbecue takes place in a long, narrow pit. A fire is built at one end and several inches or more separate the meat from it. The meat is cooked slowly at a very low temperature for up to 6 hours, during which time sauce is liberally applied from time to time.*

Season the beef brisket with black and red pepper, onion salt, and dry mustard.

Organize your smoker as indicated in the illustration.

COOKING

Sear the brisket on a grill or in a roasting pan over very high heat for 5 minutes on each side. Brown both sides thoroughly.

Place the uncovered brisket in the smoker. Allow to smoke for 1 hour.

Add the salt to the brisket and smoke for an additional 1 hour.

Cover with foil and place in a 300°F (148.9°C) oven. Cook the brisket until it is fork tender and reaches a minimum internal temperature of 145°F (62.8°C) or higher for at least 15 seconds.

Remove the roast from the oven and let it rest for 25 minutes, covered loosely with aluminum foil. Reserve the rendered fat from the brisket to use in the preparation of the barbecue sauce.

SERVING/HOLDING

Pull the meat apart to create a shredded effect or slice the brisket across the grain.

Serve the sliced brisket on hot plates and top with heated barbecue sauce.

Hold the brisket at 140°F (60°C) or higher.

COOLING/STORING

Cut the remaining brisket into smaller pieces. Cool the brisket and sauce from 140°F (60°C) to 70°F (21.1°C) or lower within 2 hours. Cool from 70°F (21.1°C) to 41°F (5°C) within an additional 4 hours for a total cooling time of 6 hours or less.

Cover brisket and sauce; label, date, and store under refrigeration at 41°F (5°C) or lower.

lid

product to
be smoked

rack

drip tray

hardwood
chips

smoke
roasting
pan

BARBECUE SAUCE

YIELD: 1 QUART · PORTION SIZE: 3 OUNCES

4 fluid ounces (120ml) rendered fat from barbecued meat

1½ ounce (45g) onion, cut into small dice

12 fluid ounces (360ml) ketchup

4 fluid ounces (120ml) Worcestershire sauce

4 fluid ounces (120ml) lemon juice

2½ ounces (75g) brown sugar

3 fluid ounces (90ml) water

Tabasco sauce, to taste

CHEF TIPS *Hot pepper sauce comes in hundreds of varieties, flavors, and level of heat. Tabasco sauce is one of the most popular hot pepper sauces available in the United States. Feel free to experiment until you find the hot sauce that yields the ideal flavor for your special barbecue sauce recipe.*

Heat the rendered fat reserved from the brisket preparation in a small saucepot.

Add the diced onions and sauté until they are translucent.

Add the ketchup, Worcestershire sauce, and lemon juice.

Place over low heat and stir in the brown sugar and water.

Simmer for 15 minutes. Do not allow the simmering sauce to fall below 140°F (60°C).

Season the sauce to taste with hot pepper sauce.

Hold the sauce at 140°F (60°C) or higher.

COOLING/STORING

Cool the sauce from 140°F (60°C) to 70°F (21.1°C) or lower within 2 hours. Cool from 70°F (21.1°C) to 41°F (5°C) within an additional 4 hours for a total cooling time of 6 hours or less.

Cover the sauce; label, date, and store under refrigeration at 41°F (5°C) or lower.

Mole de Pollo

YIELD: 6 PORTIONS · PORTION SIZE: 12 OUNCES OR 3 PIECES

3 fryer chickens 40 ounces (1200g) each, boned and cut into 6 pieces (18 pieces total)

3 fluid ounces (90ml) vegetable oil

3 ounces (90g) dried ancho chiles

3 ounces (90g) dried cascabel chile

12 ounces (360g) onion, chopped

4 cloves garlic, minced

¼ teaspoon (1g) anise seeds, toasted

6 sprigs cilantro

6 ounces (180g) tomato

1½ ounces (45g) unsalted peanuts

1 pinch cloves, ground

2 pinches cinnamon, ground

¼ teaspoon (1g) cumin, ground

24 fluid ounces (720ml) white chicken stock, prepared (see page 517)

⅓ tablespoon (5g) lard

1½ ounce (45g) unsweetened chocolate, grated

salt, to taste

black pepper, ground, to taste

1 ounce (30g) sesame seeds

CHEF TIPS *Adding the chicken breasts to the sauce after the dark cuts ensures that all of the chicken is done at the same time. Dark cuts of chicken take longer to cook than the breasts.*

Reserve the prepared chicken under refrigeration at 41°F (5°C) or lower until needed.

Heat one-third of the vegetable oil in a large pan over medium-high heat. Sear the pieces from one of the chickens until they are browned thoroughly on both sides. Hold the pieces at 140°F (60°C) or higher until needed. Repeat this process for the remaining 2 chickens, being careful to let the new oil heat up sufficiently to sear the pieces of chicken.

Rehydrate the dried chiles by simmering them in a small, covered saucepot of water for 10 minutes. Remove the chiles from the water. When the chiles have cooled enough to handle, remove the skins, stems, and seeds.

Place the chiles, onion, garlic, and seasonings, and 1 cup (240ml) of the chicken stock in a blender. Purée until smooth.

Melt the lard in a large saucepot. Stir in the purée and adjust the heat to a simmer.

Simmer for 5 minutes and add the remaining chicken stock, the dark-meat pieces of the chicken, and the chocolate.

Season the sauce to taste with salt and black pepper and simmer for 30 minutes. Do not allow the simmering sauce to fall below 140°F (60°C).

Add the chicken breasts to the sauce and continue to simmer for an additional 15 minutes. Do not allow the simmering sauce to fall below 140°F (60°C). Simmer until the chicken is done and reaches an internal temperature of 165°F (73.9°C) or higher for at least 15 seconds.

SERVING/HOLDING

Place a breast and 2 dark cuts of chicken on a heated plate. Serve the sauce over the chicken and garnish with toasted sesame seeds.

Hold the mole de pollo at 140°F (60°C) or higher.

COOLING/STORING

Cool the mole de pollo from 140°F (60°C) to 70°F (21.1°C) or lower within 2 hours. Cool from 70°F (21.1°C) to 41°F (5°C) within an additional 4 hours for a total cooling time of 6 hours or less.

Cover the mole de pollo; label, date, and store under refrigeration at 41°F (5°C) or lower.

Lone Star Chicken-Fried Steak with Cream Gravy

YIELD: 6 PORTIONS · PORTION SIZE: 10 OUNCES

8 ounces (240g) all-purpose flour

1 teaspoon (5g) salt

seasoned pepper mix, to taste

2¾ pounds (1.2kg) beef round steak, cut into 7-ounce (198g) portions, trimmed, and tenderized until very thin

2 large eggs, slightly beaten

6 fluid ounces (180ml) milk

vegetable oil, as needed

GRAVY

3 fluid ounces (90ml) pan drippings or bacon fat

3 ounces (90g) all-purpose flour

24 fluid ounces (710ml) milk

salt, to taste

black pepper, ground, to taste

CHEF TIPS *Chicken-fried steak is traditionally served with the works—white cream gravy, mashed potatoes, fresh corn kernels or green beans, and biscuits.*

Combine flour, salt, and seasoned pepper mix.

Dredge the steaks in the seasoned flour mixture until lightly coated.

Mix the eggs and milk together in a pan.

Dip the steaks into the egg mixture and then dredge in the flour again liberally, getting plenty of flour mashed into the steak.

Hold under refrigeration at 41°F (5°C) or lower until needed.

COOKING

Heat ½ inch (1.27cm) of vegetable oil in a heavy-bottomed sautoir pan. Pan-fry the steaks until they are golden brown and reach a minimum internal temperature of 155°F (68.3°C) or higher for at least 15 seconds.

Remove steaks from the oil and drain on absorbent paper towels. Season to taste with salt. Hold at 140°F (60°C) or higher until needed.

Allow the oil and pan drippings to cool slightly and discard all but 3 fluid ounces (90ml).

Return the oil to medium heat and add the flour. Blend to form a roux. Cook the roux approximately 10–12 minutes over low heat until it is a golden brown color.

Slowly blend in the milk. Bring to a boil, reduce the heat, and simmer, stirring frequently, until the sauce thickens.

Season the sauce to taste with salt and black pepper.

SERVING/HOLDING

Serve the chicken-fried steak on hot plates topped with the cream gravy.

Hold the chicken-fried steak at 140°F (60°C) or higher.

COOLING/STORING

Discard the remaining egg wash and seasoned flour.

Cool the remaining steaks and sauce from 140°F (60°C) to 70°F (21.1°C) or lower within 2 hours. Cool from 70°F (21.1°C) to 41°F (5°C) within an additional 4 hours for a total cooling time of 6 hours or less.

Cover steaks and sauce; label, date, and store under refrigeration at 41°F (5°C) or lower.

Chicken Flautas

YIELD: 6 PORTIONS · PORTION SIZE: 12 OUNCES OR 3 FLAUTAS

vegetable oil, as needed

18 corn tortillas (recipe follows)

18 ounces (540g) chicken meat, cooked
and shredded

18 ounces (540g) iceberg lettuce, cut
into chiffonade

6 ounces (180g) Monterey Jack cheese, shredded

12 ounces (360g) guacamole (see page 298)

6 ounces (180ml) sour cream

CHEF TIPS *Commercially prepared corn tortillas can easily be substituted for the homemade version called for in this recipe. Flautas
are traditionally served with refried beans
and Mexican rice.*

Heat approximately ½ inch (1.27cm) of vegetable oil until hot but not smoking.

Dip the corn tortillas, one at a time, in the hot oil for a brief period—just long enough for the tortilla to become limp. Remove from the oil and stack on absorbent paper towels. Reserve until needed.

Place approximately 1 ounce (30g) of the chicken meat in a strip on one side of each tortilla. Roll up the tortillas as tightly as possible and secure with toothpicks.

Pan-fry the flautas, a few at a time, in the hot oil for approximately 1–2 minutes or until they are crisp and reach a minimum internal temperature of 165°F (73.9°C) for at least 15 seconds. Degrease the flautas on a rack or on absorbent paper towels and remove the toothpicks.

SERVING/HOLDING

Serve 3 flautas per portion over a bed of shredded lettuce. Top the flautas with grated cheese and a dollop each of guacamole and sour cream.

Hold the flautas at 140°F (60°C) or higher.

COOLING/STORING

Cool the flautas from 140°F (60°C) to 70°F (21.1°C) or lower within 2 hours. Cool from 70°F (21.1°C) to 41°F (5°C) within an additional 4 hours for a total cooling time of 6 hours or less.

Cover the flautas; label, date, and store under refrigeration at 41°F (5°C) or lower.

CORN TORTILLAS

YIELD: 6 PORTIONS · PORTION SIZE: 3 TORTILLAS

24 ounces (720g) masa harina

48 fluid ounces (1.4L) water

1 teaspoon (5g) salt

CHEF TIPS *If the dough is sticky, it is too wet. Blend in a little more masa harina until the proper consistency is reached. If the dough is crumbly, it is too dry. Slowly blend in more water. You will not harm the dough by handling it too much—indeed, handling seems to improve it.*

Mix all the ingredients in a bowl until a smooth dough forms.

Divide evenly into 18 balls. Flatten the balls and roll them out to ⅛ inch (.3cm) thick or use a tortilla press. Tortilla dough must be cooked immediately after rolling or pressing, so have cooking materials ready.

COOKING

Heat a cast-iron skillet or comal over medium-high heat.

Place the tortilla in the hot skillet and cook it for 30–40 seconds or until the tortilla starts to bubble on top. Turn it over and cook an additional 20 seconds.

Remove the tortilla from the pan and keep warm by placing between towels until needed.

COOLING/STORING

Cover the tortillas; label, date, and store under refrigeration at 41°F (5°C) or lower.

Texas Red Chili with Jalapeño Corn Bread

16 fluid ounces (480ml) water

½ ounce (14g) ancho chile

¾ fluid ounce (22ml) vegetable oil

½ ounce (14g) butter

16 ounces (480g) beef stew meat, cut into small dice

3½ ounces (105g) onion, cut into small dice

2½ ounces (75g) green bell pepper, cut into small dice

1½ tablespoons (22g) Gebhardt's chili powder

½ tablespoon (7g) cumin, ground

1 tablespoon (15g) salt

½ tablespoon (7g) black pepper, coarsely ground

1 tablespoon (15g) garlic, minced

1 ounce (30g) all-purpose flour

9 fluid ounces (270ml) tomato sauce

1 ounce (30g) pickled jalapeños, chopped

6 ounces (180g) Longhorn cheddar cheese, grated

6 ounces (180g) onions, finely diced

24 ounces (720g) jalapeño corn bread (recipe follows)

CHEF TIPS *In Texas, the term* Texas Red *refers to beef chili without beans. End of discussion. This is a meal in itself, but adding hot, buttered jalapeño corn bread always makes it a winning combination. Chuck roast or ground beef can be substituted for the stew meat; however, if ground beef is used, the minimum internal temperature for doneness must be increased to 165°F (73.9°C). As a serving option, top the chili with finely grated longhorn cheddar cheese and raw chopped yellow onion. Serve the Texas chili with crackers and/or jalapeño cornbread.*

Bring the water to a boil in a saucepot. While it is heating, cook the ancho chile under a hot broiler for 1 minute on each side.

Remove the chile. Let cool until it can be safely handled. Remove the stem and any seeds inside the chile.

Place the chile in the boiling water. Cover and remove the pot from the heat. Let the chile steep in the water until needed.

Add the oil and butter to a large saucepot or chili pot and heat on medium-high.

When the fats become hot, sear the meat. Stir frequently until the meat is thoroughly browned and reaches a minimum internal temperature of 155°F (68.3°C) for at least 15 seconds.

Add the onions and bell peppers, stir, and add the chili powder, cumin, salt, black pepper, and garlic. Stir again.

Add the flour, a little at a time, stirring constantly until blended.

Reduce the heat to medium and cook for 5 minutes.

Strain the ancho chile from the liquid. Mince the chile. Reserve the liquid and minced chile until needed.

Add the ancho chile liquid to the beef and vegetable mixture and stir until the fond is released from the bottom of the pot. Add the tomato sauce, minced ancho chiles, and the pickled jalapeños.

Stir the chili until all ingredients are thoroughly mixed. Bring to a boil and reduce the heat to a simmer. Do not allow the simmering chili to fall below 140°F (60°C). Simmer uncovered for 1–2 hours, stirring occasionally to keep the chili from sticking, until the meat is tender and the desired consistency is reached.

SERVING/HOLDING

Carefully ladle the chili into hot bowls or soup plates, top with grated cheddar and diced onions, and serve with jalapeño corn bread.

Hold the chili at 140°F (60°C) or higher.

COOLING/STORING

Cool the chili from 140°F (60°C) to 70°F (21.1°C) or lower within 2 hours. Cool from 70°F (21.1°C) to 41°F (5°C) within an additional 4 hours for a total cooling time of 6 hours or less.

Cover chili; label, date, and store under refrigeration at 41°F (5°C) or lower.

JALAPEÑO CORN BREAD

YIELD: 6 PORTIONS · PORTION SIZE: 3 OUNCES

9½ ounces (285g) cornmeal, finely ground

4½ ounces (135g) all-purpose flour

2 teaspoons (10g) double-acting baking powder

1 teaspoon (5g) baking soda

1 teaspoon (5g) salt

4 ounces (120g) cheddar cheese, shredded

6 ounces (180g) jalapeños, seeded, chopped

2 large eggs

18 fluid ounces (540ml) buttermilk

3 tablespoons (45g) butter

Heat a seasoned 9-inch (23cm) cast-iron skillet or heavy-duty cake pan over low heat.

Sift the cornmeal, flour, baking powder, baking soda, and salt together in a bowl. Add the cheddar cheese and the jalapeños and mix thoroughly.

In a separate bowl, whisk the eggs and buttermilk together.

Melt the butter in the heated skillet or cake pan. Add the buttermilk mixture and whisk to incorporate.

Working quickly, pour the buttermilk mixture into the cornmeal mixture. Stir the mixture until the ingredients are combined and a batter forms. Pour the batter back into the heated skillet or cake pan.

Bake the corn bread in the middle of a preheated 425°F (218.3°C) oven for 25–30 minutes or until it pulls away from the side of the skillet. The top of the corn bread should be slightly brown.

SERVING/HOLDING

Let the corn bread cool a little before slicing. Cut the corn bread into squares and serve with butter on the side.

COOLING/STORING

Cover the corn bread; label, date, and store under refrigeration at 41°F (5°C) or lower.

Chiles Rellenos with Tomatillo Salsa

YIELD: 6 PORTIONS · PORTION SIZE: 4 OUNCES

24 ounces (720g) or 12 poblano chiles

6 ounces (180g) cheddar and/or Monterey Jack cheese, cut into thin slices, 1 inch (2.5cm) x 3 inches (7.6cm)

4 large eggs, separated

salt, as needed

oil, as needed

all-purpose flour, as needed

18 ounces (540g) tomatillo salsa (recipe follows)

CHEF TIPS *For the best flavor, the chiles rellenos should be fried at the last minute; however, the time-consuming roasting and peeling of the chiles can be done up to 2 days in advance. Keep the chiles covered with plastic wrap under refrigeration until needed.*

In many Tex-Mex restaurants, American cheese singles are used in place of cheddar or Jack cheese.

Roast the poblano chiles on a hot grill. Turn constantly to ensure that the skin chars evenly. As each chile is finished roasting, place it in a plastic bag and allow it to sweat in the closed bag for approximately 30 minutes.

Peel off the outer skins of the chiles and slit the chiles lengthwise along one side. Remove the seeds; this lowers the heat of the chile.

Trim the cheese slices so they fit inside the chiles and place approximately ½ ounce (14g) of cheese in each chile. Close the chiles completely.

Beat the egg yolks in a mixing machine for approximately 15 minutes or until they are thick and lemon-colored.

In a separate bowl, beat the egg whites with a pinch of salt in a mixing machine until a stiff meringue forms.

Heat approximately ½ inch (1.27cm) of oil in a sautoir pan over high heat.

Add the egg yolks to the meringue and briefly beat on low speed to incorporate the eggs. Be prepared to begin cooking the rellenos immediately, as the batter quickly begins to deflate.

Dredge the chiles rellenos in the flour. Shake off the excess flour and dip in the egg batter.

Pan-fry the chiles rellenos in the hot oil for approximately 2 minutes or until brown on one side, then turn and continue to cook until brown on the other side. Add oil to the skillet as needed or if the chiles begin to stick to the pan. Ensure that the chiles rellenos reach a minimum internal temperature of 145°F (62.8°C) for at least 15 seconds.

As the rellenos are cooked, layer them in a roasting pan with a piece of aluminum foil between each layer and hold them in a 150°F (65.6°C) oven while pan-frying the remaining chiles rellenos. Do not let the chiles rellenos fall below 140°F (60°C) or higher.

SERVING/HOLDING

Serve 2 chiles rellenos in the center of each hot plate topped with approximately 3 ounces (90g) of tomatillo salsa.

Hold the chiles rellenos at 140°F (60°C) or higher.

COOLING/STORING

Cool the chiles rellenos from 140°F (60°C) to 70°F (21.1°C) or lower within 2 hours. Cool from 70°F (21.1°C) to 41°F (5°C) within an additional 4 hours for a total cooling time of 6 hours or less.

Cover the rellenos and salsa; label, date, and store under refrigeration at 41°F (5°C) or lower.

TOMATILLO SALSA

YIELD: 6 PORTIONS · PORTION SIZE: 3 OUNCES

16 fluid ounces (480ml) water

6 ounces (180g) tomatillos, husks removed, quartered

4 cloves garlic, minced

½ ounce (15g) red jalapeño, peeled and seeded, finely diced

1½ ounces (45g) onions, finely diced

½ ounce (15g) cilantro

salt, to taste

black pepper, ground, to taste

GARNISH

½ ounce (15g) onion, finely diced

¼ ounce (7g) cilantro, chopped

Bring the water to a boil in a small saucepot. Add the tomatillos, half the garlic, the red jalapeños, and onions.

Cook over medium heat for 20 minutes. Remove from the heat. Strain the contents and reserve the liquid until needed.

In a blender, purée the remaining garlic with the cilantro and the tomatillo mixture. Add reserved liquid from the tomatillos as needed in order to achieve the desired consistency.

Season the salsa to taste with salt and black pepper.

Stir in the raw diced onions and the cilantro as a garnish for the salsa.

COOLING/STORING

Cover the salsa; label, date, and store under refrigeration at 41°F (5°C) or lower.

Colache

YIELD: 6 PORTIONS · PORTION SIZE: 4 OUNCES

5 ounces (150g) acorn squash, cut into large dice

5 ounces (150g) sweet potato, cut into large dice

3 ounces (90g) green bell peppers, cut into large dice

1 ounce (30g) poblano chile, cut into large dice

5 ounces (150g) green beans, cut into 1-inch (2.54cm) pieces

3 ounces (90g) corn kernels

½ ounce (15g) butter

2 ounces (60g) onion, cut into small dice

1 clove garlic, minced

4 ounces (120g) tomato concassée in large chunks

1 teaspoon (5g) chili powder

salt, to taste

black pepper, ground, to taste

Parboil the squash, sweet potato, pepper, poblano chile, beans, and corn individually to their respective points of doneness. Shock the vegetables in an ice-water bath as they are done and reserve until needed. Alternatively, cool the vegetables from 140°F (60°C) to 70°F (21.1°C) or lower within 2 hours. Cool from 70°F (21.1°C) to 41°F (5°C) within an additional 4 hours for a total cooling time of 6 hours or less.

Melt the butter in a medium-sized sauté pan. Sauté the onions and garlic. Add the reserved vegetables and cook until they are thoroughly heated and reach a minimum internal temperature of 165°F (73.9°C) for at least 15 seconds.

Add the tomatoes and the chili powder.

Season to taste with salt and black pepper.

SERVING/HOLDING

Hold the vegetables at 140°F (60°C) or higher.

COOLING/STORING

Cool the vegetables from 140°F (60°C) to 70°F (21.1°C) or lower within 2 hours. Cool from 70°F (21.1°C) to 41°F (5°C) within an additional 4 hours for a total cooling time of 6 hours or less.

Cover the colache; label, date, and store under refrigeration at 41°F (5°C) or lower.

Escabeche of Vegetables

3 fluid ounces (90ml) extra-virgin olive oil

2 bulbs garlic, ends trimmed

1 onion, cut into medium dice

2 carrots, cut into coins on the bias

¾ teaspoon (4g) black peppercorns

½ teaspoon (2g) dried thyme

½ teaspoon (2g) dried oregano

½ teaspoon (2g) dried marjoram

4 bay leaves

½ head cauliflower, cut into florets

2 jalapeños, seeded and chopped

¾ cup (180ml) white vinegar

½ cup (120ml) warm water

1 jicama, peeled and sliced

2 zucchini, cut into coins on the bias

salt, to taste

CHEF TIPS *Do not overcook the vegetables. They should be crunchy to the bite. This dish is best served at room temperature after resting under refrigeration overnight. The resting process allows the full extraction of flavors of the vegetables.*

Heat the olive oil in a sauté pan over medium-high heat. Sauté the whole garlic bulbs and the onions for approximately 3 minutes, stirring occasionally.

Reduce the heat to medium and add the carrots, black peppercorns, dried herbs, and bay leaves. Cover and cook for an additional 2 minutes.

Stir in the cauliflower, jalapeños, vinegar, and water. Cover and cook over medium-high heat for 5 more minutes.

Stir in the jicama and zucchini. Cover and cook over medium-high heat for an additional 5 minutes. Season to taste with salt.

COOLING/STORING

Cool the escabeche from 140°F (60°C) to 70°F (21.1°C) or lower within 2 hours. Cool from 70°F (21.1°C) to 41°F (5°C) within an additional 4 hours for a total cooling time of 6 hours or less.

Cover the escabeche; label, date, and store overnight while under refrigeration at 41°F (5°C) or lower.

SERVING

🍲 **Serve** at room temperature. Do not allow the escabeche to stand at room temperature for more than 4 hours. After this point, it must be discarded.

Refried Beans

YIELD: 6 PORTIONS · PORTION SIZE: 8 OUNCES

8 ounces (240g) dried pinto beans

40 fluid ounces (1.2L) white chicken stock, prepared (see page 517)

2 ounces (60g) bacon, cut into small dice

2 ounces (60g) onion, cut into small dice

½ clove garlic, minced

salt, to taste

black pepper, ground, to taste

2 ounces (60g) Monterey Jack or queso blanco, grated

Soak the pinto beans overnight under refrigeration.

COOKING

Drain the beans and place them in a large saucepot with the chicken stock.

Bring to a boil and turn the heat down to a simmer. Simmer for approximately 1–1½ hours or until the beans are tender. Do not allow the simmering beans to fall below 140°F (60°C).

Drain the beans and reserve the beans and liquid until needed.

Sauté the bacon in a cast-iron skillet or heavy-bottomed pan until all the fat is rendered.

Add the onions and garlic. Sweat the vegetables.

Remove the bacon, onions, and garlic. Reserve until needed.

Add the cooked pinto beans to the hot bacon fat and toss.

CHEF TIPS *The bacon fat in this recipe can be replaced with a simple vegetable oil if a more nutritionally sound dish is desired. Refried beans are commonly referred to as* refritos *and are usually made from pinto beans. The Spanish word* refritos *means "well fried" and is frequently misinterpreted as "refried" or "twice fried." Typically, pinto beans are cooked and drained, then mashed with hot lard or bacon fat, seasonings, and (sometimes) chiles. Despite their name, Tex-Mex—style refried beans are fried only once.*

In the American Southwest region, authentic refried beans call for smoking-hot lard to be poured over the cooked, mashed pinto beans and stirred in—thus the name refried beans. Due to the unusually high cholesterol content of lard, we have chosen a more up-to-date approach using a small amount of bacon fat and to refry the beans from the bottom as opposed to the traditional Southwest procedure. A cast-iron frying pan yields the best results. However, a nonstick pan will also work.

Mash the cooked beans while continuing to cook over medium heat. A food processor can also be used to mash the beans.

Add the bacon, onions, and garlic back to the mashed beans.

Blend in enough of the bean liquid to make the beans creamy. Lower the heat and cook the beans until a crust forms on the bottom of the pan.

Season the beans to taste with salt and black pepper.

SERVING/HOLDING

Serve hot with the crust up and sprinkled with grated Monterey Jack or queso blanco.

Hold the beans at 140°F (60°C) or above.

COOLING/STORING

Pour the remaining beans into small metal containers.

Cool the beans from 140°F (60°C) to 70°F (21.1°C) or lower within 2 hours. Cool from 70°F (21.1°C) to 41°F (5°C) within an additional 4 hours for a total cooling time of 6 hours or less.

Cover the beans; label, date, and store under refrigeration at 41°F (5°C) or lower.

Arroz à la Mexicana

1 fluid ounce (30ml) vegetable or corn oil

8 ounces (240ml) raw long-grain white rice, washed twice

2 ounces (60g) onion, cut into small dice

1 clove garlic, minced

1 ounce (30g) poblano chile, peeled and diced

4 ounces (120g) carrot, cut into small dice

6 ounces (180g) tomato concassée

16 fluid ounces (480ml) white chicken stock, prepared (see page 517)

salt, to taste

black pepper, ground, to taste

1½ bay leaves

1 teaspoon (5ml) cilantro, chopped

CHEF TIPS *Arroz à la Mexicana can be cooked on the stovetop as well as in the oven. However, it is much easier to burn on the stovetop and requires more attention while cooking. To cook on the stovetop, simply simmer the rice while covered. Decrease the cooking time to approximately 20 minutes. Make sure not to allow the simmering rice to fall below 140°F (60°C).*

Heat the oil in a sautoir pan over high heat.

Add the rice and sauté in the hot oil, stirring frequently, until it begins to brown.

Stir in the onion and garlic, stirring constantly, and cook until the rice is nicely browned and has a nutty aroma.

Add the poblano chiles, carrots, tomatoes, and chicken stock. Season to taste with salt and black pepper. Add the bay leaves.

Bring to a boil. Turn the heat down to a simmer. Cover the pan with a tight-fitting lid and place in a 350°F (176.7°C) oven for 40 minutes.

Remove the lid and fluff the rice with a fork. Mix in the chopped cilantro.

SERVING

Hold the rice at 140°F (60°C) or higher.

Cool the rice from 140°F (60°C) to 70°F (21.1°C) or lower within 2 hours. Cool from 70°F (21.1°C) to 41°F (5°C) within an additional 4 hours for a total cooling time of 6 hours or less.

Cover the rice; label, date, and store under refrigeration at 41°F (5°C) or lower.

Mashed Potatoes

YIELD: 6 PORTIONS · PORTION SIZE: 6 OUNCES

36 ounces (1kg) russet potatoes

salt, as needed

2 ounces (60g) butter, softened

8 fluid ounces (240ml) buttermilk, warmed but not boiled

salt, to taste

black pepper, ground, to taste

CHEF TIPS *Mashed potatoes can be made by either baking or boiling potatoes. When boiling, do not cut the potatoes too small, as they will become waterlogged and prevent the finished mashed potatoes from being light and fluffy, which is the desired texture for this starch. A ricer is a culinary tool frequently used to mash potatoes.*

Peel and cut the potatoes into 2-inch (5cm) cubes.

Boil the potatoes in a large saucepot with a generous amount of salted water until they are tender.

Drain the potatoes and return them to the pot. Cook over low heat for approximately 3 minutes to allow them to dry completely.

Mash, grind, or rice the potatoes.

Blend in the softened butter and most of the warmed buttermilk.

Adjust the consistency as desired with warm buttermilk.

Season to taste with salt and black pepper.

COOLING/STORING

Cool the potatoes from 140°F (60°C) to 70°F (21.1°C) or lower within 2 hours. Cool from 70°F (21.1°C) to 41°F (5°C) within an additional 4 hours for a total cooling time of 6 hours or less.

Cover the potatoes; label, date, and store under refrigeration at 41°F (5°C) or lower.

Flan

YIELD: 6 PORTIONS · PORTION SIZE: 3 OUNCES

14 ounces (420g) sugar

3 fluid ounces (90ml) lemon juice

7 large eggs

4 ounces (120g) sugar

1 pinch salt

1 tablespoon (15ml) vanilla

16 fluid ounces (480ml) milk, scalded

CHEF TIPS *The process of tempering is done in this recipe to prevent the eggs from cooking or scrambling when placed in the scalded milk. To temper the eggs, stir approximately 4–6 fluid ounces (118–177ml) of the scalded milk into the beaten eggs to warm them gradually, then stir the egg mixture into the remaining scalded milk.*

Caramelize the first amount of sugar with the lemon juice. Pour evenly into the bottom of 6 ovenproof cups or ramekins. Reserve until needed.

Whisk the eggs and the second amount of sugar together. Mix in the salt and vanilla.

Temper the scalded milk into the egg mixture. Strain and pour the mixture into the reserved cups with the caramelized sugar.

Place a towel on the bottom of a large roasting pan and place the custard cups on top.

Fill the roasting pan with water so that the level of the water comes to at least half the height of the cups. Cover the cups with parchment paper and bake in a preheated 350°F (176.7°C) oven until the flan is set. Times vary greatly from oven to oven. However, you can tell when the flan is done by inserting a skewer or toothpick into the flan. When the skewer comes out clean, the flan is done. The flan must reach a minimum internal temperature of 145°F (62.8°C) for at least 15 seconds.

SERVING/HOLDING

Once the flan is thoroughly cooled, run a paring knife around the perimeter of the cups.

Invert the flan onto chilled plates and allow the caramel sauce to flow over the flan.

Store the flan under refrigeration at 41°F (5°C) or lower until needed.

COOLING/STORING

Cool the flan from 140°F (60°C) to 70°F (21.1°C) or lower within 2 hours. Cool from 70°F (21.1°C) to 41°F (5°C) within an additional 4 hours for a total cooling time of 6 hours or less.

Cover the flan; label, date, and store under refrigeration at 41°F (5°C) or lower.

Does the Rocky Mountain region have its own cuisine? If so, then what is it? Beef, buffalo, elk, and trout? True, it's famous for these. But does the serving of these items constitute an entire cuisine?

If you're looking for Rocky Mountain dishes, you might start with bison (the high-end name for *buffalo*). All the Native Americans and mountain men ate it. Buff marrow, called *prairie butter*, greased many a mountain man's chin. Hump, tongue, and rib bones were favored.

With the gold seekers of 1859 came food from back home: New England, Pennsylvania, Ohio, the Deep South, Germany, Cornwall, and, later, the Scandinavian countries. Denver sported restaurants with all these foods in the 1870s and to the turn of the nineteenth century. English, Scottish, Welsh, Irish, and German miners ate "their" foods. Later, with Italian and Greek immigrants came new culinary additions to the fabric of the Rocky Mountains.

The Santa Fe, Burlington Northern, Union Pacific, and Rio Grande train companies set a concept for Colorado cuisine: It was a bit "ranchy" with Mexican overtones, as one traveler put it. Think of the thousands of tourists who have, for a century, eaten Rocky Mountain cuisine at the lodges of dude ranches: pan-fried rainbow trout, sirloin steaks and eggs, prime rib, lamb and mutton chops, roasted or fried chicken, chili con carne, and beans and tortillas.

This is what the nation thinks is Rocky Mountain cuisine. But one thread runs through it all: hearty portions, mostly unsauced, and plain, uncomplicated real food.

Sam Arnold is owner of the renowned Fort Restaurant in Denver, Colorado. He is author of several cookbooks championing the cuisine of the west.

The Rocky Mountain States

Colorado

Idaho

Montana

Nevada

Utah

Wyoming

The Rocky Mountain states of Wyoming, Colorado, Utah,

Nevada, Idaho, and Montana are known for their meat-and-potato cuisine, which

originated with the wholesome, hearty foods of the pioneers—notably, stews,

roasts, and steaks. Not only was this cuisine influenced by the Native Americans

but it also draws its heritage from the Basque and Hispanic settlers who were the

first Europeans to live in the region. The Rocky Mountains offer a variety of indige-

nous game and freshwater fish as well as an abundance of berries and mush-

rooms, which grow in the mountain forests and meadows of the plains. Grains,

potatoes, beef, and lamb are today the largest agricultural commodities produced

in this region of America.

The story of Rocky Mountain cuisine begins with the rapid settlement of the American West in the mid-1800s, before the transcontinental railroad was built. Prospectors and immigrants heading to the gold rush of California traveled two main routes: the Oregon Trail and the Santa Fe Trail. The northern route, the Oregon Trail, began in Missouri, crossed the Rocky Mountains into Utah, and veered north through Idaho and into Oregon, while the Santa Fe trail took a more southerly route through Colorado into New Mexico. Both of these routes influenced the cuisine of the Rocky Mountain region and Western American cooking as we know it today. The cooking originating from the Oregon Trail is responsible for our fondness for simmered beans, pan gravies, stews, biscuits, and quick breads. The cooking originating from the Santa Fe Trail, with its heavy Mexican and Native American influences, contributed not only to the cuisine of the Rocky Mountains but also to that of the American Southwest.

The first known group to follow the Oregon Trail, leaving Independence, Missouri, in 1842, was the Bidwell-Bartleson party. Over the next two decades, hundreds of thousands of immigrants left their homes to follow the Bidwells and Bartlesons in their quest for gold. The Mormons followed the Oregon Trail for religious freedom instead. They veered south once in the Great Basin of Utah. Many of the dishes still popular in Utah, such as hearty stews and other one-pot dishes made with beans, have roots in the foods eaten by the Mormons while traveling West. When the Mormon population chose to settle in Utah rather than continuing west, their taste and preferences prevailed in the area. The Mormons continue to influence the foods of the region today.

As did the cowboys who ate chuck wagon cooking in Texas, the pioneers and immigrant settlers on the Oregon Trail found that their daily sustenance included sourdough breads, quick breads, salt pork preparations, wild game and fish, and what could be foraged from the forests, mountain valleys, and plains. The basic storage on the typical Oregon Trail chuck wagon also included coffee, sugar, dried beans, flour and baking powder for making quick breads, and acidic sour milk to activate the leavening of breads. The Dutch oven, a cast-iron pot with a tight-fitting lid and depth of 6 inches (15.25cm), was the primary cooking vessel for most meals served on the Oregon Trail. It was used for cooking breads and stews, and roasting meat. Hot coals were placed under the pot and around the lid, making it effective for both dry and wet heat cooking methods. Many historians still argue today that the popular dish of biscuits and gravy originated on the Oregon Trail when fried bacon gravy was served over quick bread for breakfast as well as the evening meal.

In addition to prospectors and immigrants, many soldiers and fur trappers also followed the Oregon Trail. The soldiers ate a food called *cold flour*, which was a coarse, polenta-like meal made from parched corn and served with cinnamon and sugar. The soldiers ate the meal as is, or made gruel out of it by cooking it with water. Sometimes the soldiers pressed dried, sliced vegetables into cakes to eat on the long journey. The cakes must not have been tasty or popular, however, because the soldiers referred to them as *desecrated vegetables* instead of their correct name, *desiccated vegetables*. Fur trappers traveling the Oregon Trail frequently consumed a Native American dish called *pemmican*, a high-energy food made from bison meat, which was cut into thin strips and dried in the sun. It was then pounded into a fine powder between two stones and sometimes mixed with the juice of wild chokecherries. Afterward, the pemmican was placed in a bison-hide bag, typically with the hair on the outside, and sealed shut. It was consumed on long trips.

The Santa Fe Trail opened in 1821. The first expedition was completed by William Becknell, who set out from Missouri eager to begin trade with the Mexicans and Native Americans of the Southwest. Once this route proved prosperous, many Southern businesspeople and Canadian fur traders began to travel the trail, bringing with them a more sophisticated palate than those who followed the Oregon Trail. In 1835, the first trading post, called Bent's Fort, opened near the town of La Junta, Colorado. Bent's Fort was a place to rest and relax as well as to eat a proper meal, served at a table with forks and knives. Native American cooking was the primary cuisine and featured foods such as bison jerky, corn cakes, and washtunkala, a stew made from dried corn. Many travelers acquired a taste for tortillas, a Mexican unleavened flat bread made from corn masa and served during most meals with pine nuts from the piñon trees in the region. Aside from its local cuisine, Bent's Fort was also a place to purchase champagne, Bordeaux wine, ginger and other West Indian spices, and even fresh oysters, which came by train, packed in ice and sprinkled with cornmeal. One of today's most popular Rocky Mountain restaurants is The Fort, located in Morrison, Colorado. It is an exact replica of Bent's Fort and serves traditional Rocky Mountain cuisine and Native American foods.

The more affluent pioneers brought a taste for classic European cuisine to the Rocky Mountain region. At that time, the big city of the region was Denver, Colorado, where the region's first luxury hotel, the Brown Palace, was founded in the late 1800s. A Western bill-of-fare, however, was unlikely to be found on the menu at the Brown. As the guests of the hotel were generally rich miners and railroad tycoons who had already made their fortune, the menus at the Brown Palace rivaled any famous hotel in the East. Frequently, dishes such as crab, lobster, veal, and duck were on the menu, served in an opulent dining room and paired with the finest of wines. Today's popularity of classical and European cuisine in the Rocky Mountain region no doubt has roots in the foods served at this hotel over 100 years ago. The Brown Palace, named after Molly Brown, is still in business in its original location and maintains its fine reputation for serving gourmet meals to the world's most notable people.

The Basque people who immigrated from southwestern France and northern Spain came to the west as sheepherders who worked on the ranches of Idaho, Nevada, and Wyoming. In many remote areas, thriving communities of Basque descendants developed. Hearty stews of beef, chicken, and lamb flavored with onions, garlic, tomatoes, bell peppers, and herbs best describe the Basque contribution to the cooking of the region. The largest Basque community in existence today, outside of Europe, is in Boise, Idaho. Basque restaurants in America are known for their family-style service and many courses of hearty food. In many cases, Basque restaurants have long communal tables, where being seated with strangers makes for an interesting dining experience.

Much of the wild game enjoyed for its own sake today in the Rocky Mountains was first eaten out of necessity. Today, game is considered a delicacy. Abundant fowl, venison, boar, and bison are available and thrive in the mountains of the region. Today, most game served in restaurants and hotels is not wild by any means. Wild game is not inspected for consumption by the U.S. Department of Agriculture and, therefore, is typically not served in commercial foodservice establishments. The game served in commercial foodservice operations is generally farm-raised in a closely controlled environment and developed specifically for the foodservice industry. Due to the pleasing taste and low levels of fat in many game products, their popularity is rising, and the Rocky Mountain region has game farms and ranches to satisfy the needs of the American palate.

There is a variety of trout and bass in the streams, rivers, and lakes of the region, which provide ample quantities of these high-quality and tasty freshwater fish. Trout is often farm-raised specifically for the foodservice industry, as game animals are. Wild fish are generally reserved for sport and fly fishermen. Rainbow trout, originally found only in North America, are now being farm-raised in Europe and are actually the most commonly purchased fish in France. American fish farming techniques are utilized to keep the supply of trout in balance with the heavy demand for this easy-to-prepare fish.

One of the most famous foods indigenous to the Rocky Mountain region is the potato. Over 100 varieties are farmed, mostly in Idaho and Colorado. In fact, Idaho Potato is now a registered trademark. Idaho potatoes are usually grown in volcanic soil and irrigated with fresh mountain runoff water. Russet potatoes from Idaho are the most popular and common potato variety and are primarily used as baking potatoes and for the production of french fries. Colorado, while also producing russets, is known more for its specialty potatoes that come in a variety of colors, sizes, and flavors.

Dried beans, referred to as *legumes* or *pulses*, are produced in great quantity and quality in the Rocky Mountain region. Almost all brown, green, and yellow lentils consumed in America come from the Palouse Valley in northern Idaho. Colorado dried bean production is most noted for the pinto and Anasazi varieties.

Today's two largest agricultural products from the Rocky Mountain region are beef and lamb. Colorado lamb is world renowned for its excellent flavor, low fat content, and large eye in the rack, making Colorado lamb chops the envy of lamb producers worldwide. The eastern slopes of the Rocky Mountains in Wyoming and Colorado are home to many of the largest cattle ranches in the world. Needless to say, "beef is what's cooking" in the Rocky Mountains.

Genuine Rocky Mountain cuisine is rarely found in the cities of the region but instead in the small towns of the plains and mountains. In these small communities, the culture, heritage, and culinary traditions of the American pioneers and settlers continue to this day.

Typical Rocky Mountain Ingredients and Dishes

Alaskan Sweetheart Potato: A variety of potato from Colorado's San Luis Valley. Alaskan Sweethearts are slightly pink in color, with a red skin, making them an excellent choice for a colorful potato salad. They are good for both baking and boiling.

Anasazi Bean: A dry bean with a history dating back over 500 years. The Native American tribe of the same name first cultivated these beans. The Anasazi vanished mysteriously, leaving only their ruins in Mesa Verde, Colorado; however, the beans they cultivated are quite popular today. The beans are distinctively colored, with a mottled black and brown or red and white skin, and are sweet, with a full flavor. Anasazi beans contain 75 percent fewer carbohydrates, which can cause less digestive gas than most other dried beans.

Baby All Blue Potato: A variety of potato from Colorado's San Luis Valley. These potatoes are small, thin, and long, and are referred to as *fingerling potatoes*. They have a bluish-lavender flesh and are a good choice for soup. Baby All Blues are best cooked whole by steaming, roasting, or boiling.

Big Jim Chile: Grown in the plains east of Pueblo, Colorado, these chiles are grown side by side with Anaheim chiles. Big Jim chiles are a little hotter and spicier than their Anaheim cousins; however, they look almost identical. They are also referred to as *Pueblo chiles*. New Mexico green chiles are actually Anaheim green chiles grown in the state of New Mexico. The heat of Big Jim chiles is rated with 1000–1500 Scoville units and usually placed at 1 or 2 on a scale of 1 to 10.

Bison: Commonly called *buffalo*, a member of the Bovidae family and believed to be descendants of wild cattle. Bison numbered over 40 million in population in the mid-1800s; however, the population shrank to less than 1000 by 1900. Today, bison number over 150,000, as the population is strictly controlled and monitored by government activists. Bison is once again being raised for consumption and has become quite popular due to its rich, sweet taste and low level of fat compared to beef. Cook bison at lower temperatures and for less time than you would cook beef.

Buffalo: See *bison*.

Buffaloberry: A wild berry, orange or red in color, found throughout the mountains and plains. It ripens in early to late fall. Buffaloberries are somewhat bitter in flavor and are used primarily to make jams and jellies. If they are picked just after a frost, they become sweet enough to use in pies.

Chanterelle Mushroom: A wild mushroom normally associated with French cooking; however, it grows in late August in the high-altitude mountains surrounding Telluride, Colorado. These mushrooms are mustard-colored and give off an apricot scent. You can sample chanterelle recipes at the annual mushroom festival in Telluride.

Chokecherry: A small, orange-purple fruit, this member of the plum family is common throughout the Rocky Mountain region. Chokecherries are quite hardy and extremely resistant to changes in the weather. The name *chokecherry* describes its taste—very astringent—which makes it well suited for jams, jellies, and syrups. When chokecherries are at their peak of ripeness, they can be eaten from the vine, but one must take care, as the leaves and pits are poisonous.

Chorizo: A spicy sausage of Hispanic heritage that is made with pork and seasonings. Traditionally, chorizo of Mexican origin is made with fresh pork, while the Spanish tradition calls for smoked pork.

Chukar Partridge: A popular game bird from Idaho. Chukar partridges are prized among hunters due to their richly flavored meat and tender texture. They become available starting in September.

Cold Flour: A provision of the chuck wagons that traveled west along the Oregon Trail. Cold flour was a parched corn that was pounded into a coarse meal similar to polenta. The meal was either eaten as is or mixed with sugar and cinnamon and eaten as a cereal.

Crawdads: A freshwater crustacean related to its saltwater cousin, the crawfish. Crawdads are indigenous to the rivers of the Rocky Mountains and have a taste similar to lobster. Typically, the tails are sucked out of the shell while in the mouth and the remainder of the crawdad is discarded. The bodies and legs make for excellent soup or stock; however, they are a little too difficult to eat.

Cutthroat Trout: A variety of freshwater trout with distinctive markings on its neck. Cutthroat trout are commonly found in the rivers and lakes of Utah and, in 1997, replaced the rainbow trout as the state fish.

Dandelion: A wild meadow plant with a bright yellow flower, originating in France. The leaves are usually blanched and served in salads. For the best flavor, dandelions should be eaten before they flower, after which they are bitter. Dandelion roots are also used as a vegetable in Japanese cooking.

Elk: A very large relative of the deer. Smoked elk's tongue is considered a delicacy by many in the Rocky Mountain region.

Grouse: A popular game bird from Montana. Blue and ruffed grouse become available starting in September. Grouse has a distinct taste with a slightly oily texture. This depth of flavor makes it popular when in season.

Huckleberry: The most highly prized berry of the Rocky Mountain region. Huckleberries are similar to blueberries in texture, color, and flavor; however, they have a thick blue-black skin and contain several seeds in the middle. The berries have a unique astringency that is very flavorful and tasty. The mountain states of Idaho and Montana are known to produce the tastiest varieties.

Indian Flat Bread: An all-purpose flat bread made with corn flour by the Native Americans of the Four Corners region (Colorado, Utah, New Mexico, and Arizona). Indian flat bread is also referred to as *Navajo fry bread.*

Jerky: Cured and salted air- or oven-dried strips of beef or bison.

Lentil Bean: Almost all of the lentil beans produced in the United States come from a region called the Palouse in the valleys of northern Idaho and eastern Washington. These popular American beans come in three varieties: green, brown, and yellow.

Matsutaki Mushroom: A mushroom that grows within the decaying leaves and branches that cover the forest floor. It becomes available in September. Matsutaki mushrooms are favorites in Japanese cooking.

Meadow Mushroom: This wild mushroom, when mature, is tan in color, has a large, flat cap, and resembles a portobello mushroom. Meadow mushrooms grow in field grasses and are available from May through June. When they are immature, they are slightly pink in color and are dubbed *pinkbottoms.*

Montana Whitefish: This huge freshwater whitefish from Flathead Lake in Montana weighs up to 9 pounds. The Montana whitefish is known for its mild, pleasant-tasting flesh and excellent golden roe. The whitefish population in Flathead Lake was an accident. Shrimp were seeded in the lake in an attempt to lure salmon into the body of water; however, the whitefish came seeking the shrimp instead.

Oyster Mushroom: This mushroom is cultivated first in May and June, then again in September and October. Oyster mushrooms are grayish in color and grow in clusters on cottonwood trees at lower elevations along rivers and lakes.

Ozette Potato: A variety of potato from Colorado's San Luis Valley. Ozettes are yellow-skinned and yellow-fleshed fingerling potatoes. They are best cooked by roasting or baking.

Palisade Peach: A variety of peach indigenous to the western slopes of Colorado near the city of Grand Junction. Palisade peaches are world renowned for their sweet flavor and firm texture. This area is the second-largest producer of peaches in the United States, just behind Georgia.

Pemmican: An early American food made from chokecherry juice pounded with suet, mixed with powdered bison jerky, and stored in a bison-hide bag. During pioneer days, Native Americans taught the settlers to make pemmican, which helped to sustain them on the long voyage west.

Pheasant: A game bird, about the same size as a chicken, found in the mountains of Montana. Pheasant has darker meat than chicken, with a pleasant but not overwhelming flavor. Due to the popularity of pheasant, the bird is now farmed in hatcheries to make obtaining good-quality pheasants easier for chefs and restaurateurs.

Pine Nuts: Also referred to as *piñon nuts*. Pine nuts are harvested from the cones of pine trees growing in high altitudes in the Rocky Mountains and the American Southwest. Pine nuts can be roasted or ground to add a distinctive flavor to any dish.

Pinto Bean: Grown primarily in Dove Creek, in the southwestern corner of Colorado, the pinto bean is an essential ingredient of chili con carne, a favorite recipe in the Rocky Mountain region. These beans grow best in a semiarid climate in a high elevation, normally 7000 feet above sea level. Pintos are also the main ingredient in refried beans, commonly served as a starch in Tex-Mex and Southwestern cuisine.

Porcini Mushroom: A wild mushroom normally associated with French and Italian cooking; however, porcini grow in the Rocky Mountain region from July through mid-September. Also known as *cèpes* in France, these mushrooms have red caps and a white, bulbous base.

Pueblo Chile: See *Big Jim chile*.

Purple Peruvian Potato: A fingerling potato, originating in South America, with a deep purple color. The purple Peruvian potatoes have an extremely earthy flavor and are excellent either boiled or baked.

Quinoa: An ancient grain from the Andes region of South America, quinoa was referred to by the Incas as the "mother grain." Studies have shown that quinoa contains all eight amino acids required for human tissue growth. Quinoa also has a high content of vitamins and minerals. When cooked, quinoa is light and fluffy, with a subtle crunch. Quinoa comes in both brown and black varieties and cooks in just ten minutes to four times its original volume. Quinoa can be easily substituted for rice, millet, and other grains.

Rainbow Trout: A freshwater fish that begins life in the rivers of Idaho. The young fish travel many hundreds of miles to the Pacific Ocean through a network of streams and rivers to live there for approximately four years. After this time, the trout return to their spawning grounds through the same rivers and streams. Rainbow trout are the favorite fish of the region. Typically, they are cooked whole in a skillet or grilled and served with brown butter sauce.

Red Bliss Potato: A small potato from Colorado's San Luis Valley, sometimes referred to as *Cherry Red*. Red Bliss potatoes are white-fleshed, with a deep red skin and a creamy, buttery taste.

Red Sangre Potato: A medium-sized potato from Colorado. Red Sangre potatoes are named after the Sangre de Cristo Mountain Range in the southern part of the state. They are white-fleshed, with a red skin, and are excellent for both baking and boiling.

Rhubarb: Originally from the Himalaya Mountains of Tibet, this stem of a large perennial plant found its way to the Rocky Mountains. Technically, rhubarb is a vegetable, but it is used primarily as a fruit. Rhubarb is widely available and sold both fresh or canned. Fresh rhubarb is usually stewed with sugar and used for pies and jams.

Rocky Mountain Oysters: A culinary tradition of the Old West, Rocky Mountain oysters are the testicles of a sheep or young bull, roasted whole in a pan. Eating Rocky Mountain oysters was a ritual test of manhood for the cowboys of the Old West. The cowboys removed the testicles from the animal and cooked and consumed them before an audience of their peers. Today, they are usually coated, breaded, then pan- or deep-fried and served with a spicy dipping sauce in most Western-themed restaurants.

Russet Potato: The preferred potato of Americans, raised primarily in Idaho, where the volcanic soil and mountain runoff water provide excellent growing conditions. These not-very-attractive tubers are large and oblong, with a slightly rough skin. Their low moisture content makes them perfect for making light and fluffy baked potatoes. In addition, their low sugar content makes them suitable for french fries, of which Americans consume over 4.5 billion pounds annually.

Striped Bass: A freshwater bass indigenous to the streams, rivers, and lakes of the Rocky Mountains. Similar to its saltwater relatives, this smallmouth bass has a white, flaky flesh and is very flavorful. Due to the high cost of harvesting striped bass, it is rarely served outside the Rocky Mountain region.

Venison: A generic term for any variety of deer meat. Venison, one of the most popular varieties of game, needs to be hung and marinated before cooking, unless the animal is very young. The best venison comes from the buck, which is about two years old. The most popular cut is the haunch or leg, which, when boneless, is referred to as a *Denver leg.* Whitetailed deer are both common and popular in the Rocky Mountain region. The meat is tender and flavorful, without the gaminess associated with other varieties of venison.

Yellow Fin or Yukon Gold Potato: A yellow-skinned and yellow-fleshed potato developed in Finland and now grown in the San Luis Valley of Colorado. These potatoes have a creamy texture and a buttery flavor suitable for any potato preparation.

Sample Menus from Rocky Mountain Cuisine

MENU ONE

Red Potato, Corn, and Chorizo Chowder

*Spinach Salad with Toasted Pine Nuts, Smoked Bacon, Red Peppers, Goat Cheese,
and Mustard Vinaigrette Dressing*

*Grilled Flank Steak with Confetti Butter and Beer-Battered Onion Rings ·
Cowboy Beans*

MENU TWO

Buffalo Consommé with Anasazi Bean Custard

Barbecued Montana Quail with Barley Salad

Rocky Mountain Trout in Cornmeal Crust with Horseradish Butter Sauce ·

Warm Rocky Mountain Slaw · Cayenne and Honey-Glazed Carrots · Indian Flat Bread

MENU THREE

Charred Corn and Quinoa Soufflé with Mountain Crawdads

Marinated Colorado Dried Bean Salad with Red Bean Crêpes

Garlic and Rosemary Roasted Leg of Lamb with Pan Gravy · Red Chard Casserole ·

Caramelized Onions · Sweet Potato Dumplings

Red Potato, Corn, and Chorizo Chowder

YIELD: 6 PORTIONS · PORTION SIZE: 7 OUNCES

4 ounces (120g) chorizo sausage links, cut into ½-inch (1.27cm) pieces

1 tablespoon (15ml) clarified butter

4 ounces (120g) onion, cut into fine dice

1 ounce (30g) celery, cut into fine dice

½ ounce (15g) all-purpose flour

16 fluid ounces (480ml) white chicken stock, prepared (see page 517)

16 ounces (480g) Red Bliss potatoes, B size, cut into medium dice

10 ounces (30g) corn on the cob, grilled

salt, to taste

black pepper, ground, to taste

16 fluid ounces (480ml) milk

1 tablespoon (15g) parsley, chopped

2 tablespoons (30ml) cider vinegar

Cook the chorizo over medium heat until done and until it reaches an internal temperature of 155°F (68.3°C) or higher for 15 seconds.

Add the butter, diced onions, and celery and sweat until the onions are translucent.

Stir in the flour, reduce the heat, and cook the roux over low heat for 6–8 minutes.

Add the chicken stock and stir so the liquid is well incorporated into the roux.

Bring to a boil and add half of the potatoes. Boil gently, stirring frequently.

Cook the other half of the potatoes either in a steamer or in boiling salted water until done. Drain and reserve until needed.

Slice the corn kernels from the ears, add half of the corn kernels to the soup, and reserve the other half.

Season the soup to taste with salt and black pepper.

Once the potatoes in the soup are cooked, remove half the mixture to a blender and purée thoroughly.

Return the blended soup to the pot, add the milk, steamed or boiled potatoes, and the remaining corn kernels.

Adjust the seasoning as needed.

Stir in the chopped parsley and cider vinegar and serve immediately.

SERVING/HOLDING

Carefully ladle the soup into hot soup cups.

Hold the chowder at 140°F (60°C) or above.

COOLING/STORING

Pour the remaining chowder into small metal containers.

Cool the chowder from 140°F (60°C) to 70°F (21.1°C) or lower within 2 hours. Cool from 70°F (21.1°C) to 41°F (5°C) within an additional 4 hours for a total cooling time of 6 hours or less.

Cover the chowder; label, date, and store under refrigeration at 41°F (5°C) or lower.

Buffalo Consommé with Anasazi Bean Custard

YIELD: 6 PORTIONS · PORTION SIZE: 10 OUNCES

½ onion, peeled

6 egg whites

8 ounces (240g) beef, lean, ground (shank, neck, or shoulder)

8 ounces (240g) buffalo, lean, ground (shank, neck, or shoulder)

2 ounces (60g) onion, cut into medium dice

2 ounces (60g) celery, cut into medium dice

1 ounce (30g) carrots, cut into medium dice

3½ ounces (105g) tomato, seeded, diced

64 fluid ounces (1.9L) light brown beef broth or brown stock, prepared (see page 515), cold

SACHET D'ÉPICES

½ teaspoon (2g) thyme leaves

½ teaspoon (2g) black peppercorns, cracked

3–4 parsley stems

1 clove garlic, crushed

salt, to taste

white pepper, ground, to taste

dry sherry, to taste

CUSTARD

4 ounces (120g) dried Anasazi beans

salt, as needed

4 cloves garlic, peeled

1½ fluid ounces (45ml) milk

4 fluid ounces (120ml) heavy cream

2 large eggs

½ teaspoon (2g) dried thyme

CHEF TIPS *The charred onion called for in this recipe is classically referred to as an onion brûlé. Adding a well-caramelized onion to a dark consommé, broth, or stock adds color and depth of flavor to the finished product.*

The cheesecloth sack containing herbs, spices, and other aromatic vegetables is classically referred to as a sachet d'épices or, more commonly, a sachet bag. The sachet bag allows for the transference of flavor from the items inside the bag to the stock, sauce, or soup. The items can also be quickly and easily removed. The use of a sachet bag is especially advantageous when straining is not desired.

salt, to taste

white pepper, ground, to taste

1 pinch nutmeg, ground

butter, softened, as needed

Char the peeled onion on a hot flattop or griddle until its surfaces are thoroughly caramelized and very dark brown in color. Reserve until needed.

Whisk the egg whites until slightly frothy.

Combine the egg whites, ground beef, ground buffalo, diced onions, celery, carrots, and tomatoes in an appropriate size stockpot.

Add the cold beef stock or broth. Mix well and add the charred onion.

Place the thyme, peppercorns, parsley, and garlic in a small square of cheesecloth. Tie with twine and add to the simmering stock.

COOKING

Slowly bring the mixture to a simmer over medium heat, stirring occasionally. Stop stirring when the raft begins to form.

Break a hole in the center of the raft with a spoon to allow the steam to escape and the consommé to bubble through.

Simmer for approximately 1½ hours or until a full flavor and aroma develops. Do not allow the simmering soup to fall below 140°F (60°C).

Adjust the seasoning with salt, white pepper, and dry sherry.

Strain through several layers of rinsed cheesecloth.

Degrease the soup by skimming the surface with a flat spoon.

Hold the consommé at 140°F (60°C) or higher until needed.

Rinse and sort the beans, removing any stones, and cover with salted water.

Bring to a boil and reduce heat to simmer.

Simmer approximately 30–45 minutes or until tender. Do not allow the simmering beans to fall below 140°F (60°C).

Drain beans and purée in a food processor until smooth. Reserve until needed.

Place the garlic cloves in a small saucepan and add just enough water to cover.

Bring to a boil and drain the water from garlic.

Place the garlic in a blender with the milk and purée to a smooth consistency.

Add the cream, eggs, and thyme. Blend until smooth.

Season to taste with salt, white pepper, and nutmeg.

Add the anasazi bean purée and mix until thoroughly incorporated.

Lightly butter the inside of six 2-ounce (60g) ovenproof ramekins or timbale molds.

Carefully ladle the custard and bean mixture into the ramekins and bake in a water bath at 325°F (162.8°C) for 30–45 minutes or until the mixture reaches a minimum internal temperature of 145°F (62.8°C) for at least 15 seconds.

SERVING/HOLDING

Run a paring knife around the rim of the ramekins to loosen the custard from the molds. Invert and unmold one custard into the bottom-center of each hot soup bowl or plate.

Carefully ladle the finished consommé around the custard.

Hold the soup and custard at 140°F (60°C) or above.

COOLING/STORING

Pour the remaining soup into small metal containers.

Cool the consommé and custard from 140°F (60°C) to 70°F (21.1°C) or lower within 2 hours. Cool from 70°F (21.1°C) to 41°F (5°C) within an additional 4 hours for a total cooling time of 6 hours or less.

Cover soup; label, date, and store under refrigeration at 41°F (5°C) or lower.

Barbecued Montana Quail with Barley Salad

YIELD: 6 PORTIONS · PORTION SIZE: 6 OUNCES

4 ounces (120g) butter

16 fluid ounces (480ml) apple juice

2 fluid ounces (60ml) vinegar

1 teaspoon (5g) dry mustard

1 teaspoon (5g) sugar

2 teaspoons (10g) chili powder

¼ teaspoon (1g) cayenne pepper

2 teaspoons (10ml) Worcestershire sauce

4 ounces (120g) onion, finely chopped

1 clove garlic, minced

1 teaspoon (5ml) Tabasco sauce

1½ teaspoons (7g) salt

1 teaspoon (5g) black pepper, ground

1 teaspoon (5g) paprika

3 quail, boneless, split

SALAD

2 tablespoons (30ml) clarified butter

½ pound (240g) shiitake mushrooms, stemmed, sliced

½ pound (240g) button mushrooms, stemmed, sliced

2 ounces (60g) barley

2 cloves garlic, minced

2 tablespoons (30g) parsley, chopped

white chicken stock, prepared (see page 517), as needed

salt, to taste

black pepper, ground, to taste

1 ounce (30g) butter

6 red leaf lettuce leaves

CHEF TIPS *In order to keep the quail's shape while cooking and to assist with the grill marking process, the quail halves should be skewered before grilling. Once the quail is cooked, remove the skewers.*

The addition of apple, cherry, or other hardwoods to the grill while cooking enhances the flavor.

Place the butter, apple juice, and vinegar in a saucepan.

Stir in the mustard, sugar, chili powder, cayenne pepper, Worcestershire sauce, onion, garlic, Tabasco sauce, salt, black pepper, and paprika.

Bring to the sauce to a boil, simmer for 10 minutes, and cool.

Marinate the quail halves in half of the sauce for 1 hour. Reserve the quail and the other half of the sauce under refrigeration at 41°F (5°C) or lower until needed.

Grill the quail halves over medium heat for approximately 5 minutes on each side, basting them with some of the remaining sauce, until the quail reaches an internal temperature of 165°F (73.9°C) or higher for at least 15 seconds.

Hold the quail at 140°F (60°C) or higher until needed.

Cook barley by covering it with 8 ounces (240g) of water. Bring to boil. Cover, add seasonings, and bake for 45 minutes at 350°F (175°C).

Prepare the barley salad by heating the clarified butter over medium-high heat in a sauté pan. Add the sliced mushrooms and sauté for approximately 2 minutes.

Lower the heat to medium and add the cooked barley, garlic, and chopped parsley.

Continue to cook over medium heat for approximately 5 minutes or until all of the ingredients are tender and heated thoroughly.

Moisten the barley salad with a little chicken stock, if needed.

Season to taste with salt and black pepper.

Stir in the butter.

SERVING/HOLDING

Serve the quail by placing a small mound of barley salad on a red leaf lettuce liner in the center of each serving plate. Lean a grilled quail half on top of the barley salad and top with a little of the remaining sauce.

Hold the quail at 140°F (60°C) or higher.

COOLING/STORING

Cool the quail from 140°F (60°C) to 70°F (21.1°C) or lower within 2 hours. Cool from 70°F (21.1°C) to 41°F (5°C) within an additional 4 hours for a total cooling time of 6 hours or less.

Cover the quail and sauce; label, date, and store under refrigeration at 41°F (5°C) or lower.

Charred Corn and Quinoa Soufflé with Mountain Crawdads

YIELD: 6 PORTIONS · PORTION SIZE: 8 OUNCES

6 corn husks

24 ounces (720g) crawdads, in the shell

4 ounces (120g) raw quinoa

CHEF TIPS *Either freshwater crayfish or salt-water crawfish can be substituted for the crawdads.*

SAUCE

6 ounces (180g) butter

2½ ounces (75g) mushrooms, washed, sliced

¾ ounce (22g) all-purpose flour

16 fluid ounces (480ml) fish stock, prepared (see page 518)

1 tablespoon (15ml) lemon juice

1 teaspoon (5g) tomato paste

¼ teaspoon (1g) salt

¼ teaspoon (1g) white pepper, ground

¼ teaspoon (1g) cayenne pepper

4 egg yolks

6 fluid ounces (180ml) heavy cream

SOUFFLÉ

11 ounces (330g) corn kernels

½ teaspoon (2g) brown sugar

½ teaspoon (2g) paprika

2 large eggs, separated

1 ounce (30g) all-purpose flour

1 ounce (30g) butter, softened

¼ teaspoon (1g) salt

4½ fluid ounces (135ml) heavy cream

Soak the corn husks in warm water until they are soft and pliable.

Using a glass or small can as a form, tie the cornhusks into a ring shape. Reserve until needed.

Steam the crawdads for 5 minutes or until they have reached a minimum internal temperature of 145°F (62.8°C) for at least 15 seconds. Reserve 6 whole crawdads and peel the rest, reserving the shells. Chop the meat coarsely and reserve under refrigeration at 41°F (5°C) or lower until needed.

Cook 4 ounces (120g) of quinoa by covering it with 1 cup (240ml) water. Bring to a boil, reduce the heat, cover, and simmer for 12 minutes.

Remove from the heat and let steep for 10 minutes. Fluff with a fork and hold at room temperature until needed.

Melt 2 ounces (60g) of the butter in a heavy-bottomed saucepan over medium-high heat and sauté the mushrooms for approximately 3 minutes.

Stir in the flour and continue cooking for 3 additional minutes, stirring constantly.

Whisk in the fish stock a little at a time, blending thoroughly to ensure a smooth sauce.

Add the lemon juice, tomato paste, salt, white pepper, and cayenne pepper. Cook for 5 minutes, stirring constantly.

Reduce the heat, cover, and simmer for 5 additional minutes.

Remove from the heat and hold at 140°F (60°C) or higher until needed.

Crush the reserved shells in a saucepan. Add the remaining 4 ounces (120g) butter and 4 fluid ounces (120ml) water.

Bring to a boil. Reduce the heat and simmer for 10 minutes, stirring occasionally.

Place the contents of the pan in a blender and blend thoroughly.

Strain the contents through a piece of rinsed cheesecloth into another saucepan. Make sure to squeeze as much of the liquid as possible into the pan and reserve until needed.

Blend the egg yolks and cream in a bowl.

Temper the cream mixture with the warm stock and mushroom mixture by stirring approximately 2–3 ounces (60–90ml) of the warm liquid into the beaten eggs and cream to warm them gradually. Then stir the egg mixture into the remaining hot liquid.

Place this combination in the top of a double boiler and stir until thick, but do not allow it to boil.

Stir in the liquid from the strained crawdad shells and the crawdad meat.

Adjust the seasoning as needed with salt and white pepper and hold at 140°F (60°C) or higher until needed.

Toss the corn with the sugar and paprika. Char slightly in a very hot, dry pan, then cool slightly.

Beat the egg yolks from the separated eggs with the flour, softened butter, and salt. Add the heavy cream and fold in the charred corn.

Stir in the cooked quinoa and season to taste with salt and white pepper.

Beat the egg whites until stiff and immediately fold them into the egg yolk and quinoa mixture.

Place the reserved corn husk rings on a sheet pan lined with parchment paper and remove the forms. Fill the rings as full as possible with the soufflé mixture.

Bake at 375°F (190.6°C) for approximately 20 minutes in a convection over or 35 minutes in a traditional oven or until the soufflés rise and reach a minimum internal temperature of 145°F (62.8°C) for at least 15 seconds.

SERVING/HOLDING

Serve the soufflés immediately by placing them in the center of each hot plate. Drizzle the crawdad cream sauce and meat on the plate around the soufflé.

Garnish the dish with a reserved whole crawdad.

Hold the soufflés and sauce at 140°F (60°C) or higher.

COOLING/STORING

Cool the soufflés and sauce from 140°F (60°C) to 70°F (21.1°C) or lower within 2 hours. Cool from 70°F (21.1°C) to 41°F (5°C) within an additional 4 hours for a total cooling time of 6 hours or less.

Cover the soufflés and sauce; label, date, and store under refrigeration at 41°F (5°C) or lower.

Spinach Salad with Toasted Pine Nuts, Smoked Bacon, Red Peppers, Goat Cheese, and Mustard Vinaigrette Dressing

YIELD: 6 PORTIONS · PORTION SIZE: 6 OUNCES

3 ounces (90g) pine nuts, toasted

6 ounces (180g) goat cheese, rolled into a log

6 ounces (180g) thick-cut bacon, smoked

12 ounces (360g) spinach, cleaned, trimmed

10 ounces (300g) red bell peppers, minced

8 fluid ounces (240ml) mustard vinaigrette (recipe follows)

Finely chop half the toasted pine nuts. Reserve until needed.

Roll the goat cheese in the chopped toasted pine nuts. Wrap tightly in plastic wrap and reserve until needed under refrigeration at 41°F (5°C) or lower.

Cut the bacon slices into paysanne, ½ inch (1.27cm) x ½ inch (1.27cm) square.

Render the bacon over medium heat until thoroughly cooked and crispy. Drain well on absorbent paper towels. When cool, crumble and hold at room temperature until needed.

SERVING/HOLDING

Toss the spinach and red bell peppers in the vinaigrette, thoroughly coating all of the leaves. Place a small mound of the dressed salad in the center of each chilled plate.

Slice the goat cheese into ¼-inch (.64cm)-thick wheels and place 2 on each of the salads.

Garnish the salads by topping them with crisp bacon bits and the remaining toasted pine nuts.

COOLING/STORING

Cover the salad and cheese; label, date, and store under refrigeration at 41°F (5°C) or lower.

MUSTARD VINAIGRETTE

1 tablespoon (15g) Dijon mustard

2 fluid ounces (60ml) white wine vinegar

¼ teaspoon (1g) black pepper, ground

1 pinch sugar

2 fluid ounces (60ml) olive oil

2 fluid ounces (60ml) corn oil

Whisk the mustard, vinegar, pepper, and sugar together in a small bowl.

Slowly drizzle in the olive and corn oils, whisking constantly until the vinaigrette has thickened.

Adjust the seasonings as needed.

COOLING/STORING

Cover the vinaigrette; label, date, and refrigerate at 41°F (5°C) or lower.

Marinated Colorado Dried Bean Salad with Red Bean Crêpes

2 ounces (60g) dried red beans

2 ounces (60g) dried lentils

2 ounces (60g) dried pinto beans

2 ounces (60g) dried Anasazi beans

2 tablespoons (30g) sage, cut into chiffonade

4 cloves garlic, minced

2½ fluid ounces (75ml) cider vinegar

5 fluid ounces (150ml) olive oil

½ teaspoon (2g) salt

¼ teaspoon (1g) black pepper, ground

2 ounces (60g) Big Jim or New Mexico green chiles, roasted, peeled, seeded, cut into medium dice

10 ounces (300g) green bell peppers, roasted, peeled, seeded, cut into medium dice

4 ounces (120g) onion, cut into medium dice

1½ ounces (45g) cornstarch

1½ ounces (45g) all-purpose flour

3 large eggs

6 fluid ounces (180ml) milk

1 teaspoon (5ml) vegetable oil

2 ounces (60g) salt

4 fluid ounces (120ml) heavy cream

2 fluid ounces (60ml) half-and-half

1 ounce (30g) chives, finely chopped

2 teaspoons (10ml) cider vinegar

⅓ teaspoon (2g) salt

½ teaspoon (2g) black pepper, ground

10½ ounces (315g) leaf lettuce

18 ounces (540g) tomatoes, thinly sliced

Cover each type of bean with water in an individual container and soak overnight under refrigeration at 41°F (5°C) or lower.

🥣 **Simmer** each type of bean individually in 16 ounces (480ml) salted water until tender. Do not allow the simmering beans to fall below 140°F (60°C).

🥣 **Drain** the beans, reserving the liquid from the red beans. Cool from 140°F (60°C) to 70°F (21.1°C) or lower within 2 hours. Cool from 70°F (21.1°C) to 41°F (5°C) within an additional 4 hours for a total cooling time of 6 hours or less.

Reduce the red bean cooking liquid to ¾ cup (180ml) by simmering slowly. Cool and reserve until needed.

Whisk together the sage, garlic, vinegar, olive oil, salt, and first quantity of black pepper.

Toss the cooked beans, chiles, peppers, onions, and dressing. Marinate and reserve under refrigeration at 41°F (5°C) or lower for at least 1 hour or until needed.

Prepare the red bean crêpes by combining the reduced cooking liquid from the red beans, cornstarch, flour, eggs, milk, vegetable oil, and salt.

Prepare 6 small crêpes, approximately 6 inches (15cm) in diameter, in a nonstick crêpe or sauté pan over medium-high heat. Reserve the crêpes at room temperature until needed.

Combine the heavy cream, half-and-half, chives, cider vinegar, salt, and second quantity of black pepper in a bowl. Blend well.

Toss the leaf lettuce in the cream mixture. Divide the salad and roll each portion in a crêpe.

SERVING/HOLDING

On a chilled plate, shingle 5 slices of tomato from rim to rim down the center of the plate.

Season the tomatoes to taste with salt and black pepper.

Lay the filled crêpe beside the tomatoes in the same direction.

Carefully spoon 4 ounces (120g) of the marinated bean salad across the crêpe and tomatoes at a slight angle.

COOLING/STORING

🥣 **Cover** the salad, crêpes, and tomatoes; label, date, and refrigerate at 41°F (5°C) or lower.

Rocky Mountain Trout in Cornmeal Crust with Horseradish Butter Sauce

YIELD: 6 PORTIONS · PORTION SIZE: 8 OUNCES

48 ounces (1.4kg) or 6 trout, boneless

salt, to taste

black pepper, coarsely ground, to taste

9½ ounces (285g) cornmeal, finely ground

4 fluid ounces (120ml) clarified butter

6 fluid ounces (180ml) corn oil

1 tablespoon (15g) garlic, minced

5 ounces (150g) green bell pepper, minced

5 ounces (150g) red bell pepper, minced

16 fluid ounces (180ml) horseradish butter sauce (recipe follows)

Dry the surface of the trout thoroughly and season the inside to taste with salt and black pepper.

Split each trout into 2 fillets. Dredge in cornmeal until completely coated.

Heat the clarified butter and oil in a sautoir pan until very hot and pan-fry the fillets on each side for approximately 2 minutes or until crisp and golden brown. Turn the fillets only once during cooking. Cook the trout until it reaches a minimum internal temperature of 145°F (62.8°C) for at least15 seconds.

Degrease the trout fillets by patting with absorbent paper towels. Hold at 140°F (60°C) or higher until needed.

Discard the oil and butter from the pan and add the garlic and minced peppers.

Sauté over medium-high heat for 2–3 minutes.

SERVING/HOLDING

Place 2 trout fillets skinside down on each hot plate and top with some of the sautéed pepper and garlic mixture.

Carefully spoon approximately 2½ ounces (75ml) of horseradish sauce over each portion.

 Hold the trout, peppers, and horseradish sauce at 140°F (60°C) or higher.

COOLING/STORING

 Cool the fish, peppers, and horseradish sauce from 140°F (60°C) to 70°F (21.1°C) or lower within 2 hours. Cool from 70°F (21.1°C) to 41°F (5°C) within an additional 4 hours for a total cooling time of 6 hours or less.

Cover the trout, peppers, and horseradish sauce; label, date, and store under refrigeration at 41°F (5°C) or lower.

HORSERADISH BUTTER SAUCE

YIELD: 6 PORTIONS · PORTION SIZE: 2½ OUNCES

4 fluid ounces (120ml) lemon juice

4 fluid ounces (120ml) dry white wine

8 ounces (240g) shallots, chopped

1 ounce (30g) horseradish root, grated

16 ounces (480g) butter, softened

salt, to taste

white pepper, ground, to taste

4 tablespoons (60g) parsley, chopped

In a small sauté pan, reduce the lemon juice, white wine, and shallots to a syrupy consistency.

Add the grated horseradish root and whisk in the butter a little at a time over very low heat. Do not allow the sauce to come to a boil. Whisk constantly.

Strain through a chinois and hold in a warm-water bath until needed.

Season to taste with salt and white pepper.

Garnish the sauce with chopped parsley.

SERVING/HOLDING

 Hold the sauce at 140°F (60°C) or higher.

Cool the sauce from 140°F (60°C) to 70°F (21.1°C) or lower within 2 hours. Cool from 70°F (21.1°C) to 41°F (5°C) within an additional 4 hours for a total cooling time of 6 hours or less.

Cover the sauce; label, date, and store under refrigeration at 41°F (5°C) or lower.

Venison Stew

YIELD: 6 PORTIONS · PORTION SIZE: 10 OUNCES

48 ounces (1.4kg) venison, cut into 2-inch (5cm) chunks

6 ounces (180g) carrots, sliced

6 ounces (180g) onions, quartered

3 ounces (90g) celery, sliced

½ teaspoon (2g) dried thyme

salt, to taste

black pepper, ground, to taste

⅛ teaspoon (1g) cayenne pepper

48 fluid ounces (1.4L) red wine

2¼ teaspoons (11ml) red wine vinegar

3¾ tablespoons (55ml) corn oil

3 tablespoons (44g) all-purpose flour

16 fluid ounces (480g) water or brown beef stock, prepared (see page 515)

CHEF TIPS *Venison stew is typically served with boiled small potatoes.*

In a mixing bowl large enough to hold the venison and vegetables, combine the venison, carrots, onions, celery, thyme, salt, black pepper, and cayenne pepper. Cover the mixture with the wine and vinegar.

Cover and marinate under refrigeration at 41°F (5°C) or lower for 2–4 days. Turn the meat and vegetables once or twice per day.

COOKING

Drain the meat and vegetables in a colander for about 30 minutes and reserve marinade until needed.

Sort the vegetables from the meat and reserve until needed.

Dry the venison completely with absorbent paper towels.

In a large, heavy-bottomed braising pan, heat a thin coat of corn oil over medium-high heat.

Season the venison to taste with salt and black pepper and brown thoroughly in several small batches, being careful not to overcrowd the pan. Add more corn oil as needed.

Remove the venison from the pan and reserve until needed.

In the same braising pan, sauté the vegetables for approximately 5 minutes (add more corn oil if necessary).

Remove the vegetables and reserve with the browned venison until needed.

Prepare a roux by adding the flour to the oil in the braising pan. Add more corn oil if necessary to equal 2 tablespoons (30ml) of oil. Mixture should resemble wet sand.

Cook the roux over low heat for 10–12 minutes, stirring frequently. When done, the roux is dark brown in color and has a nutty aroma.

Strain the reserved marinade over the roux and quickly whisk the mixture together.

Add the water or brown beef stock and bring the mixture to a boil, stirring frequently.

Add the browned venison and vegetables to the sauce and return to a boil.

Cover the braising pan with a tight-fitting lid and cook on the middle shelf of a preheated 300°F (148.9°C) oven for approximately 1½ hours or until the venison is fork tender and reaches a minimum internal temperature of 155°F (68.3°C) for at least 15 seconds.

Using a slotted spoon, transfer the meat and vegetables to a serving dish, cover, and hold at 140°F (60°C) or higher until needed.

Degrease and reduce the sauce for approximately 30 minutes or until the desired consistency is attained. Adjust the seasoning as needed.

SERVING/HOLDING

Place approximately 8 ounces (240g) of stew and vegetables into the center of large heated soup crocks or plates. Carefully ladle the sauce over the meat and vegetables. Serve immediately.

Hold the stew at 140°F (60°C) or above.

COOLING/STORING

Cool the stew and sauce from 140°F (60°C) to 70°F (21.1°C) or lower within 2 hours. Cool from 70°F (21.1°C) to 41°F (5°C) within an additional 4 hours for a total cooling time of 6 hours or less.

Cover the stew and sauce; label, date, and store under refrigeration at 41°F (5°C) or lower.

Garlic and Rosemary Roasted Leg of Lamb with Pan Gravy

YIELD: 6 PORTIONS · PORTION SIZE: 10 OUNCES

48 ounces (1.4kg) leg of lamb, boneless

2 cloves garlic, peeled, sliced

2 tablespoons (30ml) olive oil

½ teaspoon (2g) kosher salt

¼ teaspoon (1g) black pepper, ground

½ teaspoon (2g) dried rosemary

¼ teaspoon (1g) dried thyme

SAUCE

2 ounces (60g) onion, cut into medium dice

1 ounce (30g) celery, cut into medium dice

1 ounce (30g) carrot, cut into medium dice

2 cloves garlic, crushed

½ ounce (15g) tomato paste

2 ounces (60g) all-purpose flour

8 fluid ounces (240ml) red wine

32 fluid ounces (960ml) brown beef stock, prepared (see page 515)

CHEF TIPS *If desired, root vegetables—carrots, parsnips, onions, small potatoes—can be roasted in the pan with the lamb.*

Trim the excess fat from the lamb leg.

Cut slits about ½ inch (1.27cm) deep into the lamb and insert garlic slices.

Rub the olive oil over the entire leg of lamb.

Combine salt, black pepper, rosemary, and thyme in a small bowl.

Rub the herb mixture over the lamb and let rest at room temperature for 20 minutes.

Tightly roll the lamb and truss with butcher's twine so it retains its shape while roasting and to assist it in cooking evenly.

Preheat an oven to 450°F (232.2°C) and roast the lamb on an elevated rack in a roasting pan for 15 minutes.

Turn the oven down to 350°F (176.7°C) and continue to roast until the desired degree of doneness is reached. Baste the lamb with the pan juices once or twice during the roasting process. For medium-rare, roast the lamb for approximately 1 hour. Use an instant-read thermometer to determine the exact internal temperature.

Add the onions, celery, carrots, crushed garlic, and tomato paste after the lamb has roasted 30 minutes.

Once the lamb reaches the desired internal temperature and a minimum internal temperature of 145°F (62.8°C) or higher for at least 3 minutes, remove the lamb from the pan and allow it to rest undisturbed for 15–20 minutes.

Clarify the fat from the pan drippings and stir in the flour to make a roux. Add more oil if needed.

Cook the roux in the roasting pan over low heat for approximately 5 minutes, stirring frequently.

Stir in the red wine and reduce the volume of liquid by half over medium-high heat.

Stir in the stock and continue to reduce until the desired consistency is attained.

Strain the gravy through a chinois and season to taste with salt and black pepper.

SERVING/HOLDING

Slice the lamb and serve approximately 8 ounces (240ml) on each hot plate. Carefully ladle the sauce over part of the slices.

Hold the lamb and gravy at 140°F (60°C) or higher.

COOLING/STORING

Cool the lamb and gravy from 140°F (60°C) to 70°F (21.1°C) or lower within 2 hours. Cool from 70°F (21.1°C) to 41°F (5°C) or lower.

Grilled Flank Steak with Confetti Butter and Beer-Battered Onion Rings

YIELD: 6 PORTIONS · PORTION SIZE: 10 OUNCES

3 cloves garlic, minced

2 ounces (60g) onions, cut into small dice

½ teaspoon (2g) red pepper flakes, crushed

½ teaspoon (2g) dried oregano

½ teaspoon (2g) cumin, ground

¼ teaspoon (1g) allspice, ground

2 tablespoons (30ml) honey

2 tablespoons (30g) horseradish root, grated

4 tablespoons (60ml) beer

3 tablespoons (45ml) olive oil

½ teaspoon (2g) salt

½ teaspoon (2g) black pepper, ground

32 ounces (960g) flank steaks, trimmed

CONFETTI BUTTER

4 cloves garlic, peeled

6 ounces (180g) butter, softened

2 tablespoons (30g) chives, finely chopped

3 ounces (90g) red bell peppers, cut into brunoise

¼ teaspoon (1g) salt

¼ teaspoon (1g) white pepper, ground

12 ounces (360g) beer-battered onion rings (recipe follows)

CHEF TIPS *This steak should be sliced on the bias, fanned, and served with 3 fried onion rings overlapping each other and placed along the top of the fan. Steamed broccoli can be served next to the meat at top center. Cowboy beans can flow along the right side of the meat for an effective presentation.*

In a large mixing bowl, combine the first amount of minced garlic, onions, red pepper flakes, oregano, cumin, allspice, honey, grated horseradish root, beer, olive oil, salt, and black pepper. Mix well.

Trim excess fat from the flank steaks and add to the herb marinade. Toss to coat the meat thoroughly.

Marinate under refrigeration at 41°F (5°C) or lower for at least 1 and up to 24 hours.

Roast the remaining garlic in a 350°F (176.7°C) oven for approximately 15 minutes or until soft. Mince finely.

Mix the butter, garlic, chives, red bell peppers, salt, and white pepper in a mixing machine with the paddle attachment. Maintain the compound butter until needed in this softened state to top the steak at serving time.

COOKING

Remove the steak from the marinade, pat dry, and grill for 5–8 minutes per side or until the desired level of doneness is attained and an internal temperature of 145°F (62.8°C) is reached for at least 15 seconds.

Let the steaks rest undisturbed at 140°F (60°C) or higher for approximately 10 minutes.

SERVING/HOLDING

Slice the steak very thinly across the grain and on a bias.

Serve approximately 7 ounces (210g) of the sliced steak on each hot plate, fanned from the center and covering the lower left-hand third of the plate.

Carefully spoon 1 ounce (30g) of the confetti butter over each portion of sliced steak.

Place 2 ounces (60g) of beer-battered onion rings near the center of the plate and shingle them over the upper left-hand third of the plate.

Hold the flank steak and onion rings at 140°F (60°C) or higher.

COOLING/STORING

Cool the flank steak and onion rings from 140°F (60°C) to 70°F (21.1°C) or lower within 2 hours. Cool from 70°F (21.1°C) to 41°F (5°C) within an additional 4 hours for a total cooling time of 6 hours or less.

Cover the flank steak, onion rings, and confetti butter; label, date, and store under refrigeration at 41°F (5°C) or lower.

BEER-BATTERED ONION RINGS

YIELD: 6 PORTIONS · PORTION SIZE: 2 OUNCES

12 ounces (360g) sweet onions, peeled, cut into ½-inch (1.27cm) slices

7 fluid ounces (210ml) buttermilk

4 ounces (120g) all-purpose flour

½ tablespoon (7g) baking powder

½ teaspoon (2g) salt

¼ teaspoon (1g) white pepper, ground

9 fluid ounces (270g) amber beer

2 tablespoons (30g) parsley, chopped

DREDGING FLOUR

4½ ounces (135g) all-purpose flour

½ teaspoon (2g) salt

¼ teaspoon (1g) white pepper, ground

Separate the rings of the sliced onions and select the largest rings (save the remaining slices for other uses, such as stocks or minced onions).

Soak the selected rings in buttermilk for a minimum of 15 minutes.

Combine the first quantity of flour, baking powder, salt, white pepper, beer, and parsley in a bowl. Blend well until a batter forms.

Drain the rings from the buttermilk and dredge them in flour that has been seasoned with salt and white pepper.

Shake as much of the excess flour from the rings as possible and coat the rings in the beer batter.

COOKING

Deep-fry the rings, using the swimming method, until they are golden brown.

Drain on absorbent paper towels.

SERVING/HOLDING

Serve immediately

Hold at 140°F (60°C) or higher.

COOLING/STORING

Cool the onion rings from 140°F (60°C) to 70°F (21.1°C) or lower within 2 hours. Cool from 70°F (21.1°C) to 41°F (5°C) within an additional 4 hours for a total cooling time of 6 hours or less.

Cover the onion rings; label, date, and store under refrigeration at 41°F (5°C) or lower.

Red Chard Casserole

YIELD: 6 PORTIONS · PORTION SIZE: 4 OUNCES

BÉCHAMEL SAUCE

2 fluid ounces (60ml) clarified butter

2 ounces (60g) all-purpose flour

32 fluid ounces (960ml) milk

¼ teaspoon (1g) salt

⅛ teaspoon (1g) white pepper, ground

nutmeg, ground, to taste

CHARD

40 ounces (1.2kg) red Swiss chard, chopped

2 ounces (60g) scallions, chopped

salt, to taste

white pepper, ground, to taste

4 ounces (120g) butter

4 ounces (120g) breadcrumbs, fresh

3½ ounces (104g) Parmesan cheese, grated

CHEF TIPS *To prepare the fresh bread-crumbs, use only fresh white bread with the crust removed. Slice and tear the bread into pieces and place in a clean, dry food processor. Process until the bread resembles a coarse meal. The classic name for these fresh breadcrumbs is* mis de pain.

Prepare a béchamel sauce by melting the clarified butter in a saucepan and incorporating the flour to make a roux.

Cook the roux over low heat, stirring frequently, for 5 minutes. Let stand at room temperature for 10–15 minutes.

Bring the milk to a boil and gently stir in the roux, a little at a time, until it is fully incorporated. Bring back to a boil, stirring frequently, and reduce the heat to a simmer.

Simmer over low heat for 40 minutes. Do not allow the simmering sauce to fall below 140°F (60°C). Use a wooden spoon to stir and make sure not to scrape the bottom of the pot.

Season the sauce to taste with salt, white pepper, and pinch of nutmeg.

Strain and hold in a bain marie at 140°F (60°C) or higher until needed.

Blanch the chard in boiling salted water. Drain thoroughly.

Mix the chard with the chopped scallions and season to taste with salt and white pepper.

Place the chard mixture in an ovenproof casserole or baking dish and top with 20 fluid ounces (600ml) of the reserved béchamel sauce. Set aside briefly.

Melt the butter in a saucepan over medium heat and add the breadcrumbs. Toss or stir until thoroughly coated.

Remove the breadcrumbs from the heat and stir in the Parmesan cheese.

Top the chard casserole with the breadcrumb and cheese mixture, evenly coating the surface, and bake in a preheated 375°F (190.6°C) oven for approximately 35 minutes or until hot and golden brown.

SERVING/HOLDING

Let the casserole rest for 10 minutes before serving.

Hold the casserole at 140°F (60°C) or higher.

COOLING/STORING

Cool the casserole from 140°F (60°C) to 70°F (21.1°C) or lower within 2 hours. Cool from 70°F (21.1°C) to 41°F (5°C) within an additional 4 hours for a total cooling time of 6 hours or less.

Cover the casserole; label, date, and store under refrigeration at 41°F (5°C) or lower.

Cayenne and Honey-Glazed Carrots

YIELD: 6 PORTIONS · PORTION SIZE: 4 OUNCES

18 ounces (540g) carrots, cut into julienne

2 ounces (60g) butter

½ teaspoon (2g) cayenne pepper

1 teaspoon (5g) paprika

6 ounces (180ml) honey

white chicken stock, prepared (see page 517), as needed

2 tablespoons (30g) parsley, chopped

salt, to taste

Cook carrots in boiling salted water until al dente. Drain well and shock in an ice-water bath. Reserve until needed.

Heat the butter in a sauté pan and add the cayenne pepper, paprika, and honey. If necessary, thin with a little chicken stock.

Reheat the carrots by placing them in a strainer and briefly submerging them in boiling salted water.

Drain the carrots thoroughly and sauté them in the honey-butter mixture until they are hot, thoroughly cooked, and glazed.

Toss with chopped parsley.

Season to taste with salt.

SERVING/HOLDING

Hold the carrots at 140°F (60°C) or higher.

COOLING/STORING

Cool the carrots from 140°F (60°C) to 70°F (21.1°C) or lower within 2 hours. Cool from 70°F (21.1°C) to 41°F (5°C) within an additional 4 hours for a total cooling time of 6 hours or less.

Cover the carrots; label, date, and store under refrigeration at 41°F (5°C) or lower.

Warm Rocky Mountain Slaw

YIELD: 6 PORTIONS · PORTION SIZE: 6 OUNCES

1¼ tablespoons (18g) butter

16 ounces (480g) green cabbage, shredded

8 ounces (240g) red cabbage, shredded

8 ounces (240g) carrots, shredded

3½ tablespoons (52ml) rice vinegar

1¼ teaspoons (6g) sugar

1 teaspoon (5g) dry mustard

1 teaspoon (5g) celery seeds

salt, to taste

black pepper, ground, to taste

CHEF TIPS *Adding caraway seeds as well as celery seeds spices up the slaw. This slaw makes an excellent accompaniment to pork dishes, cold cuts, and sandwiches.*

This recipe can also be easily prepared in a microwave in approximately 10 minutes. Melt the butter in a casserole dish at 100 percent power for 30 seconds. Add the cabbage and carrots with three-quarters of the rice vinegar and sugar, and all of the dry mustard and celery seeds. Microwave at 100 percent power for 1 minute. Stir and continue to cook on full power for 2 additional minutes. Add the remaining vinegar and sugar to taste. Season to taste with the remaining vinegar, sugar, salt, and pepper.

Melt the butter over medium heat in a saucepan.

Stir in the shredded green cabbage, red cabbage, and carrots. Add three-quarters of the rice vinegar and sugar, and all of the dry mustard and celery seeds.

Cook, uncovered, over medium heat, stirring occasionally, for approximately 3–5 minutes or until the cabbage is limp but still a little crisp.

Season to taste with the remaining vinegar, sugar, salt, and pepper.

SERVING/HOLDING

Hold the slaw at 140°F (60°C) or higher.

COOLING/STORING

Cool the slaw from 140°F (60°C) to 70°F (21.1°C) or lower within 2 hours. Cool from 70°F (21.1°C) to 41°F (5°C) within an additional 4 hours for a total cooling time of 6 hours or less.

Cover the slaw; label, date, and store under refrigeration at 41°F (5°C) or lower.

Caramelized Onions

YIELD: 6 PORTIONS · PORTION SIZE: 3 OUNCES

1½ fluid ounces (45ml) clarified butter

40 ounces (1200g) yellow onions,
cut into julienne

white beef stock, prepared (see page 517),
as needed

salt, to taste

white pepper, ground, to taste

CHEF TIPS *Caramelizing onions brings out their natural sugars and creates a sweet taste. The onions can be puréed and used to sweeten and thicken sauces or can be used as an accompaniment to a main item. The key to good caramelized onions is a hot pan and knowing just when to add beef stock and stir. Overstirring the onions causes them to sweat rather than caramelize.*

Heat the clarified butter in a heavy-bottomed saucepan or sautoir until almost smoking.

Add the onions all at once, spacing them evenly across the bottom of the pan. Stir every 3 minutes, but do not stir too much.

While onions are cooking, add a little beef stock in the areas that are browning the fastest to remove the fond from the bottom of the pan and incorporate it with the onions.

Continue to cook the onions for approximately 20 minutes or until they are a uniformly dark brown color.

Season to taste with salt and white pepper.

SERVING/HOLDING

Hold the onions at 140°F (60°C) or higher.

COOLING/STORING

Cool the onions from 140°F (60°C) to 70°F (21.1°C) or lower within 2 hours. Cool from 70°F (21.1°C) to 41°F (5°C) within an additional 4 hours for a total cooling time of 6 hours or less.

Cover the onions; label, date, and store under refrigeration at 41°F (5°C) or lower.

Indian Flat Bread

YIELD: 6 PORTIONS · PORTION SIZE: 2 OUNCES

13 ounces (390g) all-purpose flour

2 tablespoons (30g) baking powders

1 teaspoon (5g) salt

2 tablespoons (10g) dry milk powder

10 fluid ounces (300ml) warm water (approximately 100°F [37.8°C])

corn oil, as needed

Mix all dry ingredients together.

Add 8 ounces (240ml) of the warm water and mix just until blended.

Add the remaining water, a little at a time, until a soft, but not sticky, dough develops.

Cover and allow to rest at room temperature for 30 minutes.

Tear into 2-ounce (60g) balls and roll out flat to about 10 inches (25.4cm) in diameter and ¼ inch (.64cm) thick.

COOKING

Heat the corn oil in a heavy-bottomed pot or deep-fryer to 350°F (176.7°C).

Gently place the pieces of dough in the corn oil and cook on each side until golden brown.

When done, carefully remove the flat breads from the oil and drain on absorbent paper towels.

SERVING/HOLDING

Hold the flat breads at 140°F (60°C) or higher.

COOLING/STORING

Cool the flat breads from 140°F (60°C) to 70°F (21.1°C) or lower within 2 hours. Cool from 70°F (21.1°C) to 41°F (5°C) within an additional 4 hours for a total cooling time of 6 hours or less.

Cover the flat breads; label, date, and store under refrigeration at 41°F (5°C) or lower.

Cowboy Beans

YIELD: 6 PORTIONS · PORTION SIZE: 6 OUNCES

8 ounces (240g) dried pinto beans

6 ounces (180g) ham shank, smoked, chopped

4 ounces (120g) onion, chopped

8 ounces (240g) tomato concassée

4 ounces (120g) Big Jim or New Mexico green chiles, diced

2 ounces (60g) brown sugar

1 teaspoon (5g) chili powder

½ teaspoon (2g) salt

½ teaspoon (2g) dry mustard

1 teaspoon (5g) cumin, ground

1 teaspoon (5g) dried oregano

1 teaspoon (5g) dried cilantro

CHEF TIPS *The shank bone from which the ham was cut can be mixed with the beans in the casserole dish before baking. As the beans cook, flavor from the bone will be extracted, enhancing the overall taste of the finished beans. Be sure to remove the bone prior to serving.*

Rinse the pinto beans under cold running water and remove any stones.

Cover the pinto beans with cold water and soak overnight under refrigeration.

Combine the beans with 16 ounces (480ml) salted water and bring to a boil. Reduce the heat and simmer the beans gently until tender. Do not allow the simmering beans to fall below 140°F (60°C).

Drain the beans and reserve the liquid. Cool the beans and liquid from 140°F (60°C) to 70°F (21.1°C) or lower within 2 hours. Cool from 70°F (21.1°C) to 41°F (5°C) within an additional 4 hours for a total cooling time of 6 hours or less. Reserve until needed.

Combine ½ cup (120ml) of the bean liquid and the ham, onions, tomatoes, chiles, brown sugar, chili powder, salt, dry mustard, cumin, oregano, and cilantro and stir into the bean mixture.

Place the mixture in a casserole or baking dish. Cover and bake at 325°F (162.8°C) for approximately 1 hour.

Uncover and bake an additional 45 minutes or until the desired consistency is attained and the beans reach a minimum internal temperature of 165°F (73.9°C) for at least 15 seconds.

🍲 **Hold** the beans at 140°F (60°C) or higher.

COOLING/STORING

🍲 **Cool** the beans from 140°F (60°C) to 70°F (21.1°C) or lower within 2 hours. Cool from 70°F (21.1°C) to 41°F (5°C) within an additional 4 hours for a total cooling time of 6 hours or less.

Cover the beans; label, date, and store under refrigeration at 41°F (5°C) or lower.

Green Chile Corn Bread

YIELD: 6 PORTIONS · PORTION SIZE: 4 OUNCES

¾ **teaspoon (4g) baking powder**

4½ **ounces (135g) all-purpose flour**

3 **ounces (90g) yellow cornmeal**

¼ **teaspoon (1g) salt**

¾ **tablespoon (11g) sugar**

1 **ounce (30g) Big Jim or New Mexico green chiles, roasted, peeled, seeded, finely diced**

1 **tablespoon (15g) parsley, chopped**

3 **fluid ounces (90ml) water**

3 **fluid ounces (90ml) buttermilk**

3 **fluid ounces (90ml) butter, melted**

CHEF TIPS *Using paper muffin liners saves wear and tear on muffin pans and protects muffins until they are required for service.*

Do not wash the chiles. This removes their essential and flavorful oils.

The corn bread can be served hot, cold, or at room temperature.

Combine all the dry ingredients in a mixing bowl.

Add the diced green chiles and chopped parsley.

Mix the water and buttermilk together, then combine with the melted butter.

Add this liquid to the dry ingredients and mix on medium speed just until a batter develops. Be careful not to overmix the batter, as it will result in dry, crumbly corn bread.

Rest the batter under refrigeration for a minimum of 30 minutes before baking.

Pour the batter into an appropriately sized baking dish or muffin tin and bake for 40–50 minutes in a preheated 400°F (204.4°C) oven until golden brown.

Hold the corn bread at 140°F (60°C) or higher.

COOLING/STORING

Cool the corn bread from 140°F (60°C) to 70°F (21.1°C) or lower within 2 hours. Cool from 70°F (21.1°C) to 41°F (5°C) within an additional 4 hours for a total cooling time of 6 hours or less.

Cover the corn bread; label, date, and store under refrigeration at 41°F (5°C) or lower.

Sweet Potato Dumplings

YIELD: 6 PORTIONS · PORTION SIZE: 4 OUNCES

½ tablespoon (7ml) vegetable oil

32 ounces (960g) sweet potatoes

⅛ teaspoon (1g) chili powder

3 large eggs, whipped

3 ounces (90g) all-purpose flour

¾ ounce (21g) Parmesan cheese, grated

1½ tablespoons (22g) potato starch

salt, to taste

white pepper, ground, to taste

16 ounces (480g) croutons, prepared

2 tablespoons (30ml) butter, melted

CHEF TIPS *If desired, the dumplings can be seared in clarified butter before poaching to give them a crisper texture.*

Oil the skins of the sweet potatoes and prick holes in their surfaces with a fork or skewer.

Bake the sweet potatoes in a preheated 350°F (176.7°C) oven until thoroughly cooked.

Slightly cool the potatoes until they can be safely handled. Split the potatoes and scoop the meat from the skin into a bowl.

Blend the chili powder, whipped eggs, flour, Parmesan cheese, and potato starch into the potato meat.

Season the mixture to taste with salt and white pepper.

Form ball or dumpling shapes, each using approximately 2 ounces (60g) of the potato mixture.

Insert 2 or 3 of the croutons into the center of each dumpling, ensuring that the potato mixture completely covers the croutons.

COOKING

Bring a large saucepot of salted water to a boil. Add the dumplings, a few at a time, to the boiling water.

Cook the dumplings for approximately 15 minutes and until they reach a minimum internal temperature of 145°F (62.8°C) for at least 15 seconds. The dumplings float when they are done.

Drain well.

SERVING/HOLDING

Serve the sweet potato dumplings topped with the melted butter.

Hold the potatoes at 140°F (60°C)or higher.

COOLING/STORING

Cool the dumplings from 140°F (60°C) to 70°F (21.1°C) or lower within 2 hours. Cool from 70°F (21.1°C) to 41°F (5°C) within an additional 4 hours for a total cooling time of 6 hours or less.

Cover the dumplings; label, date, and store under refrigeration at 41°F (5°C) or lower.

Roasted Garlic Potatoes

CHOUX PASTE

    4 fluid ounces (120ml) water

    1½ ounces (45g) butter

    ½ teaspoon (2g) salt

    1 pinch black pepper, ground

    2 ounces (60g) all-purpose flour, sifted

    2 large eggs

POTATOES

    16 ounces (480g) potatoes, peeled, cut into large dice

    1 ounce (30g) garlic, peeled, roasted, mashed

    2 tablespoons (30g) parsley, minced

    salt, to taste

    black pepper, ground, to taste

    all-purpose flour, as needed

    egg wash, as needed

    breadcrumbs, dry, as needed

    frying oil, as needed

Prepare the choux paste by combining the water, butter, salt, and pepper.

Bring the mixture to a boil in a heavy-bottomed saucepan.

Remove from the heat and stir in the flour until the ingredients are thoroughly incorporated.

Place the pan over medium heat and stir constantly until the flour mixture easily pulls away from the sides of the pan. Remove from the heat.

Stir in the eggs, one at a time, blending thoroughly to incorporate the first before adding the second. Reserve until needed.

COOKING

Cook the potatoes in boiling salted water until soft and tender.

Drain and mash the potatoes.

Mix the roasted garlic into the mashed potatoes.

Blend in the chopped parsley.

Add 1 cup (237ml) choux paste to the potato mixture and mix thoroughly. Season with salt and pepper.

Form 6 slightly pear-shaped balls from the potato mixture and rest under refrigeration for at least 1 hour.

Apply the standard breading procedure to the potato shapes by dredging them in the flour, dipping them into egg wash, and, finally, thoroughly coating them with dry, finely ground breadcrumbs.

Deep- or pan-fry the croquettes in 350°F (176.7°C) oil or fat until they are golden brown and reach a minimum internal temperature of 165°F (73.9°C) for at least 15 seconds.

Drain well on absorbent paper towels.

SERVING/HOLDING
Hold the croquettes at 140°F (60°C) or higher.

COOLING/STORING
Cool the croquettes from 140°F (60°C) to 70°F (21.1°C) or lower within 2 hours. Cool from 70°F (21.1°C) to 41°F (5°C) within an additional 4 hours for a total cooling time of 6 hours or less.

Cover the croquettes; label, date, and store under refrigeration at 41°F (5°C) or lower.

Huckleberry Pie

YIELD: 6 PORTIONS · PORTION SIZE: 4 OUNCES OR 1 SLICE

2 pie crusts (recipe follows)

FILLING

8 ounces (240g) sugar

½ cup (120g) brown sugar

2 ounces (60g) tapioca, quick-cooking

½ teaspoon (2g) cinnamon, ground

48 ounces (1.4L) huckleberries, picked over, cleaned

1 tablespoon (15ml) lemon juice

2 tablespoons (30g) butter, chilled, cut into medium dice

1 tablespoon (15g) sugar

TOPPING

8 ounces (240ml) whipping cream

2 ounces (60g) powdered sugar

CHEF TIPS *Blueberries are the normal substitute for huckleberries, as fresh huckleberries can be procured from Montana and Idaho only during the late summer months. Frozen huckleberries can be purchased year-round but are rather expensive compared to other berries. When using blueberries as a substitute, add a little extra lemon juice to the recipe to simulate the unique astringent flavor of huckleberries.*

Press 1 piece of the pie dough firmly into a 9-inch (22.8cm) pie pan.

Reserve the pie pan with the dough and the second piece of the pie dough under refrigeration until needed.

Combine the first quantity of sugar, brown sugar, tapioca, and cinnamon in a large bowl.

Fold in the huckleberries and lemon juice and let stand at room temperature for 10–15 minutes.

Place the huckleberry mixture in the center of the pie dish over the lower piece of dough, mounding the mixture in the center of the pie.

Dot the top of the filling with the pieces of chilled butter.

Place the second piece of pie dough on top of the pie and seal by crimping the dough pieces together.

Cut vents in the top crust, brush the surface with water, and sprinkle it with the remaining granulated sugar.

Bake the pie in the center of a preheated 450°F (232.2°C) oven for approximately 15 minutes. Lower the heat to 350°F (176.7°C) and continue to cook for 45–50 additional minutes or until the juices are thick and bubbling and the crust is nicely browned.

While the pie is baking, prepare the sweetened whipped cream by whipping the cream with the powdered sugar in a small mixing machine on high speed. Be careful not to overmix the cream, as this small amount can quickly turn to butter in a very short period. Reserve under refrigeration until needed.

SERVING/HOLDING

Slice the huckleberry pie into wedges and serve chilled or at room temperature.

Garnish each slice with a dollop of the reserved whipped cream.

COOLING/STORING

Cool the pie from 140°F (60°C) to 70°F (21.1°C) or lower within 2 hours. Cool from 70°F (21.1°C) to 41°F (5°C) within an additional 4 hours for a total cooling time of 6 hours or less.

Cover the pie; label, date, and store under refrigeration at 41°F (5°C) or lower.

PIE CRUST

YIELD: 2 PIE CRUSTS

12 ounces (360g) all-purpose flour

½ teaspoon (2g) salt

4 ounces (120g) butter

4 fluid ounces (120ml) cold water

Combine the flour and salt.

Blend or cut the butter into the flour by rubbing the ingredients lightly between the fingers to incorporate the butter into the flour. Continue to rub until the dough resembles pea-sized balls.

Add the cold water, a little at a time, to the rubbed flour and butter.

Blend the mixture until the dough forms.

Let the dough rest under refrigeration at 41°F (5°C) or lower for at least 1 hour or until needed.

Turn the dough onto a lightly floured surface and roll out with a rolling pin into 2 round shapes approximately ¼ inch (.64cm) thick.

COOLING/STORING

Cover the dough; label, date, and store under refrigeration at 41°F (5°C) or lower.

Mark Tarbell

ON THE CUISINE OF THE AMERICAN SOUTHWEST

HOT!! That's what people seem to think of when they think of the Southwest. I moved out west thinking Frito Lays and Tabasco stood for chips and salsa. Like most outsiders, I thought Southwestern food was something you ate when you'd had too many cervesas! It didn't take long for me to realize how far off I was and to start appreciating all the complexities of the region. The ingredients were contributed by all the cultures that have trampled across the Southwest for the last two centuries, influenced by the Mayan, Spanish, Mexican, and Native American cultures, so the culinary style is about as diverse as they come. Look at the Southwest's most dominant ingredient. I'm talking chiles! There are a couple of hundred kinds of chiles, and I think they're a perfect representation of Southwestern food. They add body, earthiness, and richness to dishes while their heat quotients range from mild to blow-your-head-off, so you get a huge range of tastes from one Southwestern staple.

So what *is* Southwestern cuisine? It's new, old, fun, and greatly varied. I recommend a discovery tour—it will change your world, and it will definitely change your perception of those bubbling cheese plates.

Ultimately, I think the soul of Southwestern cuisine is borrowed from the lively, tart flavors of Mexico. The distinctly individual flavors of each state have drifted across the border and found their way into the Southwestern pantry. Such ingredients as lime juice, pumpkin seeds, tomatillos, and all those chiles add up to cooking fun, so it's an especially great cuisine for someone studying the culinary arts to cut their teeth on! Creating Southwestern dishes, with their strong flavors yet subtle character, requires striking a balance among all the herbal, earthy, smoky ingredients.

Remember, sour cream and milk are the only things that'll cool those chile fires. And from the land where it's cool to be hot, I bid you salud, amigos!

Mark Tarbell is the owner and head chef of Tarbell's and Barmouche, restaurants in Phoenix, Arizona.

The American Southwest

Arizona

New Mexico

The American Southwest region comprises the arid deserts and mountains of New Mexico and Arizona. When the Spanish first arrived in the American Southwest in the early 1600s, they found 98 Native American settlements which they called *pueblos*, along the Rio Grande. The Spanish were amazed to discover that the Native Americans had already developed an irrigation system capable of bringing enough water to the desert fields to sustain a variety of local crops, primarily consisting of corn, squash, and beans.

The largest population of Native Americans currently resides in New Mexico and Arizona. The tribes that, over the years, have most significantly influenced the cuisine of the Southwest include the Navajo, Pima, Hopi, Pueblo, and Zuni. Typically, food for the Native Americans meant much more than simple sustenance; it had religious and cultural implications as well.

The Pima tribe is known to have lived in the American Southwest region since the fourth century, when they established a highly effective irrigation system that brought water to their fields in the desert. The Pima were descendants of the ancient Hohokam tribe and were known for their expertise in growing beans—so great that they were also referred to as the *Papago*, or "bean people."

The Navajo tribe migrated to the American Southwest from the arctic region in the thirteenth century. Originally, the Navajo were nomadic hunters and gatherers, but after arriving in the Southwest region, they adapted to some of the agrarian ways of the Pueblo tribes already living in the area. When the Europeans arrived in the region and brought with them sheep, cattle, and horses, the Navajo learned to be herders as well as farmers.

Of all the Native Americans of the American Southwest, the Hopi tribe is considered to have made the most significant contributions to cooking. The Hopi, descendants of the ancient Anasazi tribe, cultivated many varieties of squash, beans, and corn. They learned to cook in beehive-shaped ovens, called *hornos*, made of adobe clay, and frequently used cooking vessels made of fired pottery ornately decorated with geometric patterns. Similar to other tribes of the American Southwest, the Hopi had a varied diet; however, they held blue corn in the highest esteem. In the Hopi creation myth, they chose blue corn as their primary food. As blue corn was more difficult to cultivate than other varieties, this choice symbolized a difficult but rewarding life. One of the oldest known towns in America is Old Oraibi, a Hopi village founded in A.D. 1150 and still occupied today.

Hunting, gathering, and cultivating foods have always had a special meaning for the Native Americans of the American Southwest. Typically, after a successful hunt, they gave thanks to the animal just killed and offered prayers to the deity associated with that particular animal. The Native Americans who farmed also had many rituals connecting their culture with the foods they cultivated. Traditional dance rituals were performed each year with regard to beans and corn, asking the gods for good growing conditions and an excellent harvest. The cultural and religious practices of the Native Americans of the Southwest region provide them a spiritual connection with their foods.

The "three sisters" of food—corn, beans, and squash—are the New World foods indigenous to the American Southwest. These foods supported the Native Americans and early European settlers of the region. These three crops were easy to dry and store for long periods and, when eaten together, provided a complete source of protein. The Native Americans of the Southwest practiced effective methods of farming these three staples. The farming techniques also proved to be harmonious. When all three crops are planted together, the tall stalks of corn provide the vertical structure to which the bean plants cling, and the squash vines help control weeds by forming ground cover.

Corn from the American Southwest comes in six colors: red, white, blue, black, yellow, and variegated, which many Native American tribes associate with the six directions of the compass. The Native Americans religiously believed that corn was given to them by the corn maiden and was bestowed on their people as a life-giving grain. The Zuni tribe believed that if dried corn kernels were scattered in the path of the Spanish conquistadors, they would be protected from the invaders. The Hopi tribe used each of the six colors of corn for distinctly different purposes, many religious in nature. The Native Americans learned to use wood ash while cooking corn bread. Unbeknownst to them at the time, this added alkaline mineral salts needed to complete the protein chain in corn and may have contributed to the good health and longevity of the peoples of the American Southwest. The Native Americans also discovered that wood ash could be used as a seasoning and leavening agent. When applied to blue corn, the color was fixed. The Native Americans invented a process called *nixtamalization*, whereby slaked lime is applied to corn kernels, making removal of the tough outer shell possible. Of these three staple foods, corn has always had the most cultural significance and, for many Native American tribes of the region, was simply life itself.

Another of the "three sisters foods" is beans. Native Americans began consuming wild beans almost 7000 years ago. Beans, when combined and eaten with grains, seeds, or nuts, provide all the amino acids needed to create complete proteins. The Hopi tribe was the first group of Native Americans to learn effective techniques for cultivating beans and have been doing so since the fifth century. The Europeans, until the fifteenth century, were familiar with only a few varieties of beans, such as fava and broad beans, but were introduced to a large variety of New World beans by the Native Americans of the Southwest region. The most common beans utilized today in the American Southwest are the pinto bean and its smaller relative, the pinquito. However, a number of ancient varieties, called *heirloom beans*, are experiencing a resurgence in the United States.

The last member of the food triad is squash. Zucchini, summer squash, yellow squash, and numerous varieties of Indian squash are all grown in the American Southwest. This culturally important food staple of the region is often referred to by its Spanish name, *calabicitas*.

The spiciness and seasoning of many of the region's traditional dishes are similar to those used in the Mexican states of Chihuahua and Sonora—typically, not simple, but rich and complex. Flavors derived from different chiles, herbs, and seasonings are generally used to attain the characteristics of American Southwest cuisine. Chiles were first grown and utilized for cooking by the ancient Aztecs of Mexico as early as 700 B.C. The Aztecs created ristras—long strings of bright red, fresh chiles all tied together. The chiles on the ristras could be used immediately or hung to dry and used later in the year. It is said that the Native Americans from the Southwest region keep one ristra for each family member in the length equivalent to the person's height.

Christopher Columbus brought chiles from the New World to Europe in the late 1400s, where their value as an ingredient became very great. In the sixteenth century, the early settlers began to cultivate and trade chiles in New Mexico and Arizona. It is suggested that eating chiles leads to a feeling of satisfaction and a sensation of well-being. In 1912, a pharmacist named Wilbur L. Scoville of the Parke-Davis Drug Co. came up with an index for measuring the heat in a food product. He worked with hot peppers using mineral oils in a product called Heettu, a muscle-soothing sauce. It was rated by a panel of people who described the heat they felt in various degrees. This is how Scoville invented his heat index. Scoville units range from 1 to 300,000; however, a simpler scale, called the Scoville scale, is often utilized. This ranges from 1 to 10, with 1 being the mildest and 10 being the hottest.

The introduction of meats other than wild game to the cuisine of the American Southwest is attributed to the Spanish, who brought livestock with them. Capitán General Juan de Oñate first introduced sheep to the region in 1598 and, by the 1880s, millions of sheep, cattle, and hogs were being raised, many of which were shipped to other regions of the United States. At about this time, the cuisine of the region began to utilize domestically raised meats due to their abundance.

Another new food introduced to the American Southwest region by the Spanish was wheat flour. This new food staple offered the Native Americans their first alternative to corn. Wheat became so popular that it was planted all over the region and, by the sixteenth century, was more common in the American Southwest than in Spain. Eventually, flour tortillas became as popular as corn tortillas, the original staple bread of the region.

In the 1820s, Mexico finalized its independence from Spain, and the Santa Fe Trail from Missouri to New Mexico opened. This caused the city of Santa Fe to become a trading hub for the region. During the Civil War, Congress passed the Homestead Act of 1862, and, with the completion of the railroads in 1882, thousands of settlers from the eastern regions of America began to arrive in masses to the American Southwest. By the 1900s, the Anglo settlers had brought with them new crops, modern tools, and farming techniques that transformed over five million acres of the region's land into fertile farms. The first restaurants in the region were opened by Fred Harvey in the late 1800s and were called Harvey Houses. With 16 restaurants located in the railroad stations of the region, the Harvey House is quite possibly the first chain restaurant of the American Southwest.

Although the foods of the American Southwest region have roots deeply embedded in Spanish history and culture, the cooking styles of today have evolved with considerable influence from the local Native American tribes. Southwestern cuisine is one of the first and oldest regional cuisines in the United States.

Typical American Southwest Ingredients and Dishes

Achiote: The seed of the tropical annatto tree. Sometimes referred to as *annatto seeds*, achiote seeds are used commercially as a natural orange coloring agent for butter and cheese. Achiote is also a useful ingredient to use when sautéing, as it imparts a vibrant yellow-orange tint to proteins. The seeds are available dried or crushed and can be used to flavor oil. Achiote oil can be drizzled over meat or shellfish for both color and subtle flavoring and can be added to salad dressings as a flavoring ingredient.

Agua Fresca: A fresh fruit drink common to the American Southwest and originating in Mexico. Aguas frescas are generally made from puréed fruit, sugar, and sparkling water. The fruits most commonly used are tamarind, watermelon, banana, strawberry, and mango. Aguas frescas are available at most of the region's specialty markets and roadside stands.

Almendrado: An almond-flavored dessert common in the American Southwest. Almendrado is made from beaten egg whites bound with gelatin and is usually served with a creamy custard sauce. The gelatin often is tinted with colors to resemble the Mexican flag.

Anasazi Bean: An heirloom bean with a history dating back over 500 years. The Native American tribe of the same name first cultivated these beans, which are quite popular today. The beans are mottled black and brown or red and white and are sweet, with a full flavor. These beans contain 75 percent fewer carbohydrates, which can cause digestive gas, than many other dried beans.

Ancho Chile: A dried poblano chile. It measures 3–4 inches (7.62cm–10.16cm) long and has a dark, reddish-brown color. It is the sweetest of all the dried chiles and has a slightly fruity flavor. Ancho chiles are frequently ground and used as the basis for commercial chili powders. The heat of ancho chiles is rated at 1000–1500 Scoville units and placed at about 1 on a scale of 1 to 10. The typical substitute for ancho chiles is pasilla chiles. (See *poblano chile*.)

Appaloosa Bean: An heirloom bean, indigenous to the American Southwest, that is black and white or red and white, with spotting resembling the breed of horse with the same name. These beans are quick to cook and are frequently used in place of pinto beans.

Atole: An ancient soup made from dried, ground corn or masa harina. When thinned and sweetened, it is used as a beverage. Atole also is commonly found in the region as a fermented beverage. In some parts of New Mexico, atole is made with blue corn.

Blue Corn: Culturally and religiously, the single most important corn variety grown by the Native Americans of the Southwest. Although used extensively by the Hopi, Navajo, and Pueblo tribes, blue corn was almost unheard of outside the region until it gained national popularity in the 1980s. Dishes made with blue corn have a flavor that is both rich and earthy. The distinctive flavor is attributed to the drying of the kernels over a piñon-wood fire. Blue corn can be substituted in most Southwest dishes that call for yellow corn, such as chips, tamales, and tortillas; however, due to its tendency to crumble, blue corn should be blended with a little wheat flour before use.

Bollito Bean: A native of the region, the bollito bean is the ancestor of the pinto bean but is slightly smaller in size.

Buñuelo: A pastry similar to a fried tortilla. Buñuelos are usually served with a scoop of ice cream and a sprinkle of cinnamon sugar. They are a holiday season tradition in Mexico, but in the American Southwest are more frequently eaten as a snack similar to doughnuts.

Capirotada: A Southwestern bread pudding made with cheese and caramel sauce. Capirotada is a traditional dish in the region during Lent; however, it is frequently found on restaurant menus throughout the year.

Cascabel Chile: A dried chile that is approximately 1½ inches (3.81cm) in diameter and shaped like an acorn. Cascabel chiles have a distinctive flavor and are dark orange to red in color, with medium heat. The seeds of the cascabel chile rattle in the pod—hence its name, which means "jingle bell" in Spanish.

Chayote: A pear-shaped member of the squash family, similar in taste to zucchini and a staple of Hispanic cuisine for centuries. In the southern part of America, chayote are referred to as *mirliton*. Chayote have a large seed in the center that needs to be removed prior to using. Chayote are frequently stuffed and baked or cut into cubes that are seasoned and used as an ingredient in salads and appetizers.

Chico: A dried kernel of corn, sometimes referred to as *parched corn*. Chicos are usually steamed and added to soups and stews.

Chilaca Chile: A fresh, dark-green chile measuring 5–6 inches (12.7cm–15.24cm) long and 1½ inches (3.81cm) wide. Chilaca chiles are mild in heat, with a distinctive flavor, and are commonly dried and referred to as *pasilla chiles*. The typical substitute for chilaca chiles is poblano chiles. (See *pasilla chile*.) The heat of chilaca chiles is rated at 2500–5000 Scoville units and placed at about 2 on a scale of 1 to 10.

Chile: A spicy, pod-shaped fruit belonging to the nightshade family and generally green, red, or yellow in color. Today, dozens of varieties of chile are grown and harvested in the Southwest, each with its own signature flavor and level of spiciness or heat. Chiles are unpredictable and can vary in heat depending on where they are grown. They even vary within the same location in different years. Contrary to popular belief, the color of chiles has nothing to do with heat level. Most chiles start out green in color, then turn red or, sometimes, yellow as they ripen. The substance *capsaicin*, located in the seeds and ribs, is the main sauce of a chile's heat. If the flavor of the chile is desired without the heat, simply remove the ribs and seeds prior to using. Chiles are naturally high in vitamins A and C and, in the past, were used for a variety of medicinal purposes. Store chiles in a cool, dry place—they usually last several weeks. Chiles are an essential ingredient, providing spice and heat in the recipes of the Southwestern region.

Chile de Árbol: A very hot chile measuring about 3 inches (7.62cm) long and ⅜ inches (.96cm) wide and usually found dried. These chiles are similar in appearance to japónes but are longer and thinner. Chiles de Árbol are frequently ground and used in chili powders. The typical substitute is cayenne pepper. The heat of the chiles de Árbol is rated at 150,000–200,000 Scoville units and placed at 8 on a scale of 1 to 10.

Chile Pequin: A very small and highly potent chile, generally round or oval in shape. Chiltepin, a smaller variety of chile pequin, is the original chile cultivated by the Native Americans prior to the arrival of the Spanish. Chiles pequins resemble miniature bullets or peas and measure less than 1 inch (2.54cm) in length and ½ inch (1.27cm) around. The substitute for chile pequin is dried habañero. The heat of chiles pequins is rated at 100,000–250,000 Scoville units and placed at 9 on a scale of 1 to 10.

Chili Powder: Ground, dried chiles, sometimes enhanced with other herbs and spices. An extensive variety of chili powders is available, ranging widely in heat and flavor. Southwest cooking professionals generally choose to blend their own chili powder by grinding a special mix of dried chiles. This technique is used to bring an exact flavor to a given recipe by carefully balancing the flavors of several chiles.

Chipotle Chile: A sun-dried and smoked chile. Jalapeño chiles are the preferred and most common chile used for making chipotles. Chipotle chiles are brick red in color and available fresh as well as canned. They are moderately hot, as chiles go, but possess a distinct, complex flavor with no equivalent substitute. The heat of chipotle chiles is rated at 2500–5000 Scoville units and placed at about 2 on a scale of 1 to 10. (See *jalapeño*.)

Cilantro: A highly aromatic herb related to parsley and frequently used in Southwest cooking. It is also referred to as *Chinese parsley*. The leaves of the herb are usually finely chopped and used as a condiment or as an ingredient. The stems can be chopped and used in soups, beans, or anything simmered. The seeds are known as *coriander* and, when dried, are referred to as *cumin* or *comino*.

Corn: A hybrid of a wild grass that originated in Mexico over 4500 years ago. This grain must be planted deliberately, as corn plants cannot naturally sow their own seed. In the Southwest, corn is used frequently in cooking and for a wide variety of traditional recipes, such as tortillas, tamales, and breads. Corn is frequently dried and is available in many forms, including hominy, posole, chicos, and masa.

Empanada: A small, half-moon–shaped pastry stuffed with meat, fish, or cheese filling. Empanadas are typically served hot as an hors d'oeuvre or appetizer.

Epazote: A strong herb whose leaves have jagged, serrated edges. Fresh baby epazote can be used like greens and cooked in a fashion similar to spinach, while more mature epazote is used as an herb. Epazote is frequently used in cooked bean recipes, as it is said to aid with digestion and to prevent bloating. There is no known substitute for epazote, which is sometimes referred by the names *ambrosia, lamb's quarters, wormseed, stinkweed*, and *pigweed*.

Flan: A dessert similar to the French crème caramel. It is usually made as a pie and served by the slice, but sometimes it is made in individual portion–sized molds.

Fried Green Jerky: A traditional dish of the Pueblo tribe. Fried green jerky is dried beef that is softened, fried with onions and chiles in lard, and simmered with fresh chopped tomatoes.

Habañero Chile: A small chile, usually about ½ inch (1.27cm) in diameter and 1 inch (2.54cm) long. Habañero chiles are bright orange, yellow, and sometimes green in color. They have a distinctly fruity aroma similar to apricots and are among the hottest chiles available. The heat of habañero chiles is rated at 100,000–300,000 Scoville units and placed at 10 on a scale of 1 to 10.

Heirloom Bean: Any of the ancient wild and cultivated beans indigenous to the Southwest once eaten by Native Americans. Heirloom beans have recently been revived in the region. Specialty farmers who support and subscribe to the techniques of preservation agriculture generally cultivate heirloom beans. Some of the many available today include Anasazi, appaloosa, bollito, Jacob's cattle, tepary, and snowcap.

Hominy: Fresh corn kernels processed with lye or slaked lime. The processing removes the tough outer hull to make the kernel more digestible. Hominy is commonly available in cans and can be found throughout the Southwest and other parts of the country.

Horchata: A sweet beverage made from milk, ground raw rice, and almonds and flavored with cinnamon. Horchata is frequently garnished with toasted pumpkin seeds, also referred to as *pepitas*. It is said that horchata can counteract the effects of eating very hot chiles, leaving only the essence of the flavor.

Huitlacoche: Also referred to as *acuitlacoche*, huitlacoche is a fungus that grows on corn. The fungus is used in fairly large pieces as an ingredient in many Southwest dishes and is prepared similarly to mushrooms.

Jacob's Cattle Bean: An heirloom bean originating in Germany, this bean is now cultivated in the American Southwest. Jacob's cattle beans have spotting similar to appaloosa beans but are white and maroon in color. They are fairly sweet in flavor and are sometimes referred to as *trout* or *Dalmatian beans*.

Jalapeño Chile: A fairly spicy, small chile that turns from green to red at maturity. Jalapeños average about 2 inches (5cm) in length. The heat comes mainly from the seeds. The heat of the chiles is rated at 2500–5000 Scoville units and placed at about 2 on a scale of 1 to 10. The jalapeño is frequently used in American Southwest cooking. The typical substitute for jalapeño chiles is serrano chiles.

Japóne: Dried serrano chile. The heat of japónes chiles is rated at 15,000–30,000 Scoville units and placed at about 4 on a scale of 1 to 10. Cayenne pepper is an appropriate substitute. Árbol chiles, which are usually thinner and longer, are often confused with japónes chiles. (See *serrano chile*.)

Jicama: A crisp and crunchy root vegetable with a thick brown skin that must be removed prior to use. The flavor of jicama is similar to a mild apple crossed with a potato, which makes it excellent for use in salads and salsas. In the Southwest, a common appetizer consists of nothing more than slices of jicama sprinkled with salt and chili powder and served with Mexican limes. Unlike apples and potatoes, the flesh of jicama does not turn brown after it is peeled. Jicama is available from November to June.

Limón: A Mexican lime, the same variety as the Key lime. This small, round lime has a yellowish skin and is one of the two main varieties of limes available in America, the other being the more common Persian lime. True limóns are usually found in the region's specialty markets.

Masa: Spanish for "dough." In the American Southwest, masa is plain corn flour dough made from dried corn that is cooked in lime water, then cooled. Masa is most commonly used to make tamales and tortillas. Nixtamal is similar to masa but is usually combined with other seasonings. (See *nixtamal*.)

Masa Harina: A commercial dried masa that has been processed into a fine powder. To make dough for tamales, reconstitute the powder by adding water to the masa harina and blending. Posole is similar to masa harina but is made from dried nixtamal, which is usually seasoned rather than plain like masa. (See *masa, posole*.)

Mexican Hot Chocolate: A drink derived from the beans of the cocoa plant. It was invented by the Aztecs and dates back thousands of years. Originally, only priests and important rulers drank chocolate for ceremonial purposes. Today, Mexican hot chocolate is a common breakfast drink of the region and frequently substitutes for coffee and tea.

Mexican Oregano: An herb common to the Mexican border with New Mexico and Arizona. It is similar in flavor to the oregano plant of the Mediterranean, but with a much stronger flavor. Mexican oregano is actually a form of wild marjoram.

Mole: Derived from the Aztec word *molli*, meaning "concoction, stew, or sauce." Mole is more than just a Mexican chocolate sauce; it is a special, complex dish woven of dried chiles, nuts, seeds, vegetables, spices, and chocolate. There are many styles of mole. Each local area has its own version, from Texas to Arizona to Mexico. The more common varieties are green mole, made with tomatillos, and red mole, made with pumpkin seeds. Mole is frequently made as a sauce and used to braise meat and poultry items.

Navajo Fry Bread: An all-purpose flat bread made with corn flour by the Navajo tribe. Navajo fry bread, also referred to as *Indian flat bread*, is commonly available either sweet or savory. It forms the wrapper for the Navajo taco, frequently found in the region's festivals and gatherings.

New Mexico Green Chile: The California green chile, also referred to as the *Anaheim chile*, when it is grown in New Mexico. Even though it is the same plant as that grown in California, the New Mexico variety is generally much hotter, similar to the Big Jim chile grown in Colorado. New Mexico green chiles are bright green, 4–8 inches (10.18cm–20.32cm) long, 1–1½ inches (2.54cm–3.81cm) in width, and medium-hot compared with their California and Colorado counterparts. The heat of New Mexico green chiles is rated at 1000–1500 Scoville units and placed 1 to 2 on a scale of 1 to 10. If a substitute is required, Big Jim chiles are appropriate. If they are not available, use half jalapeño chiles and half Anaheim chiles.

Nixtamal: Kernels of corn partially processed with slaked lime, similar to hominy. The main application of nixtamal is to grind the kernels and mix them with seasonings to make a dough, similar to masa, which is used to make tamales. Nixtamal is also used whole in soups and stews. Nixtamal is usually found packaged in bags in the refrigerated sections of Southwest markets. Posole is an excellent substitute. Hominy can also be substituted for nixtamal, but it generally has a much milder flavor. (See *hominy, masa, posole.*)

Nopales: The paddles or pads of the prickly pear cactus. Nopales are usually sold in Southwest produce markets with the spines removed; however, if the spines are still on, they can be easily removed with a vegetable peeler. Nopalitos are cactus pads that are already peeled and cut into julienne, generally available in cans and jars. Some say the cactus pads have a flavor similar to green bell peppers, while others say nopales taste like green beans. They are commonly used in the region as an ingredient in salads. Nopalitos should be rinsed under cold water several times before using.

Painted Pony Bean: An heirloom bean indigenous to the American Southwest. It is small in size and brown in color, with a single white eye.

Panocha: A rustic Southwest dessert. Panocha is a pudding originally made before sugar was available and when honey was scarce. The settlers discovered that the starch of wheat kernels, if they were moistened and left in a warm place, would convert to a form of sugar. When ground and used as an ingredient, the wheat would provide sweetness to a recipe. Today, flour made from sprouted grain is still available and commonly used to make panocha.

Pasilla Chile: A dried chilaca chile. Pasilla chiles are commonly confused with ancho chiles, which are dried poblano chiles, much different from chilacas. True pasilla chile pods are very dark in color and generally 5–6 inches (12.7cm–15.24cm) long and 1½ inches (3.81cm) wide. Pasilla chiles are mild in heat. They have a distinctive flavor and are commonly used to make mole sauce. Even though they have different tastes, the typical substitute for pasilla chiles is ancho chiles. (See *chilaca chile.*) The heat of pasilla chiles is rated at 2500–5000 Scoville units and placed at about 2 on a scale of 1 to 10.

Pepita: The Spanish name for a pumpkin or squash seed of any variety. Pepitas are typically dried and salted and eaten as a snack, used as a garnish for salads, or ground and used as a flavoring agent for regional sauces.

Piki Bread: A traditional unleavened bread made with blue corn by the Hopi tribe. Piki bread has many thin, papery layers. It is traditionally cooked on heated piki stones, which have been seasoned to perfection over many years with bone marrow or cooked sheep's brains and which function similarly to a cast-iron skillet or wok.

Piñones: Also referred to as *piñon nuts*. Piñones are nuts harvested from the cones of pine trees, which grow at high altitudes in the Rocky Mountains and the Southwest. The Pueblo tribe uses piñones as the main ingredient in a soup preparation. Today, pine nuts are frequently roasted or ground to add a distinctive flavor to any dish.

Pinquito Bean: A smaller version of the pinto bean, with the same flavor and characteristics. (See *pinto bean.*)

Pinto Bean: A native bean of the American Southwest and the most commonly used in the cooking of the region. The pinto bean, a variation of the kidney bean, is a pinkish-beige color and slightly streaked. Once cooked, the variegations of color disappear. Pinto beans are the main ingredient in refried beans, a starch commonly served with Southwest and Tex-Mex cuisine.

Poblano Chile: A large, dark-green chile often confused with the pasilla chile, which is a dried chilaca chile. When poblano chiles are dried, they are referred to as *ancho chiles*. Poblano chiles are mild to moderately hot and have a full flavor. Poblanos are usually 3–6 inches (7.62cm–15.24cm) long and 3–4 inches (7.62cm–10.16cm) in width. The heat of poblano chiles is rated at 1000–1500 Scoville units and placed at about 1 on a scale of 1 to 10. They are commonly the chile of choice when making chiles rellenos. The typical substitute for poblano chiles is the New Mexico green chile. (See *ancho chile.*)

Posole: A dried form of nixtamal, used in a similar fashion to masa harina for making tamales and tortillas. Posole is a convenient and safe way to store corn for long periods, but it needs to be reconstituted with water prior to use. Posole is generally available in four colors: blue, red, yellow, and white. A traditional Southwestern soup or stew that uses these dried kernels also goes by the same name—posole. If posole is not available, nixtamal is an excellent substitute. Hominy can also be substituted for posole, but it generally has a much milder flavor. (See *hominy, masa harina, nixtamal.*)

Queso Fresco: Spanish for "fresh cheese." In the cooking of the Southwest, freshly made goat cheese is a common ingredient. One of the defining differences between Southwest and Tex-Mex foods is the selection of cheese. In Southwest cuisine, fresh goat cheese is used for traditional dishes, whereas in the Tex-Mex region, cheddar and Jack or queso blanco are more frequently used.

Refried Beans: A well-known recipe frequently served in the American Southwest. Refried beans are commonly referred to as *refritos* and are usually made from pinto beans. The Spanish word *refrito* means "well fried," but it is frequently misinterpreted as "refried" or "twice fried." Typically, pinto beans are cooked and drained, then mashed with hot lard or bacon fat, seasonings and sometimes, chiles. In the American Southwest, authentic refried beans call for smoking-hot lard to be poured over cooked, mashed pinto beans and stirred in. A cast-iron frying pan should be used for the best results, but a nonstick pan will also work fine.

Salsa: Spanish for "sauce." In Southwest cooking, however, *salsa* generally refers to a tomato-based condiment. If the salsa is uncooked, such as pico de gallo, it is classified as salsa cruda or salsa fresca. If a salsa is blended finely in a food processor, it is usually called a chili or a picante sauce. Today, in the United States, salsa is the best-selling condiment, surpassing even ketchup.

Sangria: A wine-based beverage whose name derives from the Spanish word for blood. Sangria was first made by the Spanish priests who introduced wine grapes to the New Mexico area. It is a punch made with red wine and fresh fruit; its fruity flavor makes for an excellent accompaniment to the spicy fare of the region. In some cases, tequila is added to the recipe for extra impact.

Serrano Chile: A small fresh, hot chile measuring about 1½ inches (3.82cm) long. As they mature, serrano chiles turn from dark green to red, then yellow. Usually, the smaller a serrano chile is in size, the hotter it is. The serrano chile is almost always used when making fresh salsas. The heat of serrano chiles is rated at 25,000 Scoville units and placed at about 3 on a scale of 1 to 10. The typical substitute for serrano chiles is jalapeño chiles. (See *japóne*.)

Sopaipilla: A rectangle of wheat flour dough, deep-fried and served as a savory bread. Frequently, after sopaipillas are fried, they are filled with honey, sprinkled with powdered sugar, and served as a dessert.

Squash Blossom: The blossom attached to newly formed zucchini as it appears on the vine. In the Southwest, squash blossoms are typically stuffed and either deep-fried or baked. Squash blossoms need to be used immediately, as their quality quickly deteriorates.

Tamale: A traditional Southwestern recipe derived from the ancient Aztec word *tamalli*. Tamales are made from masa or nixtamal dough and frequently filled with shredded pork or beef. They are usually 5–6 inches (12.7cm–15.24cm) long and about 1 inch (2.54cm) thick. The tamale is wrapped in a soaked corn husk, steamed, and topped with red chili. Tamales are a Hispanic holiday tradition and are always served at Christmas and New Year's. Green tamales are a summer favorite among Native Americans and are made from fresh white field corn. Although green tamales are typically eaten in the summer, many Southwestern cooks freeze them so they can be enjoyed throughout the year.

Tepary Beans: An antique variety of heirloom bean from the American Southwest, with special religious significance for the Pima and Zuni tribes. The earthy, full-flavored beans date back to the prehistoric era and have recently been recultivated by specialty farmers of the region.

Teswin: A Native American punch made from dried corn and finely ground roasted wheat. Teswin is often flavored with anise, cloves, and cinnamon.

Tomatillo: A small green Mexican fruit of the tomato family, sometimes referred to as a *Mexican* *green tomato*. Good-quality tomatillos are tough to the touch and covered with a brown husk that needs to be removed before use. Tomatillos are mainly used in making fresh or cooked salsa. They are simmered, then blended in a food processor with spices. Green tomatillo sauce is called *salsa verde* and is often served with enchiladas. Tomatillos have a tart flavor that cannot be attained by substituting regular tomatoes.

Tortilla: Spanish for "little cake," which the conquistadors thought the Native American dish resembled. Before the European colonists introduced wheat flour to the region, tortillas were made exclusively from corn, which was the staple food for the entire native population. In Southwest cooking, a tortilla is a round thin bread made of either corn or wheat flour. Once the dough, called *masa* or *nixtamal*, is made, the tortillas are formed in a tortilla press or are hand-shaped by patting the dough into thin, round shapes. Tortillas are cooked quickly on a hot skillet or griddle, called a *comal*, and are eaten alone or with other Southwest dishes. Corn tortillas are usually about 6 inches (15.24cm) in diameter, much smaller than their flour counterparts, which can be as large as 24 inches (60.96cm) around. Tortillas are used as a wrap around a variety of the region's foods, such as beans, meats, and vegetables, and eaten like a taco.

Tunas: The fruit of the prickly pear cactus. In Europe, this cactus fruit is referred to as a *Barbary fig*. Tunas needs to be trimmed of its spines and outer skin before use. The cactus fruit is frequently used in dessert preparations and as an ingredient in salads. Tunas has an orange or red flesh with a sweet yet tart flavor. The seeds inside the raw fruit are edible and do not need to be removed.

Sample Menus from the Cuisine of the American Southwest

Grilled Vegetable Gazpacho

Spicy Pork Empanadas

Chile-Rubbed Bass with Cilantro Cream, Ancho Chile Mayonnaise, and Southwestern Coleslaw · Calabacitas con Maize ·

Achiote Rice with Wild Mushrooms and Queso Fresco

Roasted Poblano and Potato Soup

Baked Goat Cheese with Roasted Peppers, Pine Nuts, and Corn

Coriander-Cured Pork Loin with Sweet Onion Confit · Tomatillo Fritters ·

Jalapeño Sweet Potato Timbales

Quail, Roasted Pepper, and Avocado

Ensalada de Nopalitos

Tamale Tart with Roast Garlic Custard · Blue Corn and Cheese Pudding

Grilled Vegetable Gazpacho

YIELD: 6 PORTIONS · PORTION SIZE: 8 OUNCES

2½ ounces (75g) red onion, cut into ¼-inch (.64cm) slices

3 ounces (90g) zucchini, cut into ¼-inch (.64cm) slices

1 tablespoon (15ml) olive oil

8 ounces (240g) green bell peppers, roasted, peeled, diced

1 pound (480g) tomato concassée

6 ounces (180g) cucumbers, peeled, seeded, diced

3 cloves garlic, roasted, peeled, minced

1 ounce (30g) breadcrumbs, dry

2 fluid ounces (60ml) red wine vinegar

12 fluid ounces (360ml) tomato or V-8 juice

¼ ounce (8g) cilantro, minced

2 fluid ounces (60ml) olive oil

salt, to taste

black pepper, ground, to taste

GARNISH

corn tortillas, cut into julienne, deep-fried, as needed

green onions, sliced, as needed

black peppercorns, cracked, as needed

CHEF TIPS *V-8 juice is a frequent substitute for tomato juice in this recipe. Its use changes the flavor profile of the gazpacho significantly. Although the matter is one of personal preference, many American chefs favor the depth of flavor that V-8 juice brings to this type of soup.*

Gazpacho should still be chilled in ice before serving even if it was under refrigeration overnight. The flavors peak when the soup is chilled well below 41°F (5°C).

Brush the red onions and zucchini with the first quantity of olive oil and cook on a preheated grill until tender. Watch the vegetables carefully to prevent burning.

Place the grilled onions and zucchini and the roasted bell peppers in a food processor and pulse to a coarse purée. Do not overprocess, as the vegetables will become too thin and lose their natural juices and flavor.

Mix the tomatoes, cucumbers, and roasted garlic with the processed vegetables in a stainless-steel bowl.

Mix in the breadcrumbs, vinegar, tomato juice, cilantro, and the second quantity of olive oil.

Season to taste with salt and ground black pepper.

Place the soup in a bain marie and place the container in shaved or crushed ice. Stir frequently until the gazpacho is thoroughly chilled.

SERVING/HOLDING

Carefully ladle the gazpacho into well-chilled soup cups or plates.

Garnish each portion by placing a small pile of fried tortilla strips on the surface of the soup.

Sprinkle the sliced green onions and cracked black peppercorns on top of the tortilla strips.

 Hold under refrigeration at 41°F (5°C) or lower.

COOLING/STORING

Cover the soup; label, date, and store under refrigeration at 41°F (5°C) or lower.

Roasted Poblano and Potato Soup

YIELD: 6 PORTIONS · PORTION SIZE: 8 OUNCES

1 ounce (30g) bacon, cut into small dice

3 ounces (90g) onion, cut into small dice

1½ ounces (45g) carrots, cut into small dice

1½ ounces (45g) celery, cut into small dice

24 ounces (720g) potatoes, cut into large dice

48 fluid ounces (1.4L) chicken stock, prepared

1 ham hock

12 ounces (360g) potatoes, cut into small dice

1 ounce (30g) poblano chiles, peeled, seeded, cut into small dice

½ teaspoon (2g) cumin, ground

salt, to taste

black pepper, ground, to taste

Render the bacon over medium heat in a heavy-bottomed saucepot.

Remove the bacon bits when they are crisp and reserve until needed.

Add the onions, carrots, and celery to the bacon fat and cook for approximately 5 minutes or until the onions are translucent.

Add the large diced potatoes, chicken stock, and the ham hock.

Bring to a boil and reduce the heat. Simmer for approximately 30 minutes or until the potatoes are tender. Do not allow the simmering soup to fall below 140°F (60°C).

Remove the ham hock and cool briefly until it can be handled safely. Remove the meat from the bone, cut into small dice, and reserve at 140°F (60°C) or higher until needed.

Purée the soup in a blender or food processor and return it to a soup pot.

Add the reserved bacon bits, diced ham, small diced potatoes, and poblano chiles.

Bring the soup to a boil and simmer for an additional 15 minutes or until the potatoes are tender. Do not allow the simmering soup to fall below 140°F (60°C).

Stir in the cumin and season to taste with salt and black pepper.

SERVING/HOLDING

Carefully ladle the soup into hot soup cups or plates.

Hold the soup at 140°F (60°C) or higher.

COOLING/STORING

Pour the remaining soup into small metal containers.

Cool the soup from 140°F (60°C) to a temperature of 70°F (21.1°C) or lower within 2 hours. Cool from 70°F (21.1°C) to 41°F (5°C) within an additional 4 hours for a total cooling time of 6 hours or less.

Cover the soup; label, date, and store under refrigeration at 41°F (5°C) or lower.

Spicy Pork Empanadas

DOUGH

15 ounces (450g) all-purpose flour

½ teaspoon (2g) salt

6 fluid ounces (180ml) water

1 fluid ounce (30ml) olive oil

FILLING

½ fluid ounce (15ml) olive oil

2 cloves garlic, minced

1 tablespoon (15g) ginger root, grated

2 tablespoons (30g) curry powder

1 tablespoon (15ml) rice vinegar

½ teaspoon (2g) salt

10 ounces (300g) pork tenderloin, cut into small dice

1 fluid ounce (30ml) white chicken stock, prepared (see page 517)

1 teaspoon (5g) cilantro, chopped

½ teaspoon (2g) cumin, ground

VINAIGRETTE

1 tablespoon (15ml) olive oil

2 fluid ounces (30ml) corn oil

1 tablespoon (15g) shallots, minced

½ teaspoon (2g) cumin, ground

1 tablespoon (15ml) white wine vinegar

ASSEMBLY

corn or vegetable oil, as needed

6 ounces (180g) mixed baby greens

18 ounces (540g) salsa fresca (recipe follows)

CHEF TIPS *The empanadas can also be baked in a preheated 400°F (204.4°C) oven. Obtaining a crisp crust is more difficult when cooking empanadas in an oven, but the fat content of the finished product is reduced significantly.*

To prepare the dough, combine the flour and salt and place on a clean work surface. Make a well in the center of the flour and add the water and the first quantity of olive oil.

Mix thoroughly and knead for approximately 10 minutes or until a smooth, elastic dough forms.

Place the dough in a bowl and cover with plastic wrap. Let rest for at least 1 hour before using.

Prepare the filling by heating the second quantity of olive oil in a sautoir pan over medium heat. Add the garlic and ginger and sauté for 1 minute.

Stir in the curry powder, vinegar, and salt.

Add the pork and continue to cook, stirring frequently, for an additional 15 minutes and until the pork reaches a minimum internal temperature of 145°F (62.8°C) for at least 15 seconds.

Add the white chicken stock, bring to a boil, reduce the heat, and simmer for 10 minutes. Do not allow the simmering pork to fall below 140°F (60°C).

Stir in the cilantro and the first quantity of cumin.

Cool the pork from 140°F (60°C) to 70°F (21.1°C) or lower within 2 hours. Cool from 70°F (21.1°C) to 41°F (5°C) within an additional 4 hours for a total cooling time of 6 hours or less. Reserve under refrigeration at 41°F (5°C) or lower until needed.

Divide the reserved dough into 24 balls. Roll out each ball of dough into a 4-inch (10.16cm) circle.

Place 1½ teaspoons (6g) of the pork filling in the middle of each piece of dough.

Brush the edges of the dough with a little water and fold the dough over the filling into a half-moon shape.

Crimp the edges with a fork and cover with plastic wrap. Let rest under refrigeration for at least 20 minutes before using.

Prepare the salad dressing by combining the olive and corn oils, shallots, second quantity of cumin, and white wine vinegar in a bowl. Whisk briskly and reserve under refrigeration at 41°F (5°C) or lower until needed.

Heat the frying oil in a heavy-bottomed sautoir or griswold pan over medium-high heat. Pan-fry the empanadas for approximately 1–2 minutes on each side or until they are golden brown and reach a minimum internal temperature of 165°F (73.9°C) for at least 15 seconds.

Degrease the empanadas on absorbent paper towels.

SERVING/HOLDING

Briskly whisk the dressing and toss the baby greens in it until thoroughly coated.

Place a small mound of salad in the center of each warm plate.

Place 2 empanadas next to the greens and serve with approximately 3 ounces (90g) salsa fresca on the side.

🥣 **Hold** the empanadas at 140°F (60°C) or above.

COOLING/STORING

🥣 **Cool** the empanadas from 140°F (60°C) to 70°F (21.1°C) or lower within 2 hours. Cool from 70°F (21.1°C) to 41°F (5°C) within an additional 4 hours for a total cooling time of 6 hours or less.

Cover the empanadas, dressing, greens, and salsa fresca; label, date, and store under refrigeration at 41°F (5°C) or lower.

SALSA FRESCA

YIELD: 6 PORTIONS · PORTION SIZE: 3 OUNCES

12 ounces (360g) tomatoes, cut into small dice

8 ounces (240g) onions, cut into small dice

1 ounce (30g) garlic, minced

1 ounce (30g) serrano chile, minced

2 ounces (60g) cilantro, chopped

1 fluid ounce (30ml) lime juice

salt, to taste

black pepper, coarsely ground, to taste

Combine the tomatoes, onions, garlic, chiles, cilantro, and lime juice in a stainless steel bowl.

Season the salsa to taste with salt and black pepper.

SERVING/HOLDING

🥣 **Hold** under refrigeration at 41°F (5°C) or lower until needed.

COOLING/STORING

Cover the salsa; label, date, and store under refrigeration at 41°F (5°C) or lower.

Baked Goat Cheese with Roasted Peppers, Pine Nuts, and Corn

8 ounces (240g) dried heirloom beans (any variety)

6 ounces (180g) corn kernels

12 ounces (360g) goat cheese

6 ounces (180g) cream cheese

4 ounces (120g) red bell peppers, roasted, peeled, cut into small dice

4 ounces (120g) yellow bell peppers, roasted, peeled, cut into small dice

4 ounces (120g) poblano chiles, roasted, peeled, seeded, cut into small dice

1¼ ounces (37.5g) pine nuts, toasted

1 tablespoon (15g) parsley, minced

1 tablespoon (15g) thyme, minced

6 ounces (180g) breadcrumbs, dry

CHEF TIPS *Roasting peppers and chiles allows them to develop a deeper flavor from the charring of the skin. When peeling the skin from the peppers, do not rinse under water, as the additional flavor will be washed off.*

VINAIGRETTE

2 tablespoons (30ml) olive oil

4 fluid ounces (120ml) corn oil

2 tablespoons (30g) shallots, minced

2 teaspoons (10g) cilantro, chopped

2 tablespoons (30ml) cider vinegar

GARNISH

12 ounces (360g) mixed baby greens

6 fluid ounces (180ml) ancho chile and tomato coulis (recipe follows)

Rinse and sort the beans and remove any stones. Cover with water and soak overnight.

Bring to a boil and reduce the heat to a simmer.

Simmer approximately 30–45 minutes or until tender. Do not allow the simmering beans to fall below 140°F (60°C).

Cool the beans from 140°F (60°C) to 70°F (21.1°C) or lower within 2 hours. Cool from 70°F

(21.1°C) to 41°F (5°C) within an additional 4 hours for a total cooling time of 6 hours or less. Reserve under refrigeration at 41°F (5°C) or lower until needed.

Remove the kernels from the corn cobs and steam in a covered double boiler or commercial steamer for 2–3 minutes or until tender.

Cool the corn kernels from 140°F (60°C) to 70°F (21.1°C) or lower within 2 hours. Cool from 70°F (21.1°C) to 41°F (5°C) within an additional 4 hours for a total cooling time of 6 hours or less. Reserve under refrigeration at 41°F (5°C) or lower until needed.

Mix the goat cheese and cream cheese in a bowl until the mixture is smooth.

Add half the corn kernels, half the roasted bell peppers, half the poblano chiles, and all the pine nuts. Mix until the ingredients are thoroughly incorporated.

Form the cheese mixture into 6 uniform patties weighing approximately 5 ounces (150g) each.

In a separate bowl, combine the parsley, thyme, and breadcrumbs. Pat each cake with the breadcrumb mixture until thoroughly coated.

Allow the cheese patties to rest under refrigeration at 41°F (5°C) or lower for at least 20 minutes or until well chilled and firm.

Brown the cakes under a broiler for approximately 1 minute, being careful not to let them burn. Place the cakes on a baking sheet and cook in a preheated 375°F (190.6°C) oven for approximately 8–10 minutes or until warmed throughout.

Prepare the dressing by combining the olive oil, corn oil, shallots, cilantro, and vinegar in a blender or food processor. Blend until the dressing is smooth and emulsified. Reserve under refrigeration at 41°F (5°C) or lower until needed.

SERVING/HOLDING

Toss the baby greens with three-quarters of the reserved dressing and place a small mound in the center of each cold plate.

Carefully place 1 cheese patty on the side of the mound of greens. Use a spatula to transfer the cheese patties, as they are very soft and delicate.

Drizzle the ancho-tomato coulis on the plate around the cheese and greens.

Toss the cooked heirloom beans and the remaining corn, peppers, and chiles in the remaining dressing and decoratively sprinkle them around the cheese and greens.

Hold the vegetables, greens, dressing, and sauce under refrigeration at 41°F (5°C) or lower.

Hold the cheese patties at 140°F (60°C) or higher.

⚗ **Cool** the cheese patties from 140°F (60°C) to 70°F (21.1°C) or lower within 2 hours. Cool from 70°F (21.1°C) to 41°F (5°C) within an additional 4 hours for a total cooling time of 6 hours or less.

Cover the cheese patties, vegetables, greens, dressing, and sauce; label, date, and store under refrigeration at 41°F (5°C) or lower.

ANCHO CHILE AND TOMATO COULIS

YIELD: 6 PORTIONS · PORTION SIZE: 2 OUNCES

2 ounces (60g) ancho chiles

¼ fluid ounce (7ml) vegetable oil

¾ tablespoon (11g) garlic, chopped

½ ounce (14g) onions, cut into small dice

6 ounces (180g) tomatoes, cut into medium dice

1 fluid ounce (30ml) dry white wine

2 fluid ounces (60ml) white chicken stock, prepared (see page 517)

salt, to taste

black pepper, ground, to taste

CHEF TIPS *The flavor of the ancho chiles can be enhanced without adding significantly more spiciness by heating the dried chiles in a sauté pan over medium heat. Toss the chiles in the pan until they begin to soften, then follow the reconstitution procedure.*

Reconstitute the ancho chiles by steeping them in hot water for 10 minutes. Strain, scrape the flesh from the skins, discard the skins, and purée the remaining flesh. Reserve until needed.

Heat the oil in a saucepan over medium-high heat. Sauté the garlic and onions until they are translucent.

Add the tomatoes and sauté for approximately 2 more minutes or until the onions are tender.

Add the white wine and reduce the volume of liquid by half over medium heat.

⚗ **Add** the stock, bring to a boil, and reduce the heat. Simmer for 15 minutes. Do not allow the simmering sauce to fall below 140°F (60°C).

Add the reserved ancho chile purée.

Season to taste with salt and black pepper.

Purée the sauce in a blender or food processor and strain.

Cool the sauce from 140°F (60°C) to 70°F (21.1°C) or lower within 2 hours. Cool from 70°F (21.1°C) to 41°F (5°C) within an additional 4 hours for a total cooling time of 6 hours or less. Reserve under refrigeration at 41°F (5°C) or lower until needed.

SERVING/HOLDING

Hold the sauce under refrigeration at 41°F (5°C) or lower.

COOLING/STORING

Cover the sauce; label, date, and store under refrigeration at 41°F (5°C) or lower.

Ensalada de Nopalitos

YIELD: 6 PORTIONS · PORTION SIZE: 8 OUNCES

24 ounces (720ml) nopalitos, trimmed, rinsed, cut into julienne

3 tablespoons (44g) cilantro, minced

3 ounces (90g) New Mexico green chiles, minced

7½ ounces (225g) red onions, sliced ⅛ inch thick, separated into rings

½ teaspoon (2g) Mexican oregano

3 fluid ounces (90ml) sour cream

2¼ fluid ounces (67ml) olive oil

1 tablespoon (15ml) orange juice

1 tablespoon (15ml) Mexican lime juice

salt, to taste

black pepper, ground, to taste

6 leaves green leaf lettuce

3 large eggs, hard-boiled, sliced

12 ounces (360g) queso fresco, crumbled

CHEF TIPS *This salad combination holds well when prepared in advance. It is recommended, however, that if made in large quantities and held until needed, the oregano, cilantro, and green onions be added to the salad just before serving to yield the best results.*

If Mexican oregano is not available, generic oregano can be substituted. However, a larger quantity should be used, as the Mexican variety is typically much stronger than the regular version.

Toss the nopalitos, cilantro, green chiles, onions, and Mexican oregano together in a bowl.

In a separate bowl, mix the sour cream with the olive oil, orange juice, and lime juice.

Add the nopalitos mixture to the sour cream sauce and toss until the ingredients are thoroughly coated.

Season to taste with salt and black pepper.

SERVING/HOLDING

Place a lettuce leaf in the center of each cold plate.

Place approximately 5 ounces (180g) of the nopalitos mixture on top of each lettuce leaf.

Garnish each salad with 3 slices of hard-boiled egg and approximately 2 ounces (60g) of queso blanco sprinkled over the top.

Hold the nopalitos under refrigeration at 41°F (5°C) or lower.

COOLING/STORING

Cover the nopalitos salad, cheese, and eggs; label, date, and store under refrigeration at 41°F (5°C) or lower.

Quail, Roasted Pepper, and Avocado

YIELD: 6 PORTIONS · PORTION SIZE: 10 OUNCES

6 bamboo skewers

3 quails, split in half

BALSAMIC VINAIGRETTE

2 tablespoons (30ml) olive oil

4 fluid ounces (120ml) corn oil

2 tablespoons (30g) shallots, minced

2 teaspoons (10g) parsley, chopped

1½ fluid ounces (45ml) balsamic vinegar

salt, to taste

black pepper, ground, to taste

CHEF TIPS *Avocados tend to oxidize and discolor rapidly. If the avocados need to be prepared in advance, brush them lightly with a little lemon juice to prevent oxidation.*

   4 fluid ounces (120ml) white wine vinegar

   4 tablespoons (60ml) whole-grain mustard

   1 tablespoon (15ml) mustard, yellow

   2 tablespoons (30ml) chili sauce

   1 teaspoon (5ml) lemon juice

   1 tablespoon (15ml) horseradish sauce

   1 teaspoon (5g) salt

   ½ teaspoon (2g) black pepper, ground

   ¼ teaspoon (1g) cayenne pepper

   4 fluid ounces (120ml) vegetable oil

   ½ cup (120g) green onions, minced

   ¼ cup (60g) celery, minced

   3 tablespoons (44g) parsley, minced

GARNISH

   3 avocados, sliced

   6 ounces (180g) spinach, cut into chiffonade

   12 ounces (360g) red bell peppers, roasted, peeled, cut into julienne

   12 ounces (360g) yellow bell peppers, roasted, peeled, cut into julienne

   12 ounces (360g) green bell peppers, roasted, peeled, cut into julienne

   12 ounces (360g) tomato concassée

Soak the bamboo skewers in water for at least 10 minutes. Place ½ quail on each skewer in a straight line to hold shape.

Prepare the dressing by combining the olive and corn oils, shallots, parsley, and balsamic vinegar in a blender or food processor. Blend until the dressing is smooth and emulsified.

Season the dressing to taste with salt and black pepper.

Liberally brush the quail with approximately one-half of the dressing and allow to marinate under refrigeration at 41°F (5°C) or lower for 1 hour.

Reserve the remainder of the dressing under refrigeration at 41°F (5°C) or lower until needed.

COOKING

Cook the quail skewers on a preheated grill for approximately 2–3 minutes on each side or until the quail are completely cooked and reach a minimum internal temperature of 145°F (62.8°C) for at least 15 seconds. Be careful not to burn or overcook the quail.

🍲 **Cool** the quail from 140°F (60°C) to 70°F (21.1°C) or lower within 2 hours. Cool from 70°F (21.1°C) to 41°F (5°C) within an additional 4 hours for a total cooling time of 6 hours or less. Reserve under refrigeration at 41°F (5°C) or lower until needed.

Prepare the remoulade sauce by combining the white wine vinegar, mustards, chili sauce, lemon juice, horseradish sauce, salt, and black and cayenne peppers in a blender or food processor.

Blend or process until all the ingredients are thoroughly incorporated and smooth.

With processor running, drizzle in the oil in a slow, steady stream.

🍲 **Remove** from the blender and mix in the green onions, celery, and parsley. Reserve under refrigeration at 41°F (5°C) or lower until needed.

SERVING/HOLDING

Place 3 or 4 slices of avocado in a ring shape in the center of each cold plate.

Toss the spinach and roasted bell peppers with the remaining balsamic vinaigrette dressing and carefully place a small mound in the center of the avocado ring.

Remove the skewers from the quail and decoratively place a quail half on top of the spinach and pepper salad.

Sprinkle the tomato concassée on top of the salad and around the plate.

Drizzle the remoulade sauce around the perimeter of the plate.

🍲 **Hold** the quail, spinach, salad, and remoulade sauce under refrigeration at 41°F (5°C) or lower until needed.

COOLING/STORING

Cover the quail, spinach salad, and remoulade sauce; label, date, and store under refrigeration at 41°F (5°C) or lower.

Coriander-Cured Pork Loin with Sweet Onion Confit

YIELD: 6 PORTIONS · PORTION SIZE: 8 OUNCES

4 tablespoons (60g) coriander seeds

4 tablespoons (60g) black peppercorns

8 ounces (240g) shallots, minced

2 cloves garlic, minced

4½ ounces (135g) kosher salt

¼ ounce (7g) dark brown sugar

1⅓ fluid ounces (39ml) olive oil

36 ounces (1080g) pork loin, boneless, trimmed

2 fluid ounces (60ml) vegetable oil

12 ounces (360g) sweet onion confit (recipe follows)

CHEF TIPS *American cuisine dictates nutritional balance and lighter protein portions. To comply with these guidelines, serve 5-ounce portions of proteins instead of the 8-ounce stated on the recipe yield. Guidelines state to stay within nutritional balance the diet should consist of 15-20% protein, 55-60% carbohydrates, and 25-30% fats.*

Place the coriander seeds and peppercorns in a food processor and pulse for approximately 1 minute until coarsely ground.

Add the shallots, garlic, salt, and brown sugar.

While processing, drizzle in the olive oil in a thin steady stream until a thick paste develops.

Place the pork loin roast in a pan and spread the paste over the pork loin. Reserve the pork loin under refrigeration at 41°F (5°C) or lower for at least 3 hours or until needed. Turn the pork roast every hour.

COOKING

Heat the vegetable oil in a large sautoir or roasting pan over medium-high heat until the oil begins to smoke.

Remove the pork loin from the pan and remove as much of the paste as possible.

Sear the pork loin on all sides until thoroughly browned.

Transfer the pork loin to a roasting pan with an elevated rack and cook in a preheated 400°F (204.4°C) oven for approximately 18–20 minutes or until the desired degree of doneness is attained and the pork loin reaches a minimum internal temperature of 145°F (62.8°C) for at least 15 seconds.

Allow the pork loin to rest undisturbed in a warm place for at least 10 minutes before slicing and serving.

SERVING/HOLDING

Slice the pork loin into slices ½-inch (1.27cm) thick of approximately 4 ounces (120g) each.

Shingle 2 slices in the center of each hot plate.

Garnish the sliced pork with approximately 2 ounces (60g) of the sweet onion confit.

Hold the pork loin at 140°F (60°C) or higher.

COOLING/STORING

Cool the pork loin from 140°F (60°C) to 70°F (21.1°C) or lower within 2 hours. Cool from 70°F (21.1°C) to 41°F (5°C) within an additional 4 hours for a total cooling time of 6 hours or less.

Cover the pork loin and sweet onion confit; label, date, and store under refrigeration at 41°F (5°C)or lower.

SWEET ONION CONFIT

YIELD: 6 PORTIONS · PORTION SIZE: 2 OUNCES

1½ tablespoons (22g) butter

12 ounces (360g) sweet onions, thinly sliced

3 tablespoons (44g) sugar

1½ fluid ounces (44ml) white wine vinegar

1 fluid ounce (30ml) red wine or balsamic vinegar

salt, to taste

Melt the butter in a saucepan over medium-high heat.

Add the sliced onions and sauté for 1 minute.

Add the sugar and continue to cook until it dissolves. Do not let the sugar begin to caramelize.

Deglaze the pan with the two vinegars and cook for approximately 3–5 minutes until the liquid is reduced to almost dry.

Season to taste with salt.

SERVING/HOLDING

Hold the sweet onion confit at 140°F (60°C) or higher.

COOLING/STORING

Cool the sweet onion confit from 140°F (60°C) to 70°F (21.1°C) or lower within 2 hours. Cool from 70°F (21.1°C) to 41°F (5°C) within an additional 4 hours for a total cooling time of 6 hours or less.

Cover the sweet onion confit; label, date, and store under refrigeration at 41°F (5°C) or lower.

Tamale Tart with Roasted Garlic Custard

YIELD: 6 PORTIONS · PORTION SIZE: 10 OUNCES

ROASTED GARLIC CUSTARD

- 12 fluid ounces (360ml) heavy cream
- ¾ ounce (21g) garlic, peeled
- 1 teaspoon (5ml) olive oil
- 2 egg yolks
- salt, to taste
- white pepper, ground to taste

TAMALE CRUST

- 10 ounces (300g) red bell peppers, seeded, coarsely chopped
- 3 ounces (90g) ancho chiles
- 16 fluid ounces (480ml) hot water
- 10 ounces (300g) masa harina
- 2 ounces (60g) cornmeal, yellow
- ¼ teaspoon (1g) cayenne pepper
- ½ teaspoon (2g) cumin, ground
- 2 teaspoons (10g) salt
- 3 ounces (90g) vegetable shortening, room temperature

ASSEMBLY

- 1 fluid ounce (30ml) olive oil
- 2 ounces (60g) onions, finely chopped
- 2 ounces (60g) tomato concassée
- 2 ounces (60g) yellow tomato concassée
- 2 tablespoons (30g) cilantro, minced
- 2 ounces (60g) serrano chiles, seeded, minced
- 2 teaspoons (10ml) Mexican lime juice
- salt, to taste
- black pepper, ground, to taste

CHEF TIPS *If Mexican or Key limes are not available, regular Persian limes can be substituted. However, a smaller quantity should be used, as the flavor of Mexican limes is not as strong as that of their Persian cousins. When substituting Persian limes for Mexican limes, use one Persian lime for every three Mexican limes called for in the recipe.*

Place the heavy cream in a heavy-bottomed saucepot over medium heat and reduce the volume of liquid by a quarter.

Toss the garlic in the first quantity of olive oil and wrap the cloves loosely in aluminum foil. Roast the garlic in a preheated 350°F (176.7°C) oven for approximately 20 minutes or until it is soft. Reserve until needed.

Purée the roasted garlic and whisk into the reduced cream.

In a separate bowl, whisk the egg yolks and drizzle in the cream mixture, whisking briskly. Season to taste with salt and white pepper.

Cool the cream from 140°F (60°C) to 70°F (21.1°C) or lower within 2 hours. Cool from 70°F (21.1°C) to 41°F (5°C) within an additional 4 hours for a total cooling time of 6 hours or less. Reserve under refrigeration at 41°F (5°C) or lower until needed.

Steam the red bell peppers in a saucepan over boiling water until they are tender. Drain and transfer to a blender or food processor. Blend until smooth for a yield of approximately ¾ cup (177ml) red pepper purée. Reserve until needed.

Reconstitute the ancho chiles by steeping them in the hot water for 10 minutes. Strain, reserve the liquid, and scrape the flesh from the skins. Purée the flesh with the reserved liquid. Reserve until needed.

Combine the masa harina, cornmeal, cayenne, cumin, and salt. Incorporate the shortening and mix until the mixture is light and fluffy.

Gradually incorporate the masa and cornmeal mixture into the ancho chile liquid until it is smooth.

Add the red bell pepper purée and mix until thoroughly incorporated and a dough forms.

Form the dough into a disk and press it firmly into a 9-inch (22.86cm) tart pan with a removable bottom. Press the dough evenly over the bottom and up the sides of the tart pan.

Fill the tart with the reserved garlic custard batter.

Cook the tart in a preheated 325°F (162.8°C) oven for approximately 20–25 minutes or until it is set and reaches a minimum internal temperature of 145°F (62.8°C) for at least 15 seconds. Hold the tart at 140°F (60°C) or higher until needed.

Heat the second quantity of olive oil in a pan over medium-high heat until it just begins to smoke.

Add the onions and sauté until they are translucent.

Add the tomatoes, cilantro, serrano chiles, and lime juice. Continue to sauté for an additional 2 minutes. Season with salt and black pepper.

Cut the tamale tart into 6 wedges and place 1 wedge in the center of each hot plate.

Carefully top each wedge of tamale tart with the tomato mixture.

🍲 **Hold** the tamale tart mixture at 140°F (60°C) or higher.

COOLING/STORING

🍲 **Cool** the tamale tart from 140°F (60°C) to 70°F (21.1°C) or lower within 2 hours. Cool from 70°F (21.1°C) to 41°F (5°C) within an additional 4 hours for a total cooling time of 6 hours or less.

Cover the tamale tart; label, date, and store under refrigeration at 41°F (5°C) or lower.

Chile-Rubbed Bass with Cilantro Cream, Ancho Chile Mayonnaise, and Southwestern Coleslaw

YIELD: 6 PORTIONS · PORTION SIZE: 6 OUNCES

1¼ ounces (35g) coriander seeds, toasted

2¼ ounces (64g) mustard seeds, toasted

1¼ ounces (35g) cumin seeds, toasted

¼ ounce (7g) black peppercorns

½ ounce (14g) salt

2¼ pounds (1kg) bass, boneless, skinless, cut into 6-ounce fillets

1 fluid ounce (30ml) vegetable oil

GARNISH

6 fluid ounces (180ml) cilantro cream (recipe follows)

6 fluid ounces (180ml) ancho chile mayonnaise (recipe follows)

12 ounces (360g) Southwestern coleslaw (see page 412)

3 corn tortillas, cut into fine julienne, deep-fried

1 bunch chives, finely chopped

Place the coriander, mustard, and cumin seeds in a sauté pan and cook over medium-high until they are nicely toasted and release their aroma and oils.

Cool slightly and combine the toasted seeds with the peppercorns and salt. Grind the spice mixture finely, using a spice or coffee grinder.

Rub the fillets liberally with the ground spice blend.

Heat the vegetable oil in a sautoir pan over medium-high heat. Sear the fillets, skin side up, until they are lightly browned.

Carefully turn the fillets and place the pan in a preheated 350°F (176.7°C) oven for approximately 5 minutes or until the bass reaches the desired degree of doneness and a minimum internal temperature of 145°F (62.8°C) for at least 15 seconds. Hold the fillets at 140°F (60°C) or higher until needed.

SERVING/HOLDING

Squeeze approximately 1 ounce (30ml) of the cilantro cream in a zig one way on the bottom third of each warm plate and squeeze approximately 1 ounce (30g) of the ancho mayonnaise in a zag going the other direction.

Place approximately 2 ounces (60g) of the Southwestern coleslaw in the center of the plate.

Position the sautéed fillets on top of the slaw and garnish the top of the bass with a small pile of deep-fried corn tortilla strips. Sprinkle the plate with the chopped chives.

Hold the bass at 140°F (60°C) or higher.

COOLING/STORING

Cool the bass fillets from 140°F (60°C) to 70°F (21.1°C) or lower within 2 hours. Cool from 70°F (21.1°C) to 41°F (5°C) within an additional 4 hours for a total cooling time of 6 hours or less.

Cover the bass fillets, coleslaw, and sauces; label, date, and store under refrigeration at 41°F (5°C) or lower.

CILANTRO CREAM

YIELD: 6 PORTIONS · PORTION SIZE: 1 OUNCE

2 ounces (60g) cilantro, minced

16 fluid ounces (480ml) heavy cream

salt, to taste

white pepper, ground, to taste

Combine the minced cilantro with the heavy cream in a heavy-bottomed saucepan.

Cook the cream and cilantro over medium heat until the volume is reduced by half.

Season to taste with salt and white pepper.

Strain the sauce through a chinois.

Place the sauce in a squeeze bottle.

SERVING/HOLDING

Hold the cilantro cream at 140°F (60°C) or higher.

COOLING/STORING

Cool the cilantro cream from 140°F (60°C) to 70°F (21.1°C) or lower within 2 hours. Cool from 70°F (21.1°C) to 41°F (5°C) within an additional 4 hours for a total cooling time of 6 hours or less.

Cover the cilantro cream; label, date, and store under refrigeration at 41°F (5°C) or lower.

ANCHO CHILE MAYONNAISE

YIELD: 6 PORTIONS · PORTION SIZE: 1 OUNCE

1 ounce (30g) ancho chiles

1 egg yolk, pasteurized

1 tablespoon (15ml) lemon juice

1 teaspoon (5ml) Mexican lime juice

¼ teaspoon (1g) dry mustard

⅛ teaspoon (1g) cayenne pepper

4 fluid ounces (120ml) corn oil

4 fluid ounces (120ml) olive oil

salt, to taste

CHEF TIPS *Pasteurized eggs are required as a substitute for raw egg products in most commercial foodservice operations. Raw eggs are linked to the transmission of food-borne illnesses and are considered a food safety hazard. Pasteurized egg products are becoming available at the retail level and can be found in many specialty food stores and markets.*

Reconstitute the ancho chiles by steeping them in hot water for 10 minutes. Strain, scrape the flesh from the skin, and purée. Reserve until needed.

Combine the egg yolk, lemon juice, lime juice, dry mustard, and cayenne pepper with 1 teaspoon (5ml) of the corn oil in a blender or food processor and blend for 1 minute.

While processing, drizzle the remaining corn oil and the olive oil in a steady stream into the food processor or blender and process until the mixture attains the consistency of mayonnaise.

Turn processor off and fold in the ancho chile purée until thoroughly incorporated.

Season to taste with salt.

Place the sauce in a squeeze bottle.

SERVING/HOLDING

 Hold under refrigeration at 41°F (5°C) or lower until needed.

COOLING/STORING

Cover the ancho chile mayonnaise; label, date, and store under refrigeration at 41°F (5°C) or lower.

Southwestern Coleslaw

YIELD: 6 PORTIONS · PORTION SIZE: 2 OUNCES

SLAW

1 teaspoon (5ml) corn oil

1½ ounces (45g) leeks, cut into julienne

3 ounces (90g) carrots, cut into julienne

3 ounces (90g) cabbage, finely shredded

3 ounces (90g) cucumber, cut into julienne

½ tablespoon (7g) cilantro, cut into chiffonnade

½ tablespoon (7g) mint, cut into chiffonnade

DRESSING

1 fluid ounce (30ml) rice vinegar

3 fluid ounces (90ml) chipotle oil, prepared

⅛ teaspoon (1g) onion powder

⅛ teaspoon (1g) garlic powder

Mexican lime juice, to taste

salt, to taste

black pepper, ground, to taste

CHEF TIPS *Chipotle oil is made by marinating chipotle chiles in olive or vegetable oil for a minimum of 24 hours before using. The strength or heat of the oil is determined by the ratio of chipotle chiles to oil. It is recommended that once the desired strength is achieved, the ratio be recorded to ensure consistency of the finished products using this oil as an ingredient. Chipotle oil can be stored for up to a month if advance preparation is desired. Just about any variety of dried chile can be used to create flavored oils.*

Heat the corn oil in a sautoir pan over medium-high heat. Sauté the leeks until they are tender. Remove from the heat and reserve under refrigeration at 41°F (5°C) or lower until needed.

Blanch the carrots in a saucepot of boiling salted water until they are tender. Shock in an ice-water bath, drain, and reserve under refrigeration at 41°F (5°C) or lower until needed.

Combine the sautéed leeks, blanched carrots, cabbage, cucumbers, cilantro, and mint. Reserve under refrigeration at 41°F (5°C) or lower until needed.

Prepare the dressing by combining the rice vinegar, chipotle oil, onion powder, and garlic powder.

Season the dressing to taste with lime juice, salt, and black pepper. Reserve under refrigeration at 41°F (5°C) or lower until needed.

SERVING/HOLDING

Combine the reserved vegetables with the dressing just before using. Toss thoroughly until all the vegetables are coated with the dressing.

Hold under refrigeration at 41°F (5°C) or lower until needed.

COOLING/STORING

Cover the coleslaw; label, date, and store under refrigeration at 41°F (5°C) or lower.

Calabacitas con Maize

YIELD: 6 PORTIONS · PORTION SIZE: 4 OUNCES

3 tablespoons (45g) butter

4 ounces (120g) onion, cut into small dice

2 cloves garlic, peeled, crushed

16 ounces (480g) zucchini, cut into small dice

3 ounces (90g) New Mexico green chiles, cut into small dice

10 ounces (300g) corn kernels

¼ teaspoon (1g) dried mint

salt, to taste

black pepper, ground, to taste

5 ounces (150g) tomato concassée

CHEF TIPS *Calabacitas is the Spanish word for squash.*

Melt the butter in a sautoir pan over medium-high heat.

Add the onions and garlic cloves and sauté until the onions are translucent.

Remove the garlic cloves from the pan and add the zucchini, chiles, and corn kernels.

Cover, lower the heat, and cook for approximately 3–5 minutes or until the vegetables are tender.

Stir in the mint and season to taste with salt and black pepper.

Just before serving, add the tomato concassée and toss over medium heat until thoroughly heated.

SERVING/HOLDING

Hold the vegetables at 140°F (60°C) or higher.

COOLING/STORING

Cool the vegetables from 140°F (60°C) to 70°F (21.1°C) or lower within 2 hours. Cool from 70°F (21.1°C) to 41°F (5°C) within an additional 4 hours for a total cooling time of 6 hours or less.

Cover the vegetables; label, date, and store under refrigeration at 41°F (5°C) or lower.

Tomatillo Fritters

YIELD: 6 PORTIONS · PORTION SIZE: 3 OUNCES

vegetable oil, as needed

4½ ounces (135g) all-purpose flour

1½ tablespoons (22g) baking powder

1 teaspoon (5g) baking soda

1 tablespoon (15g) paprika

1 large egg

12 fluid ounces (360ml) beer

cayenne pepper, to taste

salt, to taste

18 ounces (540g) tomatillos, husked, rinsed

16 ounces (480ml) all-purpose flour

salt, to taste

black pepper, ground, to taste

Pour enough oil into a heavy-bottomed saucepan to come 1 inch (2.54cm) up the sides. Heat over medium-high to approximately 325°F (162.8°C).

Sift the first quantity of flour, baking powder, baking soda, and paprika together and reserve until needed.

In another mixing bowl, beat the egg and beer together.

Sprinkle the reserved dry ingredients into the egg and beer, whisking briskly until the ingredients are thoroughly incorporated and a batter forms.

Season the batter to taste with cayenne pepper and salt.

Cut the tomatillos into slices ¼ inch (.64cm) thick, then cut the slices into ¼-inch (.64cm) strips.

Season the second quantity of flour to taste with salt and black pepper.

Dredge the tomatillo strips in the flour and shake off the excess.

Dip the strips in the batter and let all but a thin film run off.

Pan-fry the tomatillo strips in the hot oil, stirring gently, for approximately 2 minutes or until they brown lightly and reach a minimum internal temperature of 145°F (62.8°C) for at least 15 seconds.

SERVING/HOLDING

Hold the fritters at 140°F (60°C) or above.

COOLING/STORING

Cool the fritters from 140°F (60°C) to 70°F (21.1°C) or lower within 2 hours. Cool from 70°F (21.1°C) to 41°F (5°C) within an additional 4 hours for a total cooling time of 6 hours or less.

Cover the fritters; label, date, and store under refrigeration at 41°F (5°C) or lower.

Blue Corn and Cheese Pudding

YIELD: 6 PORTIONS · PORTION SIZE: 5 OUNCES

12 ounces (360g) corn kernels

6 fluid ounces (180ml) milk

9 ounces (270g) blue cornmeal

3 fluid ounces (90ml) corn oil

1 teaspoon (5g) baking powder

1 teaspoon (5g) sugar

½ teaspoon (2g) salt

2 eggs, beaten

6 ounces (180g) New Mexico green chiles, roasted, peeled, seeded, chopped

4 ounces (120g) Longhorn cheddar cheese, grated

Combine the corn kernels and milk in a large bowl.

Add the cornmeal and corn oil. Mix thoroughly.

Combine the baking powder, sugar, and salt and add to the corn mixture.

Stir in the beaten eggs, diced green chiles, and grated cheese.

Place the mixture in a 9-inch (22.9cm) cake pan, baking dish, or casserole and bake on the middle shelf of a preheated 375°F (190.6°C) oven for approximately 45 minutes or until it reaches a minimum internal temperature of 145°F (62.8°C) for at least 15 seconds. A simple test for approximate doneness is to insert a toothpick into the center of the pudding. If it is clean when removed, the pudding is, more than likely, done.

SERVING/HOLDING

Hold the pudding at 140°F (60°C) or higher.

CHEF TIPS *Blue corn is one of the Three Sisters of Southwestern food. A Navajo legend tells us that ears of blue corn came from the sky when a giant turkey, flying high above the earth, dropped them from under its wings. To the Pueblo tribe in northern New Mexico, it is the most sacred of Southwestern corn varieties, but it was essentially unknown outside the area until Southwestern food achieved national popularity in the 1980s. The Pueblo tribe makes blue cornbread and the Hopi tribe uses blue cornmeal to make traditional piki bread. Blue corn has a rich, deep flavor achieved partly by drying the kernels over fires made from piñon wood. The distinctive flavor has contributed to the popularity of the blue corn tortilla chip throughout the United States. Blue corn also contains more protein than yellow corn.*

Blue cornmeal is now widely available. It can be made into corn bread or used as a coating for fried foods. Because it tends to be crumbly, it is often combined with wheat flour to make crêpes or pancakes. Blue corn tortillas are made with blue corn treated with slaked lime and then ground.

Cool the pudding from 140°F (60°C) to 70°F (21.1°C) or lower within 2 hours. Cool from 70°F (21.1°C) to 41°F (5°C) within an additional 4 hours for a total cooling time of 6 hours or less.

Cover the pudding; label, date, and store under refrigeration at 41°F (5°C) or lower.

Tortillas de Maize

YIELD: 6 PORTIONS · PORTION SIZE: 2 OUNCES

10½ ounces (315g) masa harina

10½ fluid ounces (3.5ml) water, hot

Combine the masa harina and water in a medium-sized bowl.

Place the mixture on a flat surface and knead until a smooth, pliable dough forms.

If the dough is sticky, add a bit more masa harina. If it seems dry, add a bit more water.

Allow the dough to rest at room temperature, covered with plastic wrap, for 30 minutes.

Divide the dough into 12 balls.

If using a tortilla press, cut two sheets of plastic wrap into rectangles slightly larger than the diameter of the tortilla press.

Place one sheet of plastic on the surface of the tortilla press. Arrange a ball of dough in the center and set the second piece of plastic over the ball of dough.

Press firmly on the lever to close the press and form a tortilla about ¹⁄₁₆ inch (.16cm) thick. Gently peel back the top layer of plastic wrap and flip the tortilla over so that it rests on the palm of the hand. While holding the tortilla, peel away the second sheet of plastic wrap.

If a tortilla press is not available, use a rolling pin to attain similar results, or try the old-fashioned method of patting the tortilla between the hands until the desired shape and thickness is

CHEF TIPS *The distinctive scent of warm, freshly cooked corn tortillas evokes a tidal wave of nostalgic memories for anyone who has ever lived in the Southwest. Before the European colonists introduced wheat flour to the region, tortillas were made only from corn.*

Today, corn tortillas are used in the role of bread with a meal or as wrappers for a variety of ingredients limited only by the imagination of the cook. Frequently, corn tortillas are folded into a crescent and used soft or crisp to hold fillings for tacos. If rolled up like a flute and deep-fried until crisp, they are called flautas. Tortillas are also used for enchiladas and tostados. Even stale tortillas have a use. Cut into strips or wedges, they are used as garnishes for soups. Tortilla chips are tortillas cut into wedges and deep-fried. Tortilla chips, accompanied by salsa and guacamole, are commonly served in Southwestern restaurants as an appetizer.

achieved. The old-fashioned method, however, requires experience and practice in order to achieve a delicious and tender tortilla.

COOKING

Heat two skillets or comals—one to medium-high heat and the other to medium-low heat.

Place one tortilla on the skillet with the lower temperature and cook for approximately 30 seconds.

Remove the tortilla with a spatula and place the uncooked side of the tortilla on the higher-temperature skillet.

Cook for 30 seconds, then turn the tortilla again so that the first side can cook for about 30 seconds more on the higher-temperature skillet.

Remove the tortilla to a plate and cover with a clean, damp towel. Repeat the process with the remaining balls of dough.

Allow the tortillas to rest, covered, in a warm place for approximately 15 minutes to allow them to soften slightly before they are used.

SERVING/HOLDING

Hold the tortillas at 140°F (60°C) or higher.

COOLING/STORING

Cool the tortillas from 140°F (60°C) to 70°F (21.1°C) or lower within 2 hours. Cool from 70°F (21.1°C) to 41°F (5°C) within an additional 4 hours for a total cooling time of 6 hours or less.

Cover the tortillas; label, date, and store under refrigeration at 41°F (5°C) or lower.

Achiote Rice with Wild Mushrooms and Queso Fresco

YIELD: 6 PORTIONS · PORTION SIZE: 4 OUNCES

5 ounces (150g) raw long-grain rice

2 fluid ounces (60ml) achiote oil (recipe follows)

2 cloves garlic, minced

3 ounces (90g) onion, cut into small dice

1½ ounces (45g) carrot, cut into small dice

1½ ounces (45g) celery, cut into small dice

2 ounces (60g) wild mushrooms, thinly sliced

2 ounces (60g) corn kernels

¼ teaspoon (1g) cinnamon, ground

15 fluid ounces (450ml) white chicken stock, prepared, hot (see page 517)

salt, to taste

3 ounces (90g) queso fresco, crumbled

1½ tablespoons (22g) cilantro, chopped

black pepper, ground, to taste

Rinse the rice under cold running water. Drain thoroughly and reserve until needed.

Heat the achiote oil in a sautoir pan over medium-high heat. Sauté the garlic, onions, carrots, and celery for approximately 2 minutes, stirring occasionally, or until the onions are translucent.

Add the mushrooms and corn and continue to cook for an additional 2 minutes.

Add the rice and cinnamon and cook, stirring frequently, for 1–2 minutes or until the rice is thoroughly coated with the oil.

Add the hot stock and bring to a boil. Reduce the heat to a simmer, season to taste with salt, and cook, uncovered, for 15 minutes.

Cover the pan and continue to cook for approximately 5 more minutes or until the rice is tender.

Remove the rice from the heat and allow to rest, covered, for 5 minutes before using.

Mix the queso fresco and cilantro into the rice while fluffing it with a fork.

Adjust the seasoning to taste with salt and black pepper.

SERVING/HOLDING

Hold the rice at 140°F (60°C) or higher.

COOLING/STORING

Cool the rice from 140°F (60°C) to 70°F (21.1°C) or lower within 2 hours. Cool from 70°F (21.1°C) to 41°F (5°C) within an additional 4 hours for a total cooling time of 6 hours or less.

Cover the rice; label, date, and store under refrigeration at 41°F (5°C) or lower.

ACHIOTE OIL

¼ cup (60g) achiote seeds

8 fluid ounces (240ml) olive oil

Heat the achiote seeds and oil in a saucepan until the oil is very hot.

Remove from the heat and let rest at room temperature for at least 3 hours to allow the flavors from the seeds to infuse the oil.

Carefully skim off and reserve the orange-colored oil on top without disturbing the bottom layer.

Discard the bottom layer of oil with the seeds.

COOLING/STORING

Store the oil in the refrigerator for up to 2 months.

Cover the achiote oil; label, date, and store under refrigeration at 41°F (5°C) or lower.

Jalapeño Sweet Potato Timbales

YIELD: 6 PORTIONS · PORTION SIZE: 4 OUNCES

24 ounces (720g) sweet potatoes

½ teaspoon (2g) butter

1 ounce (30g) onion, cut into brunoise

1 tablespoon (15g) butter, softened

1 large egg, beaten

½ tablespoon (7ml) honey

½ teaspoon (2g) jalapeños, minced

1½ fluid ounces (45ml) heavy cream, hot

salt, to taste

black pepper, ground, to taste

CHEF TIPS *The flavor of sweet potatoes is greatly enhanced by baking them in their skins. The vast majority of the potato's natural sugar is concentrated just under the skin. If the potatoes are peeled and boiled, much of the sugar is lost with the discarded skin. As a general rule, baking tubers intensifies their flavor while boiling dilutes it.*

Bake the sweet potatoes for approximately 50–60 minutes in a preheated 350°F (176.7°C) oven or until they are tender. Remove from the oven and let cool slightly until they can be safely handled.

Melt the first quantity of butter in a pan over medium heat and sauté the onions for approximately 2–3 minutes or until they are translucent. Reserve until needed.

Split the sweet potatoes and remove the flesh from the skins.

Purée the sweet potato pulp through a food mill or mash to a smooth consistency with a potato masher.

While the puréed potatoes are still hot, mix in the softened butter.

Mix in the egg very quickly so it does not become cooked and scrambled.

Add the sautéed onions, honey, jalapeños, and heavy cream and mix until all the ingredients are thoroughly incorporated.

Season to taste with salt and black pepper.

Place the sweet potato mixture in buttered 4-ounce (120ml) ramekins or timbale molds.

Bake in a preheated 350°F (176.7°C) oven for approximately 5 minutes or until the mixture is firm and reaches a minimum internal temperature of 145°F (62.8°C) for at least 15 seconds.

SERVING/HOLDING

Hold the sweet potato timbales at 140°F (60°C) or higher.

COOLING/STORING

Cool the sweet potato timbales from 140°F (60°C) to 70°F (21.1°C) or lower within 2 hours. Cool from 70°F (21.1°C) to 41°F (5°C) within an additional 4 hours for a total cooling time of 6 hours or less.

Cover the sweet potato timbales; label, date, and store under refrigeration at 41°F (5°C) or lower.

Buñuelos with Honey Syrup

YIELD: 6 PORTIONS · PORTION SIZE: 6 OUNCES

4 ounces (120g) all-purpose flour

½ teaspoon (2g) baking powder

1 teaspoon (5g) sugar

¼ teaspoon (1g) salt

1 large egg

1½ fluid ounces (45ml) milk

frying oil, as needed

HONEY SYRUP

16 fluid ounces (480ml) water

1½ fluid ounces (45ml) honey

1 stick cinnamon

GARNISH

sugar, powdered, as needed

Combine the flour, baking powder, sugar, and salt in a bowl.

In a separate bowl, mix the egg and milk together.

Stir the egg mixture into the flour mixture and gently knead until a smooth dough forms. If the dough is too dry, add more milk.

Allow the dough to rest for at least 10 minutes.

Divide the dough into 1–1½-ounce (30–45g) balls and roll or stretch them into paper-thin round discs.

Deep-fry the dough rounds, one at a time, using the swimming method, in a preheated 375°F (190.6°C) fryer. Turn the dough rounds occasionally while cooking.

Remove the buñuelos from the fryer when they are crisp and a golden brown color and they have reached a minimum internal temperature of 145°F (62.8°C) for at least 15 seconds.

Drain on absorbent paper towels and hold at 140°F (60°C) or higher until needed.

Heat the water in a saucepan over medium heat and dissolve the honey in the water.

Add the cinnamon stick, bring to a boil, and cook until the liquid is reduced to a thick, syrupy consistency.

SERVING/HOLDING

Place one of the buñuelos on each hot plate and sprinkle powdered sugar over the top.

Serve the buñuelos with approximately 2 ounces (60ml) of the honey syrup on the side.

Hold the buñuelos and honey syrup at 140°F (60°C) or higher.

COOLING/STORING

Cool the buñuelos and honey syrup from 140°F (60°C) to 70°F (21.1°C) or lower within 2 hours. Cool from 70°F (21.1°C) to 41°F (5°C) within an additional 4 hours for a total cooling time of 6 hours or less.

Cover the buñuelos and honey syrup; label, date, and store under refrigeration at 41°F (5°C) or lower.

Bert Cutino

ON THE CUISINE OF CALIFORNIA AND HAWAII

In California, there has always been an abundance of vegetables—from the fertile valleys of Salinas, many such as iceberg lettuce, tomatoes, carrots, and romaine lettuce were popularized. In Castroville, artichokes were first planted by the Spaniards. The beautiful Monterey Bay, which is historically known for its once famous sardine industry, is known also for other species of seafood that have been utilized by many ethnic groups and finally developed in cuisine as it is called today.

California cuisine's reliance on local and regional ingredients makes it what it is today. I have found it easy to draw on these local fresh ingredients and species and to incorporate them into a menu that enables customers to experience regional cuisine. We are fortunate to have available to us the abundance of all these many resources from our coastline and valleys. The fresh ingredients of the California region, and the opportunities they provide for creativity and the expression of talent, are a chef's dream.

Bert Cutino, C.E.C., A.A.C., is a Californian and chef-owner of the landmark restaurant The Sardine Factory in Monterey, California.

California and Hawaii

California

Hawaii

California and Hawaiian cuisines are distinct from one another, but the regions are similar in climate and share many agricultural products.

California

California, compared to the United States as a whole, has a relatively young cuisine, the foundation of which is innovation. California is geographically the third largest state in America and has the largest population. It has a wide variety of climates and geography, making it well suited for growing and raising foods of all kinds. In addition, California is the home of the largest irrigation systems built in America, allowing farmers even in the most remote deserts the opportunity to raise and harvest valuable crops.

Many peoples and cultures have influenced the cuisine of California, starting with the Spanish, whose cuisine had already changed from its original form over the more than 200 years of interaction with the natives of South and Central America before its arrival in California. The gold rush of the mid-1800s brought immigrants of varied ethnic backgrounds from all points of the continent seeking fortunes and laid the foundation for the cultural and culinary diversity California is known for today.

The San Francisco Bay area is a perfect example of diversity in both cuisine and culture. The first restaurant in San Francisco was the Tadich Grill, which was founded in 1849 by three Croatian immigrants and featured grilled seafood and dishes such as cioppino. Italian fishermen who settled in the North Beach area in the late 1800s brought the tradition of hearty Italian cooking. The first Italian restaurant in San Francisco was Fior d'Italia, which opened in 1886. Nearby, in Chinatown, Asian influences from Korea, Japan, China, Thailand, and Vietnam are evident. Not far away are predominantly German, Russian, and Polish neighborhoods, which add their own cultural influences to the area's cuisine. Needless to say, however, the Spanish influence had the first and greatest impact on California cuisine as a whole due to the close proximity of Mexico and other Latin American countries and to the large number of Hispanic residents who immigrated to California over the last three centuries.

Many of today's common food staples have their origin in California. One of these is the orange. The first orange grove of any size was planted in 1804 at the San Gabriel Mission, east of Los Angeles, by a group of Franciscan monks. Seedlings from the mission were used to plant several of California's first sizable crops, including the first commercial crop in 1841. After the gold rush, the brand new state, with its swelling population, created a huge demand for oranges grown in the region. By 1873, orange groves were common from San Diego in the south to Sacramento in the north. The newly established community of Riverside became famous for its unique orange crop—the navel orange. Today, California produces over 160 varieties of citrus fruits, including 18 types of navel oranges, 11 of Valencia oranges, 16 kinds of grapefruits, and 16 varieties of lemons, to name just a few.

Spanish missionaries were the first to produce wine in California from local Mission grapes. However, it was not until after the 1849 gold rush that the wine industry began to take root. In 1833, over 100 varieties of French vines were transplanted to northern California by a Frenchman from Bordeaux named Jean-Louis Vignes. Later, a Hungarian named Agoston Haraszthy took note of Vignes's success in growing French grapes and brought back from a trip to Europe over 100,000 vine cuttings representing over 300 varieties of grapes from France, Spain, Germany, Italy, and Switzerland; he planted them in Sonoma County. Haraszthy went on to establish the first California winery, Buena Vista, which still operates today. Winemaking in

California prospered until 1916, when the vines were almost wiped out by a vine-killing root louse called *phylloxera*. The California winemaking industry recovered by the 1940s; however, the grape-growing and wine-making techniques produced mainly low- to average-quality wines. After experimentation and trial and error throughout the 1950s, 1960s, and 1970s, wine-making in California has reached maturity, now yielding high-quality wines that can compete with many older, more established European wines.

Gallo, the largest winemaking company in the world, was founded in 1933 by two Italian brothers, Ernest and Julio Gallo. Today, one out of every three bottles of wine sold in America carries the Gallo label or one from its other brands. Gallo is primarily a winemaker and buys most of its grapes from California growers. At one time, it was not unusual for Gallo to purchase over 40 percent of all grapes grown in Sonoma County and 20 percent of the Napa Valley crop. Although Gallo typically produces wines that appeal to the American mass market, the company now owns five vineyards in northern California that produce high-quality wines in the artisan fashion. The largest and most famous wine-growing area of California is Napa Valley; however, high-quality wines are also produced in the Sonoma, Carneros, Monterey, Central Valley, and Santa Barbara areas.

The largest farming state in America is California and the largest of California's agricultural industries is dairy farming, which today produces over three billion dollars worth of dairy products each year. The cheese industry of California reflects the state's diversity. Small, local artisans make prize-winning, hand-crafted, high-quality cheeses that compete well with their older, more established European counterparts. At the other end of the spectrum are high-tech cheese factories, which produce hundreds of millions of pounds of cheese each year. However, only Monterey Jack, among the three cheeses invented in America, is from California.

Agricultural innovation in California began with a horticulturist named Luther Burbank, who moved to California from New England in the late 1800s. Burbank was one of the early agricultural scientists working in the state and developed many new plants, including the Shasta daisy and the Burbank potato. From this original research, California scientists began to develop new varieties of produce carefully selected for resistance to disease, bugs, and extreme weather conditions as well as for characteristics of size, color, flavor, and shelf life. Although a significant amount of controversy surrounds these selectively bred fruits and vegetables, especially now that some are being genetically modified, one thing is for certain: the technological advances started by Burbank in California allowed the state's produce industry to supply not only America but also the world.

Another California visionary was Oliver M. Wozencraft, who, in 1849, became convinced that a 2000-square-mile area of the Colorado desert in the southeast corner of the state, known as the most desolate part of California, could be irrigated and turned into a thriving farmland. By 1902, 15,000 acres of land in the Imperial and Coachella valleys were growing large amounts of carrots, lettuce, tomatoes, onions, and squash. This man-made intervention was due to Wozencraft's irrigation plan, which brought water to the valleys from the Colorado River and stored it for irrigation at the Hoover Dam. Many settlers soon moved to the valleys as farming was made easier and more profitable by the constant sunshine, inexpensive water supply, and rich soil. The settlers found that in this desert area of California they could raise crops, harvest them, and sell them in the market before their competitors in the north. The nation's only commercial date palm grove grows in this desert oasis.

Hollywood affected the cuisine of California with the opening of the Cocoanut Grove in 1921, conveniently located near the movie studios. Hollywood stars such as Charlie Chaplin, Carole Lombard, and Judy Garland patronized the restaurant. The Cocoanut Grove retained the services of a French chef who was known for creating distinctive dishes in the classic style with local ingredients. Other famous Hollywood restaurants of the era were the Brown Derby, which invented the Cobb salad, and Don the Beachcomber, Romanoff's, Perino's, Schwab's Pharmacy, and Chasen's. Chasen's chili was so popular among the rich and famous that Elizabeth Taylor had it flown to the movie set of *Cleopatra* in Rome and Richard Nixon was known to have Chasen's chili served at dinner meetings with political dignitaries at his "western White House," located in San Clemente, California. These early California restaurants learned quickly to provide unusual high-quality food with excellent service, setting the trend for today's modern California cuisine restaurants.

Few culinary professionals could dispute Alice Waters's role as the innovative source of what we know today as California cuisine. While studying in France, Waters learned about using high-quality ingredients grown by local farmers as the foundation for cooking. She returned to America and opened her own restaurant, Chez Panisse, in Berkeley in 1971. Applying this approach to ingredients from northern California, Waters partnered with local growers and created the cooking style known as California cuisine. As other restaurants began to follow her precepts, many artisan producers found opportunities to specialize in and market certain products, such as baby vegetables, varietal tomatoes, and other market-fresh vegetables.

About ten years later, an Austrian-born chef named Wolfgang Puck, the chef at Ma Maison in Los Angeles, a hangout for Hollywood celebrities, became one of America's first celebrity chefs. In 1982, Puck opened his own restaurant in Los Angeles, called Spago, and became known for his designer pizzas. He brought a somewhat lighter bill of fare to California cuisine and added a fun and energetic atmosphere, enhancing the dining experience. Recently, fusion cuisine has become a popular innovation in California. *Fusion cuisine* is a cooking term describing the combination of flavors, techniques, and ingredients of two or more cuisines. The use of fusion cuisine in restaurants got its start from California chefs, who both represent and serve the huge diversity of people and cultures that coexist there today.

California has certainly had its share of innovation with regard to food and food-related products. A few examples of firsts coming from the Golden State include the Popsicle, invented by Frank Epperson in 1905; the hot fudge sundae, first made at C.C. Browns in Hollywood in 1906; fortune cookies, made in Los Angeles in 1916; the cheeseburger, created by the Rite Spot in Pasadena in 1920; the chili fries, from Ptomaine Tommy's in Los Angeles in 1920; the double-decker hamburger, made famous by Bob's Big Boy in Glendale in 1937; doggie bags, from Lawry's Prime Rib House in 1938; the surf-and-turf meal in the 1960s; and the California sushi roll in the 1970s.

Immigration to California continues today, with a steady influx of Eastern Europeans, Asians, Africans, and South Americans. All bring new culinary traditions and techniques, which will allow California to continue to lead the nation in food innovation, from both the farming and cooking perspectives.

Hawaii

Hawaii is the youngest of the United States, achieving statehood in 1959. However, this does not mean that the cuisine of Hawaii is not mature. In fact, when Captain James Cook landed in Hawaii in 1778, he discovered that the Hawaiian culture did indeed have a cuisine based on indigenous products.

It is believed that the first voyagers to Hawaii were from the Marquesas Islands and Tahiti and arrived in approximately A.D. 800. They brought with them plants and seedlings, such as the taro plant and breadfruit, as well as small pigs, to start their new life in Hawaii. Other foods introduced to Hawaii include sweet potatoes, bananas, coconuts, sugar cane, and pineapples.

To sailors, Hawaii was originally known as the Sandwich Islands. It was a stopover point for sea voyagers traveling from the Americas to Asia. In Hawaii, sailors could rest, enjoy a luau, and resupply their ships in the middle of the Pacific Ocean. A luau is a traditional feast of celebration in Hawaii to commemorate events such as a marriage, birthday, or graduation. The Hawaiian luau, which typically features a whole roast pig as the main dish, is every bit the tradition that the clambake is in New England and the barbecue is in the Tex-Mex region. Similar to the clambake, a pit is prepared and lined with rocks heated from a fire made from the stumps of banana trees. A pig is placed in the pit and covered with banana leaves and a wet burlap cloth, then cooked slowly for several hours. Today, luaus featuring a lavish Hawaiian buffet and local entertainment are popular among tourists visiting Hawaii and can be found every weekend at most hotels and resorts.

The sailors, traders, and whalers brought with them salted meats and fish, sea biscuits, and a limited supply of fruit and vegetables, which were introduced to the Hawaiians. Later, in the 1820s, missionaries from the east coast of the United States came to Hawaii in an attempt to Christianize the natives. They brought staples they were accustomed to in New England, such as potatoes, apples, salt cod, corned beef, cheese, and butter.

In the mid-1800s, sugar became an important crop and, as the Hawaiian sugar crops grew, so did the demand for labor, encouraging tens of thousands of people to immigrate to Hawaii. Among the first immigrants were the Chinese, who brought rice, vegetables, noodles, ginger, and stir-fry cooking. Later came the Japanese, who introduced soy sauce, sticky rice, and tempura. The Portuguese arrived and contributed spicy pork dishes and breads baked in a special oven, called a *forno*, that is fueled with burning wood. The Koreans brought garlic and spicy peppers, while the Filipinos introduced the Spanish and Malaysian flair of their homeland to the cooking in Hawaii.

In the past, Hawaii dedicated the vast majority of its agricultural production to sugar and pineapples; however, today, with the economic decline of those crops, Hawaii has taken a much more diverse posture with regard to its agricultural output. Though Hawaii is a series of islands, they are not totally dependent on the outside world. The soil in Hawaii is fertile and productive, and the climate, which offers plenty of sunshine and rain, provides excellent growing conditions for agricultural products including livestock, squash, peppers, tomatoes, and lettuce. The waters contain hundreds of species of fish and seafood, many of which are considered among the best in the world. Hawaii, as a trade center in the middle of the Pacific Ocean, reaps the benefits of a diversity of cultures adding to the cuisine of the area.

Today, the foods of Hawaii are created through a combination of American, European, Asian, and local influences.

Typical Californian and Hawaiian Ingredients and Dishes

Abalone: The meat from a large mollusk that lives off the coast of California. Pacific abalone comes in four varieties: pink, red, green, and black. Regardless of the variety, the meat is extremely sweet and tasty, but it is usually tough and requires tenderizing with a mallet prior to cooking. In the mid-1800s, when abalone were plentiful, they were harvested by the Japanese almost to the brink of extinction. Their colorful shells are sometimes referred to as *mother-of-pearl*. Today, the abalone industry is highly regulated, as the mollusks continue to be the favorite food of sea otters and thus are scarce. It is not uncommon for abalone meat to be sold for as much as $50 per pound.

Ahi: Hawaiian for "tuna." Ahi is the most prized catch from the waters of the Hawaiian Islands and is sometimes auctioned at markets in Tokyo, Japan, for its popular use as an ingredient in sushi. One large sushi-grade tuna can command prices of up to $80,000 at these open-air fish auctions.

Anaheim Chile: Also referred to as the *California green chile*, the Anaheim is one of the most frequently called-for chiles in the region's cuisine. Anaheim chiles are 6–8 inches (15.24cm–20.3cm) in length and 1½ inches (3.81cm) in diameter. They are bright green in color and have mild to moderate heat. This variety of chile, when grown in New Mexico, is referred to as a *New Mexico green chile*. Due to soil and growing conditions, this chile is typically much hotter than the Anaheim. The heat of Anaheim green chiles is rated at 1000–1500 Scoville units and usually placed 1 to 2 on a scale of 1 to 10.

Artichoke: A part of the thistle group of the sunflower family, first planted in 1922 by an Italian immigrant named Angelo Del Chiaro. The Green Globe artichoke plants grow best in the Castroville area, about 100 miles (160.9km) south of Monterey along the coast, and make up almost the entire crop of the Castroville region. The heart of the artichoke has an especially appealing flavor and texture. Artichokes are served hot or cold, as a main dish, and as an ingredient in other preparations.

Asparagus: Over 70 percent of all asparagus consumed in America is produced in California, grown mainly around the Stockton area in the northern part of the San Joaquin Valley. The most popular asparagus are the Atlas, Grande, and Apollo varieties, which thrive in the Sacramento Delta region.

Avocado: Dating back to almost 8000 B.C., the avocado originated in Mexico and was considered an aphrodisiac by the Incas and the Aztecs. The native word for avocado also meant testicle, which could be the reason that the missionaries, who brought so many foods from South and Central America to California, chose to leave the avocado behind. Avocados were first introduced to California in 1848 near Los Angeles; however, the avocado industry started in 1871 in Santa Barbara, located about 80 miles (128.7km) north of Los Angeles. The avocado tree can produce up to 400 fruits per year; these can be left on the tree for almost half a year. The most popular varieties of avocados are the Hass and the Fuerte, which are known for their sweet, slightly nutty flavor. Today, California produces over 95 percent of all avocados consumed in the United States. The most popular use for the avocado is in the dish called *guacamole*. (See *guacamole*.)

Banana: A staple food in Tahiti, where many of the original Hawaiians came from. Hawaii is home to many varieties of banana trees, some of which may have been introduced by the Tahitian immigrants. Many of the varieties of banana originally found in Hawaii tasted bitter when eaten raw but improved on cooking. Today, other varieties of the banana tree brought from Brazil and China have been planted in Hawaii. These sweet varieties are generally eaten raw.

Boysenberry: An Oregon horticulturist, Rudolph Boysen, is given credit for creating the Boysenberry in the 1920's, a cross-hybrid of blackberries, loganberries, and red raspberries.

Breadfruit: A vegetable, high in carbohydrates, originally brought to Hawaii by early settlers from the Marquesas Islands. Breadfruit is somewhat bland in flavor, similar to a potato, and is cooked by steaming or baking.

Calamari: Italian for "squid." Squid is found all along the California coast and in Hawaiian waters. It can be cooked by sautéing, frying, steaming, poaching, or broiling. Large squid are generally stuffed and braised. Squid contain an ink sac in the head containing a dark brown liquid that can be used, if the squid is extremely fresh, in sauces or as a flavoring and coloring agent for fresh pasta.

California Roll: A type of sushi, invented in California, that does not utilize raw fish or seafood. It is made similar to a sushi maki roll, but avocado and mock crab legs are rolled with rice into the seaweed. High-end California rolls usually use genuine crab legs and sometimes replace the seaweed wrapper with salmon skin. Today, California rolls can be found in supermarkets and specialty stores across the United States. (See *sushi*.)

Chop Suey: An American invention created by the cooks who fed the Chinese immigrants working to construct the Western Pacific Railroad in mid-nineteenth-century California. The favorite dish of the Chinese immigrants was called *chow mein*. However, the non-Asian cooks had little or no knowledge of how to make chow mein properly. The hybrid recipe they produced to approximate chow mein came to be called *chop suey*. The Chinese workers ate the dish and, eventually, adopted it. Today, chop suey can be found in many Chinese restaurants in California.

Cobb Salad: Invented in 1934 by the owner of the Brown Derby restaurant, Robert H. Cobb. The salad calls for chicken, bacon, hard-boiled eggs, avocado, blue cheese, and tomato, all uniformly cut and decoratively placed in strips over a bed of shredded romaine lettuce.

Coconut: The fruit of the coconut palm tree, originally from Malaysia. The milk extracted from the meat by soaking it in hot milk or water is sweet and frequently used in Hawaiian and Asian recipes. Curry dishes often use coconut milk as the basis for the sauce. The coconut meat can be eaten fresh or dried and is commonly used in baked goods, pastries, and candies. The most common use for coconuts, however, is actually for the oil that is extracted from the dried meat.

Coffee: The only coffee beans that grow in the United States are grown in a small region near Kona on the island of Hawaii. Coffee was brought to Kona from Brazil by Reverend Samuel Ruggles in the early 1800s. Later in the century, coffee plants became consistent and a worthwhile crop. In 1899, the coffee market crashed, causing plantation owners to lease their land to their workers, most of whom were Japanese. Coffee was grown on 5- to 12-acre (.02-.05 square kilometers) parcels, producing large-quantity crops. Today, there are 600 independent coffee farmers, all on 3- to 7-acre (.01-.03 square kilometers) parcels; a total of 2,290 acres (9.2 square kilometers), producing just over 2 million pounds annually. Some of the plantation names are Alinalani Gardens, Halama Farms, Kona Joe's, and Kona Loa Plantation. Kona coffee is still picked by hand and the plantations where the beans are grown and processed are named for the area where the farms are located and the techniques used to process the coffee. Many pineapple farmers are exchanging their crops for coffee, as the worldwide price of coffee is significantly higher than that of pineapples and Kona coffees are prized for their robust taste and mellow flavor.

Date: The only places in the Western Hemisphere where dates are commercially grown are the Yuma Valley and Bard Yuma Arizona off of Interstate 8, and Coachella Valley near Indio, California, where the climate is similar to that of the Middle East and North Africa. The first palm date trees were planted in California in the 1900s. Date palms require a minimum of ten years from the time the tree is planted to the time fruit can be picked. The best dates are picked soft, then frozen, which does not destroy the enzymes in the fruit that produce a natural sugar powder that forms on the skin. Lower-quality dates are allowed to cure on the tree and are then softened by steaming, which does destroy the enzymes. However, this is a much less labor-intensive process.

Dry Jack: A type of Jack cheese discovered by mistake in the early 1900s by the cheese wholesaler D. F. DeBernardi, who apparently left some in storage too long. The aged Jack cheese had hardened and developed a sweet, nutty flavor. During World War I, the supply of Romano and Parmesan cheeses imported to America became sporadic and inconsistent. Dry Jack, with a texture and flavor similar to the dried Italian cheeses, immediately became popular as a substitute. After the war, when Italian cheeses became readily available again, Dry Jack lost its popularity; however, today it is making a comeback as a California artisan-style cheese.

Dungeness Crab: The largest variety of crab, found off the coast of California. Dungeness crabs have unusually sweet-tasting and tender meat. Although the crabs are found from Mexico to the Aleutian Islands near Alaska, they are most common in the waters near Monterey and San Francisco. On the wharves in these areas, Dungeness crabs are served hot or cold and are used as an ingredient in other famous dishes, such as cioppino and Crab Louie salad. Dungeness crabs are typically purchased whole and precooked.

French Dip: The house specialty of Philippe's, a Los Angeles restaurant dating back to 1908. The sandwich calls for thinly sliced beef, pork, or lamb served hot on a French bread roll and dipped in warm pan juices. It is said that this sandwich resulted from a customer complaint that the rolls at Philippe's were stale. The customer asked if the roll could be dipped in pan juices to soften it. Other guests tried this and the sandwich eventually became a big hit.

Fresno Chile: Grown only in California, the Fresno chile is very hot, conical in shape, and approximately the same size as a jalapeño. Fresno chiles are generally used to make salsas and relishes. The typical substitutes for Fresno chiles are jalapeño or serrano chiles. The heat of Fresno chiles is rated at 5000–7500 Scoville units and usually placed at 2 or 3 on a scale of 1 to 10.

Garlic: A major crop from Gilroy, California, located in the San Joaquin Valley, which supplies 90 percent of all garlic consumed in the United States. Japanese immigrants started garlic farming in the 1920s. In 1940, Kiyoshi Hirasaki partnered with Joseph Gubser of the Po River Valley, Italy's garlic-producing region, and greatly expanded garlic cultivation in California. Gilroy is also the home of Gilroy Foods, a dehydrating plant, which opened in the 1920s. Today, Gilroy Foods processes large quantities of garlic each day.

Green Goddess Dressing: A mayonnaise-based salad dressing flavored with anchovies, tarragon, chives, and parsley, invented by the chef at the Palace Hotel in San Francisco. Green Goddess dressing was created in honor of George Arliss, a guest of the hotel, who was starring in the play *The Green Goddess*, being performed in the city.

Guacamole: A dish made from the mashed pulp of avocados mixed with herbs, seasonings, and sometimes, tomatoes and onions. In California, recipes for guacamole are passed down from generation to generation and guarded as stringently as chili recipes in Texas and gumbo in New Orleans. Guacamole can be smooth or chunky, mild or spicy. It is typically served as a dip with deep-fried corn tortilla chips.

Macadamia Nut: Originally from Australia, the macadamia tree was named after John Macadam, a native of Scotland who became a speaker of some renown in nineteenth-century Australia. The tree was first brought to Hawaii by William H. Purvis in the 1800s as an ornamental tree. In the 1920s, Ernest Shelton Van Tassell began the first commercial macadamia crop on the island of Oahu. Macadamia nuts are known for their crunchy texture, rich, buttery flavor, and distinctive taste. They are labor-intensive to produce and, thus, are limited in supply and carry a high price. Macadamia nuts are high in unsaturated fat and free of cholesterol. Oil derived from these nuts has healthy properties and a high heat tolerance.

Mahi Mahi: Hawaiian for "dolphin fish." The fish has a light pink flesh, with a delicate, sweet flavor. It is best cooked either sautéed or grilled. Mahi mahi should not be confused with dolphin or porpoise, which are mammals; dolphin fish is a fish.

Martini: An alcoholic beverage said to be invented during the California gold rush by bartender Jerry "The Professor" Thomas of the Occidental Hotel in San Francisco. The cocktail was originally named the Martinez and combined gin, vermouth, bitters, and maraschino, which were then stirred with ice and strained into a long-stemmed glass. By 1890, the drink gained wide popularity and the name evolved into *martini*.

Maui Onion: A sweet onion, grown on the island of Maui, that rivals the flavor of Vidalia onions from Georgia and Walla Walla onions from Oregon. Maui onions grow on the slopes of Mount Haleakala, where they enjoy cool temperatures and fertile soil. The sweetest of all Maui onions is the Kula Maui variety, grown near the town of Kula.

Miso Paste: A thick paste made from soybeans. Miso paste has a flavor similar to soy sauce and is frequently used to flavor soups and enrich the taste of sauces. Miso paste is commonly found in Asian specialty markets.

Monterey Jack Cheese: One of the three cheeses invented in the United States—the others are Colby and brick, from the Central Plains region. Monterey Jack cheese is derived from queso blanco, a white Mexican cheese economically produced in the missions. Monterey Jack was first produced in California's second established mission in Monterey. One story has it that a Monterey businessman, David Jacks, who owned dairies that produced a white, semisoft cheese with his name on it, was the originator. As the story goes, the *s* from his name was eventually dropped and the cheese was named Jack Cheese. Today, Monterey Jack cheese frequently comes flavored with ingredients such as jalapeño, pesto, caraway seeds, onion, and garlic, which are combined with the cheese during production.

Navel Orange: Several of these orange trees, originally from Brazil, were sent by an American missionary working there to the U.S. Department of Agriculture around 1870. The USDA then propagated the trees and offered them to any farmer who desired them. Luther C. Tibbets first planted two navel orange trees in the Riverside area of California in 1873. Most of the navel oranges in the world today descend from these two trees. Navel oranges are known for their large size, sweet taste, seedless flesh, and ease of peeling.

Olive: One of the first foods introduced to California by missionaries. In addition to eating the fruit, the missionaries used the oil from the olives for cooking, lighting, machine lubricant, and even as an insecticide. The processing and curing technique used in California was different from that of Europe. The resulting flavor, color, and texture thus differed from the typical Mediterranean olive and was called the *California black olive*. Until recently, California olives were not widely used for the production of olive oil. Today, however, many superpremium cold-pressed olive oils are being produced in the Mediterranean tradition and compete with their European counterparts.

Pacific Sole: A common flatfish found along the waters of the California coast. Several varieties of Pacific sole are available, including the English or lemon sole, Rex sole, California Dover sole, rock sole, and petrale or brill sole. All varieties of sole possess a white, sweet-tasting flesh with a lean, fine texture. The Rex and the petrale sole are two of the most sought-after fish in the region. They are frequently sautéed and served with a mild sauce.

Pineapple: This fruit was first planted in Hawaii by Spanish horticulturist Francisco de Paula y Marin in 1813. In 1886, a new pineapple variety called the Smooth Cayenne was introduced to the area and resulted in the first commercial pineapple crop. In 1901, James B. Dole started the first successful pineapple plantation in Hawaii, with 12 acres of pineapples planted on the island of Oahu. By 1940, Hawaii produced 80 percent of the world's supply of pineapples and, by the 1950s, pineapple became Hawaii's second largest crop, next to sugar cane. Pineapple is available canned and fresh; however, canned pineapple production, common in past decades, has declined because modern shipping methods have made fresh pineapples readily available worldwide.

Poi: A thick gray paste pounded from the cooked root of the taro plant. It is the typical starch of Hawaii and is eaten fresh or allowed to sour for a few days prior to eating. (See *taro*.)

Purple Passion: A variety of asparagus, purple in color, invented by a researcher at the University of California at Davis. Purple Passion is derived from asparagus of that color that grow in a small river valley in Italy near the French border. Until recently, this strain of asparagus was never successfully grown beyond the 20-acre area of its origin. Purple Passion is now farmed in South Africa, South America, and Australia, in addition to California, and is marketed primarily to high-end restaurants, hotels, and country clubs.

Queso Blanco: Spanish for "white cheese." Queso blanco, the Mexican cheese from which Monterey Jack derives, is popular as an economical product made with little equipment and even when only a small amount of milk can be obtained. (See *Monterey Jack cheese*.)

Raisin: Armenian immigrants who had experience in the Old World producing dried fruits started the raisin industry in Fresno, California. As legend has it, the raisin was created by accident when a heat wave dried a farmer's grapes on the vine before he could pick them. There are, of course, other accounts. The grape industry, which occupies over 270,000 acres (1.09 square kilometers) of land in California today, devotes almost two million tons of grapes each year to the production of raisins. The popularity of raisins can also be attributed to a marketing success story. In 1986, an advertising campaign featuring animated clay figures called the California Raisins sang and danced to Motown tunes, effectively changing the American perception of raisins. Before the advertisement, Americans generally perceived raisins as boring; however, long after the ads stopped airing, they continue to think positively about the dried fruit.

Rumaki: An appetizer recipe made famous in the 1940s at the California restaurant Don the Beachcomber. Rumaki features a chicken liver and a water chestnut wrapped in a piece of bacon, skewered, and baked until crisp.

Sand Dab: A miniature relative of the flounder that is common in the waters off the California coast. These flatfish are typically between 8 and 10 ounces (240–300g) and, on the eye side, are brown in color and mottled with orange or black spots or blotches. The small fish has a sweet flesh with a fine texture and is generally prepared by pan- or deep-frying.

Shirley Temple: A nonalcoholic cocktail, named after the child actress of the same name, designed for children by a bartender at the Brown Derby restaurant in Hollywood in the 1930s. The drink calls for lemon-lime soda mixed with ginger ale and grenadine and is typically garnished with a cherry. Over the years, numerous names have attached to the beverage, driven by the popularity of succeeding children's movies. It has been called everything from the Roy Rogers to the Buzz Lightyear, depending on which characters are most popular among children.

Smoothie: A health drink invented during the health craze of California in the 1950s and typically found in juice bars. Recipes for smoothies vary; however, the essential ingredients include whole fruit, fruit juice, and yogurt, which are blended together and served in tall glasses.

Sourdough Bread: A uniquely flavored bread originally made in the San Francisco Bay area beginning in 1849 by French baker Louis Boudin. Boudin's bread had a chewy texture, crisp crust, and a distinctive sour flavor. It is said that the texture and flavor of sourdough bread cannot be replicated outside of the San Francisco area, even if the exact recipe is followed and original starter from San Francisco is used. The local bakers say that this is due to a combination of the San Francisco area's air, fog, and bay.

Sourdough Starter: A fermented leavener made from a paste of flour and water, activated by yeast, and used to make sourdough bread. Sourdough starter was so valuable to miners and prospectors, who were sustained in the wilderness by sourdough bread, that they carried it in a pouch hung from their necks. These miners and prospectors thus were called *sourdoughs*. Sourdough starter is usually used over and over again. Each time a batch of sourdough bread is made, a portion of the dough is reserved, then mixed with water and a little salt and added to the next batch of dough in order to make it rise. The process is repeated over and over again. The Boudin bakery in San Francisco, which started making sourdough bread in 1849, claims that its bread still uses a sourdough starter directly descended from the original batch of sourdough bread. (See *sourdough bread.*)

Sugar: It is believed that the first sugar came to Hawaii via early settlers from the South Pacific and that it was used as a medicine as well as a food. In 1778, when Captain Cook arrived in Hawaii, sugar was already being cultivated extensively by the Hawaiians. The world-wide popularity of cane sugar created significant growth of this industry in Hawaii from 1852 to 1930, luring almost 500,000 immigrants to Hawaii to farm and process sugar. Sugar soon became Hawaii's main export crop. The sugar industry peaked about 1965. Today, the sugar industry in Hawaii has steadily declined as a result of decades of decreases in the worldwide price of sugar as a commodity.

Sushi: A bite-sized Japanese rice and fish preparation popularized in the United States by Californians. Two main varieties of sushi exist: maki and niguri. Sushi maki calls for sweet, sticky rice that is rolled in seaweed with raw fish, seafood, or vegetables and cut into bite-sized pieces. Niguri sushi has pieces of raw fish or seafood decoratively placed on top of an oblong log of sweet, sticky rice. Sushi needs to be served freshly made from the highest-quality fish or seafood available. It is typically served with soy sauce, pickled ginger slices, and wasabi, a Japanese green horseradish.

Table Grape: About one-third of the fruit and nut revenues of California come from table grapes. The Thompson seedless grape, which is native to Iran, took its name in the United States from an Englishman named William Thompson, who planted the grapes in the Sacramento Valley in the 1860s. Today, table grapes are extensively grown from the Mexican border to many parts of the San Joaquin Valley, with over 500,000 acres (2.02 square kilometers) of land devoted to growing them. Among the many popular table grape varieties are Ribier, Flame, Emperor, Red Globe, and Calmeria.

Taro: One of the oldest food crops in the world. It is believed that the taro plant made its way to Hawaii from Southeast Asia via Polynesian immigrants, who extensively cultivated it. Since the late 1700s, taro root was the basic sustenance for Hawaiians and the basis for a starch called *poi*, which is made by cooking the root, then pounding it into a paste. (See *poi.*) The roots from inland varieties of the plant are sometimes steamed or baked and eaten like potatoes or are sliced thin and deep-fried like potato chips. The leaves and stalks can be cooked like a vegetable and have a flavor similar to chard or spinach.

Ti Leaf: The smooth green leaf of the ti plant. Originally, ti leaves were steamed and chewed for their sweet flavor, similar to sugar cane. Ti leaves were also used to thatch roofs, make sandals, and as a medicine. A strong alcoholic beverage called *okolehao* is made like beer; the roots of the ti plant are used as its base. Today, the most important cooking use for ti leaves is as a wrapper for foods to be steamed. A traditional Hawaiian dish using this technique is laulau, a package of taro leaves, pork, and fish wrapped in a ti leaf and steamed.

Valencia Orange: A variety of orange originally from Spain and grown in large quantities in southern California, specifically Riverside, San Bernadino, Orange, Ventura, and Tulare counties. The Valencia orange is best known for its flavorful juice and is one of two orange crops representing over 95 percent of the entire California orange crop production. The other main variety produced in California is the navel orange.

Wine Grape: Approximately 20 varieties of grape are used today by California wine makers, planted on more than 350,000 acres (1.4 square kilometers) of land, primarily on the north and central coasts. For the production of white wines, the most commonly grown grape varieties are the Chardonnay, French Colombard, Chenin Blanc, and Sauvignon Blanc grapes. For the production of red wines, the most common grape varieties utilized are the Zinfandel, Cabernet Sauvignon, Merlot, and Barbera grapes.

Zombie: An alcoholic beverage invented in the 1940s at the California restaurant Don the Beachcomber. The cocktail calls for three varieties of rum blended with ice, apricot brandy, and orange, pineapple, and lime juices. Typically, 151-proof rum is floated on top of the beverage and ignited just before serving.

Sample Menus from the Cuisines of California and Hawaii

MENU ONE

Cream of Garlic Soup

Baby Greens with Warm Goat Cheese and Walnut Vinaigrette

Sautéed Petaluma Duck Breast with Port Wine Reduction · Creamed Spinach ·

Spicy Roasted Eggplant · Pasta with Capers, Olives, and Pine Nuts

MENU TWO

Chilled Castroville Artichoke with Confetti Vinaigrette

Caesar Salad

San Francisco Cioppino · Rosemary Focaccia

MENU THREE

Chilled Avocado and Cucumber Soup

Deep-Fried Monterey Bay Calamari with Lemon Butter Sauce

Macadamia-Encrusted Mahi Mahi with Tropical Fruit Salsa ·

Chinese Long Beans with Sesame Seeds · Steamed California Vegetables ·

Monterey Jack and Green Chile Polenta

Cream of Garlic Soup

YIELD: 6 PORTIONS · PORTION SIZE: 8 OUNCES

2 ounces (60g) onions, cut into paysanne

2 ounces (60g) leeks, white part only, cut into paysanne

1 tablespoon (15ml) canola oil

½ pound (240g) russet potatoes, peeled, cut into medium dice

2¼ ounces (68g) garlic, peeled, sliced

48 fluid ounces (1.2L) white chicken stock, prepared (see page 517)

4 fluid ounces (120ml) heavy cream

salt, to taste

white pepper, ground, to taste

4 ounces (120g) chives, minced

CHEF TIPS *Gilroy, a small town in Central California, is the self-proclaimed garlic capital of the world. Typically, in California cuisine, the use of roux as a thickening agent is unpopular. In this recipe, the potatoes puréed into the soup act as the thickening agent.*

Chive flowers make a great garnish for this soup. They can be used in addition to the minced chives or as a replacement.

Sweat the onions and leeks in the canola oil in a saucepot over medium-high heat until the onions are tender and translucent. Do not allow the vegetables to brown.

Add the potatoes, garlic, and stock.

Bring to a boil and reduce the heat to a simmer. Simmer the soup until potatoes and garlic are tender and thoroughly cooked. Do not allow the simmering soup to fall below 140°F (60°C).

Purée the mixture in a food processor or blender.

Return the puréed soup to a saucepot and add the cream. Season to taste with salt and white pepper.

Reheat the soup, but do not bring to a boil.

SERVING/HOLDING

Carefully ladle the soup into hot soup bowls or plates.

Garnish each portion with minced chives.

🥣 **Hold** the soup at 140°F (60°C) or above.

COOLING/STORING

Pour the remaining soup into small metal containers.

🥣 **Cool** the soup from 140°F (60°C) to 70°F (21.1°C) or lower within 2 hours. Cool from 70°F (21.1°C) to 41°F (5°C) within an additional 4 hours for a total cooling time of 6 hours or less.

Cover the soup; label, date, and store under refrigeration at 41°F (5°C) or lower.

Chilled Avocado and Cucumber Soup

12 fluid ounces (360ml) heavy cream

12 ounces (360g) avocado, cubed

10 ounces (300g) cucumber, peeled, seeded, chopped

2 tablespoons (30ml) lime juice

12 fluid ounces (360ml) yogurt

2½ teaspoons (12g) garlic, minced

5 tablespoons (74g) miso paste, yellow

1 tablespoon (15g) dill

½ teaspoon (2g) parsley, chopped

¼ teaspoon (1g) white pepper, ground

half-and-half, as needed

½ ounce (14g) scallions, sliced on the bias

CHEF TIPS *If the surface of the soup oxidizes or turns brown after being chilled, simply skim off and discard the discolored surface before serving. Yellow miso paste can be found in health food stores or Asian specialty markets.*

Place all the ingredients, except the half-and-half and scallions, in a blender or food processor and blend until smooth.

Add half-and-half a little at a time and blend it in until the desired consistency of soup is attained.

Pour the soup into a plastic or stainless-steel container. Place a piece of plastic wrap on the surface of soup to prevent discoloration.

Chill the soup under refrigeration at 41°F (5°C) or lower until thoroughly chilled.

SERVING/HOLDING

Carefully ladle the soup into chilled soup bowls or plates.

Garnish each portion with the sliced scallions.

Reserve under refrigeration at 41°F (5°C) or lower until needed.

COOLING/STORING

Cover the soup; label, date, and store under refrigeration at 41°F (5°C) or lower.

Baby Greens with Warm Goat Cheese and Walnut Vinaigrette

YIELD: 6 PORTIONS · PORTION SIZE: 6 OUNCES

GOAT CHEESE PATTIES

12 ounces (360g) goat cheese

6 fluid ounces (180ml) extra-virgin olive oil

6 sprigs thyme

VINAIGRETTE

2 tablespoons (30ml) canola oil

2 fluid ounces (60ml) walnut oil

4 tablespoons (60ml) red wine vinegar

2 teaspoons (10ml) Dijon mustard

1 teaspoon (5g) sugar

salt, to taste

black pepper, ground, to taste

SALAD

2 ounces (60g) breadcrumbs, dry

2 ounces (60g) walnuts, finely ground

12 ounces (360g) baby greens

24 sourdough bread croutons, prepared

18 chives, flowering

Shape the goat cheese into 12 patties, 1 ounce (30g) each and approximately 2 inches (5cm) in diameter.

Combine the olive oil with the thyme and marinate the goat cheese patties under refrigeration for a minimum of 4 hours or, if possible, overnight.

Prepare the vinaigrette by briskly whisking the canola and walnut oils into a mixture of red wine vinegar and Dijon mustard until thick and creamy and an emulsion forms.

Season the dressing with the sugar and to taste with salt and black pepper. Reserve the dressing under refrigeration until needed.

Combine the breadcrumbs and ground walnuts and dredge each of the marinated goat cheese patties in the mixture so that they are fully coated.

Place the patties on a lightly greased baking sheet and bake in a preheated 400°F (204.4°C) oven until the cheese is hot and the coating is lightly browned. Hold at 140°F (60°C) or higher until needed.

Toss the baby greens with the walnut vinaigrette so that all the lettuce is thoroughly coated with the dressing.

SERVING/HOLDING

Place a small mound of the dressed greens in the center of each chilled plate. Place 2 warm goat cheese patties on top of each salad and garnish with sourdough croutons and flowering chives.

Hold the salad and dressing under refrigeration at 41°F (5°C).

COOLING/STORING

Cover the salad, dressing, and goat cheese; label, date, and store under refrigeration at 41°F (5°C) or lower.

Chilled Castroville Artichoke with Confetti Vinaigrette

YIELD: 6 PORTIONS · PORTION SIZE: 8 OUNCES

6 globe artichokes

1 lemon, cut into 6 wedges

128 fluid ounces (3.8L) water

1 tablespoon (15g) salt

DRESSING

6 fluid ounces (180ml) extra-virgin olive oil

2 fluid ounces (60ml) rice vinegar

4 fluid ounces (120ml) lemon juice

3 cloves garlic, minced

2 teaspoons (10g) oregano, minced

4 ounces (120g) red bell pepper, cut into fine brunoise

4 ounces (120g) yellow bell pepper, cut into fine brunoise

4 ounces (120g) green bell pepper, cut into fine brunoise

4 ounces (120g) daikon, cut into fine brunoise

salt, to taste

black pepper, ground, to taste

CHEF TIPS *Do not put baking soda or other acids into the boiling liquid, as the artichokes will turn an unattractive brown color. Artichokes come into season in the summer and are quite tasty and highly nutritious; however, care must be taken to cook them properly to retain their natural color and vitamin content. The peak of the growing season is from July to September.*

The globe artichoke is really a type of thistle and is the flower head of a perennial plant native to North Africa. It is now culti-vated in Europe as a winter vegetable and in the United States year-round. It can be pick-led whole when small, and its tender base, or heart, is also sold canned or frozen. Artichokes can be served hot or cold and can be baked, fried, boiled, and stuffed. A vari-ety of sauces or dressings are commonly served with artichokes.

Break the stem of the artichokes so that any fibers are pulled out.

Trim the base with a knife so the artichokes sit flat on the bottom. Rub the cut surface with lemon wedges to prevent oxidation or discoloration.

Trim the leaves with scissors to remove any sharp points.

With a large knife, cut off the pointed top of the artichokes parallel to the base.

Bring a large saucepot of salted water to a boil. Place the artichokes in the boiling water and weigh them down with an ovenproof plate or lay a wet cloth on top of them so that they are completely submerged.

Simmer the artichokes for approximately 35–45 minutes or until a central leaf can be pulled out easily.

Drain the artichokes and place them upside down so that the leaves do not trap any water.

Shock the cooked artichokes in an ice-water bath and cool them from 140°F (60°C) to 70°F (21.1°C) or lower within 2 hours. Cool from 70°F (21.1°C) to 41°F (5°C) within an additional 4 hours for a total cooling time of 6 hours or less.

Grasp the central core of leaves and, with a quick twist, lift it out in one piece. Reserve until needed.

Carefully scoop out the spines with a teaspoon or Parisian scoop and discard them.

Set the core of leaves upside down in the center of the artichoke.

Reserve under refrigeration until needed.

Prepare the dressing by briskly whisking together the olive oil and rice vinegar.

Mix in the lemon juice and add the minced garlic, oregano, and vegetables. Whisk thoroughly.

Season to taste with salt and black pepper.

Let the dressing rest under refrigeration for at least 30 minutes before using.

SERVING/HOLDING

Place 1 chilled artichoke on each chilled plate. Briskly whisk the dressing and carefully spoon some into the open end of the artichoke's cone.

Spoon the remaining dressing onto the plate around the base of the artichoke and serve immediately.

Hold the artichokes and dressing under refrigeration at 41°F (5°C).

COOLING/STORING

Cover the artichokes and dressing; label, date, and store under refrigeration at 41°F (5°C) or lower.

Caesar Salad

¼ teaspoon (1g) salt

6 cloves garlic

6 anchovy fillets

1½ teaspoons (7g) dry mustard

6 fluid ounces (180ml) lemon juice

3 tablespoons (44ml) red wine vinegar

6 dashes Worcestershire sauce

3 tablespoons (44g) egg yolks, pasteurized

6 tablespoons (90ml) olive oil

32 ounces (960g) or 3 heads romaine

6 ounces (180g) croutons, prepared

3 ounces (90g) Parmesan cheese, grated

black pepper, ground, to taste

Place the salt in a wooden salad bowl.

Using a fork, mash the garlic cloves with the salt in the bowl until they become a fine paste.

Add the anchovy fillets and continue to mash until a smooth paste develops.

Add the dry mustard and mix thoroughly.

Add the lemon juice. If squeezing the juice directly from the lemons, take care not to allow the seeds to fall into the bowl. Mix thoroughly.

Add the red wine vinegar, Worcestershire sauce, and egg yolks to the bowl. Whisk all of the ingredients together.

While whisking briskly, pour a steady, fine

CHEF TIPS *Caesar salad is considered the benchmark of salads prepared tableside. A wooden bowl is selected to extract the greatest amount of oil from the garlic and anchovies. It also allows for a great marriage of flavors once the dressing is completed. In a typical Caesar salad bowl, no more than three portions should be made at once.*

The recipe calls for pasteurized egg yolks. Raw eggs are generally not allowed to be served in a commercial establishment. You can now purchase eggs pasteurized in the shell, or frozen pasteurized egg yolks.

Grinding the black pepper directly onto the bare plate is recommended so you can see how much pepper has been ground. Regular olive oil is recommended for maximum flavor. Extra-virgin olive oil is more expensive, has an overpowering flavor, and is also slightly more acidic.

Caesar Cardini conceived this salad in 1924 at his restaurant in Tijuana, Mexico, just across the border from California. Due to Prohibition in America, restaurants in Tijuana were popular with Hollywood stars, as alcoholic beverages could be legally served. One evening, a group of actors entered his restaurant near closing time, and the kitchen was out of most items, including fish, chicken, and meat, although romaine lettuce, oil and vinegar, lemon, garlic, mustard, cheese, and croutons were available. In order to satisfy this Hollywood group, Caesar gathered what he had, brought it to the dining room, and assembled his new creation in front of his guests. They raved about it, and the rest is history. Shortly afterward, the International Society of Epicures in Paris named Caesar Salad the greatest recipe originating from the New World in 50 years.

stream of the olive oil into the dressing mixture and continue to whisk until a smooth, emulsified dressing forms.

Cut or tear the lettuce leaves into bite-sized pieces and add to the dressing.

Add the croutons and three-quarters of the Parmesan cheese to the dressing. Toss thoroughly to ensure that all the lettuce leaves are coated with the dressing.

SERVING/HOLDING

Grind fresh black pepper in the desired quantity directly onto chilled plates.

Place approximately 6 ounces (180g) of the salad mixture in the center of each chilled plate.

Sprinkle the remaining Parmesan cheese on top of each salad as a garnish.

Additional fresh-ground black pepper can be added on top of the salads if desired.

Serve immediately.

Hold the salad under refrigeration at 41°F (5°C).

COOLING/STORING

Cover the salad; label, date, and store under refrigeration at 41°F (5°C) or lower.

Deep-Fried Monterey Bay Calamari with Lemon Butter Sauce

YIELD: 6 PORTIONS · PORTION SIZE: 6 OUNCES

1½ fluid ounces (45ml) lemon juice

½ ounce (15g) shallots, chopped

½ ounce (15g) garlic, chopped

9 fluid ounces (270ml) dry white wine

3 ounces (90g) all-purpose flour

salt, to taste

white pepper, ground, to taste

24 ounces (720g) Monterey Bay squid, cleaned

frying oil, as needed

16 fluid ounces (480ml) lemon butter sauce (recipe follows)

6 lemon wedges

¾ teaspoon (4g) parsley, chopped

CHEF TIPS *Calamari is another name for squid. Fresh or frozen squid is cleaned by separating the tentacles and head from the body section. Remove the ink sac from the head and reserve, if desired for coloring of foods like pasta dough. Discard the head with the cuttlebone, found inside the body section. Cut the squid into small pieces or leave it whole for cooking.*

Combine the lemon juice, shallots, garlic, and white wine. Reduce the liquid over medium heat until almost dry. Transfer to a clean saucepan and reserve until needed.

Season the flour to taste with salt and white pepper. Dredge the cleaned squid in the seasoned flour and shake off any excess.

Deep-fry the squid at 375°F (190.0°C) until it is golden brown and crisp and reaches a minimum internal temperature of 145°F (62.8°C) for at least 15 seconds.

Drain the fried squid on absorbent paper towels.

Season to taste with salt and white pepper.

SERVING/HOLDING

Serve the squid immediately on hot plates.

Garnish each portion with a side dish of lemon butter sauce served in a ramekin and a lemon wedge.

Sprinkle each portion with the chopped parsley.

🍵 **Hold** the squid at 140°F (60°C) or higher.

COOLING/STORING

🍵 **Cool** the squid from 140°F (60°C) to 70°F (21.1°C) or lower within 2 hours. Cool from 70°F (21.1°C) to 41°F (5°C) within an additional 4 hours for a total cooling time of 6 hours or less.

Cover the squid and lemon butter sauce; label, date, and store under refrigeration at 41°F (5°C) or lower.

LEMON BUTTER SAUCE

YIELD: 6 PORTIONS · PORTION SIZE: 2½ OUNCES

1½ fluid ounces (45ml) dry sherry

1 fluid ounces (30ml) fish stock, prepared (see page 518)

¼ tablespoon (4g) garlic, chopped

¼ tablespoon (4g) shallot, chopped

½ tablespoon (7ml) lemon juice

12 ounces (360g) butter, softened

¼ teaspoon (1g) salt

CHEF TIPS *Incorporating the butter is the most critical step. It should be whipped in until completely smooth. If the sauce is to be made in advance, it is recommended that 1½ ounces (45g) of fish velouté be whipped in with the lemon juice before the softened butter is added. The velouté will act as a stabilizer and allow the sauce to be held for a longer period before breaking down.*

Combine the sherry, fish stock, garlic, and shallots in a heavy-bottomed saucepan. Reduce the volume of liquid by half over medium heat.

Stir in the lemon juice. Remove from the heat and incorporate the softened butter a little at a time, whisking briskly until all of the butter is blended in and a smooth emulsion forms.

Season with salt and strain through a chinois.

SERVING/HOLDING

🍵 **Hold** the lemon butter sauce at 140°F (60°C) or higher. Carefully monitor the temperature of the sauce. If the sauce begins to get too hot, the emulsion will break down quickly. Stir the sauce regularly while holding.

COOLING/STORING

🍵 **Cool** the sauce from 140°F (60°C) to 70°F (21.1°C) or lower within 2 hours. Cool from 70°F (21.1°C) to 41°F (5°C) within an additional 4 hours for a total cooling time of 6 hours or less.

Cover the sauce; label, date, and store under refrigeration at 41°F (5°C) or lower.

San Francisco Cioppino

YIELD: 6 PORTIONS · PORTION SIZE: 12 OUNCES

SAUCE

4 ounces (120g) onions, cut into medium dice

2 teaspoons (10g) garlic, minced

1 tablespoon (15ml) olive oil

2 fluid ounces (60ml) sherry

4 fluid ounces (120ml) clam juice

5 ounces (150g) green bell peppers, cut into medium dice

4 ounces (120g) tomato purée

4 ounces (120g) tomato paste

1 bay leaf

1 teaspoon (5g) dried oregano

¼ teaspoon (1g) dried basil

½ teaspoon (2g) salt

½ teaspoon (2g) black pepper, ground

1 tablespoon (15ml) Tobasco sauce

CIOPPINO

16 ounces (480g) fish, lean, cubed

18 clams, washed

18 mussels, washed, beards removed

1 Dungeness crab, cleaned, separated

12 shrimp, 16/20, peeled, deveined

18 sea scallops, 20/30

32 fluid ounces (960ml) clam juice

CHEF TIPS *Cioppino is typically served with San Francisco sourdough bread or fresh-baked focaccia. Freshly made garlic croutons dipped in fresh minced herbs are also a frequent garnish. The fish and shellfish listed in this recipe are our choices. Feel free to substitute different varieties of seasonal fresh fish and shellfish to suit your taste and preferences.*

Cioppino is a famous seafood recipe that originated in the North Beach area of San Francisco. Cioppino is basically a West Coast version of French bouillabaisse. The dish typically uses a tomato-based broth to stew a variety of local fish and seafood. Dungeness crab is usually the featured protein in cioppino. This souplike fish stew is generally served as an entrée.

Prepare the cioppino sauce by sautéing the onions and garlic in olive oil over medium-high heat until the onions are translucent.

Deglaze the pan with the sherry.

Add the first quantity of clam juice, bell peppers, tomato purée and paste, bay leaf, oregano, basil, salt, pepper, and hot pepper sauce to the sauteed onions and sherry.

Bring the mixture to a boil. Reduce the heat and simmer for approximately 5 minutes or until the vegetables are tender.

Place the fish and shellfish in a heavy-bottomed saucepot with the second quantity of clam juice and the cioppino sauce.

Bring to a boil. Reduce the heat and simmer until the clams and mussels are open and the fish is cooked and reaches a minimum internal temperature of 145°F (62.8°C) for at least 15 seconds.

SERVING/HOLDING

Divide the fish and shellfish and attractively arrange in 6 hot soup plates or large crocks.

Carefully ladle the broth over the seafood.

Hold the cioppino at 140°F (60°C) or higher.

COOLING/STORING

Cool the cioppino from 140°F (60°C) to 70°F (21.1°C) or lower within 2 hours. Cool from 70°F (21.1°C) to 41°F (5°C) within an additional 4 hours for a total cooling time of 6 hours or less.

Cover the cioppino; label, date, and store under refrigeration at 41°F (5°C) or lower.

Monterey-Style Penne Pasta with Calamari and Baby Artichokes

1½ pounds (720g) penne pasta, dry

4 fluid ounces (120ml) extra-virgin olive oil

2 tablespoons (30g) parsley, chopped

1 tablespoon (15g) cilantro, chopped

1 tablespoon (15g) basil, chopped

1 tablespoon (15g) thyme, chopped

red pepper flakes, to taste

2 ounces (60g) anchovy fillets, undrained

4 cloves garlic, crushed

12 ounces (360g) tomato concassée (juice reserved)

2½ ounces (75g) capers, drained

6 ounces (180g) calamata olives, pitted, roughly chopped

3 pounds (1.4kg) or 18 baby artichokes, cooked, hearts removed, halved or quartered

24 ounces (720g) calamari, rings and tentacles, cleaned

olive oil, as needed

2 ounces (60g) Parmesan cheese, shaved

basil sprigs, as needed

CHEF TIPS *This recipe reflects the bounty of seafood and produce of California's central coast. The dish is made in the robust style of the Italian farmers and fishermen who immigrated to this area.*

Calamari, or squid, is typically cooked for a very short period of time, usually only 30–60 seconds at a high temperature. If cooked too long, calamari can become quite tough. However, calamari can also be cooked by braising, which breaks down the natural fibers in squid during the long, slow cooking process.

Cook the penne pasta in boiling salted water until it is al dente.

Cool the pasta slightly under cold running water. Drain well and toss with a little of the olive oil to prevent the pasta from sticking together.

Toss the pasta with the fresh chopped herbs and season to taste with the red pepper flakes.

Cool the pasta from 140°F (60°C) to 70°F (21.1°C) or lower within 2 hours. Cool from 70°F (21.1°C) to 41°F (5°C) within an additional 4 hours for a total cooling time of 6 hours or less.

Reserve under refrigeration at 41°F (5°C) or lower until needed.

Place the remaining olive oil in a heavy-bottomed saucepan.

Add the anchovies and garlic. Mash thoroughly until a paste forms.

⚱ **Add** the tomatoes, capers, and olives. Stir and place over medium heat until the mixture comes to a boil. Reduce the heat to low and simmer, uncovered, stirring occasionally, until the sauce thickens to the desired consistency. Do not allow the simmering sauce to fall below 140°F (60°C).

⚱ **Add** the cooked baby artichokes and the calamari. Continue cooking for 30–60 seconds or until calamari is cooked and reaches a minimum internal temperature of 145°F (62.8°C) for at least 15 seconds. If the sauce needs more moisture, add the reserved juice from the tomato concassée to thin it slightly.

SERVING/HOLDING

Reheat the penne pasta by tossing it in a sauté pan with a little olive oil over medium heat.

Divide the pasta into 6 large, hot pasta bowls.

Carefully ladle the sauce over the pasta, taking care to distribute the artichoke hearts and calamari evenly among the portions.

Garnish each portion with shaved Parmesan cheese and sprigs of fresh basil.

⚱ **Hold** the pasta and sauce at 140°F (60°C) or higher.

COOLING/STORING

⚱ **Cool** the pasta and sauce from 140°F (60°C) to 70°F (21.1°C) or lower within 2 hours. Cool from 70°F (21.1°C) to 41°F (5°C) within an additional 4 hours for a total cooling time of 6 hours or less.

Cover the pasta and sauce; label, date, and store under refrigeration at 41°F (5°C) or lower.

Sautéed Petaluma Duck Breast with Port Wine Reduction

48 ounces (1kg) Petaluma duck breasts, boneless, 6 ounces (180g) each

2 teaspoons (10g) thyme, chopped

salt, to taste

black pepper, ground, to taste

1 tablespoon (15ml) clarified butter

1 ounce (30g) shallots, minced

16 fluid ounces (480ml) port

8 fluid ounces (240ml) brown stock, prepared (see page 515)

CHEF TIPS *Petaluma is a small dairy town north of San Francisco that is known for its artisan-style production of ducks, geese, and free-range chickens. Although Petaluma duck breast is called for in this recipe, any high-quality duck breast can be easily substituted.*

Remove the skin and excess fat from the duck breasts, leaving only a thin cap of fat approximately ⅜ inch (1cm) wide.

Season each breast with the thyme and to taste with salt and black pepper.

Heat the clarified butter in a large heavy-bottomed sauteuse pan over medium-high heat until the butter almost reaches the smoking point.

Place the duck breasts in the pan, fat side down. Do not overcrowd the pan. If all of them do not comfortably fit in the pan at once, cook them in batches.

Turn the breasts once the first side is browned nicely. Remove the duck breasts when they reach the desired degree of doneness.

Hold the duck breasts at 140°F (60°C) or higher until needed.

Add the chopped shallots and sauté them until they are translucent.

Deglaze the pan with the port and reduce the volume of liquid by three-quarters over medium-high heat.

Add the brown stock and continue to reduce until the sauce has a nappé consistency.

Adjust the seasoning to taste with salt and black pepper.

SERVING/HOLDING

Slice each of the duck breasts and fan the slices in the center of hot plates.

Carefully ladle the sauce around the fan of sliced duck breast.

⚕ **Hold** the duck breast and sauce at 140°F (60°C) or higher.

COOLING/STORING

⚕ **Cool** the duck breasts and sauce from 140°F (60°C) to 70°F (21.1°C) or lower within 2 hours. Cool from 70°F (21.1°C) to 41°F (5°C) within an additional 4 hours for a total cooling time of 6 hours or less.

Cover the duck breasts and sauce; label, date, and store under refrigeration at 41°F (5°C) or lower.

Macadamia-Encrusted Mahi Mahi with Tropical Fruit Salsa

YIELD: 6 PORTIONS · PORTION SIZE: 9 OUNCES

2¾ pounds (1.3kg) mahi mahi

salt, to taste

black pepper, ground, to taste

2 ounces (60g) macadamia nuts, ground

4 ounces (120g) Panko breadcrumbs, dried

2 ounces (60g) cornmeal, yellow

4 fluid ounces (120ml) clarified butter

SALSA

2 ounces (60g) shallots, minced

4 ounces (120g) pineapple, cut into small dice

4 ounces (120g) papaya, cut into small dice

4 ounces (120g) mango, cut into small dice

4 fluid ounces (120ml) lemon butter sauce (see page 451)

1 tablespoon (15g) chives, minced

salt, to taste

black pepper, ground, to taste

1 tablespoon (15g) coconut, shredded, toasted

CHEF TIPS *Other nuts, or a combination of nuts, can be substituted for the macadamia nuts used to coat the fish in this recipe, depending on the flavor that is desired. Hazelnuts, almonds, Brazil nuts, walnuts, and pecans all make excellent substitutes.*

Other local fish can stand in for the mahi mahi. Pacific snapper, tilapia, and orange roughy work extremely well in this recipe.

Cut the mahi mahi into 7-ounce (210g) fillets and season them lightly with salt and black pepper.

Combine the macadamia nuts and breadcrumbs with the cornmeal and grind them finely in a food processor.

Dredge the fish in the ground nut mixture, completely coating each fillet on both sides. Reserve under refrigeration until needed.

Heat approximately three-quarters of the clarified butter in a sauteuse pan over medium-high heat. Place the fillets in the pan with the skin side up.

Brown the fish fillets and degrease the pan. Place the pan in a 350°F (176.7°C) oven for approximately 8–12 minutes or until the fillets are completely cooked and reach a minimum internal temperature of 145°F (62.8°C) for at least 15 seconds. Do not overcrowd the pan. If all of them do not comfortably fit in the pan at once, cook them in batches.

When the fillets are completely cooked, remove them from the pan and reserve in a warm place until needed.

Add the remaining clarified butter to the sauté pan. Add the minced shallots and cook over medium-high heat until they are translucent.

Add the diced fruit and continue to cook for approximately 2–3 minutes or until the fruit is tender and thoroughly heated.

Remove the fruit from the heat and stir in the lemon butter sauce and minced chives.

Season to taste with the salt and black pepper.

SERVING/HOLDING

Place the cooked fish fillets on hot plates and top each portion with approximately 2 ounces (60g) of the tropical fruit salsa.

Garnish the fish by sprinkling shredded toasted coconut on top of the salsa.

Hold the fish and sauce at 140°F (60°C) or higher.

COOLING/STORING

Cool the fish and sauce from 140°F (60°C) to 70°F (21.1°C) or lower within 2 hours. Cool from 70°F (21.1°C) to 41°F (5°C) within an additional 4 hours for a total cooling time of 6 hours or less.

Cover the fish and sauce; label, date, and store under refrigeration at 41°F (5°C) or lower.

Creamed Spinach

2 pounds (960g) spinach

2 tablespoons (30g) butter

2 tablespoons (30g) all-purpose flour

10 fluid ounces (300ml) milk

2 fluid ounces (60ml) heavy cream

1 clove garlic, peeled, split

salt, to taste

black pepper, ground, to taste

2 teaspoons (10ml) Pernod or anisette

Wash the spinach, remove the stems, and wash again. Drain lightly.

Place the wet spinach leaves in a large saucepot. Cover and cook over medium heat approximately 4 minutes or until the spinach is wilted.

Drain well by pushing the spinach into a conical strainer with the back of a spoon or ladle until all the excess liquid is drained.

Squeeze the spinach by hand until as dry as possible. Chop roughly and reserve under refrigeration until needed.

Melt the butter over low heat in a saucepan. Stir in the flour to make a blond roux and cook over low heat for 2–3 minutes, stirring frequently.

Add the milk, cream, and garlic. Bring the liquid to a boil, stirring constantly. Turn the heat down and simmer slowly for 20–30 minutes or until the starchy flavor is cooked out of the béchamel sauce. Do not allow the simmering sauce to fall below 140°F (60°C).

Remove the garlic from the sauce and add the chopped spinach. Season to taste with salt and black pepper. Simmer slowly for an additional 10 minutes or until the spinach is thoroughly hot.

Stir in the Pernod or anisette and serve immediately.

Hold the creamed spinach at 140°F (60°C) or higher.

Cool the creamed spinach from 140°F (60°C) to 70°F (21.1°C) or lower within 2 hours. Cool from 70°F (21.1°C) to 41°F (5°C) within an additional 4 hours for a total cooling time of 6 hours or less.

Cover the creamed spinach; label, date, and store under refrigeration at 41°F (5°C) or lower.

Steamed California Vegetables

YIELD: 6 PORTIONS · PORTION SIZE: 4 OUNCES

8 fluid ounces (240ml) white chicken stock, prepared (see page 517)

1 pound (480g) baby bok choy, split lengthwise

6 ounces (180g) snap peas, trimmed

4 ounces (120g) red bell peppers, seeded, cut into julienne

4 ounces (120g) yellow bell peppers, seeded, cut into julienne

4 ounces (120g) crimini mushrooms, sliced

2 ounces (60g) black bean paste

2 cloves garlic, minced

2 tablespoons (30g) cornstarch

2 tablespoons (30ml) water

1 tablespoon (15ml) soy sauce

1 tablespoon (15ml) sesame oil

salt, to taste

black pepper, ground, to taste

Bring the chicken stock to a boil in a sautoir pan. Add the bok choy, cover, and steam for 1 minute.

Add the snap peas, bell peppers, mushrooms, black bean paste, and garlic. Cover and steam for an additional 1 minute. Toss to combine the vegetables.

Mix the cornstarch with the water, soy sauce, and sesame oil. Add the slurry to the vegetables and cook over high heat for about 30 seconds, tossing constantly, or until the sauce thickens and the vegetables are nicely coated with the sauce.

Season to taste with salt and black pepper and serve immediately.

SERVING/HOLDING

Hold the steamed vegetables at 140°F (60°C) or higher.

COOLING/STORING

Cool the steamed vegetables from 140°F (60°C) to 70°F (21.1°C) or lower within 2 hours. Cool from 70°F (21.1°C) to 41°F (5°C) within an additional 4 hours for a total cooling time of 6 hours or less.

Cover the steamed vegetables; label, date, and store under refrigeration at 41°F (5°C) or lower.

Chinese Long Beans with Sesame Seeds

YIELD: 6 PORTIONS · PORTION SIZE: 4 OUNCES

2¼ tablespoons (33g) sesame seeds

1½ pounds (720g) Chinese long beans, trimmed, cut into ¾-inch (1.8cm) lengths

2 tablespoons (30ml) peanut oil

1½ cloves garlic, minced

3 tablespoons (45g) ginger, peeled, minced

2 Fresno chiles, peeled, seeded, minced

1½ teaspoons (7ml) sesame oil

4 ounces (120ml) cilantro, chopped

salt, to taste

Place the sesame seeds on a baking sheet and toast in a preheated 400°F (204.4°C) oven for approximately 5 minutes or until they are fragrant and lightly browned. Reserve at room temperature until needed.

Blanch the beans in boiling salted water. Shock in an ice-water bath and drain. Reserve under refrigeration until needed.

Heat the peanut oil over medium-high heat in a large sauté pan and cook the minced garlic, ginger, and chiles for approximately 2 minutes.

Add the beans and continue to sauté, tossing frequently, until they are tender and hot.

Add three-quarters of the toasted sesame seeds, the sesame oil, and the cilantro. Toss until incorporated.

Season to taste with salt.

SERVING/HOLDING

Serve immediately, garnished with the remainder of the toasted sesame seeds.

🍲 **Hold** the beans at 140°F (60°C) or higher.

COOLING/STORING

🍲 **Cool** the beans from 140°F (60°C) to 70°F (21.1°C) or lower within 2 hours. Cool from 70°F (21.1°C) to 41°F (5°C) within an additional 4 hours for a total cooling time of 6 hours or less.

Cover the beans; label, date, and store under refrigeration at 41°F (5°C) or lower.

Spicy Roasted Eggplant

YIELD: 6 PORTIONS · PORTION SIZE: 4 OUNCES

3 pounds (1.4kg) Japanese eggplant

1½ tablespoons (22g) sugar

3 tablespoons (45ml) oyster sauce

3 tablespoons (45ml) fish sauce, Thai or Vietnamese

1½ tablespoons (22ml) soy sauce

4 tablespoons (60ml) peanut oil

6 cloves garlic, minced

2 tablespoons (30g) ginger, peeled, minced

¾ teaspoon (4g) red pepper flakes

4 ounces (120g) cilantro, chopped

1 tablespoon (15ml) sesame oil

CHEF TIPS *Oyster sauce and fish sauce can be obtained in most supermarkets and Asian specialty stores. Fish sauce comes in two varieties: nam pla from Thailand and nuoc mam from Vietnam. Either will provide an excellent flavor to the roasted eggplant.*

Prick each of the eggplants with a fork 3 or 4 times and place on a baking sheet. Cook in a pre-heated oven at 475°F (246.1°C) for approximately 25 minutes or until the eggplants are tender.

Remove the eggplants from the oven and split lengthwise.

🥣 **Cool** the eggplants from 140°F (60°C) to 70°F (21.1°C) or lower within 2 hours. Cool from 70°F (21.1°C) to 41°F (5°C) within an additional 4 hours for a total cooling time of 6 hours or less.

Once cool, scoop the meat from the eggplants with a spoon in thick long shreds and discard the skins.

Combine the sugar, oyster sauce, fish sauce, and soy sauce in a small bowl and mix until the sugar is dissolved.

Heat the peanut oil in a large sauté pan over medium-high heat. Add the garlic, ginger, and red pepper flakes. Cook, stirring constantly, for approximately 1 minute.

Add the eggplant pulp and cook, stirring constantly, for an additional 1 minute.

Add the sauce mixture and cook 2 more minutes.

Remove from the heat and stir in the chopped cilantro and sesame oil.

Let the eggplant cool slightly in the pan and serve warm or at room temperature.

SERVING/HOLDING

Hold the eggplant at 140°F (60°C) or higher.

COOLING/STORING

🥣 **Cool** the eggplant from 140°F (60°C) to 70°F (21.1°C) or lower within 2 hours. Cool from 70°F (21.1°C) to 41°F (5°C) within an additional 4 hours for a total cooling time of 6 hours or less.

Cover the eggplant; label, date, and store under refrigeration at 41°F (5°C) or lower.

Pasta with Capers, Olives, and Pine Nuts

YIELD: 6 PORTIONS · PORTION SIZE: 6 OUNCES

3 tablespoons (45ml) butter

3 fluid ounces (90ml) olive oil

3 cloves garlic, minced

3 ounces (90g) pine nuts

15 ounces (450g) California black olives, sliced

3 tablespoons (45g) capers, rinsed, minced

1 tablespoon (15g) basil, cut into chiffonade

1 teaspoon (5g) oregano, minced

1 teaspoon (5g) flat parsley, minced

1 pound (480g) pasta, any shape

salt, to taste

black pepper, ground, to taste

2 ounces (60g) Parmesan cheese, grated

Combine the butter with the oil and heat over medium heat in a large sauté pan.

Add the garlic and pine nuts, reduce the heat to low, and continue to cook until the nuts are just beginning to turn golden in color.

Add the olives, capers, and herbs. Toss until the products are incorporated and heated thoroughly.

Cook the pasta in a large saucepot of boiling salted water until al dente. Drain well.

Toss the drained pasta with the nut-olive mixture over medium heat until the products are incorporated and heated thoroughly.

Season to taste with salt and black pepper.

SERVING/HOLDING

Garnish each portion with grated Parmesan cheese.

Hold the pasta at 140°F (60°C) or higher.

🍲 **Cool** the pasta from 140°F (60°C) to 70°F (21.1°C) or lower within 2 hours. Cool from 70°F (21.1°C) to 41°F (5°C) within an additional 4 hours for a total cooling time of 6 hours or less.

Cover the pasta; label, date, and store under refrigeration at 41°F (5°C) or lower.

Monterey Jack and Green Chile Polenta

YIELD: 6 PORTIONS · PORTION SIZE: 4 OUNCES

10 fluid ounces (300ml) white chicken stock, prepared (see page 517)

8 fluid ounces (240ml) half-and-half

1¾ ounces (50g) butter

½ tablespoon (7g) superfine sugar

¼ tablespoon (4g) salt

4½ ounces (135g) yellow cornmeal

2 ounces (60g) Monterey Jack cheese, grated

1 ounce (30g) Anaheim chiles, roasted, peeled, seeded, diced

CHEF TIPS *The polenta can be cut in circles and used as layers for a grilled vegetable napoleon. Strips of polenta can be used in place of pasta in a lasagna dish. Sun-dried tomatoes, toasted pine nuts, and a chiffonade of fresh basil can be substituted for the Jack cheese and chiles if a different flavor is desired.*

Bring the chicken stock to a boil in a heavy-bottomed saucepan.

Reduce the heat to a simmer and stir in the half-and-half, butter, sugar, and salt.

Slowly add the cornmeal in a thin stream, whisking constantly. Lower the heat and continue stirring for approximately 10–20 minutes or until the mixture starts to thicken.

Stir in the Jack cheese and the chiles. Continue to stir while cooking over low heat until the mixture is thick and easily falls away from the sides of the pan.

Pour the polenta onto a small buttered baking sheet or one lined with plastic wrap.

🍲 **Cool** the polenta from 140°F (60°C) to 70°F (21.1°C) or lower within 2 hours. Cool from 70°F (21.1°C) to 41°F (5°C) within an additional 4 hours for a total cooling time of 6 hours or less.

Once the polenta is thoroughly chilled, cut it into desired shapes and sizes.

Grill, sauté, or pan-fry the polenta shapes until they are golden brown in color and have a slightly crisp crust.

🥣 **Hold** the polenta at 140°F (60°C) or higher.

🥣 **Cool** the polenta from 140°F (60°C) to 70°F (21.1°C) or lower within 2 hours. Cool from 70°F (21.1°C) to 41°F (5°C) within an additional 4 hours for a total cooling time of 6 hours or less.

Cover the polenta; label, date, and store under refrigeration at 41°F (5°C) or lower.

Rosemary Focaccia

YIELD: 6 PORTIONS · PORTION SIZE: 3 OUNCES

SPONGE

> 8 fluid ounces (240ml) water, warm
>
> 1 teaspoon (5g) active dry yeast
>
> 1 cup (240g) all-purpose flour

FOCACCIA

> 4 fluid ounces (120ml) water
>
> 2.4 ounces (72ml) dry white wine
>
> 2.4 ounces (72ml) olive oil
>
> 2 tablespoons (30g) cornmeal, yellow
>
> 1½ teaspoons (7g) kosher salt
>
> 2¾ cups (660g) all-purpose flour
>
> 5 teaspoons (25ml) extra-virgin olive oil
>
> 1 clove garlic, minced
>
> black pepper, ground, to taste
>
> 1½ teaspoons (7g) rosemary, minced
>
> kosher salt, to taste

Place the warm water (approximately 100°F [37.8°C]) in a bowl. Sprinkle the yeast over the water and let stand for approximately 2 minutes, then stir until the yeast is dissolved.

Stir in the first quantity of flour until the mixture is smooth.

Cover and let stand at room temperature for 24 hours.

COOKING

Place the sponge in the bowl of a mixing machine and, using the paddle attachment, mix on low speed.

Slowly add the second quantity of water, wine, regular olive oil, cornmeal, and first quantity of kosher salt. Mix until thoroughly incorporated.

Gradually mix in the second quantity of flour and mix on low speed until the resulting dough is soft to the touch.

Increase the speed to medium and mix for an additional 5 minutes.

Let the dough rise at room temperature for approximately 1½ hours or until it doubles in size. Cover the dough with plastic wrap to prevent the dough from drying out while it is rising.

Grease a large rimmed baking sheet with 1 teaspoon (5ml) of the olive oil.

Transfer the dough to the baking sheet and stretch it, using oiled fingers, until the dough completely fills the baking sheet. Let rest 5 minutes. The dough will shrink.

Restretch the dough to completely cover the baking sheet. If it is still too elastic to cover the sheet, let the dough rest an additional 5–10 minutes and try again.

Let the dough rise again at room temperature, uncovered, for approximately 1½ hours.

Line an oven rack with baking tiles and preheat the oven to 550°F (288°C) for at least 45 minutes.

Using a brush, dab the dough with the remaining 2 teaspoons (10ml) of olive oil.

Sprinkle the surface of the dough with the rosemary and kosher salt to taste.

Bake for approximately 15–20 minutes or until nicely browned.

SERVING/HOLDING

Cut into squares and serve while warm.

Hold the focaccia at 140°F (60°C) or higher.

COOLING/STORING

Cool the focaccia from 140°F (60°C) to 70°F (21.1°C) or lower within 2 hours. Cool from 70°F (21.1°C) to 41°F (5°C) within an additional 4 hours for a total cooling time of 6 hours or less.

Cover the focaccia; label, date, and store under refrigeration at 41°F (5°C) or lower.

Strawberry Shortcake with Cornmeal Biscuits

YIELD: 6 PORTIONS · PORTION SIZE: 6 OUNCES

FILLING

12 ounces (360g) strawberries, washed, hulled, sliced

4 tablespoons (60g) sugar

lemon juice, to taste

8 fluid ounces (240ml) whipping cream

¼ teaspoon (1ml) vanilla extract

BISCUITS

12 ounces (360g) all-purpose flour

4 ounces (120g) cornmeal, yellow

1 tablespoon (15g) baking powder

1 tablespoon (15g) sugar

½ teaspoon (2g) salt

2 tablespoons (30g) butter, chilled, cut into ½-inch (1.27cm) cubes

12 fluid ounces (360ml) whipping cream

6 springs mint

Line a baking sheet with parchment paper.

Combine the strawberries and 3 tablespoons (45g) of the sugar in a large bowl. Let stand for 15 minutes at room temperature.

Crush the strawberries about halfway using a potato masher. Add a little lemon juice to the strawberries and reserve under refrigeration until needed.

In another bowl, combine the first quantity of cream with the remaining 1 tablespoon (15g) of sugar. Add the vanilla extract and whip to soft peaks. Cover and reserve under refrigeration until needed.

Combine the flour, cornmeal, baking powder, sugar, and salt in a large bowl. Mix in the butter by hand or with a pastry blender and rub the dough until the mixture has the appearance of a coarse meal.

Add the second quantity of cream gradually, stirring with a fork until a moist dough forms. Adjust consistency as needed with more cream.

Knead the mixture by hand until the dough is moist and can be removed from the bowl in one piece.

Place the dough on a floured worktable and knead gently for another minute or two.

Roll the dough out with a floured rolling pin into a rectangle approximately 6 inches (15.24cm) x 9 inches (23cm) and about ¾ inch (2cm) thick.

Cut the dough into 6 uniform squares and place on the lined baking sheet.

Bake in a preheated 425°F (218.3°C) oven for approximately 20 minutes or until the squares have risen and are lightly brown in color.

SERVING/HOLDING

Split each biscuit in half horizontally and place the bottom side of each biscuit on a chilled dessert plate with the cut side facing up.

Spoon the berry mixture onto the biscuit bottoms in equal portions. Spoon the remaining juice over the top of the berries.

Add a large dollop of whipped cream and cover with the top of the biscuit, cut side facing down.

Garnish each portion with a sprig of fresh mint.

COOLING/STORING

Cover the shortcakes and strawberries; label, date, and store under refrigeration at 41°F (5°C) or lower.

Walter Pisano

When I arrived in Seattle in the early 1980s, I was excited about the opportunity to work with what the Northwest is known for—fresh seafood. In Idaho, where I came from, truly fresh fish (with the exception of trout) was scarce. The first thing I tried when I arrived in Seattle was a Hama Hama oyster. There was no turning back.

Regional cooking is nothing more than the use of local ingredients. It's the idea that ingredients produced by our neighbors offer the freshest and truest flavors. I often describe my cuisine as Northwest Regional Italian because, just as cooks do in Italy, I take advantage of what our local farmers, fishermen, and purveyors have to offer.

Since I've been in the Pacific Northwest, local choices have grown far beyond seafood. Now we have artisans producing delicate cheeses, exquisite cured meats, and rustic bread, and foragers who search area forests for wild morels, chanterelles, lobster mushrooms, wild peppercress, sea beans—all delicacies that would inspire any chef.

The Pacific Northwest is much more than seafood and fusion-style cooking. We are quite aware of the fortune we have and are honored to share it with our guests.

Walter Pisano is executive chef of Tulio Ristorante in Seattle, Washington.

The Pacific Northwest

Alaska

Oregon

Washington

The states of Washington, Oregon, and Alaska form, for cuisine purposes, the Pacific Northwest region, sometimes referred to as the *Pacific Rim*. The moist weather conditions and volcanic soil in Oregon and Washington, along with the unique conditions in Alaska (fast-growing crops because of extended daylight in the short summer growing season), help create one of the most fertile growing regions in the nation, famous for producing some of America's favorite foods, including berries, stone fruits, wild mushrooms, apples, and pears. In addition, the abundance and variety of fish and seafood from the Pacific Ocean and the waters of Alaska color the region's cuisine. From the beginning, Pacific Northwest cuisine has been influenced by cultural diversity.

When Russian fur traders first explored the Pacific Northwest region, they found the area populated by Native Americans. As in other regions of America, natural products were abundant. The first Europeans to settle the region were British and French fur traders employed by the Hudson Bay Company. The Native Americans taught them how to sustain themselves in what was known at the time as the wilderness of the Pacific Northwest. The settlers were introduced to oysters, clams, crab, shrimp, and salmon from Puget Sound. They were taught about the local berries and how to forage for mushrooms. The Native Americans also introduced the settlers to the potlatch, a Chinook word meaning "gift." The term *potlatch* also describes a ceremonial feast connected with native rituals and important events. Historically, the potlatch featured dishes such as salmon, clams, wild berries, and greens along with other foods that happened to be in season, each brought by a family as their contribution to the feast. The potlatch is still an American tradition; however, its name has evolved to *potluck*. The Native American potlatch, together with their tradition of smoking foods, is still very much a Pacific Northwest culinary custom today.

Although the pioneers first came to the Pacific Northwest for the fur industry, they soon discovered the bounty of the region and generated other industries, such as mining, timber, fishing, and farming. In the early 1800s, Thomas Jefferson sent the party of Lewis and Clark to explore the Northwest; about the same time, Captain George Vancouver sailed into Puget Sound through the Straits of Juan Fuca seeking safe harbor in what is now called Port Townsend. Shortly thereafter, the Alaskan gold rush began. The name *Alaska* is an Anglicized form of the Aleutian term *Alyeska*, meaning great land; the state is now America's largest. The opening of the Oregon Trail led settlers from the Central Plains to the Pacific Northwest, many of whom were first-generation Americans still deeply attached to their roots in Europe. With the gold rush of Alaska and the influx of immigrants to the Pacific Northwest came the development of the cities of Portland and Seattle, the latter possessing one of the best deep-water ports built in the United States.

A beermaking tradition in the Pacific Northwest, called microbrewing, began in the mid-1800s with the opening of the Liberty Brewing Company in Portland, Oregon, and the Steilacoom Brewery in Tacoma, Washington. German immigrants fueled the beermaking explosion throughout the remainder of the 1800s, when hundreds of additional breweries opened. The term microbrewery originated in the Pacific Northwest and, at first, indicated a brewery producing fewer than 10,000 barrels of beer per year. As technology improved and production levels increased, the definition was amended to 15,000 barrels. Today, the strict definition has been dropped, as production levels continue to increase without loss of quality or flavor. Over 100 microbreweries currently operate in Alaska, Oregon, and Washington. A brewpub should not be confused with a microbrewery. The term *brewpub* indicates a pub that makes its own beer on the premises. Typically, a brewpub serves light, casual American cuisine to accompany their beer products. *Craft brewer* is a term describing a beermaker who follows the European artisan tradition and who can produce beer in any quantity without loss of quality, integrity, or flavor.

In the mid-1800s, a significant number of Asians immigrated to the Pacific Northwest, primarily from Japan and China, with hopes of getting rich in the gold rush; however, discrimination and hostility negated their dreams and forced the Asians into low-paying careers as launderers, railroad laborers, and cooks.

Many Chinese immigrants settled in the Portland area, the terminus of the Northern Pacific Railroad, which was completed in 1882. As cooks, the Asian immigrants had a significant influence on the region's cuisine. They exposed the European settlers to new ways of cooking and eating. These Asian cooks used the ingredients indigenous to the Pacific Northwest but prepared them in a manner similar to the cooking styles of their homeland. This style of cooking, now known as *Pacific Rim cooking*, is still quite popular today.

Japanese immigrants began to arrive in the late 1800s and early 1900s, escaping the severe economic problems brought on by natural disasters that destroyed farmlands in Japan. By 1940, Japanese immigrants comprised the largest ethnic population in Seattle, which was second in size only to the Japanese population of Los Angeles. The first berry and vegetable farms established in the Puget Sound area belonged to the Japanese immigrants. The Japanese introduced teriyaki (marinated and glazed meats), sukiyaki (thinly sliced meats and vegetables simmered in broth), and yosenabe (seafood and noodles simmered in broth) to the local residents. In addition, they taught the locals how to forage in the forests for wild mushrooms and in the waters for seaweed and other coastal foods. One of the most notable contributions the Japanese immigrants made to Pacific Northwest cuisine was the introduction of oysters to the waters of Oregon and Washington State. The Pacific and Kumamoto oyster species, today's most common varieties, were first planted and harvested by the Japanese immigrants.

The Asians, who introduced fresh coriander, bok choy, bitter melon, mustard greens, and ginger to the region, populated the first open-air markets of the Pacific Northwest. Although many of these markets no longer operate, the influence they had on the region's cuisine continues today. Seattle's Chinatown is known as the International District due to the influences of Thai, Korean, Filipino, and Vietnamese cuisine.

Pike Place Market, which opened in the early 1900s, still holds true to the value of offering locally produced high-quality, fresh ingredients. Started as an experiment in 1907 as a response to high food prices in Seattle, the Pike Place Market eliminated intermediaries and allowed consumers to purchase foods directly from growers. The concept proved successful, as the farmers typically sold all of their products by noon and the consumers reaped the benefits of significantly lower prices. Seattle's farmer's market tradition provides a gathering place for all food grown in the region—foods that represent the diverse mix of people and ethnic groups who live there.

In 1930, Pike Place Market reached its peak of operation with over 600 permits issued to sell local products. In 1942, during World War II, Japanese Americans were placed in internment camps and, overnight, Pike Place Market lost more than half its farmers, many of whom never returned. In 1949, only 53 farmers applied for permits to sell their goods. The decline continued well into the 1950s as the suburban migration moved shopping families away from the market in the center of the city. In the late 1960s, Seattle's community leaders voted to demolish the Pike Place Market in favor of new developments. Due to the efforts of community activists, the Pike Place Market's value as an institution was realized and a vote in 1971 saved the market from demolition by putting it under public ownership.

About the time Pike Place Market reached its peak in the early 1930s, farmers from Michigan, Wisconsin, and Minnesota, participants in a relocation program with its roots in the Great Depression, were settling the Matanuska Valley near Anchorage, Alaska. The soil in the valley proved extremely fertile and the growing conditions ideal, so in the "Land of the Midnight Sun," vegetables grew to enormous proportions. During the summer months in Alaska, the days can have as many as 20 hours of sunshine. The growing season in Alaska is quite short— July through September—but the size, quality, and quantity of the vegetables grown and harvested are disproportionately generous. It is not uncommon for a head of Alaskan cabbage to grow to more than 20 pounds and for common vegetables such as zucchini, cucumbers, tomatoes, and squash to grow to three or four times the size of those grown in the continental United States.

Many culinary ingredients indigenous to the Pacific Northwest come from the Pacific Ocean, including several species of salmon, flatfish such as halibut and flounder, and rockfish. The Puget Sound is home to many types of shellfish and crustacean, while the Columbia River provides trout, sturgeon, and other freshwater fish. Throughout the Pacific Northwest, the waterways are home to huge populations of wildfowl and game. The fields of the region are ample and support a large livestock industry, wheat farming, fruit orchards, and the raising of other greens and vegetables. The mountains and forests yield many varieties of wild mushrooms, berries, and other ingredients that are commonly foraged. Cheese production has grown due to the excellent conditions for raising goats, sheep, and cows. The artisan cheese producers of the Pacific Northwest who follow European traditions are called farmstead cheesemakers. They use the milk of the goats, sheep, and cows they raise themselves to make their cheeses.

The cuisine of the Pacific Northwest is broad and varied, with many traditions resulting from the combination of Northern European and Asian influences with the gifts and ingredients of the Native Americans. The cultural diversity of the region has inspired an eclectic culinary mix for the people of the Pacific Northwest to enjoy.

Typical Pacific Northwest Ingredients and Dishes

Alaskan Halibut: The largest flatfish. Alaskan halibut are known to grow as large as 500 pounds and have firm, white flesh with a mild flavor, making them excellent for grilling, baking, or sautéing. Halibut fishing in the Pacific Northwest begins in the spring and continues until mid-November. Halibut cheeks, resembling large sea scallops, are a delicacy and can weigh up to 1 pound. The most common preparation of halibut cheeks is to dredge them in flour, pan-fry them, and serve them with a simple sauce.

Apples: This fruit originally came to the Pacific Northwest by way of a British fur-trading company named the Hudson Bay Company. The first apple seeds were planted in 1826 at Fort Vancouver in the state of Washington. In the 1880s, the first commercial apple orchards began production in the Yakima Valley of Washington. Today, Washington is the largest apple-growing region in America, producing between 10 and 12 billion apples per year; this yield makes apples the state's number-one agricultural commodity. While more than half the orchards are dedicated to producing Red Delicious apples, other varieties also are grown. Some of the most common apples grown in the Pacific Northwest region are described below.

Fuji: Typically yellow-green apple with red highlights. Fuji apples are crisp and sweet, with a mild flavor, and are best eaten raw; however, they can also be used for cooking.

Gala: Originally from New Zealand, this apple is red, with a yellow hue. It is sweet, has a full flavor, and is best eaten raw.

Golden Delicious: An apple usually gold to green in color, with a yellow hue. Golden Delicious is a good all-purpose apple and can be eaten raw or used in cooking. It is good baked whole or used as a filling in apple pie.

Granny Smith: A bright green apple that sometimes has a pinkish hue. Granny Smith apples are a classic, tart apple, frequently cooked and used for applesauce or in other savory dishes.

Jonathan: A red apple that sometimes has yellow stripes. Jonathan apples are slightly tart, with a crisp texture. They are typically used both raw and cooked.

Red Delicious: The most popular variety of apple in the United States. Red Delicious apples have a crisp texture and a sweet, juicy flavor. They are best eaten raw as a snack or as an ingredient in a fruit salad.

Rome Beauty: A bright red apple, usually round in shape. The Rome Beauty apple has a slightly tart flavor and is most often baked whole.

Winesap: A deep red apple with a slightly tart flavor and pleasing aroma. Winesaps are excellent raw as well as for use in baking.

Asparagus: The Yakima and Columbia River valleys of Washington produce over 80 million pounds of asparagus annually. The asparagus season runs from April to early June. The most popular asparagus in the United States are called *pencil asparagus* for their long, thin shape; however, most chefs agree that the fatter, thicker asparagus are generally more tender and flavorful.

Blackberry: Many varieties of blackberries are common to the Pacific Northwest. The largest commercial crop of blackberries is a variety also known as the *marionberry*, which is a crossbreed of the wild and cultivated varieties of the evergreen blackberry. Other varieties of wild blackberries include the evergreen blackberry, the Himalayan, and California or trailing blackberries, all of which are commonly found and make excellent pies, cobblers, and jams. Hybrids of blackberries include the loganberry, which is a cross between a raspberry and a blackberry, and the boysenberry, which is a cross between the raspberry, blackberry, and loganberry. All of these are excellent for baking.

Blueberry: Over 160 varieties of blueberries are cultivated in Washington and Oregon. Each has its own degree of flavor and sweetness; however, a rule of thumb is that the smaller the berry, the sweeter and more flavorful it is.

Caviar: The salted eggs of the sturgeon fish. Pacific Northwest caviar is made in the same tradition as Russian and Iranian sturgeon caviar, whereby the egg sacs are passed along a mesh to separate the eggs, then treated by an experienced professional who knows just how much and how long to salt the eggs. Despite an abundance of female sturgeon in the Columbia River, many regulations concerning the collection of the roe make Pacific Northwest caviar rare as well as expensive.

Cherry: Bing cherries are America's most popular variety. They were first developed in the Hood River Valley area of Oregon and were named after a Chinese orchard manager who worked there. Bing cherries have a sweet flavor and are dark red to almost black in color. Rainier cherries were developed in Washington and, although sweet, have a much more delicate flavor than the Bing cherry. Rainier cherries are larger in size and are gold, with a reddish hue. Other varieties common to the region are the Meteor cherry, which has a sour flavor and is usually used for pies, cobblers, and jams, and the Lambert cherry, which has a unique heart shape. All cherries are seasonal in nature and available only in the summer months.

Cougar Gold Cheese: A sharp, nutty white cheddar cheese, the result of an experiment in utilizing excess milk production. It was made by students on the campus at Washington State University in the 1930s. Cougar Gold was named after the university's mascot and comes in a variety of flavors, all sold in 30-ounce tins.

Cranberries: Similar to the cranberries of the New England region, these berries grow in the bogs along the Northwest Pacific coastline. Although the region grows only a small fraction of America's cranberries, they are sought after for their extremely high quality, excellent flavor, and deep red color. The annual harvest takes place in October. Cranberries are very tart and are rarely eaten raw; however, they are excellent cooked and are used as an ingredient in a number of regional dishes. Cranberries are also frequently utilized in baked goods when slightly sweetened and dried prior to use.

Dungeness Crab: Common to coastal waters from Mexico to the Aleutian Islands of Alaska, Dungeness crabs have unusually sweet-tasting, tender meat. They are served hot or cold and are typically purchased whole and precooked. Dungeness crab season in the Pacific Northwest is in the winter months, when the water is coldest.

Filbert: Another name for hazelnut. In 1986, the Oregon nut-growing industry voted to discontinue the use of the name *filbert* due to the confusion it caused among consumers and industry professionals. (See *hazelnut*.)

Geoduck: The most famous of the Pacific Northwest's clams, even though it is not the most common variety. Pronounced *gooey-duck*, this clam's name is a Native American word meaning "digging deep." The geoduck is quite large, sometimes growing up to 5 pounds, and has a long siphon that looks like a neck. It has a tendency to burrow deep in the sand, making the geoduck somewhat difficult to find. The neck meat is generally tough and is usually chopped up and used in chowder, made into fritters, or pounded and pan-fried. The meat from the interior, referred to as the *breast*, is more tender than the neck meat and excellent for sautéing. The breast of the geoduck is frequently used as an ingredient for sushi or served raw as sashimi.

Hazelnut: A retired English sailor from the Hudson Bay Company planted the first hazelnut tree in Oregon in 1858. Today, over 99 percent of America's hazelnuts are grown in the Willamette and Umpqua valleys of Oregon. Hazelnuts can be eaten whole as a snack but are more commonly used as an ingredient in cooking and in the production of baked goods and pastries. The oil derived from grinding, heating, and pressing hazelnuts is highly prized and, when combined with a more neutral-flavored oil, is excellent for use as a salad dressing or flavoring agent. Hazelnuts are also used in such specialty products as paste, butter, and flour, all frequently used in gourmet cooking.

Huckleberry: A relative of the blueberry that grows wild in the coastal and mountain regions of the Pacific Northwest. Huckleberries are bright red or deep purple in color and are very flavorful. They are generally not available in consumer outlets due to their limited quantity and short growing season. However, they are commonly picked in the wild by local residents.

Ice Wine: A regional trend in the production of late harvest wines. Ice wine was created by accident in 1978 by a winemaker at the Château Ste. Michelle winery in Washington, who found his grapes frozen on the vine after an unusually cold evening. This inventive winemaker decided to follow through with the winemaking process as if the grapes had never frozen. The wine ended up becoming a rare collector's item because this particular weather pattern did not recur until 1995. Although Château Ste. Michelle is given credit for inventing this wine in the United States, it is, in fact, a long-established tradition in Germany.

King Crab: The largest of the crab species, typically found in the waters of Alaska. Most king crabs grow to about 6 pounds (2.24kg); however, they have been known to exceed 25 pounds (9.3kg) in weight, with a leg span of over 6 feet (182.8cm). The legs are generally steamed and served either hot or cold with drawn butter. Many crab connoisseurs believe king crabs have the best-tasting meat of all crab species and should be served cold to get the best flavor from the sweet leg meat. King crab is usually fished in the middle of winter in the rough, icy waters off the Alaskan coast. The danger involved with fishing these crabs is one reason why they are so expensive. The legs of the king crab are typically purchased precooked and frozen and are the only part of the crab utilized in commercial foodservice operations.

Lamb: Oregon and Washington are home to the Pacific Northwest's favorite meat—lamb. The most popular variety is Ellensburg lamb, from eastern Washington, which is noted for its excellent balance of flavor, tenderness, and fat content. This balance is attributed to the lamb's primary diet of grass and wild herbs instead of the more common grain.

Lingonberry: A berry related to the cranberry and indigenous to the state of Alaska, where it is sometimes referred to as the *lowbush cranberry*. Although the lingonberry is not quite as tart as the cranberry, it is not consumed raw. Rather, it is cooked and used as an ingredient in other dishes, just like its cranberry cousin.

Manila Clam: Originating in Asia, the Manila clam was introduced to the Pacific Northwest by Asian immigrants in the late 1800s. This clam is the most common variety in the region and is generally eaten in chowder or served steamed. The Manila clam can be identified by its small size, usually only 1 inch (2.54cm) in diameter; it grows well both in the wild and in oyster farms.

Marionberry: A sweet blackberry made by crossbreeding the wild and cultivated varieties of the evergreen blackberry. The marionberry is the largest commercial crop of blackberries and is named after Marion County, which is in the center of the Willamette Valley in Oregon.

Mussel: The native mussel of the Pacific Northwest is the blue mussel, which grows in abundance attached to rocks and pilings along the coast. Most blue mussels are named Penn Cove mussels after Penn Cove Bay, where they are commonly grown, off Whidbey Island in Washington. Recently, the Mediterranean mussel was introduced to the Pacific Northwest waters. This species is generally larger than the blue mussel and has plumper meat. The Mediterranean mussel is flourishing in the region, offering chefs a choice for their regional recipes.

Nettle: A perennial plant indigenous to the forests of the Pacific Northwest and gathered by forage in the spring. Nettles have a peppery flavor and are used as an ingredient in cooking in a manner similar to that of sorrel and spinach. Care must be taken when picking nettles, as their stems are a skin irritant.

Oyster: The Pacific Northwest is home to four main species of oysters: Pacific, Kumamoto, European flat, and Olympia. Today, Washington produces the most oysters in the region as well as a significant percentage of the nation's crop. The various names attached to oysters do not indicate species but rather the growing area where they were harvested. Because oysters filter about 100 gallons (378.5L) of water every day, their flavor tends to take on the flavor and characteristics of the water in which they grow. Some popular Pacific oysters are the Hama Hama, shoalwater, and Wescott Bay. Pacific oysters are the most common oysters in the region's waters. Planted in the region by the Japanese, who immigrated to the area in the late 1800s, the Pacific oyster is identified by its oblong, oval shape and its deeply cupped, lightly ridged shell. The Kumamoto oyster, originally from Japan, is smaller than the Pacific oyster, with a deeply cupped, fluted shell. The meat has a smooth texture and a mild flavor. The European flat oyster, originally from Europe, has a flat, round shell. Its meat has a pronounced flavor that is usually much stronger than that of the Pacific oyster. The Olympia oyster is the only variety native to the Pacific Northwest. It is very small, measuring only about 2 inches (5cm) in diameter. The shell is round in shape and the meat has a mild, delicate flavor.

Pear: The Willamette Valley in Oregon, along with areas in Washington, is known for excellent red and green Bartlett pears. Bartlett pears are bell-shaped and have a sweet, tender flesh that makes them an excellent choice for cooking as well as eating raw. The harvest of

Bartlett pears is the region's first of the season, so they are not classified as a winter pear like many others grown in the region. The same variety of pear exists in Europe; however, there they are called the *Williams* variety. The winter pears grown in the Pacific Northwest include Anjou and comice, which are best eaten raw, and the bosc, which is used for cooking. Asian pears, also known as *apple-pears*, are grown in the Pacific Northwest on a much smaller scale. They are round in shape, with a crisp, juicy flesh, are yellow or, sometimes, yellow-orange, and are best eaten raw.

Plum: Oregon and Washington are among America's top five plum-producing states. Freestone plums, also known as *Italian plums*, are usually cooked and are commonly used in pies, tarts, and jams. Freestone plums get their name because the pit is not attached to the flesh of the plum and is easily removed. The region also produces numerous varieties of plums that are eaten raw or used in fruit salad. Plums are seasonal in nature and are available only from June to August.

Raspberry: The two largest red-raspberry–producing states are Washington and Oregon. The Pacific Northwest also grows wild red and black raspberries, but these are not quite as common as the cultivated red raspberries. Raspberry season is in July.

Razor Clam: A popular variety of clam common to the Pacific Northwest. The razor clam is long and slightly curved, resembling the straight razor used by barbers—thus the name. Due to its unique shape, the razor clam is not used for stuffing but rather served steamed or chopped and used in chowder. The razor clam is a favorite among the Japanese and is used for sushi and sashimi preparations.

Rockfish: This fish is common to the waters along the Pacific Coast, from Baja California all the way to the Gulf of Alaska. Although dozens of varieties of rockfish exist, the most common has a bright orange skin and yellow eye. Pacific rockfish are commonly referred to as *Pacific red snapper* even though the fish is only remotely related to the red snapper of the Atlantic Ocean. The meat is lean and flaky, with a mild flavor, and is generally sautéed. Other varieties of rockfish common to the region include black rockfish, quillback rockfish, canary rockfish, and Pacific Ocean perch.

Salmon: The Pacific Northwest produces 99 percent of America's supply of wild salmon, with Alaska alone responsible for 95 percent. The fish are caught two ways: in nets and on hooks during trolling. Netted salmon are caught in larger quantities, thus making the fish less expensive to purchase. However, the flesh can be damaged in the process, resulting in a lower-quality fish. Trolling for salmon results in the highest-quality fish, as only one fish at a time can be caught on each hook. Typically, salmon caught by trolling are labeled as such and bring a higher price at market. Salmon indigenous to the Pacific Northwest include the chum, king, pink, silver, and sockeye varieties. Salmon is prepared using numerous techniques. It is said that Alaskans have as many preparations for salmon as people in the "lower 48" have for beef. Descriptions of salmon indigenous to the Pacific Northwest region are listed below:

Chum: This variety of salmon weighs about 7 pounds (2.6kg) and is referred to by many other names, including *fall, dog, silverbrite,* and *calico* salmon. Chum salmon has a pale-colored flesh, with a moderate fat content and a mild flavor. It is commonly used to produce smoked salmon via both hot and cold smoking techniques.

King: The largest of the salmon varieties, weighing between 15 (5.6kg) and 20 pounds (7.5kg). King salmon, sometimes referred to as *Chinook salmon*, has a high oil content and a rich, full flavor, making it excellent for grilling. Some king salmon have no pigmentation of the flesh and are called *white king salmon*. White king salmon are expensive because they are rare; however, they have the same flavor and texture as normal king salmon.

Pink: This variety of salmon is the smallest, weighing only 3–5 pounds (1.1–1.8kg) each. Pink salmon are found in huge numbers in the Alaskan waters and are also referred to as *humpback* or *humpy salmon*. Their flesh is light and moist but is more delicate than that of other varieties of salmon. Most pink salmon is canned and used much like canned tuna.

Silver: This variety usually weighs 7 pounds (2.6kg) and is also referred to as *coho* or *hooknose salmon*. It has a red flesh, similar to the king salmon, but a much lower fat content, making it not quite as flavorful—but still an excellent-tasting fish. Silver salmon are often canned and used much like canned tuna.

Sockeye: These fish generally weigh 6 pounds (2.24kg) and have an intensely red-colored flesh. Sockeye salmon are also referred to as *red salmon* and *bluejack salmon*. The Japanese purchase the majority of the sockeye catch, as red is the color of celebration in Japan. This makes the fish more rare in the United States as well as more expensive than the other varieties of salmon.

Salmon Berry: A relative of the wild raspberry, the salmon berry is an orange-red color and usually grows in clusters resembling plump salmon eggs. Salmon berries are not available commercially and must be foraged in the mountains of the Pacific Northwest, where they grow wild.

Smoked Salmon: Originally developed to preserve salmon throughout the winter. In the Pacific Northwest, the hot smoking technique, also referred to as *kippering*, is preferred to the cold smoking technique, which leaves the salmon virtually raw. Hot smoked salmon is usually prepared by brining the fish in a wet or dry brine; the salmon is then rinsed and cooked very slowly over a smoking hardwood fire.

Snow Crab: A smaller relative of the king crab, found in the icy waters of Alaska. Snow crab is usually purchased out of the shell, precooked, and frozen; however, when in season, it is also available in the shell. Unlike the king crab's, the body meat is utilized as well as the leg meat. Typically, the meat is available in many forms—body meat only, leg meat only, and combinations of body and leg meat. Snow crabmeat is used as an ingredient in other dishes but can also be prepared by steaming, like king crab.

Stone Fruit: A fruit containing a single pit or seed. Kinds of stone fruit include cherry, plum, peach, and apricot, to name a few.

Strawberry: The most widely consumed and utilized berry in the United States, the strawberry constitutes Oregon's largest berry crop and a significant crop in Washington as well. The Pacific Northwest is the second largest commercial strawberry producer in America, next to California. The highly prized wild strawberry, with its extremely sweet taste and fragrant aroma, is more commonly found in the Pacific Northwest than in any other region.

Sturgeon: One of the oldest fish still thriving today. It is found in the waters of the Pacific Northwest. The sturgeon is a survivor of prehistoric times and can be identified by its long snout and a bone structure that is on the surface of the flesh rather than within the fish itself. Sturgeon is a meaty white fish available in the fall. It is excellent sautéed, grilled, or smoked. The egg sac of the female sturgeon is made into caviar.

Thai Black Rice: A highly glutinous rice, black in color. Thai black rice is known for its nutty flavor and distinctly pleasing aroma.

Tillamook Cheese: *Tillamook*, a Native American word meaning "land of many waters," is the name of a county in northwestern Oregon where the milk of Holstein, Jersey, and Guernsey cows is transformed into a premier cheddar cheese. A Canadian cheesemaker named Peter McIntosh, who was familiar with the cheesemaking process used in Cheddar, England, arrived in Tillamook County in the late 1800s. His contributions significantly improved the quality of the local cheeses. He founded the tradition of cheddar-style cheeses commonly produced in the area. Today, *Tillamook* is America's top-selling name-brand natural cheese, with an annual production of over 35 million pounds.

Walla Walla Onion: Sweet onions grown in Oregon. Walla Walla onions are as prized as other special onions with distinctive flavors, such as Vidalia onions from Georgia and Maui onions from Hawaii.

Wild Mushroom: Of the 2500 varieties of wild mushroom common to the Pacific Northwest, only about 35 are considered to be of choice edible quality. The prime locations for gathering wild mushrooms are in western Oregon and Washington as well as in many areas of Alaska. The spring and fall seasons are when the vast majority of wild mushrooms become available, starting with morels in April and ending with chanterelles as late as

December. Other popular varieties of wild mushroom from the Pacific Northwest include puffball, chanterelle, matsutake, and chicken-of-the-woods. Wild mushrooms need to be fully cooked before eating due to the residual toxins that exist in many varieties. The cooking process destroys the toxins, preventing food-borne illness. Descriptions of wild mushrooms indigenous to the Pacific Northwest region are listed below:

Chanterelle: The most plentiful of the wild mushrooms found in the Pacific Northwest. Chanterelles are yellow or white in color. They appear as early as July and may be available as late as December. Chanterelles have a strongly characteristic flavor and are best cooked in a simple fashion that allows the flavor to be fully appreciated.

Chicken-of-the-Woods: These mushrooms are available in fall and early winter. They are flat and do not have a stem. Their name comes from their texture and flavor, which is similar to chicken meat.

Matsutake: A wild mushroom highly prized by the Asian community. Matsutake mushrooms are available in mid-fall and are noted for their rich earthy flavor. Their shape resembles the shiitake mushroom, only with a thicker and lumpier cap.

Morel: A mushroom with an earthy flavor, generally found in April through the end of May. Morels are tan to black in color and have a cone-shaped, umbrella-capped stem. Their growing patterns are inconsistent and unpredictable, making them scarce as well as expensive. The wrinkled caps are attached to a woody stem with a hollow center that lends itself well to stuffing.

Puffball: A large, spherical mushroom found in the fall. Its large size and firm texture make it well suited for cutting into steaks and either grilling or sautéing.

Truffle: A rare fungus that grows underground among the roots of certain trees—primarily Douglas fir in the Pacific Northwest, as opposed to oak in France and Italy. Truffles indigenous to the Pacific Northwest include the tuber gibbosum, similar to the white truffles of Umbria, Italy, and two varieties of black truffles—the tuber magnatum and the melanogaster carthusianum, both commonly found in Perigord, France. Truffles are known for their unique flavor and aroma. Truffles from the Pacific Northwest are quite rare and very expensive, seldom reaching the commercial markets of the United States.

Sample Menus from Pacific Northwest Cuisine

MENU ONE

Pan Asia Dungeness Crab Cakes with Wild Rice

Buckwheat Soba Noodle Salad with Grilled Mushrooms

Roasted Ellensburg Lamb Rack with Thyme-Merlot Sauce ·

Brussels Sprouts in Hazelnut Butter

MENU TWO

Lopez Island Blue Mussels in Spicy Butter Sauce

Chilled Blackberry Yogurt Soup

Sautéed Halibut with Warm Apple and Cranberry Compote · Oven-Roasted Vegetables

· Cardamom Cornmeal Waffles

MENU THREE

Broccoli Soup with Tillamook Cheese and Toasted Hazelnuts

Watercress Salad with Oregon Blue Cheese, Hazelnuts, and Sherry Vinaigrette

Steelhead with Asparagus and Butter Sauce · Green Beans Cooked with Summer Savory

· Mashed Potato and Wheatberry Cakes

Chilled Blackberry Yogurt Soup

YIELD: 6 PORTIONS · PORTION SIZE: 7 OUNCES

16 ounces (480g) blackberries

4 fluid ounces (120ml) sweet white wine or Gewürztraminer

3 ounces (90g) honey

1 fluid ounce (30ml) lemon juice

16 ounces (480g) yogurt

3 tablespoons (45ml) half and half

3 ounces (90g) sour cream

6 sprigs mint

CHEF TIPS *Any fresh berries or combination of fresh seasonal berries, such as strawberries, blueberries, and raspberries, can substitute for the blackberries in this recipe. Use nonreactive cookware to prevent discoloration and the transfer of a metallic flavor to the soup. The most reactive cookware is made of aluminum and copper, while the least is made of porcelain and stainless steel.*

Carefully wash the berries and reserve under refrigeration at 41°F (5°C) or lower until needed.

COOKING

Combine the wine, honey, blackberries, and lemon juice in a nonreactive saucepan.

Bring to a boil, cover, and reduce the heat. Slowly simmer the mixture for 30 minutes.

Purée the blackberry mixture in a blender or food processor and strain. Chill thoroughly under refrigeration at a temperature of 41°F (5°C) or lower.

Stir in the yogurt and half and half.

 Rechill to 41°F (5°C) or lower.

SERVING/HOLDING

Carefully ladle the soup into chilled soup bowls or plates.

Garnish each portion of soup with a small dollop of sour cream, approximately ½ ounce (15g) each. Place a sprig of fresh mint on each dollop of sour cream.

 Hold the soup at 41°F (5°C) or lower.

COOLING/STORING

Cover the soup; label, date, and store under refrigeration at 41°F (5°C) or lower.

Broccoli Soup with Tillamook Cheese and Toasted Hazelnuts

YIELD: 6 PORTIONS · PORTION SIZE: 8 OUNCES

1 ounce (30g) butter

4 ounces (120g) leeks, split lengthwise, chopped

4 ounces (120g) onions, cut into small dice

16 ounces (480g) broccoli, cut into florets

4 ounces (120g) carrots, cut into small dice

32 fluid ounces (960ml) white chicken stock, prepared (see page 517)

8 fluid ounces (240ml) half-and-half

salt, to taste

white pepper, ground, to taste

4 ounces (120g) Tillamook cheddar cheese, grated

4 ounces (120g) hazelnuts, toasted, chopped

Melt the butter in a medium saucepan over medium heat. Add the leeks and onions and sauté, stirring occasionally, for approximately 8 minutes.

Place the sautéed leeks and onions and the broccoli, carrots, and stock in a saucepot.

Bring the mixture to a boil, reduce the heat, cover, and simmer for approximately 20 minutes or until the vegetables are tender. Do not allow the simmering soup to fall below 140°F (60°C).

Purée the vegetable mixture in a food processor or blender.

Return the puréed soup to the saucepot, stir in the half-and-half, and cover.

Season the soup to taste with salt and white pepper.

SERVING/HOLDING

Carefully ladle the soup into hot soup bowls or plates.

Garnish each portion with grated cheese and toasted hazelnuts.

Hold the soup at 140°F (60°C) or above.

COOLING/STORING

Place the soup in small metal containers.

Cool the soup from 140°F (60°C) to 70°F (21.1°C) or lower within 2 hours. Cool from 70°F (21.1°C) to 41°F (5°C) within an additional 4 hours for a total cooling time of 6 hours or less.

Cover the soup; label, date, and store under refrigeration at 41°F (5°C) or lower.

Lopez Island Blue Mussels in Spicy Butter Sauce

YIELD: 6 PORTIONS · PORTION SIZE: 8 OUNCES

32 ounces (960g) or 5 dozen blue mussels, whole, washed, debearded

16 fluid ounces (480ml) dry white wine

10 ounces (300g) red bell peppers, roasted, peeled, chopped

4 ounces (120g) poblano chiles, roasted, peeled, chopped

2 ounces (60g) cilantro, minced

2 ounces (60g) scallions, minced

1 clove garlic, minced

½ teaspoon (2g) red pepper flakes

1 ounce (60g) lemon grass, grated

8 ounces (240g) butter, cut into ½-inch (1.27cm) cubes

salt, to taste

black pepper, ground, to taste

CHEF TIPS *Any black mussels can substitute for the Lopez Island mussels called for in this recipe. One variety frequently used in American regional cuisine is the Prince Edward Island, or PEI, mussel. These mussels are prized for their plump meat and small or nonexistent beard.*

Place the cleaned mussels and the wine in a medium saucepan.

Bring to a boil over high heat and cover. Steam the mussels for approximately 3 minutes or just until they open and reach a minimum internal temperature of 145°F (62.8°C) for at least 15 seconds.

Remove the pan from the heat and remove the mussels. Strain the liquid through a piece of rinsed cheesecloth and hold at 140°F (60°C) or higher until needed.

Remove the top shell from each of the mussels and discard. Reserve the mussels at 140°F (60°C) or higher until needed.

Place the mussel liquid in a saucepan and add the peppers, chiles, cilantro, scallions, garlic, red pepper flakes, and lemon grass. Bring to a boil over high heat.

Lower the heat to medium-high and reduce the volume of liquid by half.

Remove the pan from the heat and whisk in the butter cubes, a few at a time, until all the butter is incorporated and the sauce is thickened.

Season to taste with salt and black pepper.

SERVING/HOLDING

Arrange 10 mussels attractively in each hot soup plate or pasta bowl.

Carefully ladle approximately 3 ounces (90ml) of the liquid over the mussels. Serve immediately.

Hold the mussels and liquid at 140°F (60°C) or higher.

COOLING/STORING

Cool the mussels and liquid from 140°F (60°C) to 70°F (21.1°C) or lower within 2 hours. Cool from 70°F (21.1°C) to 41°F (5°C) within an additional 4 hours for a total cooling time of 6 hours or less.

Cover the mussels and liquid; label, date, and store under refrigeration at 41°F (5°C) or lower.

Pan Asia Dungeness Crab Cakes with Wild Rice

YIELD: 6 PORTIONS · PORTION SIZE: 6 OUNCES

3 limes

24 ounces (720g) Dungeness crabmeat, squeezed dry

24 ounces (720g) wild rice, cooked

8 ounces (240g) red bell peppers, minced

¼ cup (60g) basil, minced

¼ cup (60g) mint, minced

1½ tablespoons (22ml) fish sauce, nam pla or nuoc cham

1½ tablespoons (22ml) sesame oil

3 large eggs, beaten

8 ounces (240g) breadcrumbs, coarsely ground

salt, to taste

black pepper, ground, to taste

8 ounces (240g) mayonnaise

3 fluid ounces (90ml) vegetable oil

3 ounces (90g) baby mixed lettuce

6 wedges lemon

CHEF TIPS *An accompaniment for this dish is Thai fish sauce usually, found in Asian specialty markets and sometimes in the international foods section of local supermarkets. Common varieties of fish sauce include nam pla, from Thailand, and nuoc mam, from Vietnam.*

Zest and juice the limes; reserve until needed.

Combine the crabmeat, cooked wild rice, bell peppers, lime zest, all but 1 tablespoon (15g) each of the basil and mint, and the fish sauce in a bowl.

In another bowl, whisk the sesame oil with the eggs, then thoroughly mix into the breadcrumbs.

Combine the breadcrumbs with the crab and rice mixture and stir gently until all ingredients are incorporated.

Season to taste with salt and black pepper. Reserve under refrigeration at 41°F (5°C) or lower until needed.

Prepare a remoulade sauce by blending the reserved basil and mint and the lime juice into the mayonnaise. Reserve under refrigeration at 41°F (5°C) or lower until needed.

COOKING

Heat the vegetable oil over medium heat in a large sautoir pan. Using a tablespoon, place 2-ounce (60g) dollops of the crabmeat mixture in the pan and quickly form them into small cakes approximately 3 inches (7.6cm) in diameter.

Pan-fry the cakes until they are golden brown on both sides and reach a minimum internal temperature of 165°F (73.9°C) for at least 15 seconds.

Remove the cakes from the oil and degrease on absorbent paper towels.

SERVING/HOLDING

Place a small mound of baby lettuce in the center of each plate. Shingle 2 crab cakes on one side of the lettuce.

Garnish the dishes with lemon wedges. Serve a 2-ounce (60ml) portion of the remoulade sauce on the side.

Hold the crab cakes at 140°F (60°C) or higher and reserve the remoulade sauce under refrigeration at 41°F (5°C).

COOLING/STORING

Cool the crab cakes from 140°F (60°C) to 70°F (21.1°C) or lower within 2 hours. Cool from 70°F (21.1°C) to 41°F (5°C) within an additional 4 hours for a total cooling time of 6 hours or less.

Cover the crab cakes, lettuce, and remoulade; label, date, and store under refrigeration at 41°F (5°C) or lower.

Watercress Salad with Oregon Blue Cheese, Hazelnuts, and Sherry Vinaigrette

4 ounces (120g) leeks, cleaned, cut into fine julienne in 3-inch (7.5cm) lengths

all-purpose flour, as needed

vegetable oil, as needed

VINAIGRETTE

2 fluid ounces (60ml) Gewürztraminer

1 fluid ounce (30ml) sherry vinegar

4 fluid ounces (120ml) extra-virgin olive oil

salt, to taste

black pepper, ground, to taste

SALAD

3 bunches watercress, stemmed

kosher salt, to taste

black pepper, ground, to taste

9 ounces (270g) Oregon blue cheese, cut into large flat rectangles, ½ ounce (15g) each

3 ounces (90g) hazelnuts, roasted, peeled, roughly chopped

Dredge the leeks with the flour and shake off the excess.

Deep-fry the leeks in 375°F (190.6°C) vegetable oil until they are crisp and golden brown.

Degrease the fried leeks on absorbent paper towels and reserve in a warm place until needed.

Prepare the vinaigrette dressing by briskly whisking the Gewürztraminer, vinegar, and olive oil together in a bowl.

Season to taste with salt and black pepper. Reserve under refrigeration at 41°F (5°C) or lower until needed.

Place the cleaned, stemmed watercress in a bowl and toss it with approximately three-quarters of the dressing.

Season the watercress to taste with kosher salt and black pepper.

Assemble the salads by fanning 3 slices of cheese per portion in a circle around the outside of each chilled plate.

Mound the watercress in the center of the cheese. Sprinkle the top of the cheese with the remaining dressing.

Garnish the salads by sprinkling with the chopped hazelnuts and topping with the fried leeks.

COOLING/STORING

Cover the salad and dressing; label, date, and store under refrigeration at 41°F (5°C) or lower.

Buckwheat Soba Noodle Salad with Grilled Mushrooms

YIELD: 6 PORTIONS · PORTION SIZE: 6 OUNCES

BLACK SESAME VINAIGRETTE

4 fluid ounces (120ml) rice wine vinegar

¾ teaspoon (4g) ginger, minced

¾ teaspoon (4g) garlic, minced

salt, to taste

black pepper, ground, to taste

6 fluid ounces (180ml) olive oil

½ tablespoon (7g) black sesame seeds

SALAD

24 ounces (720g) buckwheat soba noodles, cooked and drained

8 ounces (240g) shiitake mushrooms, grilled, cut into julienne

6 ounces (180g) red bell peppers, cut into julienne

3 ounces (90g) pickled ginger, chopped

3 ounces (90g) cilantro, minced

8 ounces (240g) Roma tomato concassée

8 ounces (240g) bean sprouts

8 ounces (240g) mango, peeled, diced

6 leaves green leaf lettuce

Prepare the vinaigrette by combining the rice wine vinegar, ginger, garlic, salt, and pepper. Mix thoroughly.

Slowly drizzle in the oil, whisking briskly until all the oil is combined and a smooth emulsion forms. Add the sesame seeds. Reserve under refrigeration at 41°F (5°C) or lower until needed.

In a separate bowl, combine the salad ingredients, except the lettuce leaves, and mix with the dressing until thoroughly coated.

SERVING/HOLDING

Place a lettuce leaf on each chilled plate and place a 6-ounce (180g) mound of the buckwheat soba noodle salad on top of each lettuce leaf.

COOLING/STORING

Cover the salad; label, date, and store under refrigeration at 41°F (5°C) or lower.

Steelhead with Asparagus and Butter Sauce

YIELD: 6 PORTIONS · PORTION SIZE: 10 OUNCES

44 ounces (1.3kg) steelhead, cut into 7-ounce (210g) fillets, skin and pin bones removed

¾ teaspoon (4g) salt

¼ teaspoon (1g) white pepper, ground

8 fluid ounces (240ml) fish stock, prepared (see page 518)

4 fluid ounces (120ml) dry white wine

2 fluid ounces (60ml) lemon juice

2 ounces (60g) shallots, minced

1 tablespoon (15g) thyme, minced

1 tablespoon (15g) oregano, minced

12 ounces (360g) celery, peeled, cut into brunoise

8 ounces (240g) asparagus, trimmed, peeled

8 ounces (240g) butter, cut into ½-inch (1.27cm) cubes

salt, to taste

white pepper, ground, to taste

CHEF TIPS *The parchment paper lid should be cut to the diameter of the pan being used to poach the steelhead, but it should fit loosely. The idea is to trap enough of the steam to cook the portion of fish that is not submerged but to allow some steam to escape so that the cooking liquid does not significantly increase in temperature.*

If the aromatic vegetables are large in shape or hard in texture, blanch them in advance so they finish cooking at the same time as the fish.

Season the steelhead fillets with salt and white pepper.

Place the fish stock, wine, lemon juice, shallots, thyme, and oregano in a large sautoir pan and bring to a boil.

Place the celery and asparagus in the liquid and spread them evenly across the bottom of the pan.

Adjust the temperature until a slow simmer is achieved.

Place the steelhead fillets, skin side down, on top of the vegetables.

Cover the pot with a parchment paper lid and gently simmer for approximately 6–8 minutes or until the desired level of doneness is attained and the fish reaches a minimum internal temperature of 145°F (62.8°C) for at least 15 seconds.

Carefully remove the steelhead fillets, asparagus, and celery from the liquid and hold at 140°F (60°C) or higher until needed.

Strain the liquid through a chinoise into a clean saucepan and quickly reduce the volume of liquid by three-quarters over medium-high heat.

Remove the liquid from the heat and whisk in the butter a little at a time, stirring constantly, until all the butter is incorporated and a smooth emulsion is formed.

Season to taste with salt and white pepper and reserve in a warm place. Stir frequently until needed.

SERVING/HOLDING

Spoon the reserved celery into the center of each hot plate.

Place 5 or 6 asparagus spears in a fan, all pointing toward one side of the plate.

Top the celery and asparagus with the fillets of steelhead and carefully ladle the sauce over one-quarter of the fish and onto the plate. Serve immediately.

Hold the steelhead at 140°F (60°C) or higher.

COOLING/STORING

Cool the steelhead, vegetables, and sauce from 140°F (60°C) to 70°F (21.1°C) or lower within 2 hours. Cool from 70°F (21.1°C) to 41°F (5°C) within an additional 4 hours for a total cooling time of 6 hours or less.

Cover the steelhead, vegetables, and sauce; label, date, and store under refrigeration at 41°F (5°C) or lower.

Alaskan King Crab Legs with Champagne Sauce

YIELD: 6 PORTIONS · PORTION SIZE: 10 OUNCES

48 ounces (1.4kg) king crab legs, frozen, split

SAUCE

2 ounces (60g) shallots, minced

2 fluid ounces (60ml) white wine vinegar

4 fluid ounces (120ml) champagne

8 ounces (240g) butter

salt, to taste

white pepper, ground, to taste

½ ounce (15g) chives, minced

CHEF TIPS *King crab is usually obtained precooked and frozen. It should be kept frozen until ready to use. If a commercial steamer is not available, cook the legs by filling a large, tall pot one-quarter full with hot water. Invert a colander or bowl and place it in the pot in such a way that the crab legs will be suspended over the water while cooking. This will allow them to steam properly once the pot is covered. King crab should never be boiled.*

To easily remove the crabmeat from the legs without using crab crackers, split the legs prior to steaming. This is done with a large French knife while the crab legs are still frozen. Although king crab legs can be purchased already split, care must be taken as the presplit legs are highly susceptible to freezer burn, which can ruin a very expensive product.

Rinse the frozen legs in cold water.

Steam the legs over boiling water in a covered pot for approximately 5–10 minutes or until heated thoroughly.

Combine the shallots and white wine vinegar in a saucepan and bring to a boil.

Reduced the volume of liquid by half.

Add the champagne and reduce the volume of liquid by half again.

Add the butter, whisking constantly until all the butter is incorporated.

Season to taste with salt and white pepper.

Sprinkle with minced chives.

SERVING/HOLDING

Serve the crab legs immediately with a side dish of champagne sauce.

Hold the crab legs and champagne sauce at 140°F (60°C) or higher.

🍲 **Cool** the crab legs and champagne sauce from 140°F (60°C) to 70°F (21.1°C) or lower within 2 hours. Cool from 70°F (21.1°C) to 41°F (5°C) within an additional 4 hours for a total cooling time of 6 hours or less.

Cover the crab legs and champagne sauce; label, date, and store under refrigeration at 41°F (5°C) or lower.

Sautéed Halibut with Warm Apple and Cranberry Compote

YIELD: 6 PORTIONS · PORTION SIZE: 10 OUNCES

3 ounces (90g) dried cranberries

4 fluid ounces (120ml) apple brandy

4 ounces (120g) butter

8 ounces (240g) Walla Walla onions, thinly sliced

10 ounces (300g) Granny Smith apples, cut into large dice

4 cloves garlic, minced

1 tablespoon (15ml) lemon juice

salt, to taste

black pepper, ground, to taste

2 tablespoons (30ml) olive oil

44 ounces (1.3kg) halibut, cut into 7-ounce (240g) fillets, skin removed

1 large egg, beaten with 1 tablespoon (15ml) water

all-purpose flour, as needed

CHEF TIPS *A variety of apple brandies are available to choose from for this recipe. Applejack and Calvados are the most common; however, a number of local brandies made from apples in the artisan style are also available in the Pacific Northwest region.*

Rehydrate the dried cranberries by simmering them in the apple brandy for 3–4 minutes. Remove from the heat, cover, and reserve until needed.

Heat three-quarters of the butter in a saucepan over medium-high heat. Sauté the onions until they are translucent.

Add the apples and garlic and continue to sauté, stirring occasionally, until the apples are tender and the onions are golden brown in color.

Stir the lemon juice into the cranberries and brandy mixture and add to the cooked apples and onions.

Season to taste with salt and black pepper. Heat thoroughly and hold at 140°F (60°C) or higher until needed.

Combine the remaining butter with the olive oil in a sauteuse pan and heat over medium-high heat.

Dip the halibut fillets in the egg wash, then dredge in flour, and shake off any excess flour.

Sauté the fish fillets until they are golden brown on both sides and reach a minimum internal temperature of 145°F (62.8°C) for at least 15 seconds.

SERVING/HOLDING

Serve each halibut fillet on a hot plate topped with approximately 3 ounces (90g) of the apple cranberry compote.

Hold the halibut fillets and apple cranberry compote at 140°F (60°C) or higher.

COOLING/STORING

Cool the halibut and apple cranberry compote from 140°F (60°C) to 70°F (21.1°C) or lower within 2 hours. Cool from 70°F (21.1°C) to 41°F (5°C) within an additional 4 hours for a total cooling time of 6 hours or less.

Cover the halibut and apple cranberry compote; label, date, and store under refrigeration at 41°F (5°C) or lower.

Roasted Ellensburg Lamb Rack with Thyme–Merlot Sauce

6 pounds (2.7kg) or 3 whole lamb racks, chimed, split, frenched (or 3 pounds [1.3kg] of top round or bottom round leg pieces)

salt, to taste

black pepper, ground, to taste

3 tablespoons (44ml) olive oil

4 ounces (120g) Dijon mustard

1 tablespoon (15g) garlic, minced

8 ounces (240g) breadcrumbs, fresh

3 tablespoons (44g) shallots, minced

4 ounces (120ml) merlot

6 ounces (180ml) brown lamb stock, prepared (see page 515)

6 ounces (180ml) brown chicken stock, prepared (see page 515)

1 teaspoon (5g) thyme, minced

4 ounces (120g) butter

Preheat an oven to 450°F (232.2°C)

Season the lamb racks to taste with salt and black pepper.

Heat the olive oil in a large, heavy-bottomed pan over high heat.

Sear the lamb racks for approximately 1–2 minutes on each side or until they are thoroughly browned.

Remove the pan from the heat and brush the top side of the meat with the mustard.

Mix the minced garlic with the fresh breadcrumbs and pat gently on top of the mustard until the top of the meat is coated with breadcrumbs.

CHEF TIPS *As Ellensburg lamb is a regional item, an appropriate substitute is lamb racks from New Zealand, which are comparable in size and flavor. Lamb racks from the Rocky Mountain region have a distinctly different flavor and are much larger than the variety from the Pacific Northwest, so the quantity of lamb in the recipe should be reduced by half if this type is used, as one frenched Rocky Mountain lamb rack will easily yield two portions.*

Chimed, split, and frenched lamb racks are called for in this recipe. These techniques are commonly used by butchers and meat fabricators. The resulting lamb racks are trimmed of all bones except the small rib bones, which are trimmed and exposed. The outside layer or cap is removed and all excess fat is trimmed, except for a ½-inch (1.27cm) strip that allows for rendered fat to baste and moisten the meat as it roasts. Frenching a lamb rack significantly reduces the original weight of the rack, sometimes up to 50 percent, doubling the cost of an already expensive cut of meat.

The lamb racks are seared before the breadcrumb and mustard coating is applied. This helps the coating better adhere to the lamb and prevents it from coming off during cooking.

Place the pan with the lamb racks in the oven and roast until the desired internal temperature is attained and the lamb reaches a minimum internal temperature of 145°F (62.8°C) for at least 15 seconds.

Remove the pan from the oven, remove the racks, and allow the meat to rest in a warm place while the sauce is prepared.

Discard all but 1 tablespoon (15ml) of the fat rendered from roasting the lamb.

Place the pan over medium-high heat and sauté the minced shallots for 1–2 minutes or until they are translucent.

Deglaze the pan with the wine. Add the lamb stock, chicken stock, and thyme.

Reduce the liquid to half its original volume.

Remove the pan from the heat and finish the sauce by briskly whisking in the butter, a little at a time, until a smooth emulsion forms. Season to taste with salt and black pepper.

SERVING/HOLDING

Carefully ladle approximately 3 ounces (90ml) of the sauce into the center of each warm plate.

Slice each rack into 3 chops and attractively arrange them with the bones pointing to the top of the plate.

Hold the lamb racks and sauce at 140°F (60°C) or higher.

COOLING/STORING

Cool the lamb and sauce from 140°F (60°C) to 70°F (21.1°C) or lower within 2 hours. Cool from 70°F (21.1°C) to 41°F (5°C) within an additional 4 hours for a total cooling time of 6 hours or less.

Cover the lamb and sauce; label, date, and store under refrigeration at 41°F (5°C) or lower.

Oven-Roasted Vegetables

YIELD: 6 PORTIONS · PORTION SIZE: 4 OUNCES

nonstick vegetable spray, as needed

7 ounces (210g) Roma tomatoes, quartered lengthwise

8 ounces (240g) red potatoes, quartered

4 ounces (120g) zucchini, cut in half lengthwise, cut into ¼-inch (.64cm) -thick slices

4 ounces (120g) green beans, stems removed, blanched

8 ounces (240g) yellow bell peppers, cut into ½-inch (1.27cm) strips

2 fluid ounces (60ml) olive oil

salt, to taste

black peppercorns, cracked, to taste

Line two sheet pans with parchment paper and spray them lightly with nonstick vegetable spray.

Lay the tomatoes on one sheet pan, avoiding overlapping, and roast slowly in a preheated 250°F (121.1°C) oven for 1½–2 hours or until the desired degree of doneness is attained. Reserve until needed.

Lay the potatoes on the other sheet pan, avoiding overlapping, and roast in a preheated 400°F (204.4°C) for 10 minutes. Reserve until needed.

Toss the zucchini, beans, and peppers with the oil and season to taste with salt and cracked black peppercorns.

Add the oiled vegetables to the sheet pan with the potatoes and roast in a 400°F (204.4°C) oven until the potatoes are tender and golden brown and all of the vegetables are thoroughly cooked.

SERVING/HOLDING

The cooked potatoes and vegetables can be combined with the tomatoes and served mixed, or they can be presented as individual components attractively arranged on the plate.

Hold the roasted vegetables at 140°F (60°C) or higher.

COOLING/STORING

Cool the roasted vegetables from 140°F (60°C) to 70°F (21.1°C) or lower within 2 hours. Cool from 70°F (21.1°C) to 41°F (5°C) within an additional 4 hours for a total cooling time of 6 hours or less.

Cover the roasted vegetables; label, date, and store under refrigeration at 41°F (5°C) or lower.

Brussels Sprouts in Hazelnut Butter

YIELD: 6 PORTIONS · PORTION SIZE: 4 OUNCES

24 ounces (720g) Brussels sprouts, trimmed

1 ounce (30g) butter

1½ ounces (45g) onion, chopped

1 ounce (30g) hazelnuts, crushed

salt, to taste

black pepper, ground, to taste

nutmeg, freshly grated, to taste

CHEF TIPS *The purpose of scoring the bottom of the Brussels sprouts with an X is to ensure that the sprouts cook evenly.*

Score an X ¼-inch (.64cm) deep in each stem end of the Brussels sprouts.

Steam the sprouts over boiling water or in a commercial steamer until they are fork tender. Remove and reserve.

Melt the butter over medium heat. Add the onions and sauté them for approximately 2 minutes or until golden in color.

Stir in the crushed hazelnuts and continue to cook for an additional 1 minute.

Add the Brussels sprouts and toss, coating thoroughly.

Season to taste with salt, black pepper, and nutmeg.

SERVING/HOLDING

Hold the Brussels sprouts at 140°F (60°C) or higher.

COOLING/STORING

Cool the Brussels sprouts from 140°F (60°C) to 70°F (21.1°C) or lower within 2 hours. Cool from 70°F (21.1°C) to 41°F (5°C) within an additional 4 hours for a total cooling time of 6 hours or less.

Cover the Brussels sprouts; label, date, and store under refrigeration at 41°F (5°C) or lower.

Green Beans Cooked with Summer Savory

YIELD: 6 PORTIONS · PORTION SIZE: 4 OUNCES

1½ ounces (45g) salt pork or bacon, cut into small dice

24 ounces (720g) green beans, stems removed, cut into 3-inch (7.6cm) lengths

4 ounces (120g) onion, minced

1 tablespoon (15g) summer savory, minced

8 fluid ounces (240ml) water

salt, to taste

black pepper, ground, to taste

1 teaspoon (5g) cornstarch

1 tablespoon (15ml) cold water

1 tablespoon (15g) parsley, chopped

CHEF TIPS *French beans, yellow wax beans, or a combination of beans, if different colors and sizes are desirable, can substitute for the green beans in this recipe.*

Thyme or other fresh herbs can substitute for the summer savory if a different flavor is desired.

Render the salt pork in a sauteuse pan over medium heat for approximately 5 minutes or until it is a pale golden color and crisp.

Sauté the beans, onions, and savory in the fat for approximately 2–3 minutes and toss until thoroughly heated.

Add the water and cook over low heat for approximately 6–8 minutes or until the beans are tender but still a little crisp.

Season the beans to taste with salt and black pepper.

Stir the cornstarch into 1 tablespoon (15ml) of cold water and add to the cooking liquid.

Bring to a boil, stir, and reduce the heat to a simmer. Simmer for an additional 2–3 minutes. The liquid will thicken slightly.

SERVING/HOLDING

Carefully spoon some of the sauce over the beans.

Garnish each portion of beans by sprinkling it with chopped parsley.

Hold the beans at 140°F (60°C) or higher.

COOLING/STORING

Cool the beans from 140°F (60°C) to 70°F (21.1°C) or lower within 2 hours. Cool from 70°F (21.1°C) to 41°F (5°C) within an additional 4 hours for a total cooling time of 6 hours or less.

Cover the beans; label, date, and store under refrigeration at 41°F (5°C) or lower.

Mashed Potato and Wheatberry Cakes

YIELD: 6 PORTIONS · PORTION SIZE: 4 OUNCES

2 ounces (60g) wheatberries, soaked overnight

16 fluid ounces (480ml) vegetable stock, prepared (see page 519)

24 ounces (720g) russet potatoes

½ teaspoon (2g) salt

¼ teaspoon (1g) black pepper, ground

½ teaspoon (2g) cumin seeds, toasted, ground

1 ounce (30g) all-purpose flour

2 ounces (60g) breadcrumbs, dry, coarsely ground

1 large egg

vegetable oil, as needed

CHEF TIPS *Wheatberries should be soaked overnight in cold water and then boiled in salted water or stock for approximately 1 hour or until they are tender. Wheatberries are eaten in the same manner as rice— served as a starch or used as an ingredient in salads or other preparations.*

Combine the wheatberries and stock in a saucepan. Bring to a boil and reduce the heat.

Simmer gently for approximately 1 hour or until the wheatberries are tender.

Cool the wheatberries from 140°F (60°C) to 70°F (21.1°C) or lower within 2 hours. Cool from 70°F (21.1°C) to 41°F (5°C) within an additional 4 hours for a total cooling time of 6 hours or less. Reserve under refrigeration at 41°F (5°C) or lower until needed.

Bake the russet potatoes in a preheated 400°F (204.4°C) oven for approximately 45 minutes or until tender.

Split the potatoes and scoop the flesh into a bowl. Mash until smooth and free of lumps.

Cool the mashed potatoes from 140°F (60°C) to 70°F (21.1°C) or lower within 2 hours. Cool from 70°F (21.1°C) to 41°F (5°C) within an additional 4 hours for a total cooling time of 6 hours or less. Reserve under refrigeration at 41°F (5°C) or lower until needed.

Sift the salt, pepper, ground cumin seeds, and flour together into a bowl.

Add the breadcrumbs and mix thoroughly.

Combine the cooled wheatberries, mashed potatoes, breadcrumb mixture, and egg. Mix gently until the ingredients are thoroughly incorporated.

Shape the mixture into small patties approximately 2 inches in diameter and ½ inch (1.27cm) thick.

Pan-fry the patties in the vegetable oil until they are golden brown on both sides and reach a minimum internal temperature of 165°F (73.9°C) for at least 15 seconds.

Drain on absorbent paper towels.

SERVING/HOLDING

Serve 2 cakes per portion.

Hold the cakes at 140°F (60°C) or higher.

COOLING/STORING

Cool the cakes from 140°F (60°C) to 70°F (21.1°C) or lower within 2 hours. Cool from 70°F (21.1°C) to 41°F (5°C) within an additional 4 hours for a total cooling time of 6 hours or less.

Cover the cakes; label, date, and store under refrigeration at 41°F (5°C) or lower.

Cardamom Cornmeal Waffles

YIELD: 6 PORTIONS · PORTION SIZE: 4 OUNCES

4 ounces (120g) raw quinoa

8 fluid ounces (240g) water

7 ounces (210g) all-purpose flour

3 ounces (90g) cornmeal, yellow, finely ground

2 teaspoons (10g) cardamom, ground

1 teaspoon (5g) baking powder

¼ teaspoon (1g) salt

1 teaspoon (5g) sugar

4 ounces (120g) chives, minced

4 fluid ounces (120ml) buttermilk

1 fluid ounce (30ml) corn oil

6 large eggs, whipped

nonstick vegetable spray, as needed

CHEF TIPS *These waffles can be made several days in advance if stored in an airtight container after preparation. If the waffles become soft or limp, crisp them in the oven for a few minutes at 250°F (121.1°C). Because of the variations in irons and in their temperatures, cooking time for waffles will vary. The best way to judge when the waffle is done is by color. Waffle should be slightly brown around the edges.*

Place the quinoa in a saucepan and cover with the water. Bring to a boil, reduce the heat, cover, and simmer for 12 minutes.

Remove from the heat and let steep for 10 minutes. Fluff with a fork and hold at room temperature until needed.

In a large mixing bowl, combine the flour, cornmeal, cardamom, baking powder, salt, and sugar. Reserve until needed.

In a separate bowl, mix the cooked quinoa, chives, buttermilk, corn oil, and whipped eggs. Mix thoroughly.

Combine the wet and dry ingredients together and mix thoroughly until a batter forms.

Lightly spray a preheated waffle iron with vegetable oil and ladle ½ cup (120ml) batter onto it. Cook until light brown in color. Remove the waffle and cut it into 6 wedges.

Repeat the step above twice more or until all the batter is made into waffles.

Transfer the wedges to a sheet pan and bake in a preheated 225°F (107.2°C) oven for 20–30 minutes or until crisp.

Serve 3 waffle wedges per portion.

🍲 Hold the cardamom waffle wedges at 140°F (60°C) or higher.

COOLING/STORING

🍲 Cool the cardamom waffle wedges from 140°F (60°C) to 70°F (21.1°C) or lower within 2 hours. Cool from 70°F (21.1°C) to 41°F (5°C) within an additional 4 hours for a total cooling time of 6 hours or less.

Cover the cardamon waffle wedges; label, date, and store under refrigeration at 41°F (5°C) or lower.

Mushroom Bread Pudding

YIELD: 6 PORTIONS · PORTION SIZE: 6 OUNCES

12 fluid ounces (360ml) white chicken stock, prepared (see page 517)

1½ ounces (45g) tree mushrooms, dried

1 ounce (30g) butter

4 ounces (120g) shallots, minced

½ ounce (14g) garlic, minced

2 large eggs

6 fluid ounces (180ml) heavy cream

½ teaspoon (2g) salt

¼ teaspoon (1g) white pepper, ground

2 ounces (57g) domestic mushrooms, minced

1 teaspoon (5g) dried thyme

1 tablespoon (15g) chives, minced

1 teaspoon (5g) rosemary, minced

32 ounces (960g) bread or brioche, cut into ½-inch (1.27cm) cubes

nonstick vegetable spray, as needed

Bring the stock to a boil in a saucepot. Add the dried tree mushrooms, cover, and remove from the heat. Let steep for 10 minutes.

🍲 **Remove** the mushrooms from the stock. Reserve both the mushrooms and liquid at 140°F (60°C) or higher until needed.

Melt the butter in another saucepan and sweat the shallots and garlic over medium heat until the onions are translucent. Remove from the heat and reserve until needed.

Combine the eggs and cream in a bowl and season with the salt and white pepper.

Stir in the reserved mushroom liquid, minced mushrooms, and herbs and add to the onions and garlic. Incorporate products thoroughly.

Stir in the cubed bread or brioche and the reconstituted tree mushrooms.

Spray a small baking pan with nonstick vegetable spray and pour in the bread pudding mixture.

🍲 **Cover** with aluminum foil and bake in a preheated 350°F (176.7°C) oven for approximately 20–30 minutes or until the bread pudding is set and reaches a minimum internal temperature of 145°F (62.8°C) for at least 15 seconds.

SERVING/HOLDING

Remove the mushroom bread pudding from the pan and cut into 6 uniform portions.

🍲 **Hold** the mushroom bread pudding at 140°F (60°C) or higher.

COOLING/STORING

🍲 **Cool** the mushroom bread pudding from 140°F (60°C) to 70°F (21.1°C) or lower within 2 hours. Cool from 70°F (21.1°C) to 41°F (5°C) within an additional 4 hours for a total cooling time of 6 hours or less.

Cover the mushroom bread pudding; label, date, and store under refrigeration at 41°F (5°C) or lower.

Mushroom and Rice Patties

YIELD: 6 PORTIONS · PORTION SIZE: 4 OUNCES

28 fluid ounces (840ml) vegetable stock, prepared (see page 519)

1 tablespoon (15ml) olive oil

1 ounce (30g) butter

7 ounces (210g) onions, cut into small dice

7 ounces (210g) raw Arborio rice

5 ounces (150g) button mushrooms, stemmed, thinly sliced

2 ounces (60g) Parmesan cheese, grated

salt, to taste

black pepper, ground, to taste

vegetable oil, as needed

Place the stock in a saucepot and bring to a boil. Reduce the heat to a simmer. Hold the stock at 140°F (60°C) or higher until needed.

Heat the oil and butter in a heavy-bottomed saucepot. Add the onions and sauté over medium heat for 3 minutes or until translucent.

Add the Arborio rice and continue to cook over medium heat for 2 minutes. Add the sliced mushrooms and cook an additional 3 minutes.

Add 4 ounces (120ml) of the vegetable stock to the rice, stirring frequently while cooking over medium heat until the liquid is completely absorbed.

Add another 4 ounces (120ml) of the stock and continue to cook, stirring frequently, until all the stock is absorbed.

Continue to repeat step above until all the stock is used and the rice is tender and creamy.

Remove from the heat and stir in the Parmesan cheese.

Season the rice to taste with salt and black pepper.

Transfer the rice to a bowl and cool from 140°F (60°C) to 70°F (21.1°C) or lower within 2 hours. Cool from 70°F (21.1°C) to 41°F (5°C) within an additional 4 hours for a total cooling time of 6 hours or less. Reserve under refrigeration at 41°F (5°C) or lower until needed.

With wet hands, shape the rice mixture into flat rounds about 2 inches (5cm) in diameter and ½ inch (1.27cm) thick.

Let the patties rest under refrigeration for at least 15 minutes.

Heat the vegetable oil in a sautoir pan over medium-high heat until it is approximately 350°F (176.7°C).

Pan-fry the patties in small batches for approximately 3 minutes on each side or until they are golden brown and reach a minimum internal temperature of 165°F (73.9°C) for at least 15 seconds.

Drain the patties on absorbent paper towels.

SERVING/HOLDING

Serve 2 patties per portion.

Hold the patties at 140°F (60°C) or higher.

COOLING/STORING

Cool the rice patties from 140°F (60°C) to 70°F (21.1°C) or lower within 2 hours. Cool from 70°F (21.1°C) to 41°F (5°C) within an additional 4 hours for a total cooling time of 6 hours or less.

Cover the rice patties; label, date, and store under refrigeration at 41°F (5°C) or lower.

Warm Flourless Chocolate Cake with Espresso Sauce

YIELD: 6 PORTIONS · PORTION SIZE: 4 OUNCES

8 fluid ounces (240ml) heavy cream

8 ounces (240g) bittersweet chocolate, chopped

2 ounces (60g) butter, softened

5 large eggs

2 ounces (60g) sugar

12 fluid ounces (360ml) espresso sauce (recipe follows)

6 sprigs mint

30 chocolate espresso beans

Heat the heavy cream to just before the boiling point in a heavy-bottomed saucepot.

Place the chopped chocolate in a large bowl and pour in the hot cream.

Stir the mixture until the chocolate is completely melted and thoroughly incorporated.

Stir in the softened butter and reserve mixture until needed.

Combine the eggs and sugar in another bowl and whisk over a double boiler until the mixture has the consistency of whipped cream.

Gently fold the chocolate mixture into the whipped eggs and sugar.

Pour the cake batter into well-greased large-size muffin pans.

Bake in a hot-water bath in a preheated 350°F (176.7°C) oven for approximately 30–45 minutes or until the cakes are set and reach a minimum internal temperature of 145°F (68.3°C) for at least 15 seconds.

SERVING/HOLDING

Cool slightly and remove the cakes from the muffin tins.

Carefully ladle approximately 2 ounces (60ml) of espresso sauce into the center of each warm plate.

Place a cake on top of the sauce and garnish the plate by placing a sprig of mint and 4–5 chocolate espresso beans in the sauce around the cake.

COOLING/STORING

🥣 **Cool** the cakes from 140°F (60°C) to 70°F (21.1°C) or lower within 2 hours. Cool from 70°F (21.1°C) to 41°F (5°C) within an additional 4 hours for a total cooling time of 6 hours or less.

Cover the cakes and sauce; label, date, and store under refrigeration at 41°F (5°C) or lower.

ESPRESSO SAUCE

YIELD: 6 PORTIONS · PORTION SIZE: 2 OUNCES

8 fluid ounces (240ml) milk

1 fluid ounce (30ml) espresso, prepared

¼ vanilla bean

1¾ ounces (50g) sugar

3 egg yolks

Heat the milk, espresso, and vanilla bean to the boiling point in a stainless-steel saucepot.

Blend the sugar and egg yolks in a bowl and mix thoroughly.

Temper the hot liquid by gradually pouring ¼ cup (60ml) of the hot milk into the egg mixture, stirring constantly.

Gradually pour the egg and milk mixture back into the saucepan with the remaining hot milk, stirring constantly.

🥣 **Continue** to cook over medium heat, stirring constantly, until the milk begins to thicken, but do not allow the sauce to come to a boil. Cook until the sauce reaches a minimum internal temperature of 145°F (62.8°C) for at least 15 seconds. The sauce will thicken to a nappé consistency.

Strain the sauce.

COOLING/STORING

🥣 **Cool** the sauce from 140°F (60°C) to 70°F (21.1°C) or lower within 2 hours. Cool from 70°F (21.1°C) to 41°F (5°C) within an additional 4 hours for a total cooling time of 6 hours or less.

Cover the sauce; label, date, and store under refrigeration at 41°F (5°C) or lower.

Brown Stock

YIELD: 1 GALLON (3.8L)

Brown stock is a flavorful liquid made from caramelized beef, veal, chicken, or game bones and vegetables, simmered in water with seasonings for 6–8 hours (3–4 hours for chicken). This stock should be a rich, dark color, highly aromatic, and gelatinous when finished. The standard ratio of ingredients for brown stock is 8 pounds (3.6kg) of beef, veal, poultry, or game bones, 6 quarts (5.7L) of cold water, 1 pound (60g) of mirepoix, and 1 sachet d'épices or bouquet garni per gallon of finished stock.

128 ounces (3.6kg) beef, veal, chicken, or game bones

2 fluid ounces (60ml) vegetable oil

192 fluid ounces (5.7L) cold water

MIREPOIX

8 ounces (240g) onions, cut into large dice

4 ounces (120g) carrots, cut into large dice

4 ounces (120g) celery, cut into large dice

4 ounces (120g) tomato paste

SACHET D'ÉPICES

½ teaspoon (2g) thyme leaves

½ teaspoon (2g) black peppercorns, cracked

3–4 stems parsley

1 clove garlic, crushed

CHEF TIPS *For any type of brown stock, be careful to thoroughly and evenly brown the bones and mirepoix. Remember, the difference between browned and burned bones is only a brief amount of time.*

Coat the bones with the oil and roast them in a pre-heated 400°F (204.4°C) oven, stirring frequently until well browned.

Place the bones in a 10-quart (9.5L) stockpot and cover with the cold water (keep roasting pan at hand). Bring to a simmer.

Skim the surface, removing and discarding any impurities. Do not allow the simmering stock to fall below 140°F (60°C).

While the stock comes to a simmer, heat the roasting pan used to brown the bones to clarify the fat. Drain the fat and reserve.

Deglaze the roasting pan with 8 ounces (240ml) of the liquid from the stockpot. After the roasting pan is deglazed, add the remaining liquid to the simmering stock.

For the mirepoix, lightly coat the onions, carrots, and celery with some of the reserved fat, place them in the roasting pan, and brown thoroughly in a 400°F (204.4°C) oven, stirring regularly.

Combine the tomato paste with the vegetables and return to the oven. Continue to roast the vegetables, stirring regularly, until the tomato paste starts to brown (pincé).

Add the roasted, browned vegetables to the simmering stock.

Deglaze the roasting pan again with 4 ounces (120ml) of the liquid from the stockpot and add to the simmering stock.

To create the sachet d'épices, place the thyme, peppercorns, parsley, and garlic in a small square of cheesecloth and tie with twine. Add the sachet to the simmering stock.

🥄 Continue to simmer gently for 6–8 hours (3–4 hours for chicken). Skim the surface regularly, discarding the impurities. Do not allow the simmering stock to fall below 140°F (60°C).

Add water as needed to keep the bones from becoming exposed as the stock evaporates.

Degrease (degraisse) the stock and strain through several layers of cheesecloth that have been rinsed in cold water and placed in a conical strainer.

🥄 **Hold** the stock at 140°F (60°C) or higher.

White Stock

YIELD: 1 GALLON (3.8L)

White stock is a flavorful liquid made from beef, veal, or chicken bones simmered in water with vegetables and seasonings for 6–8 hours (3–5 hours for chicken bones). The resulting liquid should be clear and without color, highly aromatic, and gelatinous. For a neutral flavor, veal bones are suggested. The standard ratio of ingredients used to prepare white stock is 8 pounds (3.6kg) of beef, veal, or poultry bones, 6 quarts (5.7L) of cold water, 1 pound (460g) of mirepoix, and 1 sachet d'épices or bouquet garni per gallon of finished stock.

192 fluid ounces cold water (5.7L)

8 pounds (3.6kg) beef, veal, or chicken bones

MIREPOIX

8 ounces (240g) onions, cut into large dice

4 ounces (120g) carrots, cut into large dice

4 ounces (120g) celery, cut into large dice

SACHET D'ÉPICES

½ teaspoon (2g) thyme leaves

½ teaspoon (2g) black peppercorns, cracked

3–4 stems parsley

1 clove garlic, crushed

Bring the water to a boil in a 10-quart (9.5L) stockpot. Place the bones in the stockpot, return to a boil, then immediately remove from the heat.

CHEF TIPS *Blanching the bones before making a white stock is an optional step. Chefs today disagree on whether or not this is necessary; the question has to do with the loss of flavor during the blanching process. Although the process does take away a little flavor from the resulting product, blanching the bones gives the finished stock extra clarity. If the bones are very fresh, blanching is certainly not necessary, as extremely fresh bones provide both maximum flavor and clarity to stocks made with them. If the bones are frozen or a few days old, they should be blanched. If you choose to blanch the bones, do so with water that is boiling so that as little flavor as possible is lost.*

Strain the bones, discard the liquid, and rinse the bones under cold running water.

Clean the stockpot, add the rinsed bones to water to cover, bring to a boil, and simmer over low heat.

Skim the surface, removing and discarding any impurities. Simmer the stock for 6–8 hours (3–4 hours for chicken bones). Continue to skim the surface regularly, discarding the impurities. Do not allow the simmering stock to fall below 140°F (60°C).

Add the mirepoix ingredients.

Place the sachet d'épices ingredients in a small square of cheesecloth, tie with twine, and add to the simmering stock.

Continue to simmer gently for 1 additional hour. Do not allow the simmering stock to fall below 140°F (60°C).

Strain the stock through several layers of cheesecloth that have been rinsed in cold water and placed in a conical strainer.

Hold the stock at 140°F (60°C) or above.

Fish Stock

YIELD: 1 GALLON (3.8L)

Fish stock is a flavorful liquid made from fish or shellfish bones simmered with vegetables in water and seasonings for approximately 30–45 minutes. Good-quality fish stock is highly aromatic and colorless. The standard ratio of ingredients used to prepare fish or shellfish stock is 176 ounces (5kg) of bones or shells, 160 fluid ounces (4.7L) of cold water, 1 pound of mirepoix (454g), and 1 sachet d'épices or bouquet garni per gallon of finished stock.

> 176 ounces (5kg) fish bones
>
> 4 ounces (120g) celery, cut into large dice
>
> 8 ounces (240g) onions, cut into large dice
>
> 4 ounces (120g) leeks, green portion, chopped
>
> 10 ounces (300g) mushroom stems
>
> 160 fluid ounces (4.8L) cold water

½ teaspoon (2g) thyme leaves

¼ teaspoon (1g) black peppercorns, crushed

1 bay leaf

3–4 stems parsley

2–3 leeks, green portion, cut into 2-inch (5cm) pieces

Rinse the fish bones thoroughly under cold running water.

In a small stockpot, add the bones, diced celery, onions, chopped leeks, and mushroom stems to the cold water.

Place the ingredients for the sachet d'épices in a small square of cheesecloth, tie with twine, and add to the liquid.

Slowly bring the stock to a gentle simmer and continue to simmer for 30–45 minutes while regularly skimming the surface, removing and discarding any impurities. Do not allow the simmering stock to fall below 140°F (60°C).

Strain the stock through several layers of cheesecloth that have been rinsed in cold water and placed in a conical strainer.

Hold the stock at 140°F (60°C) or above.

Vegetable Stock

YIELD: 1 GALLON (3.8L)

Vegetable stock is a flavorful liquid made from vegetables that are simmered in water, wine, and seasonings for approximately 45 minutes. The resulting liquid should be clear, with a light color, and highly aromatic. Including just two or three vegetables in addition to mirepoix produces better results than a vegetable stock made with a larger variety of vegetables.

2 fluid ounces (60ml) vegetable oil

MIREPOIX

16 ounces (480g) onions, cut into small dice

8 ounces (240g) carrots, cut into small dice

8 ounces (240g) celery, cut into small dice

8 ounces (240g) leeks, white and green, chopped

2 ounces (60g) turnips, cut into small dice

2 ounces (60g) tomatoes, diced

4 cloves garlic, chopped

128 fluid ounces (3.8L) cold water

8 fluid ounces (240ml) dry white wine

SACHET D'ÉPICES

½ teaspoon (2g) thyme leaves

1 bay leaf

6–8 stems parsley

¼ teaspoon (1g) black peppercorns, crushed

CHEF TIPS *Any type of vegetables can be used for vegetable stock, but the number of vegetable types in a single stock should be limited. Too many vegetables can create a confusing flavor. The selection of vegetables should complement the intended purpose or finished product of the stock. If the vegetable stock is being used to make a mushroom sauce, for example, mushroom stems would be an excellent choice to include as one of the flavors in the stock. Fennel, however, would not be appropriate because its strong flavor would overpower the taste of the mushrooms.*

Heat the oil in a medium saucepot.

Sweat the mirepoix, leeks, turnips, tomatoes, and garlic until the onions are translucent, approximately 8–10 minutes.

Add the water and wine.

Place the sachet d'épices ingredients in a small square of cheesecloth, tie with twine, and add to the liquid.

Slowly bring the stock to a gentle simmer and continue to simmer for 45 minutes while regularly skimming the surface, removing and discarding any impurities. Do not allow the simmering stock to fall below 140°F (60°C).

Strain the stock through several layers of cheesecloth that have been rinsed in cold water and placed in a conical strainer.

Hold the stock at 140°F (60°C) or above.

Hollandaise Sauce

One of the five grand sauces, hollandaise sauce is a rich, hot emulsion sauce made from egg yolks and butter flavored with vinegar and lemon juice. A variety of small sauces are made from hollandaise sauce, the most common being béarnaise sauce. An example of hollandaise sauce used in American regional cuisine is demonstrated in the recipe for Corn Crêpes with Smoked Shrimp and Asparagus, featured in The Cuisine of the Mid-Atlantic States (page 64).

REDUCTION

1 teaspoon (5g) black peppercorns

4 tablespoons (60ml) cold water

2 tablespoons (30ml) distilled vinegar

½ teaspoon (2g) salt

SAUCE

5 egg yolks

18 fluid ounces (540ml) clarified butter, warm (not hot)

lemon juice, to taste

salt, to taste

CHEF TIPS *A well-made hollandaise sauce is smooth and free of lumps. The flavor is primarily of butter, but not so much that the butter overpowers the egg and lemon flavors. The consistency of hollandaise should not be heavy but rather light and fluffy.*

Many professionals choose to use softened whole butter instead of clarified butter in their hollandaise sauce because whole butter has much more flavor. If using whole butter, make sure that the initial reduction is cooked until almost dry because whole butter contains a lot of natural moisture, which can lead to a thinner sauce. This problem is countered by cooking the reduction longer to decrease liquid.

Hollandaise sauce is an emulsion sauce, which means the fat molecules of the butter are temporarily suspended in the eggs. This emulsion is not permanent and is subject to breaking down. A hollandaise may break for a variety of reasons, including exposure to heat, exposure to cold, the technique used to prepare the sauce, or simply because the sauce was not stirred from time to time.

RECOVERY INSTRUCTIONS

Before attempting to recover a broken hollandaise, perform a few diagnostics. First, feel the bottom of the bowl to determine whether the sauce is too hot or too cold. If the hollandaise is too cold, reheat it over a double boiler before following the recovery instructions. If the sauce is too hot, let it cool slightly and add an egg yolk to the water in the recovery instructions. If the hollandaise is the correct temperature, follow the recovery instructions as written.

Place 1 tablespoon (15ml) of warm water in a stainless-steel bowl and whisk in the broken sauce, 1 ounce (30ml) at a time, with a vigorous back-and-forth motion until all the broken hollandaise has reemulsified. This process is highly effective in recovery of broken hollandaise sauce.

Crack the peppercorns in the bottom of a saucepan.

Add the water, vinegar, and first quantity of salt. Bring to a boil and reduce the volume of liquid by two-thirds. Remove from the heat and reserve until needed.

Place the egg yolks in a stainless-steel bowl. Strain the liquid from the reduction into the bowl with the egg yolks.

Cook over a double boiler, whisking constantly and vigorously. Cook the egg yolks until the mixture reaches a minimum of 150°F (65.6°C). This process takes only 3–5 minutes. Typically, the egg mixture thins, then starts to thicken. At 160°F (71.1°C), the egg mixture should have a nappé consistency. Be careful to stir constantly so the eggs do not congeal.

Once the egg yolks are cooked, immediately remove the bowl from the double boiler.

Whisk in the warm clarified butter, 1 ounce (30ml) at a time, with a vigorous back-and-forth motion, in order to incorporate as much air as possible. Make sure the clarified butter is warm, as hot butter will cause the emulsion to break down.

Season the sauce to taste with lemon juice and salt.

If the sauce is too thick, adjust the consistency with a little warm water.

If the sauce appears to have small pieces of congealed egg in it, strain it through a chinois before using.

SERVING/HOLDING

Hold the sauce at 140°F (60°C) or above, stirring from time to time. An insulated thermos is an excellent storage vessel for hollandaise sauce.

COOLING/STORING

Due to potential food safety hazards, it is recommended that hollandaise sauce be discarded after 4 hours. Do not attempt to store or reuse hollandaise sauce.

Basic Culinary Vocabulary

Al Dente Cooked firm—not soft or mushy. Another way of saying al dente is "to the bite."

Albumin The primary protein found in egg whites. Albumin is available powdered and granulated and is frequently used as an edible glue for sealing foods together.

Allumette A classic vegetable cut that results in shapes measuring ⅛ inch (.32cm) x ⅛ inch (.32cm) x 2 inches (5cm). The term is used in reference to potatoes only. All other vegetables cut into this shape are referred to as *julienne*.

Appareil A prepared mixture of ingredients used by itself or as an ingredient in other preparations. Examples of appareils are due duxelles and pâte à choux.

Aromatics Spices, herbs, and certain vegetables added to preparations to enhance their flavor or aroma.

Aspic A clear jelly made from clarified stock and thickened with gelatin. Aspic is sometimes referred to as *aspic jelly* and *aspic gelée* and is used primarily to coat foods. In some cases, aspic is cut into uniform shapes and used as a garnish for pâtés and other charcuterie items.

Au Gratin Describes foods finished under a broiler or salamander and served with a browned top. Frequently, the topping for gratinée items is made from breadcrumbs, cheese, or sauce.

Au Sec Describes food cooked until almost dry.

Bain Marie A container that holds foods in a hot-water bath. *Bain marie* is also the name for a hot-water bath used to slowly cook foods or to hold them at a hot temperature until needed.

Base A widely used, commercially produced flavor base usually available in powdered, granulated, and paste forms. Bases are typically mixed with water to create instant stock or used in small quantities to enhance the flavor of soups and sauces. A number of convenient food bases are available today. The application of these convenience products is highly dependent on the type of foodservice establishment and the desired flavor outcomes. Some factors to consider when using bases are time, cost, storage, and flavor. Be sure to read the product's label carefully so that you know its ingredients. Taste the product to ensure that its flavor meets your expectations.

Batonnet A classic vegetable cut that results in shapes measuring ¼ inch (.64cm) x ¼ inch (.64cm) x 2 inches (5cm).

Blanching The process of quickly and partially cooking food items in boiling water or hot fat. Blanching is generally done as a part of a combination cooking method or to aid in the preparation of a food item. Examples of blanching uses are to remove the skin from tomatoes, to prepare french fries for final cooking, to ready food items for freezing, and to remove undesirable flavors from foods.

Bouillon French for "broth." (See *broth*.)

Bouquet Garni A selection of fresh vegetables and herbs tied into a bundle with twine. A bouquet garni is typically submerged in stocks, sauces, soups, and stews and used as a flavoring agent.

Broth The culinary definition of broth is "a flavorful liquid derived by simmering meat, vegetables, and aromatics in water." To make beef, veal, or chicken broth, simmer meat in water with vegetables and seasonings for 2–4 hours.

Brunoise A classic vegetable cut that results in shapes measuring ⅛ inch (.32cm) x ⅛ inch (.32cm) x ⅛ inch (.32cm).

Brunoise Fine A classic vegetable cut that results in shapes measuring 1/16 inch (.16cm) x 1/16 inch (.16cm) 1/16 inch (.16cm).

Caramelization The process of browning the sugars found on the surface of many foods to enhance their flavor and appearance. Browning vegetables or protein items is also referred to as caramelizing.

Carryover Cooking What happens when roasted foods, small or large, continue to cook after being removed from the oven. Carryover cooking is normal and can dramatically alter the degree of doneness once the product is removed from the oven. The larger the food item, the greater the amount of heat it retains and the more its internal temperature rises.

Château A classic vegetable cut resulting in a small seven-sided football shape approximately 1½ inches (3.81cm) in diameter.

Cheesecloth Cotton gauzelike cloth with a number of culinary uses, including straining liquids, enclosing spices, herbs, and other flavoring agents to be applied in a cooking process, and binding ingredients together during the cooking process. The cloth's loose weave allows for the distribution of flavor and moisture during cooking while the structural integrity of the product it encloses is maintained.

Chiffonade A vegetable cut applied to leafy greens and herbs, such as spinach and basil. It results in long, very thin strips typically used as a garnish or as a bed on which other food items are placed. This cut is accomplished by stacking the leaves, rolling the stack into a cylinder, and slicing the roll into fine strips.

Chinois A conical strainer. While this term applies to all such strainers, it is generally used to describe those that use a fine mesh rather than perforated metal to strain.

Clarification The process of turning a cloudy liquid into a clear one by removing the solid impurities or sediment from it. This process turns broth or stock into consommé by trapping the impurities in a mixture of ground meat, egg whites, and acidic product and aromatics. The term *clarification* is applied to this clarifying mixture, or clearmeat, as well as the process itself.

Clarified Butter Pure butterfat rendered from whole butter (a process that removes milk solids and water). Clarified butter has a higher smoking point, or temperature at which it burns, than whole butter. This property makes it suitable for cooking food at higher temperatures and for cooking processes such as sautéing. Clarified butter has less butter flavor than whole butter and may be kept for a longer period without becoming rancid.

Clearmeat The mixture of egg white, ground meat, acidic ingredient, mirepoix, and other aromatics used in the process of clarifying stock or broth into consommé. (See *clarification*.)

Cocotte A classic vegetable cut that results in a small seven-sided football shape approximately ¾ inch (1.9cm) in diameter.

Compote A preparation of chilled fresh or dried fruit previously cooked slowly in a sugar syrup. Compotes are often flavored with spices or liqueur.

Concassée To pound or coarsely chop. The term is most often applied to peeled, seeded, and coarsely chopped tomatoes. The term describes the result as well as the action. For example, a chef may concassée a tomato to produce tomato concassée.

Confit Meat or poultry slowly cooked and preserved in its own fat. Classically, goose, duck, and, sometimes, pork is used to make confit.

Conical Strainer Specifically, a conical strainer made of perforated metal rather than mesh. (See *chinois*.)

Consommé A rich, clear soup made by clarifying broth or stock. Consommés are served hot or cold. A consommé reduced by half to intensify its flavor is known as a double consommé.

Coulis A thick sauce made from raw or cooked fruit or vegetables. The term *purée* is sometimes used interchangeably.

Deglaze To add a liquid, usually stock or wine, to a pot or pan after it has been used to cook a food item in order to remove the cooked food particles and their flavor from the surface of the cooking vessel. These flavorful food particles are called the *fond* and, once lifted from the pan, are used to enhance the flavor of a stock or sauce. (See *fond*.)

Degraisse A French term referring to the process of removing the fat from the surface of a stock, soup, or sauce.

Depouillage A French term referring to the process of skimming the surface of a stock to remove the impurities that naturally rise to the surface while simmering.

Double and Triple Stocks Stocks made with a prepared stock rather than water. Double and triple stocks are not recommended, as the product cost increases significantly and the flavor is not much different from that of a properly made regular stock.

Dredge To dip or submerge an item in a dry ingredient in order to coat it. Food products are often dredged in flour to coat them prior to sautéing, pan-frying, or deep-frying them. The coating keeps the product from sticking to the pan and promotes the development of a crust on the surface of the product. This crust may enhance the product by developing an appealing brown appearance and by encasing the product in a way that retains flavor and moisture.

Duxelles An appareil composed of mushrooms, shallots, and butter. The mushrooms and shallots are finely chopped and cooked in the butter until a dry, thick paste forms. Duxelles are often used to flavor items such as soups or sauces or as stuffing or a component of stuffing.

Emulsion The suspension of one liquid within another when those liquids generally do not mix. The combination of oil (or fat) and water-based liquids into a smooth mixture is the classic culinary emulsion. An emulsion has a thicker consistency than that of either liquid separately. This characteristic provides mouthfeel, cling, and general structural benefits. Emulsions may be temporary, permanent, or semipermanent. Emulsions are often aided by the addition of emulsifiers or stabilizers such as mustard or the lecithin found in egg yolks.

Enriched Stock A stock made with meat as well as bones, creating a hybrid of stock and broth. For 1 gallon (38L) of chicken stock, it is recommended that 2 whole chickens be added to the recipe. When done, the chickens should be reserved and utilized in another recipe or preparation. For beef or veal stock, it is recommended that a 2-pound (1.8kg) piece of shank meat be added to enrich the stock. Enriched stock yields a much richer flavor than plain stock and, as long as the meat is utilized in another preparation, should not increase cost.

Essence The fusion of a particular flavor, such as mushrooms or fennel, into a stock to derive a characteristic flavor or aroma.

Fond French for "base." In French cooking, *fond* refers to a stock, typically the basis for many classic and modern recipes. *Fond* is also used to describe the residue attached to the bottom of a cooking vessel after a food ingredient has been roasted or sautéed. A great deal of flavor is usually retained in the fond, which is removed from the cooking vessel through the process of deglazing. (See *deglaze*.)

Fondant A classic vegetable cut that results in a small seven-sided football shape approximately 2 inches (5cm) in diameter.

Garnish A food item added for appearance, taste, and texture. Garnish can be integral to the dish or added as an embellishing accompaniment. The term also applies to the act of adding a garnish to a dish.

Gelatin A mixture of proteins derived from boiling bones, connective tissues, and other animal parts. Gelatin, when dissolved and cooked in a hot liquid, adds a jelly-like texture to the product. It is flavorless and odorless and comes in granular and sheet forms. It is used to thicken and stabilize food products.

Gelatinous Describes a liquid with jelly-like properties. A gelatinous product is semisolid when cold and liquid when hot. Gelatinous properties are important for stocks and sauces due to the characteristics of richness, body, substance, and mouthfeel they provide to the food products.

Glace A quality stock reduced slowly over a prolonged period until it reaches a thick and syrupy consistency. Glace can be used to enhance or enrich soups and sauces and as a glaze to add a sheen to broiled and grilled proteins. Although some commercial food bases have a similar appearance, they may or may not achieve the same results as a fresh-made glace. Today, glace can be purchased already made, but the products vary widely in flavor and quality by manufacturer.

Glazing The process of adding sheen to a food item. Glazing can be accomplished by many means. Examples include brushing a grilled steak with glace before serving, coating an hors d'oeuvre with aspic gelée, and sautéing foods in butterfat and granulated sugar.

Grand Sauce A basic classic sauce from which a number of small sauces are produced. There are five recognized grand sauces: espagnole (brown), velouté, béchamel (white), hollandaise, and tomato. In recent years, many culinarians argue that demi-glace has replaced espagnole in common use as the foundation sauce, though classic demi-glace is made from espagnole. Grand sauce is also known as *mother sauce* and *lead sauce*.

Griswold A cast-iron skillet. This heavy-gauge pan requires a seasoning process to seal it, which involves coating the pan with oil and heating it to a high temperature. The griswold is important to the production of many regional dishes. For example, it is the traditional pan used for blackening Cajun dishes, baking corn breads, and pan-frying Southern fried chicken. Its heavy gauge maintains temperature evenly once heated.

Julienne A classic vegetable cut that results in shapes measuring ⅛ inch (.32cm) x ⅛ (.32cm) x ½ inches (1.27cm).

Julienne Fine A classic vegetable cut that results in shapes measuring ¹⁄₁₆ inch (.16cm) x ¹⁄₁₆ inch (.16cm) x ½ inches (1.27cm).

Large Dice A classic vegetable cut that results in cubes measuring ¾ inch (1.9cm) x ¾ inch (1.9cm) x ¾ inch (1.9cm).

Liaison A mixture of cream and egg yolk used to finish soups and sauces. The use of a liaison enriches, slightly thickens, and gives sheen to the completed soup or sauce. A liaison must be carefully incorporated into the hot product through tempering. A product containing a liaison cannot be boiled or the yolk will scramble and the item will have a curdled or broken appearance.

Marmite A stockpot, often made of earthenware. This large pot is taller than it is wide to allow prolonged periods of simmering while minimizing evaporation. Marmites sometimes have legs.

Matignon An edible mirepoix. Matignon uses the same ratio and variety of vegetables as a traditional mirepoix, but because it is intended to be consumed, the matignon should be cut into uniform shapes before cooking.

Medium Dice A classic vegetable cut that results in cubes measuring ½ inch (1.27cm) x ½ inch (1.27cm) x ½ inch (1.27cm).

Mince To cut or chop into very small pieces.

Mirepoix A combination of vegetables frequently used in cooking. Mirepoix typically includes 50 percent onions, 25 percent carrots, and 25 percent celery. The size to which mirepoix ingredients are cut varies with the intended use and is determined by the amount of time the mirepoix will be cooked. For a brown stock that cooks for 6–8 hours, a large dice is preferred, but for a fish stock, which cooks for 45 minutes only, a small dice yields better results.

Mise en Place A culinary term meaning "everything in its place." It connotes a state of preparedness. *Mise en place* applies to the assembly of ingredients and equipment prior to undertaking food production. It is also a mindset brought about by thorough forethought and planning.

Nappé A liquid consistency that just coats a spoon. The term *nappé* also refers to the act of lightly coating a food item with sauce.

Oblique A classic vegetable cut made by cutting the vegetable on a bias. Between each cut, the vegetable is rolled 180 degrees. This cut is used primarily for carrots, but other vegetables, such as broccoli stems and asparagus, can be prepared this way.

Olivette A classic vegetable cut resulting in a small seven-sided football shape approximately ½ inch (1.27cm) in diameter.

Onion Brûlée A peeled onion cut in half and charred on the sliced side. Onion brûlée is added to stocks, soups, and sauces for added caramel color and enhanced flavor. French for burnt onion.

Onion Piqué A whole peeled onion to which a bay leaf is tacked with whole cloves. Another approach is to make a slice into the onion and secure the bay leaf within the slice, then stick cloves into the onion separately. Onion piqué is used to flavor sauces, generally white sauces such as béchamel and velouté, and soups. French for pricked onion.

Parboil To par-cook food in boiling or simmering water.

Par-cook To partially cook a food by any method. This technique is used to bring food to a state where it can be quickly cooked to finish, especially in the case of dense foods. Par-cooking is also used to prepare a number of individual foods, which take various amounts of time to cook, to a degree of doneness whereby they can be completed together in the same amount of time.

Parisienne A classic vegetable cut resulting in perfectly round shapes. No diameter is specified, but it is very important that each of the vegetables used for the same preparation is uniform in size.

Pâte à Choux A paste or batter made of milk or water, flour, butter, and eggs. It is also known as *choux paste, cream-puff dough,* and *éclair paste.* Pâte à choux is used to produce a number of hollow pastries that are often filled. It is also used as a binder or appareil for other preparations.

Paysanne A classic vegetable cut that results in shapes measuring ½ inch (1.27cm) x ½ inch (1.27cm) x ⅛ inch (.32cm). Paysanne cuts can be round, triangular, or square.

Peel To remove the outer layer or peel from fruits and vegetables. The term *peel* also describes a long-handled, spade-shaped tool used by bakers to remove baked items from the oven.

Pincé To caramelize a product by sautéing. This term is most often applied to tomato products.

Purée A sauce or soup made from ingredients, especially fruits or vegetables, that have been blended, processed, or sieved until a thick smooth consistency is achieved. The term *purée* also refers to the act of blending, processing, or sieving a food item to such a consistency.

Raft Congealed clearmeat that settles at the top of a consommé during clarification.

Reduction The product resulting when a liquid, such as a stock or sauce, is simmered or boiled to evaporate its water, reduce its volume, and concentrate its flavor. Stocks and sauces made with commercial food bases, which do not contain gelatin, will not benefit from the process of reduction.

Refresh To submerge or run a blanched product under cold water to stop the cooking process and set the color. This is also known as *shocking.*

Remouillage French for "rewetting." Remouillage is a stock made with bones previously used to make stock. The procedure for making remouillage is the same as for a regular stock, but the product is not as clear or flavorful. Remouillage is frequently used to make glace and, in the past, was used instead of regular stock to make double-strength stocks. (See *double stock, glace.*)

Rendering The process of heating fatty animal products to melt and separate the fat from the remaining tissue. This process produces clear liquid fat, useful for many cooking applications, and brown, crisp connective tissue. This crisp tissue is often crumbled or cut and used as a garnish known as *cracklings.*

Rondeau A heavy, wide, shallow, straight-sided pot with two loop handles.

Rondelle A classic vegetable cut that results in round shapes, ⅛ inch (.32cm) thick. The rondelle cut is sometimes referred to as *coins.*

Roux A mixture of cooked fat and flour used to thicken soups and sauces. Often, the fat used is butter. Other fats, such as rendered animal fat and various oils, are sometimes used for their flavor and temperature characteristics. The general ratio of fat to flour is 1:1 by weight. A roux may be cooked to various degrees of doneness for desired flavor and color characteristics.

Sachet d'Épices A bag of spices used to flavor soups, stocks, and sauces. The spices are generally wrapped in a piece of cheesecloth, tied with a long string, and fastened with one end of the string to the pot of the product to which it is applied. This allows the sachet ingredients to be easily added and removed when desired. A standard sachet d'épices contains cracked black peppercorns, parsley stems, bay leaf, dry thyme, and, sometimes, a clove of crushed garlic.

Sauteuse A single-handled sauté pan with rounded, sloping sides.

Sautoir A single-handled sauté pan with straight sides.

Shock To submerge or run a blanched product under cold water to stop the cooking process and set the color. This is also known as *refreshing*.

Sieve A wire mesh kitchen utensil used to strain liquids or sift dry ingredients, such as flour. The term also applies to the act of straining liquid or particles through a sieve.

Small Dice A classic vegetable cut that results in cubes measuring ¼ inch (.64cm) x ¼ inch (.64cm) x ¼ inch (.64cm).

Small Sauce A derivative sauce made by altering a grand sauce with additional ingredients. Many classic small sauces can be made from each of the grand sauces.

Standard Breading Procedure The sequential process of coating a food product with breadcrumbs by first dredging it in flour, then egg wash, and, finally, the crumbs. This process is also used with other dry coatings, such as cracker crumbs, ground nuts, and cornmeal. Such a coating is often applied to an item before it is pan- or deep-fried.

Stir-frying A hot, quick, dry-heat cooking method done in a skillet on the stovetop with very little fat. Traditionally, this method employs a wok as the cooking vessel. Larger items to be stir-fried are generally cut into small pieces. The method is similar to sautéing, but the food is constantly kept moving.

Sweating The process of cooking food in a pan without browning or adding color to the food. Sweating should be done over low heat until the items are tender and begin to release moisture. The purpose of sweating is to help the food release its flavor quickly when combined and cooked with other foods. Onions are an example of a food item commonly sweated. They turn almost translucent when properly sweated.

Tempering A process of adjustment employed when heat or acid may cause an ingredient or combination of ingredients to curdle. Heat or acid is applied to the ingredients gradually in order to adapt them to the change. Hot liquids are added slowly to a liaison, for example, to bring the temperature of the eggs up slowly so they do not scramble. This term also applies to the stabilization of chocolate through a melting and cooling process.

Tomato Concassée A rough cut or chop of peeled and seeded tomato.

Tourné A classic vegetable cut that results in a small football shape with seven even sides.

Tranche An angled portion slice from a fillet of fish.

Translucent Semitransparent. The term often describes the appearance of onion products cooked to the point where they are somewhat limp.

Tuber A fleshy, usually oblong or rounded thickening or outgrowth of a root, stem, or shoot beneath the ground. A common tuber is the potato.

Whisk A looped wire kitchen utensil, also called a *whip*, used for whipping and stirring. The term *whisk* also applies to the action of whipping vigorously to incorporate ingredients or air into ingredients.

White Mirepoix Standard mirepoix in which the proportion of carrots is replaced with parsnips, leeks, and mushrooms. White mirepoix is used in fish stock and fish fumet and is sometimes used in white stock when a lighter product is desired. (See *mirepoix*.)

Zest The thin outer layer of the peel of citrus fruit. Zest is used as a flavoring agent. The term *zest* also refers to the action of cutting the zest from the citrus fruit.

References

CHAPTER 1

Beard, J. *American Cookery*. Boston: Little, Brown, 1972.

Dowell, P. and A. Bailey. *Cooks' Ingredients*. New York: William Morrow, 1980.

Konemann, V. *Culinaria The United States: A Culinary Discovery*. New York: Konemann Publishers, 1998.

CHAPTER 2

Adams, Marcia. *Cooking from Quilt Country: Hearty Recipes from Amish and Mennonite Kitchens*. New York: Clarkson Potter, 1989.

Shields, John. *Chesapeake Bay Cooking*. New York: Broadway Books, 1998.

CHAPTER 3

Overton, R. *The South: New American Cooking*. Alexandria, Va.: Time-Life Books, 2000.

CHAPTER 4

Grigas, Catherine Enns. *The Art of Cracker Cooking*. http://www.waters-edge.com/dining/din_cracker.shtml. 31 October 2000.

Parkinson, Rosemary. *Culinaria the Caribbean: A Culinary Discovery*. New York: Konemann Publishers, 1999.

Stuart, Caroline. *The Food of Miami: Authentic Recipes from South Florida and the Keys*. Boston: Periplus, 1999.

CHAPTER 5

Alexander, George. *The Clash of Cultures Carl Walker*, http://www.houstonpress.com/issues/2000-08-24/toque.html.

Collin, Rima, and Richard Collin. *The New Orleans Cookbook*. New York: Alfred A. Knopf, 1975.

DeMers, John. *The Food of New Orleans: Authentic Recipes from the Big Easy*. Boston: Periplus, 1997.

Deutsch, Hermann B. *Brennan's New Orleans Cookbook*. New Orleans, La.: Robert Crager, 1982.

Folse, John. *Hot Beignets and Warm Boudoirs: A Collection of Recipes from Louisiana's Bed and Breakfasts*. Gonzales, La.: Chef John Folse and Company, 1999.

Folse, John. *The Evolution of Cajun and Creole Cuisine*. Donaldsonville, La., Chef John Folse and Company, 1989.

CHAPTER 6

Midwest Living Magazine. *Favorite Recipes from Great Midwest Cooks*. Des Moines, Iowa: Meredith Books, 1992.

CHAPTER 7

Lee, Hilde Gabriel. *Taste of the States: A Food History of America*. Charlottesville, Va.: Howell Press, 1992.

Perini, T. *Texas Cowboy Cooking*. Alexandria, Va.: Time-Life Books, 2000.

CHAPTER 8

The Volunteers of the Colorado Historical Society. *Across Colorado: Recipes and Recollections.* Niwot, Colo.: Roberts Reinhart Publishers, 1997.

CHAPTER 9

DeWitt, Dave. *The Food of Santa Fe: Authentic Recipes from the American Southwest.* Boston: Periplus, 1998.

Greer, Anne Lindsey. *Cuisine of the American Southwest.* New York: Harper and Row, 1983.

Sedlar, John. *Modern Southwest Cuisine.* New York: Simon and Schuster, 1986.

CHAPTER 10

Fletcher, Janet. *California: New American Cooking.* Alexandria, Va.: Time-Life Books, 2000.

Josselin, Jean-Marie. *A Taste of Hawaii: New Cooking from the Crossroads of the Pacific.* New York: Stewart, Tabori, and Chang, 1992.

Worthington, Diane Rossen. *The California Cook.* New York: Bantam Books, 1994.

CHAPTER 11

Johnson, Ronald. *The American Table.* New York: William Morrow, 2000.

Index